American Experiences

American Experiences

Readings in American History

Volume II From 1877

Fifth Edition

■

Randy Roberts
Purdue University

■

James S. Olson
Sam Houston State University

New York   San Francisco   Boston
London   Toronto   Sydney   Tokyo   Singapore   Madrid
Mexico City   Munich   Paris   Cape Town   Hong Kong   Montreal

Publisher: Priscilla McGeehon
Senior Acquisitions Editor: Jay O'Callaghan
Development Director: Lisa Pinto
Executive Marketing Manager: Sue Westmoreland
Supplements Editor: Kelly Villella
Production Manager: Joseph Vella
Project Coordination, Text Design, and Electronic Page Makeup: Shepherd, Inc.
Photo Research: Photosearch, Inc.
Senior Cover Design Manager/Designer: Nancy Danahy
Cover Collage: Michael Staats
Cover Photos: Woman on bicycle and early airplane: Dover Books; Flags and old family photo: Photodisc, Inc.; Packard Automobile advertisement: Corbis-Bettmann; John F. Kennedy: UPI Corbis-Bettmann; Rosa Parks memorial: AP/Wide World Photos; Oklahoma City Bomb building: Lisa Hokel Blackstar.
Senior Manufacturing Buyer: Dennis J. Para
Printer and Binder: The Maple-Vail Book Manufacturing Group
Cover Printer: Coral Graphics Services, Inc.

For permission to use copyrighted material, grateful acknowledgment is made to the copyright holders on p. 361, which are hereby made part of this copyright page

Library of Congress Cataloging-in-Publication Data

American experiences : readings in American history / [edited by]
   Randy Roberts, James S. Olson. — 5th ed.
       p.   cm.
   Includes bibliographical references.
   Contents: v. 1. To 1877 — v. 2. Since 1865.
   ISBN 0-321-07990-6 (v. 1) — ISBN 0-321-08679-1 (v. 2)
   1. United States—History.   I. Roberts, Randy, 1951–   .
II. Olson, James Stuart, 1946–   .

E178.6 .A395   2001
973—dc21   2001126431

Please visit our website at http://www.ablongman.com

ISBN 0-321-08679-1

1 2 3 4 5 6 7 8 9 10—MA—04 03 02 01

To Our Families

Contents

Preface

American History instructors enjoy talking about the grand sweep of the American past. Many note the development of unique traditions such as the American political tradition and the American diplomatic tradition. They employ the article *the* so often that they depict history as a seamless garment and Americans as all cut from the same fabric. Nothing could be further from the truth. America is a diverse country, and its population is the most ethnically varied in the world—white and black, Indian and Chicano, rich and poor, male and female. No single tradition can encompass this variety. *American Experiences* shows the complexity and richness of the nation's past by focusing on the people—how they coped with, adjusted to, or rebelled against America. The readings examine Americans as they worked and played, fought and made love, lived and died.

We designed *American Experiences* as a supplement to the standard textbooks used in college survey classes in American History. Unlike other readers, it covers ground not usually found in textbooks. For example, instead of a discussion of the political impact of the Populist movement, we explore *The Wizard of Oz* as a Populist parable. In short, *American Experiences* presents different slants on standard and not-so-standard topics.

We have tested each essay in classrooms so that *American Experiences* reflects not only our interest in social history but also student interests in American history in general. We have selected essays that are readable, interesting, and help illuminate important aspects of America's past. For example, to show the nature of the class system in the South and to introduce the topic of southern values, we selected one essay on gambling and horse racing in the Old South and another on gouging matches in the southern backcountry. As an introduction to the conventional and medical view of women in the late nineteenth century, we selected an essay about Lizzie Borden. Each essay, then, serves at least two purposes: to tell a particular story well, and to help illustrate the social or political landscape of America.

This reader presents a balanced picture of the experiences of Americans. The characters in these volumes are not exclusively white males from the Northeast, whose eyes are continually focused on Boston, New York, and Washington. Although their stories are certainly important, so too are the stories of blacks adjusting with dignity to a barbarous labor system, Chicanos coming to terms with Anglo society, and women striving for increased opportunities in a gender-restricted society. We have looked at all of these stories and, in doing so, we have assumed that Americans express themselves in a variety of ways: through work, sex, and games, as well as politics and diplomacy.

Changes to the New Edition

During the past three years, we have solicited a variety of opinions from colleagues and students about the selections for Volume II of *American Experiences*. Based on that feedback, we have made a number of changes in the fifth edition, always with the intent of selecting articles that undergraduate students will find interesting and informative. The new articles for the second volume of this edition are:

- Stephen R. Lowe, "Demarbleizing Bobby Jones"
- Arthur Schlesinger, Jr., "The Man of the Century"
- James T. Patterson, "Smoking and Cancer"
- James H. Jones, "Dr. Yes"
- Jon Wiener, "The Beatles Revolution"

American Experiences is divided into standard chronological and topical parts. Each part is introduced by a brief discussion of the major themes of the period or topic. In turn, each individual selection is preceded by a short discussion of how it fits into the part's general theme. We employed this method to give students some guidance through the complexity of the American experience. At the conclusion of each selection is a series of study questions and a brief bibliographic essay. These are intended to further the usefulness of *American Experiences* for students as well as teachers.

Randy Roberts
James S. Olson

American Experiences

PART ONE

Reconstruction and the West

Although the Civil War did not begin as a crusade against slavery, it ended that way. The Emancipation Proclamation and Thirteenth Amendment to the Constitution made human bondage in the United States illegal, and during Reconstruction Republicans worked diligently to extend full civil rights to southern blacks. Despite the concerted opposition of President Andrew Johnson, the Radical Republicans in Congress pushed through a strong legislative program. The Civil Rights Act of 1866 and the Fourteenth and Fifteenth Amendments to the Constitution were all basically designed to bring the emancipated slaves into the political arena and build a respectable Republican party in the South. Both of these goals were stillborn, however, When Congress removed the troops from the last southern states in 1877, the old planter elite resumed its control of southern politics. They disfranchised and relegated blacks to second-class citizenship, and the South became solidly Democratic. The South had indeed been brought back into the Union, but the grandiose hopes for a true reconstruction of southern life would not be realized for more than a century.

Genuine change in the southern social structure required more than most Northerners could accept. Confiscation and redistribution of the plantations among poor whites and former slaves was too brazen an assault on property rights; northern businessmen feared that someday their own workers might demand similar treatment. Nor were Northerners prepared for real social change. Advocating political rights for blacks was one thing; true social equality was quite another. Prejudice ran deep in the American psyche, too deep in the 1870s to allow for massive social change. Finally, most Americans were growing tired of the debate over civil rights and becoming preoccupied with business, money, and economic growth. Heavy industry in the East and vacant land in the West were absorbing their energies.

Just as Reconstruction was coming to an end, out west, ambitious farmers were rapidly settling the frontier, anxious to convert the land into an agricultural empire. Civilization was forever replacing a wilderness mentality with familiar political, economic, and social institutions. Already the "Old West" was becoming the stuff of which nostalgia is made. Normal, if somewhat eccentric, people were being transformed into larger-than-life heroes as American society tried to maintain its rural, individualistic roots. Back East, cities and factories were announcing a future of bureaucracies, interest groups, crowds, and enormous industrial production. America would never be the same again. The cult of Western heroes helped people forget the misery of the Civil War and vicariously preserve a disappearing way of life.

'GOOD ANGELS': CONFEDERATE WIDOWHOOD IN VIRGINIA

Jennifer Lynn Gross

The Civil War remains today, by far, the bloodiest conflict in United States history, killing more Americans than World War I, World War II, the Korean War, and the Vietnam War combined. Out of a total population of 33 million people, more than 600,000 people died, most of them young men and many of them with wives and children. Left behind were hundreds of thousands of widows forced to survive in an economy and a legal system biased against unmarried women. As Jennifer Lynn Gross writes, they were "no longer part of traditional households. Such women had to become the moral, social, and economic leaders of their families in a patriarchal society in which women were supposed to be helpmates, not heads of households." The challenges were even greater for the widows of Confederate soldiers because southern culture defined the latitude of women even more narrowly than in the North.

The widow & the orphan are, far more significant terms, than they once were to us.

—David Comfort III to Charlotte Comfort, 3 October 1874

In 1848 the Rawlings and Kelly families celebrated the marriage of their children, John and Susan. After the wedding, the newlyweds moved to a rented cottage in the small town of Lawrenceville, Virginia, not far from the North Carolina border. There, John worked as a harnessmaker while Susan helped make ends meet by taking in mending and other sewing work. Over the next twelve years, they had three children. But the outbreak of the Civil War in 1861 abruptly shattered their household. Like so many other Southern husbands, John joined the Confederate ranks soon after the firing on Fort Sumter and Virginia's secession from the Union. Fighting with Company I of the Fifty-ninth Virginia, more familiarly known as the Brunswick Blues, John saw only a year of action before he was captured and imprisoned in the notoriously lethal Union prison in Elmira, New York. He died there in 1862 from battle wounds and smallpox. John's sudden death left Susan a middle-aged widow with three young children to support and very few options in a region devastated by the war.

Throughout the South there were tens of thousands of women like Susan Rawlings who were no longer part of traditional households. Such women had to become the moral, social, and economic leaders of their families in a patriarchal society in which women were supposed to be helpmates, not heads of households. In the Old South, the roles that young white women had re-

Jennifer Lynn Gross, " 'Good Angels': Confederate Widowhood in Virginia," in Catherine Clinton, ed., *Southern Families at War: Loyalty and Conflict in the Civil War South* (New York: Oxford University Press, 2000), 133–48.

spectably played were limited to the dependent positions of daughter, wife, and mother. Daughters relied completely on their fathers for their public identities, and this dependence transferred to their husbands upon marriage. A woman's legal, social, and economic identity was always attached to the man in her life. According to white Southern social rules, marriage was the only truly acceptable place for a woman. As one scholar has noted, "Women [who] were neither the wives nor the slaves of white men . . . had no place or function in southern society." There was no place for widows; they were expected to remarry, especially if they were young and still in their childbearing years. Yet many Civil War widows could not avail themselves of the traditional solution to the "widow problem"—remarriage. Too many eligible, white Southern men had died in the war—at least 260,000—and those who had survived generally either were already married or chose to marry younger women who did not bring with them the "emotional baggage" of a previous marriage. Widowed and alone, Confederate widows faced difficult choices in their efforts to define a place for themselves and survive on their own.

Every Confederate widow shared the pain and grief of losing a husband; however, a close study of the social and economic situations of seventy Confederate widows in Brunswick County, Virginia, including Susan Rawlings, reveals that there was no single experience of the emotional and practical realities of widowhood. Factors such as prewar wealth, postwar opportunity, the presence or absence of helpful kin or dependent children, and support from the state and larger societal attitudes toward Confederate widows all affected the way that widows dealt with their widowhood and the strategies they employed to survive. Among Virginia's Confederate widows were women who remarried, women who thrived as *femmes soles,* women who just barely made it on their own, and women who became dependent on friends, family members, or the state.

The drama of Confederate widows' joys and sorrows, struggles and opportunities, and successes and failures is compelling in and of itself, yet Confederate widowhood did not exist in a vacuum. During the war, the absence of fathers and husbands from the home front allowed or forced many women to experience expanded opportunities for autonomy. For the war's duration, wives regularly assumed the role of household head. But upon their spouses' homecomings, most wives returned to their prewar positions of subordination within the home, enabling their husbands to reassert their manly "rights" as household heads within a patriarchal system. By virtue of their "manlessness," however, the thousands of widows who could not remarry continued to have access to wartime liberties. The existence of so many women who could no longer conform to the ideals of traditional Southern womanhood—combined with the South's military defeat and the end of slavery—threw a wrench in elite white Southerners' postwar efforts to build a "New South" in the image of the Old. Southern men, desperate to reassert their elevated prewar social status, which was already threatened by the loss of their authority over emancipated black men, needed to control white women, especially unattached white women. For white men to imagine themselves as proper patriarchs, white women could not be independent, just as African American men could not be equal. As the former slaves had to be controlled through discriminatory black codes, unfair labor contracts, and eventually the infamous Jim Crow system, white women, if not in reality, then at least in theory, had to be ensconced within proper patriarchal homes, provided for and protected by their menfolk. To accomplish this, Southerners had to expand their definitions of Southern womanhood to make room for Confederate widows, and to make this new attitude more palatable, they collectively imagined all Confederate widows as good and noble women who had sacrificed mightily for the cause.

When the Civil War ended in 1865, Susan Rawlings and other widows like her began the often difficult task of rebuilding their lives. For many widows, the shock and grief of suddenly losing their spouses further complicated their efforts to survive on their own. One widow's reaction to the "terrible announcement" of her husband's death in a Petersburg hospital "was as a thunderbolt at [her] very feet," recalled Judith Brockenbrough McGuire in her diary. "Oh, how she made that immense building ring with her bitter lamentations! . . . She could hear no voice of sympathy." Yet it was not grief alone that complicated widows' lives; they also had to face new familial responsibilities even while they were still in mourning. For some women, it was all they could do to get by. "I know it must have been hard for you to keep up & take that interest in your duties which your children & domestic cares call for, & I don't wonder that you yielded to these feelings [of grief]," Mary Louise Comfort wrote sympathetically to her daughter-in-law in Georgia.

For most widows, grief was accompanied by intense economic distress that varied according to the family's financial situation before the death of the household head. Generally, the more real estate a family owned before a husband's death, the better off a widow would be when her husband was gone. Conversely, widows from families with small amounts of property often suffered extreme hardship and deprivation. Although there were extremely wealthy Southerners, most white Southerners fell among the yeoman classes. And before the war almost all of Brunswick's future Confederate widows were married to yeomen—middling farmers and artisans. There were also Brunswick widows who came from poorer, less economically established families. Twenty-five Brunswick women who would become widows were married to men who, though in agricultural occupations, owned no land. Additionally, ten women's husbands were artisans—boot and shoemakers, carpenters, tailors, harnessmakers, or wheelwrights. Like the twenty-five landless "farmers," these working-class men rarely owned substantial real estate. A woman whose subsistence depended entirely on her husband's labor suffered a tremendous economic loss upon his death because she no longer had either the income from his labor or the means to perform his job in his absence.

Dead Confederate Soldiers

Even if a woman had enjoyed economic stability before her husband's death through the ownership of land, the added complication of an economy devastated by the war could often leave her facing a harrowing economic situation. With the end of slavery, all money invested in human property disappeared. Additionally, because Brunswick lay right in the path of both armies, most cattle, horses, and other livestock, as well as any stored tobacco or cotton, was likely to have been confiscated or impressed for military use. Within five years of the war's end, one-third of the widows, both those whose husbands had owned land and those whose husbands had not, held either less property or significantly depreciated property than they had before their husbands' deaths.

Although the bleak condition of the postwar South and the widows' prewar economic positions certainly contributed to the hardships that Confederate widows faced, the existing legal system could also threaten a widow's economic existence. If a woman's husband died without leaving a will—and most did, because wills were rare during this period except among men of considerable property—Virginia estate law limited a woman's access to and control over the family's possessions. Since 1662 Virginia statute law had provided that when a husband died without a will, his widow was entitled only to a "dower" portion of his property. Dower rights gave a widow only the use of the dower real estate during her lifetime ("life interest"), which meant that she did not have the power to sell or give away the property or to alter it in any way. If a widow altered the dower property, even in an effort to increase profits, the law considered this "wasting" another person's property, and the rightful heirs could sue her. From 1790 until about 1890, dower constituted only a one-third life interest in any real estate and one-third of any personal property that her husband had owned during their marriage. If there were children from the marriage, they received equal portions of the remaining two-thirds of the real and personal property. If the couple had no children, the widow still received only a one-third life interest in the real estate, but her share of the personal estate increased to one-half. Virginia law dictated that inheritance of the other two-thirds pass as follows: the eldest brother of the deceased received the entire two-thirds; if there were no brothers, it was divided equally between any sisters of the decedent; if there were no siblings at all, the inheritance passed to the "issue of the decedent's paternal grandfather, the eldest male of the nearest degree succeeding first." For personal estate, the line was identical except that the decedent's parents were considered heirs before the siblings. Under Virginia law, a widow was *never* entitled to all of her husband's estate unless there were no legal kin. Because most Confederate widows were married to yeomen, not wealthy planters, one-third of a husband's property would not allow them to support themselves. Of the seventy Brunswick husbands, only five left wills stipulating how they wished their estates disbursed. Like countless other widows in the South, the other sixty-five Brunswick widows, including Susan Rawlings, found themselves at the mercy of Virginia's estate laws.

The postwar period was trying for many Southerners, but widows faced especially daunting circumstances because inheritance laws discriminated against them, and there were few options open to unattached women in the traditional South. Those widows who could chose the traditional solution to the widowhood question— remarriage. For these women, a new spouse could

provide the emotional support and economic stability that they would perhaps be unable to achieve on their own. Only 30 percent of the seventy Brunswick widows were able to remarry.

A woman's decision to remarry generally reflected "a tangled component of need, opportunity, and desire." Financial concerns overwhelmingly influenced many decisions to remarry. It was, as one widow said of her decision to remarry, "the only chance I saw for myself."A widow who did not inherit a significant amount of property after her first husband's death might choose to seek a second husband to gain economic stability. For example, Prudence Dean, a propertyless widow at the age of twenty-one, saw advantage in a marriage to George Lippincott, a Northerner she probably met as the Union army passed through Brunswick. Because Prudence was young and penniless, remarriage was probably her best option. At the time of their marriages to Brunswick widows, over one-half of the second husbands owned real estate and/or significant amounts of personal property.

A woman's age, along with the absence or presence of children from her first marriage and their ages, also affected her decision and opportunities regarding remarriage. Older widows had a much more difficult time finding prospective new husbands. Moreover, if a widow was older and had adult children, she might be less likely to remarry because she could rely on her adult children for support. Mary Epperson, for example, had seven children, two of whom were adults within five years of the war's end. The presence of these adult children, along with her inheritance of a 240-acre farm, probably contributed to her decision to remain single. By contrast, if a widow was young and had small children, she might seek out a new spouse to provide for her family. Mary Jane Wilmoth was a twenty-five-year-old mother of three young children when her husband died, leaving her with only a small inheritance. When Charles Thompson, a prosperous forty-eight-year-old farmer with a 444-acre farm came courting, Mary Jane likely saw not only a possible love interest but also an attractive marriage partner for a widow with three young children to support. Like the presence of young children, childlessness might also compel a widow to choose remarriage. Because motherhood was one of the most important tenets of Southern womanhood, women who were childless might seek fulfillment of their "motherly nature" through a second marriage. Susan Seward, whose first marriage left her with neither great wealth nor children, was probably thrilled to accept the marriage proposal of John Dunn, a prosperous farmer with four children. He represented not only a second chance for love and economic stability but also a chance for her to be a mother.

While remarriage was the most traditional answer to the widow question, it was not always possible. Indeed, even if it was possible, it might not be desirable. During the antebellum period, "the wealthier the widow, the less likely she was to remarry." Similarly, the few Brunswick widows who inherited significant amounts of property generally chose to remain single and retain control of their wealth. Julietta Cheely, for example, likely decided against remarriage because she could support herself comfortably on the property she acquired after her husband's death. When Needham Cheely died in 1863, his will bequeathed his entire estate worth $11,965.35 to his wife, stipulating that she could receive her inheritance only if she remained unmarried. Failing to specifically designate the property as a "life estate," Needham inadvertently left Julietta in outright possession of his entire estate, opening the door for her economic autonomy. Until after 1890, Julietta maintained ownership and management of her inherited estate, hiring laborers to aid her sons in farming the land. Though several of her adult sons resided in her household, the census-taker and the community at large regarded her as the legitimate head of the household. Julietta's postwar success as one of the wealthiest and most successful of the Brunswick widows resulted from a combination of her prewar social position among the upper strata of the yeomen, a

flair for financial management probably acquired during the war, and a legal loophole in her husband's will.

A widow might also prefer to remain single because of the advantages provided by her *femme sole* status. According to Virginia law, single women, including widows, were *femmes soles*. Theoretically, they possessed all the same legal privileges as men—they could enter into contracts, bring lawsuits against debtors, sell or convey property by deed, and plan for the distribution of their property by executing wills. A few of the Brunswick widows, like Narcissa Faris, took full advantage of their *femme sole* status after their husbands' death. Although Narcissa's husband, Peter, had owned no real estate and only $100 of personal property when he died, Narcissa assumed the responsibility of administering his estate which was her right under inheritance law. As part of her responsibilities as executrix, on 22 September 1866 she filed a petition with the County Court of Brunswick requiring W. A. Faris to repay a bond to her late husband's estate in the amount of $325.60 plus $97.68 in interest. Though she likely had no experience in collecting debts or petitioning the court, Narcissa succeeded in her efforts and settled her husband's estate to her advantage.

While some widows took advantage of the opportunities offered by *femme sole* status to administer their husbands' estates and execute their own wills, many widows made decisions in concert with advice from male family members, often willingly but sometimes with reluctance. Quite often, relatives or in-laws took it upon themselves to advise a "helpless" widow as to the best course of action after her husband's death. Alice Harrison's mother-in-law counseled her to let her brother take care of her affairs after her husband's death. "Oh you know not enough of human nature to have such to deal with, and your life will become more and more labourious and miserable." Similarly, Mangus Jones admonished his sister-in-law, Frances, of King William County, Virginia, to sell the farm that her husband had left her, taking out only her dower third, as a way to disencumber herself from debt. He advised, "I think you would be benefitted by this course—in fact I don't see how it is possible for you to arrest the sale." Certainly Mangus's advice may have been Frances's most prudent course of action; the remaining evidence does not reveal any further specifics. But while her brother-in-law clearly did not regard her as capable of managing her own financial affairs, Frances's husband obviously had, because he bequeathed her his entire estate, not just her dower third. Such doubts and interference alone could make a widow's efforts to cake care of herself all the more troubling. Combined with the difficult environment of the postwar period, they could most certainly take their toll on a woman's ability or desire to make fruitful choices in the future.

Deprived of their husbands' labor and left with almost no land or personal property because of Virginia's estate laws, many widows in the predominantly agricultural South had to make difficult decisions in order to survive. Most found it necessary to enter the paid labor force after their husbands' deaths. Of course, this was not always easy, as there were few jobs open to women, and none of them paid very well. Although women could certainly work in the fields, as many yeoman wives had done on their own farms before the war, most white Southerners considered hiring out for such labor "beneath" them and their children. "How often I wished then that of all the land their father had owned, I had only a few acres on which I could live with my children and try to make a living. That would have been independence, and none of us would have shrunk from labour," lamented Cornelia Peake McDonald. "It almost broke my heart. Others worked, the first young men of Virginia went cheerfully to the plough; but the land was their own, the farms they had been born and bred on, and that was so different." Widows could also obtain work as domestics or washerwomen, but these jobs were generally reserved for African American women because, like hired agricultural labor, they were considered too indelicate for respectable white women. A more acceptable and traditional way for women to earn money was through the sale of food or other homemade products in the marketplace. Just as many yeoman families had undoubtedly benefited from women's labor in the fields before the war, many also profited from women's marketing activities in the prewar period. Even before her husband's death, Marie Hubard of Richmond sold strawberries in the marketplace to supplement her husband's income as a cannon-caster for the Confederacy. Apparently, casting cannons did not pay well enough to support a family, although it eventually cost William Hubard his life.

Though many widows were forced into menial labor just to scrape by, others were lucky enough to find work in a traditionally female "profession." Many Confederate widows, including two from Brunswick County, worked as seamstresses after the war. Additionally, women could find employment in one of the new female professions opened by the war. Such new "professional" opportunities were by no means vast, however; they were essentially limited to teaching and nursing. Even so, two Brunswick widows took advantage of them and the higher pay they provided. Mary Thomas supported her family after her husband's death by working as a teacher, most likely in the new public school system that was established in Brunswick in 1870, while Sarah, the widow of James Maitland, became a nurse.

Despite working, many widows were still unable to support themselves and their children without assistance. Maria Hubard despaired, "It seemed as if there was nothing left for us in the world but to starve or descend to the lowest level by working as labourers; and even then we could expect nothing but squalid poverty." Though almost two-thirds of the Brunswick widows were the heads of their own households in 1870, about one-third of the widows lived in other peoples' households at one time or another after becoming widows. Most of them resided with their parents, in-laws, or adult children. After Napoleon Taylor's death, his wife, Mary Jane, and their nine-year-old daughter, Pocahontas, never lived on their own. At first they shared a home with her in-laws, John W. Taylor, a seventy-three-year-old retired carpenter, and Eliza, his sixty-four-year-old wife. By 1880 the elderly Taylors had apparently died, and Mary Jane and Pocahontas moved in with Bassett Rawlings, Mary Jane's brother, and his family on a 459-acre farm. For other widows like Caroline Nash, dependency on friends and relatives was only temporary. In 1870 Caroline and her young daughter, Nancy, shared Lucretia Rawlings's home, but by 1880 they had established their own household.

Not all widows ended up living with relatives or even had such an opportunity. Many, however, faced pressure from family members who feared that they could not make it as "manless women." Charlotte Comfort received a letter from her father-in-law pleading with her to come live with them: "We . . . often wish that you were near us, that we might aid & encourage you in all your cares & responsibilities." And if a widow could not or would not move to be with family members, they often came to her, even if only for visits. Emma Garnett, the widow of General Thomas S. Garnett, received the news shortly after her husband's death that her mother-in-law would be arriving soon: "Mother will go to you very soon. She loved you as her own child, and will do all she can to give you comfort." Other widows faced well-meaning pleas that they send their children away to live with the families of "more stable" relatives. Cornelia McDonald recalled that after the death of her husband, numerous friends and relatives attempted to convince her to send her children away where they could be better provided for, since her situation was "perfectly hopeless":

Some days passed and many discussions arose with regard to the future of myself and the children. . . . All thought that the children ought to be distributed among the older members of the family. . . . I listened, but was resolved no matter what happened not to part with my

children; but often when pressed, and reminded how hopeless my condition was, and indeed how unreasonable, it was to persist in refusing to do what was the only thing that could be done, as far as any one could see, if my heart was inclined to yield for fear I would not be doing the best for the children, the thought of my poor little lonely ones . . . that thought would nerve me for resistance.

Though they could be intrusive, parents, in-laws, and other family or friends generally thought they were doing what was best for their widowed relative.

Until the 1880s, widows had been limited to finding new husbands, making it on their own, or relying on friends and relatives in their efforts to survive. Beginning in 1888, though, a new option arose: they could turn to the state for support. Such financial aid was not without precedent in Virginia. Almost from the beginning of the war, Virginia's various counties had actively raised and distributed money and food for the poverty-stricken families of soldiers. Eventually, such aid activities grew so expansive that state legislators decided to step in. Although Southern lawmakers and citizens regarded such state-sponsored aid as necessary and legitimate, most aid during the war came from local governments or churches and "ladies' aid societies."

In the years after the war, widows could also obtain assistance from memorial groups like the United Daughters of the Confederacy. Referring to their Home for Needy Confederate Women, they argued, "It is a *sacred duty* . . . to care for these women." (my emphasis). Proponents of widows' aid frequently used phrases like "sacred duty," "no charity is sweeter and saner," "their claim is strong and true, and, above all, just," and "unselfish solicitude" to describe and validate their cause, while the widows themselves were always characterized as "worthy recipients" "noble women," and "good women" to further highlight the rightness of such aid. Southern men and women considered it their inviolable responsibility to care for the widows of deceased Confederate soldiers.

Besides wartime aid, the Virginia General Assembly had since 1874 discussed postwar aid to Confederate widows. In 1880, Virginia legislators for the first time extended a one-time cash payment for the loss of a limb to a Confederate widow. Although it was not a pension, the General Assembly voted to "allow commutation for [an] artificial arm to Josephine Robinson, widow of Walter Robinson, deceased." Apparently, Walter had died before he could receive either the artificial arm or a commutation. This was not an official policy, however, and Josephine Robinson was the first and only widow to receive money from state funds until 1888, when the Virginia Assembly first extended yearly pensions to its former soldiers and their widows.

Though the Virginia Assembly began discussing the extension of yearly pensions to Confederate veterans and widows in 1874, it took fourteen long years before they approved such a measure. The political and economic climate of the postwar period contributed to the delay in awarding pensions to soldiers and their widows. From 1867 to 1871, Republicans, who were not exactly friendly toward the idea of rewarding Confederates for their role in the Civil War, ruled Virginia's General Assembly. Also, the state was still recovering from the economic devastation of the war, and the economic depression of the mid-1870s hit Virginia and the South especially hard.

In 1888, Virginia, "redeemed" by Southern Democrats, enacted its first pension law. According to this statute, any widow whose husband had died while in the Confederate armed forces was eligible to receive a pension if her yearly income was less than $300 and she had no more than $1,000 worth of property. Such limits were high enough that they excluded only elite women. More important than the financial limits, however, a widow had to be unmarried when she applied and remain unmarried to receive a Confederate pension. The 1888 statute, set at $30 per annum, was amended in 1900 and 1902 to increase the amount of payment and to broaden the scope of those who were eligible. In 1900 the General Assembly voted to give $40 to widows

who had lost their husbands in the war. Additionally, widows whose husbands had been "true and loyal soldiers" but had not died from their wartime injuries or diseases until well after the war's end were given $25. In both cases, widows could receive aid "only so long as [they] remain[ed] unmarried." In 1902 the law was further expanded to provide for women whose husbands had served in the war but had died from causes unrelated to the war. Even if a husband had died simply from old age, under this law, his widow could still receive a pension.

Although the dire financial situations of many Confederate widows were certainly compelling when Virginians took up the issue of pensions in the 1880s, their marital status was vitally important as well. The 1888 and subsequent laws each required that in order for a widow to receive a pension, she must be unmarried when she applied and remain unmarried to qualify. And Virginia was not the only Southern state to use such language. The pension systems of every other Southern state also required that a widow be unmarried to qualify for aid. Additionally, the Virginia Assembly dealt with specific claims by widows whose husbands had died after the war's end. In every case, the act mentions not only that the widow was destitute and deserving of state aid but also that she was unmarried and had no one else to take care of her. When Virginia lawmakers awarded Emma Guy of Campbell County, Virginia, an annual pension because she was "the widow of Samuel R. Guy . . . who died . . . leaving a widow and infant children in indigent circumstances, who still remains unmarried;" the state indicated that it was willing to step into the voids left by the deaths of its veteran and play the role of provider for their widows. But if a widow remarried, she did not need the state to be a substitute patriarch, because she was back in a traditional household with a patriarch of her own.

As Linda Gordon has argued regarding the development of the modern welfare system in the twentieth century, there have always been single mothers and poverty, but it is not until the patriarchal family and community system are perceived as breaking down that they become viewed as a "problem." Single mothers, when measured against the "norm" of the breadwinner husband/father and a domestic, economically dependent wife/mother, come up short. In an effort to buttress the norm, governmental aid is distributed in a way that preserves the status of unemployed men as the breadwinner. Aid to single mothers, on the other hand, is aimed at preventing them from becoming comfortable as single women. Like Gordon's twentieth-century single mothers, Confederate widows who were unable to remarry came up short when measured against the norm of the patriarchal family. In order to incorporate them back into the system, the state had to make sure they did not grow comfortable in their positions as single women. Thousands of Virginia widows, including Susan Rawlings and thirty-two other women from Brunswick, applied for and received pensions. The amount of pensions that widows received was certainly not enough to make a woman excessively comfortable in her widowhood, but for Rawlings and other widows who owned small amounts of property, pensions were an important source of income.

As recent historians have pointed out, the postbellum period was a period in which everything, including gender roles, was up for debate. The emancipation of thousands of slaves, the South's military loss in the war, and the political and economic conditions of Reconstruction, along with some of the war's direct effects—the "creation" of capable, independent women, the increase in the number of single women who could not marry and widows who could not remarry—cast doubt on the validity of traditional white Southern gender roles. In order for white Southern men to reassert their masculinity, they had to restake their claim to power. They did so by reaffirming the inferiority of black men and women and the dependent status of white women who needed protection and provision from white men. Because pensions were based on the premise that the patriarchal family was the norm, offering pensions to widows served to reinforce traditional gender roles in which men provided for women.

Confederate pension systems differentiated widows' pensions from veterans' pensions. Unlike in the federal system, where a widow collected a pension based on her husband's military rank, each of the Southern pension systems put widows in their own category, emphasizing the importance of aid for widows as a separate matter from providing for veterans. In a sense Confederate widows "earned" their pension simply by virtue of their widowhood. Setting widows apart in their own category reveals the importance in Southern men's eyes of providing for women, especially those who needed it the most. Through widows' pensions, Southern men could again imagine themselves as proper patriarchs. Although they turned over the antebellum responsibility of provision to the state, Southern men could still see themselves as providing for women because it was their state governments that were doing the providing.

Confederate pensions served not only the practical needs of provision but also the ideological needs of patriarchy. The willingness of state legislators in 1900 to grant pensions by individual legislation to women who did not meet the qualifications specified by the pension laws of 1888 and 1900 with language such as "without property and without means of support, *save from her own labor*," and "*is dependent upon her own labor and exertions for a living*" (my emphasis) indicates an affirmation of the traditional image of white Southern womanhood as too good for manual labor as well as the duty of white men to provide for white women. Moreover, by 1902 the Virginia Assembly was willing to provide for widows of soldiers who had simply died from old age, indicating that, for unmarried widows who had no one to support them, regardless of whether or not their men gave their lives for "the Cause," Southern men were willing to use the state to take on the role of substitute patriarch. Finally, there was the debate surrounding federal pensions for Confederates.

In 1894 several Southern Congressmen proposed a bill in the United States Congress that would have allowed Confederate veterans and widows to receive pensions from the federal government the same way that Union pensioners did. Justification for the bill generally fell along the lines that Southerners had contributed to the federal pension system through indirect taxes for years and therefore should benefit from it. Although several versions of the bill were proposed, it never passed. Even so, it engendered a lively debate among Southerners, producing both proponents and opponents in Virginia and the rest of the South. Not surprisingly, opinions on the bill generally broke down along class lines— elite white Southern men opposed the bill, while yeoman and lower-class veterans supported it. One opponent's position reveals what was at stake for elite Southern men in providing for their own. He states, "The failure of the Government of the United States to provide for our disabled soldiers has resulted most fortunately for the manhood and womanhood of the South. . . . Shall we barter this for gold? . . . No! A thousand times, no!" This bill "is inconsistent with our self-respect, and stains the record, to whose purity we devote and consecrate ourselves, our lives, our fortunes, and our sacred honor." Another opponent concurs, "A Federal pension is worse than Confederate poverty." Of course, when made by someone who does not suffer from poverty, such a statement is not all that convincing. Numerous proponents of the bill noted the hypocrisy in such proclamations, arguing that opponents were "not authorized to speak for the great body of ex-Confederates *who move in the more humble walks of life*" (emphasis added).

Confederate pensions, though ostensibly created for the very practical need of providing for needy Southern veterans and widows, also fulfilled the ideological need of buttressing traditional Southern patriarchy. The "willingness to vote pensions and constantly increase them under those circumstances [the postwar economy] indicates a popular and deliberate approval of the expenditure and a desire to make it," wrote William Glasson, a late-nineteenth-century commentator. Southerners—that is, elite Southerners, those who ran the General Assembly—recognized the value

of pensions for Southern society, both practical and ideological, and accordingly supported them.

On a wintry Sunday night, 14 December 1924, just eleven days before Christmas, Brunswick County residents mourned the loss of their oldest citizen—Confederate widow Susan Rawlings. Known to everyone as "Grandma," Susan had lived out her life, after John's death, in the same tiny cottage they had first rented in 1848. She had never remarried, and she and her children scraped by for years on the meager income that sewing and other odd jobs provided in a small Southern town. In 1888, twenty-seven years after John's death, Susan applied for and received a yearly pension of $30 from the state of Virginia because her husband had given his life for the ill-fated Confederacy. She was beloved by her family, including fifty-nine great-grandchildren and fifteen great-great-grandchildren, as well as countless friends. As one local newspaper reported, she was a woman who had "a very presence that seemed to radiate sunshine and good cheer. . . . No one ever went to her in distress or in need of sympathy without being helped," one member of her church fondly remembered. "The news of her death will be heard with regret by hundreds. . . . She was frequently a 'good angel:' " Even as late as Mother's Day 1941, "Grandma" Rawlings's family and friends memorialized her as the epitome of Southern womanhood, gracing the Mother's Day bulletin of Lawrenceville Methodist Church with her picture.

In the postbellum period, Southern society had to come to terms with the tens of thousands of Confederate widows who, like Susan Rawlings, could not remarry and therefore fell outside the traditional definitions of Southern womanhood. Eventually, Southern society solved this dilemma by collectively imagining them as noble women or, as in Susan Rawlings's case, "good angels," who sacrificed tremendously for "the Cause." They thereby expanded the boundaries of appropriate womanhood to include women who were legally autonomous as long as they were socially and economically dependent. In a New South trying to rebuild itself in the image of its past, the existence of so many manless women could have challenged the reestablishment of traditional gender assumptions. In providing wartime and postwar assistance and pensions with the justification that it was a "sacred duty" to "worthy recipients," elite Southerners effectively ensconced widows like Susan Rawlings under the banner of "good angels," thereby mollifying their potential as a threat to traditional Southern gender roles.

STUDY QUESTIONS

1. How does the author use the term "good angels" and in what ways was the term ironic?

2. Define the meaning of the term *femmes soles* and how did that legal status affect the lives of Confederate widows?

3. Describe the problems faced by a Confederate widow, and what were her options?

4. What was the state of the southern economy after the Civil War and how did that effect the adjustment of confederate widows?

5. How did the widows support themselves?

6. What does the article teach us about the social, economic, and legal environment in which southern women lived?

BIBLIOGRAPHY

For family life in the Confederate South, see Catherine Clinton, ed., *Southern Families at War: Loyalty and Conflict in the Civil War South* (2000) and Wayne K. Durrill, *War of Another Kind; A Southern Community in the Great Rebellion* (1990). The plight of southern women can be seen in George C. Rable, *Civil Wars: Women and the Crisis of Southern Nationalism* (1989). Dated but still useful are Charles W. Ramsdell, *Behind the Lines in the Southern Confederacy* (1944) and Bell I. Wiley, *The Plain People of the Confederacy* (1943). For more general social histories of Confederate life, see James L. Roark, *Masters without Slaves: Southern Planters in the Civil War and Reconstruction* (1978) and Maris A. Vinokskis, ed., *Toward a Social History of the American Civil War: Exploratory Essays* (1990). For African-American life during the Civil War, see Pauli Murray, *Proud Shoes: The Story of an American Family* (1956).

A ROAD THEY DID NOT KNOW

Larry McMurtry

The battle remains even today, over 125 years later, shrouded in mystery and a pop culture fog. The great Sioux warrior chiefs—Crazy Horse and Sitting Bull—took on one of the United States Army's most flamboyant officers, and when the dust settled, all of the white soldiers, including Lt. Col. George Armstrong Custer, were dead, killed in a tactical blunder of epic proportions. The death of Custer and the troops in his 7th Cavalry captured the American imagination in the 1870s; and since then, it has continued to inspire curiosity, awe, and inquiry. It has spawned a scholarly literature and a mythology unequaled in United States history. In the following article, one of America's most gifted novelists—Larry McMurtry—deciphers exactly what happened on June 25-26, 1876, at the Battle of the Little Big Horn, why it happened, and what it has meant to Americans.

By the summer of 1875 a crisis over the Black Hills of South Dakota could no longer be postponed. Lt. Col. George Armstrong Custer had made a grand announcement that there was gold in the hills, and it caught the nation's attention. After that miners could not be held back. The government was obviously going to find a way to take back the Black Hills, but just as obviously, it was not going to be able to do so without difficulty and without criticism. The whites in the peace party were vocal; they and others of various parties thought the government ought to at least *try* to honor its agreements, particularly those made as solemnly and as publicly as the one from 1868 giving the Sioux the Black Hills and other lands. So there ensued a period of wiggling and squirming, on the part of the government and the part of the Sioux, many of whom had become agency Indians by this time. The free life of the hunting Sioux was still just possible, but only in certain areas: the Powder River, parts of Montana, and present-day South Dakota west of the Missouri River, where the buffalo still existed in some numbers.

By this time most of the major Indian leaders had made a realistic assessment of the situation and drawn the obvious conclusion, which was that their old way of life was rapidly coming to an end. One way or another they were going to have to walk the white man's road—or else fight until they were all killed. The greatest Sioux warriors, Crazy Horse and Sitting Bull, were among the most determined of the hostiles; two others, Red Cloud and Spotted Tail, rivals at this point, both had settled constituencies. They were administrators essentially, struggling to get more food and better goods out of their respective agents. As more and more Indians came in and enrollment lists swelled, this became a full-time job, and a vexing and frustrating one at that.

There were of course many Indians who tried to walk a middle road, unwilling to give up the old

ways completely but recognizing that the presence of whites in what had once been their country was now a fact of life. Young Man Afraid of His Horses, son of the revered Old Man Afraid of His Horses, was one of the middle-of-the-roaders.

The whites at first tried pomp and circumstance, bringing the usual suspects yet again to Washington, hoping to tempt them—Red Cloud, Spotted Tail, anyone—to sell the Black Hills. They would have liked to have had Sitting Bull and Crazy Horse at this grand parley, or even a moderate, such as Young Man Afraid of His Horses, but none of these men or any of the principal hostiles wanted anything to do with this mini-summit. Red Cloud and Spotted Tail had no authority to sell the Black Hills, or to do anything about them at all, a fact the white authorities should have realized by this time. There were still thousands of Sioux on the northern plains who had not given their consent to anything. The mini-summit fizzled.

Many Indians by this time had taken to wintering in the agencies and then drifting off again once the weather improved. Thousands came in, but when spring came, many of them went out again.

Crazy Horse, who was about thirty-five years old, enjoyed in 1875–76 what was to be his last more or less unharassed winter as a free Indian. How well or how clearly he realized that his time was ending, we don't know. Perhaps he still thought that if the people fought fiercely and didn't relent, they could beat back the whites, not all the way to the Platte perhaps, but at least out of the Powder River country. We don't really know what he was thinking and should be cautious about making him more geopolitically attuned than he may have been. At this juncture nobody had really agreed to anything, but as the spring of 1876 approached, the Army directed a number of its major players toward the northern plains. To the south, on the plains of Texas, the so-called Red River War was over. The holdouts among the Comanches and the Kiowas had been defeated and their horse herd destroyed. Ranald S. Mackenzie and Nelson A. Miles both distinguished themselves in the Red River War and were soon sent

Larry McMurtry, "A Road They Did Not Know," *American Heritage,* 50 (February–March 1999), 52–65.

Sitting Bull

Lt. Col. George Armstrong Custer

north to help subdue the Cheyennes and the northern Sioux. Gen. George Crook was already in the field, and Col. John Gibbon, Gen. Alfred Terry, and, of course, George Armstrong Custer were soon on their way.

By March of 1876 a great many indians were moving north, toward Sitting Bull and the Hunkpapa band of Sioux, ready for a big hunt and possibly for a big fight with the whites, if the whites insisted on it, as in fact they did. The Little Bighorn in eastern Montana was the place chosen for this great gathering of native peoples, which swelled with more and more Indians as warmer weather came.

General Crook—also known as Three Stars, or the Grey Fox—struck first. He located what the scout Frank Grouard assured him was Crazy Horse's village, made a dawn attack, captured the village, destroyed the ample provender it contained (some of which his own hungry men could happily have eaten), but killed few Indians. Where Crazy Horse actually was at this time is a matter much debated, but the camp Crook destroyed seems not to have been his. For Crook the

encounter was more vexation than triumph. The Sioux regrouped that night and got back most of their horses, and the fight drove these peace-seeking Indians back north toward Sitting Bull. Crook continued to suppose that he had destroyed Crazy Horse's village; no doubt some of the Indian's friends were there, but the man himself was elsewhere.

A vast amount had been written about the great gathering of Indians who assembled in Montana in the early summer of 1876. It was to be the last mighty grouping of native peoples on the Great Plains of America. For the older people it evoked memories of earlier summer gatherings—reunions of a sort—such as had once been held at Bear Butte, near Crazy Horse's birthplace. Many of these Indians probably knew that what was occurring was in the nature of a last fling; there might be no opportunity for such a grand occasion again. Most of the Indians who gathered knew that the soldiers were coming, but they didn't care; their numbers were so great that they considered themselves invincible. Many Indians, from many tribes, remembered it as a last great meeting and mingling, a last good time. Historically, from this point on, there is a swelling body of reminiscence about the events of the spring and summer of 1876. Indeed, from the time the armies went into the field in 1876 to the end of the conflict, there is a voluminous memoir literature to be sifted through—most of it military memoirs written by whites. Much of this found its way into the small-town newspapers that by then dotted the plains. These memoirs are still emerging. In 1996 four letters written by the wife of a captain who was at Fort Robinson when Crazy Horse was killed were discovered and published. The woman's name was Angie Johnson. It had taken more than a century for this literature to trickle out of the attics and scrapbooks of America, and it is still trickling. Of course it didn't take that long for the stately memoirs of Generals Sheridan and Sherman and Miles and the rest to be published.

Though the bulk of this memoir literature is by white soldiers, quite a few of the Sioux and the Cheyennes who fought at the Little Bighorn managed to get themselves interviewed here and there. It is part of the wonder of the book *Son of the Morning Star* that Evan S. Connell has patiently located many of these obscurely published reminiscences from both sides of the fight and placed them in his narrative in such a way as to create a kind of mosaic of firsthand comment. These memoirs don't answer all the questions, or even very many of them, but it is still nice to know what the participants *thought* happened, even if what we're left with is a kind of mesquite thicket of opinion, dense with guessing, theory, and speculation. Any great military conflict— Waterloo, Gettysburg, et cetera—leaves behind a similar confusion, a museum of memories but an extremely untidy one. Did the general say that or do this? Was Chief Gall behind Custer or in front of him or nowhere near him? The mind that is troubled by unanswered and possibly unanswerable questions should perhaps avoid military history entirely. Battles are messy things. Military historians often have to resort to such statements as "it would at this juncture probably be safe to assume. . . ." Stephen E. Ambrose is precisely

right (and uncommonly frank) when he says plainly that much of the fun of studying the Battle of the Little Bighorn is the free rein it offers to the imagination. Once pointed toward this battle, the historical imagination tends to bolt; certainly the field of battle that the Indians called the Greasy Grass has caused many imaginations to bolt.

What we know for sure is that when June rolled around in 1876, there were a great many Indians, of several tribes, camped in southern Montana, with a fair number of soldiers moving west and north to fight them. Early June of that year may have been a last moment of confidence for the Plains Indians: They were many, they had meat, and they were in *their* place. Let the soldiers come.

This buildup of confidence was capped by what was probably the best-reported dream vision in Native American history—namely, Sitting Bull's vision of soldiers falling upside down into camp. This important vision did not come to the great Hunkpapa spontaneously; instead it was elaborately prepared for. Sitting Bull allowed a friend to cut one hundred small pieces of flesh from his arms, after which he danced, staring at the sun until he fainted. When he came out of his swoon, he heard a voice and had a vision of soldiers as numerous as grasshoppers falling upside down into camp. There were some who were skeptical of Sitting Bull—he could be a difficult sort—but this vision, coming as it did at the end of a great Sun Dance, convinced most of his people that if the soldiers did come, they would fall. (It is worth mentioning that Sitting Bull had mixed luck with visions. Not long before his death a meadowlark, speaking in Sioux, told him that his own people would kill him—which is what occurred.)

Shortly after this great vision of soldiers falling had been reported and considered, some Cheyenne scouts arrived with the news that General Crook was coming from the south with a lot of soldiers and a considerable body of Crow and Shoshone scouts. This was a sign that Sitting Bull had not danced in vain, although Crook never got very close to the great encampment, because

Crazy Horse, Sitting Bull, and a large force immediately went south to challenge him on the Rosebud Creek, where the first of the two famous battles fought that summer was joined.

When the Indians attacked, Crook's thousand-man force was very strung out, with soldiers on both sides of the river, in terrain that was broken and difficult. Crow scouts were the first to spot the great party from the north; by common agreement the Crows and Shoshones fought their hearts out that day, probably saving Crook from the embarrassment of an absolute rout. But Crazy Horse, Black Twin, Bad Heart Bull, and many others were just as determined. Once or twice Crook almost succeeded in forming an effective battle line, but Crazy Horse and the others kept dashing right into it, fragmenting Crook's force and preventing a serious counterattack. There was much close-quarter, hand-to-hand fighting. In a rare anticipation of women in combat, a Cheyenne woman rushed in at some point and saved her brother, who was surrounded. (The Cheyennes afterward referred to the Battle of the Rosebud as the Battle Where the Girl Saved Her Brother.) Crook struggled all day, trying to mount a strong offensive, but the attackers were so persistent that they thwarted him. Finally the day waned, and shadows began to fall across the Rosebud. The Indians, having enjoyed a glorious day of battle, went home. They had turned Three Stars back, allowing him nowhere near the great gathering on the Little Bighorn.

Because the indians left the field when the day was over, Crook claimed a victory, but nobody believed him, including, probably, himself. The Battle of the Rosebud was one of his most frustrating memories. It was indeed a remarkable battle between forces almost equally matched; in some ways it was more interesting than the fight at the Little Bighorn eight days later. Neither side could mount a fully decisive offensive, and both sides suffered unusually high casualties but kept fighting. The whites had no choice, of course; their adversaries in this case fought with extreme determination. The body count for the two sides varies with the commentator. Among historians who have written about the battle, George Hyde puts Crook's loss as high as fifty-seven men, a number that presumably includes many Crows and Shoshones who fell that day. Stephen Ambrose says it was twenty-eight men; Stanley Vestal says it was ten; and Robert Utley and Evan Connell claim it was nine. The attacking Sioux and Cheyennes may themselves have lost more than thirty men, an enormous casualty rate for a native force. Accustomed as we are to the wholesale slaughter of the two world wars, or even of the Civil War, it is hard to keep in mind that when Indian fought Indian, a death count of more than three or four was unusual.

At the end of the day, General Crook at last accepted the advice his scouts had offered him earlier, which was that there were too many Indians up ahead for him to fight.

Had the full extent of Crook's difficulties on the Rosebud been known to the forces moving west into Montana, the sensible officers—that is, Gibbon and Terry—would have then proceeded with extreme caution, but it is unlikely that any trouble of Crook's would have slowed Custer one whit. Even if he had known that the Indians had sent Crook packing, it is hard to imagine that he would have proceeded differently. He had plenty of explicit—and, at the last, desperate—warnings from his own scouts, but he brushed these aside as he hurried the 7th Cavalry on to its doom. He plainly did not want to give his pessimistic scouts the time of day. He refused the offer of extra troops and also refused a Gatling gun, for fear that it might slow him down and allow the Indians to get away. It was only in the last minutes of his life that Custer finally realized that the Indians were fighting, not running. Custer was convinced that he could whip whatever body of Indians he could persuade to face him. He meant to win, he meant to win alone, and he meant to win rapidly, before any other officers arrived to dilute his glory.

Custer, that erratic egotist, has been studied more than enough; he has even been the subject of one of the best books written about the West, Evan Connell's *Son of the Morning Star*. Historians have speculated endlessly about why he did what he did at the Little Bighorn on the twenty-fifth of June, 1876; and yet what he did was perfectly in keeping with his nature. He did what he had always done: push ahead, disregard orders, start a fight, win it unassisted if possible, then start another fight. He had seldom done otherwise, and there was no reason at all to expect him to do otherwise in Montana that summer.

It may be true, as several writers have suggested, that he was covertly running for President that summer. The Democratic National Convention was just convening; a flashy victory and a timely telegram might have put him in contention for the nomination. Maybe, as Connell suggests, he thought he could mop up on the Sioux, race down to the Yellowstone River, hop on the steamer *Far West,* and make it to the big opening of the Philadelphia Centennial Exposition on July 4. So he marched his men most of the night and flung them into battle when—as a number of Indians noted—they were so tired their legs shook as they dismounted. As usual, he did only minimal reconnaissance, and convinced himself on no evidence whatever that the Indians must be running away from him, not toward him. The highly experienced scouts who were with him—the half-breed Mitch Bouyer and the Arikara Bloody Knife and the Crow Half Yellow Face—all told Custer that they would die if they descended into the valley where the Indians were. None of them, in all their many years on the plains had ever seen anything to match this great encampment. All the scouts knew that the valley ahead was for them the valley of death. Half Yellow Face, poetically, told Custer that they would all go home that day by a road they did not know. The fatalism of these scouts is a story in itself. Bouyer, who knew exactly what was coming, sent the young scout Curly away but then himself rode on with Custer, to his death.

Whatever they said, what wisdom they offered, Custer ignored. It may be that he *was* running for President, but it is hard to believe that he would have done anything differently even if it had been an off year politically. Maj. Marcus Reno and Capt. Frederick Benteen, whom he had forced to split off, both testified much later that they didn't believe Custer had any plan when he pressed his attack. He was—and long had been—the most aggressive general in the American army. It didn't matter to him how many Indians there were. When he saw an enemy, he attacked, and would likely have done so even if he had had no political prospects.

In the week between the fight on the Rosebud and the one at the Little Bighorn, Crazy Horse went back to the big party. The great General Crook had been whipped; the Indians felt invincible again. Everyone knew that more soldiers were coming, but no one was particularly concerned. These soldiers could be whipped in turn.

Some commentators have suggested that a sense of doom and foreboding hung over the northern plains during this fatal week; Indian and soldier alike were said to feel it. Something dark and terrible was about to happen—and yet it was high summer in one of the most beautiful places in Montana, the one time when that vast plain is usually free of rain clouds or snow clouds. But this summer, Death was coming to a feast, and many felt his approach. On the morning of the battle, when most of the Sioux and Cheyennes were happily and securely going about their domestic business, never supposing that any soldiers would be foolish enough to attack them, Crazy Horse, it is said, marked a bloody hand in red pigment on both of his horse's hips and drew an arrow and a bloody scalp on both sides of his horse's neck. Oglala scouts had been keeping watch on Custer, following his movements closely. Crazy Horse either knew or sensed that the fatal day had come.

The Battle of the Little Bighorn, June 25 and 26, 1876, is one of the most famous battles in world history. I doubt that any other American battle—not the Alamo, not Gettysburg—has spawned a more extensive or more diverse literature. There are books, journals, newsletters, one or another of which has by now printed every scrap of reminiscence that has been dredged up. Historians, both professional and amateur, have poured forth voluminous speculations, wondering what would have happened if somebody—usually the unfortunate Major Reno—had done something differently, or if Custer hadn't foolishly split his command, or if and if and if. Though the battle took place more than 120 years ago, debate has not much slackened. In fact the sudden rise in Native American studies has resulted in increased reprinting of Indian as opposed to white reminiscences; now the Sioux and the Cheyennes are pressing the debate.

A number of white historians have argued that one or another Indian leader made the decisive moves that doomed Custer and the 7th; for these historians the battle was decided by strategy and generalship, not numbers. Both Stephen Ambrose and Mari Sandoz have written many pages about the brilliance of Crazy Horse in flanking Custer and seizing the high ground—today called Custer Hill—thus ending Custer's last hope of establishing a defensive position that might have held until reinforcements arrived. Others argue for their favorite chief, whether Gall, Two Moon, or another. Evan Connell, in his lengthy account of the battle, scarcely mentions Crazy Horse's part in it. All these arguments, of course, depend on Indian memory, plus study of the battleground itself. To me they seem to be permanently ambiguous, potent rather than conclusive. It is indeed an area of study where historians can give free rein to their imaginations; what Stephen Ambrose doesn't mention is that the Sioux and the Cheyennes, in remembering this battle, might be giving *their* imaginations a little running room as well. A world in which all whites are poets and all Indians sober reporters is not the world as most of us know it.

We are likely never to know for sure who killed Custer. He had his famous hair short for this campaign; had it still been long, many Indians might have recognized him. It is as well to keep in mind that as many as two thousand horses may have been in motion during this battle; between the dust they raised and the gun smoke, the scene would have become phantasmagorical; it would have been difficult for anyone

to see well, or far. It is thus little wonder that no one recognized Custer. At some sharp moment Custer must have realized that his reasoning had been flawed. The Indians he had assumed were running away were actually coming to kill him, and there were a lot of them. Whether he much regretted his error is doubtful. Fighting was what Custer did, battle thrilled him, and now he was right in the dead thick of the biggest Indian fight of all. He may have enjoyed himself right up to the moment he fell.

For his men, of course, it was a different story. They had been marching since the middle of the night; a lot of them were so tired they could barely lift their guns. For them it was dust, weariness, terror, and death.

No one knows for certain how many Indians fought in this battle, but two thousand is a fair estimate, give or take a few hundred. Besides their overpowering numbers they were also highly psyched by the great Sun Dance and their recent victory over Crook. When Major Reno and his men appeared at the south end of the great four-mile village, the Indians were primed. Reno might have charged them and produced, at least, disarray, but he didn't; the Indians soon chased him back across the Little Bighorn and up a bluff, where he survived, just barely. A lucky shot hit Bloody Knife, the Arikara scout, square in the head; Major Reno, standing near, was splattered with his brain matter. Some think this gory accident undid Major Reno, but we will never know the state of his undoneness, if any. Gall, the Hunkpap warrior, who, by common agreement, was a major factor in this battle, soon had fifteen hundred warriors mounted and ready to fight. If Reno *had* charged the south end of the village, he might have been massacred as thoroughly as Custer.

Exactly when Crazy Horse entered the battle is a matter of debate. Some say he rode out and skirmished a little with Reno's men; others believe he was still in his lodge when Reno arrived and that he was interested only in the larger fight with Custer. Most students of the battle think that when it dawned on Custer that he was in a fight for survival, not glory, he turned north, toward the high ground, hoping to establish a defensive redoubt on the hill, or rise, that is now named for him. But Crazy Horse, perhaps at the head of as many as a thousand warriors himself, flanked him and seized that high ground, sealing Custer's doom while, incidentally, making an excellent movie role for Errol Flynn and a number of other leading men.

So Crazy Horse may have done, but it was Gall and *his* thousand or so warriors who turned back Reno and then harried Custer so hard that the 7th Cavalry—the soldiers who fell into camp, as in Sitting Bull's vision—could never really establish *any* position. If Crazy Horse did flank Custer, it was of course good quarter-backing, but it hardly seems possible now to insist that any one move was decisive. Gall and his men might have finished Custer without much help from anyone; Gall had lost two of his wives and three of his children early in the battle and was fighting out his anger and his grief.

From this distance of years the historians can argue until their teeth rot that one man or another was decisive in this battle, but all these arguments are unprovable now. What's certain is that George Armstrong Custer was very foolish, a glory hound who ignored orders, skipped or disregarded his reconnaissance, and charged, all but blindly, into a situation in which, whatever the quality of Indian generalship, he was quickly overwhelmed by numbers.

What I think of when I walk that battleground is dust. Once or twice in my life I rode out with as many as thirty cowboys; I remember the dust that small, unhurried group made. The dust of two thousand milling, charging horses would have been something else altogether; the battleground would soon have been a hell of dust, smoke, shooting, hacking; once the two groups of fighting men closed with each other, visibility could not have been good. Custer received a wound in the breast and one in the temple, either of which would have been fatal. His corpse was neither scalped nor mutilated. Bad Soup, a Hunkpapa, is said to have pointed out Custer's corpse to White Bull. "There he lies," he said. "He thought he was going to be the greatest man in the world. But there he is."

Most of the poetic remarks that come to us from this battle are the work of writers who interviewed Indians, or those who knew Indians, who thought they remembered Bad Soup saying something, or Half Yellow Face making (probably in sign) the remark about the road we do not know, or Bloody Knife staring long at the sun that morning, knowing that he would not be alive to see it go down behind the hills that evening. All we can conclude now is that Bloody Knife and Bad Soup and Half Yellow Face were right, even if they didn't say the words that have been attributed to them.

Hundreds of commentators, from survivors who fought in the battle to historians who would not be born until long years after the dust had settled in the valley of the Little Bighorn, have developed opinions about scores of issues that remain, in the end, completely opaque. Possibly Crazy Horse fought as brilliantly as some think—we will never really know—but he and Sitting Bull and Two Moon survived the battle and Custer didn't. General Grant, no sentimentalist, put the blame for the defeat squarely on Custer, and said so bluntly. The Indians made no serious attempt to root out and destroy Reno, though they could have. Victory over Long Hair was enough; Custer's famous 1868 dawn attack on the Cheyenne chief Black Kettle was well avenged.

The next day, to Major Reno's vast relief, the great gathering broke up, the Indians melting away into the sheltering vastness of the plains.

What did the Sioux and Cheyenne leaders think at this point? What did they feel? Several commentators have suggested that once the jubilation of victory subsided, a mood of foreboding returned. Perhaps the tribes recognized that they were likely never to be so unified again, and they were not. Perhaps the leaders knew that they were likely never to have such a one-sided military victory again either—a victory that was thrown them because of the vainglory of one white officer.

Or perhaps they didn't think in these terms at all—not yet. With the great rally over, the great battle won, they broke up and got on with their hunting. Perhaps a few did reckon that something was over now, but it is doubtful that many experienced the sense of climax and decline as poetically as Old Lodge Skins in Thomas Berger's novel *Little Big Man:* "Yes, my son," he says, "it is finished now, because what more can you do to an enemy than beat him? Were we fighting red men against red men—the way we used to, because that is a man's profession, and besides it is enjoyable—it would now be the turn of the other side to whip us. We would fight as hard as ever and perhaps win again, but they would definitely start with an advantage, because that is the *right* way. There is no permanent winning or losing when things move, as they should, in a circle. . . .

"But white men, who live in straight lines and squares, do not believe as I do. With them it is everything or nothing: Washita or Greasy Grass. . . . Winning is all they care about, and if they can do that by scratching a pen across a paper or saying something into the wind, they are much happier. . . ."

Old Lodge Skins was right about the Army's wanting to win. Crook's defeat at the Rosebud had embarrassed the Army, and the debacle at the Little Bighorn shamed it. The nation, of course, was outraged. By August of 1876 Crook and Terry were lumbering around with a reassuring force of some four thousand soldiers. Naturally they found few Indians. Crazy Horse was somewhere near Bear Butte, harrying the miners in the Black Hills pretty much as the mood struck him. There was a minor engagement or two, of little note. The Indians were not suicidal; they left the massive force alone. Crook and Terry were such respecters now that they were bogged down by their own might.

In the fall of that year, the whites, having failed to buy the Black Hills, simply took them, with a travesty of a treaty council at which the Indians lost not only the Black Hills but the Powder River, the Yellowstone, the Bighorns. By the end of what was in some ways a year of glory, 1876, Crazy Horse had to face the fact that his people had come to a desperate pass. It was a terrible winter, with subzero temperatures day after day. The Indians were ragged and hungry; the soldiers who opposed them were warmly clothed and well equipped. The victories of the previous summer were, to the Sioux and the Cheyennes, now just memories. They had little ammunition and were hard pressed to find game enough to feed themselves.

During this hard period, with the soldiers just waiting for spring to begin another series of attacks, Sitting Bull decided to take himself and his people to Canada. Crazy Horse perhaps considered this option and then rejected it because in Canada the weather was even colder, or maybe he just didn't want to leave home. But in early May of 1877, he had eleven hundred people with him, and more than two thousand horses, when he came into Red Cloud agency at Fort Robinson in northwestern Nebraska. Probably neither the generals nor Crazy Horse himself ever quite believed that a true surrender had taken place, but this august event, the surrender of "Chief" Crazy Horse was reported in *The New York Times* on May 8, 1877.

STUDY QUESTIONS

1. What happened to Native Americans on the Great Plains in the nineteenth century and why did so many Indian leaders feel that they had no choice but to "either walk the white man's road" or die fighting?

2. Describe Crazy Horse and Sitting Bull.

3. What role did General George Crook play in the events leading up to Little Big Horn?

4. Why, in early June 1876, did the Indians consider themselves invincible in face of the invading white army?

5. Describe the personality of Lieutenant Colonel George Armstrong Custer?

6. When Custer's troops went into battle, what disadvantages did they face? How did Custer's personality contribute to their problems? What miscalculations did Custer make just prior to the battle?

7. What happened to the Sioux and to the Black Hills after the battle?

BIBLIOGRAPHY

For general surveys of the "conquest" of the American West, see Patricia Nelson Limerick, *The Legacy of Conquest: The Unbroken Past of the American West* (1987) and *"It's Your Misfortune and None of My Own": A History of the American West* (1991). Excellent studies of the Plains Indians include Morris W. Foster, *Being Comanche: A Social History of an American Indian Community* (1991) and Catherine Price, *The Oglala People, 1841-1879* (1996). For biographies of the major figures involved in the Battle of the Little Big Horn, see John G. Neihardt, *Black Elk Speaks: Being the Life Story of a Holy Man of the Oglala Sioux* (1961); Mari Sandoz, *Crazy Horse: The Strange Man of the Oglalas* (1961); Robert M. Utley, *Cavalier in Buckskin: George Armstrong Custer and the Western Military Frontier* (1988) and *The Lance and the Shield: The Life and Times of Sitting Bull* (1993).

PART TWO

The Gilded Age

Change dominated the American scene during the last quarter of the nineteenth century. Noted throughout most of the century for its agricultural output, America suddenly became an industrial giant, and by 1900 it led the world in industrial production. Unfettered by governmental codes and regulations, industrialists created sprawling empires. In 1872, Scottish immigrant Andrew Carnegie built his first steel mill, and his holdings steadily expanded until, almost 30 years later, he sold his steel empire to J. Pierpont Morgan for close to a half-billion dollars. In oil, meat packing, and other industries the pattern was the same—a handful of ruthless, efficient, and farsighted men dominated and directed America's industrial growth.

Just as important as the ambitious industrialists were the millions of men and women who provided the muscle that built the industries and ran the machines. Some came from the country's farmlands, victims of dropping agricultural prices or of the loneliness and boredom of farm life. Others were immigrants who came to the United States to escape poverty and political oppression. Crowded into booming cities, the workers—native and immigrant alike—labored long and hard for meager rewards.

The changes wrought by industrial growth and urban expansion created an atmosphere characterized by excitement and confusion. Some people, like Andrew Carnegie and John D. Rockefeller, moved from relatively humble origins to fabulous wealth and impressive social standing. Each symbolized the possibility of rising from rags to riches. New opportunities created new wealth, and the important older American families were forced to make room for the new. As a result, wealthy Americans went to extraordinary lengths to display their status. J. P. Morgan bought yachts and works of art, while other industrialists built mansions along the rocky shore of Newport, Rhode Island. Both the boats and houses marked the owners as men who had "arrived." The clubs, restaurants, and resorts of the late nineteenth century were part of an attempt to define the new American aristocracy.

Other people suffered during this time of change. For example, the social and economic positions of farmers declined during the late nineteenth century. Once considered the "salt of the earth" and "the backbone of America," they were instead

viewed as ignorant rubes and country bumpkins. Outmatched by unpredictable weather, expanding railroads, and declining prices produced by overexpansion, they consistently tried to overcome their problems by working harder, organizing cooperatives, and forming political parties. They labored heroically, but most of their efforts and organizations ended in failure.

Minority and ethnic Americans similarly faced difficult battles. Most of them were locked out of the opportunities available to educated white male Americans. It was also difficult for women to improve their social and economic positions. They experienced the excitement of the period from a distance, but they knew the pain and frustration firsthand.

AMERICAN ASSASSIN: CHARLES J. GUITEAU

James W. Clarke

Abraham Lincoln, James Garfield, William McKinley, Huey Long, John Kennedy, Robert Kennedy, Martin Luther King, Jr.—our history has been too often altered by an assassin's bullet. Some of America's political assassins were clearly insane, others were motivated by political beliefs or dark personal desires. Normally it is difficult to determine where political partisanship ends and insanity begins. In "American Assassin," James W. Clarke recounts the case of Charles J. Guiteau, a tireless self-promoter who shot President James A. Garfield on July 2, 1881. Guiteau was certainly unusual; part con man, part religious fanatic, he believed he was destined for some sort of greatness. But was he insane? And if so, was his insanity a legal defense for his actions? These and other questions had to be answered by the jurors who sat in judgment of Guiteau. In an age before Sigmund Freud's work, when individuals were held responsible for their own actions, these questions were difficult, if not impossible, to fully answer.

With the single exception of Richard Lawrence, there has been no American assassin more obviously deranged than Charles Guiteau. Unlike Lawrence [who attempted to assassinate Andrew Jackson], however, who could be described as a paranoid schizophrenic, Guiteau was not paranoid. Indeed, he possessed a rather benign view of the world until shortly before he was hanged. On the gallows, he did lash out at the injustice of his persecutors, but even then his anger was tempered by a sense of martyrdom, glories anticipated in the next world, and a dying man's belief that in the future a contrite nation would erect monuments in his honor.

That Lawrence was confined in mental hospitals for the remainder of his life and Guiteau hanged can be attributed primarily to two facts: Jackson survived; Garfield did not. For certainly the symptoms of severe mental disturbance in Guiteau's case, although of a different sort, were as striking as in Lawrence's. As we will see, the convenient label and implied motive—"disappointed office-seeker"—that has been attached to Guiteau by writers and historians confuses symptoms with causes.

Religion, Law, and Politics

Charles Julius Guiteau was born on September 8, 1841, in Freeport, Illinois. His mother, a quiet, frail woman, died seven years later of complications stemming from a mind-altering "brain fever" she had initially contracted during her pregnancy with Charles. In addition to Charles, she was survived by her husband, Luther, an intensely religious man and Charles' older brother and sister, John and Frances.

From the beginning, people noticed that little Julius, as he was called (until he dropped the name in his late teens because "there was too much of the Negro about it"), was different.

Clarke, James W., *American Assassins: The Darker Side of Politics.* Copyright © 1982 by Princeton University Press. Excerpt. pp. 198–214, reprinted by permission of Princeton University Press.

Luther Guiteau soon became exasperated with his inability to discipline his unruly and annoying youngest son and, as a result, Julius was largely raised by his older sister and her husband, George Scoville. Years later, in 1881, Scoville would be called to represent the accused assassin at his trial.

Although plagued by a speech impediment, for which he was whipped by his stern father, Guiteau was, in his fashion, a rather precocious youngster who learned to read quickly and write well. An annoying aversion to physical labor was observed early and remained with him the rest of his life. At the age of eighteen, Charles became interested in furthering his education and, against his father's will, used a small inheritance he had received from his grandfather to enter the University of Michigan.

His father, who was scornful of secular education, had urged his son to seek a scripture-based education at the utopian Oneida Community in New York. The curriculum there focused on study of the Bible. The elder Guiteau had hopes that his errant son might also acquire some self-discipline in a more authoritarian God-fearing environment.

After a couple of semesters at Ann Arbor, Charles, as he was now called, decided to heed his father's advice and transfer to Oneida where, in addition to religious instruction, he had recently learned that they practiced free love. With sex and the Lord on his mind, he enthusiastically entered the New York commune in June 1860. Like his father, Charles now believed that Oneida was the first stage in establishing the Kingdom of God on Earth.

Not long after his arrival, Charles came to believe that he had been divinely ordained to lead the community because, as he announced with a typical lack of humility, he alone possessed the ability. Since no one else had received this revelation, Charles soon found himself at odds with the community leadership. Moreover, the Oneida leaders believed that Charles' vigorously protested need of increasing periods for contemplative pursuits was merely evidence of the slothfulness his father had hoped they would correct.

Other tensions also began to build. Young Charles was becoming increasingly frustrated because the young women of the community were not responding to his amorous overtures. Convinced of his personal charm, this nervous, squirrel-like little man was annoyed because these objects of his intended affection were so unresponsive. Adding insult to injury they soon laughingly referred to him as Charles "Gitout."

As his position within the community continued to deteriorate, Charles became more isolated and alienated until, in April 1865, he left for New York City. He wrote to his father to explain his decision after arriving in Hoboken:

Dear Father:

I have left the community. The cause of my leaving was because I could not conscientiously and heartily accept their views on the labor question. They wanted to make a hard-working businessman of me, but I could not consent to that, and therefore deemed it expedient to quietly withdraw, which I did last Monday. . . .

I came to New York in obedience to what I believed to be the call of God for the purpose of pursuing an independent course of theological and historical investigation. With the Bible for my textbook and the Holy Ghost for my schoolmaster, I can pursue my studies without interference from human dictation. In the country [Oneida] my time was appropriated, but now it is at my own disposal, a very favorable change. I have procured a small room, well furnished, in Hoboken, opposite the city, and intend to fruitfully pursue my studies during the next three years.

Then he announced a new scheme:

And here it is proper to state that the energies of my life are now, and have been for months, pledged to God, to do all that within me lies to extend the sovereignty of Jesus Christ by placing at his disposal a powerful daily paper. I am persuaded that theocratic presses are destined, in due time, to supersede to a great extent pulpit oratory. There are hundreds of thousands of ministers in the world but not a single daily theocratic press. It appears to me that there is a splendid chance for some one to do a big thing for God, for humanity and for himself.

With a new suit of clothes, a few books, and a hundred dollars in his pocket, he planned to publish his own religious newspaper that would, he was convinced, spearhead a national spiritual awakening.

In another lengthy letter to his father, Charles continued to detail his plans for the "Theocratic Daily" that would "entirely discard all muddy theology, brain philosophy and religious cant, and seek to turn the heart of men toward the living God." Buoyed with an ill-founded sense of well-being and enthusiasm, Charles went on euphorically: "I claim that I am in the employ of Jesus Christ and Co., the very ablest and strongest firm in the universe, and that what I can do is limited only by their power and purpose." And knowing full well that *he* would edit the paper, he announced confidently:

Whoever edits such a paper as I intend to establish will doubtless occupy the position of Target General to the Press, Pulpit, and Bench of the civilized world; and if God intends me for that place, I fear not, for I know that He will be "a wall of fire round me," and keep me from all harm.

Confidently expecting to promote the Kingdom of God without the restrictions of the Oneida Community and, not incidentally, also enjoy wealth and fame in the process, Guiteau sought financial backing for the paper in New York City. In a flurry of optimistic salesmanship, he scurried about presenting his proposal to prospective subscribers and advertisers; they, as it turned out, were not impressed with this odd little entrepreneur and his religious views. Soon finding himself short of money, somewhat discouraged, and tiring of a diet of dried beef, crackers, and lemonade that he ate in his dingy Hoboken room, Charles returned to Oneida after only three months in the big city.

But his return only confirmed his original reservations about the place, and he soon left again—this time more embittered by his experiences there than ever before. Again without money, Charles wrote to the Community requesting a $9,000 reimbursement—$1,500 a year for the six years he had spent there. When the community refused to pay, Charles sued, threatening to make public the alleged sexual, as well as financial, exploitation employed by the Oneida leadership—especially its founder, John Humphrey Noyes.

Undoubtedly bitter about the rejection he had endured in this sexually permissive environment, Charles lashed out in an unintentionally amusing attack on both Noyes and the Oneida women. Charging that Noyes lusted after little girls, Guiteau angrily told a reporter: "All the girls that were born in the Community were forced to cohabit with Noyes at such an early period it dwarfed them. The result was that most of the Oneida women were small and thin and homely."

Obviously stung by such criticism, Noyes threatened to bring extortion charges against Guiteau. In a letter to Charles' father, who was mortified by his son's behavior, he advised that Charles had admitted to, among other sins, stealing money, frequenting brothels, and being treated for a venereal ailment. Noyes added that Charles also had apparently thrown in the towel, so to speak, in an uninspired battle with masturbation. Such appraisals confirmed his father's sad suspicion that Charles' real purpose in going to Oneida was "the free exercise of his unbridled lust." Charles' "most shameful and wicked attack" and subsequent episodes convinced Luther Guiteau that his prodigal son was "absolutely insane." In despair, he wrote to his oldest son John that, unless something stopped him, Charles would become "a fit subject for the lunatic asylum."

Having thus incurred his father's anger and facing the prospects of a countersuit for extortion, Charles abandoned his legal claim and left New York for Chicago. There, given the standards of the day, he began to practice law, after a fashion. In 1869, he married a young woman he had met at the Y.M.C.A., a Miss Annie Bunn. After only one memorably incoherent attempt to argue a case, his practice of law was reduced to collecting delinquent bills for clients. By 1874, the law practice and marriage had both failed, the latter as a result of his adultery with a "high toned" prostitute and the occasional beatings he used to discipline his beleaguered wife.

When his marriage ended, Charles wandered back to New York. Continually borrowing small sums of money that he never repaid voluntarily, Guiteau soon found himself, as usual, in trouble with creditors. Resentful of such unseemly harassment, he wrote an indignant letter to his brother John addressing him as "Dear Sir." This and other letters reveal the unfounded arrogance and unintentional humor of a man with only the most tenuous grasp of the reality of his position:

Your letter from Eaton . . . dated Nov. 8, '72, received. I got the $75 on my supposed responsibility as a Chicago lawyer. I was introduced to Eaton by a gentleman I met at the Young Men's Christian Association, and it was only incidentally that your name was mentioned.

I wrote to Eaton several times while at Chicago, and he ought to have been satisfied, but he had the impertinence to write you and charge me with fraud, when he knew he let me have the money entirely upon my own name and position. Had he acted like a "white" man, I should have tried to pay it long ago. I hope you will drop him.

Yours truly,
CHARLES J. GUITEAU.

A few days after this letter was written, Charles' exasperated brother himself became the target of an angry response when he requested a repayment of a small loan:

J. W. GUITEAU: NEW YORK, March 13th, 1873
   Find $7 enclosed. Stick it up your bung-hole and wipe your nose on it, and that will remind you of the estimation in which you are held by
                              CHARLES J. GUITEAU

   Sign and return the enclosed receipt and I will send you $7, but not before, and that, I hope, will end our acquaintance.

Disdainful of the pettiness of such small lenders, Charles confidently launched another major venture in the publishing business: he wanted to purchase the Chicago *Inter-Ocean* newspaper. But businessmen and bankers, from whom he sought financial backing, were unimpressed and not a little skeptical about this seedy little man with a confidential manner. Frustrated but ever the undaunted optimist, Charles turned again to religion.

Impressed with the bountiful collection plates at the Chicago revival meetings of Dwight Moody where he served as an usher in the evening services, Charles decided to prepare himself for the ministry. After a short period of voracious reading in Chicago libraries, he soon had himself convinced that he alone had ascertained the "truth" on a number of pressing theological questions. With familiar enthusiasm, he launched his new career with pamphlets and newspaper advertisements. Adorned with sandwich board posters, Charles walked the streets inviting all who would listen to attend his sermons on the physical existence of hell, the Second-Coming, and so forth. The self-promotion campaign was repeated in one town after another as he roamed between Milwaukee, Chicago, New York, and Boston.

In handbills, Charles proclaimed himself "the Eloquent Chicago Lawyer." His performances, in fact, followed a quite different pattern: a bombastic introduction that soon deteriorated into a series of incoherent nonsequiturs, whereupon he would end inconclusively and abruptly dash from

the building amid the jeers and laughter of his audiences—the whole episode lasting perhaps ten to fifteen minutes. With his dubious reputation as an evangelist growing, Charles darted from one town to another leaving in his path a growing accumulation of indignant audiences and unpaid bills. Often arrested, he was periodically jailed for short periods between 1877 and 1880 when he again turned his attention to politics.

The Garfield Connection

Describing himself as a "lawyer, theologian, and politician," Guiteau threw himself into the Stalwart faction's fight for the 1880 Republican presidential nomination in New York. When a third term was denied the Stalwart's choice, Ulysses S. Grant, the nomination went to a darkhorse, James A. Garfield. Guiteau quickly jumped on the Garfield bandwagon. In New York, he began to hang around the party headquarters and, as he was to remind people later, he did work on the "canvass" for the candidate. In his view, his most noteworthy contribution to the campaign and Garfield's subsequent election, however, was an obscure speech he wrote (and may have delivered once in Troy, New York) entitled, "Garfield vs. Hancock." A few weeks before, the same speech had been entitled "Grant vs. Hancock." Undeterred by the change in candidates, the speech, Guiteau later claimed, originated and developed the issue that won the election for Garfield. That issue, in brief, was the claim that if the Democrats gained the presidency it would mean a resumption of the Civil War because the Democrats had only sectional, rather than national, loyalties. In a personal note, dated March 11, 1881, to the newly appointed secretary of state, James G. Blaine, Guiteau explained his claim:

I think I have a right to claim your help on the strength of this speech. It was sent to our leading editors and orators in August. It was the first shot in the rebel war claim idea, and it was their idea that elected Garfield. . . . I will talk with you about this as soon as I can get a chance. There is nothing against me. I claim to be a gentlemen and a Christian.

Indeed, from the moment the election results were in, Guiteau had begun to press his claims in letters to Garfield and Blaine. He also became a familiar figure at the Republican party headquarters in New York, confident that he would be rewarded for his efforts with a consulship appointment; the only question remaining, he believed, was the location. Would it be Paris, Vienna, or some other post of prominence? With this in mind, he moved from New York to Washington on March 5, 1881, where he began to badger not only the President's staff but Blaine and the President himself in the corridors of the White House. Striking a posture of gallingly unwarranted familiarity with those he encountered, he also let loose a barrage of "personal" notes written in the same annoying style. Typical is the following:

[Private]
GEN'L GARFIELD
From your looks yesterday I judge you did not quite understand what I meant by saying "I have not called for two or three weeks." I intended to express my sympathy for you on account of the pressure that has been on you since you came into office.

I think Mr. Blaine intends giving me the Paris consulship with your and Gen. Logan's approbation, and I am waiting for the break in the Senate.

I have practiced law in New York and Chicago, and presume I am well qualified for it.

I have been here since March 5, and expect to remain some little time, or until I get my commission.

Very respectfully,
CHARLES GUITEAU.
AP'L 8.

Shortly before he had written to the secretary of state to inquire whether President Hayes' appointments to foreign missions would expire in March 1881, as he expected. Learning that they would, Guiteau became more persistent in pressing his claims for an appointment to the missions of either Vienna, Paris, or possibly Liverpool. Earlier he had written again to Garfield, whom he had never met, to advise him of his plans to wed a wealthy and cultured woman (whose acquaintance, also, he had not at that time, or ever, made). Such unknowingly ludicrous acts were intended, in the bizarre judgment of Charles J. Guiteau, to enhance his already eminent qualifications for a foreign ministry.

In the meantime, the newspapers were filled with the controversy that had developed between the new President and the boss-dominated Stalwart faction of the Republican party over patronage appointments in New York. Finally, on May 13, 1881, the two most powerful of the Stalwart bosses, Roscoe Conkling and Tom "Me Too" Platt of New York, resigned their Senate seats in protest over the President's failure to follow their preferences in his patronage appointments. In so doing, they discounted the fact that Garfield had accepted their man, "Chet" Arthur, as his running mate and vice-president. Angrily condemning the beleaguered Garfield's disloyalty and traitorous tactics, the resignations triggered numerous editorial attacks and denunciations of the President and his mentor Blaine, which were to continue until July 2, 1881.

On the same day the resignations were announced, Guiteau once again approached Blaine with his by now familiar blandishments, only to have the exasperated secretary roar, "Never bother me again about the Paris consulship as long as you live!" But Guiteau persisted. A week later, he wrote again to the President:

[Private]
General GARFIELD:
I have been trying to be your friend; I don't know whether you appreciate it or not, but I am moved to call your attention to the remarkable letter from Mr. Blaine which I have just noticed.

According to Mr. Farwell, of Chicago, Blaine is "a vindictive politician" and "an evil genius," and you will "*have no peace till you get rid of him.*"

This letter shows Mr. Blaine is a wicked man, and you ought to demand his immediate resignation; otherwise you and the Republican party will come to grief. I will see you in the morning, if I can, and talk with you.

Very respectfully
CHARLES GUITEAU.
May 23.

If past behavior is any clue to the future, at this point Guiteau would have begun to consider yet another occupational change, returning again perhaps with his typical enthusiastic optimism to theology or law. Previously, Guiteau had accepted failure with remarkable equanimity, sustained always by the exalted opinion he had of himself. As one scheme after another collapsed—his leadership aspirations at Oneida, his journalistic ventures, the law practice, and the evangelistic crusade—his bitterness and disappointment were short-lived as he moved on to other careers. His confidence in his own ability and the Horatio Alger-like opportunities that abounded in nineteenth-century America remained unshaken. Even his angry exchanges with the Oneida establishment possessed the tone of someone who enjoyed the battle as well as the spoils; certainly these exchanges reflected none of the desperation of the all-time loser that he, in fact, was. In Guiteau's delusional world, these frustrations were merely temporary set backs in a career that was, he remained convinced, destined for wealth and fame.

Now, for the first time in his oddly chaotic life, Guiteau found himself sharing his outsider status with men he admired: Conkling and Platt and the other Stalwarts. And it was in this realization—not the denial of the various appointments he had sought—that his assassination scheme germinated. Indeed, a month later, on June 16, he wrote in his "Address to the American People":

I conceived of the idea of removing the President four weeks ago. Not a soul knew of my purpose. I conceived the idea myself. I read the newspapers carefully, for and against the administration, and gradually the conviction settled on me that the President's removal was a political necessity, because he proved a traitor to the men who made him, and thereby imperiled the life of the Republic. At the late Presidential election, the Republican party carried every Northern State. Today, owing to the misconduct of the President and his Secretary of State, they could hardly carry ten Northern States. They certainly could not carry New York, and that is the pivotal State.

Ingratitude is the basest of crimes. That the President, under the manipulation of his Secretary of State, has been guilty of the basest ingratitude to the Stalwarts admits of no denial. . . . In the President's madness he has wrecked the once grand old Republican party; and for this he dies. . . .

I had no ill-will to the President.

This is not murder. It is a political necessity. It will make my friend Arthur President, and save the Republic. I have sacrificed only one. I shot the President as I would a rebel, if I saw him pulling down the American flag. I leave my justification to God and the American people.

I expect President Arthur and Senator Conkling will give the nation the finest administration it has ever had. They are honest and have plenty of brains and experience.

[signed] Charles Guiteau [Emphasis added.]

Later, on June 20, he added this even more bizarre postscript:

The President's nomination was an act of God. The President's election was an act of God. The President's removal is an act of God. I am clear in my purpose to remove the President. Two objects will be accomplished: It will unite the Republican party and save the Republic, and it will create a great demand for my book, "The

Charles J. Guiteau, assassin of President James Garfield (1881). Much of the public viewed his insanity plea as a dodge, arguing that Guiteau's methodical planning and self-seeking motives could not be the product of a disturbed mind.

Truth," This book was written to save souls and not for money, and the Lord wants to save souls by circulating the book.

Charles Guiteau

It is unlikely that Guiteau would have chosen the course of action he did without the sense that he was in good company—"a Stalwart of the Stalwarts," as he liked to describe himself. In his distorted mind, to "remove" the President, as he euphemistically described it, would provide the same status and recognition he had sought in a consulship appointment, and, more importantly, in every hare-brained scheme he had botched since the time he first entered the Oneida Community to establish the Kingdom of God on Earth. In this last grandly deluded plan, his aspirations in theology, law, and politics were to culminate in a divinely inspired and just act "to unite the Republican party and save the Republic" and, not incidentally, launch a new career for Charles Guiteau

not only as a lawyer, theologian, and politician, but as a national hero with presidential aspirations.

With this in mind, on June 8, Guiteau borrowed fifteen dollars and purchased a silver-mounted English revolver. He planned to have it, along with his papers, displayed after the assassination at the Library of the State Department or the Army Medical Museum. To prepare for the big event, he began target practice on the banks of the Potomac. After stalking the President for several weeks and bypassing at least two opportunities to shoot him, Guiteau rose early on Saturday, July 2, 1881. He had rented a room a few days before at the Riggs House and, on this morning, began preparations to meet the President at the Baltimore and Potomac Railroad Station. The President was scheduled to leave that morning for a vacation trip. Downing a hearty breakfast, which he charged to his room, he pocketed the last of a series of bizarre explanations:

July 2, 1881

To the White House:

The President's tragic death was a sad necessity, but it will unite the Republican party and save the Republic. Life is a fleeting dream, and it matters little when one goes. A human life is of small value. During the war thousands of brave boys went down without a tear. I presume the President was a Christian, and that he will be happier in Paradise than here.

It will be no worse for Mrs. Garfield, dear soul, to part with her husband this way than by natural death. He is liable to go at any time anyway.

I had no ill-will towards the President. His death was a political necessity. I am a lawyer, a theologian, a politician. I am a Stalwart of the Stalwarts. I was with General Grant and the rest of our men in New York during the canvass. I have some papers for the press, which I shall leave with Byron Andrews and his co-journalists at 1440 N.Y. Ave., where all the reporters can see them. I am going to jail.

[signed] Charles Guiteau

Guiteau then walked to the banks of the Potomac where after taking a few final practice shots he proceeded to the railroad station to await the President's arrival. Once at the station, he used the men's room, had his shoes shined, and, after estimating that his assignment would be completed shortly before the President's train was scheduled to leave, he reserved a hackman for an anticipated 9:30 arrest and departure to the District Prison. He had already checked the prison's security, lest in the emotion of the moment he might be attacked by crowds who had not had time to realize what a great patriotic service he had just rendered. He was convinced that after his explanation was published the wisdom and justice of his act would be appreciated. Until such time, however, he had taken a further precaution of drafting a letter requesting that General Sherman see to his safekeeping in jail. The letter, which fell from his pocket during the scuffle that followed the shooting, read as follows:

TO GENERAL SHERMAN:

I have just shot the President. I shot him several times, as I wished him to go as easily as possible. His death was a political necessity. I am a lawyer, theologian and politician. I am a Stalwart of the Stalwarts. I was with General Grant and the rest of our men in New York during the canvass. I am going to jail. Please order out your troops and take possession of the jail at once.

Very respectfully,
[signed] Charles Guiteau

So it was with this completely distorted view of reality that Charles Guiteau fired two shots into the President's back as he walked arm-in-arm with Secretary Blaine toward the waiting train. The President, failing to respond to treatment, lingered two and a half months before dying on September 19, 1881.

The Trial

Throughout his lengthy seventy-two-day trial, Guiteau's delusional state was apparent to anyone inclined to acknowledge it. His brother-in-law, George Scoville, represented him at the trial and entered a plea of insanity. In Scoville's opening statement for the defense, he described in some detail the history of mental illness in the Guiteau family: at least two uncles, one aunt, and two cousins, not to mention his mother who died of "brain fever" but was probably insane. He went on to mention the highly eccentric behavior of his father that, at least one physician thought, properly qualified him for this category. It should also be noted that Guiteau's sister, Frances, the wife of George Scoville, behaved so strangely during her brother's trial that her probable insanity was noted by one participating physician who had occasion to observe her closely. And indeed, her husband later had her declared insane and institutionalized in October 1882, after her brother's execution.

This seemingly overwhelming evidence of an hereditary affliction was ignored or discounted by expert witnesses and finally the jury. Also discounted were the defendant's own delusional symptoms evident in the past schemes, bizarre letters to prominent persons he had never met, and his distorted conception of reality, which was apparent in his remarks throughout the trial and to the day he was executed. Scoville's line of defense was rejected by the defendant himself and greatly resented by John W. Guiteau, Charles' older bother. In a letter to Scoville, dated October 20, 1881, shortly after the trial began, John denied the history of family insanity described by the defense. Rather than heredity, he argued indignantly, most of the cases Scoville cited could be explained by self-induced factors such as inso-briety and "mesmerism"; the others, specifically his parents' symptoms, he categorically denied. Falling into line with previous diagnoses of the causes of Charles' problems, most notably that of leaders of the Oneida Community, John Guiteau wrote: "I have no doubt that masturbation and self-abuse is at the bottom of his [Charles'] mental imbecility."

As for Charles himself, thoroughly contemptuous of his brother-in-law's legal abilities, he drafted his own plea, which read as follows:

I plead not guilty to the indictment and my defense is threefold:

1. Insanity, in that it was God's act and not mine. The Divine pressure on me to remove the President was so enormous that it destroyed my free agency, and therefore I am not legally responsible for my act.

Throughout his trial, Guiteau would acknowledge only this interpretation of insanity; that is, he was insane only in the sense that he did something that was not his will but God's. He did not accept the idea that he was in any way mentally deficient. Typical of his remarks on this issue made throughout the trial is the following:

. . . the Lord interjected the idea [of the President's removal] into my brain and then let me work it out my own way. That is the way the Lord does. He doesn't employ fools to do his work; I am sure of that; he gets the best brains he can find.

His plea continued describing two rather novel circumstances that, he claimed, were the Lord's will just as the assassination:

2. The President died from malpractice. About three weeks after he was shot his physicians, after careful examination, decided he would recover. Two months after this official announcement he died. Therefore, I say he was not fatally shot. If he had been well treated he would have recovered.

The third circumstance had to do with the court's jurisdiction:

3. The President died in New Jersey and, therefore, beyond the jurisdiction of this Court. This malpractice and the President's death in New Jersey are special providences, and I am bound to avail myself of them in my trial in justice to the Lord and myself.

He went on to elaborate:

I undertake to say that the Lord is managing my case with eminent ability, and that he had a special object in allowing the President to die in New Jersey. His management of this case is worthy of Him as the Deity, and I have entire confidence in His disposition to protect me, and to send me forth to the world a free and innocent man.

The jury's guilty verdict notwithstanding, it was clear that Guiteau had no grasp of the reality of his situation. Almost to the last, he believed he would be acquitted, at which point, he planned to begin a lecture tour in Europe and later return to the United States in time to re-enter politics as a presidential contender in 1884. He was confident that the jury, like the great majority of Americans, would recognize that Garfield's "removal" was divinely ordained and that the Almighty himself was responsible. He was convinced they would recognize that he was only an instrument in the Master's hands.

Contrary to some assessments, there was no evidence of paranoia in his behavior. Buoyed by a delusion-based optimism, he mistook the crowds of curious on-lookers at the jail as evidence of respect and admiration: bogus checks for incredible sums of money and ludicrous marriage proposals that were sent to him by cranks were sincerely and gratefully acknowledged; and promotional schemes evolved in his distorted mind to market his ridiculous books and pamphlets—all this while anticipating a run for the presidency in 1884! Meanwhile, in high spirits, the poor wretch ate heartily and slept well in a small cell located both literally and figuratively in the shadow of the gallows.

The Execution

When at the very last he realized that there was no hope for survival, his anger was, considering the circumstances, tempered much as it had been during his dispute with the Oneida Community. There were warnings of divine retribution for the ungrateful new president, Chester Arthur, the unfair prosecuting attorneys, and the jury, but again his anger lacked the intensity and desperation of someone facing death. As the execution date approached, Charles, realizing failure once again, simply set his sights elsewhere as he had on many previous occasions. Eschewing politics, the presidency, the Stalwarts, and the law that had failed him, the lawyer and politician once again became the theologian. Anticipating an other-worldly position at the side of the Almighty, Charles walked serenely to the gallows. Earlier he had given the letter below to the chaplain who stood by him at the last:

> *Washington, D.C.*
> *June 29, 1882*
> TO THE REV. WILLIAM W. HICKS:
>
> *I, Charles Guiteau, of the City of Washington, in the District of Columbia, now under sentence of death, which is to be carried into effect between the hours of twelve and two o'clock on the 30th day of June, A.D., 1882, in the United States jail in the said District, do hereby give and grant to you my body after such execution; provided, however, it shall not be used for any mercenary purposes.*
>
> *And I hereby, for good and sufficient considerations, give, deliver and transfer to said Hicks my book entitled "The Truth and Removal" and copyright thereof to be used by him in writing a truthful history of my life and execution.*

> *And I direct that such history be entitled "The Life and Work of Charles Guiteau"; and I hereby solemnly proclaim and announce to all the world that no person or persons shall ever in any manner use my body for any mercenary purpose whatsoever.*
>
> *And if at any time hereafter any person or persons shall desire to honor my remains, they can do it by erecting a monument whereon shall be inscribed these words: "Here lies the body of Charles Guiteau, Patriot and Christian. His soul is in glory."*
>
> *[signed] Charles Guiteau*
> *Witnesses: Charles H. Reed*
> *James Woodward*

Before the noose was placed around his neck, he was given permission to read his "last dying prayer" to the crowd of faces gazing up at him from the prison yard below. Comparing his situation to that of Christ at Calvary, Guiteau condemned President Arthur's ingratitude "to the man that made him and saved his party and land" and warned of divine retribution.

After completing his prayer, he again looked thoughtfully out over the crowd before announcing in a loud clear voice:

> *I am now going to read some verses which are intended to indicate my feelings at the moment of leaving this world. If set to music they may be rendered effective. The idea is that of a child babbling to his mamma and his papa. I wrote it this morning about 10 o'clock.*

Then with childlike mournfulness, Guiteau read:

> *I am going to the Lordy. I am so glad.*
> *I am going to the Lordy. I am so glad.*
> *I am going to the Lordy. Glory,*
> *   hallelujah; glory hallelujah.*
> *I am going to the Lordy;*
> *I love the Lordy with all my soul; glory,*
> *   hallelujah.*

*And that is the reason I am going to
the Lord.*
*Glory, hallelujah; glory, hallelujah. I
am going to the Lord.*
*I saved my party and my land; glory,
hallelujah.*
*But they have murdered me for it, and
that is the reason*
I am going to the Lordy.
*Glory, hallelujah; glory, hallelujah. I
am going to the Lordy.*
*I wonder what I will do when I get to
the Lordy;*
*I guess that I will weep no more when
I get to the Lordy.*
Glory, hallelujah!
*I wonder what I will see when I get to
the Lordy,*

*I expect to see most splendid things, be-
yond all earthly conception.*

As he neared completion, he raised his voice to a
very high pitch and concluded with

*When I am with the Lordy, glory,
hallelujah!*
Glory, hallelujah! I am with the Lord.

Whereupon attendants strapped his legs, adjusted
the noose, and placed a black hood over his head
as Rev. Hicks prayed, "God the Father be with
thee and give thee peace evermore." Guiteau, according to his own request, signaled the hangman
by dropping a slip of paper from his fingers. As the
trap sprung, Charles Guiteau slipped confidently
into eternity with "Glory, Glory, Glory" on his lips.

CONCLUSIONS

Although the debate on the true state of Guiteau's mental condition was to continue
among physicians for some years afterward, a brief article in the *Medical News* a day
after the execution seems to have been representative of the prevailing view of the
medical profession. While conceding that the neurologists who testified to the assassin's obvious insanity may have been correct, society would still be better, the editors
reasoned, for having rid itself of such persons. As a further practical matter, it is unlikely that in 1881 any jury in the country would have acquitted the President's assassin whatever his mental condition.

STUDY QUESTIONS

1. Was Guiteau's life before the assassination consistent with his plea of insanity?

2. What were the political motivations for Guiteau's actions?

3. What were the problems with evaluating the evidence presented by the experts
   on insanity? Did Guiteau, according to the author, actually suffer from paranoia?

4. How would you describe Guiteau's religious beliefs? In your opinion, did those values inhibit his ability to interpret reality?

5. Was the verdict of the jury just? Could any other verdict have been reasonably
   justified?

BIBLIOGRAPHY

The most thoughtful and thought-provoking exploration of the Guiteau episode is Charles E. Rosenberg, *The Trial of the Assassin Guiteau* (1968). However, some contemporary articles also make interesting reading. John P. Gray, a leading late nineteenth-century American expert on insanity and an important witness in the Guiteau trial, presented his conclusions in "The United States vs. Charles J. Guiteau," *American Journal of Insanity,* 38 (1882). Edward C. Spitzka, the other major expert in the case, offered his opinion in "A Contribution to the Question on the Mental Status of Guiteau and the History of His Trial," *Alienist and Neurologist,* 4 (1883). The most recent work on American political assassinations is James W. Clarke, *American Assassins: The Darker Side of Politics* (1982). Clarke provides a good general bibliography on the subject. For the politics of the period see H. Wayne Morgan, *From Hayes to McKinley: National Party Politics, 1877–1896* (1969) and John M. Taylor, *Garfield of Ohio: The Available Man* (1970).

THE WIZARD OF OZ: PARABLE ON POPULISM

Henry M. Littlefield

The late nineteenth century was not a period known for its social justice. Angry and exploited workers found little sympathy in the halls of government. During strikes, federal authorities consistently intervened on the side of management rather than labor, even though strikes were usually responses to wage cuts. In the 1894 Pullman strike, for example, President Grover Cleveland sided with the rights of property over the rights of labor and crushed the strike. Thus the newly formed unions won few concessions for their members. At the end of the century, the work week for the "average" industrial worker was almost 60 hours. The average skilled worker earned 20 cents an hour, twice as much as the average unskilled worker.

Life on the farms in the Midwest and South was probably even worse than life in the northern industries. Technological innovations and scientific farming techniques led to increased production, which in turn sent prices spiraling downward. Discriminatory railroad rates and the government's tight money policies further weakened the economic positions of farmers. As a result, farmers faced an economic depression that cost many their farms. Returning to his midwestern home in 1889, writer Hamlin Garland noted, "Nature was as bountiful as ever . . . but no splendor of cloud, no grace of sunset could conceal the poverty of these people; on the contrary, they brought out, with a more intolerable poignancy, the gracelessness of these homes, and the sordid quality of the mechanical routine of these lives." In the following essay, Henry M. Littlefield takes a fascinating look at Lyman Frank Baum's *The Wonderful Wizard of Oz* and the light it shed on the workers' and farmers' plight in the late nineteenth century.

On the deserts on North Africa in 1941 two tough Australian brigades went to battle singing,

Have you heard of the wonderful
  wizard,
The wonderful Wizard of Oz,
And he is a wonderful wizard,
If ever a wizard there was.

It was a song they had brought with them from Australia and would soon spread to England. Forever afterward it reminded Winston Churchill of those "buoyant days." Churchill's nostalgia is only one symptom of the worldwide delight found in an American fairy-tale about a little girl and her odyssey in the strange land of Oz. The song he reflects upon came from a classic 1939 Hollywood production of the story, which introduced millions of people not only to the land of Oz, but to a talented young lady named Judy Garland as well.

Ever since its publication in 1900 Lyman Frank Baum's *The Wonderful Wizard of Oz* has been immensely popular, providing the basis for a profitable musical comedy, three movies and a number of plays. It is an indigenous creation, curiously warm and touching, although no one really knows why. For despite wholehearted acceptance by generations of readers, Baum's tale has been accorded neither critical acclaim, nor extended critical examination. Interested scholars, such as Russell B. Nye and Martin Gardiner, look upon *The Wizard of Oz* as the first in a long and delightful series of Oz stories, and understandably base their appreciation of Baum's talent on the totality of his works. *The Wizard of Oz* is an entity unto itself, however, and was not originally written with a sequel in mind. Baum informed his readers in 1904 that he had produced *The Marvelous Land of Oz* reluctantly and only in answer to well over a thousand letters demanding that he create another Oz tale. His original effort remains unique and to some degree separate from the books which follow. But its uniqueness does not rest alone on its peculiar and transcendent popularity.

Professor Nye finds a "strain of moralism" in the Oz books, as well as "a well-developed sense of satire," and Baum stories often include searching parodies on the contradictions in human nature. The second book in the series, *The Marvelous Land of Oz,* is a blatant satire on feminism and the suffragette movement. In it Baum attempted to duplicate the format used so successfully in *The Wizard,* yet no one has noted a similar play on contemporary movements in the latter work. Nevertheless, one does exist, and it reflects to an astonishing degree the world of political reality which surrounded Baum in 1900. In order to understand the relationship of *The Wizard* to turn-of-the-century America, it is necessary first to know something of Baum's background.

Born near Syracuse in 1856, Baum was brought up in a wealthy home and early became interested in the theater. He wrote some plays which enjoyed brief success and then, with his wife and two sons, journeyed to Aberdeen, South Dakota, in 1887. Aberdeen was a little prairie town and there Baum edited the local weekly until it failed in 1891.

For many years Western farmers had been in a state of loud, though unsuccessful, revolt. While Baum was living in South Dakota not only was the frontier a thing of the past, but the Romantic view of benign nature had disappeared as well. The stark reality of the dry, open plains and the acceptance of man's Darwinian subservience to his environment served to crush Romantic idealism.

Hamlin Garland's visit to Iowa and South Dakota coincided with Baum's arrival. Henry Nash Smith observes,

Garland's success as a portrayer of hardship and suffering on Northwestern farms was due in part to the fact that his personal experience happened to parallel the shock which the entire West received in the later 1880s from the combined effects of low prices, . . . grasshoppers, drought, the terrible blizzards of the winter of 1886–1887, and the juggling of freight rates. . . .

From Henry M. Littlefield, "The Wizard of Oz: Parable on Populism" in *American Quarterly,* Vol. 16 (Spring 1964). © The Johns Hopkins University Press. Reprinted by permission.

As we shall see, Baum's prairie experience was no less deeply etched, although he did not employ naturalism to express it.

Baum's stay in South Dakota also covered the period of the formation of the Populist party, which Professor Nye likens to a fanatic "crusade." Western farmers had for a long time sought governmental aid in the form of economic panaceas, but to no avail. The Populist movement symbolized a desperate attempt to use the power of the ballot. In 1891 Baum moved to Chicago where he was surrounded by those dynamic elements of reform which made the city so notable during the 1890s.

In Chicago Baum certainly saw the results of the frightful depression which had closed down upon the nation in 1893. Moreover, he took part in the pivotal election of 1896, marching in "torch-light parades for William Jennings Bryan." Martin Gardiner notes besides, that he "consistently voted as a Democrat . . . and his sympathies seem always to have been on the side of the laboring classes." No one who marched in even a few such parades could have been unaffected by Bryan's campaign. Putting all the farmers' hopes in a basket labeled "free coinage of silver," Bryan's platform rested mainly on the issue of adding silver to the nation's gold standard. Though he lost, he did at least bring the plight of the little man into national focus.

Between 1896 and 1900, while Baum worked and wrote in Chicago, the Great Depression faded away and the war with Spain thrust the United States into world prominence. Bryan maintained Midwestern control over the Democratic party, and often spoke out against American policies toward Cuba and the Philippines. By 1900 it was evident that Bryan would run again, although now imperialism and not silver seemed the issue of primary concern. In order to promote greater enthusiasm, however, Bryan felt compelled once more to sound the silver leitmotif in his campaign. Bryan's second futile attempt at the presidency culminated in November 1900. The previous winter Baum had attempted unsuccessfully to sell a rather original volume of children's fantasy, but that April, George M. Hill, a small Chicago publisher, finally agreed to print *The Wonderful Wizard of Oz*.

Baum's allegiance to the cause of Democratic Populism must be balanced against the fact that he was not a political activist. Martin Gardiner finds through all of his writings "a theme of tolerance, with many episodes that poke fun at narrow nationalism and ethnocentrism." Nevertheless, Professor Nye quotes Baum as having a desire to write stories that would "bear the stamp of our times and depict the progressive fairies of today."

The Wizard of Oz has neither the mature religious appeal of a *Pilgrim's Progress,* nor the philosophic depth of a *Candide*. Baum's most thoughtful devotees see in it only a warm, cleverly written fairy tale. Yet the original Oz book conceals an unsuspected depth, and it is the purpose of this study to demonstrate that Baum's immortal American fantasy encompasses more than heretofore believed. For Baum created a children's story with a symbolic allegory implicit within its story line and characterizations. The allegory always remains in a minor key, subordinated to the major theme and readily abandoned whenever it threatens to distort the appeal of the fantasy. But through it, in the form of a subtle parable, Baum delineated a Midwesterner's vibrant and ironic portrait of this country as it entered the twentieth century.

We are introduced to both Dorothy and Kansas at the same time:

Dorothy live in the midst of the great Kansas prairies, with Uncle Henry, who was a farmer, and Aunt Em, who was the farmer's wife. Their house was small, for the lumber to build it had to be carried by wagon many miles. There were four walls, a floor and a roof, which made one room; and this room contained a rusty-looking cooking stove, a cupboard for the dishes, a table, three or four chairs, and the beds.

When Dorothy stood in the doorway and looked around, she could see nothing but the great gray prairie on every side. Not a tree nor a house broke the broad sweep of flat country that reached to the edge of the sky in all directions. The sun had baked the plowed land into a gray mass, with little cracks running through it. Even the grass was not green, for the sun had burned the tops of the long blades until they were the same gray color to be seen everywhere. Once the house had been painted, but the sun blistered the paint and the rains washed it away, and now the house was as dull and gray as everything else.

When Aunt Em came there to live she was a young, pretty wife. The sun and wind had changed her, too. They had taken the sparkle from her eyes and left them a sober gray; they had taken the red from her cheeks and lips, and they were gray also. She was thin and gaunt, and never smiled now. When Dorothy, who was an orphan, first came to her, Aunt Em had been so startled by the child's laughter that she would scream and press her hand upon her heart whenever Dorothy's merry voice reached her ears; and she still looked at the little girl with wonder that she could find anything to laugh at.

Uncle Henry never laughed. He worked hard from morning till night and did not know what joy was. He was gray also, from his long beard to his rough boots, and he looked stern and solemn, and rarely spoke.

It was Toto that made Dorothy laugh, and saved her from growing as gray as her other surroundings. Toto was not gray; he was a little black dog, with long silky hair and small black eyes that twinkle merrily on either side of his funny, wee nose. Toto played all day long, and Dorothy played with him, and loved him dearly.

Dorothy and her friends prepare to "follow the yellow brick road." The spectacularly successful 1939 film based on The Wizard of Oz came out during another Great Depression and prefigured happiness in "Somewhere Over the Rainbow."

Hector St. John de Crèvecoeur would not have recognized Uncle Henry's farm; it is straight out of Hamlin Garland. On it a deadly environment dominates everyone and everything except Dorothy and her pet. The setting is Old Testament and nature seems grayly impersonal and even angry. Yet it is a fearsome cyclone that lifts Dorothy and Toto in their house and deposits them "very gently—for a cyclone—in the midst of a country of marvelous beauty." We immediately sense the contrast between Oz and Kansas. Here there are "stately trees bearing rich and luscious fruits . . . gorgeous flowers . . . and birds with . . . brilliant plumage" sing in the trees. In Oz "a small brook rushing and sparkling along" murmurs "in a voice very grateful to a little girl who had lived so long on the dry, gray prairies."

Trouble intrudes. Dorothy's house has come down on the wicked Witch of the East, killing her. Nature, by sheer accident, can provide benefits, for indirectly the cyclone has disposed of one of the two truly bad influences in the Land of Oz. Notice that evil ruled in both the East and the West; after Dorothy's coming it rules only in the West.

The wicked Witch of the East had kept the little Munchkin people "in bondage for many years, making them slave for her night and day." Just what this slavery entailed is not immediately clear, but Baum later gives us a specific example. The Tin Woodman, whom Dorothy meets on her way to the Emerald City, had been put under a spell by the Witch of the East. Once an independent and hardworking human being, the Woodman found that each time he swung his axe it chopped off a different part of his body. Knowing no other trade he "worked harder than ever," for luckily in Oz tinsmiths can repair such things. Soon the Woodman was all tin. In this way Eastern witchcraft dehumanized a simple laborer so that the faster and better he worked the more quickly he became a kind of machine. Here is a Populist view of evil Eastern influences on honest labor which could hardly be more pointed.

There is one thing seriously wrong with being made of tin; when it rains rust sets in. Tin Woodman had been standing in the same position for a year without moving before Dorothy came along and oiled his joints. The Tin Woodman's situation has an obvious parallel in the condition of many Eastern workers after the depression of 1893. While Tin Woodman is standing still, rusted solid, he deludes himself into thinking he is no longer capable of that most human of sentiments, love. Hate does not fill the void, a constant lesson in the Oz books, and Tin Woodman feels that only a heart will make him sensitive again. So he accompanies Dorothy to see if the Wizard will give him one.

Oz itself is a magic oasis surrounded by impassable deserts, and the country is divided in a very orderly fashion. In the North and South the people are ruled by good witches, who are not quite as powerful as the wicked ones of the East and West. In the center of the land rises the magnificent Emerald City ruled by the Wizard of Oz, a successful humbug whom even the witches mistakenly feel "is more powerful than all the rest of us together." Despite these forces, the mark of goodness, placed on Dorothy's forehead by the Witch of the North, serves as protection for Dorothy throughout her travels. Goodness and innocence prevail even over the powers of evil and delusion in Oz. Perhaps it is this basic and beautiful optimism that makes Baum's tale so characteristically American—and Midwestern.

Dorothy is Baum's Miss Everyman. She is one of us, levelheaded and human, and she has a real problem. Young readers can understand her

quandary as readily as can adults. She is good, not precious, and she thinks quite naturally about others. For all of the attractions of Oz Dorothy desires only to return to the gray plains and Aunt Em and Uncle Henry. She is directed toward the Emerald City by the good Witch of the North, since the Wizard will surely be able to solve the problem of the impassable deserts. Dorothy sets out on the Yellow Brick Road wearing the Witch of the East's magic Silver Shoes. Silver shoes walking on a golden road; henceforth Dorothy becomes the innocent agent of Baum's ironic view of the Silver issue. Remember, neither Dorothy, nor the good Witch of the North, nor the Munchkins understand the power of these shoes. The allegory is abundantly clear. On the next to last page of the book Baum has Glinda, Witch of the South, tell Dorothy, "Your Silver Shoes will carry you over the desert. . . . If you had known their power you could have gone back to your Aunt Em the very first day you came to this country." Glinda explains, "All you have to do is to knock the heels together three times and command the shoes to carry you wherever you wish to go." William Jennings Bryan never outlined the advantages of the silver standard any more effectively.

Not understanding the magic of the Silver Shoes, Dorothy walks the mundane—and dangerous— Yellow Brick Road. The first person she meets is a Scarecrow. After escaping from his wooden perch, the Scarecrow displays a terrible sense of inferiority and self doubt, for he has determined that he needs real brains to replace the common straw in his head. William Allen White wrote an article in 1896 entitled "What's the Matter with Kansas?" In it he accused Kansas farmers of ignorance, irrationality and general muddle-headedness. What's wrong with Kansas are the people, said Mr. White. Baum's character seems to have read White's angry characterization. But Baum never takes White seriously and so the Scarecrow soon emerges as innately a very shrewd and very capable individual.

The Scarecrow and the Tin Woodman accompany Dorothy along the Yellow Brick Road, one seeking brains, the other a heart. They meet next the Cowardly Lion. As King of Beasts he explains, "I learned that if I roared very loudly every living

thing was frightened and got out of my way."
Born a coward, he sobs, "Whenever there is danger my heart begins to beat fast." "Perhaps you
have heart disease," suggests Tin Woodman, who
always worries about hearts. But the Lion desires
only courage and so he joins the party to ask help
from the Wizard.

The Lion represents Bryan himself. In the election of 1896 Bryan lost the vote of Eastern labor,
though he tried hard to gain their support. In
Baum's story the Lion, on meeting the little group,
"struck at the Tin Woodman with his sharp
claws." But, to his surprise, "he could make no impression on the tin, although the Woodman fell
over in the road and lay still." Baum here refers to
the fact that in 1896 workers were often pres-
sured into voting for McKinley and gold by their
employers. Amazed, the Lion says, "he nearly
blunted my claws," and he adds even more appro-
priately, "When they scratched against the tin it
made a cold shiver run down my back." The King
of Beasts is not after all very cowardly, and Bryan,
although a pacifist and an anti-imperialist in a time
of national expansion, is not either. The magic Silver Shoes belong to Dorothy, however. Silver's
potent charm, which had come to mean so much
to so many in the Midwest, could not be entrusted
to a political symbol. Baum delivers Dorothy from
the world of adventure and fantasy to the real
world of heartbreak and desolation through the
power of Silver. It represents a real force in a land
of illusion, and neither the Cowardly Lion nor
Bryan truly needs or understands its use.

All together now the small party moves toward
the Emerald City. Coxey's Army of tramps and in-
digents, marching to ask President Cleveland for
work in 1894, appears no more naively innocent
than this group of four characters going to see a
humbug Wizard, to request favors that only the
little girl among them deserves.

Those who enter the Emerald City must wear
green glasses. Dorothy later discovers that the
greenness of dresses and ribbons disappears on
leaving, and everything becomes a bland white.
Perhaps the magic of any city is thus self imposed.
But the Wizard dwells here and so the Emerald

City represents the national Capital. The Wizard,
a little bumbling old man, hiding behind a facade
of papier mâché and noise, might be any President from Grant to McKinley. He comes straight
from the fairgrounds in Omaha, Nebraska, and he
symbolizes the American criterion for leadership—he is able to be everything to everybody.

As each of our heroes enters the throne room
to ask a favor the Wizard assumes different
shapes, representing different views toward national leadership. To Dorothy, he appears as an
enormous head, "bigger than the head of the
biggest giant." An apt image for a naive and innocent little citizen. To the Scarecrow he appears to
be a lovely, gossamer fairy, a most appropriate
form for an idealistic Kansas farmer. The Woodman sees a horrible beast, as would any exploited
Eastern laborer after the trouble of the 1890s. But
the Cowardly Lion, like W. J. Bryan, sees a "Ball of
Fire, so fierce and glowing he could scarcely bear
to gaze upon it." Baum then provides an additional analogy, for when the Lion "tried to go
nearer he singed his whiskers and he crept back
tremblingly to a spot nearer the door."

The Wizard has asked them all to kill the Witch
of the West. The golden road does not go in that
direction and so they must follow the sun, as
have many pioneers in the past. The land they
now pass through is "rougher and hillier, for
there were no farms nor houses in the country of
the West and the ground was untilled." The
Witch of the West uses natural forces to achieve
her ends; she is Baum's version of sentient and
malign nature.

Finding Dorothy and her friends in the West,
the Witch sends forty wolves against them, then
forty vicious crows and finally a great swarm of
black bees. But it is through the power of a magic
golden cap that she summons the flying monkeys.
They capture the little girl and dispose of her
companions. Baum makes these Winged Monkeys
into an Oz substitute for the plains Indians. Their
leader says, "Once . . . we were a free people, living happily in the great forest, flying from tree to
tree, eating nuts and fruit, and doing just as we
pleased without calling anybody master." "This,"

he explains, "was many years ago, long before Oz came out of the clouds to rule over this land." But like many Indian tribes Baum's monkeys are not inherently bad; their actions depend wholly upon the bidding of others. Under the control of an evil influence, they do evil. Under the control of goodness and innocence, as personified by Dorothy, the monkeys are helpful and kind, although unable to take her to Kansas. Says the Monkey King, "We belong to this country alone, and cannot leave it." The same could be said with equal truth of the first Americans.

Dorothy presents a special problem to the Witch. Seeing the mark on Dorothy's forehead and the Silver Shoes on her feet, the Witch begins "to tremble with fear, for she knew what a powerful charm belonged to them." Then "she happened to look into the child's eyes and saw how simple the soul behind them was, and that the little girl did not know of the wonderful power the Silver Shoes gave her." Here Baum again uses the Silver allegory to state the blunt homily that while goodness affords a people ultimate protection against evil, ignorance of their capabilities allows evil to impose itself upon them. The Witch assumes the proportions of a kind of western Mark Hanna or Banker Boss, who, through natural malevolence, manipulates the people and holds them prisoner by cynically taking advantage of their innate innocence.

Enslaved in the West, "Dorothy went to work meekly, with her mind made up to work as hard as she could; for she was glad the Wicked Witch had decided not to kill her." Many Western farmers have held these same grim thoughts in less mystical terms. If the Witch of the West is a diabolical force of Darwinian or Spencerian nature, then another contravening force may be counted upon to dispose of her. Dorothy destroys the evil Witch by angrily dousing her with a bucket of water. Water, that precious commodity which the drought-ridden farmers on the Great Plains needed so badly, and which if correctly used could create an agricultural paradise, or at least dissolve a wicked witch. Plain water brings an end to malign nature in the West.

When Dorothy and her companions return to the Emerald City they soon discover that the Wizard is really nothing more than "a little man, with a bald head and a wrinkled face." Can this be the ruler of the land?

Our friends looked at him in surprise and dismay.

"I thought Oz was a great Head," said Dorothy. . . . "And I thought Oz was a terrible Beast," said the Tin Woodman. "And I thought Oz was a Ball of Fire," exclaimed the Lion. "No; you are all wrong," said the little man meekly. "I have been making believe."

Dorothy asks if he is truly a great Wizard. He confides, "Not a bit of it, my dear; I'm just a common man." Scarecrow adds, "You're more than that . . . you're a humbug."

The Wizard's deception is of long standing in Oz and even the Witches were taken in. How was it accomplished? "It was a great mistake my ever letting you into the Throne Room," the Wizard complains. "Usually I will not see even my subjects, and so they believe I am something terrible." What a wonderful lesson for youngsters of the decade when Benjamin Harrison, Grover Cleveland and William McKinley were hiding in the White House. Formerly the Wizard was a mimic, a ventriloquist and a circus balloonist. The latter trade involved going "up in a balloon on circus day, so as to draw a crowd of people together and get them to pay to see the circus." Such skills are as admirably adapted to success in late-nineteenth-century politics as they are to the humbug wizardry of Baum's story. A pointed comment on Midwestern political ideals is the fact that our little Wizard comes from Omaha, Nebraska, a center of Populist agitation. "Why that isn't very far from Kansas," cries Dorothy. Nor, indeed, are any of the characters in the wonderful land of Oz.

The Wizard, of course, can provide the objects of self-delusion desired by Tin Woodman, Scarecrow and Lion. But Dorothy's hope of going home fades when the Wizard's balloon leaves too soon. Understand this: Dorothy wishes to leave a green and fabulous land, from which all evil has disappeared, to go back to the gray desolation of the Kansas prairies. Dorothy is an orphan, Aunt Em and Uncle Henry are her only family. Reality is never far from Dorothy's consciousness and in the most heartrending terms she explains her reasoning to the Good Witch Glinda,

Aunt Em will surely think something dreadful has happened to me, and that will make her put on mourning; and unless the crops are better this year than they were last I am sure Uncle Henry cannot afford it.

The Silver Shoes furnish Dorothy with a magic means of travel. But when she arrives back in Kansas she finds, "The Silver Shoes had fallen off in her flight through the air, and were lost forever in the desert." Were the "her" to refer to America in 1900, Baum's statement could hardly be contradicted.

Current historiography tends to criticize the Populist movement for its "delusions, myths and foibles," Professor C. Vann Woodward observed recently. Yet *The Wonderful Wizard of Oz* has provided unknowing generations with a gentle and friendly Midwestern critique of the Populist rationale on these very same grounds. Led by naive innocence and protected by good will, the farmer, the laborer and the politician approach the mystic holder of national power to ask for personal fulfillment. Their desires, as well as the Wizard's cleverness in answering them, are all self-delusion. Each of these characters carries within him the solution to his own problem, were he only to view himself objectively. The fearsome Wizard turns out to be nothing more than a common man, capable of shrewd but mundane answers to these self-induced needs. Like any good politician he gives the people what they want. Throughout the story Baum poses a central thought; the American desire for symbols of fulfillment in illusory. Real needs lie elsewhere.

Thus the Wizard cannot help Dorothy, for of all the characters only she has a wish that is self-less, and only she has a direct connection to honest, hopeless human beings. Dorothy supplies real fulfillment when she returns to her aunt and uncle, using the Silver Shoes, and cures some of their misery and heartache. In this way Baum tells us that the Silver crusade at least brought back Dorothy's lovely spirit to the disconsolate plains farmer. Her laughter, love and good will are no small addition to that gray land, although the magic of Silver has been lost forever as a result.

Noteworthy too is Baum's prophetic placement of leadership in Oz after Dorothy's departure. The Scarecrow reigns over the Emerald City, the Tin Woodman rules in the West and the Lion protects smaller beasts in "a grand old forest." Thereby farm interests achieve national importance, industrialism moves West and Bryan commands only a forest full of lesser politicians.

Baum's fantasy succeeds in bridging the gap between what children want and what they should have. It is an admirable example of the way in which an imaginative writer can teach goodness and morality without producing the almost inevitable side effect of nausea. Today's children's books are either saccharine and empty, or boring and pedantic. Baum's first Oz tale—and those which succeed it—are immortal not so much because the "heart-aches and nightmares are left out" as that "the wonderment and joy" are retained.

Baum declares, "The story of 'the Wonderful Wizard of Oz' was written solely to pleasure children of today." In 1963 there are very few children who have never heard of the Scarecrow, the Tin Woodman or the cowardly Lion, and whether they know W. W. Denslow's original illustrations of Dorothy, or Judy Garland's whimsical characterization, is immaterial. *The Wizard* has become a genuine piece of American folklore because, knowing his audience, Baum never allowed the consistency of the allegory to take precedence over the theme of youthful entertainment. Yet once discovered, the author's allegorical intent seems clear, and it gives depth and lasting interest even to children who only sense something else beneath the surface of the story. Consider the fun in picturing turn-of-the-century America, a difficult era at best, using these ready-made symbols provided by Baum. The relationships and analogies outlined above are admittedly theoretical, but they are far too consistent to be coincidental, and they furnish a teaching mechanism which is guaranteed to reach any level of student.

The Wizard of Oz says so much about so many things that it is hard not to imagine a satisfied and mischievous gleam in Lyman Frank Baum's eye as he had Dorothy say, "And oh, Aunt Em! I'm so glad to be at home again!"

STUDY QUESTIONS

1. Why was Lyman Frank Baum in a good position to understand the problems of workers in the late nineteenth century?

2. What sort of picture does *The Wonderful Wizard of Oz* paint of farm life? What was the effect of agrarian labor on the farmers themselves?

3. How does the story detail the complexities of the silver issue? Does Baum seem to feel that the gold standard was the major problem facing the farmers?

4. How does the Tin Woodman dramatize the plight of the northern industrial worker? How does the Scarecrow symbolize the plight of the farmers?

5. In what ways is the Cowardly Lion similar to William Jennings Bryan?

6. What roles do the good and bad witches play in the story?

7. Is *The Wonderful Wizard of Oz* an effective parable?

BIBLIOGRAPHY

Martin Gardiner and Russell B. Nye, *The Wizard of Oz and Who He was* (1957), examine Baum and his works. The best studies of the Populist movement are John D. Hicks, *The Populist Revolt* (1931); C. Vann Woodward, *Tom Watson: Agrarian Rebel* (1938); Lawrence Goodwyn, *Democratic Promise: The Populist Movement in America* (1976); Robert C. McMath, Jr., *Populist Vanguard: A History of the Southern Farmers' Alliance* (1975); and Stanley B. Parsons, *The Populist Context: Rural Versus Urban Power on a Great Plains Frontier* (1973). Paul W. Glad, *McKinley, Bryan, and the People* (1964) and Robert F. Durden, *The Climax of Populism: The Election of 1896* (1965) examine the crucial election of 1896. For industrial working conditions in the late nineteenth century see Herbert G. Gutman, *Work, Class, and Society in Industrializing America* (1976); David Brody, *Steelworkers in America: The Nonunion Era* (1960); and Albert Rees, *Real Wages in Manufacturing, 1890–1914* (1961). Also see Steven Hahn, *The Roots of Southern Populism* (1983).

SHE COULDN'T HAVE DONE IT, EVEN IF SHE DID

Kathryn Allamong Jacob

There is something infinitely compelling and fascinating about an unsolved murder. England has Jack the Ripper, and although it has been more than 100 years since the last Ripper murder was committed, historians of the crimes still speculate on the identity of the murderer. The American equivalent to Jack the Ripper is Lizzie Borden, who very likely killed her father and stepmother on August 2, 1892. Although she was judged innocent of the murders, strong circumstantial evidence points toward her guilt. However, in a larger sense the jury was more concerned with the physical and psychological nature of upper-class womanhood than with the actual crimes. As Kathryn Allamong Jacob writes, during the summer of 1893 "the entire Victorian conception of womanhood was on trial for its life." The question most commonly asked that summer was to the point: How could a well-bred woman, who by her very nature was innocent, childlike, and moral, commit such a horrible crime? The answer of most well-bred men, and of all 12 of the prosperous, Yankee jurors, was that she could not. An examination of the case thus illuminates an entire cultural landscape, casting light especially on American attitudes toward women. Were women, as a writer for *Scribner's* believed, "merely large babies . . . shortsighted, frivolous, and [occupying] an intermediate stage between children and men . . ."? Or was there something more to the issue?

During the summer of 1893, Americans riveted their attention on the town of New Bedford, Massachusetts, where Lizzie Andrew Borden was being tried for the gruesome ax murder of her father and stepmother. All other news paled in comparison, for here, in south-eastern Massachusetts, not only a particular woman, but the entire Victorian conception of womanhood, was on trial for its life.

The drama began in August of 1892 at Number 92 Second Street in Fall River, Massachusetts, the home of Andrew Jackson Borden, whose family coat of arms prophetically bore a lion holding a battle-ax. The household consisted of Andrew, seventy; Abby Gray Borden, sixty-five, his wife; his two daughters, Lizzie Andrew and Emma Lenora, aged thirty-two and forty-two; and Bridget Sullivan, twenty-six, an Irish servant who had been with the family for nearly three years.

Andrew Borden began his business career as an undertaker. It was rumored that he had cut the feet off corpses to make them fit into undersized coffins, but however ill-gotten his initial profits, Borden invested them wisely. By 1892 he was worth nearly half a million dollars, served as a director of several banks and as a board member of three woolen mills, and had built the imposing A. J. Borden Building on Main Street as a testimony to his business acumen. To keep his fortunes increasing, Borden foreclosed, undercut, overcharged, and hoarded without flinching.

Borden's first wife, Sarah, had died in 1862 after bearing him three daughters, only two of whom survived past infancy. Two years later, he married Abby Gray, a thirty-eight-year-old spinster. Nothing suggests that Abby was anything but kind to the two little girls whose stepmother she became, but they never returned her affection. After her marriage, Abby became a compulsive eater. Only a little over five feet tall, by 1892 she weighed more than two hundred pounds.

She Couldn't Have Done It, Even If She Did" by Kathryn Allamong Jacob, from *American Heritage* 29 (February/March, 1978) pp. 42–53. Reprinted by permission.

Emma, the older daughter, still lived at home at age forty-two. By all accounts, she was dowdy and narrow-minded. Lizzie Borden, ten years younger, also lived at home. Otherwise tightfisted, Andrew Borden doted on his younger daughter: over the years he lavished on Lizzie expensive gifts—a diamond ring, a sealskin cape, even a Grand Tour of Europe. Lizzie worshiped her father in return, and even gave him her high school ring to wear as a token of her affection.

Like her sister, Lizzie had evidently given up hope of marriage, but she led a more active life, centered around good works and the Central Congregational Church, where she taught a Sunday-school class of Chinese children, the sons and daughters of Fall River laundrymen. Though she loathed doing housework, she enthusiastically helped cook the church's annual Christmas dinner for local newsboys. In addition to being secretary-treasurer of the Christian Endeavor, Lizzie was active in the Ladies' Fruit and Flower Mission, the Women's Christian Temperance Union, and the Good Samaritan Charity Hospital.

Lizzie's Christian charity did not extend to her own home. The Border family was not happy. While Emma tolerated her stepmother, Lizzie openly disliked her. Ill feelings increased in 1887, when Andrew gave Abby a house for the use of her sister. Seeking peace, Andrew gave his daughters a house of greater value to rent out, but they were not placated. A dressmaker later remembered making the mistake of referring to Abby as Lizzie's "mother," causing Lizzie to snap, "Don't call her that to me. She is a mean thing and we hate her."

Even the house Lizzie lived in vexed her. Its Grant-era furnishings contrasted sharply with her stylish clothes. There was no bath and no electricity, though such conveniences were common elsewhere in town. Beside the water closet in the basement stood a pile of old newspapers for sanitary purposes. No interior space was wasted on hallways. Rooms simply opened into one another, making it difficult for anyone to pass through unnoticed. Lizzie longed to live "on the hill," Fall River's most elegant neighborhood and the symbol of the social prominence she craved. While her father's wealth entitled her to live there, Andrew insisted on living on déclassé Second Street.

On Tuesday, August 2, 1892, strange things began to happen in the Borden house. Mr. and Mrs. Borden and Bridget suffered severe vomiting; Lizzie later claimed she felt queasy the next day. Emma, on vacation in Fairhaven, was spared. Over Andrew's objections, Abby waddled across the street to Dr. Bowen's to tell him she feared they had been poisoned. When he learned that the previous night's dinner had been warmed-over fish, the doctor laughingly sent her home.

The next day, Uncle John Morse, brother of the first Mrs. Borden, arrived unexpectedly on business. Like Andrew, Morse was single-minded in his pursuit of wealth, and the two men had remained friends. That evening, Lizzie visited Miss Alice Russell, a friend of Emma's. Miss Russell later testified that their conversation had been unsettling. Lizzie had spoken of burglary attempts on the Borden home, of threats against her father from unknown enemies. "I feel as if something was hanging over me that I cannot throw off . . .," she said. "Father has so much trouble. . . ." Though Miss Russell tried to reassure her, Lizzie Left on an ominous, but prescient, note: "I am afraid somebody will do something."

On Thursday morning, August 4, Bridget rose about six and lit the breakfast fire. Around seven, the elder Bordens and their guest sat down to eat in the dining room. Lizzie did not appear downstairs till nine. By then, Mrs. Borden had begun dusting the downstairs and Morse had left the house to visit relatives across town. Lizzie told Bridget she did not feel well enough to eat breakfast, but sat in the kitchen sipping coffee. About twenty after nine, Andrew, too, left the house, setting off downtown to oversee his investments. Perhaps ten minutes later, Abby Borden went upstairs to tidy the guest room, and Bridget went outside to begin washing the downstairs windows. Only Lizzie and Abby remained in the house; Abby was never seen alive again.

Perhaps because of the oppressive heat, Andrew broke his long-established routine by coming home for lunch at a quarter of eleven, an hour and a half early. Bridget later testified that she had just begun scrubbing the inside of the windows when she heard him struggling with the front-door lock and let him in. Lizzie, by her own admission, was coming down the stairs from the second floor where Abby's body lay. (At the Borden trial the following year, the prosecution would produce witnesses who testified that Abby's body, lying on the guest-room floor, was clearly visible from the staircase, while the defense claimed it was almost completely obscured by a bed). Andrew asked Lizzie about Abby's whereabouts, according to Bridget, and Lizzie told him that Abby had received a note asking her to attend a sick friend.

Bridget finished her windows and climbed the back stairs to her attic room to rest at about eleven. Andrew lay down on the parlor sofa to nap. On the guest-room floor above him lay Abby's bleeding corpse. The house was hot and silent. Within minutes, Bridget recalled, she was awakened by Lizzie calling, "Come down quick; father's dead; somebody came in and killed him."

Little was left of Andrew's face. Half an eye hung from its socket. Doctors testified that a single ax blow had killed him; nine others had been gratuitous. Shortly after the police arrived, Bridget and a neighbor ventured upstairs for a sheet to cover the hideous sight, and there they found Abby. Her plump body lay face down in a pool of blood, her head and neck a bloody mass. Those first on the scene noted that Lizzie remained remarkably calm throughout the ordeal. While one woman claimed that there were tears in her eyes, several others testified that Lizzie's eyes were dry and her hands steady.

News traveled fast from neighbor to neighbor and even before the evening presses rolled, everyone in Fall River seemed to know of the horrifying incident. A local reporter recalled that "The cry of murder swept through the city like a typhoon . . . murder committed under the very glare of the midday sun within three minutes walk of the City Hall. . . ." By the next day, the story was front-page news throughout the country and when, after two days, no crazed ax-wielder was produced, newspapers which had praised the police began to question their competence. Trial transcripts suggest that the police did err on the side of caution. If the victims had not been so prominent, matters, would have been simpler. The *New York Times* appreciated this fact, and on August 6 noted that "The police are acting slowly and carefully in the affair giving way, no doubt, to feelings of sentiment because of the high social standing of the parties involved." No systematic search of the Borden house was conducted until thirty-two hours after the murders. Out of deference to the bereaved daughters, neither Lizzie nor Emma, who had been summoned home from her vacation, was closely questioned for nearly three days.

Yet, by Saturday, the day of the funerals, the police felt that they had little choice but to arrest Lizzie. She alone, they felt, had had the opportunity to commit the murders. They found it hard to believe that anyone could have passed through the house unseen by Lizzie, who claimed to have been on the first floor while Abby was being murdered above. It also strained credibility to assert, as Lizzie did, that Abby's 210-pound body had crashed to the floor without a sound. Furthermore, despite a reward offered by the Borden sisters, no sender of the note that Lizzie claimed had called Abby to town could be found.

Lizzie's own contradictory answers to the first questions put to her by police were highly damaging. When asked her whereabouts when her father was killed, she gave different answers to different interrogators: "In the back yard"; ". . . in the loft getting a piece of iron for sinkers"; ". . . up in the loft eating pears." The closed barn loft would have been so insufferably hot that day that few would have visited it voluntarily, much less lingered to eat pears. Furthermore, an officer who claimed to have been the first to examine the loft after the crimes testified that the dust on the floor was undisturbed by footprints or trailing skirts.

In Lizzie's favor was the fact that she had been neat and clean when first seen after the murders. The police were certain that the murderer would have been covered with blood. (Medical experts would later examine the trajectories of the spurting blood and argue otherwise, but belief in a blood-drenched killer persisted.)

Though puzzled by Lizzie's cleanliness, police were certain that they had found the murder weapon. Lying in a box of dusty tools, stored high on a chimney jog in the basement, was a hatchet head. It was neither rusty nor old, though it had been freshly rubbed in ashes, perhaps to make it appear so. Moreover, its wooden handle, from which blood would have been difficult to remove, had been broken off near the head.

When the news broke that Lizzie was under suspicion, newspaper readers were horrified—not over the possibility that Lizzie might have murdered her parents, but that the police would harbor such horrid thoughts. The Boston *Globe* expressed its readers' indignation: "The only person that the government can catch is one whose innocence placed her in its power; the poor, defenseless child, who ought to have claimed by very helplessness their protection."

Angry letters denouncing the police flooded newspaper offices from New York to Chicago. Editorials appeared castigating the brutish officers who would suspect a grieving daughter of such a crime. Americans were certain that well-brought-up daughters could not commit murder with a hatchet on sunny summer mornings. And their reaction was not entirely without rationale.

Throughout the 1890s nearly every issue of *Forum, Arena, Scribner's, North American Review, Popular Science Monthly,* and *Harper's* (one of Lizzie's favorites) carried at least one article attesting to the gentleness, physical frailty, and docility of the well-bred American woman. Many of these articles were written in response to the growing number of women who were demanding equal rights, and were written with the intention of proving women hopelessly unable to handle the sacred privileges of men. After having read many such articles written by "learned gentlemen"—and antifeminist women—by the summer of 1892, men and women, regardless of how they stood on women's rights, felt certain that Lizzie Borden could not have hacked her parents to death. Physical and psychological frailties simply made it impossible.

Popular theories about women's physiological and psychological make-up took on new importance to followers of the Borden case. After detailed anatomical analysis, scientists confidently declared that the women of their era differed little from their prehistoric sisters. They spoke with assurance of women's arrested evolution. The fault, they agreed, lay in her reproductive capacity, which sapped vital powers that in men contributed to ever-improving physique and intellect.

The defects of the female anatomy included sloping shoulders, broad hips, underdeveloped muscles, short arms and legs, and poor coordination. To those who believed Lizzie innocent, evidence was abundant that no short-armed, uncoordinated, weakling of a woman could swing an ax with enough force to crash through hair and bone almost two dozen times.

But there was more to it than that. Having already noted woman's smaller frame, anatomists should hardly have been surprised to find her skull proportionately smaller than man's, yet they held up this revelation, too, as further proof of her inferiority. Rather than follow intellectual pursuits, for which they were woefully ill-equipped, women were advised to accept their intended roles as wives and mothers. After all, they were reminded, "Woman is only womanly when she sets herself to man `like perfect music unto noble works.' "

Spinsters like Lizzie were, as one author charitably put it, "deplorable accidents," but they were not wholly useless. The nation's old maids were urged to devote themselves to Christian charities and to teaching—a "reproductive calling." Lizzie's devotion to good works and the church followed this prescription precisely. Compelling indeed was the image of this pious daughter serving steaming bowls of soup to indigent newsboys and diligently trying to bring the gospel to the heathen Chinese of Fall River.

While anatomists studied the size of woman's skull, psychologists examined its contents. Among the qualities found to be essentially female were spiritual sensitivity, a good memory for minutiae, and a great capacity for "ennobling love." These positive attributes, however, could not obscure the psychologists' basic premise; women were illogical, inconsistent, and incapable of independent thought.

It is not accident that these traits bore striking resemblance to those attributed to children. As one psychologist pointed out in *Scribner's:* "Women are merely large babies. They are short-sighted, frivolous and occupy an intermediate stage between children and men. . . ."

Several authors manfully chuckled over woman's inability to plan and think things through. Clearly the murderer of the Bordens had planned things quite well. Not only had "he" managed to murder two people and elude the police, but "he" had shown remarkable tenacity by hiding for more than an hour after murdering Abby in order to do the same to Andrew.

Woman was considered man's superior in one area only: the moral sphere. She was thought to possess more "natural refinement," "diviner instincts," and stronger "spiritual sensibility" than man. She was inherently gentle, and abhorred cruelty—hardly the virtues of an ax murderer. Woman was also truthful, though some authors attributed her inability to lie to a lack of intelligence rather than to innate goodness. When reporters interviewed Lizzie's friends, the young women repeatedly mentioned her honesty.

Lizzie benefited greatly from the prevailing stereotypes of feminine delicacy and docility: her cause was also served by the widely accepted stereotype of the female criminal. Ironically, the same periodicals which carried articles about women's gentle nature also carried enough sordid stories of crimes committed by them to cast considerable doubt on their moral superiority. But writers did not find the situation paradoxical. To them, there were clearly two types of women: the genteel ladies of their own class and those women beneath them. Gentlemen authors believed that the womanly instincts of gentleness and love were the monopoly of upper-class women.

Scientists could hardly charge women of their own class with propensities toward violence without casting doubt on their own good breeding. For lower-class women with whom they had no intimate ties (at least none to which they would admit), the situation was quite different. These writers made it very clear that no woman servant, housekeeper, prostitute, nurse, washerwoman, barmaid, or factory girl could be above suspicion.

Several authors even believed that the female criminal had to look the part. In an article in *North American Review,* August, 1895, one criminologist thoughtfully provided the following description: "[She] has coarse black hair and a good deal of it. . . . She has often a long face, a receding forehead, overjutting brows, prominent cheek-bones, an exaggerated frontal angle as seen in monkeys and savage races, and nearly always square jaws."

She could also be marked by deep wrinkles, a tendency toward baldness, and numerous moles. Other authors noted her long middle fingers, projecting ears, and overlapping teeth. While Lizzie had a massive jaw, her hair was red, her teeth were straight, and her ears flat. Perhaps fortunately for Bridget, a member of the suspect servant class, she was mole-free and brown-haired, and she did not have protruding middle fingers.

Criminal women supposedly exhibited neither the aversion to evil nor the love of mankind which ennobled their upper-class sisters. Among their vices were said to be great cruelty, passionate temper, a craving for revenge, cunning greed, rapacity, contempt for truth, and vulgarity. Such women were thought to be "erotic," but incapable of devoted love. Certainly the Bordens' murderer had been exceedingly cruel. But, while Lizzie was admittedly fond of money and volunteered her dislike of her stepmother, few would have called her rapacious or vengeful, and erotic was hardly an adjective one would have applied to the chaste treasurer of the Fruit and Flower Mission.

The ferocity of the criminal woman fascinated many authors. A favorite murderess was Catherine Hayes, who, in 1890, stabbed her husband to death, cut off his head with a penknife, and boiled it. But then, Mrs. Hayes was a mill worker. One writer did admit that murders might be committed by well-bred women; their weapon would be poison, however, rather than a penknife or an ax, because its passivity appealed to their nature.

Lizzie's attorneys skillfully exploited these two stereotypes—the genteel young woman and the wart-ridden murderess—to their client's advantage throughout the Borden trial. Even before the case reached court, the press had firmly implanted in the public mind a clear picture of Lizzie as bereaved daughter. The image-making began with the very first—and entirely false—story about Lizzie printed in the Boston *Globe* on the day after the murders; "The young woman, with her customary cheery disposition, evidenced her feelings in the tuneful melody from *Il Trovatore,* her favorite opera, which she was singing as she returned to the house. . . . One glance into the living room changed her from a buoyant-spirited young woman into a nervous wreck, every fiber of her being palpitating with the fearful effects of that look. . . ."

In the dozens of articles that followed, Lizzie became the embodiment of genteel young womanhood. A reporter who interviewed her friends found "not one unmaidenly nor a single deliberately unkind act." Voicing the belief of many, he concluded, "Miss Borden, without a word from herself in her own defense, is a strong argument in her own favor."

The attributes of womanliness which vindicated Lizzie did not apply to Bridget. A servant, semiliterate, nearly friendless, Catholic and Irish, Bridget was the perfect target for suspicion. To the dismay of many, no evidence or motive ever could be found to implicate her in the deaths of her employers. Nevertheless, the police received dozens of letters urging her arrest. One man wrote demanding that Bridget and "her Confessor"—that is, her priest—be thrown into prison until she admitted her guilt.

The inquest began in Fall River on August 9. Two pharmacists from Smith's Drug Store testified that Lizzie had been shopping for poison on the afternoon before the murders. She had not asked for arsenic, which was sold over the counter, they said, but for the more lethal prussic acid, claiming she needed it to clean her sealskin cape. On the stand, Lizzie steadfastly denied the pharmacists' story, even denied knowing where Smith's Drug Store was, though it had been there for fourteen years on a street not five minutes from the house in which she had lived since childhood.

Lizzie's own testimony was full of contradictions. Discrepancies in her story might have been explained by hysteria or grief, but she had displayed neither. On August 5, a reporter at the murder scene for the Providence *Journal* noted: "She wasn't the least bit scared or worried. Most women would faint at seeing their father dead, for I never saw a more horrible sight. . . . She is a woman of remarkable nerve and self-control."

Such self-control seemed unnatural in an age when women were expected to swoon, and many people were alarmed by it. The reverend Mr. Buck, Lizzie's minister, reassured her champions that "her calmness is the calmness of innocence." Her lawyer, Mr. Jennings, sought to explain away her inconsistent answers by noting that "she was having her monthly illness" on the day of the murders, thereby evoking embarrassed nods of understandings.

Public sentiment on Lizzie's behalf rose to extraordinary heights. In full agreement with their pastor, her church declared her innocent. Ecclesiastical supporters were joined by several noted feminists. Mary Livermore, Susan Fessenden (president of the Women's Christian Temperance Union), and Lucy Stone took up the cudgels on Lizzie's behalf. Livermore declared her arrest to be another outrage perpetrated by "the tyrant man." Lizzie became the sacrificial lamb, the simple, warmhearted girl offered up by corrupt police to the altar of a power-hungry district attorney.

Nonetheless, the judge ordered her arrest at the inquest's end.

Reporters found Lizzie disappointingly composed after the indictment. With no tears to report, they concentrated on her cherry trimmed hat and the two ministers on whose arms she leaned as she went off to jail in Taunton, the county seat. The horrible cell that awaited her was described in detail. In fact, Lizzie was not confined to a cell, but spent much of her time in the matron's room. Little mention was made of the flowers that graced the prison's window sill, or the lace-edged pillow slips brought by Emma, or of the meals which Lizzie had sent over from Taunton's best hotel.

When the preliminary hearing before Judge Blaisdell began in late November, reporters from more than forty out-of-town newspapers attended. Police held back huge crowds while ladies and gentlemen from Fall River's elite filed into the courtroom to claim the best seats.

A new piece of evidence, damaging to Lizzie's cause, was introduced. She had turned over to the police a spotlessly clean, fancy, blue bengaline dress that she swore she had worn on the day of the murders. Women in New England were surprised. No one wore party dresses of bengaline, a partly woolen fabric, around the house in the August heat. While witnesses swore that Lizzie was indeed wearing blue that day, none could swear that this dress was the one they had seen. To confound the problem, Alice Russell reluctantly admitted that she had seen Lizzie burn a blue cotton dress in the kitchen stove three days after the murders. The dress was soiled, she said Lizzie had told her, with brown paint—a color, noted the prosecutor, not unlike that or dried blood.

Except for rubbing her shoe buttons together, Lizzie sat quietly and displayed little interest. On the very last day, however, she broke into sobs as she heard her lawyer declare that no "person could have committed that crime unless his heart was black as hell." Delighted newspaper artists sketched a tearful Lizzie listening to Mr. Jennings as he asked: "Would it be the stranger, or would it be the one bound to the murdered man by ties of love? . . . what does it mean when we say the youngest daughter? The last one whose baby fingers have been lovingly entwined about her father's brow? Is there nothing in the ties of love and affection?"

Lizzie Borden, accused of the ax murders of her father and stepmother in Fall River, Massachusetts (August 1892), was acquitted by an all-male jury that refused to believe that a well-bred woman could be capable of such an act.

Judge Blaisdell listened to all the evidence. It was no stranger who sat before him, but the daughter of a family he knew well. Jennings' image of the twining baby fingers was compelling, but so was the evidence prosecutor Hosea Knowlton produced. The judge finally began to speak: "Suppose for a single moment that *a man* was standing there. He was found close by that guestchamber which to Mrs. Borden was a chamber of death. Suppose that *a man* had been found in the vicinity of Mr. Borden and the only account he could give of himself was the unreasonable one that he was out in the barn looking for sinkers, that he was in the yard. . . . Would there be any question in the minds of men what should be done with such a man?" The

judge's voice broke, but he continued: ". . . the judgment of the court is that you are probably guilty and you are ordered to wait the action of the Superior Court."

The trial began in New Bedford, Massachusetts, on June 5, 1893. Reporters from all over the East Coast converged on the town. Every hotel room within miles was reserved. Fences had to be erected around the courthouse to control the crowds.

Lizzie's newly inherited fortune of several hundred thousand dollars bought her excellent counsel. George Robinson, former governor of the state, was a masterful orator with a politician's shrewd sense of public opinion: at his suggestion, Lizzie went into mourning for the first time since the murders. Laboring against him were District Attorneys Hosea Knowlton and William Moody (a future U.S. Supreme Court justice), as able as Robinson, but with a distaste for flamboyance. Among the three judges who would hear Lizzie's case was Justice Justin Dewey, whom Robinson had elevated to the bench while governor.

One hundred and forty-eight men awaited jury selection. It was assumed that all had formed opinions; they were asked only if their minds were still open enough to judge the evidence fairly. The first man called claimed he could never convict a woman of a capital offense and was dismissed. Of the final twelve, the foreman was a real estate broker and sometime politician, two were manufacturers, three were mechanics, and six were farmers with considerable acreage. Not one foreign-sounding name was among them. Nearly all were over fifty: all were good Yankees.

The first blow to the prosecution came when Judge Dewey ruled Lizzie's damaging inquest testimony inadmissible and barred evidence regarding the alleged attempt to buy poison. While these rulings made Knowlton's task more difficult, his biggest worry was that jury men believed, as did the Boston *Globe,* in the "moral improbability that a woman of refinement and gentle training . . . could have conceived and executed so bloody a butchery." As he repeatedly reminded the jury, "We must face this case as men, not gallants."

Knowlton produced medical experts from Harvard who testified that any average-sized woman could have swung an ax with force enough to commit the murders, and that the trajectory of blood would have been away from the assailant: Lizzie's tidy appearance minutes after the crimes had no bearing on her guilt or innocence. Robinson blithely discounted their testimony by asking the jurymen whether they put more store in Harvard scientists than in their own New England common sense.

Though Lizzie later professed to be shocked at his bill of $25,000, Robinson was worth every penny. As she sat before the jury, a Sunday-school teacher and loving youngest daughter, the jurymen, nearly all of whom were fathers themselves, heard Robinson conclude: "If the little sparrow does not fall unnoticed, then indeed in God's great providence, this woman has not been alone in this court room."

The jury was sent off to deliberate with what one reporter called Judge Dewey's "plea for the innocent." The other two judges were said to have been stunned by his lack of objectivity. Though Dewey was indeed grateful to Robinson for his judgeship, a more compelling reason for his unswerving belief in Lizzie's innocence may have been the three daughters he had at home, the eldest of whom was Lizzie's age.

The jurors who filed out with Dewey's plea ringing in their ears were bewhiskered, respectable, family men. If they could believe that a gentlewoman could pick up a hatchet such as surely lay in their own basements, and by murdering her parents become an heiress, what could they think next time they looked into their own girls' eyes?

They returned in one hour. The *New York Times* reported that Lizzie's "face became livid, her lips were compressed as she tottered to her feet to hear the verdict!" Before the clerk could finish asking for it, the foreman cried, "Not guilty!" Lizzie dropped to her seat as an enormous cheer went up from the spectators who climbed onto the benches, waving hats and handkerchiefs and weeping.

It would have been difficult for any jury to convict "beyond all reasonable doubt" on the circumstantial evidence presented. However, in the nearby bar to which the jurors dashed, a reporter learned that there had been no debate at all among the twelve. All exhibits were ignored. Their vote had been immediate and unanimous. It was only to avoid the impression that their minds had been made up in advance that they sat and chatted for an hour before returning with their verdict.

The following morning, Americans found reflected in the headlines their own joy that the jury had been so wise. Lizzie and Emma returned to Second Street.

Fall River society, which had defended her throughout her ordeal, fell away thereafter, and Lizzie was left pretty much alone. Undaunted, she determined to have all the things she had missed in her youth. With what some considered indiscreet haste, she bought a large house on the hill and named it Maplecroft. She also asked to be called Lisbeth and stopped going to the church whose parishioners had defended her so energetically. Matters were not improved when townspeople learned that she had bought and destroyed every available copy of local reporter Edwin Porter's *The Fall River Tragedy*, which had included portions of her inquest testimony.

Lizzie sealed her isolation in 1904 by striking up a friendship with Nance O'Neil, a Boston actress. The following year, to her neighbors' horror, Lizzie gave a party—complete with caterers and potted palms—for Miss O'Neil and her troupe. That night, Emma quietly moved out and never spoke to or saw Lizzie again.

Lizzie continued to live at Maplecroft in increasing isolation. Undoubtedly, she heard the nasty rhyme children began to sing to the tune of "Ta-Ra-Ra Boom-De-Ay!":

Lizzie Borden took an ax
And gave her mother forty whacks;
When she saw what she had done,
She gave her father forty-one!

Lizzie Borden died on June 1, 1927, at the age of sixty-six in Fall River. Emma died ten days later in New Hampshire. Few gravestones conceal a puzzle more intricate than that sealed away by the imposing Borden monument in Oak Grove Cemetery. The truth about the events on Second street lies buried there along with Andrew, Abby, Emma, and Lizzie, but back then, in the summer of 1893, most Americans knew in their hearts that no young lady like Lizzie could have murdered her parents with an ax. Reputable authors in respectable magazines assured them their intuition was correct. They did not even want to think that it could be otherwise.

STUDY QUESTIONS

1. How did Lizzie Borden's class and social standing influence the way she was treated by legal authorities?

2. What were the physical, psychological, intellectual, and moral characteristics that popular magazines in the late nineteenth century attributed to well-bred women? How closely did Lizzie conform to these expectations?

3. What did late nineteenth-century writers mean by such concepts as "arrested evolution" and "deplorable accidents"? How do these concepts indicate a sexually biased society?

4. In what area were women considered superior to men? Why was this so?

5. How did popular attitudes toward upper-class and lower-class women differ? Why were many people more inclined to suspect Bridget Sullivan than Lizzie Borden of the crime?

6. How was Lizzie's behavior during the entire episode interpreted?

7. Why was the trial politically and symbolically significant?

BIBLIOGRAPHY

The Borden murder case has been examined and reexamined. Victoria Lincoln, *Lizzie Borden, a Private Disgrace* (1967) and Robert Sullivan, *Goodbye Lizzie Borden* (1974) argue that she was indeed guilty of the crimes. Edward D. Radin, *Lizzie Borden: The Untold Story* (1961) views the case from a different perspective. Recent historical scholarship has only begun to explore the complexities of American attitudes toward women. Lois W. Banner, *Women in Modern America: A Brief History* (1974, second edition 1984) presents a fine introduction to the topic and a good bibliography. Other useful studies on women in the late nineteenth century include John S. Haller, Jr., and Robin M. Haller, *The Physician and Sexuality in Victorian America* (1974); G. J. Barker-Benfield, *The Horrors of the Half-Known Life: Male Attitudes Toward Women and Sexuality in Nineteenth-Century America* (1976); Linda Gordon, *Woman's Body, Woman's Right: A Social History of Birth Control in America* (1976); and Lois Banner, *American Beauty* (1983). Two other books present different views of the role of women in America. Kate Chopin, *The Awakening* (1980) is a wonderful novel written with depth and sensitivity. Questions of isolation and alienation in a small American town are touched upon in Michael Lesy, *Wisconsin Death Trip* (1973).

THE FIRST CHAPTER OF CHILDREN'S RIGHTS

Peter Stevens and Marian Eide

Today it is sadly common, a story whose ending is so often tragic. It is a story set in some of America's worst slums, and in some of the country's wealthiest neighborhoods. In the late 1980s the case of Joel Steinberg and Hedda Nussbaum focused the public consciousness on the issue of child abuse. In the mid-1980s, Steinberg, a New York criminal lawyer, and Nussbaum, a former editor and writer of children's books, illegally "adopted" two children. Soon a cycle of physical and mental abuse began. In the early morning of November 2, 1987, Nussbaum's 911 call brought paramedics to their apartment. On the floor the paramedics found six-year-old Lisa, naked, bruised, emaciated, and unable to breathe. She was in a coma. Tied to a "playpen" they discovered 16-month-old Mitchell, whose body also displayed clear signs of physical abuse.

Lisa never recovered, dying less than a week later. Examinations of her body told a tale of violent and prolonged abuse. The horror of her short life became evident during the sensational trial of Steinberg (all charges against Nussbaum were dropped in return for her testimony). In the end, Steinberg was found guilty and sentenced to serve 8 1/2 to 25 years in prison, and the state of New York passed new legislation—the "Lisa Law"—to end some of the loopholes in private adoptions. But perhaps even more importantly, it reminded Americans that child abuse knew no economic or social boundaries.

In "The First Chapter of Children's Rights," Peter Stevens and Marian Eide show that child abuse is not the product of the twentieth century. The issue of a child's rights versus the rights of parents to raise a child was as pressing in the 1870s as in the 1990s. It is important to keep in mind that in the decade before the Mary Ellen McCormack case, Congress abolished slavery in the United States and passed the Fourteenth Amendment, making it unlawful to deprive any American "of life, liberty, or property, without due process of law; nor deny to any person . . . the equal protection of the laws."

In the quiet New York courtroom, the little girl began to speak. "My name is Mary Ellen McCormack. I don't know how old I am. . . . I have never had but one pair of shoes, but can't recollect when that was. I have had no shoes or stockings on this winter. . . . I have never had on a particle of flannel. My bed at night is only a piece of carpet, stretched on the floor underneath a window, and I sleep in my little undergarment, with a quilt over me. I am never allowed to play with any children or have any company whatever. Mamma has been in the habit of whipping and beating me almost every day. She used to whip me with a twisted whip, a raw hide. The whip always left black and blue marks on my body. I have now on my head two black and blue marks which were made by mamma with the whip, and a cut on the left side of my forehead which was made by a pair of scissors in mamma's hand. She struck me with the scissors and cut me. I have no recollection of ever having been kissed, and have never been kissed by mamma. I have never been taken on my mamma's lap, or caressed or petted. I never dared to speak to anybody, because if I did I would get whipped. . . . Whenever mamma went out I was locked up in the bedroom. . . . I have no recollection of ever being in the street in my life."

At the beginning of 1874 there were no legal means in the United States to save a child from abuse. Mary Ellen's eloquent testimony changed that, changed our legal system's view of the rights of the child.

Yet more than a century later the concerns that arose from Mary Ellen's case are still being battled over in the courts. The classic dilemmas of just how deeply into the domestic realm the governmental arm can reach and what the obligations of public government are to the private individual take on particular urgency in considering child abuse.

"The First Chapter of Children's Rights" by Peter Stevens and Marian Eide in *American Heritage,* Vol. 41/No. 5, July/August 1990, pp. 84–91. Reprinted by permission of *American Heritage* Magazine, a division of Forbes, Inc. © Forbes, Inc., 1990.

Early in 1989, in the case of *DeShaney* v. *Winnebago County,* the Supreme Court declared that the government is not obligated to protect its citizens against harm inflicted by private individuals. DeShaney brought the case before the court in a suit against county social service agencies that had failed to intervene when her estranged husband abused their son, Joshua, who, as a result of his father's brutality, suffered permanent brain damage. The father was convicted, but his former wife believes that fault also lies with the agencies, whose failure to intercede violated her son's Fourteenth Amendment right not to be deprived of life or liberty without due process of the law. Chief Justice William H. Rehnquist wrote that intervening officials are often charged with "improperly intruding into the parent-child relationship." Justice William J. Brennan, Jr., dissenting, wrote: "Inaction can be every bit as abusive of power as action, [and] oppression can result when a State undertakes a vital duty and then ignores it."

The difficulty in bringing Mary Ellen McCormack into the New York Supreme Court in 1874 grew from similar controversy over the role of government in family matters, and Mary Ellen's sad history is not so different from Joshua DeShaney's.

When Mary Ellen's mother, Frances Connor, immigrated to the United States from England in 1858, she took a job at the St. Nicholas Hotel in New York City as a laundress. There she met an Irishman named Thomas Wilson who worked in the hotel kitchen shucking oysters. They were married in April 1862, shortly after Wilson had been drafted into the 69th New York, a regiment in the famous Irish Brigade. Early in 1864 she gave birth to their daughter, whom she named Mary after her mother and Ellen after her sister.

The birth of her daughter seems to have heralded the beginning of Frances Wilson's own decline. Her husband was killed that same year in the brutal fighting at Cold Harbor, Virginia, and with a diminished income she found it necessary to look for a job. In May 1864, unable to pay someone to watch the baby while she was at work, she gave Mary Ellen over to the care of a woman named Mary Score for two dollars a week, the whole of her widow's pension. Child farming was a common practice at that time, and many women made a living taking in unwanted children just as others took in laundry. Score lived in a tenement in the infamous warrens of Mulberry Bend, where thousands of immigrants crowded into small, airless rooms, and it is likely that providing foster care was her only means of income.

Finally Frances Wilson became unable to pay for the upkeep of her child; three weeks after the payments ceased, Score turned Mary Ellen over to the Department of Charities. The little girl—whose mother was never to see her again—was sent to Blackwells Island in July 1865. Her third home was certainly no more pleasant than Mulberry Bend. Mary Ellen was among a group of sick and hungry foundlings; fully two-thirds of them would die before reaching maturity.

The same slum-bred diseases that ravaged the children on Blackwells Island had also claimed all three children of a couple named Thomas and Mary McCormack. So when Thomas frequently bragged of the three children he had fathered by another woman, his wife was more receptive to the idea of adopting them than she might otherwise have been. Those children, he told her, were still alive, though their mother had turned them over to the care of the city.

On January 2, 1866, the McCormacks went to the Department of Charities to reclaim one of the children Thomas's mistress had abandoned. The child they chose as their own was Mary Ellen Wilson. Because the McCormacks were not asked to provide any proof of relation to the child and gave only the reference of their family doctor, there is no evidence that Thomas was in any way related to the child he brought home that day. More than a month later an indenture was filed for Mary Ellen in which the McCormacks promised to report on her condition each year. There were no other requirements.

Shortly after bringing the child home, Thomas McCormack died, and his widow married a man named Francis Connolly. Little more than that is known of the early childhood of Mary Ellen. She came to her new home in a flannel petticoat, and

when her clothing was removed from Connolly's home as evidence six years later, there was barely enough to fill a tiny suitcase. She was beaten, set to work, deprived of daylight, and locked in closets for days at a time; she was rarely bathed, never kissed, and never addressed with a gentle word. During the six years she lived with Connolly, only two reports on her progress were filed with the Commissioners of Charities and Correction.

Late in 1873 Etta Angell Wheeler, a Methodist caseworker serving in the tenements of New York City, received a disturbing report. It came from Margaret Bingham, a landlord in Hell's Kitchen, and told of a terrible case of child abuse. The child's parents had been tenants of Bingham for about four years, and almost immediately after they moved in, Bingham began to observe how cruelly they treated their child, Mary Ellen. They confined her in close quarters during hot weather, kept her severely underdressed in cold, beat her daily, and left her unattended for hours at a time. On several occasions Bingham tried to intervene; each time the child's mother said she would call upon the fullest resources of the law before she would allow any interference in her home. Finally Bingham resorted to threat: The beatings and ill treatment would have to stop, or the family would be evicted. When her plan backfired and the family left, Bingham, in a last-ditch effort, sent for Etta Wheeler. In order to observe Mary Ellen's predicament, Wheeler went to the Connollys's neighbor, an ailing tubercular woman named Mary Smitt. Enlisting Smitt's aid, she proposed that Mary Ellen be sent over each day to check on the patient. Smitt reluctantly agreed, and on the pretext of inquiring about this sick neighbor, Wheeler knocked on Mary Connolly's door.

Inside she saw a "pale, thin child, bare-foot, in a thin, scanty dress so tattered that I could see she wore but one garment besides.

"It was December and the weather bitterly cold. She was a tiny mite, the size of five years, though, as afterward appeared, she was then nine. From a pan set upon a low stool she stood washing dishes, struggling with a frying pan about as heavy as herself. Across the table lay a brutal whip of twisted leather strands and the child's meager arms and legs bore many marks of its use. But the saddest part of her story was written on her face in its look of suppression and misery, the face of a child unloved, of a child that had seen only the fearsome side of life. . . . I never saw her again until the day of her rescue, three months later. . . ."

Though social workers often witnessed scenes of cruelty, poverty, and grief, Wheeler found Mary Ellen's plight especially horrifying. She went first to the police; they told her she must be able to furnish proof of assault in order for them to act. Charitable institutions she approached offered to care for the child, but first she must be brought to them through legal means. There were none. Every effort Wheeler made proved fruitless. Though there were laws to protect children—laws, in fact, to prevent assault and battery to any person—there were no means available for intervention in a child's home.

Finally Wheeler's niece had an idea. The child, she said, was a member of the animal kingdom; surely Henry Bergh, the founder of the American Society for the Prevention of Cruelty to Animals, who was famous for his dramatic rescue of mistreated horses in the streets of New York, might be willing to intervene. Within the hour Wheeler had arranged a meeting with Bergh. Despite its apparent strangeness, this sort of appeal was not new to Bergh. Once before he had tried to intervene in a case of child abuse and had failed. This time he was more cautious.

"Very definite testimony is needed to warrant interference between a child and those claiming guardianship," Bergh told Wheeler. "Will you not send me a written statement that, at my leisure, I may judge the weight of the evidence and may also have time to consider if this society should interfere? I promise to consider the case carefully."

Wheeler provided a statement immediately, including in it the observations of neighbors to whom she had spoken. Bergh was convinced. "No time is to be lost," he wrote his lawyer, Elbridge T. Gerry. "Instruct me how to proceed."

The next day Wheeler again visited the sick woman in Hell's Kitchen and found in her room a young man who, on hearing Wheeler's name, said, "I was sent to take the census in this house. I have been in every room." Wheeler then knew him to be a detective for Bergh.

On the basis of the detective's observations and the testimony provided by Etta Wheeler, Bergh's lawyers, Gerry and Ambrose Monell, appeared before Judge Abraham R. Lawrence of the New York Supreme Court to present a petition on behalf of Mary Ellen. They showed that Mary Ellen was held illegally by the Connollys, who were neither her natural parents nor her lawful custodians, and went on to describe the physical abuse Mary Ellen endured, the marks and bruises on her body, and the general state of deprivation that characterized her existence. They offered a list of witnesses willing to testify on behalf of the child and concluded by stating that there was ample evidence to indicate that she was in clear danger of being maimed or even killed. The lawyers requested that a warrant be issued, the child removed from her home and placed in protective custody, and her parents brought to trial.

Bergh testified that his efforts on behalf of the child were in no way connected to his work with abused animals and that they did not make use of the special legal provisions set up for that purpose. Because of Bergh's association with animal rescue, to this day the case is often described as having originated in his conviction that the child was a member of the animal kingdom. Bergh, however, insisted that his actions were merely those of any humane citizen and that he intended to prevent cruelties inflicted on children through any legal means available.

Judge Lawrence issued a warrant under Section 65 of the Habeas Corpus Act as requested. This provision read in part: "Whenever it shall appear by satisfactory proof that any one is held in illegal confinement or custody, and that there is good reason to believe that he will . . . suffer some irreparable injury, before he can be relieved by the issuing of a *habeas corpus* or *certiorari*, any court or officer authorized to issue such

Many children, like these girls in the garment industry, grew up in factories. In 1874, Henry Bergh, Elbridge Gerry, and James Wright founded the New York Society for the Prevention of Cruelty to Children and eventually secured passage of a bill that made labor by children under the age of fourteen illegal.

writs, may issue a warrant . . . [and] bring him before such court or officer, to be dealt with according to law."

The press of the day hailed Gerry's use of Section 65 of the Habeas Corpus Act as brilliant. The act was rarely invoked, and the legal means for removing a child from its home were nonexistent. In using the little-known law, Gerry created a new method for intervention.

That same day, April 9, 1874, Mary Ellen was taken from her home and brought into Judge Lawrence's court. Having no adequate clothing of her own, the child had been wrapped in a carriage blanket by the policemen who held her in custody. A reporter on the scene described her as "a bright little girl, with features indicating unusual mental capacity, but with a care-worn, stunted, and prematurely old look. . . . No change of custody or condition could be much for the worse."

The reporter Jacob Riis was present in the court. "I saw a child brought in . . . at the sight of which men wept aloud, and I heard the story of little Mary Ellen told . . . that stirred the soul of a city and roused the conscience of a world that had forgotten, and as I looked, I knew I was where the first chapter of children's rights was being written." Her body and face were terribly bruised; her hands and feet "showed the plain marks of great exposure." And in what almost instantly seemed to condemn Mrs. Connolly before the court, the child's face bore a fresh gash through her eyebrow and across her left cheek that barely missed the eye itself. Mary Ellen was to carry this scar throughout her life.

Interestingly, there is no further mention in the ample reports surrounding Mary Ellen's case of her foster father, Francis Connolly. He was never brought into court, never spoke publicly concerning the child. All her life Mary Ellen exhibited a frightened timidity around men, yet it was against her foster mother that she testified.

On the evening of her detention, Mary Ellen was turned over to the temporary custody of the matron of police headquarters. The next day, April 10, the grand jury read five indictments against Mary Connolly for assault and battery, felonious assault, assault with intent to do bodily harm, assault with intent to kill and assault with intent to maim. Once the stepmother had been brought into the legal system, there were ample means to punish her.

Mary Ellen herself was brought in to testify against the woman she had called her mother. On her second appearance in court she seemed almost wholly altered. She was clothed in a new suit, and her pale face reflected the kindness that surrounded her. She carried with her a new picture book, probably the first she had ever owned. She acted open and uninhibited with strangers, and interestingly, seemed to show no great fear of her mother or any apparent enmity toward her.

The lawyers Gerry and Monell gathered several witnesses against Mary Connolly, among them neighbors, Wheeler, and Mary Ellen herself. Margaret Bingham said she had seen the child locked up in a room and had told other neighbors, but they said there was no point in interfering since the police would do nothing. Bingham had tried to open the window of the child's room to let in some air, but it would not lift more than an inch. As a constant presence and reminder, a cowhide whip was locked in the room with the child. Wheeler recounted her first visit to Mary Ellen, during which the child washed dishes that seemed twice her size and was apparently oblivious of the visitor's presence. The whip lay on the table next to her. The next day, when Wheeler came by again, the child was sewing, and the whip lay on a chair near her.

Then it was the mother's turn to testify. On the witness stand Mary Connolly showed herself to be a woman of some spirit. Despite her treatment of the child, there is something compelling in Connolly's strength and humor. At one point the prosecutor asked if she had an occupation be-

yond house-keeping. "Well," she said, "I sleep with the boss." As the trial wore on, she became enraged at Gerry's prodding questions; finally she accused him of being "ignorant of the difficulties of bringing up and governing children." Yet she admitted that contrary to regulations, in the six years she had Mary Ellen in her custody, she had reported on her condition to the Commissioners of Charities and Correction only twice.

Two indictments were brought against Connolly, the first for her assault on the child with scissors on April 7, the second for the continual assault inflicted on the child throughout the years 1873 and 1874. After twenty minutes of deliberation the jury returned a verdict of guilty of assault and battery. Connolly was sentenced to one year of hard labor in the city penitentiary, then known as the Tombs. In handing down this sentence, the judge defined it not only as a punishment to Connolly but also as a statement of precedence in child abuse cases.

Mary Ellen never returned to the Connollys's home. In the ensuing months the publicity that her case received brought in many claims of relation. But on investigating, her guardian, Judge Lawrence, discovered the stories were fictions, and he finally placed the child in the Sheltering Arms, a home for grown girls; soon after, she was moved to the Woman's Aid Society and Home for Friendless Girls. This mirrors another critical problem in the system's treatment of minors. All juveniles were handled by the Department of Charities and Correction, and whether they were orphaned or delinquent, their treatment was the same. And so it was that the ten-year-old Mary Ellen was placed in a home with mostly delinquent adolescents.

Etta Wheeler knew this was wrong for Mary Ellen, and she expressed her hesitations to Judge Lawrence. He, in turn, consulted with Henry Bergh, and eventually they agreed to turn the girl over the Etta Wheeler herself. Unable to imagine giving up her work in the slums of New York City but believing that Mary Ellen deserved a better environment, Wheeler brought the child to her mother in North Chili, New York, Wheeler's mother became ill shortly afterward, and Mary Ellen was raised mostly by Wheeler's sister.

"Here began a new life," Wheeler wrote. "The child was an interesting study, so long shut within four walls and now in a new world. Woods, fields, `green things growing,' were all strange to her, she had not known them. She had to learn, as a baby does, to walk upon the ground,—she had walked only upon floors, and her eye told her nothing of uneven surfaces. . . . But in this home there were other children and they taught her as children alone can teach each other. They taught her to play, to be unafraid, to know her rights and to claim them. She shared their happy, busy life from the making of mud pies up to charming birthday parties and was fast becoming a normal child."

The happiness of her years in the upstate New York countryside lies in stark contrast to her early childhood. And indeed, as Wheeler wrote, she learned by example the ways of normal childhood. She grew up strong and well, learning how to read and playing with friends and pet kittens. In 1875 Wheeler reported to Gerry that Mary Ellen was growing up as a normal child. "She has some faults that are of the graver sort. She tells fibs and sticks to them bravely, steals lumps of sugar & cookies and only confesses when the crumbs are found in her pocket—in short she is very much like other children, loving—responding to kindness & praise, hating a task unless there be a play, or a reward thereof, and inevitably `forgetting' what she does not wish to remember—what children do not do some or all of these forbidden things! She is a favorite with nearly all the people who have come to know her."

When she was twenty-four, Mary Ellen married a widower named Louis Schutt and with him had two children, Etta—named after the woman who had rescued her—and Florence. She adopted a third, orphaned child, Eunice. She also raised Louis Schutt's three children from his first wife.

In 1911 Wheeler visited her protégé in her home, "finding her well and happy. . . . The family income is small, but Mary Ellen is a prudent housewife and they are comfortable. The two

daughters are promising girls." The eldest daughter, Etta, worked industriously through that summer, finished high school, and became a teacher. Florence followed her sister's path, teaching first grade for thirty-eight years. When she retired, the elementary school in North Chili was renamed in her honor. Eunice earned a business degree, married, and raised two sons.

Florence remembers her mother as a solemn woman who came alive whenever she listened to Irish jigs and especially to "The Irish Washerwoman." She was unfailingly generous with her time and her affection. Her years in North Chili had saved her from the vicious cycle abused children often suffer of becoming abusers themselves. According to Florence her mother was capable of sternness and certainly willing to punish her daughters, but the terrible experiences of her early childhood never spilled into her own child rearing. As Etta Wheeler wrote, "To her children, two bright, dutiful daughters, it has been her joy to give a happy childhood in sharp contrast to her own."

Etta and Florence often asked their mother about the Connollys, but Mary Ellen was reluctant to speak of her early years. She did show her daughters the scars on her arms where she had been burned with a hot iron, and of course they could see the scissors scar across her face. Florence distinctly recalls that in the few times they spoke of her mother's years in New York City, she never mentioned a woman inflicting her injuries; it was always a man.

In October of 1913 Mary Ellen Schutt attended a meeting of the American Humane Society in Rochester. She was accompanied by Etta Wheeler, who was there to present a paper entitled "The Finding of Mary Ellen." The paper concluded: "If the memory of her earliest years is sad, there is this comfort that the cry of her wrongs awoke the world to the need of organized relief for neglected and abused children."

Mary Ellen died on October 30, 1956, at the age of ninety-two. She was survived by her two daughters, her adopted daughter, three stepchildren, three grandchildren, and five great-grandchildren. More important, she was survived by the beginning of a movement to prevent the repetition of tragedies like her own. On December 15, 1874, Henry Bergh, Elbridge Gerry, and James Wright founded the New York Society for the Prevention of Cruelty to Children (SPCC) with the ample assistance of Cornelius Vanderbilt. It was the first organization of its kind in America. At the outset of their work the founders signed a statement of purpose: "The undersigned, desirous of rescuing the unprotected children of this city and State from the cruelty and demoralization which neglect and abandonment engender, hereby engage to aid, with their sympathy and support, the organization and working of a Children's Protective Society, having in view the realization of so important a purpose."

The SPCC saw its role essentially as a legal one. As an agent or a friend of the court, the society endeavored to intervene on the behalf of children, enforcing the laws that were in existence to prevent cruelty toward them and at the same time introducing new legislation on their behalf.

At the first meeting of the SPCC on December 16, 1874, Gerry stressed the fact that the most crucial role of the society lay in the rescue of children from abusive situations. From there, he pointed out, there were many excellent groups available to care for and shelter children and many state laws to punish abusive parents. He went on to predict that as soon as abusers learned that the law could reach them, there would be few cases like that of Mary Ellen.

Bergh was less optimistic. At the same meeting, he pointed out that neglected and abused children were to become the mothers and fathers of the country and that unless their interests were defended, the interests of society in general would suffer.

In its first year the SPCC investigated more than three hundred cases of child abuse. Many people felt threatened by the intrusion of the government into their private lives; discipline, they believed, was a family issue, and outside influence was not only unwelcome but perhaps even unconstitutional. When, with the aid of a state senator, James W. Booth, Gerry introduced in the New York legislature a law entitled "An Act to Prevent and Punish Wrongs to Children," the proposal was immediately and vigorously attacked. The New York *World* wrote that Bergh was to be authorized to "break into the garrets of the poor and carry off their children upon the suspicion of spanking." According to the *World,* the law would give Bergh "power to discipline all the naughty children of New York. . . . We sincerely hope that it may not be finally kicked out of the legislature, as it richly deserves to be, until the public mind shall have had time to get itself thoroughly enlightened as to the state of things in which it has become possible for such a person as Mr. Bergh to bring the Legislature to the point of seriously entertaining such an impudently senseless measure. This bill is a bill to supersede the common law in favor of Mr. Bergh, and the established tribunals of justice in favor of an irresponsible private corporation." The bill was passed in 1876, however, and became the foundation upon which the SPCC performed its work.

From its initial concentration on preventing abuse in the home, the society broadened its franchise to battle neglect, abandonment, and the exploitation of children for economic gain. In 1885, after considerable effort by the SPCC and in the face of yet more opposition, Gerry secured passage of a bill that made labor by children under the age of fourteen illegal.

As the explosive story of the death of Lisa Steinberg in the home of her adoptive parents revealed to the nation in 1987, abuse still haunts American society. There are still legal difficulties in removing a child from an abusive situation. In 1987 the House Select Committee on Children, Youth, and Families reported that the incidence of child abuse, particularly sexual abuse and neglect, is rising; in 1985 alone almost two million children were referred to protective agencies. In part, the committee said, this increase was due to a greater awareness of the issue, and there has also been an increased effort to educate children themselves about situations that constitute abuse or molestation and about ways to get help.

Despite a plethora of programs designed to address abuse, the committee concluded that not enough is being done. The most effective programs were found to be those that worked to prevent the occurrence of abuse at the outset through education in parenting techniques, through intervention in high-risk situations, such as unwanted pregnancies, and through screening for mental and emotional difficulties. However, funding for public welfare programs has fallen far below the demands, and what funding there is must frequently be diverted to intervene in more and more sensational and hopeless cases.

If there is still much hard, sad work ahead, there is also much that has been accomplished. And all of it began when Mary Ellen McCormack spoke and, in speaking, freed herself and thousands of other children from torment.

STUDY QUESTIONS

1. What issues did the case of Mary Ellen McCormack raise? What role should the state and federal governments play in the private lives of citizens?

2. What was the practice of "child farming"?

3. What problems did Etta Angell Wheeler face when she attempted to help Mary Ellen McCormack? Why did she turn to Henry Bergh? What role did Bergh play in the case and in Mary Ellen's life?

4. What can you tell about the life of Mary Connolly from this essay?

5. What happened to Mary Ellen after she was separated from Mary Connolly?

6. How did the case of Mary Ellen McCormack lead to new laws to benefit children? How did the laws change the problem of child abuse and exploitation?

BIBLIOGRAPHY

Only recently have historians begun a serious study of the private lives of American families, and the connections between private behavior and public policy. An excellent place to start is Steven Mintz and Susan Kellogg, *Domestic Revolutions: A Social History of American Family Life* (1988), as well as Steven Mintz, *A Prison of Expectations: The Family in Victorian Culture* (1983). The career of Henry Bergh is covered in Gerald Carson, "The Great Meddler," *American Heritage* (December, 1967). Social conditions of New York's slums are explored in the writings of Jacob Riis, especially *How the Other Half Lives* (1890). An outstanding study of the problems of social reform in the cities is Paul Boyer, *Urban Masses and Moral Reform in America. 1820–1920* (1978).

PART THREE

War and Peace in a New Century

The period between the assassination of William McKinley in 1901 and America's entry into the Great War in 1917 has been labeled as the Progressive Era. In character and tone the years mirrored the first Progressive president, Theodore Roosevelt. Animated and energetic, T. R. used the presidency as a "bully pulpit," readily giving his opinion on a variety of subjects, ranging from literature and politics to football and divorce. Roosevelt believed that America's greatness was the result of its Anglo-Saxon heritage. Although he hoped to bring a "Square Deal" to all Americans, his reforming impulse was conservative in nature; he maintained that only through moderate reform could America preserve its traditional social, economic, and political structure. He had no sympathy for such "radical fanatics" as socialists or anarchists, nor did he trust the masses of American people who lacked his breeding and education. His answer for any sort of mob action was "taking ten or a dozen of their leaders out, standing . . . them against a wall, and shooting them dead."

Despite their ethnocentricity and self-righteousness, Roosevelt and the next two Progressive presidents—William Howard Taft and Woodrow Wilson—did attempt to curb some of the worst abuses of the urban-industrial society. They saw legislation through Congress that limited the number of hours that women and children could work and enacted the Pure Food and Drug Act (1906) and the Meat Inspection Act (1906). However, other Progressives, often with the support of the president, supported prohibition and antidivorce legislation, thereby seeking to regulate the private lives of millions of Americans.

A major shortcoming of the Progressive movement was the general reluctance to support minority and ethnic groups. Such Progressives as James K. Vardaman and Theodore G. Bilbo, both from Mississippi, supported forward-looking legislation for whites but were violent race-baiters. Progressives rarely attacked the Jim Crow system in the South or introduced antilynching legislation in Congress. Segregation within the federal government expanded under Woodrow Wilson.

Similarly, vocal and independent labor unions and women's rights organizations seldom found support among influential Progressives. Margaret Sanger's birth control movement met strong opposition from middle-class men and women who saw it as a threat to family and morality. Such radical working-class organizations as the Industrial Workers of the World (the IWW, or "Wobblies") were not embraced by the mainstream of the Progressive movement.

The Progressive movement, however, did not really survive World War I. As a result of the Spanish-American War of 1898, the United States had acquired new territories in the distant Pacific, requiring a two-ocean navy and leaving Americans with global responsibilities. Those responsibilities eventually complicated and compromised the reform spirit. The Great War of 1914–1918 damaged the reform impulses of Progressivism. It inspired skepticism, pessimism, and ultimately cynicism, and in the death-filled trenches of Western Europe, the Progressive movement met its demise.

The following essays deal with different characteristics of the Progressive movement. Confronted by the powerful forces of urbanization and industrialization, Americans attempted—sometimes successfully, often unsuccessfully—to come to terms with their changing society. Amidst that attempt, World War I complicated Progressivist dreams with the reality of horror, stupidity, and mass death.

TEDDY ROOSEVELT AND THE ROUGH RIDERS

Robert J. Maddox

Anchored off the coast of Cuba, aboard the *Yucatan,* Theodore Roosevelt received news on the evening of June 21, 1898 that he and his men, a volunteer cavalry regiment dubbed the Rough Riders, should disembark from the safety of the ship and join the fighting ashore. It was a welcomed invitation, celebrated with cheers, war dances, songs, boasts, and toasts. "To the officers—may they get killed, wounded, or promoted," urged one toast that captured the mood aboard ship.

Who were these Rough Riders who seemed so bent on winning glory? As one of them told Roosevelt, "Who would not risk his life for a star?" And who was Theodore Roosevelt, the energetic rich kid who lusted after fame and perhaps had his eyes—albeit nearsighted—focused on the presidency? Robert J. Maddox retells this story of Theodore Roosevelt, the Rough Riders, and America's "splendid little war" with Spain. In the process he tells a great deal about the future president and the nation that made him its hero.

The war against Spain in 1898 was one of the more popular conflicts in American history. Victory came easily, there were relatively few casualties, and the cause seemed just in the minds of most people. From it the United States acquired the Philippine Islands, Puerto Rico, Guam, and a virtual protectorate over Cuba. The nation acquired several heroes as well, Admiral Dewey to name one, but none more colorful than the flamboyant Teddy Roosevelt. His exploits in Cuba, at the head of his Rough Riders, made him a legend in his own lifetime and helped make him President of the United States.

Roosevelt was in the prime of his life when the war broke out. Not yet forty years old, he possessed an imposing if somewhat overweight physique which he kept fit by almost daily exercise. In this regard he was a self-made man. Spindly and a trifle owlish as a youngster, Roosevelt, through what one of his biographers termed the "Cult of Strenuosity," had built up his body by relentless physical activity. Only one of his faculties had failed to respond—his eyesight. Cursed from boyhood with extreme nearsightedness, which grew worse over the years, Roosevelt was very self-conscious about this weakness in an otherwise healthy organism. During the war he was so worried it would betray him in combat that he had at least a half-dozen pairs of spectacles sewn in various parts of his uniform as insurance.

Mentally, Roosevelt was a complex individual. Exceedingly bright, he read voraciously, and penned his own books and articles without the help of a ghostwriter. He was, or would become, friendly with some of the leading intellectuals of the era. One side of him, however, remained boyish until the day he died. "You must always remember," a British diplomat wrote a friend some years later, "that the President [Roosevelt] is about six." Without in any way belittling his patriotism, it

An 1889 photo shows Teddy Roosevelt as colonel of the Rough Riders. Teddy's uniforms, which had extra spectacles sewn into them, were tailored by Brooks Brothers to ensure a proper fit.

seems safe to say that Teddy's enthusiasm for fighting the Spaniards stemmed at least as much from his desire to have a "bully" time doing it.

No one ever accused Roosevelt of being a pacifist. During the 1880s and 1890s the United States had gotten into a number of scrapes with other nations over issues large and small. Almost invariably T. R. had called for the most militant actions in response to these situations, and had denounced those who urged caution. War to him was not a catastrophe to be avoided; it could be a tonic to the nation's bloodstream. A country too long at peace, he believed, tended to grow soft and effeminate, while war encouraged "manliness," a characteristic he prized above all else.

Teddy Roosevelt and the Rough Riders" by Robert J. Maddox. This article is reprinted from the November 1977 issue of *American History Illustrated* 12, pp. 8–15, 18–19, with the permission of Cowles History Group, Inc. Copyright *American History Illustrated* magazine.

Before 1897 Roosevelt had held no office which dealt directly with military or foreign affairs. He had served in the New York state legislature as federal Civil Service Commissioner, and as a commissioner of the New York City Police Department. Despite having held such prestigious jobs for a man of his years, Roosevelt's political future was clouded by his tendency to alienate some of those who could help him and by the strident views on foreign policy which he never hesitated to voice—often to the great embarrassment of his own party. When, as a reward for his services in the election of 1896, T. R.'s friends began pushing for his appointment as Assistant Secretary of the Navy in the new Republican administration, they encountered stiff opposition. The President-elect himself had reservations about Teddy, but named him anyway. "I hope he has no preconceived plans," McKinley said wistfully, "which he would wish to drive through the moment he got in."

McKinley hoped in vain. Within two months of his appointment, Roosevelt wrote the well-known naval expert, Captain Alfred Thayer Mahan, that:

If I had my way, we would annex those islands [Hawaii] tomorrow. If that is impossible, I would establish a protectorate . . . . I believe we should build the Nicaraguan Canal at once, and should build a dozen new battleships, half of them on the Pacific Coast. I am fully alive to the danger from Japan.

These and similar sentiments clearly demonstrated that T. R. had no intention of vanishing into the bureaucracy. Nor did he. A short time later, when Secretary of the Navy John D. Long went on vacation, one newspaper reported that Roosevelt soon had "the whole Navy bordering on a war footing. It remains only to sand down the decks and pipe to quarters for action." Teddy did not try to conceal his delight in being left to mind the store. "The Secretary is away," he wrote in one letter, "and I am having immense fun running the Navy." One story had it that when asked about his Assistant Secretary, Long dourly responded "Why 'Assistant'?"

Sticking pins in maps and running around on inspection tours must have amused him, but Roosevelt wanted some real action. Spain provided the most likely source. Once the possessor of a world empire, Spain by this time was a minor power clinging grimly to its few remaining territories. One of these, Cuba, lay less than 100 miles from American shores, and for several years had smoldered with insurrection against Spanish domination. Though he refrained from speaking out publicly, Roosevelt, in private talks and correspondence, recommended war against Spain almost from the day he became Assistant Secretary. American honor demanded it, he said, and a brief war would help rekindle martial instincts which had flagged through years of peace. There would be an additional dividend, he wrote on one occasion, that being "the benefit done our military forces by trying both the Army and Navy in actual practice."

Roosevelt did not bring on the war with Spain, of course, however much he tried. Cuban propaganda, sensationalist American newspapers, and jingoes in and outside Congress, combined to keep talk of war before the pubic. Still, through 1897, President McKinley refused to be stampeded, and the Spanish Government (which very much wished to avoid war) repeatedly gave in to American demands over the treatment of Cuba.

Then, early in 1898, two events occurred which made war virtually inevitable. First, a letter critical of McKinley, written by the Spanish minister in Washington, was stolen from the mails and reprinted in the American press. Trivial in itself, this blunder enraged many Americans. More important, the warship *Maine* blew up in a Cuban harbor with the loss of more than 200 sailors. Though not a shred of evidence has ever emerged to indicate that the Spanish were responsible, most Americans (abetted by much of the press) assumed that they were and demanded revenge. McKinley simply was not strong enough to stand against this pressure. On April 10 he asked Congress for what amounted to a declaration of war.

Well before the war began Roosevelt had told others that if it came he would not be content to remain in Washington. He was true to his word. By March he was beseeching New York state officials to permit him to raise a regiment of volunteers, which unit, he promised, would be "jim-dandy." That he had never served in the military, let alone seen combat, fazed Teddy not at all. He was greatly miffed when his generous offer was spurned.

Roosevelt, as usual, had other irons in the fire. Due to the minuscule size of the Regular Army, Congress had authorized the recruitment of three volunteer cavalry regiments from the Southwest. Because of his political connections, which he used to the utmost, Roosevelt was offered the command of one of these units. Modesty suddenly descended upon him. Estimating that it might take him a month or so to familiarize himself thoroughly with military procedures and tactics, T. R. asked that his friend, Captain Leonard Wood (at that time a military surgeon), be promoted to colonel and given command of the regiment. He would be satisfied with a mere lieutenant-colonelcy and would serve under Wood. Roosevelt's light could not be hidden, however, and from the start the First Volunteer Cavalry was known as "Roosevelt's Rough Riders."

Teddy was eager to get going. Quickly ordering the appropriate uniforms from Brooks Brothers (to ensure a proper fit), he began complaining that the war might be over before he could get into it—"it will be awful if we miss the fun." At last, in early May, he set out for San Antonio, Texas, where the First Volunteers were undergoing preliminary training. He arrived to the welcome of a brass band and "his boys."

And what a group it was. "Mingling among the cowboys and momentarily reformed bad men from the West," Henry Pringle has written, "were polo players and steeplechase riders from the Harvard, Yale, and Princeton clubs of New York City." Though from time to time Roosevelt protested against the carnival atmosphere which pervaded the camp, he enjoyed himself hugely. After one period of mounted drill, for instance, he told his men to "drink all the beer they want, which I will pay for" and had a few himself. Colonel Wood admonished Teddy for this kind of behavior, which the latter admitted was out of place. "Sir," Roosevelt replied, "I consider myself the damnedest ass within ten miles of this camp."

Two weeks after Teddy arrived in San Antonio, the Rough Riders were ordered to report to the Tampa, Florida staging area for the expedition against Cuba. By this time they had been transformed from an undisciplined group in civilian clothes to an undisciplined group in uniform. Tampa was, if possible, even more chaotic than San Antonio had been. Units of Regulars, National Guard, and volunteers milled about with little over-all direction and inadequate facilities. Some units were without arms, others had arms but no ammunition, still others lacked uniforms, bedding, or tents. It was a mess. "No head," Roosevelt wrote angrily in his diary, "a breakdown of both the railroad and military systems of the country."

With an aroused public clamoring for action, the War Department ordered the expedition to sail despite its obvious lack of preparation. At this point the Rough Riders had what amounted to their first engagement of the war—against other American soldiers. Port Tampa lay about nine miles from Tampa, where the troops were quartered, with only a single track railway connecting them. The orders sent to individual regiments included no scheduling, so it was up to each unit to get to the port as best it could. A mad scramble ensued to commandeer whatever rolling stock was available: The Rough Riders were lucky enough to come upon an engine with some coal cars which they promptly seized. But the excitement was not yet over. Arriving at the port, Roosevelt and Wood found that the ship allotted to them was also designated for two regiments and there was not enough space for all three. As Teddy later recounted the episode:

Accordingly, I ran at full speed to our train; and leaving a strong guard with the baggage I double-quicked the rest of the regiment up to the boat just in time to board her as she came into the quay and then to hold her against the 2d Regulars and the 71st, who had arrived a little too late. . . . There was a good deal of expostulation, but we had possession.

It was a false alarm. On the eve of departure another message arrived from the War Department. "Wait until you get further orders before you sail," it read. "Answer quick." As things turned out the officers and men of the expeditionary force spent almost two weeks sweating and cursing in the tightly packed ships at anchor under the Florida sun. At last, on June 14, thirty-two steamers moved out of Port Tampa heading slowly toward Cuba. The Fifth Army Corps, as it was designated, consisted of two divisions and an independent brigade of infantry, a division of dismounted cavalry, four batteries of field artillery, and some auxiliary troops. The Rough Riders were aboard, of course, but like the other cavalry units they had nothing to ride. Because of the lack of space, the only animals brought along were horses for the officers and mules for carrying supplies.

Eventually the flotilla reached Cuba and landings were made virtually unopposed in several places. The debarkations resembled the disorder which had reigned at Tampa Bay. The men and equipment were brought ashore in helter-skelter fashion by an assortment of launches and other small boats. The animals were even less fortunate: They were driven off the sides of ships and left to fend for themselves. Some reached shore safely, others swam to watery graves. Once again, teddy was unwilling to trust luck. Recognizing the captain of a small vessel which drew alongside as a man he had known in the Navy Department. Roosevelt directed that the ship be used solely for getting the rough Riders ashore as quickly as possible. After spending weeks aboard what they referred to as "prison hulks," the men must have appreciated the initiative of their second-in-command.

The course of the Cuban campaign cannot be recounted in detail here. The most charitable single word to describe it is "muddled." The commander of the Fifth Corps was General William R. Shafter, a rather lethargic man who weighed well over 300 pounds. Suffering from the heat since arriving in Florida, Shafter, during the latter part of the fighting, had to be transported reclining on a barn door. His immediate subordinates were three other general officers, who seemed at least as much concerned with outdoing one another as with fighting the Spaniards. One of them, "Fighting Joe" Wheeler, had last seen combat as a Confederate officer during the Civil War. During moments of stress, it was reported, he became confused as to who his opponents were and several times referred to them as "those Yankees." Fortunately for the Americans, the Spanish were in even worse shape. Although some individual Spanish troops and units fought well, they were badly led and defeatism permeated the defending forces.

Once a semblance of order was created on the beach, preparations were made for the expedition's advance against the main target, the harbor city of Santiago, less than twenty miles west along the coastline. The only available overland route, however, swung inland through jungles which provided excellent concealment for defenders. The movement took place in fits and starts and was not without incident—and losses. The Spanish fought a brief rearguard action at a place called Las Guásimas, for instance, during which sixteen Americans were killed and another fifty wounded. The Rough Riders took part in this engagement, as did some regular units, and there is evidence to indicate that Wood and Roosevelt led their men into an ambush. In later years Roosevelt indignantly denied any such thing and claimed that "every one of the officers had full knowledge of where he would find the enemy." In any event, Teddy boasted, ". . . we wanted the first whack at the Spaniards and we got it."

Finally, by the end of June, American forces were within striking distance of Santiago. Their way was blocked by a series of fortifications and trenches located on a chain of hills surrounding the city—the most prominent of which was San Juan Hill. The difficulty in moving supplies and ammunition by pack animal along narrow jungle trails caused the troops to remain before Santiago for several days. The plan of attack was simple. One division would move several miles north to attack a stronghold at El Caney, the rest of the units would march head-on against the San Juan and nearby hills. Both assaults began on the morning of July 1.

From where they had grouped, American troops had to push through several miles of jungle and ford a stream before reaching clear ground in front of the hills. They began taking losses while still in the jungle. There were only two trails they could use and Spanish artillery had these zeroed in. One column had at its head an observation balloon pulled along by men holding guy ropes. It proved to be of little help to the Americans, but showed Spanish artillery-men exactly where the enemy was. Fortunately for the men underneath it, the bag was pierced several times and settled gently to the ground before it could cause even greater damage.

The jungle ended abruptly at a stream which ran along its edge roughly parallel to the Spanish lines on the ridges. Across the stream there were several hundred yards of meadowlands before reaching the slopes. As the troops emerged from the jungle, therefore, they were exposed to withering Spanish rifle fire from above. What little order there was broke down as the advancing columns began clogging up at the jungle's edge. Some units refused to cross the stream, others became disorganized as they tried to move through and get into position. The situation presented a cruel dilemma to American commanders. To attack with insufficient numbers of men would be to risk defeat. To wait until all units were deployed would mean exposing those who crossed the stream first to an extended period under the crippling fire. Finally, a little past noon and before elements in the rear had left the jungle, the assault began.

San Juan Hill was the main objective. Somewhat to the right and much closer to American lines lay Kettle Hill, assigned to the dismounted cavalry. Since Colonel Wood earlier had taken command of a brigade, Roosevelt now led the Rough Riders. This was what he had been waiting for, and he would not be found wanting. Showing complete disdain for enemy bullets, Teddy galloped around on his horse, Little Texas, exhorting his men to form up for attack. They were joined by elements from several other regiments, including black troops from the 10th Cavalry. Roosevelt

waved his hat and the men moved forward. "By this time we were all in the spirit of the thing and greatly excited by the charge," he wrote later, "the men cheering and running forward between shots. . . . I . . . galloped toward the hill. . . ."

According to his own account Roosevelt quickly moved ahead of the men, preceded only by his orderly, Henry Bardshar, "who had run ahead very fast in order to get better shots at the Spaniards. . . ." About forty yards from the crest Teddy encountered a wire fence and jumped off Little Texas, letting the horse run free. Almost immediately he saw Bardshar shoot down two Spaniards who emerged from the trenches. Soon Roosevelt and Bardshar were surrounded by the rest of the men as they swarmed over the hill, capturing or killing the few Spanish troops who had not retreated. The charge up Kettle Hill was over.

From their newly won position, Roosevelt and his men had an excellent view of the assault against San Juan Hill. Earlier artillery barrages had failed to cause much damage to the breastworks, and the black powder used in American guns produced smoke which drew Spanish counterfire. Now, however, three Gatling guns opened up with good effect. "They went b-r-r-r, like a lawn mower cutting grass over our trenches," a Spanish officer said later. "We could not stick a finger up when you fired without getting it cut off." Still the Spaniards held their positions as the ragged blue lines moved forward. Despite heavy losses, the Americans pushed doggedly up the hill. At last, just before they reached the top, the Spanish defenders fired a last volley and fled.

Beyond Kettle Hill and to the right of San Juan lay another ridge from which the enemy kept shooting. Rallying his men again, Roosevelt led them down the far side of Kettle, across the intervening valley, and up the slopes. "I was with Henry Bardshar, running up at the double," Teddy later recalled, "and two Spaniards leaped from the trenches and fired at us, not ten yards away. As they turned to run I closed in and fired twice, missing the first and killing the second. My revolver was from the sunken battleship *Maine*." Again the Americans drove the Spanish before them. When they took possession of these crests, "we found ourselves overlooking Santiago."

Although the Americans had won the day, the battle for Santiago was not yet over. The Spanish had about 16,000 men to defend the city, the Americans an equal number to take it. The latter were exhausted from their attacks and lacked reserves, food, and ammunition. By July 3, two days after the initial assaults, the Americans had lost 224 men killed and 1,370 wounded. The result was a stand-off. Spanish units did not attempt to break out of the ring; the Americans were in no shape to move against the city's defenses. "Tell the President for Heaven's sake to send us every regiment and above all every battery possible," Roosevelt wrote a friend. "We have won so far at a heavy cost, but the Spaniards fight very hard and charging these intrenchments against modern rifles is terrible. . . . We *must* have help—thousands of men, batteries, and *food* and ammunition." Fortunately, the Spanish launched no major counter attacks.

While the men dug themselves into the hills, the battle for Santiago was decided by another engagement—at sea. A Spanish fleet had been bottled up in Santiago Harbor for some time: Shafter's expedition was supposed to take the city, thereby forcing the Spanish ships to leave the harbor or surrender. At 9:30 A.M. on July 3, Spanish ships began coming out singly under the guns of the blockaders. It was a courageous but futile effort. Despite some bungling on the part of the U. S. Navy, all the opposing ships were sunk or disabled. After two weeks of negotiation Shafter received the surrender of Santiago, and less than a month after that the Spanish Government sued for peace.

Although the war had ended in complete victory for the United States, it came in for a great deal of criticism in the period following. Charges of incompetence were leveled against the top echelons, there were undignified exchanges between generals and admirals over who deserved credit for which victory, and the condition of the men returning from Cuba caused a public outcry. Many troops died from tropical illnesses, and still others from food poisoning caused by tainted meat.

It was probably for these reasons that Roosevelt's star came to shine so brightly. He had performed heroically, after all, and he was sufficiently subordinate in rank to escape any blame about the war's mismanagement.

Teddy himself was not loath to accept the limelight; indeed, he eagerly sought it. Almost immediately he began campaigning for the governorship of New York state and, lest anyone forget his exploits, kept the Rough Rider bugler at his side during his speeches. Roosevelt had other assets, of course, but being the "Hero of San Juan Hill" (he was not disposed to argue about which hill he had climbed) did him no harm. He had become fixed in the national mind as Colonel Teddy Roosevelt of the Rough Riders.

"I would honestly rather have my position of colonel," Roosevelt had told his men at their mustering-out ceremony, "than any other position on earth." No doubt he meant it at the time. As governor of New York, and later as President of the United States, he looked back fondly on his days in Cuba and the men who had served with him. In both positions he tried to accommodate as many as possible of the former Rough Riders who petitioned him for a job. His loyalty, if not his judgment, could scarcely be questioned. In one case he tried to have appointed as territorial marshal a man who, it was found, was serving time in prison for homicide. Undaunted, Teddy later tried to have the person installed as warden of the very prison in which he had been confined. "When I told this to John Hay," Roosevelt said, "he remarked (with a brutal absence of feeling) that he believed the proverb ran, `Set a Rough Rider to catch a thief.' "

For once in his life, Teddy was at a loss for a reply.

STUDY QUESTIONS

1. What character traits inclined Roosevelt toward war? What events led the United States to war with Spain?

2. What sorts of men joined the Rough Riders?

3. What problems did the United States have mobilizing for war?

4. What role did the Battles of Kettle Hill and San Juan Hill play in the war in Cuba?

5. How did Roosevelt capitalize on his newly won fame?

BIBLIOGRAPHY

The best overview of the Spanish-American War is David Trask, *The War with Spain in 1898* (1981). Shorter, but still useful is Frank Freidel, *The Splendid Little War* (1958). Theodore Roosevelt's own account of his moments of glory is *The Rough Riders* (1899). Among the more readable biographies of Roosevelt are Edmund Morris, *The Rise of Theodore Roosevelt* (1979) and David McCullough, *Mornings on Horseback* (1981). More scholarly biographies are G. Wallace Chessman, *Theodore Roosevelt and the Politics of Power* (1969) and Howard K. Beals, *Theodore Roosevelt and the Rise of America to World Power* (1956). On the war also see Gerald F. Linderman, *The Mirror of War: American Society and the Spanish-American War* (1974) and H. Wayne Morgan, *America's Road to Empire* (1965). Also see Stuart C. Miller, *"Benevolent Assimilation": The American Conquest of the Philippines, 1899–1903* (1982).

READING 8

LIVING AND DYING IN PACKINGTOWN, CHICAGO from *THE JUNGLE*

Upton Sinclair

In the late fall of 1904, Upton Sinclair, a young ambitious novelist imbued with a zealous sense of socialism, traveled to Chicago to gather information about the horrors and abuses of the meatpacking industry. For the next seven weeks, as a cold fall gave way to a brutal winter, Sinclair lived in the workers' ghetto of Packingtown, talked with workers, and studied the meatpacking industry.

On Christmas Day of 1904 he began writing *The Jungle,* the story of Jurgis Rudkus. A Lithuanian immigrant of great strength, Rudkus came to America full of hope—only to be used, abused, and discarded by the unfeeling powers of Packingtown. Sinclair wrote frantically for three months, stopping only occasionally to eat or sleep. He poured all his emotions into Rudkus's story, hoping to show Americans how evil the industry—and by extension, capitalism—had become. He recorded the stench and unhealthy conditions of Packingtown and the dangers of working in the packinghouses. Of the work, one historian wrote, "Each job had its own dangers: the dampness and cold of the packing rooms and hide cellar, the sharp blade of the beef boner's knife, the noxious dust of the wood department and fertilizer plant, the wild charge of a half-crazed steer on the killing floor." The following selection from *The Jungle* describes some of the working and living conditions in Packingtown.

During this time that Jurgis was looking for work occurred the death of little Kristoforas, one of the children of Teta Elzbieta. Both Kristoforas and his brother, Juozapas, were cripples, the latter having lost one leg by having it run over, and Kristoforas having congenital dislocation of the hip, which made it impossible for him ever to walk. He was the last of Teta Elzbieta's children, and perhaps he had been intended by nature to let her know that she had had enough. At any rate he was wretchedly sick and undersized; he had the rickets, and though he was over three years old, he was no bigger than an ordinary child of one. All day long he would crawl around the floor in a filthy little dress, whining and fretting; because the floor was full of draughts he was always catching cold, and snuffling because his nose ran. This made him a nuisance, and a source of endless trouble in the family. For his mother, with unnatural perversity, loved him best of all her children, and made a perpetual fuss over him—would let him do anything undisturbed, and would burst into tears when his fretting drove Jurgis wild.

And now he died. Perhaps it was the smoked sausage he had eaten that morning—which may have been made out of some tubercular pork that was condemned as unfit for export. At any rate, an hour after eating it, the child had begun to cry with pain, and in another hour he was rolling about on the floor in convulsions. Little Kotrina, who was all alone with him, ran out screaming for help, and after a while a doctor came, but not until Kristoforas had howled his last howl. No one was really sorry about this except poor Elzbieta, who was inconsolable. Jurgis announced that so far as he was concerned the child would have to be buried by the city, since they had no money for a funeral; and at this the poor woman almost went out of her senses, wringing her hands and screaming with grief and despair. Her child to be buried in a pauper's grave! And her stepdaughter to stand by and hear it said without protesting! It

was enough to make Ona's father rise up out of his grave to rebuke her! If it had come to this, they might as well give up at once, and be buried all of them together! . . . In the end Marija said that she would help with ten dollars; and Jurgis being still obdurate, Elzbieta went in tears and begged the money from the neighbors, and so little Kristoforas had a mass and a hearse with white plumes on it, and a tiny plot in a graveyard with a wooden cross to mark the place. The poor mother was not the same for months after that; the mere sight of the floor where little Kristoforas had crawled about would make her weep. He had never had a fair chance, poor little fellow, she would say. He had been handicapped from birth. If only she had heard about it in time, so that she might have had the great doctor to cure him of his lameness! . . . Some time ago, Elzbieta was told, a Chicago billionaire had paid a fortune to bring a great European surgeon over to cure his little daughter of the same disease from which Kristoforas had suffered. And because this surgeon had to have bodies to demonstrate upon, he announced that he would treat the children of the poor, a piece of magnanimity over which the papers became quite eloquent. Elzbieta, alas, did not read the papers, and no one had told her; but perhaps it was as well, for just then they would not have had the car-fare to spare to go every day to wait upon the surgeon, nor for that matter anybody with the time to take the child.

All this while he was seeking for work, there was a dark shadow hanging over Jurgis; as if a savage beast were lurking somewhere in the pathway of his life, and he knew it, and yet could not help approaching the place. There are all stages of being out of work in Packingtown, and he faced in dread the prospect of reaching the lowest. There is a place that waits for the lowest man—the fertilizer-plant!

The men would talk about it in awe-stricken whispers. Not more than one in ten had ever really tried it; the other nine had contented themselves with hearsay evidence and a peep through the door. There were some things worse than even starving to death. They would ask Jurgis if

Upton Sinclair, "Living and Dying in Packingtown, Chicago." From Upton Sinclair, *The Jungle*. Chicago, 1905.

he had worked there yet, and if he meant to; and Jurgis would debate the matter with himself. As poor as they were and making all the sacrifices that they were, would he dare to refuse any sort of work that was offered to him, be it as horrible as ever it could? Would he dare to go home and eat bread that had been earned by Ona, weak and complaining as she was, knowing that he had been given a chance, and had not had the nerve to take it?—And yet he might argue that way with himself all day, and one glimpse into the fertilizer-works would send him away again shuddering. He was a man, and he would do his duty; he went and made application—but surely he was not also required to hope for success.

The fertilizer-works of Durham's lay away from the rest of the plant. Few visitors ever saw them, and the few who did would come out looking like Dante, of whom the peasants declared that he had been into hell. To this part of the yards came all the "tankage" and waste products of all sorts; here they dried out the bones—and in suffocating cellars where the daylight never came you might see men and women and children bending over whirling machines and sawing bits of bones into all sorts of shapes, breathing their lungs full of the fine dust, and doomed to die, every one of them, within a certain definite time. Here they made the blood into albumen, and made other foul-smelling things into things still more foul-smelling. In the corridors and caverns where it was done you might lose yourself as in the great caves of Kentucky. In the dust and the steam the electric lights would shine like far-off twinkling stars—red and blue, green and purple stars, according to the color of the mist and the brew from which it came. For the odors in these ghastly charnel-houses there may be words in Lithuanian, but there are none in English. The person entering would have to summon his courage as for a cold-water plunge. He would go on like a man swimming under water; he would put his handkerchief over his face, and begin to cough and choke; and then, if he were still obstinate, he would find his head beginning to ring, and the veins in his forehead to throb, until finally

he would be assailed by an overpowering blast of ammonia fumes, and would turn and run for his life, and come out half-dazed.

On top of this were the rooms where they dried the "tankage," the mass of brown stringy stuff that was left after the waste portions of the carcasses had had the lard and tallow dried out of them. This dried material they would then grind to a fine powder, and after they had mixed it up well with a mysterious but inoffensive brown rock which they brought in and ground up by the hundreds of carloads for that purpose, the substance was ready to be put into bags and sent out to the world as any one of a hundred different brands of standard bone-phosphate. And then the farmer in Maine or California or Texas would buy this, at say twenty-five dollars a ton, and plant it with his corn; and for several days after the operation the fields would have a strong odor, and the farmer and his wagon and the very horses that had hauled it would all have it too. In Packingtown the fertilizer is pure, instead of being a flavoring, and instead of a ton or so spread on several acres under the open sky, there are hundreds and thousands of tons of it in one building, heaped here and there in haystack piles, covering the floor several inches deep, and filling the air with a choking dust that becomes a blinding sandstorm when the wind stirs.

It was to this building that Jurgis came daily, as if dragged by an unseen hand. The month of May was an exceptionally cool one, and his secret prayers were granted; but early in June there came a record-breaking hot spell, and after that there were men wanted in the fertilizer-mill.

The boss of the grinding room had come to know Jurgis by this time, and had marked him for a likely man; and so when he came to the door about two o'clock this breathless hot day, he felt a sudden spasm of pain shoot through him—the boss beckoned to him! In ten minutes more Jurgis had pulled off his coat and overshirt, and set his teeth together and gone to work. Here was one more difficulty for him to meet and conquer!

His labor took him about one minute to learn. Before him was one of the vents of the mill in

Chicago's meatpacking industry grew up with little or no government control. These sausage makers at Armour & Co. worked in extreme temperatures and without adequate ventilation, causing many to faint or to vomit from the stench.

which the fertilizer was being ground—rushing forth in a great brown river, with a spray of the finest dust flung forth in clouds. Jurgis was given a shovel, and along with half a dozen others it was his task to shovel this fertilizer into carts. That others were at work he knew by the sound, and by the fact that he sometimes collided with them; otherwise they might as well not have been there, for in the blinding dust-storm a man could not see six feet in front of his face. When he had filled one cart he had to grope around him until another came, and if there was none on hand he continued to grope till one arrived. In five minutes he was, of course, a mass of fertilizer from head to feet; they gave him a sponge to tie over his mouth, so that he could breathe, but the sponge did not prevent his lips and eyelids from caking up with it and his ears from filling solid. He looked like a brown ghost at twilight—from hair to shoes he became the color of the building and of everything in it, and for that matter a hundred yards outside it. The building had to be left open,

and when the wind blew Durham and Company lost a great deal of fertilizer.

Working in his shirt-sleeves, and with the thermometer at over a hundred, the phosphates soaked in through every pore of Jurgis's skin, and in five minutes he had a headache, and in fifteen was almost dazed. The blood was pounding his brain like an engine's throbbing; there was a frightful pain in the top of his skull, and he could hardly control his hands. Still, with the memory of his four months' siege behind him, he fought on, in a frenzy of determination; and half an hour later he began to vomit—he vomited until it seemed as if his innards must be torn to shreds. A man could get used to the fertilizer-mill, the boss had said, if he would only make up his mind to it; but Jurgis now began to see that it was a question of making up his stomach.

At the end of that day of horror, he could scarcely stand. He had to catch himself now and then, and lean against a building and get his bearings. Most of the men, when they came out, made straight for a saloon—they seem to place fertilizer and rattlesnake poison in one class. But Jurgis was too ill to think of drinking—he could only make his way to the street and stagger on to a car. He had a sense of humor, and later on, when he became an old hand, he used to think it fun to board a streetcar and see what happened. Now, however, he was too ill to notice it—how the people in the car began to gasp and sputter, to put their handkerchiefs to their noses, and transfix him with furious glances. Jurgis only knew that a man in front of him immediately got up and gave him a seat; and that half a minute later the two people on each side of him got up; and that in a full minute the crowded car was nearly empty—those passengers who could not get room on the platform having gotten out to walk.

Of course Jurgis had made his home a miniature fertilizer-mill a minute after entering. The stuff was half an inch deep in his skin—his whole system was full of it, and it would have taken a week not merely of scrubbing, but of vigorous exercise, to get it out of him. As it was, he could be compared with nothing known to men, save that newest discovery of the savants, a substance which emits energy for an unlimited time, without being itself in the least diminished in power. He smelt so that he made all food at the table taste, and set the whole family to vomiting; for himself it was three days before he could keep anything upon his stomach—he might wash his hands, and use a knife and fork, but were not his mouth and throat filled with the poison?

And still Jurgis stuck it out! In spite of splitting headaches he would stagger down to the plant and take up his stand once more, and begin to shovel in the blinding clouds of dust. And so at the end of the week he was a fertilizer man for life—he was able to eat again, and though his head never stopped aching, it ceased to be so bad that he could not work.

So there passed another summer. It was a summer of prosperity, all over the country, and the country ate generously of packinghouse products, and there was plenty of work for all the family, in spite of the packers' efforts to keep a su-

perfluity of labor. They were again able to pay their debts and to begin to save a little sum; but there were one or two sacrifices they considered too heavy to be made for long—it was too bad that the boys should have to sell papers at their age. It was utterly useless to caution them and plead with them; quite without knowing it, they were taking on the tone of their new environment. They were learning to swear in voluble English; they were learning to pick up cigar-stumps and smoke them, to pass hours of their time gambling with pennies and dice and cigarette-cards; they were learning the location of all the houses of prostitution on the "Levée," and the names of the "madames" who kept them, and the days when they gave their state banquets, which the police captains and the big politicians all attended. If a visiting "country-customer" were to ask them, they could show him which was "Hinkydink's" famous saloon, and could even point out to him by name the different gamblers and thugs and "hold-up men" who made the place their headquarters. And worse yet, the boys were getting out of the habit of coming home at night. What was the use, they would ask, of wasting time and energy and a possible car-fare riding out to the stockyards every night when the weather was pleasant and they could crawl under a truck or into an empty doorway and sleep exactly as well? So long as they brought home a half dollar for each day, what mattered it when they brought it? But Jurgis declared that from this to ceasing to come at all would not be a very long step, and so it was decided that Vilimas and Nikalojus should return to school in the fall, and that instead Elzbieta should go out and get some work, her place at home being taken by her younger daughter.

Little Kotrina was like most children of the poor, prematurely made old; she had to take care of her little brother, who was a cripple, and also of the baby; she had to cook the meals and wash the dishes and clean house, and have supper ready when the workers came home in the evening. She was only thirteen, and small for her age, but she did all this without a murmur; and her mother went out, and after trudging a couple of days about the yards, settled down as a servant of a "sausage-machine."

Elzbieta was used to working, but she found this change a hard one, for the reason that she had to stand motionless upon her feet from seven o'clock in the morning till half-past twelve, and again from one till half-past five. For the first days it seemed to her that she could not stand it—she suffered almost as much as Jurgis had from the fertilizer—and would come out at sundown with her head fairly reeling. Besides this, she was working in one of the dark holes, by the electric light, and the dampness, too, was deadly—there were always puddles of water on the floor, and a sickening odor of moist flesh in the room. The people who worked here followed the ancient custom of nature, whereby the ptarmigan is the color of dead leaves in the fall and of snow in winter, and the chameleon, who is black when he lies upon a stump and turns green when he moves to a leaf. The men and women who worked in this department were precisely the color of the "fresh country sausage" they made.

The sausage-room was an interesting place to visit, for two or three minutes, and provided that you did not look at the people; the machines were perhaps the most wonderful things in the entire plant. Presumably sausages were once chopped and stuffed by hand, and if so it would be interesting to know how many workers had been displaced by these inventions. On one side of the room were the hoppers, into which men shoveled loads of meat and wheelbarrows full of spices; in these great bowls were whirling knifes that made two thousand revolutions a minute, and when the meat was ground fine and adulterated with potato-flour, and well mixed with water, it was forced to the stuffing-machines on the other side of the room. The latter were tended by women; there was a sort of spout, like the nozzle of a hose, and one of the women would take a long string of "casing" and put the end over the nozzle and then work the whole thing on, as one works on the finger of a tight glove. This string would be twenty or thirty feet long, but the woman would have it all on in a jiffy;

and when she had several on, she would press a lever, and a stream of sausage-meat would be shot out, taking the casing with it as it came. Thus one might stand and see appear, miraculously born from the machine, a wriggling snake of sausage of incredible length. In front was a big pan which caught these creatures, and two more women who seized them as fast as they appeared and twisted them into links. This was for the uninitiated the most perplexing work of all; for all that the woman had to give was a single turn of the wrist; and in some way she contrived to give it so that instead of an endless chain of sausages, one after another, there grew under her hands a bunch of strings, all dangling from a single centre. It was quite like the feat of a prestidigitator—for the woman worked so fast that the eye could literally not follow her, and there was only a mist of motion, and tangle after tangle of sausages appearing. In the midst of the mist, however, the visitor would suddenly notice the tense set face, with the two wrinkles graven in the forehead, and the ghastly pallor of the cheeks; and then he would suddenly recollect that it was time he was going on. The woman did not go on; she stayed right there—hour after hour, day after day, year after year, twisting sausage-links and racing with death. It was piece-work, and she was apt to have a family to keep alive; and stern and ruthless economic laws had arranged it that she could only do this by working just as she did, with all her soul upon her work, and with never an instant for a glance at the well-dressed ladies and gentlemen who came to stare at her, as at some wild beast in a menagerie.

With one member trimming beef in a cannery, and another working in a sausage factory, the family had a first-hand knowledge of the great majority of Packingtown swindles. For it was the custom, as they found, whenever meat was so spoiled that it could not be used for anything else, either to can it or else to chop it up into sausage. With what had been told them by Jonas, who had worked in the pickle-rooms, they could now study the whole of the spoiled-meat industry on the inside, and read a new and grim meaning into that old Packingtown jest—that they use everything of the pig except the squeal.

Jonas had told them how the meat that was taken out of pickle would often be found sour, and how they would rub it up with soda to take away the smell, and sell it to be eaten on free-lunch counters; also of all the miracles of chemistry which they performed, giving to any sort of meat, fresh or salted, whole or chopped, any color and any flavor and any odor they chose. In the pickling of hams they had an ingenious apparatus, by which they saved time and increased the capacity of the plant—a machine consisting of a hollow needle attached to a pump; by plunging this needle into the meat and working with his foot, a man could fill a ham with pickle in a few seconds. And yet, in spite of this, there would be hams found spoiled, some of them with an odor so bad that a man could hardly bear to be in the room with them. To pump into these the packers had a second and much stronger pickle which destroyed the odor—a process known to the workers as "giving them thirty percent." Also, after the hams had been smoked, there would be found some that had gone to the bad. Formerly these had been sold as "Number Three Grade," but later on some ingenious person had hit upon a new device, and now they would extract the bone, about which the bad part generally lay, and insert in the hole a white-hot iron. After this invention there was no longer Number One, Two, and Three Grade—there was only Number One Grade. The packers were always originating such schemes—they had what they called "boneless hams," which were all the odds and ends of pork stuffed into casing; and "California hams," which were the shoulders, with big knuckle-joints, and nearly all the meat cut out; and fancy "skinned hams," which were made of the oldest hogs, whose skins were so heavy and coarse that no one would buy them—that is, until they had been cooked and chopped fine and labelled "head cheese"!

It was only when the whole ham was spoiled that it came into the department of Elzbieta. Cut up by the two-thousand-revolutions-a-minute flyers, and mixed with half a ton of other meat, no odor that ever was in a ham could make any difference. There was never the least attention paid to what was cut up for sausage; there would come all the way back from Europe old sausage that had been rejected, and that was mouldy and white—it would be dosed with borax and glycerine, and dumped into the hoppers, and made over again for home consumption. There would be meat that had tumbled out on the floor, in the dirt and sawdust, where the workers had tramped and spit uncounted billions of consumption germs. There would be meat stored in great piles in rooms; and the water from leaky roofs would drip over it, and thousands of rats would race about on it. It was too dark in these storage places to see well, but a man could run his hand over these piles of meat and sweep off handfuls of the dried dung of rats. These rats were nuisances, and the packers would put poisoned bread out for them; they would die, and then rats, bread, and meat would go into the hoppers together. This is no fairy story and no joke; the meat would be shovelled into carts, and the man who did the shovelling would not trouble to lift out a rat even when he saw one—there were things that went into the sausage in comparison with which a poisoned rat was a tidbit. There was no place for the men to wash their hands before they ate their dinner, and so they made a practice of washing them in the water that was to be ladled into the sausage. There were the butt-ends of smoked meat, and the scraps of corned beef, and all the odds and ends of the waste of the plants, that would be dumped into old barrels in the cellar and left there. Under the system of rigid economy which the packers enforced, there were some jobs that it only paid to do once in a long time, and among these was the cleaning out of the waste-barrels. Every spring they did it; and in the barrels would be dirt and rust and old nails and stale water—and cart load after cart load of it would be taken up and dumped into the hoppers with fresh meat, and sent out to the public's breakfast. Some of it they would make into "smoked" sausage—but as the smoking took time, and was therefore expensive, they would call upon their chemistry department, and preserve it with borax and color it with gelatine to make it brown. All of their sausage came out of the same bowl, but when they came to wrap it they would stamp some of it "special," and for this they would charge two cents more a pound.

Such were the new surroundings in which Elzbieta was placed, and such was the work she was compelled to do. It was stupefying, brutalizing work; if left her no time to think, no strength for anything. She was part of the machine she tended, and every faculty that was not needed for the machine was doomed to be crushed out of existence. There was only one mercy about the cruel grind—that it gave her the gift of insensibility. Little by little she sank into a torpor—she fell silent. She would meet Jurgis and Ona in the evening, and the three would walk home together, often without saying a word. Ona, too, was falling into the habit of silence—Ona, who had once gone about singing like a bird. She was sick and miserable, and often she would barely have strength enough to drag herself home. And there they would eat what they had to eat, and afterwards, because there was only their misery to talk of, they would crawl into bed and fall into a stupor and never stir until it was time to get up again, and dress by candlelight, and go back to the machines. They were so numbed that they did not even suffer much from hunger, now; only the children continued to fret when the food ran short.

Yet the soul of Ona was not dead—the souls of none of them were dead, but only sleeping; and now and then they would waken, and these were cruel times. The gates of memory would roll open—old joys would stretch out their arms to them, old hopes and dreams would call to them, and they would stir beneath the burden that lay upon them, and feel its forever immeasurable weight. They could not even cry out beneath it; but anguish would seize them, more dreadful than the agony of death. It was a thing scarcely to be spoken—a thing never spoken by all the world, that will not know its own defeat.

They were beaten; they had lost the game, they were swept aside. It was not less tragic because it was so sordid, because that it had to do with wages and grocery bills and rents. They had dreamed of freedom; of a chance to look about them and learn something; to be decent and clean, to see their child grow up to be strong. And now it was all gone—it would never be! They had played the game and they had lost. Six years more of toil they had to face before they could expect the least respite, the cessation of the payments upon the house; and how cruelly certain it was that they could never stand six years of such a life as they were living! They were lost, they were going down—and there was no deliverance for them, no hope; for all the help it gave them the vast city in which they lived might have been an ocean waste, a wilderness, a desert, a tomb. So often this mood would come to Ona, in the nighttime, when something wakened her; she would lie, afraid of the beating of her own heart, fronting the blood-red eyes of the old primeval terror of life. Once she cried aloud, and woke Jurgis, who was tired and cross. After that she learned to weep silently—their moods so seldom came together now! It was as if their hopes were buried in separate graves.

Jurgis, being a man, had troubles of his own. There was another spectre following him. He had never spoken of it, nor would he allow any one else to speak of it—he had never acknowledged its existence to himself. Yet the battle with it took all the manhood that he had—and once or twice, alas, a little more. Jurgis had discovered drink.

He was working in the steaming pit of hell; day after day, week after week—until now there was not an organ of his body that did its work without pain, until the sound of ocean breakers echoed in his head day and night, and the buildings swayed and danced before him as he went down the street. And from all the unending horror of this there was a respite, a deliverance—he could drink! He could forget the pain, he could slip off the burden; he would see clearly again, he would be master of his brain, of his thoughts, of his will. His dead self would stir in him, and he would find himself laughing and cracking jokes with his companions—he would be a man again, and master of his life.

It was not an easy thing for Jurgis to take more than two or three drinks. With the first drink he could eat a meal, and he could persuade himself that that was economy; with the second he could eat another meal—but there would come a time when he could eat no more, and then to pay for a drink was an unthinkable extravagance, a defiance of the age-long instincts of his hunger-haunted class. One day, however, he took the plunge, and drank up all that he had in his pockets, and went home half "piped," as the men phrase it. He was happier than he had been in a year; and yet, because he knew that the happiness would not last, he was savage, too—with those who would wreck it, and with the world, and with his life; and then again, beneath this, he was sick with the shame of himself. Afterward, when he saw the despair of his family, and reckoned up the money he had spent, the tears came into his eyes, and he began the long battle with the spectre.

It was a battle that had no end, that never could have one. But Jurgis did not realize that very clearly; he was not given much time for reflection. He simply knew that he was always fighting. Steeped in misery and despair as he was, merely to walk down the street was to be put upon the rack. There was surely a saloon on the corner—perhaps on all four corners, and some in the middle of the block as well; and each one stretched out a hand to him—each one had a personality of its own, allurements unlike any other. Going and coming—before sunrise and after dark—there was warmth and a glow of light, and the steam of hot food, and perhaps music, or a friendly face, and a word of good cheer. Jurgis developed a fondness for having Ona on his arm whenever he went out on the street, and he would hold her tightly, and walk fast. It was pitiful to have Ona know of this—it drove him wild to think of it; the thing was not fair, for Ona had never tasted drink, and so could not understand. Sometimes, in desperate hours, he would find himself wishing that she might learn what it was, so that he need not be ashamed in her presence. They might drink together, and escape from the horror—escape for a while, come what would.

So there came a time when nearly all the conscious life of Jurgis consisted of a struggle with the craving for liquor. He would have ugly moods, when he hated Ona and the whole family, because they stood in his way. He was a fool to have married; he had tied himself down, and made himself a slave. It was all because he was a married man that he was compelled to stay in the yards; if it had not been for that he might have gone off like Jonas, and to hell with the packers. There were single men in the fertilizer-mill—and those few were working only for a chance to escape. Meantime, too, they had something to think about while they worked—they had the memory of the last time they had been drunk, and the hope of the time when they would be drunk again. As for Jurgis, he expected to bring home every penny; he could not even go with the men at noontime—he was supposed to sit down and eat his dinner on a pile of fertilizer dust.

This was not always his mood, of course; he still loved his family. But just now was a time of trial. Poor little Antanas, for instance—who had never failed to win him with a smile—little Antanas was not smiling just now, being a mass of fiery red pimples. He had had all the diseases that babies are heir to, in quick succession—scarlet fever, mumps, and whooping-cough in the first year, and now he was down with the measles. There was no one to attend him but Kotrina; there was no doctor to help him because they were too poor, and children did not die of the measles—at least not often. Now and then Kotrina would find time to sob over his woes, but for the greater part of the time he had to be left alone, barricaded upon the bed. The floor was full of draughts, and if he caught cold he would die. At night he was tied down, lest he should kick the covers off him, while the family lay in their stupor of exhaustion. He would lie and scream for hours, almost in convulsions; and then when he was worn out, he would lie whimpering and wailing in his torment. He was burning up with fever, and his eyes were running sores; in the daytime he was a thing uncanny and impish to behold, a plaster of pimples and sweat, a great purple lump of misery.

Yet all this was not really cruel as it sounds, for sick as he was, little Antanas was the least unfortunate member of that family. He was quite able to bear his sufferings—it was as if he had all these complaints to show what a prodigy of health he was. He was the child of his parents' youth and joy; he grew up like the conjurer's rose bush, and all the world was his oyster. In general, he toddled around the kitchen all day with a lean and hungry look—the portion of the family's allowance that fell to him was not enough, and he was unrestrainable in his demand for more. Antanas was but little over a year old, and already no one but his father could manage him.

It seemed as if he had taken all of his mother's strength—had left nothing for those that might come after him. Ona was with child again now, and it was a dreadful thing to contemplate; even Jurgis, dumb and despairing as he was, could not but understand that yet other agonies were on the way, and shudder at the thought of them.

For Ona was visibly going to pieces. In the first place she was developing a cough, like the one that had killed old Dede Antanas. She had had a trace of it ever since that fatal morning when the greedy street-car corporation had turned her out into the rain; but now it was beginning to grow serious, and to wake her up at night. Even worse than that was the fearful nervousness from which she suffered; she would have frightful headaches and fits of aimless weeping; and sometimes she would come home at night shuddering and moaning, and would fling herself down upon the bed and burst into tears. Several times she was quite beside herself and hysterical; and then Jurgis would go half mad with fright. Elzbieta would explain to him that it could not be helped, that woman was subject to such things when she was pregnant; but he was hardly to be persuaded, and would beg and plead to know what had happened. She had never been like this before, he would argue—it was monstrous and unthinkable. It was the life she had to live, the accursed work she had to do, that was killing her by inches. She was not fitted for it—no woman was fitted for it, no woman ought to be allowed to do such work; if the world could not keep them alive any other way it ought to kill them at once and be done with it. They ought not to marry, to have children; no working-man ought to marry—if he, Jurgis, had known what a woman was like, he would have had his eyes torn out first. So he would carry on, becoming half hysterical himself, which was an unbearable thing to see in a big man; Ona would pull herself together and fling herself into his arms, begging him to stop, to be still, that she would be better, it would be all right. So she would lie and sob out her grief upon his shoulder, while he gazed at her, as helpless as a wounded animal, the target of unseen enemies.

STUDY QUESTIONS

1. What was health care like for children in Packingtown?

2. What sort of men worked in the fertilizer plants? What were the hazards of the job?

3. How did the constant demand for money affect families?

4. What were the abuses of the "spoiled-meat" industry?

5. What response was Upton Sinclair hoping to achieve with *The Jungle?*

BIBLIOGRAPHY

On the life of Upton Sinclair, see Floyd Dell, *Upton Sinclair: A Study in Social Protest* (1927); Jon Yoder, *Upton Sinclair* (1975); Leon Harris, *Upton Sinclair, American Rebel* (1975); and his own *The Autobiography of Upton Sinclair* (1962). Three good books on the literature of the period are Daniel Aaron, *Writers of the Left* (1969); James Burkhart Gilbert, *Writers and Partisans: A History of Literary Radicalism in America* (1968); and Larzer Ziff, *The American 1890s: Life and Times of a Lost Generation* (1966). On the meatpacking industry, Packingtown, and the lives of the workers, consult Louis Carroll Wade, *Chicago's Pride: The Stockyards, Packingtown, and Environs in the Nineteenth Century* (1987) and James R. Barrett, *Work and Community in the Jungle: Chicago's Packinghouse Workers* (1988).

ROSE SCHNEIDERMAN AND THE TRIANGLE SHIRTWAIST FIRE

Bonnie Mitelman

The progress Americans made during the Progressive Era depended on one's perspective. For middle-class Americans, progress was everywhere visible. Real income rose and the government worked to ensure order and efficiency in the industrial world. For their part, most large industrialists cooperated with the government's effort to impose order, which often resulted in the elimination of bothersome competition. For example, leading meatpackers supported the Meat Inspection Act of 1906. The act raised inspection standards, thereby driving out small competitors and guaranteeing the quality of American meat on the competitive world market.

America's working class, however, had reason to question the nature of the "progress" that was being made. The men and women who labored in industrial America often performed uncreative, repetitive tasks at a pace set by machines. Possibly worse than the monotony of industrial life was the danger of it. Machines were blind and uncaring; they showed no sympathy for tired or bored workers who allowed their fingers to move too close to moving cogs. Injuries were common, and far too often industrialists were as unsympathetic as their machines. And for most unskilled workers, labor unions were weak and unrecognized by leading industrialists and manufacturers. In the following essay, Bonnie Mitelman discusses the 1911 Triangle Waist Company fire, a tragedy in which 146 workers died. The fire and its results raise serious questions about the extent and nature of progress during the early twentieth century.

On Saturday afternoon, March 25, 1911, in New York City's Greenwich Village, a small fire broke out in the Triangle Waist Company, just as the 500 shirtwaist employees were quitting for the day. People rushed about, trying to get out, but they found exits blocked and windows to the fire escape rusted shut. They panicked.

As the fire spread and more and more were trapped, some began to jump, their hair and clothing afire, from the eighth and ninth floor windows. Nets that firemen held for them tore apart at the impact of the falling bodies. By the time it was over, 146 workers had died, most of them young Jewish women.

A United Press reporter, William Shepherd, witnessed the tragedy and reported, "I looked upon the heap of dead bodies and I remembered these girls were the shirtwaist makers. I remembered their great strike of last year in which these same girls had demanded more sanitary conditions and more safety precautions in the shops. These dead bodies were the answer."

The horror of that fire touched the entire Lower East Side ghetto community, and there was a profuse outpouring of sympathy. But it was Rose Schneiderman, an immigrant worker with a spirit of social justice and a powerful way with words, who is largely credited with translating the ghetto's emotional reaction into meaningful, widespread action. Six weeks following the tragedy, and after years of solid groundwork, with one brilliant, well-timed speech, she was able to inspire the support of wealthy uptown New Yorkers and to swing public opinion to the side of the labor movement, enabling concerned civic, religious, and labor leaders to mobilize their efforts for desperately needed safety and industrial reforms.

"Rose Schneiderman and the Triangle Fire" by Bonnie Mitelman, from *American History Illustrated* 16 (July, 1981), pp. 38–47. Copyright © 1981 by Historical Times, Inc. Reprinted through the courtesy of Historical Times, Inc., publishers of *American History Illustrated*.

The Triangle fire, and the deaths of so many helpless workers, seemed to trigger in Rose Schneiderman an intense realization that there was absolutely nothing or no one to help working women except a strong union movement. With fierce determination, and the dedication, influence, and funding of many other people as well, she battled to regulate hours, wages, and safety standards and to abolish the sweatshop system. In so doing, she brought dignity and human rights to all workers.

The dramatic "uprising of the 20,000" of 1909–1910, in which thousands of immigrant girls and women in the shirtwaist industry had endured three long winter months of a general strike to protest deplorable working conditions, had produced some immediate gains for working women. There had been agreements for shorter working hours, increased wages, and even safety reforms, but there had not been formal recognition of their union. At Triangle, for example, the girls had gained a 52-hour-week, a 12–15 percent wage increase, and promises to end the grueling subcontracting system. But they had not gained the only instrument on which they could depend for lasting change: a viable trade union. This was to have disastrous results, for in spite of the few gains that they seemed to have made, the workers won no rights or bargaining power at all. In fact, "The company dealt only with its contractors. It felt no responsibility for the girls."

There were groups as well as individuals who realized the workers' impotence, but their attempts to change the situation accomplished little despite long years of hard work. The Women's Trade Union League and the International Ladies' Garment Workers' Union, through the efforts of Mary Dreier, Helen Marot, Leonora O'Reilly, Pauline Newman, and Rose Schneiderman had struggled unsuccessfully for improved conditions: the futility that the union organizers were feeling in late 1910 is reflected in the WTUL minutes of December 5 of that year.

A scant eight months after their historic waistmakers' strike, and three months before the deadly Triangle fire, a Mrs. Malkiel (no doubt

Theresa Serber Malkiel, who wrote the legendary account of the strike, *The Diary of a Shirtwaist Striker: A Story of the Shirtwaist Makers' Strike in New York,*) is reported to have come before the League to urge action after a devastating fire in Newark, New Jersey killed twenty-five working women. Mrs. Malkiel attributed their loss to the greed and negligence of the owners and the proper authorities. The WTUL subsequently demanded an investigation of all factory buildings and it elected an investigation committee from the League to cooperate with similar committees from other organizations.

The files of the WTUL contain complaint after complaint about unsafe factory conditions; many were filled out by workers afraid to sign their names for fear of being fired had their employers seen the forms. They describe factories with locked doors, no fire escapes, and barred windows. The *New York Times* carried an article which reported that fourteen factories were found to have no fire escapes, twenty-three had locked doors, and seventy-eight had obstructed fire escapes. In all, according to the article, 99 percent of the factories investigated in New York were found to have serious fire hazards.

Yet no action was taken.

It was the Triangle fire that emphasized, spectacularly and tragically, the deplorable safety and sanitary conditions of the garment workers. The tragedy focused attention upon the ghastly factories in which most immigrants worked; there was no longer any question about what the strikers had meant when they talked about safety and sanitary reform, and about social and economic justice.

The grief and frustration of the shirtwaist strikers were expressed by one of them, Rose Safran, after the fire: "If the union had won we would have been safe. Two of our demands were for adequate fire escapes and for open doors from the factories to the street. But the bosses defeated us and we didn't get the open doors or the better fire escapes. So our friends are dead."

The families of the fire victims were heartbroken and hysterical, the ghetto's *Jewish Daily For-*

ward was understandably melodramatic, and the immigrant community was completely enraged. Their Jewish heritage had taught them an emphasis on individual human life and worth; their shared background in the *shtetl* and common experiences in the ghetto had given them a sense of fellowship. They were, in a sense, a family—and some of the most helpless among them had died needlessly.

The senseless deaths of so many young Jewish women sparked within these Eastern Europeans a new determination and dedication. The fire had made reform absolutely essential. Workers' rights were no longer just socialist jargon: They were a matter of life and death.

The Triangle Waist Company was located on the three floors of the Asch Building, a 10-story, 135-foot-high structure at the corner of Greene Street and Washington Place in Greenwich Village. One of the largest shirtwaist manufacturers, Triangle employed up to 900 people at times, but on the day of the fire, only about 500 were working.

Leon Stein's brilliant and fascinating account of the fire, entitled simply *The Triangle Fire,* develops and documents the way in which the physical facilities, company procedures, and human behavior interacted to cause this great tragedy. Much of what occurred was ironic, some was cruel, some stupid, some pathetic. It is a dramatic portrayal of the eternal confrontation of the "haves" and the "havenots," told in large part by those who survived.

Fire broke out at the Triangle Company at approximately 4:45 P.M. (because time clocks were reportedly set back to stretch the day, and because other records give differing times of the first fire alarm, it is uncertain exactly what time the fire started), just after pay envelopes had been distributed and employees were leaving their work posts. It was a small fire at first, and there was a calm, controlled effort to extinguish it. But the fire began to spread, jumping from one pile of debris to another, engulfing combustible shirtwaist fabric. It became obvious that the fire could not be snuffed out, and the workers tried to reach the elevators or stairway. Those who reached the one open stairway raced down eight flights of stairs to safety; those who managed to climb onto the available passenger elevators also got out. But not everyone could reach the available exits. Some tried to open the door to a stairway and found it locked. Others were trapped between long working tables or behind the hordes of people trying to get into the elevators or out through the one open door.

Under the work tables, rags were burning; the wooden floors, trim, and window frames were also afire. Frantically, workers fought their way to the elevators, to the fire escape, and to the windows—to any place that might lead to safety.

Fire whistles and bells sounded as the fire department raced to the building. But equipment proved inadequate, as the fire ladders reached only to the seventh floor. And by the time the firemen connected their hoses to douse the flames, the crowded eighth floor was completely ablaze.

For those who reached the windows, there seemed to be a chance for safety. The *New York World* describes people balancing on window sills, nine stories up, with flames scorching them from behind, until firemen arrived: "The nets were spread below with all promptness. Citizens were commandeered into service, as the firemen necessarily gave their attention to the one engine and hose of the force that first arrived. The catapult force that the bodies gathered in the long plunges made the nets utterly without avail. Screaming girls and men, as they fell, tore the nets from the grasp of the holders, and the bodies struck the sidewalks and lay just as they fell. Some of the bodies ripped big holes through the life nets."

One reporter who witnessed the fire remembered how:

A young man helped a girl to the window sill on the ninth floor. Then he held her out deliberately, away from the building, and let her drop. He held out a second girl the same way and let her drop. He held out a third girl who did not resist. They were all as unresisting as if he were helping them into a street car instead of into eternity. He saw that a terrible death awaited them in the flames and his was only a terrible chivalry. He brought around another girl to the window. I saw her put her arms around him and kiss him. Then he held her into space— and dropped her. Quick as a flash, he was on the window sill himself. His coat fluttered upwards—the air filled his trouser legs as he came down. I could see he wore tan shoes.

Those who had rushed to the fire escape found the window openings rusted shut. Several precious minutes were lost in releasing them. The fire escape itself ended at the second floor, in an airshaft between the Asch Building and the building next door. But too frantic to notice where it ended, workers climbed on to the fire escape one after another until, in one terrifying moment, it collapsed from the weight, pitching the workers to their death.

Those who had made their way to the elevators found crowds pushing to get into the cars. When it became obvious that the elevators could no longer run, workers jumped down the elevator shafts, landing on the tops of the cars, or grabbing for cables to ease their descent. Several died, but incredibly, some did manage to save themselves this way. One man was found, hours after the fire, beneath an elevator car in the basement of the building, nearly drowned by the rapidly rising water from the firemen's hoses.

Several people, among them Triangle's two owners, raced to the roof, and from there were led to safety. Others never had that chance. "When Fire Chief Croker could make his way into the [top] three floors," states one account of the fire, "he found sights that utterly staggered . . . he saw as the smoke drifted away bodies burned to the bare bones. There were skeletons bending over sewing machines."

The day after the fire, the *New York Times* announced that "the building was fireproof. It shows hardly any signs of the disaster that overtook it. The walls are as good as ever, as are the

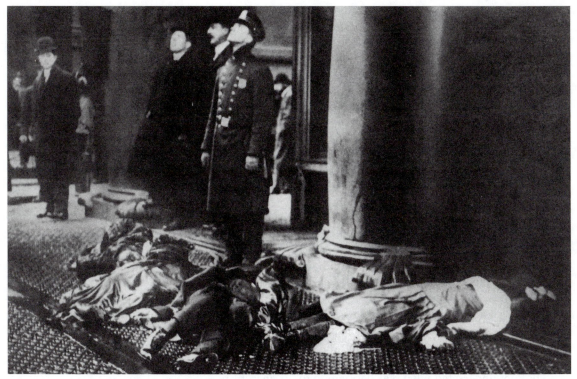

An unsafe work environment at the Triangle Waist Company caused the deaths of 146 workers when a fire broke out in the building in 1911. The tragedy brought labor issues to national attention.

floors: nothing is worse for the fire except that furniture and 14 [*sic*] of the 600 men and girls that were employed in its upper three stories."

The building *was* fireproof. But there had never been a fire drill in the factory, even though the management had been warned about the possible hazard of fire on the top three floors. Owners Max Blanck and Isaac Harris had chosen to ignore these warnings in spite of the fact that many of their employees were immigrants who could barely speak English, which would surely mean panic in the event of a crisis.

The *New York Times* also noted that Leonora O'Reilly of the League had reported Max Blanck's visit to the WTUL during the shirtwaist strike, and his plea that the girls return to work. He claimed a business reputation to maintain and told the Union leaders he would make the necessary im-

provements right away. Because he was the largest manufacturer in the business, the League reported, they trusted him and let the girls return.

But the improvements were never made. And there was nothing that anybody could or would do about it. Factory doors continued to open in instead of out, in violation of fire regulations. The doors remained bolted during working hours, apparently to prevent workers from getting past the inspectors with stolen merchandise. Triangle had only two staircases where there should have been three, and those two were very narrow. Despite the fact that the building was deemed fireproof, it had wooden window frames, floors, and trim. There was no sprinkler system. It was not legally required.

These were the same kinds of conditions which existed in factories throughout the garment industry; they had been cited repeatedly in the complaints filed with the WTUL. They were not unusual nor restricted to Triangle; in fact, Triangle was not as bad as many other factories.

But it was at Triangle that the fire took place.

The *Jewish Daily Forward* mourned the dead with sorrowful stories, and its headlines talked of "funerals instead of weddings" for the dead young girls. The entire Jewish immigrant community was affected, for it seemed there was scarcely a person who was not in some way touched by the fire. Nearly everyone had either been employed at Triangle themselves, or had a friend or relative who had worked there at some time or another. Most worked in factories with similar conditions, and so everyone identified with the victims and their families.

Many of the dead, burned beyond recognition remained unidentified for days, as searching family members returned again and again to wait in long lines to look for their loved ones. Many survivors were unable to identify their mothers, sisters, or wives; the confusion of handling so many victims and so many survivors who did not understand what was happening to them and to their dead led to even more anguish for the community. Some of the victims were identified by the names on the pay envelopes handed to them at quitting time and stuffed deeply into pockets or stockings just before the fire. But many bodies remained unclaimed for days, with bewildered and bereaved survivors wandering among them, trying to find some identifying mark.

Charges of first- and second-degree manslaughter were brought against the two men who owned Triangle, and Leon Stein's book artfully depicts the subtle psychological and sociological implications of the powerful against the oppressed, and of the Westernized, German-Jewish immigrants against those still living their old-world, Eastern European heritage. Ultimately, Triangle owners Blanck and Harris were acquitted of the charges against them, and in due time they collected their rather sizable insurance.

The shirtwaist, popularized by Gibson girls, had come to represent the new-found freedom of females in America. After the fire, it symbolized

death. The reaction of the grief-stricken Lower East Side was articulated by socialist lawyer Morris Hillquit:

The girls who went on strike last year were trying to readjust the conditions under which they were obliged to work. I wonder if there is not some connection between the fire and that strike. I wonder if the magistrates who sent to jail the girls who did picket duty in front of the Triangle shop realized last Sunday that some responsibility may be theirs. Had the strike been successful, these girls might have been alive today and the citizenry of New York would have less of a burden upon its conscience.

For the first time in the history of New York's garment industry there were indications that the public was beginning to accept responsibility for the exploitation of the immigrants. For the first time, the establishment seemed to understand that these were human beings asking for their rights, not merely trouble-making anarchists.

The day after the Triangle fire a protest meeting was held at the Women's Trade Union League, with representatives from twenty leading labor and civic organizations. They formed "a relief committee to cooperate with the Red Cross in its work among the families of the victims, and another committee . . . to broaden the investigation and research on fire hazards in New York factories which was already being carried on by the League."

The minutes of the League recount the deep indignation that members felt at the indifference of a public which had ignored their pleas for safety after the Newark fire. In an attempt to translate their anger into constructive action, the League drew up a list of forceful resolutions that included a plan to gather delegates from all of the city's unions to make a concerted effort to force safety changes in factories. In addition, the League called upon all workers to inspect factories and then report any violations to the proper city authorities and to the WTUL. They called upon the city to immediately appoint organized workers as unofficial inspectors. They resolved to submit the following fire regulations suggestions: compulsory fire drills, fireproof exits, unlocked doors, fire alarms, automatic sprinklers, and regular inspections. The League called upon the legislature to create the Bureau of Fire Protection and finally, the League underscored the absolute need for all workers to organize themselves at once into trade unions so that they would never again be powerless.

The League also voted to participate in the funeral procession for the unidentified dead of the Triangle fire.

The city held a funeral for the dead who were unclaimed. "More than 120,000 of us were in the funeral procession that miserable rainy April day," remembered Rose Schneiderman. "From ten in the morning until four in the afternoon we of the Women's Trade Union League marched in the procession with other trade-union men and women, all of us filled with anguish and regret that we had never been able to organize the Triangle workers."

Schneiderman, along with many others, was absolutely determined that this kind of tragedy would never happen again. With single-minded dedication, they devoted themselves to unionizing the workers. The searing example of the Triangle fire provided them with the impetus they needed to gain public support for their efforts.

They dramatized and emphasized and capitalized on the scandalous working conditions of the immigrants. From all segments of the community came cries for labor reform. Stephen S. Wise, the prestigious reform rabbi, called for the formation of a citizens' committee. Jacob H. Schiff, Bishop David H. Greer, Governor John A. Dix, Anne Morgan (of *the* Morgans) and other leading civic and religious leaders collaborated in a mass meeting at the Metropolitan Opera House on May 2 to protest factory conditions and to show support for the workers.

Several people spoke at the meeting on May 2, and many in the audience began to grow restless and antagonistic. Finally, 29-year-old Rose Schneiderman stepped up to the podium.

In a whisper barely audible, she began to address the crowd.

I would be a traitor to these poor burned bodies, if I came here to talk good fellowship. We have tried you good people of the public and we have found you wanting. The old Inquisition had its rack and its thumbscrews and its instruments of torture with iron teeth. We know what these things are today: the iron teeth are our necessities, the thumbscrews the high-powered and swift machinery close to which we must work, and the rack is here in the fireproof structures that will destroy us the minute they catch on fire.

This is not the first time girls have burned alive in the city. Every week I must learn of the untimely death of one of my sister workers. Every year thousands of us are maimed. The life of men and women is so cheap and property is so sacred. There are so many of us for one job it matters little if 140-odd are burned to death.

We have tried you, citizens, we are trying you now, and you have a couple of dollars for the sorrowing mothers and daughters and sisters by way of a charity gift. But every time the workers come out in the only way they know to protest against conditions which are unbearable, the strong hand of the law is allowed to press down heavily upon us.

Public officials have only words of warning to us—warning that we must be intensely orderly and must be intensely peaceable, and they have the workhouse just back of all their warnings. The strong hand of the law beats us back when we rise into the conditions that make life bearable.

I can't talk fellowship to you who are gathered here. Too much blood had been spilled. I know from my experience it is up to the working people to save themselves. The only way they can save themselves is by a strong working-class movement.

Her speech has become a classic. It is more than just an emotional picture of persecution; it reflects the persuasive sadness and profound understanding that comes from knowing, finally, the cruel realities of life, the perspective of history, and the nature of human beings.

The devastation of that fire and the futility of the seemingly successful strike that had preceded it seemed to impart an undeniable truth to Rose Schneiderman: they could not fail again. The events of 1911 seemed to have made her, and many others, more keenly aware than they had ever been that the workers' fight for reform was absolutely essential. If they did not do it, it would not be done.

In a sense, the fire touched off in Schneiderman an awareness of her own responsibility in the battle for industrial reform. This fiery socialist worker had been transformed into a highly effective labor leader.

The influential speech she gave did help swing public opinion to the side of the trade unions, and the fire itself had made the workers more aware of the crucial need to unionize. Widespread support for labor reform and unionization emerged. Pressure from individuals, such as Rose Schneiderman, as well as from groups like the Women's Trade Union League and the International Ladies' Garment Workers' Union, helped form the New York State Factory Investigating Commission, the New York Citizens' Committee on Safety, and other regulatory and investigatory bodies. The League and Local 25 (the Shirtwaist Makers' Union of the ILGWU) were especially instrumental in attaining a new Industrial Code for New York State, which became "the most outstanding instrument for safeguarding the lives, health, and welfare of the millions of wage earners in New York State and . . . in the nation at large."

It took years for these changes to occur, and labor reform did not rise majestically, Phoenix-like, from the ashes of the Triangle fire. But that fire, and Rose Schneiderman's whispered plea for a strong working-class movement, had indeed become the loud, clear call for action.

STUDY QUESTIONS

1. How successful had workers at the Triangle Waist Company been in gaining better working conditions before the fire? What had been their major successes and failures?

2. What were the major labor concerns of the female immigrant workers?

3. Why did the fire lead to so many deaths? How did the design of the building contribute to the tragedy?

4. What was the Jewish community's reaction to the fire? How did the funeral help unify reform-minded people in New York City?

5. What role did Rose Schneiderman play in the aftermath of the tragedy? How did the fire influence the American labor movement?

BIBLIOGRAPHY

As Mitelman indicates, the best treatment of the tragedy is Leon Stein, *The Triangle Fire* (1962). Leslie Woodcock Tentler, *Wage-Earning Women: Industrial Work and Family Life in the United States, 1900-1930* (1979), treats the difficulties faced by working women. Useful treatments of the same theme are Susan Estabrook Kennedy, *If All We Did Was to Weep at Home: A History of White Working Class Women in America* (1979), and Barbara Mayer Wertheimer, *We Were There: The Story of Working Women in America* (1977). Two excellent introductions to general issues that concerned workers are Herbert Gutman, *Work, Culture and Society in Industrializing America* (1977), and David Montgomery, *Workers' Control in America: Studies in the History of Work, Technology, and Labor Struggles* (1979). Moses Rischin, *The Promised City: New York's Jews, 1870-1940* (1970); Arthur S. Goren, *New York Jews and the Quest for Community: The Kehillah Experiment, 1908-1922* (1970); and Irving Howe, *World of our Fathers: The Journey of the Eastern European Jews to America and the Life They Found and Made* (1976), treat the Jewish experience in America.

READING 10

JACK JOHNSON WINS THE HEAVYWEIGHT CHAMPIONSHIP

Randy Roberts

For the most part, the Progressive movement was a for-whites-only affair. During the first twenty years of the twentieth century, Asian and black Americans faced open and violent discrimination. On the West Coast, Japanese and Chinese immigrants confronted a humiliating series of discriminatory laws, while in the South and even North blacks were equally hardpressed. Neither presidents Theodore Roosevelt nor Woodrow Wilson made any attempt to alter the social structure of the Jim Crow South, where the lives of the blacks were unequal to the lives of the whites. Although blacks retained some political and civil rights in the North, they still suffered from social and economic discrimination.

Some blacks responded to the injustice. Booker T. Washington was willing to forego social and political equality for economic opportunities. W. E. B. Du Bois demanded more; he worked for full equality. Other blacks lodged less articulate protests through their actions. They refused to live within the narrow borders proscribed for them by white society. Often these blacks were labeled "bad niggers." White authorities hated and punished them, but in black communities they were regarded as heroes and legends. The most famous of these real-life renegades was Jack Johnson, the first black heavyweight champion. He defeated white boxers, married white women, enraged white authorities, and lived by his own laws. In the following selection, historian Randy Roberts uses Johnson's fight with Tommy Burns as an opportunity to examine the racial attitudes of the early twentieth century.

fterwards concerned whites said it should never have taken place. John L. Sullivan, who by 1908 had quit drinking and become a moral crusader, said, "Shame on the money-mad Champion! Shame on the man who upsets good American precedents because there are Dollars, Dollars, Dollars in it." A dejected sports columnist wrote, "Never before in the history of the prize ring has such a crisis arisen as that which faces the followers of the game tonight." The sadness these men felt could only be expressed in superlatives—greatest tragedy, deepest gloom, saddest day, darkest night. The race war had been fought. Armageddon was over. The Caucasian race had lost. Twenty years after the event, and after a few more such Armageddons, Alva Johnston tried to explain the mood of the day: "The morale of the Caucasian race had been at a low ebb long before the great blow fell in 1908. The Kaiser had been growing hysterical over the Yellow Peril. Africa was still celebrating the victory of Emperor Menelik of Abyssinia over the Italians. Dixie was still in ferment because Booker T. Washington . . . had had a meal at the White House. Then . . . Jack Johnson won the World Heavyweight Championship from Tommy Burns. The Nordics had not been so scared since the days of Tamerlane."

Black ghetto dwellers and sharecroppers rejoiced. In cities from New York to Omaha, blacks smiled with delight. "Today is the zenith of Negro sports," observed a *Colored American Magazine* editor. Other black publications felt such qualifications were too conservative. The *Richmond Planet* reported that "no event in forty years has given more genuine satisfaction to the colored people of this country than has the signal victory of Jack Johnson." Joy and pride spilled over into arrogance, or so some whites believed. The cotton-buying firm of Logan and Bryan predicted that Johnson's victory would encourage other blacks

to enter boxing, thereby creating a shortage of field labor. Independent of Logan and Bryan's report, the black writer Jim Nasium counseled black youths to consider seriously a boxing career—where else could they face whites on an equal footing? In that last week of 1908 social change seemed close at hand. The implication of most reports was that Jack Johnson had started a revolution.

How had it all come about? When Burns arrived in Perth in August 1908, the world did not seem in any immediate danger. He was treated like a conquering hero. From Perth to Sydney he was cheered and fêted. Mayors and members of Parliament courted Burns as if he were visiting royalty. When the train made its normal 6 A.M. stop at Abury, men stood shivering in the cold to greet Burns. And at Sydney, at a more civilized hour, more than 8,000 people cheered the champion. Speeches were made and applause modestly received. An Australian politician, Colonel Ryrie, extolled the virtues of boxing, telling the gathering that the sport produced sturdy young men needed for battle, "not those milksops who cry out against it."

At these August occasions Burns was frequently asked about Johnson. Would he fight the black champion? If so, where? When? Burns patiently answered the questions like a saint repeating a litany. He would fight Johnson when the right purse was offered. The place was not important. In fact, Australia was as good as—if not better than—any other place. As Burns told a Melbourne reporter: "There are a lot of newspaper stories that I don't want to fight Johnson. I do want to fight him, but I want to give the white boys a chance first." And since the early English settlers had exterminated the Tasmanians, there were a lot of white boys in Australia.

Listening to Burns was an ambitious promoter. Hugh D. "Huge Deal" McIntosh was an American success story with an Australian setting. As a boy he worked in the Broken Hill mines and as a rural laborer, but early in life he realized that a man could make more money using his brain than his back. His fortune was made as a pie salesman in

Australian parks and sporting events, but his career included tours as a racing cyclist, a boxer, a waiter, a newspaper publisher, a member of parliament, a theatrical impresario, and other assorted jobs. All these stints equipped him with enough gab and gall to become a first-rate boxing promoter. It was McIntosh who had invited Burns to Australia to defend his title against Aussie boxers. A student of maps and calendars, he knew that when Teddy Roosevelt's Great White Fleet, then cruising about the Pacific, dropped anchor in Australia a heavyweight championship fight would prove a good draw. With this in mind, he rented a market garden at Rushcutter's Bay, on the outskirts of Sydney, and built an open-air stadium on it. By mid-summer he was ready for Burns.

In June he matched Burns against Bill Squires, whom the champion had already knocked out twice, once in the United States and once in France. In defense of Squires, however, it was noted by the press that in his second fight with Burns he had lasted eight rounds, seven longer than the first fight. On his home continent Squires did even better. He was not knocked out until the thirteenth round. Though the fight was not particularly good, the overflowing stadium pleased McIntosh mightily. More than 40,000 people showed up for the fight, including American sailors from the Great White Fleet, but only 15,000 could be seated in the stadium. The 25,000 others milled about outside, listening to the noise made by lucky spectators watching the fight.

Less than two weeks later Burns again defended his title, this time against Bill Lang in Melbourne before 19,000 spectators. Like the stadium at Rushcutter's Bay, South Melbourne Stadium had been hurriedly constructed on McIntosh's orders—it was built in twelve days—and the result had been worth the effort. In the two fights Burns made more than $20,000 and McIntosh grossed about $100,000, half of which was clear profit. In addition, both fights had been filmed, and revenue from this pioneering effort was much greater than anticipated. Burns, McIntosh, and the Australian boxing public were all exceedingly pleased.

In late October Johnson arrived, and the pulse of Australia picked up a beat. The fight had already been arranged. McIntosh guaranteed Burns $30,000. Before such a sum the color line faded. Therefore, when Johnson landed at Perth he was in an accommodating mood. "How does Burns want it? Does he want it fast and willing? I'm his man in that case. Does he want it flat footed? Goodness, if he does, why I'm his man again. Anything to suit; but fast or slow, I'm going to win." After eight years of trying Johnson was about to get his chance to fight for the heavyweight title.

Short of money, Johnson and Fitzpatrick set up their training quarters in the inexpensive Sir Joseph Banks Hotel in Botany, far less plush than the Hydro Majestic Hotel at Medlow Bath, where Burns trained. Yet Johnson, like Burns, trained in earnest. Johnson looked relaxed—he joked, smiled, made speeches, and played the double bass—but the men and women who watched him train failed to notice that he was also working very hard. Each morning he ran; each afternoon he exercised and sparred with Bill Lang, who imitated Burns's style. Johnson knew that Burns—short, inclined toward fatness, addicted to cigars and strong drink—was nonetheless a very good boxer. In Bohum Lynch's opinion, Burns was a "decidedly good boxer" who, though unorthodox, had a loose and easy style. And in the weeks before the fight Johnson showed by his training that he did not take Burns lightly.

Nor did he disregard the power of Australian racism. He feared that in the emotionally charged atmosphere of an interracial championship fight he might not be given an even break. His concern was not unfounded. An editorial in Sydney's *Illustrated Sporting and Dramatic News* correctly indicated the racial temper of Australian boxing fans: "Citizens who have never prayed before are supplicating Providence to give the white man a strong right arm with which to belt the coon into oblivion." But of more concern to Johnson than white men's prayers were his suspicions of McIntosh as promoter and self-named referee. Several times the two quarreled in public, and they nearly came to blows when Johnson greeted the promoter with "How do, Mr. McIntosh? How do you drag yourself away from Tahmy?" McIntosh, a big, burly, muscular man, thereafter began carrying a lead pipe wrapped in sheet music. As he told his friend Norman Lindsay, it was in case "that black bastard" ever "tries any funny business."

As the bout drew closer, the racial overtones destroyed the holiday atmosphere. It seemed as if all Australia were edgy. In the name of civilization, Protestant reformers spoke words that fell on deaf ears. The fight, said the Sydney Anglican Synod, with "its inherent brutality and dangerous nature" would surely "corrupt the moral tone of the community." But the community was worried less about being corrupted than about the implication of a Johnson victory. Lindsay, whom McIntosh hired to draw posters to advertise the fight, visually portrayed the great fear. Across Sydney could be seen his poster showing a towering black and a much smaller white. As Richard Broome has suggested, "Thus must have evoked the deepest feelings Australians held about the symbols of blackness and whiteness and evoked the emotiveness of a big man versus a small man and the populous coloured races versus the numerically smaller white race." Clearly, the *Australian Star* editors had this in mind when they printed a cartoon showing the fight being watched by representatives of the white and black races. Underneath was a letter that predicted that "this battle may in the future be looked back upon as the first great battle of an inevitable race war. . . . There is more in this fight to be considered than the mere title of pugilistic champion of the world."

Racial tension was nothing new to Australia. Race had mattered since the colony's founding. Partly it was an English heritage, passed down from the conquerors of Ireland, Scotland, and Wales—and absolute belief in the inferiority of everything and everyone non-English. In Australia, however, it had developed its own unique characteristics. There common English prejudices had been carried to extremes, and when confronted with dark-skinned natives, the Australians did not shrink from the notion of geno-

cide. The most shocking example of racial relations was the case of the small island of Tasmania off the southeast coast of Australia. When the English first settled the island there were perhaps a few thousand Tasmanians. Short but long-legged, these red-brown people were described as uncommonly friendly natives. But the friendliness soon died, as British colonists hunted, raped, enslaved, abducted, or killed the Tasmanians. Slowly the race died off, until in 1876 Truganini, the very last survivor, died. Her passing struck many Australians as sad—but inevitable. As a correspondent for the *Hobart Mercury* wrote, "I regret the death of the last of the Tasmanian aborigines, but I know that it is the result of the *fiat* that the black shall everywhere give place to the white."

For Australia the problem was that other darker races had not given way fast enough in the generation after the death of Truganini. Though Social Darwinists preached the virtues of the light-skinned, by 1909 Australians felt threatened by the "lower" races. Increasingly after 1900 Australians demonstrated anxiety over their Oriental neighbors. Immigration restrictions aimed at keeping the country white were proposed and adopted. So bitter had the struggle become that in 1908, the year of the Johnson-Burns fight, the *Australia Bulletin* changed its banner from "Australia for Australians" to "Australia for the white men."

Johnson and Burns became both an example of and a contribution to the fears of white Australians. Small, white Burns became the symbol of small, white Australia, nobly battling against the odds. Burn's defense was his brain and pluck, his desire to stave off defeat through intelligence and force of will. Johnson became the large, vulgar, corrupt, and sensual enemy. Reports said that he ignored training and instead wenched and drank. He had strength and size but lacked heart—in fact, he *should* win but probably would not. This last report gave rise to the rumor that the fight was fixed. Even the *New York Times* endorsed this view, as did the betting line that made Burns a 7 to 4 favorite.

Cool rains washed Sydney on Christmas night, the eve of the fight. To allow filming, the fight was not scheduled to begin until 11 A.M., but by 6 A.M. an orderly crowd of more than 5,000 was waiting at the gate. The stadium would be filled to capacity; yet interest was much more widespread. Throughout Australia men milled around newspaper offices hoping to hear a word about the progress of the fight. Inside the stadium at Rushcutter's Bay all Christmas cheer had vanished. The mood and tone of the day, from the gray, overcast sky to the uneasy quiet of the spectators, was eulogistic.

Johnson entered the ring first. Despite his dull gray robe his mood was almost carefree. There were a few cheers—though not many—as he slipped under the upper strand of the ropes, but calls of "coon" and "nigger" were more common. He smiled, bowed grandly, and threw kisses in every direction. He liked to strut the stage, and the vicious insults did not outwardly affect him. If anything, his smile became broader as he was more abused. In a country exhilarated by the discovery of gold, Johnson's gold-toothed smile ironically attracted only hate. Satisfied that he was not the crowd's favorite, he retired to his corner, where Sam Fitzpatrick massaged his shoulders and whispered words of assurance into an unlistening ear.

By contrast, when Burns climbed into the ring, the stadium was filled with sound. Burns did not seem to notice. For a time it looked as if he had come into the ring expecting something other than a fight. He was dressed in a worn blue suit, more appropriate for a shoe salesman than the heavyweight champion. Methodically he removed the suit, folded it neatly, and put it in a battered wicker suitcase. Yet even in his short, tight boxing trunks he looked out of place. Jack London, covering the fight for the *New York Herald,* wrote that Burns looked "pale and sallow, as if he had not slept all night, or as if he had just pulled through a bout with fever." Pacing nervously in his corner, he avoided looking across the ring at Johnson.

Burns examined the bandages on Johnson's hands. He did this carefully, looking for hard tape or other unnatural objects. Satisfied, he returned to his corner. Johnson, however, was upset by the tape on Burns's elbows. He asked Burns to remove it. Burns refused. Johnson—suddenly serious—said he would not fight until the tape was removed. Still Burns refused. McIntosh tried to calm the two fighters. He was unsuccessful. The crowd, sensing an unexpected confrontation but not aware of the finer details, sided with Burns and used the moment as a pretext to shout more insults at Johnson, who smiled as if complimented on a new necktie but still refused to alter his protest. Finally, Burns removed the tape. Johnson nodded, satisfied.

McIntosh called the fighters to the center of the ring. He went over the do's and don'ts and the business of what punches would or would not be allowed. Then he announced that in the event that the police stopped the fight, he would render a decision based on who was winning at the time. The unpopular "no decision" verdict would not be given. Both Johnson and Burns had earlier agreed to this procedure. The fighters returned to their corners. A few moments later the bell rang. The color line in championship fights was erased.

Watching films of Johnson boxing is like listening to a 1900 recording of Enrico Caruso played on a 1910 gramophone. When Johnson fought Burns, film was still in its early days, not yet capable of capturing the subtleties of movement. Nuance is lost in the furious and stilted actions of the figures, which move about the screen in a Chaplinesque manner, as if some drunken cutter had arbitrarily removed three of every four frames. When we watch fighters of Johnson's day on film, we wonder how they could have been considered even good. That some of them were champions strains credulity. They look like large children, wrestling and cuffing each other, but not actually fighting like real boxers, not at all like Ali captured in zoom-lensed, slow-motion, technological grace. But the film misleads.

It was no Charlie Chaplin that shuffled out of his corner in round one to meet Tommy Burns. It was a great boxer who at age thirty was in his physical prime. No longer thin, Johnson was well-muscled, with a broad chest and thick arms and legs. His head was shaved in the style of the eighteenth-century bare-knuckle fighters, and his high cheekbones gave his face a rounded appearance. Although he had fought often, his superb defensive skills had kept his face largely unmarked. Like his mother he had a broad, flat nose and full lips, but his eyes were small and oddly Oriental when he smiled. He was famous for his clowning, but this stereotype of a black man obscured the more serious reality. He was often somber, and even when he smiled and acted like a black-faced minstrel, he could be serious. What he thought, he believed, was his own affair. His feelings could not be easily read on his face.

Both boxers began cautiously. Johnson flicked out a few probing jabs, designed more to test distance than to do any physical damage. Although Burns was much smaller than Johnson, he was considered a strong man with a powerful punch. Johnson clinched, tested Burns's strength, then shifted to long-range sparring. He allowed Burns to force the action, content to parry punches openhanded. Burns tried to hit Johnson with long left hooks, which fell short. Johnson feinted a long left of his own, but in the same motion he lowered his right shoulder, pivoted from the waist, stepped forward with his right foot, and delivered a perfect right uppercut. It was Johnson's finest weapon, and some ring authorities claim there never has been a fighter who could throw the punch as well as Johnson. Burns was caught flatfooted, leaning into the punch. His momentum was stopped and he fell backward. His head hit heavily on the floor. He lay still. The referee started to count.

"The fight," Jack London wrote only hours after it ended, "there was no fight. No Armenian massacre could compare with the hopeless slaughter that took place in the Sydney stadium today." From the opening seconds of the first round it was clear who would win. At least it was clear to London. It was a fight between a "colossus and a toy automation," between a "playful Ethiopian and a small and futile white man," between a "grown man and a naughty child." And through it all, London and the 20,000 white sup-

The first African American man to gain the heavyweight boxing championship of the world was Jack Johnson, who held the title from 1908 to 1915.

porters of Burns watched in horror as their worst fears materialized.

"Hit the coon in his stomach." Burns needed no reminder. After surviving the first-round knockdown, he shifted to a different strategy, one he had thought about before. In the days before the fight, when reporters asked about his battle plan, he had smiled knowingly at his white chroniclers and said he would move in close and hit the black fighter where all black fighters were weak—in the stomach. This theory was hardly novel; it had long been considered axiomatic that black boxers had weak stomachs and hard heads. So thoroughly was the view accepted that black boxers took it for granted that white fighters would attack the body. Peter Jackson once told Fred Dartnell, "They are all after my body. Hit a nigger in the stomach and you'll settle him, they say, but it never seems to occur to them that a white man might just as quickly be beaten by a wallop in the same region." Sam Langford agreed: blacks hated to be hit by a hard punch to the stomach, but so too did whites.

Boxing was not immune to the scientific explanations of the day. Polygenists believed—and Darwinists did not deny—that the black race was an "incipient species." Therefore, whites maintained, physically blacks and whites were very different. Burns, for example, assumed that Johnson not only had a weak stomach but lacked physical endurance. So he believed that the longer the fight lasted the better were his chances. Behind these stereotypes rested the science of the day. Writing only a year before in the *North American Review,* Charles F. Woodruff claimed that athletes raised in Southern climates lacked endurance: "The excessive light prods the nervous system to do more than it should, and in time such constant stimulation is followed by irritability and finally by exhaustion." Only athletes from the colder Northern latitudes had enough stamina to remain strong during the course of a long boxing match. Therefore, Burns, a Canadian, had reason to remain hopeful. By contrast, Johnson, raised about as far south as one could travel in the United States and only a generation or two removed from Africa, had to win quickly or not at all. At least, this was what Burns and his white supporters hoped.

Burns's strategy was thus founded on the racist belief that scientists, armed with physiological and climatological evidence, had proved that blacks were either inferior to whites, or—as in the case of harder heads—superior because of some greater physiological inferiority; that is to say, blacks had thicker skulls because they had smaller brains. Burns never questioned that his abdominal strength and his endurance were superior to Johnson's. Nor did he doubt that his white skin meant that his desire to win and willingness to accept pain were greater than Johnson's. But above all, he was convinced that as a

white he could outthink Johnson, that he could solve the problems of defense and offense more quickly than his black opponent. Burns's faith, in short, rested ultimately on the color of his skin.

Burns forgot, however, that he was facing a boxer liberated from the myths of his day. Johnson's stomach was not weak, and, more important, he knew it was not. As the fight progressed, he exposed the fallacy of Burns's theory. He started to taunt Burns. "Go on, Tommy, hit me here," Johnson said pointing to his stomach. When Burns responded with a blow to Johnson's midsection, Jack laughed and said to try again. "Is that all the better you can do, Tommy?" Another punch. "Come on, Tommy, you can hit harder than that, can't you?" And so it continued; Johnson physically and verbally was destroying the white man's myths.

Burns fought gamely, but without success. Johnson did not try for a knockout; he was content to allow the fight to last until the later rounds. Partly his decision was based on economics. The bout was being filmed, and few boxing fans in America would pay to watch pictures of pressmen, seconds, and other boxers for five minutes as a build-up for a fight that lasted only half a minute. But more important was Johnson's desire for revenge. He hated Burns and wanted to punish him. And he did. By the second round Burns's right eye was discolored and his mouth was bloody. By the middle rounds Burns was bleeding from a dozen minor facial cuts. Blood ran over his shoulders and stained the canvas ring. Before the white audience, Johnson badly punished Burns. And he enjoyed every second of it.

But punishment was not enough. Johnson wanted also to humiliate Burns. He did this verbally. From the very first round Johnson insulted Burns, speaking with an affected English accent, so that "Tommy" became "Tahmy." Mostly what Johnson said was banal: "Poor little Tahmy, who told you you were a fighter?" Or, "Say little Tahmy, you're not fighting. Can't you? I'll have to show you how." Occasionally, when Burns landed a punch, Johnson complimented him: "Good boy, Tommy; good boy, Tommy." In almost every taunt Johnson referred to Burns in the diminutive. It was always "Tommy Boy"; or "little Tommy." And always a derisive smile accompanied the words.

Sometimes Johnson sought to emasculate Burns verbally. Referring to Burns's wife, Johnson said, "Poor little boy, Jewel won't know you when she gets you back from this fight." Once when Burns landed what looked to be an effective punch, Johnson laughed: "Poor, poor Tommy. Who taught you to hit? Your mother? You a woman?" Crude, often vulgar and mean, Johnson's verbal warfare was nevertheless effective.

Burns responded in kind. Bohum Lynch, who was a great fan of Burns, admitted that his champion's ring histrionics included baleful glaring, foot stomping, and mouth fighting. He often called Johnson a "cur" or a "big dog." At other times, when he was hurt or frustrated, he said, "Come on and fight, nigger. Fight like a white man." Burns's comments, however, were self-defeating. When Johnson insulted Burns, the champion lost control and fought recklessly. But Burns's taunts pleased Johnson, who responded by fighting in an even more controlled way than before. Johnson gained particular strength from Burns's racist statements. It was like playing the Dozens, where accepting abuse with an even smile and concealing one's true emotions were the sign of a sure winner.

When Johnson was not insulting Burns, he was talking to ringsiders. Usually he just joked about how easy the fight was and what he would do with the money he won from betting on the bout. That the ringsiders hated Johnson and screamed racial insults did not seem to bother him. Only rarely did Johnson show his disgust with the white audience. Once as he moved from his corner at the start of a round he spat a mouthful of water toward the press row, but such actions were unusual. More common was the smile—wide, detached, inscrutable. In describing the grin, Jack London came closest to the truth: it was "the fight epitomized." It was the smile of a man who has mastered the rules to a slightly absurd game.

After a few rounds the only question that remained unanswered was not who would win but how much punishment Burns could take. By the middle rounds that too was evident—he could survive great amounts of punishment. His eyes were bruised and discolored, his mouth hung open, his jaw was swollen and looked broken, and his body was splotched with his own blood. In the corner between rounds his seconds sponged his face with champagne, which was popularly believed to help revive hurt fighters. It did not help Burns. Yet at the bell he always arose to face more punishment and insults. For the white spectators, Burns's fortitude was itself inspiring. As Bohum Lynch wrote, "To take a beating any time, even from your best friend, is hard work. But to take a beating from a man you abhor, belonging to a race you despise, to know that he is hurting you and humiliating you with the closest attention to detail, and the coldest deliberation . . . this requires pluck."

By the thirteenth round everyone but Burns and Johnson was surfeited with the carnage. Spectators, left with nothing and nobody to cheer, now yelled for the fight to be stopped. After the thirteenth round police entered the ring. They talked with McIntosh, then with Burns. The white champion refused to concede. He insisted that he could win. But in the fourteenth Burns was again severely punished. A hard right cross knocked him to the canvas. He arose at the count of eight but was wobbly. Again policemen climbed into the ring, only this time there was no talking. The fight was stopped, although Burns—dazed, covered with blood, but still game—screamed at the police to give him another chance.

Everywhere was a stunned silence as the spectators accepted that the inevitable was now the actual. It had happened. A black man now wore the crown that had once belonged to Sullivan, Corbett, and Jeffries. As far as Australia was concerned, an "archetypal darkness" had replaced sweetness and light; the barbarian had defeated the civilized man. As the *Daily Telegraph* observed in doggerel:

And yet for all we know and feel,
For Christ and Shakespeare,
  knowledge, love,
We watch a white man bleeding reel,
We cheer a black with bloodied glove.

The imagery in which the fight was reported clearly reflects the white Australian attitude toward Johnson. He was portrayed as a destructive beast. *Fairplay,* the liquor trades weekly, called Johnson "a huge primordial ape," and the *Bulletin's* cartoons likened him to a shaven-headed reptile. He was the discontented black and yellow masses that haunted the Australian mind. Journalist Randolph Bedford, perhaps the most unabashedly racist reporter at the fight, depicted it in ominous terms: "Yet the white beauty faced the black unloveliness, forcing the fight, bearing the punishment as if it were none . . . weight and reach were ebbing against intrepidity, intelligence and lightness. . . . His courage still shone in his eyes; his face was disfigured and swollen and bloodied. He was still beauty by contrast—beautiful but to be beaten; clean sunlight fighting darkness and losing."

In America the fight was not viewed in quite so maudlin a manner. Certainly the white American press was not pleased by the result, but it generally tried to dismiss it in a light-hearted mood. Perhaps, reporters reasoned, all was not lost. "Br'er Johnson is an American anyway," commented a reporter for the *Omaha Sunday Bee.* Then, too, boxing had declined so much in recent years that some experts wondered if the fight meant anything at all. Though John L. Sullivan criticized Burns for fighting Johnson, he added that "present day bouts cannot truly be styled prize fights, but only boxing matches." A fine distinction, but Sullivan believed it was enough to invalidate Johnson's claim as heavyweight champion. And certainly even if Johnson were the champion, reporters all agreed that he was far below the likes of Sullivan, Corbett, or Jeffries.

Though the mood had not yet reached a crisis stage, the fight's portent was still most unsettling to American whites. This was especially true about the manner in which blacks celebrated Johnson's victory. It was reported that the Manassas Club, a Chicago organization of wealthy blacks who had

white wives, hired white waiters to serve the food at their banquet. And one of their members said that "Johnson's victory demonstrates the physical superiority of the black over the Caucasian. The basis of mental superiority in most men is physical superiority. If the negro can raise his mental standard to his physical eminence, some day he will be a leader among men." In other parts of the country blacks were reported as acting rude to whites and being swelled by false pride.

Johnson's actions in Australia did little to calm Caucasian fears. Turning against the sportsman-like tradition of praising one's opponent, Johnson openly said that Burns was a worthless boxer: "He is the easiest man I ever met. I could have put him away quicker, but I wanted to punish him. I had my revenge." Nor was Johnson discreet about the company with whom he was seen in public. Hattie McClay, his companion who had remained in the background during the weeks before the fight, was now prominently on display. Dressed in silk and furs, she seemed as prized a possession of Johnson's as his gold-capped teeth.

Johnson now seemed more apt to emphasize racial issues that irritated whites. Interviewed during the days after the fight, he told reporters that he had the greatest admiration for the aboriginal Australians. Commenting on their weapons, he said, "Your central Australian natives must have been men of genius to have turned out such artistic and ideal weapons." Nor, he hinted, was he any less a genius. He understood human nature: because he defeated Burns he could expect to be hated by all whites. But, he added, he could find solace in his favorite books—*Paradise Lost, Pilgrim's Progress* and *Titus Andronicus.* His comments achieved their purpose; everywhere white Australians snorted in disgust. But his choice of books certainly did not reflect his own attitude. Unlike Milton's Adam, Johnson did not practice the standard Christian virtues.

Burns left Australia soon after the fight. A richer man by some $30,000, he nevertheless was bitter and filled with hatred. Johnson, however, decided to stay for a while in Australia. His side of the purse, a mere $5,000, was hardly enough to make the venture profitable. He hoped instead to capitalize on his fame by touring Australia as a vaudeville performer. It was common for any famous boxer to make such tours. In 1908 he had toured in America and Canada with the Reilly and Woods Big Show and had enjoyed the experience. He loved the limelight and, unlike other boxers, put on a good show. He demonstrated a few boxing moves, sang several songs, danced, and played the bass fiddle. During his Australian tour he actually made more money than he had in his fight with Burns. Not until mid-February was he ready to go home.

He had changed. The Johnson who left Australia in February was not the same man who had arrived in October. Inwardly, perhaps, he was much the same. But outwardly he was different. He was more open about his beliefs and his pleasures, less likely to follow the advice of white promoters and managers. Undoubtedly he believed the title of world champion set him apart from others of his race. And in this he was right. He would never be viewed as just another black boxer. But he was wrong in his assumption that the crown carried with it some sort of immunity against the dictates of whites and traditions of white society. Now more than ever Johnson was expected to conform. And now more than ever Johnson felt he did not have to. The collision course was set.

STUDY QUESTIONS

1. How did the promoters of≈ the Johnson-Burns fight use racism to build up the gate? How did the racial attitudes of white Australians compare with those of white Americans?

2. How did Burns demonstrate racial stereotypes by the manner in which he fought Johnson?

3. What was the reaction of white Australians and Americans to Jack Johnson's victory?

4. What was Johnson's attitude toward white society?

5. How else might one use sports or popular culture to demonstrate racial attitudes?

BIBLIOGRAPHY

The section is taken from Randy Roberts, *Papa Jack: Jack Johnson and the Era of White Hopes* (1983). Finis Farr, *Black Champion: The Life and Times of Jack Johnson* (1965), provides a readable popular history of the boxer, and Al-Tony Gilmore, *Bad Nigger! The National Impact of Jack Johnson* (1975), traces the newspaper reaction to Johnson. Johnson's image in black folklore is treated by William Wiggins, "Jack Johnson as Bad Nigger: The Folklore of His Life," *Black Scholar* (1969), and Lawrence W. Levine, *Black Culture and Black Consciousness: Afro-American Folk Thought from Slavery to Freedom* (1977). A number of books trace the evolution of white attitudes toward blacks. Among the best are George M. Fredrickson, *The Black Image in the White Mind: The Debate on Afro-American Character and Destiny, 1817-1914* (1971); Thomas F. Gossett, *Race: The History of an Idea in America* (1965); and John S. Haller, Jr., *Outcasts from Evolution: Scientific Attitudes of Racial Inferiority, 1859-1900* (1971).

READING 11

THE TRENCH SCENE

Paul Fussell

For the generation that fought it, World War I was the Great War. It came after almost one hundred years of general European peace, and it shattered not only nations and people but also a system of thought, a world view. Before the Great War, intellectuals talked seriously and earnestly about human progress and the perfectability of societies and individuals. Men and women, they agreed, were reasonable creatures, fully capable of ordering their lives and environment. The terrible slaughter of Verdun and the Somme, the mud and lice and rats of the trenches, the horrors of poison gases and bullet-torn bodies draped over barbed-wire barriers—these unspeakable barbarities silenced talk of progress. Ernest Hemingway spoke for his generation when he wrote about the impact of the Great War: "I was always embarrassed by the words *sacred, glorious,* and *sacrifice* and the expression *in vain* . . . I had seen nothing sacred, and the things that were glorious had no glory and the sacrifices were like the stockyards at Chicago if nothing was done with the meat except to bury it. There were many words that you could not stand to hear and finally only the names of places had dignity. . . . Abstract words such as *glory, honor, courage,* or *hallow* were obscene beside the concrete names of villages, the number of roads, the names of rivers, the numbers of regiments and the dates."

In the following essay literary historian Paul Fussell discusses the Great War as experienced by millions of soldiers who served time in the trenches of the Western Front. In these ditches some 7,000 British soldiers were killed or wounded daily between 1914 and 1918. Though not in such horrendous numbers, Americans too died in the trenches of France, and the experience of mass death transformed American society. The United States went into the war to "make the world safe for democracy" but emerged from the war pessimistic, cynical, and discouraged. As Fussell observes, "To be in the trenches was to experience an unreal, unforgettable enclosure and constraint, as well as a sense of being unoriented and lost." This was the aspect of the Great War that changed the temper of Western culture.

The idea of "the trenches" has been assimilated so successfully by metaphor and myth ("Georgian complacency died in the trenches") that it is not easy now to recover a feeling for the actualities. *Entrenched,* in an expression like *entrenched power,* has been a dead metaphor so long that we must bestir ourselves to recover its literal sense. It is time to take a tour.

From the winter of 1914 until the spring of 1918 the trench system was fixed, moving here and there a few hundred yards, moving on great occasions as much as a few miles. London stationers purveying maps felt secure in stocking "sheets of 'The Western Front' with a thick wavy black line drawn from North to South alongside which was printed 'British Line.' " If one could have gotten high enough to look down at the whole line at once, one would have seen a series of multiple parallel excavations running for 400 miles down through Belgium and France, roughly in the shape of an *S* flattened at the sides and tipped to the left. From the North Sea coast of Belgium the line wandered southward, bulging out to contain Ypres, then dropping down to protect Béthune, Arras, and Albert. It continued south in front of Montidier, Compiégne, Soissons, Reims, Verdun, St. Mihiel, and Nancy, and finally attached its southernmost end to the Swiss border at Beurnevisin, in Alsace. The top forty miles—the part north of Ypres—was held by the Belgians; the next ninety miles, down to the river Ancre, were British; the French held the rest, to the south.

Henri Barbusse estimates that the French front alone contained about 6,250 miles of trenches. Since the French occupied a little more than half the line, the total length of the numerous trenches occupied by the British must come to about 6,000 miles. We thus find over 12,000 miles of trenches on the Allied side alone. When we add the trenches of the Central Powers, we arrive at a figure of about 25,000 miles, equal to a trench

sufficient to circle the earth. Theoretically it would have been possible to walk from Belgium to Switzerland entirely below ground, but although the lines were "continuous," they were not entirely seamless: occasionally mere shell holes or fortified strong-points would serve as a connecting link. Not a few survivors have performed the heady imaginative exercise of envisioning the whole line at once. Stanley Casson is one who, imagining the whole line from his position on the ground, implicitly submits the whole preposterous conception to the criterion of the "normally" rational and intelligible. As he remembers, looking back from 1935:

Our trenches stood on a faint slope, just overlooking German ground, with a vista of vague plainland below. Away to right and left stretched the great lines of defense as far as eye and imagination could stretch them. I used to wonder how long it would take for me to walk from the beaches of the North Sea to that curious end of all fighting against the Swiss boundary; to try to guess what each end looked like; to imagine what would happen if I passed a verbal message, in the manner of the parlor game, along to the next man on my right to be delivered to the end man of all up against the Alps. Would anything intelligible at all emerge?

Another imagination has contemplated a similar absurd transmission of sound all the way from north to south. Alexander Aitken remembers the Germans opposite him celebrating some happy public event in early June, 1916, presumably either the (ambiguous) German success at the naval battle of Jutland (May 31–June 1) or the drowning of Lord Kitchener, lost on June 5 when the cruiser *Hampshire* struck a mine and sank off the Orkney Islands. Aitken writes, "There had been a morning in early June when a tremendous tin-canning and beating of shell-gongs had begun in the north and run south down their lines to end, without doubt, at Belfort and Mulhausen on the Swiss frontier." Impossible to believe, really, but in this mad setting, somehow plausible.

The British part of the line was normally populated by about 800 battalions of 1,000 men each. They were concentrated in the two main sectors of the British effort: the Ypres Salient in Flanders and the Somme area in Picardy. Memory has given these two sectors the appearance of two distinguishable worlds. The Salient, at its largest point about nine miles wide and projecting some four miles into the German line, was notable for its terrors of concentrated, accurate artillery fire. Every part of it could be covered from three sides, and at night one saw oneself almost surrounded by the circle of white and colored Very lights set up by the Germans to illuminate the ground in front of their trenches or to signal to the artillery behind them. The "rear area" at Ypres was the battered city itself, where the troops harbored in cellars or in the old fortifications built by Vauban in the seventeenth century. It was eminently available to the German guns, and by the end of the war Ypres was flattened to the ground, its name a byword for a city totally destroyed. Another war later, in 1940, Colin Perry—who was not born until four years after the Great War—could look at the ruins of London and speak of "the Ypres effect of Holborn." If the character of the Ypres sector was concentration and enclosure, inducing claustrophobia even above ground, the Somme was known—at least until July 1, 1916—for its greater amplitude and security. German fire came generally from only one direction; and troops at rest could move further back. But then there was the Somme mud; although the argument about whether the mud wasn't really worse at Ypres was never settled.

Each of these two sectors had its symbolic piece of ruined public architecture. At Ypres it was the famous Cloth Hall, once a masterpiece of medieval Flemish civic building. Its gradual destruction by artillery and its pathetic final dissolution were witnessed by hundreds of thousands, who never forgot this eloquent emblem of what happens when war collides with art. In the Somme the memorable ruined work of architecture, connoting this time the collision of the war with religion and the old pieties, was the battered

Basilica in the town of Albert, or "Bert," as the troops called it. The grand if rather vulgar red and white brick edifice had been built a few years before the war, the result of a local ecclesiastic's enthusiasm. Together with his townsmen he hoped that Albert might become another Lourdes. Before the war 80,000 used to come on pilgrimages to Albert every year. The object of veneration inside the church was a statue of the Virgin, said to have been found in the Middle Ages by a local shepherd. But the statue of the Virgin never forgotten by the hordes of soldiers who passed through Albert was the colossal gilded one on top of the battered tall tower of the Basilica. This figure, called Notre Dame des Brebiéres, originally held the infant Christ in outstretched arms above her; but now the whole statue was bent down below the horizontal, giving the effect of a mother about to throw her child—in disgust? in sacrifice?—into the debris-littered street below. To Colonel Sir Maurice Hankey, Secretary of the War Committee, it was "a most pathetic sight." Some said that the statue had been bent down by French engineers to prevent the Germans from using it to aim at. But most—John Masefield among them—preferred to think it a victim of German artillery. Its obvious symbolic potential (which I will deal with later) impressed itself even on men who found they could refer to it only facetiously, as "The Lady of the Limp."

The two main British sectors duplicated each other also in their almost symbolic road systems. Each had a staging town behind: for Ypres it was Poperinghe (to the men, "Pop"); for the Somme, Amiens. From these towns troops proceeded with augmenting but usually well-concealed terror up a sinister road to the town of operations, either Ypres itself or Albert. And running into the enemy lines out of Ypres and Albert were the most sinister roads of all, one leading to Menin, the other to Bapaume, both in enemy territory. These roads defined the direction of ultimate attack and the hoped-for breakout. They were the goals of the bizarre inverse quest on which the soldiers were ironically embarked.

But most of the time they were not questing. They were sitting or lying or squatting in places below the level of the ground. "When all is said and done," Sassoon notes, "the war was mainly a matter of holes and ditches." And in these holes and ditches extending for ninety miles, continually, even in the quietest times, some 7,000 British men and officers were killed and wounded daily, just as a matter of course. "Wastage," the Staff called it.

There were normally three lines of trenches. The front-line trench was anywhere from fifty yards or so to a mile from its enemy counterpart. Several hundred yards behind it was the support trench line. And several hundred yards behind that was the reserve line. There were three kinds of trenches: firing trenches, like these; communication trenches, running roughly perpendicular to the line and connecting the three lines; and "saps," shallower ditches thrust out into No Man's Land, providing access to forward observation posts, listening posts, grenade-throwing posts, and machine gun positions. The end of a sap was usually not manned all the time: night was the favorite time for going out. Coming up from the rear, one reached the trenches by following a communication trench sometimes a mile or more long. It often began in a town and gradually deepened. By the time pedestrians reached the reserve line, they were well below ground level.

A firing trench was supposed to be six to eight feet deep and four or five feet wide. On the enemy side a parapet of earth or sandbags rose about two or three feet above the ground. A corresponding "parados" a foot or so high was often found on top of the friendly side. Into the sides of trenches were dug one- or two-man holes ("funk-holes"), and there were deeper dugouts, reached by dirt stairs, for use as command posts and officers' quarters. On the enemy side of a trench was a fire-step two feet high on which the defenders were supposed to stand, firing and throwing grenades, when repelling attack. A well-built trench did not run straight for any distance: that would have been to invite enfilade fire. Every few yards a good trench zigzagged. It had frequent traverses designed to contain damage within a

limited space. Moving along a trench thus involved a great deal of weaving and turning. The floor of a proper trench was covered with wooden duckboards, beneath which were sumps a few feet deep designed to collect water. The walls, perpetually crumbling, were supported by sandbags, corrugated iron, or bundles of sticks or rushes. Except at night and in half-light, there was of course no looking over the top except through periscopes, which could be purchased in the "Trench Requisites" section of the main London department stores. The few snipers on duty during the day observed No Man's Land through loopholes cut in sheets of armor plate.

The entanglements of barbed wire had to be positioned far enough out in front of the trench to keep the enemy from sneaking up to grenade-throwing distance. Interestingly, the two novelties that contributed most to the personal menace of the war could be said to be American inventions. Barbed wire had first appeared on the American frontier in the late nineteenth century for use in restraining animals. And the machine gun was the brainchild of Hiram Stevens Maxim (1840–1916), an American who, disillusioned with native patent law, established his Maxim Gun Company in England and began manufacturing his guns in 1889. He was finally knighted for his efforts. At first the British regard for barbed wire was on a par with Sir Douglas Haig's understanding of the machine gun. In the autumn of 1914, the first wire Private Frank Richards saw emplaced before the British positions was a single strand of agricultural wire found in the vicinity. Only later did the manufactured article begin to arrive from England in sufficient quantity to create the thickets of mock-organic rusty brown that helped give a look of eternal autumn to the front.

The whole British line was numbered by sections, neatly, from right to left. A section, normally occupied by a company, was roughly 300 yards wide. One might be occupying front-line trench section 51; or support trench S 51, behind it; or reserve trench SS 51, behind both. But a less formal way of identifying sections of trench was by place or street names with a distinctly London

Trench warfare was a common practice during World War II. Here, U.S. troops set up trench artillery in France.

flavor. *Piccadilly* was a favorite; popular also were *Regent Street* and *Strand;* junctions were *Hyde Park Corner* and *Marble Arch*. Greater wit—and deeper homesickness—sometimes surfaced in the naming of the German trenches opposite. Sassoon remembers "Durley's" account of the attack at Delville Wood in September, 1916: "Our objective was Pint Trench, taking Bitter and Beer and clearing Ale and Vat, and also Pilsen Lane." Directional and traffic control signs were everywhere in the trenches, giving the whole system the air of a parody modern city, although one literally "underground".

The trenches I have described are more or less ideal, although not so ideal as the famous exhibition trenches dug in Kensington Gardens for the edification of the home front. These were clean, dry, and well furnished, with straight sides and sandbags neatly aligned. R. E. Vernède writes his wife from the real trenches that a friend of his has just returned from viewing the set of ideal ones. He "found he had never seen anything at all like it before." And Wilfred Owen calls the Kensington Gardens trenches "the laughing stock of the army." Explaining military routines to civilian readers, Ian Hay labors to give the impression that the real trenches are identical to the exhibition

ones and that they are properly described in the language of normal domesticity a bit archly deployed:

The firing-trench is our place of business—our office in the city, so to speak. The supporting trench is our suburban residence, whither the weary toiler may betake himself periodically (or, more correctly, in relays) for purposes of refreshment and repose.

The reality was different. The British trenches were wet, cold, smelly, and thoroughly squalid. Compared with the precise and thorough German works, they were decidedly amateur, reflecting a complacency about the British genius for improvisation. Since defense offered little opportunity for the display of pluck or swank, it was by implication derogated in the officers' *Field Service Pocket Book*. One reason the British trench system was so haphazard and ramshackle was that it had originally taken form in accord with the official injunction: "The choice of a [defensive] position and its preparation must be made with a view to economizing the power expended on defense in order that the power of offense may be increased." And it was considered really useless to build solid fortifications anyway: "An occasional shell may strike and penetrate the parapet, but in the case of shrapnel the damage to the parapet will be trifling, while in the case of a shell filled with high explosive, the effect will be no worse on a thin parapet than on a thick one. It is, therefore, useless to spend time and labor on making a thick parapet simply to keep out shell." The repeatedly revived hopes for a general breakout and pursuit were another reason why the British trenches were so shabby. A typical soldier's view is George Coppard's:

The whole conduct of our trench warfare seemed to be based on the concept that we, the British, were not stopping in the trenches for long, but were tarrying awhile on the way to Berlin and that very soon we would be chasing Jerry across country. The result, in the long term, meant that we lived a mean and impoverished sort of existence in lousy scratch holes.

In contrast, the German trenches, as the British discovered during the attack on the Somme, were deep, clean, elaborate, and sometimes even comfortable. As Coppard found on the Somme, "Some of the [German] dugouts were thirty feet deep, with as many as sixteen bunk-beds, as well as door bells, water tanks with taps, and cupboards and mirrors." They also had boarded walls, floors, and ceilings; finished wooden staircases; electric light; real kitchens; and wallpaper and overstuffed furniture, the whole protected by steel outer doors. Foreign to the British style was a German dugout of the sort recalled by Ernst Jünger:

At Monchy . . . I was master of an underground dwelling approached by forty steps hewn in the solid chalk, so that even the heaviest shells at this depth made no more than a pleasant rumble when we sat there over an interminable game of cards. In one wall I had a bed hewn out. . . . At its head hung an electric light so that I could read in comfort till I was sleepy. . . . The whole was shut off from the outer world by a dark-red curtain with rod and rings. . . .

As these examples suggest, there were "national styles" in trenches as in other things. The French trenches were nasty, cynical, efficient, and temporary. Kipling remembered the smell of delicious cooking emanating from some in Alsace. The English were amateur, vague, *ad hoc,* and temporary. The German were efficient, clean, pedantic, and permanent. Their occupants proposed to stay where they were.

Normally the British troops rotated trench duty. After a week of "rest" behind the lines, a unit would move up—at night—to relieve a unit in the front-line trench. After three days to a week or more in that position, the unit would move back for a similar length of time to the support trench, and finally back to the reserve. Then it was time for a week of rest again. In the three lines of trenches the main business of the soldier was to exercise self-control while being shelled. As the poet Louis Simpson has accurately remembered:

Being shelled is the main work of an infantry soldier, which no one talks about. Everyone has his own way of going about it. In general, it means lying face down and contracting your body into as small a space as possible. In novels [The Naked and the Dead is an example] you read about soldiers, at such moments, fouling themselves. The opposite is true. As all your parts are contracting, you are more likely to be constipated.

Simpson is recalling the Second War, but he might be recalling the First. While being shelled, the soldier either harbored in a dugout and hoped for something other than a direct hit or made himself as small as possible in a funk-hole. An unlucky sentry or two was supposed to be out in the open trench in all but the worst bombardments, watching through a periscope or loophole for signs of an attack. When only light shelling was in progress, people moved about the trenches freely, and we can get an idea of what life there was like if we posit a typical twenty-four hours in a front-line trench.

The day began about an hour before first light, which often meant at about 4:30. This was the moment for the invariable ritual of morning stand-to (short for the archaic formal command for repelling attack, "Stand to Arms"). Since dawn was the favorite time for launching attacks, at the order to stand-to everyone, officers, men, forward artillery observers, visitors, mounted the fire-step, weapon ready, and peered toward the German line. When it was almost full light and clear that the Germans were not going to attack that morning, everyone "stood down" and began preparing breakfast in small groups. The rations of tea, bread, and bacon, brought up in sandbags during the night, were broken out. The bacon was fried in mess-tin lids over small, and if possible smokeless, fires. If the men were lucky enough to be in a division whose commanding general permitted the issue of the dark and strong government rum, it was doled out from a jar with the traditional iron spoon, each man receiving about two tablespoonful. Some put it into their tea, but most swallowed it straight. It was a precious thing, and serving it out was almost like a religious ceremonial, as David Jones recalls in *In Parenthesis,* where a corporal is performing the rite:

> *O have a care—don't spill the precious*
> *O don't jog his hand—ministering; do*
>   *take care.*
> *O please—give the poor bugger elbow*
>   *room.*

Larger quantities might be issued to stimulate troops for an assault, and one soldier remembers what the air smelled like during a British attack: "Pervading the air was the smell of rum and blood." In 1922 one medical officer deposed before a parliamentary committee investigating the phenomenon of "shell shock": "Had it not been for the rum ration I do not think we should have won the war."

During the day the men cleaned weapons and repaired those parts of the trench damaged during the night. Or they wrote letters, deloused themselves, or slept. The officers inspected, encouraged, and strolled about looking nonchalant to inspirit the men. They censored the men's let-

ters and dealt with the quantities of official inquiries brought them daily by runner. How many pipe-fitters had they in their company? Reply immediately. How many hairdressers, chiropodists, bicycle repairmen? Daily "returns" of the amount of ammunition and the quantity of trench stores had to be made. Reports of the nightly casualties had to be sent back. And letters of condolence, which as the war went on became form letters of condolence, had to be written to the relatives of the killed and wounded. Men went to and fro on sentry duty or working parties, but no one showed himself above the trench. After evening stand-to, the real work began.

Most of it was above ground. Wiring parties repaired the wire in front of the position. Digging parties extended saps toward the enemy. Carrying parties brought up not just rations and mail but the heavy engineering materials needed for the constant repair and improvement of the trenches: timbers, A-frames, duckboards, stakes and wire, corrugated iron, sandbags, tarpaulins, pumping equipment. Bombs and ammunition and flares were carried forward. All this antwork was illuminated brightly from time to time by German flares and interrupted very frequently by machine gun or artillery fire. Meanwhile night patrols and raiding parties were busy in No Man's Land. As morning approached, there was a nervous bustle to get the jobs done in time, to finish fitting the timers, filling the sandbags, pounding in the stakes, and then returning mauls and picks and shovels to the Quartermaster Sergeant. By the time of stand-to, nothing human was visible above ground anywhere, but every day each side scrutinized the look of the other's line for significant changes wrought by night.

Flanders and Picardy have always been notorious for dampness. It is not the least of the ironies of the war for the British that their trenches should have been dug where the water-table was the highest and the annual rainfall the most copious. Their trenches were always wet and often flooded several feet deep. Thigh-boots or waders were issued as standard articles of uniform. Wilfred Owen writes his mother from the Somme at the beginning of 1917: "The waders are of course indispensable. In 2 1/2 miles of trench which I waded yesterday there was not one inch of dry ground. There is a mean depth of two feet of water." Pumps worked day and night but to little effect. Rumor held that the Germans not only could make it rain when they wanted it to—that is, all the time—but had contrived some shrewd technical method for conducting the water in their lines into the British positions—perhaps piping it underground. Ultimately there was no defense against the water but humor. "Water knee deep and up to the waist in places," one soldier notes in his diary. "Rumors of being relieved by the Grand Fleet." One doesn't want to dwell excessively on such discomforts, but here it will do no harm to try to imagine what, in these conditions, going to the latrine was like.

The men were not the only live things in the line. They were accompanied everywhere by their lice, which the professional delousers in rest positions behind the lines, with their steam vats for clothes and hot baths for troops, could do little to eliminate. The entry *lousy* in Eric Partridge's *Dictionary of Slang and Unconventional English* speaks volumes: "Contemptible; mean; filthy. . . . Standard English till 20th C, when, especially after the Great War, colloquial and used as a mere pejorative." *Lousy with,* meaning *full of,* was "originally military" and entered the colloquial word-hoard around 1915: "That ridge is lousy with Fritz."

The famous rats also gave constant trouble. They were big and black, with wet, muddy hair. They fed largely on the flesh of cadavers and on dead horses. One shot them with revolvers or coshed them to death with pick handles. Their hunger, vigor, intelligence, and courage are recalled in numerous anecdotes. One officer notes from the Ypres Salient: "We are fairly plagued with rats. They have eaten nearly everything in the mess, including the table-cloth and the operations orders! We borrowed a large cat and shut it up at night to exterminate them, and found the place empty next morning. The rats must have

eaten it up, bones, fur, and all, and dragged it to their holes."

One can understand rats eating heartily there. It is harder to understand men doing so. The stench of rotten flesh was over everything, hardly repressed by the chloride of lime sprinkled on particularly offensive sites. Dead horses and dead men—and parts of both—were sometimes not buried for months and often simply became an element of parapets and trench walls. You could smell the front line miles before you could see it. Lingering pockets of gas added to the unappetizing atmosphere. Yet men ate three times a day, although what they ate reflected the usual gulf between the ideal and the actual. The propagandist George Adam announced with satisfaction that "the food of the army is based upon the conclusions of a committee, upon which sat several eminent scientists." The result, he asserted, is that the troops are "better fed than they are at home." Officially, each man got daily: 1 1/4 pounds fresh meat (or 1 pound preserved meat), 1 1/4 pounds bread, 4 ounces bacon, 3 ounces cheese, 1/2 pound fresh vegetables (or 2 ounces dried), together with small amounts of tea, sugar, and jam. But in the trenches there was very seldom fresh meat, not for eating, anyway; instead there was "Bully" (tinned corned-beef) or "Maconochie" (ma-cón-o-chie), a tinned meat-and-vegetable stew named after its manufacturer. If they did tend to grow tedious in the long run, both products were surprisingly good. The troops seemed to like the Maconochie best, but the Germans favored the British corned beef, seldom returning from a raid on the British lines without taking back as much as they could carry. On trench duty the British had as little fresh bread as fresh meat. "Pearl Biscuits" were the substitute. They reminded the men of dog biscuits, although, together with the Bully beef, they were popular with the French and Belgian urchins, who ran (or more often strolled) alongside the railway trains bringing troops up to the front, soliciting gifts by shouting, "Tommee! Bull-ee! Bee-skee!" When a company was out of the line, it fed better. It was then serviced by its company cookers—stoves on wheels—and often got something approaching the official ration, as it might also in a particularly somnolent part of the line, when hot food might come up at night in the large covered containers known as Dixies.

Clothing and equipment improved as the war went on, although at the outset there was a terrible dearth and improvisation. During the retreat from Mons, as Frank Richards testifies, "A lot of us had no caps: I was wearing a handkerchief knotted at the four corners—the only headgear I was to wear for some time." Crucial supplies had been omitted: "We had plenty of small-arm ammunition but no rifle-oil or rifle-rag to clean our rifles with. We used to cut pieces off our shirts . . . and some of us who had bought small tins of vaseline . . . for use on sore heels or chafed legs, used to grease our rifles with that." At the beginning line officers dressed very differently from the men. They wore riding-boots or leather puttees; melodramatically cut riding breeches; and flare-skirted tunics with Sam Browne belts. Discovering that this costume made them special targets in attacks (German gunners were instructed to fire first at the people with the thin knees), by the end they were dressing like the troops, wearing wrap puttees; straight trousers bloused below the knee; Other Ranks' tunics with inconspicuous insignia, no longer on the cuffs but on the shoulders; and Other Ranks' web belts and haversacks. In 1914 both officers and men wore peaked caps, and it was rakish for officers to remove the grommet for a "Gorblimey" effect. Steel helmets were introduced at the end of 1915, giving the troops, as Sassoon observed, "a Chinese look." Herbert Read found the helmets "the only poetic thing in the British Army, for they are primeval in design and effect, like iron mushrooms." A perceptive observer could date corpses and skeletons lying on disused battlefields by their evolving dress. A month before the end of the war, Major P. H. Pilditch recalls, he

spent some time in the old No Man's Land of four years' duration. . . . It was a morbid but intensely interesting occupation tracing the various battles amongst the hundreds of skulls, bones and remains scattered thickly about. The progress of our successive attacks could be clearly seen from the types of equipment on the skeletons, soft cloth caps denoting the 1914 and early 1915 fighting, then respirators, then steel helmets marking attack in 1916. Also Australian slouch hats, used in the costly and abortive attack in 1916.

To be in the trenches was to experience an unreal, unforgettable enclosure and constraint, as well as a sense of being unoriented and lost. One saw two things only: the walls of an unlocalized, undifferentiated earth and the sky above. Fourteen years after the war J. R. Ackerley was wandering through an unfrequented part of a town in India. "The streets became narrower and narrower as I turned and turned," he writes, "until I felt I was back in the trenches, the houses upon either side being so much of the same color and substance as the rough ground between." That lost feeling is what struck Major Frank Isherwood, who writes his wife in December, 1914. "The trenches are a labyrinth, I have already lost myself repeatedly. . . . You can't get out of them and walk about the country or see anything at all but two muddy walls on each side of you." What a survivor of the Salient remembers fifty years later are the walls of dirt and the ceiling of sky, and his eloquent optative cry rises as if he were still imprisoned there: "To be out of this present, ever-present, eternally present misery, this stinking world of sticky, trickling earth ceilinged by a strip of threatening sky." As the only visible theater of variety, the sky becomes all-important. It was the sight of the sky, almost alone, that had the power to persuade a man that he was not already lost in a common grave.

STUDY QUESTIONS

1. What was the effect of World War I on the landscape of Europe?

2. In theory, how were the trenches supposed to be constructed? What was life supposed to be like in the ideal trench? How did reality differ from theory?

3. What national differences were there in the construction and maintenance of trenches? What do the differences tell us about the different national characters and war aims?

4. Describe the sights, sounds, and smell of life in the trenches. How did trench life affect the soldiers?

5. What does Fussell mean when he describes the experience as "unreal"? How did trench life breed "a sense of being unoriented and lost"?

BIBLIOGRAPHY

The above selection is taken from Fussell's award-winning *The Great War and Modern Memory* (1975), the best discussion of the impact of the war on modern culture. Robert Wohl, *The Generation of 1914* (1979), recreates the experiences of the men who fought and wrote about the war. Three good military overviews of the war are James L. Stokesbury, *A Short History of World War I* (1981); B. H. Liddell Hart, *The Real War, 1914-1918* (1930); and Cyril Falls, *The Great War* (1959). S. B. Fay, *The Origins of World War* (2 vols., 1928–1930); L. Albertini, *The Origins of the War of 1914* (3 vols., 1952-1957); and Fritz Fischer, *Germany's Aims in the First World War* (1967), discuss the complex origins of the war. The best studies of America's entry into the war are E. R. May, *The First World War and American Isolation* (1957); P. Devlin, *Too Proud to Fight: Woodrow Wilson's Neutrality* (1975); and Barbara Tuchman, *The Zimmerman Telegram* (1958). Military studies that give the reader a sense of the problems faced by the typical soldier include Martin Middlebrooks, *The First Day on the Somme* (1971); Alister Horne, *The Price of Glory: Verdun, 1916* (1962); Leon Wolff, *In Flanders Field* (1958); Barrie Pitt, *The Last Act* (1962); and John Keegan, *The Face of Battle: A Study of Agincourt, Waterloo, and the Somme* (1976). Two recent books are especially good: John Keegan, *The First World War* (2000) and Gary Mead, *The Doughboys: America and the First World War* (2000).

PART FOUR

Heroes and Society in the 1920s

The year 1920 ushered in a decade that historians steadfastly refuse to discuss in anything less than superlative terms. The decade brings to mind Charles Dickens's description of the revolutionary years of the eighteenth century in his novel *A Tale of Two Cities:* "It was the best of times, it was the worst of times . . . it was the season of Light, it was the season of Darkness, it was the spring of hope, it was the winter of despair, we had everything before us, we had nothing before us." If a decade may be said to have a personality, then the 1920s had the personality of a child; sometimes laughing and playful, at other times brooding, brutal, and ugly.

The first and perhaps most widely read book about the decade was Frederick Lewis Allen's *Only Yesterday: An Informal History of the 1920s.* Published in 1931 during the midst of the Great Depression, *Only Yesterday* describes a carefree decade that began with the end of the Great War and ended with the stock market crash. Allen paints a decade that roars with excitement, a decade brimming with bathtub gin, bootleg liquor, and bubbling champagne. Gangsters, movie sex goddesses, athletic heroes, and fabulous moneymakers seem to come alive on the pages of *Only Yesterday.* In sweeping terms Allen examines the "revolution in manners and morals," the "aching disillusionment" of intellectuals, and the crass materialism of millions of Americans.

Allen was not necessarily wrong. The sexual mores of the youth were changing, and there was evidence of intellectual disillusionment and crass materialism. The problem with the book is that its sweeping generalizations are simply too sweeping. In addition, too much of the activity of the decade is left out. The economic plight of rural Americans, the rise of the Ku Klux Klan, urban-rural tensions, racial injustice, nativism, and religious revivalism are just a few of the subjects that Allen does not treat. As a result, *Only Yesterday* is a flawed and unbalanced classic.

THE AMERICAN
FLAPPER · 1927

In recent years historians have explored the areas where Allen did not venture. And they have presented a different view of the 1920s, viewing the decade as a period of transition where older rural and newer urban attitudes uneasily coexisted. Although the country was becoming increasingly urban and bureaucratic, many Americans clung tightly to the more traditional values of their parents and grandparents. In an effort to preserve these values, they supported a variety of movements such as the Society for the Preservation of New England Antiquities, the Ku Klux Klan, and the National Origins Act of 1924.

If rural America resisted change, most of urban America accepted it. Spectators filled movie theaters and athletic stadiums to watch others perform, and entertainment became a product that was packaged and marketed by business executives. Millions of Americans worshipped at the altar of business efficiency and organization. Even crime became more organized and efficient. By 1929 the debate between rural and urban America was decided. The future belonged to the cities.

READING 12

DEMARBLEIZING BOBBY JONES
Stephen R. Lowe

In the 1920s, athletes were elevated to national heroes, placed on nearly untouchable altars and endowed with mythical attributes. Journalists generally only recorded the positive sides of their careers, turning a blind eye and a deaf ear to anything negative, and millions of Americans greedily followed the exploits of such athletes as boxer Jack Dempsey, football player Red Grange, baseball player Babe Ruth, and tennis player Bill Tilden. They were America's champions, knocking out opponents, zig-zagging toward the end zone, crushing a baseball over a fence, or smashing a back-hand down a line. They were the answer to anyone who suggested that America had grown flabby or that all gods were dead and all faiths in man shaken. Americans be-lieved that their athletic heroes demonstrated the greatness of America itself.

In this age of heroes, no hero was more revered than Robert Tyre "Bobby" Jones, the greatest amateur golfer who ever lived. His accomplishments during the decade were staggering. From 1923 to 1930 he dominated amateurs and professionals alike, winning five United States Amateurs, four United States Opens, three British Opens, and one British Amateur. In 1930 he did what no golfer before or after has accom-plished by winning the Grand Slam—the United States Open and Amateur and the British Open and Amateur. But what made Jones stand above the other athletic idols was how he won. He refused to give up his amateur status, as if money would some-how tarnish the purity of his sport and efforts. Americans thought of him as the Am-ateur Champion, the southern lawyer and gentleman who represented the best of America. In the following essay, Stephen R. Lowe, author of *Sir Walter and Mr. Jones: Walter Hagen, Bobby Jones, and the Rise of American Golf* (2000), examines the myths and realities behind the Jones legend.

For Georgians the name Robert Tyre "Bobby" Jones is synonymous with golf; many uninitiated Americans learn as much each spring through CBS's telecast of the sport's first major event, the Masters. Even casual observers quickly discover that Jones, along with Clifford Roberts and Dr. Alister Mackenzie, was a founder of Augusta National. Viewers are usually reminded about Jones's winning the Grand Slam (the U.S. Amateur, U.S. Open, British Amateur, and British Open in 1930), as well as his other notable golf achievements in the 1920s, the so-called Golden Age of American sports. What is always stressed, however, is his amateurism, the notion that he competed purely out of a love for competition and not for material gain. Moreover, it is almost impossible to watch ABC's coverage of the British Open without hearing commentator Jim McKay say that Jones never played the game more than six months out of any calendar year, putting his clubs away in November and not touching them again until April. Indeed, there is a lot of myth surrounding Jones's amateurism; commentators most often emphasize how unimportant golf really was to the Atlantan. He was a lawyer first and foremost, we are usually told, and golf was far down his list of priorities.

Above all, Jones is portrayed as a sportsman and a gentleman, an image rooted in his role as an amateur golfer and the way in which he handled the final years of his life. In 1948 Jones was stricken with a rare spinal disorder called syringomyelia. He played his last round of golf that year and was soon reduced from walking with braces to using a wheelchair and eventually to being completely immobile. Through it all Jones publicly displayed remarkable steadfastness, even good cheer. He remained as active as possible until his death in 1971 and became a symbol of individual strength and character. Such behavior, coupled with his amateur career and the rise of the Masters Tournament, made him golf's and, arguably, the entire sports world's greatest paragon.

From Stephen R. Lowe, "Demarbleizing Bobby Jones" in *The Georgia Historical Quarterly,* vol. 83 (Winter 1999).

Jones lived an admirable, extraordinary life, even for a famous athlete. Not surprisingly, golf fans have tended to "marbleize" him. As always, such efforts distort the record and, more importantly, unintentionally dehumanize the hero, in this case making Bobby Jones into something that he did not care to be, a "golf machine." The purpose of this essay is to highlight the historical record in two ways, by sketching Jones's background, life, and golf achievements, and then discussing some of the realities of his competitive career. Ultimately, by placing Jones into proper cultural and historical context, this essay will serve to chip away a little of the marble. That, though, is a good thing, for Jones is much more valuable and admirable as a man than as a myth.

Georgia fans, in particular, know that the Jones family's rise to prominence did not begin with Bobby or with golf. In fact, it began with Bobby's grandfather, the original Robert Tyre Jones of Canton, Georgia, who would himself be worthy of a scholarly article, if not a book. Born in 1849 to William Green Jones and Emily Chafin Jones, R. T. (as he was called) grew up on the family farm near Covington, Georgia. It seems that from the beginning, R. T. Jones was a devoutly religious man; he joined the Presbyterian church as an eighteen-year-old in 1867 and a few years later transferred his membership to the Baptist church. His strapping 6′ 5″, 235-pound frame was baptized on the second Sunday of August 1870. The next year he enrolled at Moores Business College. R. T. married in 1878; a short time later he and his new wife, Susan Walker, left the familiar surroundings of Covington for the hills of Canton. There he made a name and a good deal of money for himself by opening a general store and eventually a textile manufactory. Within a few years, R. T. Jones was one of the wealthiest men in town.

But Jones became the leading citizen of Canton for more than just his substantial business interests; he never abandoned his religious faith and, indeed, served as the Sunday School superintendent of the First Baptist Church for more than forty years, teaching the largest adult class. He occasionally wrote articles for the local paper, the

Cherokee Advance. R. T. revealed his Victorian, theistic world view in an October 1920 piece entitled "Christianity as Related to Business." "The first thing to be considered by the Christian in any line of endeavor is—how will this serve as a factor in God's Kingdom?" he admonished. It was not enough for a business "to simply succeed from a money profit standpoint"; it must also "glorify our Lord." In other words, if any business was to be truly successful, "Christianity should be the dominating power and . . . govern its operation."

In sum, R. T. Jones was like so many other Americans of his generation. He was guided by a series of "absolutes" that were based on an unwavering Christian faith and a literal reading of the Bible. He fathered a large family which, along with church and business, became the focal point of his life. In all of his relationships, R. T. was fair and honest but also disciplined and even stern. More than most southerners of his day, he did not have much use for people who disagreed with him and was not particularly open-minded about anything. R. T. Jones had a recipe for success that served him in very good stead: old-fashioned religion and hard work.

R. T. could not bring himself to drink even a Coca-Cola; he certainly did not have much use for sports. That was one of the many sticking points between R. T. Jones and his eldest son, Robert Purmedus. R. P. was born in 1879 and was never comfortable with the fact that he had not been named after his father. Lewis Jones, Jr., Bobby's cousin, recalled that the withholding of his father's name left R. P. with a sense of disappointment and personal inadequacy. It quickly became obvious that father and son were little alike in personality as well. Whereas R. T. was stern and serious, R. P. was affable, gregarious, and generally fun-loving. One might say that R. P. was more concerned about enjoying this life than was his father and much less concerned about preparing for the next one. R. P. drank, danced, and related adult jokes. In addition, Bobby Jones once described his father as an "expert in profanity."

R. P. was no slacker, however, and he easily understood the value of formal education. So he took

classes at the University of Georgia and Mercer University before studying law and passing the bar exam. While in college, R. P. engaged vigorously in athletics, especially baseball. He even flirted with the idea of pursuing a professional baseball career; when R. T. learned of it, he supposedly threatened to disown his son. On one occasion, a baseball authority noticed R. P.'s prowess on the ball diamond. R. T. simply responded, "You could not pay him a poorer compliment."

Like so many other young people at the turn of the century, R. P. Jones simply rebelled against the formalism of his father's generation. He genuinely respected and admired his father, but their world views were very different. It was only reasonable that, given the opportunity, R. P. Jones would move from Canton. The opportunity came in 1901, just after R. P. finished his education and got married. That year his wife, Clara Thomas of Auburn, Alabama, gave birth to a son named William. The child was frail like his mother and survived less than three months. By the fall, Clara Jones was pregnant again and, believing that Atlanta would be a much safer place than Canton to bear a child, convinced her husband to move to the big city. R. P. Jones thought that Atlanta, a burgeoning center of southern commerce, was a very good place to begin his law practice and so accommodated his wife's wishes. Before the year was out, the couple was living in Atlanta.

On March 19, 1902, the *Atlanta Constitution* quietly announced: "A little son has come to brighten the home of Mr. and Mrs. Robert Jones." Two days earlier, on the 17th, Robert Tyre Jones II had been born. (He would later refer to himself as "junior" out of respect for his father.) Like William, he was weak and sickly. O. B. Keeler, Bobby Jones's biographer and close friend, aptly described Jones's early childhood as "not much of a start." Little Bob (as everyone called him to distinguish him from his father, who became known as Big Bob or The Colonel) was afflicted with a variety of stomach-digestive problems that made it impossible for him to retain solid foods. Jones later wrote that for the first few years he was never out of the watch of his understandably hyper-protective mother or the family's black nursemaid, Camilla.

By 1907, R. P. Jones was doing well enough in his law practice, including work for Coca-Cola, that the family moved from their house on Willow Street to an apartment on affluent West Peachtree Street. The Joneses also spent most of the summer of 1907 in the country, leasing several rooms in a large house that was adjacent to the East Lake Club. East Lake, owned by the Atlanta Athletic Club (AAC), had one of the country's finest golf courses. Big Bob and Clara Jones immediately took to the links that summer, as did their five-year-old son. A fellow renter named Fulton Colville introduced Bobby Jones to the game. Little Bob was too small to hit around the big course, so he and some friends laid out a pitch-and-putt affair in front of the house.

The following year Big Bob joined the AAC's board of directors, and every summer thereafter the family lived at East Lake. With each passing year, Little Bob gained strength and balance. Although he enjoyed swimming, tennis, and baseball, he soon decided that the links was his favorite place, and there were few days in the summers after 1908 that he was not seen on the East Lake course. Family friends and fellow club members George and Perry Adair once told reporters that Little Bob "virtually 'lived on the links.' "

The game came relatively easy for young Jones; in fact, a convincing case may be made that he was the most naturally gifted golfer ever. In 1911 he won the AAC's junior championship, and by 1915 he had won several other local events and had played in his first Southern Amateur Championship. Although he was eliminated in the second round, *Golfers Magazine* considered the thirteen-year-old Jones the "sensation of the tournament." Later that summer *American Golfer* declared that "in the course of a few years in which [Jones] can gain the necessary experience . . . he will develop into one of the very best golfers in the country."

In 1916 Jones confirmed the confidence of golf writers by winning the Georgia State Amateur Championship and faring remarkably well in his first national competition, the U.S. Amateur held at the Merion Cricket Club outside Philadelphia. It was at Merion that Jones first stepped onto the national stage, and a big step it was. He advanced into the third round, defeating a former national champion in the first round and the reigning Pennsylvania state champion in the second. Jones lost his third-round match with defending champion Robert Gardner but took the Chicagoan to the thirty-third hole. "Not even Bob Gardner, who is the last word in courage, could outgame the little fellow," noted the *New York Times.*

Thus began one of the greatest golf careers ever. Like so much else in Jones's life, his competitive career had a certain symmetry about it. For example, he started and finished it at Merion, winning the final leg of the Grand Slam there in the fall of 1930. He also won his first U.S. Amateur title at Merion in 1924. By 1917 fans were well aware of Jones's hot temper; the worst manifestation of it occurred at St. Andrews during the 1921 British Open, when an angry, frustrated nineteen-year-old Jones picked up his ball and quit, figuratively "tearing up" his scorecard. Six years later, however, Jones returned to St. Andrews to win his second British Open, and it was at the mecca of golf that Jones won his only British Amateur and the first leg of the Grand Slam. Indeed, few athletic careers contain so many dramatic coincidences.

Jones's career is also interesting because on the surface it appears to be two careers in one. From 1916 through 1922, Jones failed to win a major tournament, and from 1923 through 1930, he enjoyed rare dominance, winning thirteen major championships, including five U.S. Amateurs, four U.S. Opens, three British Opens, and one British Amateur. Using the biblical allusion that was popular in sportswriting of the period, O. B. Keeler wrote that Jones, like Egypt as recorded in Genesis, endured seven lean years and thrived throughout seven fat years. Though oft-repeated, Keeler's description breaks down on several levels. For one thing, in the Genesis account the seven fat years preceded the seven lean

Bobby Jones was only fourteen years old when this photograph was made at the Merion Cricket Club near Philadelphia. The "new kid from Dixie" became the "Dixie Wonder," narrowly losing to the reigning champion, Robert Gardner, in the quarter finals. *Photograph from Sidney L. Matthew, Life and Times of Bobby Jones: Portrait of a Gentleman (Chelsea, Mich., 1995).*

years, and, for another, Jones experienced eight fat years, not seven.

Beyond these technicalities, Keeler was wrong on a more substantive ground; that is, there was really nothing lean about Jones's career between 1916 and 1920. He progressed nicely as a competitive golfer during that period, narrowly losing the U.S. Amateur in 1919 at Oakmont to local favorite S. Davidson Herron. Only seventeen when he lost to Herron, he had not yet entered a

U.S. Open, which he did a year later at Inverness in Toledo, finishing a respectable eighth place. Golf insiders realized both Jones's potential and lack of experience; in December 1919, the *New York Times* ranked Jones the number-two amateur in the country, behind Herron but ahead of Charles "Chick" Evans and Francis Ouimet. The 1921 and 1922 seasons were understandably disappointing for Jones, who could not "break through" in the National Amateur, despite steadily improving his U.S. Open record during those years. By then the expectations to win were tremendous; those expectations, though, clouded what had been a steadily and naturally progressing golf career.

The turning point came at the 1923 U.S. Open, which Jones won after an exciting playoff with Bobby Cruickshank. For the next eight years, the Atlantan was never without a national title, and he capped his competitive career in 1930 with the Grand Slam. That achievement, however, may not have been his greatest on the links; it certainly does not underscore his dominance of the period as does his U.S. Open record. In eleven U.S. Opens, Jones finished out of the top ten only once (eleventh place at Oakmont in 1927), and in his nine starts between 1922 and 1930, Jones bagged four victories and four runner-ups.

And he did it all without compromising sportsmanship; indeed, Jones would have won the 1925 U.S. Open had he not been so determined to uphold the rules and so considerate of his opponents. Jones called a penalty on himself in that tournament for a rules infraction that no one but he witnessed. The one-stroke penalty made the difference because he finished the tournament proper in a tie with Willie MacFarlane and lost the 36-hole playoff by one stroke the next day. Final tallies through the 108 holes of the 1925 U.S. Open: MacFarlane, 438; Jones, 439. Keeler later reported that when Jones was praised for his honesty, the amateur golfer replied, "You'd as well praise me for not breaking into banks. There is only one way to play this game."

Having "completed the cycle" (as some sportswriters initially described the Grand Slam), the twenty-eight-year-old Jones announced his retirement from competitive golf in November 1930. Few people were surprised; for years Jones had seemed uncomfortable in the limelight, and he was tired of putting his family through the travel and rigors of a competitive career. Jones had married Mary Malone in 1924; in early 1931 the couple's third and last child was born. Moreover, Jones had graduated from the Georgia Institute of Technology in 1922, had taken a second bachelor's degree from Harvard University in 1924, had enrolled in classes at Emory University in 1926, and had passed the Georgia bar exam late in 1927. In 1928, following a three-year stint in real estate, Jones began practicing law in between golf events. In other words, he had a growing family, one of the finest formal educations of any athlete ever, and plenty of interests and career paths other than golf. So, Jones "cashed in" immediately after his retirement by signing a motion-picture deal with Warner Brothers for an estimated $250,000 and then declared that he would not pursue professional golf.

Nonetheless, it became obvious, as the *Professional Golfer* put it in early 1931, "that Jones and golf in one form or another are destined to be inseparable." Jones later admitted that he became "deeply involved in enough golf projects to preclude, at least for many years, my taking any serious interest in other activities." Such "golf projects" included designing and endorsing a line of golf equipment for A. G. Spalding & Brothers. Soon after, Jones began his longest lasting and most famous golf project, the creation of the Augusta National Golf Club and its annual tournament, the Masters.

The Masters was successful because it was Bobby Jones's tournament. Without him, the club and tournament would not have happened. The early events were viable largely because of his own entry; between 1934 and 1948, when he became too ill to play, Jones competed in the Masters. Co-founder Clifford Roberts believed that the success of the inaugural event depended on Jones's presence, and he convinced the Atlantan to come out of retirement once a year and to play against the nation's best amateurs and professionals.

Although it is an episode in his career that is often overlooked or at least glossed over, in 1934 Jones made a semi-serious comeback effort. The record shows that he practiced long and hard and that he harbored sincere hopes of winning the inaugural Masters. But despite the crowd's rebel yells and the use of his mother's edition of his famous putter, Calamity Jane, Jones could do no better than a 294, ten shots behind winner Horton Smith. When it was over, Jones said, "I have no idea of returning to open competition. I hope to have this masters' tournament become an annual affair and I will limit my competition to playing in it for the fun I get out of it." In 1935 Jones finished in twenty-sixth place, fifteen shots behind Gene Sarazen and Craig Wood. The following year he shot a non-competitive course-record 64 and was quoted at 6-1 odds prior to the event. But he posted a dismal 306, good enough only for thirty-third place. By then it had become painfully clear that Jones had lost his putting touch and that not even he could compete once a year and seriously challenge the nation's top players. Yet, most people probably concurred with the *Atlanta Constitution's* Ralph McGill: "I can't see where it was a comeback. Comeback from what? Jones wasn't coming back in the sense that he was seeking to regain anything. He had beaten the world. He had everything."

Despite Jones's lackluster showing in the early Masters, the period between 1931 and 1948 was probably the happiest of his life. In those years he became the game's most revered figure. Providing legal advice to friends and family, Jones spent most of his time developing his interests in Augusta, in A. G. Spalding & Brothers, and in his increasingly profitable Coca-Cola distributorships. When the public called, Jones graciously responded; in 1936 he served as a consultant to President Franklin D. Roosevelt's Works Progress Administration. Jones aided the New Deal agency in its construction and refurbishment of more than six hundred municipal golf courses. The Great Depression had little effect on the Jones family, who moved into a beautiful mansion named Whitehall at 3425 Tuxedo Road in Atlanta. Bob and Mary Jones furnished their eighteen-room home in elegant style with European antiques, Waterford chandeliers, and Aubusson rugs. It was the perfect dwelling for a retired athlete who fancied himself a southern gentleman.

When World War II broke out, Jones again felt compelled by duty. Unlike the majority of public figures, Jones refused to sit on the sidelines or spend his time playing exhibitions to raise money. Instead, he fought for a position in the armed forces and then fought for his country in Great Britain and northern France. Jones never spoke much about his military career—he served as an intelligence officer and took part in the invasion of Normandy—yet when the Atlantan left the service in 1944, he had been promoted from captain to major to lieutenant colonel and had earned the World War II Victory Medal and Army of Occupation Medal. He did not serve on the front lines, but his record was nonetheless admirable, particularly given his age and the legitimate excuses available to him for avoiding military service.

A few years after the war, Jones's life took an abrupt turn. In the summer of 1948, he began experiencing regular neck and shoulder pain, as well as difficulties in the movements of his right hand and leg. He endured several operations, but by the end of 1950 Jones realized that his condition would only worsen. In 1956 he was diagnosed with syringomyelia, a spinal disorder that seems similar but is actually quite different from Lou Gehrig's disease.

Jones spent the last twenty years of his life in constant pain, yet he always kept a stiff upper lip in public and even expressed surprising good cheer. In 1949, for instance, he told one reporter, "Now I can stand around the first tee and make a nuisance of myself by giving golfing advice to my friends. And the funny part is they cannot get back at me since I can no longer play." A few years later, however, Jones privately confessed to good friend and fellow golfer Alexa Stirling: "I fight it every day. When it first happened to me I was pretty bitter, and there were times when I didn't want to go on living, [but] I decided I'd just do the very best I could."

But as his body deteriorated, Jones's public image grew stronger. By 1950 the Masters was on

the eve of major tournament status. Coincidentally, the country elected General Dwight D. Eisenhower to the presidency in 1952; Ike loved golf and Augusta, and he was also a good friend of Jones and Roberts. A few years later the youthful professional Arnold Palmer began competing at Augusta, helping to elevate the Masters and to establish golf as a televised sport. The rise of the Masters, the election of Eisenhower, and Jones's relationship to both strengthened the Atlantan's position as golf's idol. His presence at Augusta for the green-jacket closing ceremonies of the Masters became popular television viewing by the late 1950s, allowing golf fans around the globe a glimpse of their hero.

Jones's everyday life in the 1950s and 1960s was less dramatic and quite challenging. Each day around 11:00 A.M. his chauffeur would drive him in his tan Cadillac to his law office at the firm of Jones, Bird, and Howell in downtown Atlanta. Once inside the building on Poplar Street, Jones would spend several hours answering mail or conducting an interview. He corresponded with friends, players, golf writers, and family, especially cousin Lewis Jones, Jr., who was in charge of the Canton businesses. Sometime between 4:00 and 4:30, Jones would be driven back to Whitehall. He sustained that routine until the last year of his life.

By late 1970 Jones could no longer make regular visits to his office. Within six months, he became essentially bedridden, except for a few hours each day when he was propped up in a chair. In early December 1971 Jones's heart finally collapsed to an aneurysm, a by-product of years of laboring under syringomyelia. On the 15th, he asked his wife to call her priest, and later that day he converted to Catholicism. On December 18, 1971, Robert Tyre Jones, Jr., died quietly at the age of sixty-nine. He was buried at Atlanta's Oakland Cemetery on the 21st in unseasonably warm air and under gloomy skies. The funeral was private; only the immediate family attended. More than one reporter noted that it was an ironic way for one of America's most lauded athletes to finish his life. But, as Bob Jones III assured everyone, "That's the way dad wanted it. He didn't want any great fuss."

Throughout the following days, the golf world mourned. Eulogies came pouring in from around the world. Some discussed Jones's outstanding competitive career, but many more reflected on his immense public stature and character. The *New York Times* took the opportunity to repeat one of Jones's favorite axioms: "First come my wife and children. Next comes my profession— the law. Finally, and never as a life in itself, comes golf." The *Constitution and Journal* simply observed that Jones's "golf fame [was] transcended by human qualities." Fellow golfer Ben Hogan, whose record was most often compared to Jones's, summed him up: "Jones was a winner. But anyone can be a winner. It was the way he won that made him stand out above all others." Paul Gallico, former sportswriter and long-time friend, may have put it best: "He was a gentleman, and he loved his friends. . . . He was the best golf player the world has ever known."

Since his death, the life and times of Bobby Jones have been told and retold, usually by golf commentators or journalists. Because of his outstanding, unprecedented record and personal triumphs, Jones's story has often been mistold, miswritten, and exaggerated. Myths, some of which were passed along as early as 1923, have attached themselves to the collective memory of Jones. To be sure, like most myths, the Jones stories are exaggerations of the truth; they do have some basis in reality but are in the end essentially false. While Jones was a rare and truly admirable public figure, mythologizing him is not only unnecessary but ultimately does him an injustice.

There are many misconceptions about Bobby Jones's competitive career, some of which are occasionally and regularly broadcast by so-called golf experts who ought to know better. Two of the most common are that in his prime, when he was winning major events, Jones played little more golf than the average weekend hacker, and that Jones played the sport purely for the love of it and not for any personal material gain. Both misconceptions are rooted in Jones's amateurism, the quality in his career that provided the foundation for his public appeal.

The first myth is the easier of the two to debunk. The historical record, particularly newspaper and golf journal accounts, is clear: in the period between 1915 and 1930, Jones rarely went more than a few weeks, much less as long as six months, without playing a round of golf. In other words, the suggestion that he was a six-month, half-time, or weekend golfer who could put his clubs in the closet in November, pick them up in April, and then go out and win a U.S. Open is misleading and wildly inaccurate.

In fact, Jones played far more golf as a youngster than did most professionals. From an early age, he had access to East Lake, one of the finest, most challenging layouts in the country, and, according to his friends, "virtually 'lived on the links.'" Few professional golfers in the 1920s, men like Walter Hagen or Gene Sarazen, who had working-class, immigrant backgrounds, could say as much about their childhoods. That good fortune allowed Jones to play the game for hours during his formative years, developing balance, rhythm, timing, and skill that would last a lifetime. Indeed, from 1914 through 1918 (when Jones entered Georgia Tech), he played as often as he liked and, in addition, competed in numerous tournaments and charity exhibitions.

The 1919–1924 seasons, Jones's college days, were little different. To be sure, he studied hard and made excellent grades. He even structured his golf schedule around academic requirements (a rarity in contemporary collegiate athletics). Jones only traveled abroad once during that period, in 1921 when he embarrassed himself at the British Open. Yet Jones played for the Georgia Tech "Golden Tornado," an unofficial golf squad, and, although not a member of the university's team, he traveled with the Harvard University linksmen, playing many practice rounds and scheduled exhibitions. Indeed, some credited his "break through" victory at Inwood to his long hours of practice on the North's fast, bent-grass greens. When Jones emerged from Harvard in 1924, he probably had played as much golf as any other twenty-two-year-old in the world.

The amount of golf that Jones played did change during the last seven years of his career, and it reached both extremes; that is, in his competitive prime Jones had periods where he played a great deal and other periods in which he played the least number of rounds in his life. Commentators never mention it, but Jones spent the winters of 1925 and 1926 playing golf with professionals in Florida. In 1926 he played his famous 72-hole match against Walter Hagen, the leading professional of the era. Jones did not simply visit Florida for a week to play that match; he lived there for the winter, promoting real estate, especially the Whitfield Estates Golf Club in Sarasota. He also played dozens of exhibitions and entered several open events, including the Florida West Coast Opens of 1925 and 1926. Rumors even circulated prior to the 1926 winter season that Jones would team up with Tommy Armour, his usual exhibition partner, and compete in the short-lived Professional Winter Golf League. Of course Jones never went that far, but he did play his share of winter golf.

It is true that in the winters of 1927, 1928, and 1929, Jones played much less golf. During those seasons, he probably averaged no more than a dozen rounds, or one round per week between the months of December and February. O. B. Keeler claimed that Jones played only two and a half rounds in the winter of 1927. Given Jones's performance in the U.S. Open that year, Keeler may have been telling the truth. Those winters probably gave rise to the "clubs in the closet in November and not touched again until April" stories. Yet even in the late 1920s, Jones played winter golf, albeit sparingly and much less than usual. And as all Jones fans know, the Atlantan took the 1930 season very seriously, playing more practice rounds and entering a couple of professional winter tournaments to tune up his game. Finally, it is worth repeating that for at least six months out of every year between 1915 and 1930, during the spring and summer, golf was indeed Jones's priority, and he played a great deal of it.

What does all of this mean? Was Jones not such a naturally gifted golfer after all? Did he play just as often as the professionals? It is all a matter of perspective. Jones worshippers, for example,

would argue that there is little difference between leaving the clubs in the closet from November to April and playing only a few rounds between December and February, as Jones did in 1927, or playing only a dozen rounds in that three-month period, as Jones did in 1929. Some golfers, particularly those who know the difference between a perfectly timed, balanced swing and a loose, inefficient one, might argue otherwise. In any case, it is true that during the 1927–1929 seasons Jones played much less golf than the professionals he was beating in the U.S. Open, which would suggest that Jones had extraordinary balance, timing, body control, and physical abilities necessary to play golf; in light of that and his tournament record, it is fair to conclude that Jones was indeed a natural golf genius, probably the most naturally endowed golfer ever.

Even Jones, though, said that it took him at least "a month's hard practice" to prepare for an event. He never claimed to have taken six months off, to have picked up his clubs, and to have so easily beaten the world's best golfers. It seemed that way at times, so sportswriters began referring to Jones as "the Atlanta golf machine"; only a machine, not a mere man, they implied, was capable of such performances. Jones never liked being compared to a machine, and he probably would have found many of the statements made about him by today's commentators ridiculous, specifically concerning his amount of play.

Another common misconception concerning Jones is that he played the game purely for the love of the sport and competition. The truth is that Jones never did accept any prize money. It is also true that Jones did not endorse golf equipment or other products before November 1930. Neither did Jones give lessons. In those ways, Jones was a simon-pure amateur. On the other hand, in 1927 Jones began writing a series of syndicated newspaper articles for which he eventually received some $25,000. The year before, moreover, he accepted a Pierce-Arrow sedan from the city of Sarasota, a gift of thanks for his help in promoting the young city. To be sure, other amateur athletes had accepted gifts and signed similar writing contracts, and neither act violated the USGA's amateur code. Still, those opportunities and gifts would not have been bestowed on Jones were he not a top amateur golfer.

In January 1928 Jones received resounding adulation when he returned a gift of $50,000 to the citizens of Atlanta. Civic boosters had given Jones the money a few months earlier to recognize his contributions to the city and to help him purchase a house. The USGA advised Jones that his acceptance of the gift would not be in the best interests of amateur golf, and Jones agreed. Had he so desired, he could have resisted the authority of the USGA. Other amateur athletes, especially in tennis, defied their ruling bodies. The fact that Jones did not reveals much about his personality. Conservative by nature, he found it fairly easy to submit to golf's authorities and traditions.

Yet Bobby Jones was hardly a financial simpleton. He understood perfectly that his unique and strong public image rested on his amateurism. If he exercised discipline in the short run and turned back the $50,000, he would later be in a position to retire and make much more money. Jones obviously had no way of knowing just how successful he would be, but even in 1928 he was confident of his ability to cash in. He already had compiled an impressive competitive record and there was no reason to believe that he would not continue to dominate his sport. So as a young superstar, he was in a position to profit any time that he wanted to. Most importantly, if Jones waited and turned down the $50,000, he would maintain his spotless image, the respect of the public, and the admiration of the USGA. The entire episode underscores Jones's impeccable judgment, financial and otherwise.

The returned $50,000 gift contributed to an estimated $250,000 motion-picture deal. Eventually, Jones also made thousands of dollars from his contract with A. G. Spalding & Brothers, the sale of his autobiographies, a series of radio interviews, and Augusta National. It is, then, patently false to suggest that as an amateur Jones profited little from his sport; in fact, he probably made much more money from golf in the long run, having

played as an amateur, than he ever would have made in the short run as a professional, accepting purse money and thus transforming—or diluting—his image. Walter Hagen, the nation's top professional and exhibitionist, is widely considered to be the first golfer to make a million dollars. True, but Hagen was never offered a $250,000 contract for anything, much less for a dozen film shorts a year after the stock market crashed.

Some would have us believe that all of this happened to Jones by accident—that he unwittingly came into all of this money. A few continue to argue ludicrously that, despite all of his golf dealings, Jones did not really profit from the sport. Some fans seem almost incapable of believing that the Atlantan could ever have been motivated by economic self-interest. Those notions provide comfort in a contemporary era in which there are seemingly no pure amateurs, not even in the collegiate ranks or in the Olympics, and in which professional athletes sign multi-million-dollar contracts before playing a single game. If comforting, though, such an image of Jones is dishonest.

The mythologizing of Jones has been understandable and probably inevitable, given his life and accomplishments. Nonetheless, it is unfortunate for at least two reasons. First, Jones never made any pretenses to perfection—moral, ethical, athletic, or otherwise—and it is simply unfair to burden him with such an image. Second, the myths obscure the man, who in reality reveals much about his times and still generally offers an admirable example.

In 1927, just as he was rising to superstardom, Jones confessed to a reporter, "Of course, it's nice to have people say nice things about you, but honestly, when New York papers make me out such a glowing example of moral discipline I don't know what to make of it." The most remarkable quality of Jones's character was his humility; he had a rare sense of his importance in relation to others. He was never accused of being rude or inconsiderate or a braggart. Jones's most bitter rival was Charles "Chick" Evans; the Chicago amateur grew to despise and envy Jones, but the worst thing that he ever accused Jones of was signing a contract with Warner Brothers a few weeks before he retired (a charge, incidentally, that was never substantiated). Not even Evans suggested that Jones was an egomaniac.

Because of his sense of humility, Jones did not want to be considered a paragon—which in some ways he was not. He made inconsistent statements. For example, in the summer of 1929, having just won the U. S. Open, Jones told reporters that he was going to give Calamity Jane a rest for a couple of months and focus on his law practice until the U.S. Amateur in the fall. Two days later he shot a 66 at East Lake, and over the next three weeks, he played in no less than six publicized exhibitions. Like every other amateur athlete of the period, he was sometimes disingenuous about his standing.

Beyond that, Jones engaged in several of the traditional vices. In the 1920s he drank regularly, if usually not heavily, and thus, in the age of Prohibition consistently broke the law. Despite popular belief, not everyone did that. There were plenty of traditionally valued Americans who shunned the alcohol that Jones so easily consumed. He also liked to gamble. Jones was not addicted to either vice, but, as a chain smoker, he was thoroughly addicted to tobacco, and although he eventually learned to control it, Jones had a fiery temper, as well as his father's proclivity for profanity.

In addition, Jones was characteristically conservative on social questions. In recent years, Augusta National and the Masters have come in for much criticism for their exclusivity and perceived insensitivity to black Americans. It is not fair to saddle Jones with all that has been wrong about Augusta and the Masters, and neither is it accurate to credit him with all that is admirable about the club and its tournament. The fact is that by the mid-1950s, when the Masters became a major tour event, Jones was becoming physically weaker by the month, so Clifford Roberts assumed power, shaping the club and tournament for good and bad. Moreover, there are absolutely no incidents of racial hatred in the lives of R. T., R. P., or Bobby Jones; if never unmindful of their superior racial status, the Joneses were very popular among blacks they knew personally.

That said, Jones did not lend public support to progressive civil rights policies. He campaigned for President Dwight D. Eisenhower and seemed satisfied with Ike's social conservatism. In truth, Jones never seemed anything but comfortable in the New South's segregated society. Still, if the Atlantan held values and engaged in behavior that were less than admirable, he seemed to have understood that much better than his legions of worshippers.

Bobby Jones was simply a product of the era in which he came of age. Since at least the mid-1960s, professional historians have discarded the interpretation of the 1920s as being a frivolous interlude between the deadly serious World War I and the onset of the Great Depression. Scholars of the period have concluded that it was a much more important and complicated decade than once believed. It was a period in which Americans struggled to assimilate a generation of intense socioeconomic development marked by the rise of an urban, modern society. Many Americans were caught between the old and the new, wanting to preserve the best of the past, while carefully moving into the future. The generation that cheered Jones on to victory was plagued by a sense of insecurity and ambivalence, the result of rapid change.

Placed in his proper historical context, Jones reflects the temper of his times. His lineage and background were emblematic of broader changes in social thought. Through grandfather R. T. and father R. P., Bobby Jones received a mixture of Victorian and modern values. His father, like so many other American youths in the 1890s, had essentially rebelled against the moral absolutism of R. T.'s Victorian age. Both men and their generations heavily influenced the life and thought of Bobby Jones; indeed, his commitment to family, education, duty to country, personal modesty, and, of course, amateurism and sportsmanship are all indicative of the traditional values of his grandfather's generation. On the other hand, his willingness to violate Prohibition, his heavy smoking, and his decision to organize so much of his life around a sport, even if as an amateur, are manifestations of the modern values of his father's generation. Racial views were representative of the generations and cultures of every Jones.

There is too much myth surrounding Jones, particularly his competitive career. One may argue that the myths do more harm than simply misrepresent history. Ultimately, the "clubs in the closet" stories and the unwillingness to acknowledge Jones's natural and savvy economic motivations idealize the Atlantan to an unhealthy extreme. The Jones image often loses touch with reality. Jones becomes a symbol or a monument, revered but somehow unreal and essentially irrelevant to everyday life. But Bobby Jones is too important to be dismissed and too complex to be trivialized. His life and legacy are a rich example to a contemporary society that all too often seems plagued by infidelity, shameless self-promotion, and an obsession with expediency, winning, and material gain. We should not be careless of his memory; we should be its honest caretakers.

STUDY QUESTIONS

1. Considering the Jones family history given by the author, did Bobby Jones exist as an anomaly or a reflection of the evolving South?

2. Why did Bobby Jones remain an amateur?

3. What image is the author "demarbleizing" and what are its essential components? What role did this image play in American culture from 1920 to 1948 and beyond?

4. How did the rise of the Masters in the postwar golf scene reflect the relationship between the South and the rest of the nation?

5. The 1920s, a period of "insecurity and ambivalence," produced both Babe Ruth and Bobby Jones. What are their similarities and differences?

BIBLIOGRAPHY

For a recent look at the mythical Bobby Jones, see Sidney Matthews, *Life and Times of Bobby Jones* (1995) and "Atlanta's Immortal Bobby Jones" *Atlanta History* 43 (1999): 6–20. To explore the roles of the two greatest golfers of the study period, see Lowe's recent work, *Sir Walter and Mr. Jones: Walter Hagen, Bobby Jones, and the Rise of American Golf* (2000). That Jones played a crucial part in making the Masters a revered event and Augusta National a golfing landmark is established in Charles Price's *A Golf Story: Bobby Jones, Augusta National and the Masters Tournament* (2001). H.W. Wind presents a general history of golf in *The Story of American Golf,* 3rd rev. ed. (1975). The best general history of sports remains Benjamin G. Rader's *American Sports: From the Age of Folk Games to the Age of Televised Sports,* 4th ed. (1999). For histories on the South and America during this period, respectively, see George Tindall, *The Emergence of the New South 1913–1945* (1967) and Michael E. Parrish, *Anxious Decades: America in Prosperity and Depression, 1920–1941* (1992).

READING 13

THE MOOD OF THE PEOPLE

Roderick Nash

No decade in American history has been more studded with heroes and idols than the 1920s. Such athletic heroes as Babe Ruth, Jack Dempsey, Red Grange, Bill Tilden, and Bobby Jones are still household names. In Hollywood, they were rivaled by stars such as Rudolph Valentino, Mary Pickford, Douglas Fairbanks, Clara Bow, and Charlie Chaplin. Heroes even came from the worlds of business, finance, and government. Herbert Hoover and Edward Bok demonstrated the appeal of self-made millionaires. The greatest hero, however, was Charles Lindbergh, who captured the public's imagination in 1927 by making the first solo flight across the Atlantic.

Nor has there been a decade that has been more acclaimed for its literary output. Novelists F. Scott Fitzgerald and Ernest Hemingway and poets e. e. cummings, T. S. Eliot, and Edna St. Vincent Millay are among the most talented America ever produced. More people, however, read the stories of such popular novelists as Gene Stratton-Porter, Harold Bell Wright, Zane Grey, and Edgar Rice Burroughs.

In the following essay historian Roderick Nash probes the meaning behind the heroes people chose and the novels they read. Heroes, Nash claims, reflect the "mood of the people"; they mirror the aspirations, longings, and fears of millions of unheralded Americans. Similarly, popular novelists' success depends on their ability to interpret and tap the mood of the nation. That mood, Nash feels, was not bold and carefree, as Frederick Lewis Allen believed, but rather timid and nervous. Americans chose heroes and read novels that glorified their rural past and eased their minds concerning their urban future.

eroes abounded in the American 1920s. Their names, especially in sports, have been ticked off so frequently they have become clichés. Less often have commentators paused to probe for explanations. Why were the twenties ripe for heroism? And why did the heroics follow a predictable pattern? Such questions lead to an understanding of the mood of the people, because heroism concerns the public as well as the individual. It depends on achievement but even more on recognition. In the final analysis the hopes and fears of everyday Americans create national heroes.

The nervousness of the post-World War I generation provided fertile soil for the growth of a particular kind of heroism. Many Americans felt uneasy as they experienced the transforming effects of population growth, urbanization, and economic change. On the one hand, these developments were welcome as steps in the direction of progress. Yet they also raised vague fears about the passing of frontier conditions, the loss of national vigor, and the eclipse of the individual in a mass society. Frederick Jackson Turner and Theodore Roosevelt, among others, had pointed to the liabilities of the transformation at the turn of the century. World War I underscored the misgivings and doubts. By the 1920s the sense of change had penetrated to the roots of popular thought. Scarcely an American was unaware that the frontier had vanished and that pioneering, in the traditional sense, was a thing of the past. Physical changes in the nation were undeniable. They occurred faster, however, than intellectual adjustment. Although Americans, in general, lived in a densely populated, urban-industrial civilization, a large part of their values remained rooted in the frontier, farm, and village. Exposure of this discrepancy only served to increase the tightness with which insecure people clung to the old certainties. Old-style pioneering was impossible, but Americans proved ingenious in finding equivalents. The upshot in the twenties was the cult of the hero—the man who provided living testimony of the power of courage, strength, and honor and of the efficacy of the self-reliant, rugged individual who seemed on the verge of becoming as irrelevant as the covered wagon.

Sports and the star athlete were the immediate beneficiaries of this frame of mind. The American sports fan regarded the playing field as a surrogate frontier; the athletic hero was the twentieth-century equivalent of the pathfinder or pioneer. In athletic competition, as on the frontier, people believed, men confronted tangible obstacles and overcame them with talent and determination. The action in each case was clean and direct; the goals, whether clearing forests or clearing the bases, easily perceived and immensely satisfying. Victory was the result of superior ability. The sports arena, like the frontier, was pregnant with opportunity for the individual. The start was equal and the best man won. Merit was rewarded. True or not, such a credo was almost instinctive with Americans. They packed the stadiums of the 1920s in a salute to time-honored virtues. With so much else about America changing rapidly, it was comforting to find in sports a ritualistic celebration of the major components of the national faith.

Writing in the *North American Review* for October 1929, A. A. Brill, a leading American psychologist of the Freudian school, took a closer look at the meaning of athletics. Why, he wondered, do men play and why do they select the particular kinds of play they do? Brill was also interested in the reasons spectators came to games. His main point was that sports were not idle diversions but intensely serious endeavors rooted in the values and traditions of a civilization. "The ancestry of sport," Brill declared, "is written very plainly in the fact that the first games among all nations were simple imitations of the typical acts of warriors and huntsmen." The primary motivation of play, according to Brill, was the "mastery impulse"—and inherent aggressiveness in man stemming from the Darwinian struggle for existence. Modern man had largely transcended direct physical struggle, but the need for it persisted in the human psyche. Sports were contrived as substitutes for actual fighting, mock struggles that satisfied the urge to conquer. Brill did not suggest a relationship between American sports and the American frontier, but his argument suggested one. So did the fact that the rise of mass spectator sports and the decline of the frontier were simultaneous in the United States.

By the 1920s the nation went sports crazy. It seemed to many that a golden age of sport had arrived in America. Football received a large portion of the limelight. As they had in the declining days of Rome, fans thronged the stadiums to witness contact, violence, bloodshed, man pitted against man, strength against strength. The vicarious element was invariably present. For a brief, glorious moment the nobody in the bleachers *was* the halfback crashing into the end zone with the winning touchdown. For a moment he shared the thrill of individual success and fought off the specter of being swallowed up in mass society.

Big-time professional football began on September 17, 1920, when the American Football Association was organized with the great Indian athlete Jim Thorpe as its first president. When the Green Bay Packers joined the Association in 1921, the saga of pro football was solidly launched. Attendance rose dramatically. On November 21, 1925, the presence on the playing field of the fabled Harold "Red" Grange helped draw 36,000 spectators to a game. A week later 68,000 jammed the Polo Grounds in New York to watch Grange in action. The names of the pro teams were suggestive. As on the frontier of old, it was cowboys versus Indians, or giants versus bears— with the names of cities prefixed.

The twenties was also the time of the emergence of college football on an unprecedented scale. Heroes appeared in good supply: Red Grange at Illinois, Knute Rockne's "Four Horsemen" at Notre Dame in 1924, Harold "Brick" Muller who began a dynasty at California that extended through fifty consecutive victories in the

seasons 1919 through 1925. Hundreds of thousands attended the Saturday games, an estimated twenty million during the season. Millions more followed the action over their radios and made a Sunday morning ritual of devouring the newspaper accounts of the games of the previous day. To accommodate the crowds colleges and universities built huge new stadiums. Yale's and California's seated eighty thousand; Illinois, Ohio State, and Michigan were not far behind. The number of Americans who attended games doubled between 1921 and 1930. A *Harper's* writer caught the spirit of college football in 1928: "It is at present a religion, sometimes it seems to be almost our national religion." So, once, had been westward expansion.

Despite its popularity, football tended to obscure the heroic individual. It was, after all, a team sport. Even Red Grange received an occasional block on his long runs. But in sports pitting man against man or against the clock the heroism latent in competition achieved its purest expression. Americans in the 1920s had a glittering array of well-publicized individuals from which to choose their idol. In golf Robert T. "Bobby" Jones, Walter Hagen, and Gene Sarazen were the dominant figures. Tennis had "Big" Bill Tilden and "Little" Bill Johnson whose epic duels on the center court at Forest Hills filled the stands. The competition was even more direct in boxing with its "knockout," the symbol of complete conquest. During the twenties promoters like Tex Rickard built boxing into a big business. Jack Dempsey and Gene Tunney proved so attractive to the sporting public that a ticket sale of a million dollars for a single fight became a reality. By the end of the decade the figure was two million. Fifty bouts in the twenties had gates of more than $100,000. More than 100,000 fans came to Soldiers' Field in Chicago on September 22, 1927, to see the second Dempsey-Tunney fight with its controversial "long count" that helped Tunney retain the championship and earn $990,000 for thirty minutes of work. In a nation not oblivious to the approach of middle age, it was comforting to count the heavyweight champion of the world among the citizenry. Here was evidence, many reasoned, that the nation remained strong, young, and fit to survive in a Darwinian universe. Record-breaking served the same purpose, and in Johnny Weismuller, premier swimmer, and Paavo Nurmi, Finnish-born track star, the United States had athletes who set world marks almost every time they competed. Gertrude Ederle chose a longer course when she swam the English Channel in 1926, but she too set a record and was treated to one of New York's legendary ticker-tape parades.

And there was the Babe. No sports hero of the twenties and few of any decade had the reputation of George Herman Ruth. Baseball was generally acknowledged to be the national game, and Ruth played with a superb supporting cast of New York Yankees, but when he faced a pitcher Babe Ruth stood as an individual. His home runs (particularly the 59 in 1921 and the 60 in 1927) gave him a heroic stature comparable to that of legendary demigods like Odysseus, Beowulf, or Daniel Boone. Ruth's unsavory background and boorish personal habits were nicely overlooked by talented sportswriters anxious to give the twenties the kind of hero it craved. The payoff was public adulation of the Babe and of baseball.

The twenties also saw the public exposure of corruption in baseball and confronted Americans with the necessity of reviewing their entire hero complex. On September 28, 1920, three members of the Chicago White Sox appeared before a grand jury to confess that they and five other players had agreed to throw the 1919 World Series to Cincinnati for a financial consideration. Gradually the unhappy story of the "Black Sox" unfolded. Big-time gamblers had persuaded selected players to make sure that a bet on the underdog Cincinnati team would pay off. Some of the greatest names in the game were involved, preeminently that of "Shoeless" Joe Jackson. An illiterate farm boy from South Carolina, Jackson's natural batting eye helped him compile a .356 average in ten seasons as a major leaguer. In the process he became one of the most idolized players in baseball. It was Jackson's exit from the grand jury chamber on September 28 that allegedly precipitated the

agonized plea from a group of boys: "Say it ain't so, Joe!" According to the newspapers, Jackson, shuffling, head down, replied, "Yes, boys, I'm afraid it is."

Reaction to the Black Sox testified to the importance baseball had for many Americans. One school of thought condemned the "fix" in the strongest terms and agitated for the restoration of integrity to the game. It was a serious matter. The Philadelphia *Bulletin* compared the eight players with "the soldier or sailor who would sell out his country and its flag in time of war." Suggesting the link between sports and the national character, the *New York Times* declared that bribing a ballplayer was an offense "which strikes at the very heart of this nation." If baseball fell from grace, what could be honest in America? The question haunted journalists and cartoonists. *Outlook* for October 13, 1920, carried a drawing of a crumpled statue of a ballplayer whose torn side revealed a stuffing of dollar bills. The statue bore the inscription "The National Game." A small boy wept in the foreground; the caption to the cartoon read "His Idol."

Baseball officials and club owners were similarly dismayed at the revelation of corruption and determined to clean up the game. Charles A. Comiskey, owner of the Chicago White Sox, led the way with a public statement that no man involved in the fix would ever wear the uniform of his club again. Other owners followed suit until all organized baseball, even the minor leagues, was closed to the Black Sox. On November 12, 1920, Kenesaw Mountain Landis, a former federal judge, was appointed commissioner of baseball with full control over the game and a charge to safeguard its integrity.

The everyday fans' response to the fix differed sharply from that of the sportswriters and owners. Many Americans seemed determined to deny the entire affair; more precisely, they didn't *want* to believe anything could be wrong with something as close to the national ideal as baseball. Like the boys of the "say it ain't so" episode, they begged for evidence that the old standards and values still applied. Especially in

1920 in the United States sports heroes were needed as evidence of the virtues of competition, fair play, and the self-reliant individual. Consequently, when confronted with the scandal, the average American simply closed his eyes and pretended nothing was wrong. The heroes remained heroes. When the Black Sox formed an exhibition team, it received enthusiastic support. Petitions were circulated in the major league cities to reinstate the players in organized baseball. But the most remarkable demonstration of the public's feeling came at the conclusion of the Black Sox trial on August 2, 1921. After deliberating two hours and forty-seven minutes, the jury returned a verdict of *not* guilty. According to the *New York Times* reporter at the scene, the packed courtroom rose as one man at the good news, cheering wildly. Hats sailed and papers were thrown about in the delirium. Men shouted "hooray for the clean sox." The bailiffs pounded for order until, as the *Times* reported, they "finally noticed Judge Friend's smiles, and then joined in the whistling and cheering." Finally the jury picked up the acquitted ballplayers and carried them out of the courtroom on their shoulders!

Baseball officials and journalists regarded the acquittal of the Black Sox as a technical verdict secured by the lenient interpretation of the Illinois statute involved. The fans in the courtroom, however, and, presumably, many elsewhere were on the side of the players regardless, and viewed the verdict as a vindication. They were not prepared to believe that baseball or its heroes could become tarnished. The game was too important to the national ego. Following baseball gave Americans an opportunity to pay tribute to what many believed was the best part of their heritage. The game was a sacred rite undertaken not merely to determine the winner of league championships but to celebrate the values of a civilization. As one newspaper account of the scandal put it, to learn that "Shoeless" Joe Jackson had sold out the world series was like discovering that "Daniel Boone had been bought by the Indians to lose his fights in Kentucky."

In the gallery of popular heroes in the United States the only rival of the frontiersman and his athletic surrogate was the self-made man. In the 1920s the archetype was Herbert Hoover, a hero-President hewn out of the traditional rags-to-riches mold. Left an orphan in 1884 at the age of ten, Hoover launched an international career in mining that made him rich. During World War I he became famous, heading the American Relief Commission abroad and the Food Administration at home. A genius in matters of large-scale efficiency, Hoover neatly executed apparent miracles. After the decline of Woodrow Wilson in the wake of the Versailles Treaty, Hoover was easily the foremost American beneficiary of war-caused popularity. In 1922, while Secretary of Commerce under Warren G. Harding, he set forth his creed in a slender book entitled *American Individualism.* Apparently oblivious of the doubts that beset intellectuals at the time, Hoover professed his "abiding faith in the intelligence, the initiative, the character, the courage, and the divine touch in the individual." But he also believed that individuals differed greatly in energy, ability, and ambition. Some men inevitably rose to the top of the heap, and for Hoover this was entirely right and proper. It was necessary, moreover, if society were to progress. Hoover's philosophy was the old American one of rugged individualism and free enterprise that the Social Darwinists had decorated with scientific tinsel after the Civil War. Intellectually, Hoover was a bedfellow with Benjamin Franklin and William Graham Sumner.

Hoover's social, political, and economic ideas followed from these assumptions. He staunchly defended the unregulated profit system. Society and government owed the people only three things: "liberty, justice, and equality of opportunity." Competition took care of the rest, carrying the deserving to their just rewards and the failures to deserved defeat. Any interference, such as philanthropy to the poor or favoritism to the rich, only dulled *"the emery wheel of competition."* To be sure, Hoover paid lip service to restricting the strong in the interest of the society, but the main thrust of his thought awarded the victors their spoils. Critics were disarmed with three words—"equality of opportunity." The state should interfere to preserve it; otherwise, hands off! An exponent of the gospel of efficiency in economic affairs, Hoover believed that the road to the good life lay in the direction of more and better production. His mind equated material success with progress.

In the concluding chapter of *American Individualism,* Hoover drew the connection between his philosophy and the frontier. "The American pioneer," he declared, "is the epic expression of . . . individualism and the pioneer spirit is the response to the challenge of opportunity, to the challenge of nature, to the challenge of life, to the call of the frontier." Undismayed by the ending of the geographical frontier in the United States, Hoover declared that "there will always be a frontier to conquer or to hold to as long as men think, plan, and dare. . . . The days of the pioneer are not over."

When Hoover was elected President in 1928, these ideals were accorded the nation's highest accolade. They dominated popular thought as they had for three centuries of American history. In fact, all the men who occupied the Presidency from 1917 to 1930 were distinctly old-fashioned in their beliefs and in their public image. The traits are so familiar as to require listing only: Wilson the moralist and idealist; Harding the exemplar of small-town, "just folks" normalcy; Coolidge the frugal, farm-oriented Puritan; and Hoover the self-made man. If there was any correlation between a people's taste and its Presidents, then the record of this period underscored nostalgia.

Rivalling Hoover in the public mind of the early 1920s as an exponent of self-help and individualism was Edward Bok, the Dutch boy who made good and wrote about it in *The Americanization of Edward Bok* (1920). The book described Bok's immigration from Holland in 1870 at the age of six and his rise from a fifty-cents-a-week window cleaner to editor of the magazine with the largest circulation in the nation, the *Ladies Home Journal.* Bok's autobiography reads as a paean to the American ideal of success. Through luck, pluck, and clean living, he became

a confidant and friend of Presidents. Thrift and determination made him rich. Bok played the rags to riches theme to the hilt. "Here was a little Dutch boy," he wrote in his preface, "unceremoniously set down in America . . . yet, it must be confessed, he achieved." His book, Bok promised, would describe "how such a boy, with every disadvantage to overcome, was able . . . to 'make good.' "

In the final chapters of his autobiography, Bok stepped back to comment on the liabilities and advantages of America. He did not slight the former, yet in "What I Owe to America" Bok brushed all debits aside in order to celebrate America's gift of "limitless opportunity: here a man can go as far as his abilities will carry him." For anyone "endowed with honest endeavor, ceaseless industry, and the ability to carry through, . . . the way is wide open to the will to succeed."

The public reception of *The Americanization of Edward Bok* suggests how much Americans in the 1920s wanted to confirm old beliefs. Bok was a hero in the Benjamin Franklin-Horatio Alger mold. His success story demonstrated that passing time and changing conditions had not altered hallowed ideals. His pages suggested no troubling doubts, and, after receiving the Pulitzer Prize for biography in 1921, Bok's book became a bestseller. An inexpensive eighth edition issued in July 1921 enabled it to attain third place on the 1922 lists. But the primary reason for Bok's popularity as hero-author was his ability to tell a nervous generation what it wanted to hear.

It has long puzzled students of the Great Crash of 1929 why even the most informed observers in education and government as well as business did not recognize and heed the prior economic danger signals that in retrospect seem so apparent. Part of the explanation possibly lies in the depth of the general commitment to the ideals of rugged individualism and free enterprise that Hoover and Bok articulated and symbolized. This commitment, in turn, lay in the nervousness of the American people. So much about the twenties was new and disturbing that Americans tended to cling tightly to familiar economic forms. They just could not bear to admit that the old business premises based on individualism and free enterprise might be fraught with peril. With Herbert Hoover leading the way, they chose to go down with the economic ship rather than question and alter its suicidal course.

Respect for the old-time hero was evident in other aspects of postwar thought. The vogue of the Boy Scouts is an example. Although the movement began in 1910, the twenties was the time of its flowering. There were 245,000 Scouts at the beginning of 1917, 942,500 at the end of 1929. In addition, 275,000 adults volunteered their services as leaders. No youth club and few adult organizations matched this record. The Boy Scout Handbook, a manual of ideals and instruction, sold millions of copies. Scouting, apparently, tapped fertile soil in its embodiment of the old-time idea of good citizenship and expertise in the outdoors. The Scout, standing straight in his shorts or knickers and doing the daily good deed that his oath required, was the epitome of the traditional American model of heroic young manhood.

In the late 1920s the Boy Scout Handbook featured an unusual drawing. In the foreground was a clean-cut Scout, eyes fixed on adventure. Behind him, signifying the heritage from which he sprang, were the figures of Daniel Boone, Abraham Lincoln, and Theodore Roosevelt, men who were staples in the annals of American heroism. But there was also a new face, that of Charles A. Lindbergh of Minnesota. At the age of just twenty-five Lindbergh rose to the status of an American demigod by virtue of a single feat. On May 20, 1927, he took off in a tiny single-engine airplane from New York City and thirty-three hours later landed in Paris. The nonstop, solo run across the Atlantic catapulted the average American into a paroxysm of pride and joy. Overnight Lindbergh became the greatest hero of the decade. There was but little exaggeration in the contention of one journalist that Lindbergh received "the greatest ovation in history." Certainly his return from Paris to the United States generated a reception extraordinary even for an age that specialized in ballyhoo. The *New York Times* devoted more

space to Lindbergh's return than it had to the Armistice ending World War I. A virtual national religion took shape around Lindbergh's person. A 1928 poll of schoolboys in a typical American town on the question of whom they most wanted to be like produced the following results: Gene Tunney, 13 votes; John Pershing, 14; Alfred E. Smith, 16; Thomas A. Edison, 27; Henry Ford, 66; Calvin Coolidge, 110; Charles A. Lindbergh, 363. If the amount of national adulation is meaningful, adults everywhere would likely have responded in similar proportions.

The explanation of Lindbergh's popularity lies less in his feat (pilots had flown across the Atlantic before) and more in the mood of the people at the time it occurred. The typical American in 1927 was nervous. The values by which he ordered his life seemed in jeopardy of being swept away by the force of growth and change and complexity. Lindbergh came as a restorative tonic. He reasserted the image of the confident, quietly courageous, and self-reliant individual. He proved to a generation anxious for proof that Americans were still capable of pioneering. Even in an age of machines the frontier was not dead—a new one had been found in the air.

The reaction to Lindbergh's flight in the national press stressed these ideas. "Lindbergh served as a metaphor," wrote one commentator in *Century.* "We felt that in him we, too, had conquered something and regained lost ground." A writer in *Outlook* made the point more explicitly: "Charles Lindbergh is the heir of all that we like to think is best in America. He is the stuff out of which have been made the pioneers that opened up the wilderness first on the Atlantic coast, and then in our great West." A newspaper cartoon showed a covered wagon leaving for California in 1849 and next to it Lindbergh's plane taking off for Paris in 1927. Colonel Theodore Roosevelt, the son of the President, remarked that Lindbergh "personifies the daring of youth. Daniel Boone, David Crockett, and men of that type played a lone hand and made America. Lindbergh is their lineal descendant." Calvin Coolidge, who personally welcomed Lindbergh home, simply said that

In an age of mechanization, Charles Lindbergh represented a comforting continuation of the pioneering spirit and of self-reliance. His flight was well publicized, and Lindbergh returned to a wildly enthusiastic America as a popular hero.

he was "a boy representing the best traditions of this country."

For one journalist the most significant part of the Lindbergh phenomenon was not the flight but the character of the man: "his courage, his modesty, his self-control, his sanity, his thoughtfulness of others, his fine sense of proportion, his loyalty, his unswerving adherence to the course that seemed right." His unassuming manner fit the traditional hero's mold. Many observers of the postflight celebration noted how the hero refused to capitalize financially on his popularity. It was telling evidence as an essayist put it, that the American people "are *not* rotten at the core, but morally sound and sweet and good!" The generalization from the individual to society was easily acceptable because Americans in 1927 desperately wanted to keep the old creed alive. Lind-

bergh's flight was popularly interpreted as a flight of faith—in the American experience and in the American people.

Looking back over the 1920s F. Scott Fitzgerald remembered in 1931 that "in the spring of 1927, something bright and alien flashed across the sky. A young Minnesotan who seemed to have nothing to do with his generation did a heroic thing, and for a moment people set down their glasses in country clubs and speakeasies and thought of their old best dreams." Also in 1931 Frederick Lewis Allen recalled that Lindbergh had been "a modern Galahad for a generation which had foresworn Galahads." Both Fitzgerald and Allen were right in their assessment of the public reaction to Lindbergh's flight, but wrong about the dreams he engendered being foreign to the 1920s. Fitzgerald notwithstanding, Lindbergh had a great deal to do with his generation. Allen to the contrary, the Lindbergh craze was not a case of Americans returning to ideals they had forsaken; they had never left them.

Popular books as well as heroes revealed the American mind in the 1920s, and the great majority of the best-sellers of the decade were decidedly old-fashioned. Frontier and rural patterns of thought and action dominated the popular novels. Their plots and protagonists operated according to time-honored standards of competition, loyalty, and rugged individualism. Complications were few and usually resolved, in the final pages, with an application of traditional morality. The total effect was a comforting reaffirmation of the old American faith. Such novels, to be sure, made slight contribution to serious American literature. But they were read—by millions! And they both influenced and reflected the mood of Americans who had never even heard of Fitzgerald and Hemingway. Indeed in comparison to best-selling authors, the Fitzgeralds and Hemingways were highly esoteric.

Exact figures are elusive, but it would be difficult to dispute Gene (Geneva) Stratton-Porter's claim to preeminence among popular novelists in the first three decades of the twentieth century. Her vogue began with *Freckles* in 1904 and continued right through the war, into the twenties, and beyond. In 1932 a *Publisher's Weekly* survey of the best-selling novels of the century revealed Porter in the top four positions with *Freckles, The Girl of the Limberlost* (1909), *The Harvester* (1911), and *Laddie* (1913). Each had sold well over a million copies. With other titles Porter made the "top ten" list in 1918, 1919, 1921, and 1925. Most of her sales were in fifty-cent reprint editions, suggesting that her public consisted or relatively unsophisticated readers.

Gene Stratton-Porter found a publishing bonanza by articulating the values to which a large part of the American reading public subscribed. Chief among them was a belief in the virtue of close association with nature. As a girl Porter ran in the swamps, woods, and fields around Wabash, Indiana, and the characters in her novels do likewise. The experience was represented as inspirational in the highest sense. Nature was not only a source of beauty and contentment but a repository of moral and religious truth. The outdoors provided a constant backdrop in Porter's stories. Indeed the margins of her books were sometimes adorned with pen and ink drawings of birds, animals, and flowers. *The Harvesters* was dedicated to Henry David Thoreau.

Second only to nature in Porter's scale of values was cheerfulness. Her stories expound the benefits of optimism, confidence, courage, and keeping a stiff upper lip. Typically the plots involve the protagonist, frequently a child, in a series of adversities. But looking for the silver lining and heeding the teachings of nature eventually resolve all problems. *Freckles,* for instance, describes a boy who believes himself an orphan, wanders in the Limberlost swamp, and is ultimately found and claimed by his wealthy father. Eleanora of *A Girl of the Limberlost* defies poverty by selling the moths she collected in the swamp. In *Michael O'Halloran* Porter copied the Horatio Alger formula, taking a little newsboy up the success ladder on the wings of determination and pluck.

Porter's novels appealed to the kind of American whose eyes glazed and even dampened when they thought of the good old days when life was simple and generally lived in close proximity to nature. In Porter one basked momentarily in an uncomplicated world where virtue triumphed and right prevailed. Much of Porter's public seemed to consist of people displaced or crushed by modern American civilization. Letters of appreciation poured in to her from sanitariums, rest homes, reform schools, and jails. But in a larger sense the uncertainties and nervousness of the age in general provided a milieu in which her kind of writing could flourish.

William Lyon Phelps once wrote of Gene Stratton-Porter, "She is a public institution, like Yellowstone Park, and I should not think she would care any more than a mountain for adverse criticism." In fact, Porter did care. She habitually replied to her unfavorable reviewers in lengthy letters. In one she responded to a critic who had labeled her writing "molasses fiction." This was really a compliment, rejoined Porter: "Molasses is more necessary to the happiness of human and beast then vinegar. . . . I am a molasses person myself. . . . So I shall keep straight on writing of the love and joy of life . . . and when I have used the last drop of my molasses, I shall stop writing." She closed the letter with a hint of conceit: "God gave me a taste for sweets and the sales of the books I write prove that a few other people are similar to me in this."

Harold Bell Wright rivaled Gene Stratton-Porter as a dispenser of wholesomeness, optimism, and the arcadian myth. His *The Winning of Barbara Worth* (1911) had a half million copies in print within a month of its initial publication and maintained sufficient popularity to rank fifth, behind Porter's four books, in the 1932 best-selling novels of the century poll. After *Barbara Worth* Wright produced a novel every other year for two decades. Americans seemed as eager to buy and read his books after the war as before. His first twelve books enjoyed an average sale of nearly 750,000 each.

A sometime minister, Wright sermonized constantly in his novels. Until the final typing no character in any had a name except that of his main trait—Hypocrisy, Greed, Ambition, and so on. Wright's message was the familiar one: clean living, hard work, and contact with God's great open spaces could save a man from the physical and moral deterioration city life engendered. *When a Man's a Man* of 1916, for example, features a millionaire who goes west to escape the effete, artificial, decadent East. Its setting on an Arizona cattle ranch reflected Wright's own enthusiasm for the Southwest that led him to make his home there. Wright also loved Missouri's Ozark Mountains, and the region figured in a number of his stories. *The Re-Creation of Brian Kent,* third on the best-seller list for 1920, employs an Ozark setting to tell the story of a human wreck who is redeemed by the beauty of nature, the challenge of work, and a woman's love. An

elderly schoolmarm, identified only as Auntie Sue, supervises the transformation and extracts the moral.

The stereotyped plots and characters, the wooden dialogue, and the commonplace preaching in Wright's books elicited a barrage of unfavorable criticism. According to one reviewer in 1924, Wright was guilty of perpetuating "the shibboleths and superstitions of our fathers, making old creeds and antique fables sacred in the eyes of all." And so he did. Yet his stories sold millions of copies. A large number of American readers found his message comfortable and meaningful. "Harold," one critic punned, "is always Wright." But for the popular mind of the teens and twenties ethical certainty was highly valued, and traditional mores seemed the most certain. The intellectuals might scoff, but Wright, like Porter, found the goldmine of popular favor.

The western novel, which Owen Wister introduced into American writing in 1902 with *The Virginian,* increased in popularity as the nation moved increasingly further from frontier conditions. The foremost practitioner of the art in the decade after World War I was a one-time dentist from Zanesville, Ohio, named Zane Grey. Blending minor literary talent with a keen sense of the public taste, Grey produced over fifty westerns and provided the basis for dozens of motion pictures, many of which were produced in the early 1920s before the advent of sound tracks. The total sale of all his writings approaches twenty million. From 1917 to 1924 Grey was never *off* the national list of the top ten best-sellers. Twice, 1918 and 1920, he ranked first. He may well have been the most widely read author in the American twenties.

The Zane Grey magic was a blend of violence, heroism, and the frontier. His stories lacked sophistication, but they juxtaposed good and evil in unmistakable terms. Titanic struggles might be waged, but the issues were always clearly defined and the outcome, as Grey fans came to learn, never really in doubt. A simple code of conduct suffused Grey's books. It emphasized courage, self-reliance, fair play, and persistence—the traditional frontier virtues. Those who violated the code always paid the price.

As a mythmaker for the multitudes in the 1920s, Zane Grey became as legendary as his protagonists. Many people believed he spoke for the best parts of the national heritage. John Wanamaker, the department store mogul, addressed him directly: "Never lay down your pen, Zane Grey. . . . You are distinctively and genuinely American. You have borrowed none of the decadence of foreign writers. . . . The good you are doing is incalculable." Even the critics treated Grey more tolerantly than they did Porter and Wright. "We turn to him," one commentator wrote, "not for insight into human nature and human problems nor for refinements of art, but simply for crude epic stories, as we might to an old Norse skald, maker of the sagas of the folk."

The concept of escape from the present, so important in the appeal of many of the best-selling popular novels in the twenties, reached a climax in the writing of Edgar Rice Burroughs. A failure for years in business and pulp magazine writing, Burroughs turned to a new theme in 1914 and struck pure gold. *Tarzan of the Apes* has probably sold more copies to date (over five million) than any other American book. Over thirty other stories of the English orphan reared in the African jungle by apes followed. As early as 1920 the Tarzan cult was nationwide. Burroughs was syndicated in newspapers; his motion pictures reached millions of people. With his superhuman prowess and his mate, Jane, Tarzan entered public thought and speech to an astonishing degree. For people vaguely repressed by civilization, Tarzan was a potent symbol of freedom, power, and individuality. A new wild man on a new frontier, Tarzan helped sustain traditional American values.

American readers seemed to have an insatiable appetite for nature novels for the first three decades of the twentieth century. In addition to Porter, Wright, Grey, and Burroughs, a host of others rode the theme to publishing successes that were minor only in comparison. The names of Rex Beach, Peter B. Kyne, Emerson Hough, and James Oliver Curwood were quite familiar to readers and moviegoers of the postwar decade even if they are not to most literary historians. Curwood, for instance, published between 1908 and 1926 twenty-six novels that dramatized the theme of courage in the wilderness. The motion pictures made from his books, such as *Back to God's Country* (1919), were intended, so an advertisement ran, for those who "love God's great out-of-doors, the land of frozen forests and everlasting snows where the gaunt wolf stalks its prey, where men loom large and life is big." In 1923 Hough's *The Covered Wagon* became the basis for the most famous western movie of the decade. Stewart Edward White rivaled both Curwood and Hough with books such as *The Blazed Trail, The Silent Places,* and *The Rules of the Game.* And that was it precisely—the game had rules that were at once easily perceived and rooted in the national character. If changing conditions were eroding the old certainties, that was only more reason to grasp them more tightly.

In popular fiction Americans of the 1920s were still inhabitants of the nineteenth century. The sexy novels of flaming youth and the risqué movies satisfied only part of the taste of the twenties. The other, and larger, part thrilled to old-time heroics such as those provided by the man Douglas Durkin sketched in *The Lobstick Trail* of 1922: "His blood was clean, his body knit of fibre woven in God's out-of-doors, his mind fashioned under a clear sky in a land of wide horizons."

STUDY QUESTIONS

1. What caused the nervousness that many American experienced in the 1920s?

2. What values were characteristic of America's pioneering past? How did the heroes of the 1920s demonstrate these values?

3. Why were sports so popular during the decade? How did athletic heroes help ease Americans' minds about the national character?

4. How were the popular images of Herbert Hoover and Charles Lindbergh similar? Why were both men considered heroes during the 1920s?

5. What were the characteristics of many popular novels during the 1920s? What types of stories did people enjoy reading?

6. How were the novels of Gene Stratton-Porter, Harold Bell Wright, Zane Grey, and Edgar Rice Burroughs similar or different?

BIBLIOGRAPHY

The selection comes from Roderick Nash, *The Nervous Generation: American Thought, 1917–1930* (1970), which presents a view of the 1920s vastly different from Frederick Lewis Allen's. A good overview of the role of the hero in American culture is Leo Lowenthal, *Literature, Popular Culture and Society* (1961). The most important athletic heroes of the decade are discussed in Randy Roberts, *Jack Dempsey: The Manassa Mauler* (1979); Robert Creamer, *Babe* (1974); Marshall Smelser, *The Life that Ruth Built* (1975); Paul Gallico, *The Goddess People* (1965); and Frank Deford, *Big Bill Tilden: The Triumphs and the Tragedy* (1975). John W. Ward, "The Meaning of Lindbergh's Flight," *American Quarterly,* 10 (1958), is a classic study of the importance of heroism in the 1920s. On Lindbergh also see Walter S. Ross, *The Last Hero: Charles Lindbergh* (1976).

THE BLACK SOX SCANDAL

Dean Smith

Every few years or so, fat-bellied, middle-aged journalists start complaining that base-ball "isn't what it used to be," that the American pastime is "in trouble," that the game is "in a crisis from which it may never recover." And yet, in spite of their nostalgic re-flections about "the good old days," baseball is alive and well. Men's and women's softball leagues fill city recreation parks every night of the week, and Little Leaguers are playing more baseball than ever before. Fantasy baseball groups have sprouted in small towns and large cities all over the country, and junior high school boys have turned baseball cards into big business. America still loves baseball.

But there was a time when baseball was in real trouble. In 1921, headlines in news-papers across the country let Americans know that eight members of the Chicago White Sox were accused of conspiring to lose the 1919 World Series. The ensuing in-vestigation and trial became symbolic of American life in the post-World War I years, when doubts about the country's future seemed endemic. It became known as the Black Sox Scandal, and in the following article Dean Smith describes the controversy and its significance in the 1920s.

When Jim Crusinberry, the *Chicago Tribune's* ace baseball writer, entered the lobby of the Sinton Hotel in Cincinnati that evening of September 30, 1919, he stumbled onto one of the most remarkable scenes of his career.

Perched atop a chair in the lobby was a wildly gesturing man whom he immediately recognized as Abe Attell, former world featherweight boxing champion and consort of New York gamblers. Attell had $1,000 bills in both hands and he was screaming his head off to anyone who would listen, offering to bet on the Cincinnati Reds to beat the Chicago White Sox—any amount, and at even money—in the World Series which was to open the following day at Redland Park.

Crusinberry's nose for news twitched like a bloodhound's. Even in those free-wheeling days of American sport, gamblers usually exercised more discretion than Attell was displaying. And why was he betting against the White Sox? The awesome Sox, one of the finest teams ever assembled up to that time, were top-heavy favorites to crush the so-so Reds in the Series. In most quarters, one had to offer at least 4-to-1 odds to bet on Chicago. Yet here was Attell betting big on Cincinnati, and at even money!

For most of the next two years, Crusinberry pursued his big story. Although thwarted repeatedly by baseball officialdom, underworld silence, and his cautious sports editor, he put the pieces together at last. With other tenacious reporters, he forced a Chicago grand jury to investigate the case that exploded over the sporting world as the Black Sox Scandal.

For nearly six decades American sports buffs have been discussing and analyzing the Black Sox legend, and still the complete story may never be told. What has been established is that eight members of the 1919 White Sox team conspired

"The Black Sox Scandal" by Dean Smith. This article is reprinted from the January 1977 issue of *American History Illustrated* 11, pp. 16–25, with the permission of Cowles History Group, Inc. Copyright *American History Illustrated* magazine.

with two combinations of gamblers to throw the World Series to the Reds, and that the White Sox did indeed lose, five games to three. None of the sinning players, forever tarred in history as the Black Sox, ever received all the money promised for the fix, and several may have gotten no money at all.

What they did get was lifetime exile from organized baseball—an edict decreed and enforced by Commissioner Kenesaw Mountain Landis—despite the fact that the jury in a Cook County trial found them all innocent.

The Black Sox Scandal had an immense impact on a nation struggling to resume "normalcy" in the wake of World War I. To many Americans in that era of innocence, baseball was an almost religious rite, and the World Series was its most holy sacrament. The heroes of the Great American Game were assumed to be as pure as saints—despite considerable evidence to the contrary—and the heresy of desecrating the game for gambler's gold was unthinkable. When the stink of the Black Sox sellout fouled the air, an entire nation was sickened.

This early 20th-century scandal did incalculable damage to America's self-image as a moral nation, disillusioned millions of youthful fans, and helped set the tone for the licentious decade of the 1920's. Teapot Dome, the Prohibition era, corruption in high places, and the public acceptance of "everybody's doing it" raised questions about the value of personal integrity that remain to the present.

To reconstruct the story of the Black Sox tragedy, return to the Sinton Hotel and September 30, 1919. Jim Crusinberry was only one of many who had heard the rumor of an impending White Sox sellout. Hugh Fullerton, syndicated columnist of the Chicago Herald and Examiner, wired this cryptic warning to his newspaper clients: "Don't bet on Series. Ugly rumors afloat."

Jack Doyle, whose New York billiard academy was one of the nation's biggest gambling centers, estimated that $2,000,000 was wagered in his establishment the night before the Series opener. "You couldn't miss it . . . the thing had an odor," he said later. "I saw smart guys take even money on the Sox who should have been asking for 5-to-1 odds."

The Series fix was one of the worst-kept secrets in the history of infamy. As the betting odds shifted dramatically, Cincinnati was buzzing with rumors. Chick Gandil, the Chicago first baseman and admitted ringleader of the sellout, recalled in a Sports Illustrated confession nearly four decades later that even a clerk in a downtown stationary store whispered to him on the eve of the opener, "I have it firsthand that the Series is in the bag."

Everybody knew, and yet nobody knew for sure. Who was bribing whom—and to do what? To complicate the situation, a story popped up that some Chicago gamblers were out to insure a White Sox victory by getting ace Cincinnati pitcher Dutch Ruether drunk the night before the opener.

The White Sox should have needed no help at all. Owner Charles Comiskey, revered as "The Old Roman," had built a magnificent ball club in Chicago. There was Eddie Collins, probably the best second baseman in baseball, and Buck Weaver, without a peer at third base. "Shoeless Joe" Jackson was a virtual illiterate, but there was no better hitter and left fielder in the game. Happy Felsch in center and Shano Collins in right rounded out a great Chicago outfield. Chick Gandil at first base was so tough he could play his position without a glove. And Swede Risberg was one of the great shortstops of the era. Behind the plate was the superb Ray Schalk.

The pitching staff was a little thin, especially with Red Faber on the injured list, but Eddie Cicotte, Claude Williams, and Dickie Kerr were a match for anything Cincinnati could throw against them. As for manager Kid Gleason, he was a canny veteran who knew the game inside out and did a passable job of welding his moody and contentious athletes into a team that had dominated the American League.

The first post-World War Series had been lengthened to best five games of nine to insure a bigger box office take (it was returned to best four-of-seven shortly thereafter), and a nation weary of war and sacrifice was eager for the spectacle to begin.

The tragic prelude to the opener at Cincinnati on October 1, 1919, is still difficult to piece together. Conflicting grand jury and court testimony, countless published revelations and "authentic" analyses—but a paucity of reliable source material—combine to create a knotty problem for the historian. Eliot Asinof's *Eight Men Out,* generally regarded as the most comprehensive book on the subject, says the Black Sox plot had its beginning when Gandil contacted Boston gambler Joseph (Sport) Sullivan some three weeks before the 1919 Series and offered to "put the Series in the bag" for $80,000. Gandil, in his 1956 revelation, declared it was Sullivan who first suggested to him that the Series might be fixed.

At any rate, Gandil first enlisted pitcher Eddie Cicotte in the plot and then shortstop Swede Risberg and pitcher Claude Williams. The team's top three hitters—Buck Weaver, Joe Jackson, and Happy Felsch—were reluctant enlistees. Gandil felt sure that those seven could guarantee a White Sox defeat. They could ground out in crucial spots, feed a fat pitch to a slugger with men on base, barely miss a fly ball—all without detection. The seven were soon joined by an eighth conspirator through sheer accident. Utility infielder Fred McMullin, a man hardly in a position to affect the Series outcome, was lying behind a locker one afternoon and overheard Gandil discussing the plan with Risberg. McMullin demanded a part of the action, and he was included to buy his silence.

Consorting with gamblers was not a new occupation for Gandil, who for years had sold information on starting pitchers and other useful baseball tips to the betting fraternity. "We all mixed with gamblers," Gandil explained later, "and most of them were honest." Such shady associations were a fact of baseball life in 1919, and nobody seemed to care very much.

The eight Chicago players assembled in Gandil's room at the Ansonia Hotel in New York City on the evening of September 21st to discuss strategy. The eight were not particularly good friends and were united on only one subject: their

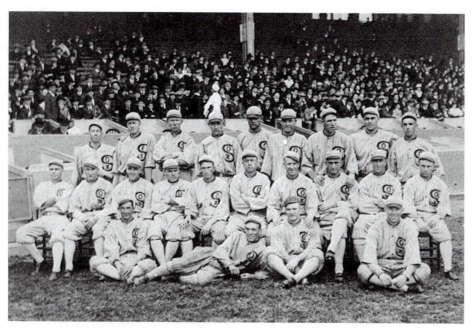

"Shoeless" Joe Jackson and seven other players on the Chicago White Sox were charged with accepting money to throw the 1919 World Series.

common hatred for Comiskey, whom they regarded as a tight-fisted tyrant who paid his players less than did any other owner in major league baseball.

Gandil and Felsch, for example, were earning only a little more than $4,000 a year; Cicotte's 1919 salary was about $5,000 (and he a 29-game winner with an earned run average of 1.82!); and the great Jackson, batting .375 for the season, earned only $6,000—compared with the $10,000 Cincinnati paid its leading hitter, Ed Roush.

The eight agreed to deal with the gamblers, although Weaver is said to have suggested that they take the fix money and win the Series, anyhow. The evidence is conclusive that the superlative third baseman never threw a game or received a dime from the gamblers. He spent the rest of his life protesting his innocence and trying to restore his good name.

Even before arrangements could be made with Sullivan, word of the fix attempt leaked out. Cicotte was approached by gambler William T.

(Sleepy Bill) Burns, a former pitcher who had made money in Texas oil, to let him bid on the action. Soon two gambling combinations— unknown to each other—were negotiating with the Chicago eight.

It was common knowledge in the far-flung American gambling community that only one man, Arnold Rothstein of New York City, could put up enough money to engineer a project as grandiose as the fixing of a World Series. Burns hurriedly consulted with a small-time gambler named Billy Maharg in Philadelphia, and together they rushed to Rothstein with the proposition.

Rothstein would not see them personally, but told his ambitious lieutenant, Abe Attell, to check it out. Attell was entranced with the sheer audacity of the idea, so Rothstein agreed to discuss the matter with Burns. But the gambling king, known far and wide as "The Big Bankroll," turned Burns down flat and advised him to forget this wild scheme.

Attell could not put the lucrative idea out of his mind, however, and he decided to step into the big time on his own. He called Burns and told him a lie that could have bought Abe a concrete casket: Rothstein had changed his mind, said Attell, and would put up $100,000 if Burns could get the eight White Sox to go along. It was sheer bluff on Attell's part. Certainly he could not lay his hands on the money the players were demanding, but he put up a confident front and prayed he could get the cash somewhere.

Meanwhile, Sullivan was busy, too. He also sought out Rothstein and somehow made a better impression on the shrewd New Yorker than had Burns. Rothstein assigned an aide named Nat Evans to work out the details of the Series fix with Sullivan and the players.

So Gandil and his co-conspirators began their comic opera dealings with two sets of gamblers, holding clandestine meetings in hotel rooms and hoping the rival fixers would never meet. The players demanded cash in advance, but the gamblers were untrusting souls who refused payment except after each game Chicago lost. Only Cicotte held out for his money beforehand, so Sullivan gave Gandil $10,000 to clinch the deal. The money mysteriously appeared under Cicotte's pillow at the Sinton Hotel the night before the Series opener.

According to the Black Sox legend, Rothstein demanded that Cicotte "give a sign" that the fix was on by hitting the first Cincinnati batter with a pitch. Whether or not Cicotte agreed, we will never know for sure, but for whatever reason— the heat of the 90-degree afternoon, the screaming throng of 30,500 in Redland Park, nerves made jumpy by his Judas role, or a shouted threat from the stands that "there's a guy looking for you with a rifle"—Cicotte's second pitch to Cincinnati leadoff hitter Maurice Rath strayed inside and hit him in the small of the back.

It was not Cicotte's day. He was driven from the mound in the fourth inning as the Reds waltzed to a 9-1 victory. Even the Cincinnati pitcher, Dutch Ruether, connected for two triples to the humiliation of the proud Sox. The next day Claude Williams, a left-hander famous for his control, was shockingly wild and the Reds won again, 4-2.

Meanwhile, rumors of the fix had reached manager Gleason and owner Comiskey. Late at night after the first game, according to one version of the story, Comiskey woke John Heydler, president of the National League and a member of baseball's National Commission, and poured out his fears that the White Sox had sold out to the gamblers. Heydler then woke Ban Johnson, president of the American League and a bitter enemy of Comiskey's, and relayed the Chicago owner's apprehensions.

"That's the yelp of a beaten cur!" sneered Johnson, who terminated the conversation abruptly and went back to bed.

The gamblers were equally indisposed to conversation. Sullivan disappeared after the first game. Attell was in town, but he was very vague about specifics of the payoff to Gandil. "The money is all out on bets," he told the ringleader. "You'll have to give me another day."

According to Asinof's version, Attell did come up with $10,000 after the second game, the money going to Gandil. Gandil later denied receiving any of the money for himself, but he did manage somehow to buy a big new car immediately after the Series.

Chicago had lost the first two games and, aside from Gandil and Cicotte, none of the White Sox conspirators had received so much as a "thank you" from either gambling combination. Understandably, they were now ready to forget the entire arrangement and play to win. With rookie Dickie Kerr pitching a three-hit shutout before 29,126 rabid fans at Chicago's Comiskey Park, the White Sox cruised to a 3-0 triumph. Gandil himself drove in two of the Chicago runs.

Unfortunately for Attell, Burns, and their colleagues, the news of the White Sox rebirth of spirit had not reached them. As they ruefully reported later, they lost all their previous winnings betting on the Reds in the third game and had no further participation in the Series machinations. But Sullivan was still very much in the game. Fearful that the White Sox players had revolted, he came up with $20,000, part of the bankroll reportedly supplied by Rothstein.

Now it was time for the fourth game and Cicotte's chance to redeem himself. The spitball ace pitched a strong five-hitter, but his mates were powerless at the plate and Cincinnati walked away with a 2-0 win. Williams gave up only four hits in the fifth game, but again the White Sox bats were silent and the Reds had their fourth victory, 5-0.

At this point Sullivan made the last of the gamblers' payments, this one purportedly $15,000.

Only one game away from losing the Series, the White Sox miraculously returned to their regular season form in the sixth game. Kerr won it, 5-4, with Gandil's hit providing the winning margin in the 10th inning. Cicotte was brilliant in the seventh game, winning 4-1, and suddenly the White Sox looked like winners again.

The gamblers were more than a little nervous, even with the paid-off Williams slated to pitch the eighth game in Chicago. To be sure of his position, Sullivan (according to Williams' wife) employed a professional persuader to remind Williams of the unpleasant consequences in store for him and his family if he should win.

A well-known gambler telephoned reporter Fullerton before the game and told him to "watch out for the biggest first inning you ever saw." It arrived on schedule, with Williams surrendering four runs in the first frame. The fired-up Reds raced off to a 10-1 lead before Chicago scored four in the eighth to close the final Cincinnati victory margin to 10-5.

The lowly Reds had pulled off the baseball upset of the decade. But had they really outplayed the White Sox, or had the eight Chicago conspirators handed the Series to them in return for tainted money?

The debate continues to this day.

One of the leading advocates of the "no fix" theory, Victor Luhrs, in his book *The Great Baseball Mystery,* declares the indications are overwhelming that Cincinnati would have won the Series anyhow. In his summary Luhrs admits that Williams' poor pitching cost the White Sox the second and eighth games and that he quite probably was an intentional loser. Gandil and Risberg, he says, did not give their best efforts and McMullin (who appeared only twice as a pinch hitter) did not play enough to permit a judgment. But

he stoutly defends Jackson, Weaver, Felsch, and Cicotte, crediting all four with playing their best.

Dr. Harold Seymour, in his book *Baseball—The Golden Age,* concluded that the box scores do not indicate that the Series was thrown. "In fact," says he, "the Black Sox on the whole actually made a better showing in the games than the Clean Sox (the other Chicago players)."

Joe Jackson, for example, led both teams at the plate with a .375 average, and Weaver ended with a .324 batting effort. Gandil's timely hitting won two games, and both Weaver and Jackson played errorless ball. Clean Eddie Collins, on the other hand, made two errors and batted an anemic .224; the other unblemished Chicago regulars did little better.

The rumors of a fix continued for many months, despite the best efforts of investigative reporters to dig out the truth. Comiskey offered a $20,000 reward (soon reduced to $10,000) for information on any skullduggery. But he ignored tips supplied by at least one gambler and never answered a letter from the remorseful Jackson, written by his wife, offering to tell what he knew. Apparently baseball officialdom had decided to sweep the dirt under the rug and hope it would be forgotten.

But the Chicago *Tribune*'s Jim Crusinberry would not forget.

Crusinberry devoted every spare moment to tracking down leads, and at last—on a rainy New York afternoon in July 1920—the first crack in the wall of silence appeared. The telephone rang in the hotel room when Crusinberry was relaxing with columnist Ring Lardner. It was Kid Gleason, and he spoke in an excited whisper.

"I'm at Dinty Moore's," he told Crusinberry, "and Abe Attell is at the bar, drinking and starting to talk. Come on over and get close enough to listen." Within minutes, Crusinberry and Lardner were eavesdropping on a fascinating conversation.

"So it was Arnold Rothstein who put up the dough for the fix," they heard Gleason say. "That was it, Kid," answered Attell. "You know, Kid, I hated to do that to you, but I thought I was going to make a lot of money and I needed it, and then the big guy double-crossed me, and I never got but a small part of what he promised."

Attell rambled on for half an hour, naming the participants. At last Crusinberry had the information for his block-busting story. But his sports editor, wary of a libel suit, refused to print it. Frustrated and angry, Crusinberry decided to take matters into his own hands. He wrote an open letter to the *Tribune,* demanding a grand jury investigation of the Series fix, and persuaded Chicago businessman Fred M. Loomis to sign it. The strategy worked. The Cook County grand jury agreed to the probe, and on September 21, 1920 subpoenas were sent to baseball owners, managers, players, writers, and gamblers.

Six days later the first sensational revelation hit the newspapers. Enterprising Jimmy Isaminger, a writer for the Philadelphia *North American,* tracked down gambler Billy Maharg—a cohort of Burns and Attell—and got him to talk. Maharg knew only part of the story, of course, but his statement exploded like a bombshell. He implicated Cicotte as the chief fixer, said Attell had betrayed Burns and himself, and declared that the first, second, and eighth Series games had been thrown by the Chicago eight—who immediately became known as the Black Sox.

The ink was still damp on the Isaminger story when Gleason sought out the tormented Cicotte and persuaded him to confess. Weeping through much of his sensational testimony before the grand jury the following day, Cicotte admitted receiving $10,000, confessed that he had served up pitches that anyone could hit, and said he did it for his wife and children.

Jackson next took the stand, nervously admitting that he got $5,000 of the $20,000 promised him. As he was leaving the courthouse following his testimony, the most poignant incident of the whole sordid scandal took place. Several ragged youngsters crowded around him and one asked pleadingly, "Say it ain't so, Joe!"

All America fervently joined in that plea.

Historians may note with some amusement that the original Associated Press quote of the remark was a more grammatical "It isn't true, is it, Joe?" But several other reporters who were there quoted it in the street jargon in which it was probably uttered.

Williams testified next, admitting that he got

$5,000 for his part in the fix. Then came Felsch, who also confessed $5,000, but insisted that he had done nothing to throw any of the games.

Although the White Sox were battling for the American League pennant in the final week of the season, Comiskey immediately suspended all seven active players. (Gandil had "retired" from baseball before the start of the 1920 season.) With the Chicago team decimated, Cleveland breezed to the league championship.

The grand jury indicted all eight Chicago players, along with gamblers Attell, Burns, Hal Chase, and "Rachael Brown," the name used by Rothstein aide Nat Evans. Rothstein himself escaped indictment. The New York gambling king made an appearance before the grand jury, storming in outraged innocence, and somehow convinced everyone that he had not participated in any way.

When the Black Sox trial finally began, on June 27, 1921, the prosecution made an electrifying announcement: All the players' signed confessions had mysteriously disappeared from the files! American League President Ban Johnson accused Rothstein of paying $10,000 to arrange the theft, upon which Rothstein threatened him with a $250,000 slander suit. He never carried out the threat.

Free of the damning confessions, the players all denied their earlier testimony and pleaded innocent. None testified during the trial.

All through a blazing hot July the sensational trial dragged on in the sweltering Chicago courtroom. The defense was conducted by several of the most expensive lawyers of the day (who paid them was never proved), and the crowded courtroom was noisily in support of the players. Burns turned state's evidence, and the other gamblers all avoided prosecution through legal maneuvers.

The outcome teetered in the balance as the mountain of testimony piled up. Then, on August 2d, both legal teams rested their cases and Judge Hugo Friend made his charge to the jury:

The State must prove that it was the intent of the ballplayers and gamblers charged with conspiracy through the throwing of the World Series to defraud the public and others, and not merely to throw ball games.

The tricky bit of semantics was all the jury needed. The judge said taking bribes was not enough—throwing ball games was not enough. To be legally guilty, the players must have intended to defraud the public. How could anybody prove that?

In just two hours, forty-seven minutes the jury brought in "not guilty" verdicts on all concerned. The hushed courtroom erupted in wild cheering and, incredibly, members of the jury hoisted several of the Black Sox to their shoulders and paraded them triumphantly around the courtroom. Flushed with victory, Gandil spotted Ban Johnson, rushed to his side, and declared: "Goodbye, good luck, and to hell with you!"

The Black Sox celebrated their triumph at an Italian restaurant after the verdict was read—the same restaurant, incidentally, where the jurors dined and congratulated themselves—and toasted the immediate resumption of their baseball careers. But they did not reckon with the stern morality of white-haired Judge Kenesaw Mountain Landis, who had been installed as Commissioner of Baseball following the grim days of the grand jury investigation. Landis had said upon taking office that the Black Sox would never play again, but that was before the trial. Surely, the players reasoned, the judge would not dare to overrule a court of law.

But he did just that. Landis's statement after the trial was a verdict of doom:

Regardless of the verdict of juries, no player that throws a ball game . . . [or] sits in a conference with a bunch of crooked players and gamblers where the ways and means of throwing games are planned and discussed, and does not promptly tell his club about it, will ever play professional baseball.

He added one more shocker: In addition to the eight Black Sox, he slapped a lifetime ban on Joe Gedeon of the St. Louis Browns, who had told the grand jury he made money betting on Cincinnati at the suggestion of Swede Risberg.

The players screamed, hired lawyers, and got petitions signed—but all to no avail. None of them ever played in organized baseball again. Landis was as unbending as iron, and many years later

he went so far as to deny Jackson's petition to manage the Greenville, South Carolina, club in the low-low minors.

Part of the Black Sox legend is that Landis's stiff punishments saved baseball in its darkest hour. A glance at the soaring major league gate receipts in 1920 and 1921, however, seems to show that the sporting public would have supported the game whether or not the Black Sox had been punished. But the old judge's decision undoubtedly discouraged future cozy dealings between players and gamblers. Baseball never has suffered another scandal.

So the chastened Black Sox were cast out to make a living the best way they could. Weaver ran a Chicago drug store. Cicotte farmed near Detroit and then worked at an automobile plant. Williams ran a Chicago poolroom for a time and then started a nursery business in California. Felsch opened a tavern in Milwaukee. Risberg worked on a Minnesota dairy farm before opening a tavern in northern California. Gandil became a plumber in California. McMullin took one job and then another. Jackson operated a restaurant, and later a liquor store, in South Carolina.

All eight are now dead.

Though most of them protested varying degrees of innocence throughout their lives, Gandil declared in his 1956 confession, "To this day, I feel that we got what we had coming."

Baseball survived and thrived, but it was never again the gloriously pure American rite it once had been. Too many little boys—of all ages—had suffered sobering disillusionment.

Perhaps Nelson Algren, who had idolized Swede Risberg, said it best many years later in his superb short story "The Silver-Colored Yesterday":

I traded off my Risberg bat . . . and I flipped the program from that hot and magic Sunday when Cicotte was shutting out everybody forever, and a triumphant right-hander's wind had blown all the score cards across home plate, into the Troy Street gutter. I guess that was one way of learning what Hustletown, sooner or later, teaches all its sandlot sprouts. "Everybody's out for The Buck. Even big leaguers."

Even Swede Risberg.

STUDY QUESTIONS

1. Why did the little boy's comment "Say it ain't so, Joe" come to symbolize the public's reaction to the entire scandal?

2. What actually happened? Did the players really throw the World Series?

3. Who were the major characters in the scandal?

4. What decision did Judge Landis reach? Do you agree with the decision?

5. How would you compare the punishment given to the players in 1921 with contemporary professional athletes who gamble or find themselves with drug problems?

BIBLIOGRAPHY

In recent years the history of sport in the United States has enjoyed increasing scholarly respectability. For a general survey, see Benjamin Rader, *American Sports: From the Age of Folk Games to the Age of Spectators* (1983). Stephen Reiss, *Touching Base: Professional Baseball and American Culture in the Progressive Era* (1980) is an especially useful examination of baseball in early twentieth-century America. Also see David Q. Voigt, *American Baseball. Vol. 1: From Gentlemen's Sport to the Commissioner System* (1966). On the scandal itself, see Eliot Asinof, *Eight Men Out: The Black Sox and the 1919 World Series* (1963). For a discussion of the mood of the 1920s in the United States, see Roderick Nash, *The Nervous Generation: American Thought, 1917–1930* (1970). Organized crime in the 1920s has also generated a scholarly literature. Herbert Asbury, *Sucker's Progress: An Informal History of Gambling in America* (1938) is a good, if dated, survey. Also see Jenna Joselit, *Our Gang: Jewish Crime and Politics in One American Community* (1983) and Humbert S. Nelli, *The Business of Crime: Italians and Syndicate Crime in the United States* (1981).

ORGANIZED CRIME IN URBAN SOCIETY: CHICAGO IN THE TWENTIETH CENTURY

Mark Haller

In 1919 Congress adopted the Eighteenth Amendment, which prohibited "the manufacture, sale, or transportation of intoxicating liquors." Prohibition, however, did not stop Americans from manufacturing, selling, or transporting alcohol; it simply made the actions illegal. During the 1920s and early 1930s, criminals rather than businessmen supplied the public's thirst, and often the distinction between the two occupations grew fuzzy. As "Scarface" Al Capone once noted, "I make my money by supplying a public demand. If I break the law, my customers, who number hundreds of the best people in Chicago, are as guilty as I am. . . . Everybody calls me a racketeer. I call myself a businessman. When I sell liquor it's bootlegging. When my patrons serve it on a silver tray on Lake Shore Drive, it's hospitality."

For many Americans, Capone's point was well taken. As a result, criminals achieved a certain social respect and were able to spread their influence into legitimate business. A 1926 congressional investigation demonstrated that organized crime had made significant inroads into the worlds of labor unions, industry, and city governments. By 1933 when Congress repealed the Eighteenth Amendment, organized crime had become a permanent part of the American scene.

In the following essay, historian Mark H. Haller examines the role of crime in ethnic communities and urban society. Like sports and entertainment, crime served as an avenue out of the ethnic ghettoes and played an important role in the complex urban environment.

Many journalists have written exciting accounts of organized crime in American cities and a handful of scholars have contributed analytical and perceptive studies. Yet neither the excitement in the journalistic accounts nor the analysis in the scholarly studies fully captures the complex and intriguing role of organized criminal activities in American cities during the first third of the twentieth century. The paper that follows, although focusing on Chicago, advances hypotheses that are probably true for other cities as well. The paper examines three major, yet interrelated, aspects of the role of organized crime in the city: first, the social worlds within which the criminals operated and the importance of those worlds in providing social mobility from immigrant ghettos; second, the diverse patterns by which different ethnic groups became involved in organized criminal activities and were influenced by those activities; and third, the broad and pervasive economic impact of organized crime in urban neighborhoods, and the resulting influence that organized crime did exert.

Crime and Mobility

During the period of heavy immigrant movement into the cities of the Northeast and Midwest, organized crime provided paths of upward mobility for many young men raised in ethnic slums. The gambling kings, vice lords, bootleggers and racketeers often began their careers in the ghetto neighborhoods; and frequently these neighborhoods continued to be the centers for their entrepreneurial activities. A careful study of the leaders of organized crime in Chicago in the late 1920s found that 31 percent were of Italian background, 29 percent of Irish background, 20 percent Jewish, and 12 percent black; none were native white of native white parents. A recognition of the eth-

"Organized Crime in Urban Society: Chicago in the Twentieth Century" by Mark Haller, from *Journal of Social History 5* (Winter, 1971-1972). pp. 210-234. Copyright © 1971 by The Regents of the University of California. Reprinted by permission.

nic roots of organized crime, however, is only a starting point for understanding its place in American cities.

At a risk of oversimplification, it can be said that for young persons in the ethnic ghettos three paths lay open to them. The vast majority became, to use the Chicago argot, "poor working stiffs." They toiled in the factories, filled menial service and clerical jobs, or opened mom-and-pop stores. Their mobility to better jobs and to homeownership was, at best, incremental. A second, considerably smaller group followed respectable paths to relative success. Some of this group went to college and entered the professions; others rose to management positions in the business or governmental hierarchies of the city.

There existed, however, a third group of interrelated occupations which, although not generally regarded as respectable, were open to uneducated and ambitious ethnic youths. Organized crime was one such occupational world, but there were others.

One was urban machine politics. Many scholars have, of course, recognized the function of politics in providing mobility for some members of ethnic groups. In urban politics, a person's ethnic background was often an advantage rather than a liability. Neighborhood roots could be the basis for a career that might lead from poverty to great local power, considerable wealth, or both.

A second area consisted of those businesses that prospered through political friendships and contacts. Obviously, construction companies that built the city streets and buildings relied upon government contracts. But so also did banks in which government funds were deposited, insurance companies that insured government facilities, as well as garbage contractors, fraction companies and utilities that sought city franchises. Because political contacts were important, local ethnic politicians and their friends were often the major backers of such enterprises.

A third avenue of success was through leadership in the city's labor unions. The Irish in Chicago dominated the building trade unions and most of the other craft unions during the first

25 years of this century. But persons of other ethnic origins could also rise to leadership positions, especially in those unions in which their own ethnic group predominated.

Another path of mobility was sports. Boxing, a peculiarly urban sport, rooted in the neighborhood gymnasiums, was the most obvious example of a sport in which Irish champions were succeeded by Jewish, Polish and black champions. Many a fighter, even if he did not reach national prominence, could achieve considerable local fame within his neighborhood or ethnic group. He might then translate this local fame into success by becoming a fight manager, saloon keeper, politician or racketeer.

A fifth area often dominated by immigrants was the entertainment and night life of the city. In Chicago, immigrants—primarily Irish and Germans—ran the city's saloons by the turn of the century. During the 1920s, Greek businessmen operated most of the taxi-dance halls. Restaurants, cabarets and other night spots were similarly operated by persons from various ethnic groups. Night life also provided careers for entertainers, including B-girls, singers, comedians, vaudeville and jazz bands. Jewish comedians of the 1930s and black comedians of our own day are only examples of a larger phenomenon in which entertainment could lead to local and even national recognition.

The organized underworld of the city, then, was not the only area of urban life that provided opportunities for ambitious young men from the ghettos. Rather, it was one of several such areas. Part of the pervasive impact of organized crime resulted from the fact that the various paths were interrelated, binding together the worlds of crime, politics, labor leadership, politically related businessmen, sports figures and the night life of the city. What was the nature of the interrelationships?

To begin with, organized crime often exerted important influences upon the other social worlds. For aspiring politicians, especially during the early years after an ethnic group's arrival in a city, organized crime was often the most important source of money and manpower. (By the turn of the century, an operator of a single policy wheel in Chicago could contribute not only thousands of dollars but also more than a hundred numbers writers to work the neighborhoods on election day.) On occasion, too, criminals supplied strongarm men to act as poll watchers, they organized repeat voters, and they provided other illegal but necessary campaign services. Like others engaged in ethnic politics, members of the organized underworld often acted from motives of friendship and common ethnic loyalties. But because of the very nature of their activities, criminal entrepreneurs required and therefore sought political protection. It would be difficult to exaggerate the importance of organized crime in the management of politics in many of the wards of the city.

Furthermore, it should not be thought that the politics of large cities like Chicago was peculiarly influenced by organized crime. In a large and heterogeneous city, there were always wards within which the underworld exercised little influence and which could therefore elect politicians who would work for honest government and law enforcement. But in the ethnic and blue-collar industrial cities west or southwest of Chicago, the influence of organized crime sometimes operated without serious opposition. In Cicero, west of Chicago along major commuting lines, gambling ran wide open before the 1920s; and after 1923 Capone's bootlegging organization safely had its headquarters there. In other towns, like Stickney and Burnham, prostitution and other forms of entertainment often operated with greater openness than in Chicago. This symbiotic relationship, in which surrounding blue-collar communities provided protected vice and entertainment for the larger city, was not limited to Chicago. Covington, Kentucky, had a similar relationship to Cincinnati, while East St. Louis serviced St. Louis.

The organized underworld was also deeply involved in other areas of immigrant mobility. Organized criminals worked closely with racketeering labor leaders and thus became involved in shakedowns, strike settlements and decisions concerning union leadership. They were participants in the night life, owned many of the night spots in the entertainment districts, and hired and promoted many of the entertainers. (The comedian Joe E. Lewis started his career in Chicago's South Side vice district as an associate and employee of the underworld; his case was not atypical.) Members of the underworld were also sports fans and gamblers and therefore became managers of prize fighters, patrons at the race tracks and loyal fans at ball games. An observer who knew many of Chicago's pimps in the 1920s reported:

The pimp is first, last and always a fight fan. He would be disgraced if he didn't go to every fight in town. . . .
   They hang around gymnasiums and talk fight. Many of them are baseball fans, and they usually get up just about in time to go to the game. They know all the players and their information about the game is colossal. Football is a little too highbrow for them, and they would be disgraced if they played tennis, but of late the high grade pimps have taken to golf, and some of them belong to swell golf clubs.

However, criminals were not merely sports fans; some ran gambling syndicates and had professional interests in encouraging sports or predicting the outcome of sports events. Horse racing was a sport conducted primarily for the betting involved. By the turn of the century, leading gamblers and bookmakers invested in and controlled most of the race tracks near Chicago and in the rest of the nation. A number of successful gamblers had stables of horses and thus mixed business with pleasure while becoming leading figures in horse race circles. At a less important level, Capone's organization in the late 1920s owned highly profitable dog tracks in Chicago's suburbs.

The fact that the world of crime exerted powerful influences upon urban politics, business, labor unions, sports and entertainment does not adequately describe the interrelations of these worlds. For many ambitious men, the worlds were tied together because in their own lifetimes

they moved easily from one area to another or else held positions in two or more simultaneously. In some ways, for instance, organized crime and entertainment were barely distinguishable worlds. Those areas of the city set aside for prostitution and gambling were the major entertainment districts of the city. Many cabarets and other night spots provided gambling in backrooms or in rooms on upper floors. Many were places where prostitutes solicited customers or where customers could find information concerning local houses of prostitution. During the 1920s, places of entertainment often served liquor and thus were retail outlets for bootleggers. In the world of entertainment, the distinction between legitimate and illegitimate was often blurred beyond recognition.

Take, as another example, the career of William Skidmore. At age fourteen, Billie sold racing programs at a race track near Chicago. By the time he was twenty-one, in the 1890s, he owned a saloon and cigar store, and soon had joined with others to operate the major policy wheels in Chicago and the leading handbook syndicate on the West Side. With his growing wealth and influence, he had by 1903 also become ward committeeman in the thirteenth ward and was soon a leading political broker in the city. In 1912 he was Sergeant-at-Arms for the Democratic National Convention and, afterwards, aided Josephus Daniels in running the Democratic National Committee. Despite his success as gambler and politician, his saloon, until well into the 1920s, was a hangout for pickpockets and con men; and "Skid" provided bail and political protection for his criminal friends. In the twenties Skidmore branched into the junk business and made a fortune selling junk obtained through contracts with the county government. Not until the early 1940s did he finally go to prison, the victim of a federal charge of income tax evasion. In his life, it would be impossible to unravel the diverse careers to determine whether he was saloon keeper, gambler, politician or businessman.

The various social worlds were united not simply by the influence of organized crime and by in-

Ben Shahn's "Prohibition Alley" portrays whiskey barrels, delivered by ship, being stacked under a portrait of Chicago gangster Al Capone, a victim of gang warfare at lower left, and patrons outside a speakeasy at lower right.

terlocking careers; the worlds also shared a common social life. At local saloons, those of merely local importance met and drank together. At other restaurants or bars, figures of wider importance had meeting places. Until his death in 1920, Big Jim Colossimo's restaurant in the South Side vice district brought together the successful from many worlds; the saloon of Michael (Hinky Dink) Kenna, first ward Alderman, provided a meeting place in the central business district. Political banquets, too, provided opportunities for criminals, police, sports figures and others to gather in honor of a common political friend. Weddings and funerals were occasions when friends met to mark the important passages through life. At the funeral of Colossimo—politician, vice lord and

restauranteur—his pallbearers included a gambler, two keepers of vice resorts, and a bailbondsman. Honorary pallbearers were five judges (including the chief judge of the criminal courts), two congressmen, nine resort keepers or gamblers, several aldermen and three singers from the Chicago Opera. (His good friend, Enrico Caruso, was unable to be present.) Such ceremonial events symbolized the overlapping of the many worlds of which a man like Colossimo was a part.

Thus far we have stressed the social structure that linked the criminal to the wider parts of the city within which he operated. That social world was held together by a system of values and beliefs widely shared by those who participated in crime, politics, sports and the night life of the city. Of central importance was the cynical—but not necessarily unrealistic—view that society operated through a process of deals, friendships and mutual favors. Hence the man to be admired was the smart operator and dealer who handled himself well in such a world. Because there was seen to be little difference between a legal and an illegal business, there was a generally tolerant attitude that no one should interfere with the other guy's racket so long as it did not interfere with one's own. This general outlook was, of course, widely shared, in whole or in part, by other groups within American society so that there was no clear boundary between the social world of the smart operators and the wider society.

In a social system held together by friendships and favors, the attitude toward law and legal institutions was complex. A basic attitude was a belief that criminal justice institutions were just another racket—a not unrealistic assessment considering the degree to which police, courts and prosecutor were in fact used by political factions and favored criminal groups. A second basic attitude was a belief that, if anyone cooperated with the law against someone with whom he was associated or to whom he owed favors, he was a stoolpigeon whose behavior was beneath contempt. This does not mean that criminal justice institutions were not used by members of organized crime. On a day-to-day basis, members of the underworld were tied to police, prosecutors and politicians through payments and mutual favors. Criminal groups often used the police and courts to harass rival gangs or to prevent the development of competition. But conflicts between rival groups were also resolved by threats or violence. Rival gambling syndicates bombed each others' places of business, rival union leaders engaged in bombing and slugging, and rival bootlegging gangs after 1923 turned to assassinations that left hundreds dead in the streets of Chicago. The world of the rackets was a tough one in which a man was expected to take his knocks and stand up for himself. Friendship and loyalty were valued; but so also were toughness and ingenuity.

Gangsters, politicians, sports figures and entertainers prided themselves for being smart guys who recognized how the world operated. They felt disdain mixed with pity for the "poor working stiffs" who, ignorant of how the smart guys operated, toiled away at their menial jobs. But if they disdained the life of the working stiffs, they also disdained the pretensions of those "respectable" groups who looked askance at the world within which they operated. Skeptical that anyone acted in accordance with abstract beliefs or universalistic principles, the operators believed that respectable persons were hypocrites. For instance, when Frank J. Loesch, the distinguished and elderly lawyer who headed the Chicago Crime Commission, attacked three criminal court judges for alleged political favoritism, one politician declared to his friends:

Why pick on these three judges when every judge in the criminal court is doing the very same thing, and always have. Who is Frank Loesch that he should holler? He has done the same thing in his day. . . . He has asked for plenty of favors and has always gotten them. Now that he is getting older and is all set and doesn't have to ask any more favors, he is out to holler about every one else. . . . There are a lot of these reformers who are regular racketeers, but it won't last a few years and it will die out.

In short, the world view of the operators allowed them to see their world as being little different from the world of the respectable persons who looked down upon them. The whole world was a racket.

Ethnic Specialization

Some have suggested that each ethnic group, in its turn, took to crime as part of the early adjustment to urban life. While there is some truth to such a generalization, the generalization obscures more than it illuminates the ethnic experiences and structure of crime. In important respects, each ethnic group was characterized by different patterns of adjustment; and the patterns of involvement in organized crime often reflected the particular broader patterns of each ethnic group. Some ethnic groups—Germans and Scandinavians, for instance—appear not to have made significant contributions to the development of organized crime. Among the ethnic groups that did contribute, there was specialization within crime that reflected broader aspects of ethnic life.

In Chicago by the turn of the century, for example, the Irish predominated in two areas of organized crime. One area was labor racketeering, which derived from the importance of the Irish as leaders of organized labor in general.

The second area of Irish predominance was the operation of major gambling syndicates. Irish importance in gambling was related to a more general career pattern. The first step was often ownership of a saloon, from which the owner might move into both politics and gambling. Many Irish saloon keepers ran handbooks or encouraged other forms of gambling in rooms located behind or over the saloon. Those Irishmen who used their saloon as a basis for electoral politics continued the gambling activities in their saloons and had ties to larger gambling syndicates. Other saloon keepers, while sometimes taking important but backstage political positions such as ward committeeman, developed the gambling syndicates. Handbooks required up-to-the-minute information from race tracks across the country. By establishing poolrooms from which information was distributed to individual handbooks, a single individual could control and share in the profits of dozens or even hundreds of handbooks.

The Irish also predominated in other areas of gambling. At the turn of the century they were the major group in the syndicates that operated the policy games, each with hundreds of policy writers scattered in the slum neighborhoods to collect the nickels and dimes of the poor who dreamed of a lucky hit. They also outfitted many of the gambling houses in the Loop which offered roulette, faro, poker, blackjack, craps and other games of chance. Furthermore, many top police officers were Irish and rose through the ranks by

attaching themselves to the various political factions of the city. Hence a complex system of Irish politicians, gamblers and police shared in the profits of gambling, protected gambling interests and built careers in the police department or city politics. Historians have long recognized the importance of the Irish in urban politics. In Chicago, at any rate, politics was only part of a larger Irish politics-gambling complex.

The Irish politics-gambling complex remained intact until about World War I. By the 1920s, however, the developing black ghetto allowed black politicians and policy operators to build independent gambling and political organizations linked to the Republicans in the 1920s and the Democratic city machine in the 1930s. By the 1920s, in addition, Jewish gamblers became increasingly important, both in the control of gambling in Jewish neighborhoods and in operations elsewhere. Finally, by the mid-1920s, Italian bootleggers under Capone took over gambling in suburban Cicero and invested in Chicago gambling operations. Gambling had become a complex mixture of Irish, Negro, Jewish and Italian entrepreneurship.

Although the Irish by the twentieth century played little direct role in managing prostitution, Italians by World War I had moved into important positions in the vice districts, especially in the notorious Levee district on the South Side. (Political protection, of course, often had to be arranged through Irish political leaders.) Just as the Irish blocked Italians in politics, so also they blocked Italians in gambling, which was both more respectable and more profitable than prostitution. Hence the importance of prohibition in the 1920s lay not in initiating organized crime (gambling continued both before and after prohibition to be the major enterprise of organized crime); rather, prohibition provided Italians with an opportunity to break into a major field of organized crime that was not already monopolized by the Irish.

This generalization, to some extent, oversimplifies what was in fact a complex process. At first, prohibition opened up business opportunities for large numbers of individuals and groups, and the situation was chaotic. By 1924, however, shifting coalitions had emerged. Some bootleg-ging gangs were Irish, including one set of O'Donnell brothers on the far West Side and an-other set on the South Side. Southwest of the stockyards, there was an important organization, both Polish and Irish, coordinated by "Pollack" Joe Saltis. And on the Near North Side a major group—founded by burglars and hold-up men—was led by Irishmen . . . and Jews. . . . There were, finally, the various Italian gangs, including the Gennas, the Aiellos, and, of course, the Capone organization.

The major Italian bootlegging gang, that asso-ciated with the name of Al Capone, built upon roots already established in the South Side vice district. There John Torrio managed houses of prostitution for Big Jim Colossimo. With Colos-simo's assassination in 1920, Torrio and his assis-tant, Capone, moved rapidly to establish a boot-legging syndicate in the Loop and in the suburbs south and west of the city. Many of their associ-ates were persons whom they had known during humbler days in the South Side vice district and who now rose to wealth with them. Nor was their organization entirely Italian. Very early, they worked closely with Irishmen like Frankie Lake and Terry Druggan in the brewing of beer, while Jake Guzik, a Jew and former South Side pimp, be-came the chief business manager for the syndi-cate. In the bloody bootlegging wars of the 1920s, the members of the Capone organization gradu-ally emerged as the most effective organizers and most deadly fighters. The success of the organiza-tion brought wealth and power to many ambi-tious Italians and provided them with the means in the late 1920s and early 1930s to move into gambling, racketeering and entertainment, as well as into a broad range of legitimate enter-prises. Bootlegging allowed Italians, through en-trepreneurial skills and by assassination of rivals, to gain a central position in the organized under-world of the city.

Although Jewish immigrants in such cities as Cleveland and Philadelphia were major figures in bootlegging and thus showed patterns similar to Italians in Chicago, Jews in Chicago were some-what peripheral figures. By World War I, Chicago Jews, like Italians, made important inroads into vice, especially in vice districts on the West Side. In the 1920s, with the dispersal of prostitution, several Jewish vice syndicates operated on the South and West Sides. Jews were also rapidly in-vading the world of gambling. Although Jews took part in vice, gambling and bootlegging, they made a special contribution to the organized un-derworld by providing professional or expert ser-vices. Even before World War I, Jews were be-coming a majority of the bailbondsmen in the city. By the 1920s, if not before, Jews constituted over half the fences who disposed of stolen goods. (This was, of course, closely related to Jewish predominance as junk dealers and their importance in retail selling.) Jews were also heav-ily overrepresented among defense attorneys in the criminal courts. It is unnecessary to empha-size that the entrepreneurial and professional ser-vices of Jews reflected broader patterns of adap-tation to American urban life.

Even within relatively minor underworld posi-tions, specialization by ethnicity was important. A study of three hundred Chicago pimps in the early 1920s, for instance, found that 109 (more than one-third) were black, 60 were Italian, 47 Jew-ish and 26 Greek. The large proportion of blacks suggests that the high prestige of the pimp among some elements of the lower-class black commu-nity is not a recent development but has a rela-tively long tradition in the urban slum. There has, in fact, long been a close relationship of vice ac-tivities and Negro life in the cities. In all probabil-ity, the vice districts constituted the most inte-grated aspect of Chicago society. Black pimps and madams occasionally had white girls working for them, just as white pimps and madams some-times had black girls working for them. In addi-tion, blacks held many of the jobs in the vice dis-tricts, ranging from maids to entertainers. The location of major areas of vice and entertainment around the periphery and along the main busi-ness streets of the South Side black neighborhood gave such activities a pervasive influence within the neighborhood.

Black achievements in ragtime and jazz had their roots, at least in part, in the vice and entertainment districts of the cities. Much of the early history of jazz lies among the talented musicians—black and white—who performed in the famous resorts in the Storyville district of New Orleans in the 1890s and early 1900s. With the dissolution of Storyville as a segregated vice district, many talented black musicians carried their styles to Chicago's South Side, to Harlem, and to the cabarets and dance halls of other major cities. In the 1920s, with black performers like King Oliver and Louis Armstrong and white performers like Bix Beiderbecke, Chicago was an important environment for development of jazz styles. Just as Harlem became a center for entertainment and jazz for New Yorkers during prohibition, so the black and tan cabarets and speakeasies of Chicago's South Side became a place where blacks and whites drank, danced and listened to jazz music—to the shock of many respectable citizens. Thus, in ways that were both destructive and productive, the black experience in the city was linked to the opportunities that lay in the vice resorts, cabarets and dance halls of the teeming slums. In the operation of entertainment facilities and policy rackets, black entrepreneurs found their major outlet and black politicians found their chief support.

Until there has been more study of comparative ethnic patterns, only tentative hypotheses are possible to explain why various ethnic groups followed differing patterns. Because many persons involved in organized crime initiated their careers with customers from their own neighborhood or ethnic group, the degree to which a particular ethnic group sought a particular illegal service would influence opportunities for criminal activities. If members of an ethnic group did not gamble, for instance, then ambitious members of that ethnic group could not build gambling syndicates based upon local roots. The general attitude toward law and law enforcement, too, would affect opportunities for careers in illegal ventures. Those groups that became most heavily involved in organized crime migrated from regions in

which they had developed deep suspicions of government authority—whether the Irish fleeing British rule in Ireland, Jews escaping from Eastern Europe, Italians migrating from southern Italy or Sicily, or blacks leaving the American South. Within a community suspicious of courts and government officials, a person in trouble with the law could retain roots and even respect in the community. Within a community more oriented toward upholding legal authority, on the other hand, those engaged in illegal activities risked ostracism and loss of community roots.

In other ways, too, ethnic life styles evolved differently. Among both Germans and Irish, for instance, friendly drinking was part of the pattern of relaxation. Although the Irish and Germans by 1900 were the major managers of Chicago's saloons, the meaning of the saloon was quite different for the two groups. German saloons and beer gardens were sometimes for family entertainment and generally excluded gambling or prostitution; Irish saloons, part of an exclusively male social life, often featured prostitution or gambling and fit more easily into the world of entertainment associated with organized crime. Finally, it appears that south Italians had the highest homicide rate in Europe. There was, in all probability, a relationship between the cultural factors that sanctioned violence and private revenge in Europe and the factors that sanctioned the violence with which Italian bootleggers worked their way into a central position in Chicago's organized crime.

There were, at any rate, many ways that the immigrant background and the urban environment interacted to influence the ethnic experience with organized crime. For some ethnic groups, involvement in organized crime was not an important part of the adjustment to American urban life. For other groups, involvement in the organized underworld both reflected and influenced their relatively unique patterns of acculturation.

Economic Impact

The economic role of organized crime was an additional factor underlying the impact of organized crime upon ethnic communities and urban society. Organized crime was important because of the relatively great wealth of the most successful criminals, because of the large numbers of persons directly employed by organized crime, and because of the still larger numbers who supplemented their income through various part-time activities. And all of this does not count the multitude of customers who bought the goods and services offered by the bootleggers, gambling operators and vice lords of the city.

During the first thirty or forty years after an immigrant group's arrival, successful leaders in organized crime might constitute a disproportionate percentage of the most wealthy members of the community. In the 1930s at least one-half of the blacks in Chicago worth more than $100,000 were policy kings; Italian bootleggers in the 1920s may have represented an even larger proportion of the very wealthy among immigrants from southern Italy. The wealth of the successful criminals was accompanied by extensive political and other contacts that gave them considerable leverage both within and outside the ethnic community. They had financial resources to engage in extensive charitable activities, and often did so lavishly. Projects for improvement of ethnic communities often needed their support and contacts in order to succeed. Criminals often invested in or managed legitimate business enterprises in their communities. Hence, despite ambiguous or even antagonistic relations that they had with "respectable" members of their ethnic communities, successful leaders in organized crime were men who had to be reckoned with in the ethnic community and who often represented the community to the outside world.

In organized crime, as in other economic activities, the very successful were but a minority. To understand the economic impact of crime, it is necessary to study the many persons at the middle and lower levels of organization. In cities like Chicago the number of persons directly employed in the activities of organized crime was considerable. A modest estimate of the number of full-time prostitutes in Chicago about 1910 would be 15,000—not counting madams, pimps, procurers and others in managerial positions. Or take the policy racket. In the early 1930s an average policy wheel in the black ghetto employed 300 writers; some employed as many as 600; and there were perhaps 6,000 policy writers in the ghetto. The policy wheels, in this period of heavy unemployment, may have been the major single source of employment in the black ghetto, a source of employment that did not need to lay off workers or reduce wages merely because the rest of the economy faced a major depression. Finally, during the 1920s, bootlegging in its various aspects was a major economic activity employing thousands in manufacture, transportation and retailing activities.

Yet persons directly employed constituted only a small proportion of those whose income derived from organized crime. Many persons supplemented their income through occasional or part-time services. While some prostitutes walked the streets to advertise their wares, others relied upon intermediaries who would direct customers in return for a finder's fee. During certain periods, payments to taxi drivers were sufficiently lucrative so that some taxi drivers would pick up only those passengers seeking a house of prostitution. Bellboys, especially in the second-class hotels, found the function of negotiating between guests and prostitutes a profitable part of their service. (Many of the worst hotels, of course, functioned partly or wholly as places of assignation.) Bartenders, newsboys and waiters were among the many helpful persons who provided information concerning places and prices.

Various phases of bootlegging during the 1920s were even more important as income supplements. In the production end, many slum families prepared wine or became "alky cookers" for the bootlegging gangs—so much so that after the mid-1920s, explosions of stills and the resulting fires were a major hazard in Chicago's slum neighborhoods. As one observer reported:

During prohibition times many respectable Sicilian men were employed as "alky cookers" for the Capones, the Aiellos or for personal use. Many of these people sold wine during prohibition and their children delivered it on foot or by streetcar without the least fear that they might be arrested. . . .

During the years of 1927 to 1930 more wine was made than during any other years and even the "poorest people" were able to make ten or fifteen barrels each year—others making sixty, seventy, or more barrels.

Other persons, including policemen, moonlighted as truck drivers who delivered booze to the many retail outlets of the city. Finally, numerous persons supplemented their income by retailing booze, including bellboys, janitors in apartment buildings and shoe shine boys.

The many persons who mediated between the underworld and the law were another group that supplemented its income through underworld contacts. Large numbers of policemen, as well as bailiffs, judges and political fixers, received bribes or political contributions in return for illegal cooperation with the underworld. Defense attorneys, tax accountants and bailbondsmen, in return for salaries or fees, provided expert services that were generally legal.

For many of the small businessmen of the city, retailing the goods or services of the underworld could supplement business income significantly. Saloons, as already mentioned, often provided gambling and prostitution as an additional service to customers. Large numbers of small businesses were outlets for handbooks, policy, baseball pools, slot machines and other forms of gambling. A substantial proportion of the cigar stores, for example, were primarily fronts for gambling; barber shops, pool halls, newsstands, and small hotels frequently sold policy or would take bets on the horses. Drug stores often served as outlets for cocaine and, during the 1920s, sometimes sold liquor.

The organized underworld also influenced business activity through racketeering. A substantial minority of the city's labor unions were racketeer-controlled; those that were not often used the assistance of racketeer unions or of strongarm gangs during strikes. The leaders of organized crime, as a result, exercised control or influence in the world of organized labor. Not so well known was the extensive racketeering that characterized small business organizations. The small businesses of the city were generally marginal and intensely competitive. To avoid cutthroat competition, businessmen often formed associations to make and enforce regulations illegally limiting competition. The Master Barbers Association, for example, set minimum prices, forbad a shop to be open after 7:30 P.M., and ruled that no shop could be established within two blocks of another shop. Many other types of small businesses formed similar associations: dairies, auto parts dealers, garage owners, candy jobbers, butcher stores, fish wholesalers and retailers, cleaners and dyers, and junk dealers. Many of the associations were controlled, or even organized, by racketeers who levied dues upon association members and controlled the treasuries; they then used a system of fines and violence to insure that all businessmen in the trade joined the association and abided by the regulations. In return for control of the association's treasury, in short, racketeers performed illegal services for the association and thereby regulated much of the small business activity of the city.

Discussion of the economic influence of organized crime would be incomplete without mentioning the largest group that was tied economically to the underworld, namely, the many customers for the illegal goods and services. Like other retailers in the city, some leaders of organized crime located their outlets near the center of the city or along major transportation lines and serviced customers from the entire region; others were essentially neighborhood businessmen with a local clientele. In either case, those providing illegal goods and services usually attempted to cultivate customer loyalty so that the same customers would return on an ongoing basis and advertise among their friends. Organized crime existed because of wide customer demand, and a large proportion of the adult population of the city was linked to organized crime on a regular basis for purchase of goods and services.

Heroism and Ambiguity

Because of the diverse ways that successful criminal entrepreneurs influenced the city and ethnic communities, many of them became heroes—especially within their own communities. There were a variety of reasons for the admiration that they received. Their numerous philanthropies, both large and small, won them reputations as regular guys who would help a person in need. Moreover, they were often seen as persons who fought for their ethnic communities. They aided politicians from their communities to win elections in the rough and often violent politics of the slums and thereby advanced their ethnic group toward political recognition. Sometimes they were seen as fighters for labor unions and thus as friends of labor. And, on occasion, they fought directly for their ethnic group. There was, for instance, the case of the three Miller brothers from Chicago's West Side Jewish ghetto. In typical ghetto pattern, one became a boxer, one a gangster and one a policeman. The boxer and gangster were heroes among Jews on the West Side, where for many years Jewish peddlers and junk dealers had been subjected to racial slurs and violent attacks by young hoodlums from other ethnic groups. "What I have done from the time I was a boy," Davy Miller told a reporter,

was to fight for my people here in the Ghetto against Irish, Poles or any other nationality. It was sidewalk fighting at first. I could lick any five boys or men in a sidewalk free-for-all.

When the Miller brothers and their gang protected the Jews of the West Side, the attacks against them abated.

Particularly for youngsters growing up in the ghettos, the gangsters were often heroes whose exploits were admired and copied. Davy Miller modestly recognized this when he said:

Maybe I am a hero to the young folks among my people, but it's not because I'm a gangster. It's because I've always been ready to help all or any of them in a pinch.

An Italian student at the University of Chicago in the early 1930s remembered his earlier life in the Italian ghetto:

For 26 years I lived in West Side "Little Italy," the community that has produced more underworld limelights than any other area in Chicago. . . .

I remember these men in large cars, with boys and girls of the neighborhood standing on the running board. I saw them come into the neighborhood in splendor as heroes. Many times they showered handfuls of silver to youngsters who waited to get a glance at them—the new heroes—because they had just made headlines in the newspapers. Since then I have seen many of my playmates shoot their way to the top of gangdom and seen others taken for a ride.

Nevertheless, despite the importance of gangsters and the world within which they moved, their relations to ethnic groups and the city were always ambiguous. Because many of their activities were illegal, they often faced the threat of arrest and, contrary to common belief, frequently found themselves behind bars. Furthermore, for those members of the ethnic community who pursued respectable paths to success, gangsters gave the ethnic group a bad name and remained a continuing source of embarrassment. St. Clair Drake and Horace R. Cayton, in their book on the Chicago black ghetto, describe the highly ambiguous and often antagonistic relations of the respectable black middle class and the policy kings. In his book on Italians in Chicago, Humbert S. Nelli explains that in the 1920s the Italian language press refused to print the name of Al Capone and covered the St. Valentine's Day massacre without suggesting its connection with bootlegging wars.

The respectable middle classes, however, were not the only ones unhappy about the activities or notoriety of gangsters. Organized crime sometimes contributed to the violence and fear of violence that pervaded many of the ghetto neighborhoods. Often local residents feared to turn to the police and lived with a stoical acceptance that gangs of toughs controlled elections, extorted money from local businesses and generally lived outside the reach of the law. Some immigrant parents, too, resented the numerous saloons, the open prostitution and the many gambling dens—all of which created a morally dangerous environment in which to raise children. Especially immigrant women, who watched their husbands

squander the meager family income on liquor or gambling, resented the activities of organized crime. Within a number of neighborhoods, local churches and local leaders undertook sporadic campaigns for better law enforcement.

Organized crime, then, was an important part of the complex social structure of ethnic communities and urban society in the early twentieth century. For certain ethnic groups, organized crime both influenced and reflected the special patterns by which the groups adjusted to life in urban America. Through organized crime, many members of those ethnic groups could achieve mobility out of the ethnic ghettos and into the social world of crime, politics, ethnic business, sports, and entertainment. Those who were successful in organized crime possessed the wealth and contacts to exercise broad influence within the ethnic communities and the city. The economic activities of the underworld provided jobs or supplemental income for tens of thousands. Despite the importance of organized crime, however, individual gangsters often found success to be ambiguous. They were not always able to achieve secure positions or to translate their positions into respectability.

STUDY QUESTIONS

1. What were the primary occupational paths out of the ghetto for uneducated but ambitious ethnic youths? How were the paths interrelated?

2. How did organized crime exert influence upon other social worlds? What in particular was the relationship between organized crime and urban politics?

3. What social values did criminals share with the leaders in politics, sports, labor unions, entertainment, and business? What was the attitude of the men in these professions toward law and legal institutions?

4. What does Haller mean by "ethnic specialization" in crime? What factors account for the criminal specialization of the different ethnic groups?

5. What was the economic impact of organized crime on the ethnic and urban environment?

6. Why did a number of criminals become ethnic heroes? What role did the "criminal heroes" play in their ethnic neighborhoods?

BIBLIOGRAPHY

Because of the secretive nature of organized crime, it has proven an elusive subject for scholars. Nevertheless historians and sociologists have produced several valuable studies. Andrew Sinclair, *Prohibition: The Era of Excess,* (1962), examines the impact of the Eighteenth Amendment on the rise of organized crime. Works by Humbert S. Nelli, *The Italians in Chicago, 1880–1930: A Study in Ethnic Mobility* (1970) and *The Business of Crime* (1976), deal admirably with the subject of ethnic crime. John A. Gardiner, *The Politics of Corruption: Organized Crime in the American City* (1970), is also valuable. William F. Whyte, *Street Corner Society: The Social Structure of an Italian Slum* (1955), is a classic sociological study of an ethnic urban environment. Finally, Daniel Bell, *The End of Ideology* (1961), considers crime as a means of social and economic mobility.

PART FIVE

Depression and War

Despite all the talk about prosperity and progress in the 1920s, there were disturbing signs that the economy was not as healthy as people assumed. Throughout the decade agricultural prices steadily declined as production rose, in what many called a "poverty of abundance." In face of high protective tariffs, foreign trade gradually declined and the production of durable, domestic goods peaked in 1927. When the bubble burst with the crash of the stock market in October 1929, most Americans were shocked. The shock soon turned to despair as banks failed in record numbers, small businesses closed their doors, and unemployment reached unheard-of levels. How could it have been? For three centuries the world viewed America as the land of opportunity. Suddenly, people were losing their jobs, homes, and life savings. The American dream had become a nightmare.

Bewildered with their plight, most Americans were desperate for answers. Socialists and Communists blamed capitalism, arguing that, just as Karl Marx had predicted, the system was collapsing under the weight of its own corruption and exploitation. The technocrats claimed that industrialization had run its course and that a new social order, based on science and technology, would soon emerge out of the rubble of the depression. Businessmen blamed politicians for the trouble. Farmers saw bogeymen in bankers and commodities speculators. Some Americans even blamed Jews for the collapse. Abandoning laissez-faire economics, Hoover modestly tried to reorganize the federal government to fight the depression, but his efforts failed. In the next presidential election Americans put Franklin D. Roosevelt into the White House.

Roosevelt was an unlikely hero for an impoverished nation. Born to old wealth and raised in splendor, he had little understanding of economics and no empathy for poverty. But he did have keen political instincts and few philosophical inhibitions. In a whirlwind of activity, the New Deal greatly increased relief spending, attacked specific problems in the money markets, and tried, usually in a haphazard way, to stimulate an industrial recovery. Although it took World War II to finally lift the country out of the depression, Franklin D. Roosevelt nevertheless became one of the most beloved presidents in American history, popular enough to win reelection in 1936,

170

1940, and 1944. People remembered him for the spark in his eye, his smiling face and cocked head, and his uncompromising exuberance. To men working on government projects, it was Roosevelt who took them away from the soup lines. To farm wives living in poverty, it was Roosevelt who brought the electric transmission lines, the subsidy check, and the refinanced mortgage. To mass production workers, it was Roosevelt who sanctioned their labor unions and brought minimum wages. And to old people, it was Roosevelt who provided for their futures with Social Security.

But just as Roosevelt was easing fears about the economic future, political developments in Europe were bringing new tensions to a weary nation. Adolf Hitler's designs on Austria, Czechoslovakia, and Poland in 1938 and 1939 convinced many that another war was imminent and that the problems of the depression, as bad as they were, would only be child's play compared to a new global conflagration. Hitler's conquest of France and the Low Countries in 1940, the assault on Great Britain, and the invasion of the Soviet Union in 1941 only confirmed those fears. For a brief time, the United States was caught between its historic need for isolation and its responsibilities as a global leader. On December 7, 1941, Japan resolved America's uncertain position.

THE MAN OF THE CENTURY

Arthur M. Schlesinger, Jr.

When President Franklin D. Roosevelt collapsed and died of a stroke on April 12, 1945, the nation went into a state of depression unknown since the death of Abraham Lincoln. Like Lincoln, Roosevelt had become inseparably linked with a series of national crises—in his case the Great Depression and World War II. And like Lincoln, Roosevelt was viewed as a savior, a man who had redeemed his people, first from starvation and then from the specter of fascist oppression. Put simply, FDR enjoyed the elusive charisma so prized by politicians. Blessed with enormous self-confidence and an ingratiating personality, he inspired tremendous loyalty among most Americans. They loved him and put him in the White House on four separate occasions—1932, 1936, 1940, and 1944. But like all charismatic leaders, Roosevelt also generated tremendous hostility in some circles, particularly in corporate boardrooms and the parlors of the well-to-do. They viewed him as a "traitor to his class," a politician so seduced by power that he posed a threat to property and the social order.

Franklin D. Roosevelt was a complicated man, a beloved acquaintance of thousands but an intimate of very few. Born rich and raised in pampered splendor, he nevertheless led a virtual revolution in public policy, giving ethnic minorities, labor unions, and poor people their first taste of influence at the federal level. Although Roosevelt inspired a legion of intellectuals to invest their energies in public service, he was not an innovative thinker himself. He preferred the give and take of politics, and the inherent excitement of its risks, to the intricate nuts and bolts of social and economic policy. In the following essay Arthur Schlesinger, a historian who has defended Roosevelt and the Roosevelt legacy for decades, presents why he believes that FDR was one of America's greatest presidents and, even more importantly, how FDR shaped the world we live in today.

After half a century it is hard to approach Franklin D. Roosevelt except through a minefield of clichés. Theories of FDR, running the gamut from artlessness to mystification, have long paraded before our eyes. There is his famous response to the newspaperman who asked him for his philosophy: "Philosophy? I am a Christian and a Democrat—that's all"; there is Robert E. Sherwood's equally famous warning about "Roosevelt's heavily forested interior"; and we weakly conclude that both things were probably true.

FDR's Presidency has commanded the attention of eminent historians at home and abroad for fifty years or more. Yet no consensus emerges, especially in the field of foreign affairs. Scholars at one time or another have portrayed him at every point across a broad spectrum: as an isolationist, as an internationalist, as an appeaser, as a warmonger, as an impulsive decision maker, as an incorrigible vacillator, as the savior of capitalism, as a closet socialist, as a Machiavellian intriguer plotting to embroil his country in foreign wars, as a Machiavellian intriguer avoiding war in order to let other nations bear the brunt of the fighting, as a gullible dreamer who thought he could charm Stalin into postwar collaboration and ended by selling Eastern Europe down the river into slavery, as a tightfisted creditor sending Britain down the road toward bankruptcy, as a crafty imperialist serving the interests of American capitalist hegemony, as a high-minded prophet whose vision shaped the world's future. Will the real FDR please stand up?

Two relatively recent books illustrate the chronically unsettled state of FDR historiography—and the continuing vitality of the FDR debate. In *Wind Over Sand* (1988) Frederick W. Marks III finds a presidential record marked by ignorance, superficiality, inconsistency, random prejudice, erratic impulse, a man out of his depth, not waving but drowning, practicing a diplomacy as insubstantial and fleeting as wind blowing over sand. In *The Juggler* (1991), Warren F. Kimball finds a record marked by intelligent understanding of world forces, astute maneuver, and a remarkable consistency of purpose, a farsighted statesman

facing dilemmas that defied quick or easy solutions. One-third of each book is given over to endnotes and bibliography, which suggests that each portrait is based on meticulous research. Yet the two historians arrive at diametrically opposite conclusions.

So the debate goes on. Someone should write a book entitled *FDR: For and Against,* modeled on Pieter Geyl's *Napoleon: For and Against.* "It is impossible," the great Dutch historian observed, "that two historians, especially two historians living in different periods, should see any historical personality in the same light. The greater the political importance of a historical character, the more impossible this is." History, Geyl (rightly) concluded, is an "argument without end."

I suppose we must accept that human beings are in the last analysis beyond analysis. In the case of FDR, no one can be really sure what was going on in that affable, welcoming, reserved, elusive, teasing, spontaneous, calculating, cold, warm, humorous, devious, mendacious, manipulative, petty, magnanimous, superficially casual, ultimately decent, highly camouflaged, finally impenetrable mind. Still, if we can't as historians puzzle out what he *was,* we surely must as historians try to make sense out of what he *did.* If his personality escapes us, his policies must have some sort of pattern.

What Roosevelt wrote (or Sam Rosenman wrote for him) in the introduction to the first volume of his *Public Papers* about his record as governor of New York goes, I believe, for his foreign policy too: "Those who seek inconsistencies will find them. There were inconsistencies of methods, inconsistencies caused by ceaseless efforts to find ways to solve problems for the future as well as for the present. There were inconsistencies born of insufficient knowledge. There were inconsistencies springing from the need of experimentation. But through them all, I trust that there also will be found a consistency and continuity of broad purpose."

Now purpose can be very broad indeed. To say that a statesman is in favor of peace, freedom, and security does not narrow things down very much.

Meaning resides in the details, and in FDR's case the details often contradict each other. If I may invoke still another cliché, FDR's foreign policy seems to fit Churchill's description of the Soviet Union: "a riddle wrapped in a mystery inside an enigma." However, we too often forget what Churchill said next: "But perhaps there is a key. That key is Russian national interest." German domination of Eastern Europe, Churchill continued, "would be contrary to the historic life-interests of Russia." Here, I suggest, may be the key to FDR, the figure in his carpet: his sense of the historic life-interests of the United States.

Of course, "national interest" narrows things down only a little. No one, except a utopian or a millennialist, is against the national interest. In a world of nation-states the assumption that governments will pursue their own interests gives order and predictability to international affairs. As George Washington said, "No nation is to be trusted farther than it is bound by [its] interest." The problem is the substance one pours into national interest. In our own time, for example, Lyndon Johnson and Dean Rusk thought our national interest required us to fight in Vietnam; William Fulbright, Walter Lippmann, Hans Morgenthau thought our national interest required us to pull out of Vietnam. The phrase by itself settles no arguments.

How did FDR conceive the historic life-interests of the United States? His conception emerged from his own long, if scattered, education in world affairs. It should not be forgotten that he arrived in the White House with an unusual amount of international experience. He was born into a cosmopolitan family. His father knew Europe well and as a young man had marched with Garibaldi. His elder half-brother had served in American legations in London and Vienna. His mother's family had been in the China trade; his mother herself had lived in Hong Kong as a little girl. As FDR reminded Henry Morgenthau in 1934, "I have a background of a little over a century in Chinese affairs."

FDR himself made his first trip to Europe at the age of three and went there every summer from his ninth to his fourteenth year. As a child he learned French and German. As a lifelong stamp collector he knew the world's geography and politics. By the time he was elected President, he had made thirteen trips across the Atlantic and had spent almost three years of his life in Europe. "I started . . . with a good deal of interest in foreign affairs," he told a press conference in 1939, "because both branches of my family have been mixed up in foreign affairs for a good many generations, the affairs of Europe and the affairs of the Far East."

Now much of his knowledge was social and superficial. Nor is international experience in any case a guarantee of international wisdom or even of continuing international concern. The other American politician of the time who rivaled FDR in exposure to the great world was, oddly, Herbert Hoover. Hoover was a mining engineer in Australia at twenty-three, a capitalist in the Chinese Empire at twenty-five, a promoter in the City of London at twenty-seven. In the years from his Stanford graduation to the Great War, he spent more time in the British Empire than he did in the United States. During and after the war he supervised relief activities in Belgium and in Eastern Europe. Keynes called him the only man to emerge from the Paris Peace Conference with an enhanced reputation.

Both Hoover and Roosevelt came of age when the United States was becoming a world power. Both saw more of that world than most of their American contemporaries. But international experience led them to opposite conclusions. What Hoover saw abroad soured him on foreigners. He took away from Paris an indignant conviction of an impassable gap between his virtuous homeland and the European snake pit. Nearly twenty years passed before he could bring himself to set foot again on the despised continent. He loathed Europe and its nationalist passions and hatreds. "With a vicious rhythm," he said in 1940, "these malign forces seem to drive [European] nations like the Gadarene swine over the precipice of war." The less America had to do with so degenerate a place, the Quaker Hoover felt, the better.

The patrician Roosevelt was far more at home in the great world. Moreover, his political genealogy instilled in him the conviction that the United States must at last take its rightful place among the powers. In horse breeder's parlance, FDR was by Woodrow Wilson out of Theodore Roosevelt. These two remarkable Presidents taught FDR that the United States was irrevocably a world power and poured substance into his conception of America's historic life-interests.

FDR greatly admired TR, deserted the Democratic party to cast his first presidential vote for him, married his niece, and proudly succeeded in 1913 to the office TR had occupied fifteen years earlier, Assistant Secretary of the Navy. From TR and from that eminent friend of both Roosevelts, Admiral Mahan, young Roosevelt learned the strategic necessities of international relations. He learned how to distinguish between vital and peripheral interests. He learned why the national in-

terest required the maintenance of balances of power in areas that, if controlled by a single power, could threaten the United States. He learned what the defense of vital interests might require in terms of ships and arms and men and production and resources. His experience in Wilson's Navy Department during the First World War consolidated these lessons.

But he also learned new things from Wilson, among them that it was not enough to send young men to die and kill because of the thrill of battle or because of war's morally redemptive qualities or even because of the need to restore the balance of power. The awful sacrifices of modern war demanded nobler objectives. The carnage on the Western Front converted FDR to Wilson's vision of a world beyond war, beyond national interest, beyond balances of power, a world not of secret diplomacy and antagonistic military alliances but of an organized common peace, founded on democracy, self-determination, and the collective restraint of aggression.

Theodore Roosevelt had taught FDR geopolitics. Woodrow Wilson now gave him a larger international purpose in which the principles of power had a strong but secondary role. FDR's two mentors detested each other. But they joined to construct the framework within which FDR, who cherished them both, approached foreign affairs for the rest of his life.

As the Democratic vice presidential candidate in 1920, he roamed the country pleading for the League of Nations. Throughout the twenties he warned against political isolationism and economic protectionism. America would commit a grievous wrong, he said, if it were "to go backwards towards an old Chinese Wall policy of isolationism." Trade wars, he said, were "symptoms of economic insanity." But such sentiments could not overcome the disillusion and disgust with which Americans in the 1920s contemplated world troubles. As President Hoover told the Italian foreign minister in 1931, the deterioration of Europe had led to such "despair . . . on the part of the ordinary American citizen [that] now he just wanted to keep out of the whole business."

Depression intensified the isolationist withdrawal. Against the national mood, the new President brought to the White House in 1933 an international outlook based, I would judge, on four principles. One was TR's commitment to the preservation of the balance of world power. Another was Wilson's vision of concerted international action to prevent or punish aggression. The third principle argued that lasting peace required the free flow of trade among nations. The fourth was that in a democracy foreign policy must rest on popular consent. In the isolationist climate of the 1930s, this fourth principle compromised and sometimes undermined the first three.

Diplomatic historians are occasionally tempted to overrate the amount of time Presidents spend in thinking about foreign policy. In fact, from Jackson to FDR, domestic affairs have always been, with a few fleeting exceptions—perhaps Polk, McKinley, Wilson—the presidential priority. This was powerfully the case at the start for FDR. Given the collapse of the economy and the anguish of unemployment, given the absence of obvious remedy and the consequent need for social experiment, the surprise is how much time and energy FDR did devote to foreign affairs in these early years.

He gave time to foreign policy because of his acute conviction that Germany and Japan were, or were about to be, on the rampage and that unchecked aggression would ultimately threaten vital interests of the United States. He packed the State Department and embassies abroad with unregenerate Wilsonians. When he appointed Cordell Hull Secretary, he knew what he was getting; his brain trusters, absorbed in problems at hand, had warned him against international folly. But there they were, Wilsonians all: Hull, Norman Davis, Sumner Welles, William Phillips, Francis B. Sayre, Walton Moore, Breckinridge Long, Josephus Daniels, W. E. Dodd, Robert W. Bingham, Claude Bowers, Joseph E. Davies. Isolationists like Raymond Moley did not last long at State.

Roosevelt's early excursions into foreign policy were necessarily intermittent, however, and in his own rather distracting personal style. Economic diplomacy he confided to Hull, except when Hull's free-trade obsessions threatened New Deal recovery programs, as at the London Economic Conference of 1933. He liked, when he found the time, to handle the political side of things himself. He relished meetings with foreign leaders and found himself in advance of most of them in his forebodings about Germany and Japan. He invited his ambassadors, especially his political appointees, to write directly to him, and nearly all took advantage of the invitation.

His diplomatic style had its capricious aspects. FDR understood what admirals and generals were up to, and he understood the voice of prophetic statesmanship. But he never fully appreciated the professional diplomat and looked with some disdain on the career Foreign Service as made up of tea drinkers remote from the realities of American life. His approach to foreign policy, while firmly grounded in geopolitics and soaring easily into the higher idealism, always lacked something at the middle level.

At the heart of Roosevelt's style in foreign affairs was a certain incorrigible amateurism. His off-the-cuff improvisations, his airy tendency to throw out half-baked ideas, caused others to underrate his continuity of purpose and used to drive the British especially wild, as minutes scribbled on Foreign Office dispatches make abundantly clear. This amateurism had its good points. It could be a source of boldness and creativity in a field populated by cautious and conventional people. But it also encouraged superficiality and dilettantism.

The national mood, however, remained FDR's greatest problem. Any U.S. contribution to the deterrence of aggression depended on giving the government power to distinguish between aggressors and their victims. He asked Congress for this authority, first in cooperating with League of Nations sanctions in 1933, later in connection with American neutrality statutes. Fearing that aid to one side would eventually involve the nation in war, Congress regularly turned him down. By rejecting policies that would support victims against aggressors, Congress effectively nullified the ability of the United States to throw its weight in the scales against aggressors.

Roosevelt, regarding the New Deal as more vital for the moment than foreign policy and needing the support of isolationists for his domestic program, accepted what he could not change in congressional roll calls. But he did hope to change public opinion and began a long labor of popular education with his annual message in January 1936 and its condemnation of "autocratic institutions that beget slavery at home and aggression abroad."

It is evident that I am not persuaded by the school of historians that sees Roosevelt as embarked until 1940 on a mission of appeasement, designed to redress German grievances and lure the Nazi regime into a constructive role in a reordered Europe. The evidence provided by private conversations as well as by public pronouncements is far too consistent and too weighty to permit the theory that Roosevelt had illusions about coexistence with Hitler. Timing and maneuver were essential, and on occasion he tacked back and forth like the small-boat sailor that Gaddis Smith reminds us he was. Thus, before positioning the United States for entry into war, he wanted to make absolutely sure there was no prospect of negotiated peace: hence his interest in 1939–40 in people like James D. Mooney and William Rhodes Davis and hence the Sumner Welles mission. But his basic course seems pretty clear: one way or another to rid the world of Hitler.

I am even less persuaded by the school that sees Roosevelt as a President who rushed the nation to war because he feared German and Japanese economic competition. America "began to go to war against the Axis in the Western Hemisphere," the revisionist William Appleman Williams tells us, because Germany was invading U.S. markets in Latin America. The Open Door cult recognizes no geopolitical concerns in Washington about German bases in the Western Hemisphere. Oddly, the revisionists accept geopolitics as an O.K. motive for the Soviet Union but deny it to the United States. In their view American foreign policy can never be aimed at strategic security but must forever be driven by the lust of American business for foreign markets.

In the United States, of course, as any student of American history knows, economic growth has been based primarily on the home market, not on foreign markets, and the preferred policy of American capitalists, even after 1920, when the United States became a creditor nation, was protection of the home market, not freedom of trade. Recall Fordney-McCumber and Smoot-Hawley. The preference of American business for high tariffs was equally true in depression. When FDR proposed his reciprocal trade agreements program in 1934, the American business community, instead of welcoming reciprocal trade as a way of penetrating foreign markets, denounced the whole idea. Senator Vandenberg even called the bill "Fascist in its philosophy, Fascist in its objectives." A grand total of two Republicans voted for reciprocal trade in the House, three in the Senate.

The "corporatism" thesis provides a more sophisticated version of the economic interpretation. No doubt we have become a society of large organizations, and no doubt an associational society generates a certain momentum toward coordination. But the idea that exporters, importers, Wall Street, Main Street, trade unionists, and farmers form a consensus on foreign policy and impose that consensus on the national government is hard to sustain.

It is particularly irrelevant to the Roosevelt period. If Roosevelt was the compliant instrument of capitalist expansion, as the Open Door ideologies claim, or of corporate hegemony, as the corporatism thesis implies, why did the leaders of American corporate capitalism oppose him so viciously? Business leaders vied with one another in their hatred of "that man in the White House." The family of J. P. Morgan used to warn visitors against mentioning Roosevelt's name lest fury raise Morgan's blood pressure to the danger point. When Averell Harriman, one of that rare breed, a pro-New Deal businessman, appeared on Wall Street, old friends cut him dead. The theory that Roosevelt pursued a foreign policy dictated by the same corporate crowd that fought him domestically and smeared him personally belongs, it seems to me, in the same library with the historiography of Oliver Stone.

What was at stake, as FDR saw it, was not corporate profits or Latin American markets but the security of the United States and the future of democracy. Basking as we do today in the glow of democratic triumph, we forget how desperate the democratic cause appeared half a century ago. The Great War had apparently proved that democracy could not produce peace; the Great Depression that it could not produce prosperity. By the 1930s contempt for democracy was widespread among elites and masses alike: contempt for parliamentary methods, for government by discussion, for freedoms of expression and opposition, for bourgeois individualism, for pragmatic muddling through. Discipline, order, efficiency, and all-encompassing ideology were the talismans of the day. Communism and fascism had their

acute doctrinal differences, but their structural similarities—a single leader, a single party, a single body of infallible dogma, a single mass of obedient followers—meant that each in the end had more in common with the other than with democracy, as Hitler and Stalin acknowledged in August 1939.

The choice in the 1930s seemed bleak: either political democracy with economic chaos or economic planning with political tyranny. Roosevelt's distinctive contribution was to reject this either/or choice. The point of the New Deal was to chart and vindicate a middle way between laissez-faire and totalitarianism. When the biographer Emil Ludwig asked FDR to define his "political motive," Roosevelt replied, "My desire[is] to obviate revolution. . . . I work in a contrary sense to Rome and Moscow."

Accepting renomination in 1936, FDR spoke of people under economic stress in other lands who had sold their heritage of freedom for the illusion of a living. "Only our success," he continued, "can stir their ancient hope. They begin to know that here in America we are waging a great and successful war. It is not alone a war against want and destitution and economic demoralization. It is more than that: it is a war for the survival of democracy. We are fighting to save a great and precious form of government for ourselves and for the world."

Many people around the world thought it a futile fight. Let us not underestimate the readiness by 1940 of Europeans, including leading politicians and intellectuals, to come to terms with a Hitler-dominated Europe. Even some Americans thought the downfall of democracy inevitable. As Nazi divisions stormed that spring across Scandinavia, the Low Countries, and France, the faint-hearted saw totalitarianism, in the title of a poisonous little book published in the summer by Anne Morrow Lindbergh, a book that by December 1940 had rushed through seven American printings, as "the wave of the future." While her husband, the famous aviator, predicted Nazi victory and opposed American aid to Britain, the gentle Mrs. Lindbergh lamented "the beautiful things . . . lost in the dying of an age," saw totalitarianism as democracy's predestined successor, a "new, and perhaps even ultimately good, conception of humanity trying to come to birth," discounted the evils of Hitlerism and Stalinism as merely "scum on the wave of the future," and concluded that "the wave of the future is coming and there is no fighting it." For a while Mrs. Lindbergh seemed to be right. Fifty years ago there were only twelve democracies left on the planet.

Roosevelt, however, believed in fighting the wave of the future. He still labored under domestic constraints. The American people were predominantly against Hitler. But they were also, and for a while more strongly, against war. I believe that FDR himself, unlike the hawks of 1941— Stimson, Morgenthau, Hopkins, Ickes, Knox— was in no hurry to enter the European conflict. He remembered what Wilson had told him when he himself had been a young hawk a quarter-century before: that a President could commit no greater mistake than to take a divided country into war. He also no doubt wanted to minimize American casualties and to avoid breaking political promises. But probably by the autumn of 1941 FDR had finally come to believe that American participation was necessary if Hitler was to be beaten. An increasing number of Americans were reaching the same conclusion. Pearl Harbor in any case united the country, and Hitler then solved another of FDR's problems by declaring war on the United States.

We accepted war in 1941, as we had done in 1917, in part because, as Theodore Roosevelt had written in 1910, if Britain ever failed to preserve the European balance of power, "the United States would be obliged to get in . . . in order to restore the balance." But restoration of the balance of power did not seem in 1941, any more than it had in 1917, sufficient reason to send young men to kill and die. In 1941 FDR provided higher and nobler aims by resurrecting the Wilsonian vision in the Four Freedoms and the Atlantic Charter and by proceeding, while the war was on, to lay the foundations for the postwar reconstruction of the world along Wilsonian lines.

I assume that it will not be necessary to linger with a theory that had brief currency in the immediate postwar years, the theory that Roosevelt's great failing was his subordination of political to military objectives, shoving long-term considerations aside in the narrow interest of victory. FDR was in fact the most political of politicians, political in every reflex and to his fingertips—and just as political in war as he had been in peace. As a virtuoso politician he perfectly understood that there could be no better cloak for the pursuit of political objectives in wartime than the claim of total absorption in winning the war. He had plenty of political objectives all the same.

The war, he believed, would lead to historic transformations around the world. "Roosevelt," Harriman recalled, "enjoyed thinking aloud on the tremendous changes he saw ahead—the end of colonial empires and the rise of newly independent nations across the sweep of Africa and Asia." FDR told Churchill, "A new period has opened in the world's history, and you will have to adjust yourself to it." He tried to persuade the British to leave India and to stop the French from returning to Indochina, and he pressed the idea of UN trusteeships as the means of dismantling empires and preparing colonies for independence.

Soviet Russia, he saw, would emerge as a major power. FDR has suffered much criticism in supposedly thinking he could charm Stalin into postwar collaboration. Perhaps FDR was not so naive after all in concentrating on Stalin. The Soviet dictator was hardly the helpless prisoner of Marxist-Leninist ideology. He saw himself not as a disciple of Marx and Lenin but as their fellow prophet. Only Stalin had the power to rewrite the Soviet approach to world affairs; after all, he had already rewritten Soviet ideology and Soviet history. FDR was surely right in seeing Stalin as the only lever capable of overturning the Leninist doctrine of irrevocable hostility between capitalism and communism. As Walter Lippmann once observed, Roosevelt was too cynical to think he could charm Stalin. "He distrusted everybody. What he thought he could do was to outwit Stalin, which is quite a different thing."

Roosevelt failed to save Eastern Europe from communism, but that could not have been achieved by diplomatic methods alone. With the Red Army in control of Eastern Europe and a war still to be won against Japan, there was not much the West could do to prevent Stalin's working his will in countries adjacent to the Soviet Union. But Roosevelt at Yalta persuaded Stalin to sign American-drafted Declarations on Liberated Europe and on Poland—declarations that laid down standards by which the world subsequently measured Stalin's behavior in Eastern Europe and found it wanting. And FDR had prepared a fallback position in case things went wrong: not only tests that, if Stalin failed to meet them, would justify a change in policy but also a great army, a network of overseas bases, plans for peacetime universal military training, and the Anglo-American monopoly of the atomic bomb.

In the longer run Roosevelt anticipated that time would bring a narrowing of differences between democratic and Communist societies. He once told Sumner Welles that marking American democracy as one hundred and Soviet communism as zero, the American system, as it moved away from laissez-faire, might eventually reach sixty, and the Soviet system, as it moved toward democracy, might eventually reach forty. The theory of convergence provoked much derision in the Cold War years. Perhaps it looks better now.

So perhaps does his idea of making China one of the Four Policemen of the peace. Churchill, with his scorn for "the pigtails," dismissed Roosevelt's insistence on China as the "Great American Illusion." But Roosevelt was not really deluded. As he said at Teheran, he wanted China there "not because he did not realize the weakness of China at present, but he was thinking farther into the future." At Malta he told Churchill that it would take "three generations of education and training . . . before China could become a serious factor." Today, two generations later, much rests on involving China in the global web of international institutions.

As for the United States, a great concern in the war years was that the country might revert to iso-

lationism after the war just as it had done a quarter-century before—a vivid memory for FDR's generation. Contemplating Republican gains in the 1942 midterm election, Cordell Hull told Henry Wallace that the country was "going in exactly the same steps it followed in 1918." FDR himself said privately, "Anybody who thinks that isolationism is dead in this country is crazy."

He regarded American membership in a permanent international organization, in Charles Bohlen's words, as "the only device that could keep the United States from slipping back into isolationism." And true to the Wilsonian vision, he saw such an organization even more significantly as the only device that could keep the world from slipping back into war. He proposed the Declaration of the United Nations three weeks after Pearl Harbor, and by 1944 he was grappling with the problem that had defeated Wilson: how to reconcile peace enforcement by an international organization with the American Constitution. For international peace enforcement requires armed force ready to act swiftly on the command of the organization, while the Constitution requires (or, in better days, required) the consent of Congress before American troops can be sent into combat against a sovereign state. Roosevelt probably had confidence that the special agreements provided for in Article 43 of the UN Charter would strike a balance between the UN's need for prompt action and Congress's need to retain its war-making power and that the great-power veto would further protect American interests.

He moved in other ways to accustom the American people to a larger international role—and at the same time to assure American predominance in the postwar world. By the end of 1944 he had sponsored a series of international conferences designed to plan vital aspects of the future. These conferences, held mostly at American initiative and dominated mostly by American agendas, offered the postwar blueprints for international organization (Dumbarton Oaks), for world finance, trade, and development (Bretton Woods), for food and agriculture (Hot Springs), for relief and rehabilitation (Washington), for civil aviation (Chicago). In his sweeping and sometimes grandiose asides, FDR envisaged plans for regional development with environmental protection in the Middle East and elsewhere, and his Office of the Coordinator for Inter-American Affairs pioneered economic and technical assistance to developing countries. Upon his death in 1945 FDR left an imaginative and comprehensive framework for American leadership in making a better world—an interesting achievement for a President who was supposed to subordinate political to military goals.

New times bring new perspectives. In the harsh light of the Cold War some of FDR's policies and expectations were condemned as naive or absurd or otherwise misguided. The end of the Cold War may cast those policies and expectations in a somewhat different light.

FDR's purpose, I take it, was to find ways to safeguard the historic life-interests of the Republic—national security at home and a democratic environment abroad—in a world undergoing vast and fundamental transformations. This required policies based on a grasp of the currents of history and directed to the protection of U.S. interests and to the promotion of democracy elsewhere. From the vantage point of 1994, FDR met this challenge fairly well.

Take a look at the Atlantic Charter fifty years after. Is not the world therein outlined by Roosevelt and Churchill at last coming to pass? Consider the goals of August 1941—"the right of all peoples to choose the form of government under which they will live," equal access "to the trade and to the raw materials of the world," "improved labor standards, economic advancement and social security," assurance that all "may live

their lives in freedom from fear and want," relief from "the crushing burden of armaments," establishment of a community of nations. Is this not the agenda on which most nations today are at last agreed?

Does not most of the world now aspire to FDR's Four Freedoms? Has not what used to be the Soviet Union carried its movement toward the West even more rapidly than FDR dared contemplate? Has not China emerged as the "serious factor" FDR predicted? Did not the Yalta accords call for precisely the democratic freedoms to which Eastern Europe aspires today? Has not the UN, at last liberated by the end of the Cold War to pursue the goals of the founders, achieved new salience as the world's best hope for peace and cooperation?

Consider the world of 1994. It is manifestly not Adolf Hitler's world. The thousand-year Reich turned out to have a brief and bloody run of a dozen years. It is manifestly not Joseph Stalin's world. That world disintegrated before our eyes, rather like the Deacon's one-hoss shay. Nor is it Winston Churchill's world. Empire and its glories have long since vanished into the past.

The world we live in today is Franklin Roosevelt's world. Of the figures who, for good or for evil, bestrode the narrow world half a century ago, he would be the least surprised by the shape of things at the end of the century. Far more than the rest, he possessed what William James called a "sense of futurity." For all his manifold foibles, flaws, follies, and there was a sufficiency of all of those, FDR deserves supreme credit as the twentieth-century statesman who saw most deeply into the grand movements of history.

STUDY QUESTIONS

1. Why has it been difficult for historians to define a singular FDR?

2. How does Schlesinger "understand" FDR? Why?

3. What events/influences shaped FDR's perception of "national interest?" What historical contexts made this important?

4. How have historians disagreed in their explanations of FDR's involvement in the "global community?" What does Schlesinger propose as an explanation?

5. What were FDR's goals for World War II? What did American involvement achieve? Describe his legacy for American foreign diplomacy.

BIBLIOGRAPHY

Classic works that remain invaluable to the study of FDR include Arthur M. Schlesinger's three volume series "The Age of Roosevelt." See *The Crisis of the Old Order* (1957), *The Coming of the New Deal* (1959), and *The Politics of Upheaval* (1960). Also, for a general survey of the Roosevelt years, see William E Leuchtenburg, *Franklin D. Roosevelt and the New Deal, 1932-1940* (1963). For FDR's legacy and postwar America, see Dewey Grantham *Recent America: The United States Since 1945* (1987). Works on American foreign diplomacy include, Robert H. Ferrell, *America as a World Power, 1872-1945* (1971), Gaddis Smith, *American Diplomacy During the Second World War, 1941-1945* (1985), and Gary Donaldson, *America at War Since 1945: Politics and Diplomacy in Korea, Vietnam, and the Gulf War* (1996). Finally, two competing interpretations of the war at home, John M. Blum, *V was for Victory: Politics and American Culture during World War II* (1976) and Richard Polenburg, *War and Society: The United States, 1941-1945* (1972).

READING 17

THE BLACK BLIZZARDS ROLL IN
Donald Worster

Early in 1935 clouds black as night began to rumble across the southern plains. These waves of dirt rose from the ground, sometimes to a height of 7,000 or 8,000 feet, and they obscured the sun. They filled streets and houses with dirt, sand-blasted paint from automobiles, covered the exposed faces of men and women with a layer of grime. All the while they kept moving, some making their way to the Atlantic seaboard and the ocean beyond. The year before they had dumped millions of pounds of dirt on Boston, New York, Washington, and Atlanta; ship captains 300 miles out in the Atlantic reported decks coated with dust. They were part of the worst ecological disaster in the 1930s—the "dirty thirties"—part of what came to be known simply as the Dust Bowl.

Nature helped form the Dust Bowl, but humans made it. The ecology of the high plains had always been fragile, but farmers had moved into the area and exploited the land, transforming millions of acres of grasslands into wheat fields. They over-planted, used the wrong sort of plows, and prayed for plenty of rain. But in an area known more for drought than rain, they badly miscalculated. Soon strong winds lifted the dry top soil and sent it east, leaving dust pneumonia, ruined crops, and shattered lives in its wake.

While Franklin D. Roosevelt's New Deal confronted the economic and physical costs of the Dust Bowl, artists focused on the human suffering. Pare Lorentz's documentary *The Plow That Broke the Plains,* Woody Guthrie's song "The Great Dust Bowl," Alexandre Hogue's painting "Drouth Survivors," and John Steinbeck's novel *The Grapes of Wrath* were all inspired by the Dust Bowl. In the following essay historian Donald Worster eloquently describes what the dust storms looked, tasted, smelled, and felt like. People who lived through such a storm, where, as one writer observed, "Lady Godiva could ride thru streets without even the horse seeing her," did not soon forget the experience.

The thirties began in economic depression and in drought. The first of those disasters usually gets all the attention, although for the many Americans living on farms drought was the more serious problem. In the spring of 1930 over 3 million men and women were out of work. They had lost their jobs or had been laid off without pay in the aftermath of the stock market crash of the preceding fall. Another 12 million would suffer the same fate in the following two years. Many of the unemployed had no place to live, nor even the means to buy food. They slept in public toilets, under bridges, in shantytowns along the railroad tracks, or on doorsteps, and in the most wretched cases they scavenged from garbage cans—a Calcutta existence in the richest nation ever. The farmer, in contrast, was slower to feel the impact of the crash. He usually had his own independent food supply and stood a bit aloof from the ups and downs of the urban-industrial system. In the twenties that aloofness had meant that most farm families had not fully shared in the giddy burst of affluence—in new washing machines, silk stockings, and shiny roadsters. They had, in fact, spent much of the decade in economic doldrums. Now, as banks began to fail and soup lines formed, rural Americans went on as before, glad to be spared the latest reversal and just a little pleased to see their proud city cousins humbled. Then the droughts began, and they brought the farmers to their knees, too.

During the spring and summer of 1930, little rain fell over a large part of the eastern United States. A horizontal band on the map, from Maryland and Virginia to Missouri and Arkansas, marked the hardest hit area of wilting crops, shrinking groundwater supplies, and uncertain income. Over the summer months in this drought band the rainfall shortage was 60,000 tons for each 100-acre farm, or 700 tons a day. Seventeen million people were affected. In twelve states the drought set record lows in precipitation, and

among all the Eastern states only Florida was above normal. Three years earlier the Mississippi River had overflowed its banks and levees in one of the most destructive floods in American history. Now captains there wondered how long their barges would remain afloat as the river shrank to a fraction of its average height.

During the thirties serious drought threatened a great part of the nation. The persistent center, however, shifted from the East to the Great Plains, beginning in 1931, when much of Montana and the Dakotas became almost as arid as the Sonoran Desert. Farmers there and almost everywhere else watched the scorched earth crack open, heard the gray grass crunch underfoot, and worried about how long they would be able to pay their bills. Around their dried-up ponds the willows and wild cherries were nearly leafless, and even the poison ivy dropped. Drought, of course, is a relative term: it depends upon one's concept of "normal." But following the lead of the climatologists of the time, we can use a precipitation deficiency of at least 15 percent of the historical mean to qualify as drought. By that standard, of all the American states only Maine and Vermont escaped a drought year from 1930 to 1936. Twenty states set or equaled record lows for their entire span of official weather data. Over the nation as a whole, the 1930s drought was, in the words of a Weather Bureau scientist, "the worst in the climatological history of the country."

Intense heat accompanied the drought, along with economic losses the nation could ill afford. In the summer of 1934, Nebraska reached 118 degrees, Iowa, 115. In Illinois thermometers stuck at over 100 degrees for so long that 370 people died—and one man, who had been living in a refrigerator to keep cool, was treated for frostbite. Two years later, when the country was described by *Newsweek* as "a vast simmering caldron," more than 4,500 died from excessive heat, water was shipped into the West by diverted tank-cars and oil pipelines, and clouds of grasshoppers ate what little remained of many farmers' wheat and corn—along with their fence posts and the washing on their clotheslines. The financial cost of the

From *The Dust Bowl: Southern Plains 1930's* by Daniel Worster, © 1979 Oxford University Press, Inc. Used by permission of the publisher.

1934 drought alone amounted to one-half the money the United States had put into World War I. By 1936, farm losses had reached $25 million a day, and more than 2 million farmers were drawing relief checks. Rexford Tugwell, head of the Resettlement Administration, who toured the burning plains that year, saw "a picture of complete destruction"—"one of the most serious peacetime problems in the nation's history."

As the decade reached its midpoint, it was the southern plains that experienced the most severe conditions. During some growing seasons there was no soil moisture down to three feet over large parts of the region. By 1939, near Hays, Kansas, the accumulated rainfall deficiency was more than 34 inches—almost a two-year supply in arrears. Continued long enough in such a marginal, semiarid land, a drought of that magnitude would produce a desert. Weathermen pointed out that there had been worse single years, as in 1910 and 1917, or back in the 1890s, and they repeatedly assured the people of the region that their records did not show any modern drought lasting more than five years, nor did they suggest any long-range adverse climatic shift. But farmers and ranchers did not find much comfort in statistical charts; their cattle were bawling for feed, and their bank credit was drying up along with the soil. Not until after 1941 did the rains return in abundance and the burden of anxiety lift.

Droughts are an inevitable fact of life on the plains, an extreme one occurring roughly every twenty years, and milder ones every three or four. They have always brought with them blowing dust where the ground was bare of crops or native grass. Dust was so familiar an event that no one was surprised to see it appear when the dry weather began in 1931. But no one was prepared for what came later: dust storms of such violence that they made the drought only a secondary problem—storms of such destructive force that they left the region reeling in confusion and fear.

"Earth" is the word we use when it is there in place, growing the food we eat, giving us a place to stand and build on. "Dust" is what we say when it is loose and blowing on the wind. Nature en-compasses both—the good and the bad from our perspective, and from that of all living things. We need the earth to stay alive, but dust is a nuisance, or, worse, a killer. On a planet such as ours, where there is much wind, where there are frequent dry spells, and where we encounter vast expanses of bare soil, dust is a constant presence. It rises from the hooves of animals, from a wagon's wheels, from a dry riverbed, from the deserts. If all the continents were an English greensward, there would be no dust. But nature has not made things so. Nor has man, in many times and places.

Dust in the air is one phenomenon. However, dust storms are quite another. The story of the southern plains in the 1930s is essentially about dust storms, when the earth ran amok. And not once or twice, but over and over for the better part of a decade: day after day, year after year, of sand rattling against the window, of fine powder caking one's lips, of springtime turned to despair, of poverty eating into self-confidence.

Explaining why those storms occurred requires an excursion into the history of the plains and an understanding of the agriculture that evolved there. For the "dirty thirties," as they were called, were primarily the work of man, not nature. Admittedly, nature had something to do with this disaster too. Without winds the soil would have stayed put, no matter how bare it was. Without drought, farmers would have had strong, healthy crops capable of checking the wind. But natural factors did not make the storms—they merely made them possible. The storms were mainly the result of stripping the landscape of its natural vegetation to such an extent that there was no defense against the dry winds, no sod to hold the sandy or powdery dirt. The sod had been destroyed to make farms to grow wheat to get cash. But more of that later on. It is the storms themselves we must first comprehend: their magnitude, their effect, even their taste and smell. What was it like to be caught in one of them? How much did the people suffer, and how did they cope?

Weather bureau stations on the plains reported a few small dust storms throughout 1932, as many as 179 in April 1933, and in November of that year a large one that carried all the way to Georgia and New York. But it was the May 1934 blow that swept in a new dark age. On 9 May, brown earth from Montana and Wyoming swirled up from the ground, was captured by extremely high-level winds, and was blown eastward toward the Dakotas. More dirt was sucked into the airstream, until 350 million tons were riding toward urban America. By late afternoon the storm had reached Dubuque and Madison, and by evening 12 million tons of dust were falling like snow over Chicago—4 pounds for each person in the city. Midday at Buffalo on 10 May was darkened by dust, and the advancing gloom stretched south from there over several states, moving as fast as 100 miles an hour. The dawn of 11 May found the dust settling over Boston, New York, Washington, and Atlanta, and then the storm moved out to sea. Savannah's skies were hazy all day 12 May; it was the last city to report dust conditions. But there were still ships in the Atlantic, some of them 300 miles off the coast, that found dust on their decks during the next day or two.

"Kansas dirt," the New York press called it, though it actually came from farther north. More would come that year and after, and some of it was indeed from Kansas—or Nebraska or New Mexico. In a later spring, New Hampshire farmers, out to tap their maples, discovered a fresh brown snow on the ground, discoloration from transported Western soil. Along the Gulf Coast, at Houston and Corpus Christi, dirt from the Llano Estacado collected now and then on windowsills and sidewalks. But after May 1934 most of the worst dust storms were confined to the southern plains region; less frequently were they carried by those high-altitude currents moving east or southeast. Two types of dusters became common then: the dramatic "black blizzards" and the more frequent "sand blows." The first came with a rolling turbulence, rising like a long wall of muddy water as high as 7,000 or 8,000 feet. Like the winter blizzards to which they were compared, these dusters were caused by the arrival of a polar continental air mass, and the atmospheric electricity

it generated helped lift the dirt higher and higher in a cold boil, sometimes accompanied by thunder and lightning, other times by an eerie silence. Such storms were not only terrifying to observers, but immensely destructive to the region's fine, dark soils, rich in nutrients. The second kind of duster was a more constant event, created by the low sirocco-like winds that blew out of the southwest and left the sandier soils drifted into dunes along fence rows and ditches. Long after New York and Philadelphia had forgotten their taste of the plains, the people out there ate their own dirt again and again.

In the 1930s the Soil Conservation Service compiled a frequency chart of all dust storms of regional extent, when visibility was cut to less than a mile. In 1932 there were 14; in 1933, 38; 1934, 22; 1935, 40; 1936, 68; 1937, 72; 1938, 61—dropping as the drought relented a bit— 1939, 30; 1940, 17; 1941, 17. Another measure of severity was made by calculating the total number of hours the dust storms lasted during a year. By that criterion 1937 was again the worst: at Guymon, in the panhandle of Oklahoma, the total number of hours that year climbed to 550, mostly concentrated in the first six months of the year. In Amarillo the worst year was 1935, with a total of 908 hours. Seven times, from January to March, the visibility there reached zero—all complete blackouts, one of them lasting eleven hours. A single storm might rage for one hour or three and a half days. Most of the winds came from the southwest, but they also came from the west, north, and northeast, and they could slam against windows and walls with 60 miles-per-hour force. The dirt left behind on the front lawn might be brown, black, yellow, ashy gray, or, more rarely, red, depending upon its source. And each color had its own peculiar aroma, from a sharp peppery smell that burned the nostrils to a heavy greasiness that nauseated.

In the memory of older plains residents, the blackest year was 1935, particularly the early spring weeks from 1 March to mid-April, when the Dust Bowl made its full-blown debut. Springtime in western Kansas can be a Willa Cather world of meadowlarks on the wing, clean white curtains dancing in the breeze, anemones and wild verbena in bloom, lilacs by the porch, a windmill spinning briskly, and cold fresh water in the bucket—but not in 1935. After a February heat wave (it reached 75 degrees in Topeka that month), the dust began moving across Kansas, Oklahoma, and Texas, and for the next six weeks it was unusual to see a clear sky from dawn until sundown. On 15 March, Denver reported that a serious dust storm was speeding eastward. Kansans ignored the radio warnings, went about their business as usual, and later wondered what had hit them. Small-town printer Nate White was at the picture show when the dust reached Smith Center: as he walked out the exit, it was as if someone had put a blindfold over his eyes; he bumped into telephone poles, skinned his shins on boxes and cans in an alleyway, fell to his hands and knees, and crawled along the curbing to a dim houselight. A seven-year-old boy wandered away and was lost in the gloom; the search party found him later, suffocated in a drift. A more fortunate child was found alive, tangled in a barbed wire fence. Near Colby, a train was derailed by dirt on the tracks, and the passengers spent twelve dreary hours in the coaches. The Lora-Locke Hotel in Dodge City overflowed with more than two hundred stranded travelers; many of them bedded down on cots in the lobby and ballroom. In the following days, as the dust kept falling, electric lights burned continuously, cars left tracks in the dirt-covered streets, and schools and offices stayed closed. A reporter at Great Bend remarked on the bizarre scene: "Uncorked jug placed on sidewalk two hours, found to be half filled with dust. Picture wires giving way due to excessive weight of dust on frames. Irreparable loss in portraits anticipated. Lady Godiva could ride thru streets without even the horse seeing her."

The novelty of this duster, so like a coffee-colored winter snow, made it hard for most people to take it seriously. But William Allen White, the Emporia editor, called it "the greatest show" since Pompeii was buried in ashes. And a Garden City woman described her experience for the *Kansas City Times*:

All we could do about it was just sit in our dusty chairs, gaze at each other through the fog that filled the room and watch that fog settle slowly and silently, covering everything— including ourselves—in a thick, brownish gray blanket. When we opened the door swirling whirlwinds of soil beat against us unmerci- fully. . . . The door and windows were all shut tightly, yet those tiny particles seemed to seep through the very walls. It got into cupboards and clothes closets; our faces were as dirty as if we had rolled in the dirt; our hair was gray and stiff and we ground dirt between our teeth.

By the end of the month conditions had become so unrelenting that many Kansans had begun to chew their nails. "Watch for the Second Coming of Christ," warned one of Topeka's unhinged, "God is wrathful." Street-corner sects in Hill City and other towns warned pedestrians to heed the signs of the times. A slightly less frenetic Concordian jotted in her log: "This is ultimate darkness. So must come the end of the world." The mood of the people had begun to change, if not to apocalyptic dread in every case, at least to a fear that this was a night-mare that might never end.

By 24 March southeastern Colorado and west-ern Kansas had seen twelve consecutive days of dust storms, but there was worse to come. Near the end of March a new duster swept across the southern plains, destroying one-half the wheat crop in Kansas, one-quarter of it in Oklahoma, and all of it in Nebraska—5 million acres blown out. The storm carried away from the plains twice as much earth as men and machines had scooped out to make the Panama Canal, deposit-ing it once again over the East Coast states and the Atlantic Ocean. Then the wind slackened off a bit, gathering strength, as it were, for the spec-tacular finale of that unusual spring season— Black Sunday, 14 April.

Dawn came clear and rosy all across the plains that day. By noon the skies were so fresh and blue that people could not remain indoors; they remembered how many jobs they had been postponing, and with a revived spirit they rushed outside to get them done. They went on picnics, planted gardens, repaired henhouses, attended funerals, drove to the neighbors for a visit. In midafternoon the summery air rapidly turned colder, falling as many as 50 degrees in a few hours, and the people noticed then that the yards were full of birds nervously fluttering and chattering—and more were arriving every moment, as though fleeing from some unseen enemy. Suddenly there appeared on the northern horizon a black blizzard, moving toward them; there was no sound, no wind, nothing but an immense "boogery" cloud. The storm struck Dodge City at 2:40 p.m. Not far from there John Garretson, a farmer in Haskell County, Kansas, who was on the road with his wife, Louise, saw it coming, but he was sure that he could beat it home. They had almost made it when they were engulfed; abandoning the car, they groped for the fencewire and, hand over hand, followed it to their door. Down in the panhandle Ed and Ada Phillips of Boise City, with their six-year-old daughter, were on their way home too, after an outing to Texline in their Model A Ford. It was about five o'clock when the black wall appeared, and they still had fifteen miles to go. Seeing an old adobe house ahead, Ed realized that they had to take shelter, and quickly. By the time they were out of the car the dust was upon them, making it so dark that they nearly missed the door. Inside they found ten other people, stranded, like themselves, in a two-room hut, all fearing that they might be smothered, all unable to see their companions' faces. For four hours they sat there, until the storm let up enough for them to follow the roadside ditch back to town. By then the ugly pall was moving south across the high plains of Texas and New Mexico.

Older residents still remember Black Sunday in all its details—where they were when the storm hit, what they did then. Helen Wells was the wife of the Reverend Rolley Wells, the Methodist minister in Guymon. Early that morning she had

helped clean the accumulated dust from the church pews, working until she was choking and exhausted. Back in the parsonage she switched on the radio for some inspiring music, and what she heard was the hymn "We'll Work Till Jesus Comes." "I just had to sit down and laugh," she recalls; she had worn out her sweeper but still had a broom if that was needed. Later that day her husband, partly to please two visiting *Saturday Evening Post* reporters, held a special "rain service," which concluded in time for the congregation to get home before the dust arrived.

A Kansas cattle dealer, Raymond Ellsaesser, almost lost his wife that day. She had gone into Sublette with her young daughter for a Rebekah lodge meeting. On the way home she stopped along the highway, unable to see even the winged hood ornament on her car. The static electricity in the storm then shorted out her ignition, and, foolishly, she determined to walk the three-quarters of a mile home. Her daughter plunged ahead to get Raymond's help, and he quickly piled into a truck and drove back down the road, hallooing out the window. Back and forth he passed, but his wife had disappeared into the fog-like dust, wandering straight away from the car into the field, where she stumbled about with absolutely no sense of direction. Each time she saw the truck's headlights she moved that way, not realizing her husband was in motion too. It was only by sheer luck that she found herself at last standing in the truck's beams, gasping for air and near collapse.

The last of the major dust storms that year was on 14 April, and it was months before the damages could be fully calculated. Those who had been caught outside in one of the spring dusters were, understandably, most worried about their lungs. An epidemic of respiratory infections and something called "dust pneumonia" broke out across the plains. The four small hospitals in Meade County, Kansas, found that 52 percent of their April admissions were acute respiratory cases—thirty-three patients died. Many dust victims would arrive at a hospital almost dead, after driving long distances in a storm. They spat up clods of dirt, washed the mud out of their mouths, swabbed their nostrils with Vaseline, and rinsed their bloodshot eyes with boric acid water. Old people and babies were the most vulnerable to the dusters, as were those who had chronic asthma, bronchitis, or tuberculosis, some of whom had moved to the plains so they might breathe the high, dry air.

Doctors could not agree on whether the dust caused a new kind of pneumonia, and some even denied that there were any unusual health problems in their communities. But the Red Cross thought the situation was so serious that it set up six emergency hospitals in Kansas, Colorado, and Texas, and it staffed them with its own nurses. In Topeka and Wichita volunteers worked in high school sewing rooms to make dust masks of cheesecloth; over 17,000 of those masks were sent to the plains, especially to towns where goggles had been sold out. Chewing tobacco was a better remedy, snorted some farmers, who thought it was too much of a bother to wear such gadgets when driving their tractors. But enough wore the Red Cross masks or some other protection to make the plains look like a World War I battlefield, with dust instead of mustard gas coming out of the trenches.

On 29 April the Red Cross sponsored a conference of health officers from several states. Afterward the representatives of the Kansas Board of Health went to work on the medical problem in more detail, and eventually they produced a definitive study on the physiological impact of the dust storms. From 21 February to 30 April they counted 28 days of "dense" dust at Dodge City and only 13 days that were "dust free." Dirt deposited in bakepans during the five biggest storms gave an estimated 4.7 tons of total fallout per acre. Agar plate cultures showed "no pathogenic organisms" in the accumulation, only harmless soil bacteria, plant hair, and microfungus spores. But the inorganic content of the dust was mainly fine silicon particles, along with bits of feldspar, volcanic ash, and calcite; and "silica," they warned, "is as much a body poison as is lead"—"probably the most widespread and insid-

ious of all hazards in the environment of mankind," producing, after sufficient contact, silicosis of the lungs. These scientists also found that a measles outbreak had come with the black blizzards, though why that happened was not clear; in only five months there were twice as many cases as in any previous twelve-month period. The death rate from acute respiratory infections in the 45 western counties of Kansas, where the dust was most intense, was 99 per 100,000, compared with the statewide average of 70; and the infant mortality was 80.5, compared with the state's 62.3.

The medical remedies for the dust were at best primitive and makeshift. In addition to wearing light gauze masks, health officials recommended attaching translucent glasscloth to the inside frames of windows, although people also used cardboard, canvas, or blankets. Hospitals covered some of their patients with wet sheets, and housewives flapped the air with wet dish towels to collect dust. One of the most common tactics was to stick masking tape, felt strips, or paraffin-soaked rags around the windows and door cracks. The typical plains house was loosely constructed and without insulation, but sometimes those methods proved so effective that there was not enough air circulation inside to replenish the oxygen supply. Warren Moore of southwestern Kansas remembers watching, during a storm, the gas flame on the range steadily turn orange and the coal-oil lamp dim until the people simply had to open the window, dust or no dust. But most often there was no way to seal out the fine, blowing dirt: it blackened the pillow around one's head, the dinner plates on the table, the bread dough on the back of the stove. It became a steady part of one's diet and breathing. "We thrived on it," claim some residents today; it was their "vitamin K." But all the same they prayed that they would not ingest so much it would maim them for life, or finish them off, as it had a neighbor or two.

Livestock and wildlife did not have even those crude defenses. "In a rising sand storm," wrote Margaret Bourke-White, "cattle quickly become blinded. They run around in circles until they fall and breathe so much dust that they die. Autopsies show their lungs caked with dust and mud." Newborn calves could suffocate in a matter of hours, and the older cattle ground their teeth down to the gums trying to eat the dirt-covered grass. As the dust buried the fences, horses and cattle climbed over and wandered away. Where there was still water in rivers, the dust coated the surface and the fish died too. The carcasses of jackrabbits, small birds, and field mice lay along roadsides by the hundreds after a severe duster; and those that survived were in such shock that they could be picked up and their nostrils and eyes wiped clean. In a lighter vein, it was said that prairie dogs were now able to tunnel upward several feet from the ground.

Cleaning up houses, farm lots, and city stores after the 1935 blow season was an expensive matter. People literally shoveled the dirt from their front yards and swept up bushel-basketfuls inside. One man's ceiling collapsed from the silt that had collected in the attic. Carpets, draperies, and tapestries were so dust-laden that their patterns were indiscernible. Painted surfaces had been sandblasted bare. Automobile and tractor engines operated in dust storms without oil-bath air cleaners were ruined by grit, and the repair shops had plenty of business. During March alone, Tucumcari, New Mexico, reported over $288,000 in property damage, although most towns' estimates were more conservative than that: Liberal, Kansas, $150,000; Randall County, Texas, $10,000; Lamar, Colorado, $3,800. The merchants of Amarillo calculated from 3 to 15 percent damage to their merchandise, not to mention the loss of shoppers during the storms. In Dodge City a men's clothing store advertised a "dust sale," knocking shirts down to 75 cents. But the heaviest burdens lay on city work crews, who had to sweep dirt from the gutters and municipal swimming pools, and on housewives, who struggled after each blow to get their houses clean.

The emotional expense was the hardest to accept, however. All day you could sit with your hands folded on the oilcloth-covered table, the wind moaning around the eaves, the fine, soft, talc sifting in the keyholes, the sky a coppery gloom; and when you went to bed the acrid dust crept into your dreams. Avis Carlson told what it was like at night:

A trip for water to rinse the grit from our lips. And then back to bed with washcloths over our noses. We try to lie still, because every turn stirs the dust on the blankets. After a while, if we are good sleepers, we forget.

After 1935 the storms lost much of their drama; for most people they were simply a burden to be endured, and sometimes that burden was too heavy. Druggists sold their supplies of sedatives quickly. An Oklahoman took down his shotgun, ready to kill his entire family and himself—"we're all better off dead," he despaired. That, to be sure, was an extreme instance, but there were indeed men and women who turned distraught, wept, and then, listless, gave up caring.

The plains people, however, then as now, were a tough-minded, leather-skinned folk, not easily discouraged. Even in 1935 they managed to laugh a bit at their misfortunes. They told about the farmer who fainted when a drop of water struck him in the face and had to be revived by having three buckets of sand thrown over him. They also passed around the one about the motorist who came upon a ten-gallon hat resting on a dust drift. Under it he found a head looking at him. "Can I help you some way?" the motorist asked, "Give you a ride into town maybe?" "Thanks, but I'll make it on my own," was the reply, "I'm on a horse." They laughed with Will Rogers when he pointed out that only highly advanced civilizations—like ancient Mesopotamia—were ever covered over by dirt, and that California would never qualify. Newspaper editors could still find something to joke about, too: "When better dust storms are made," the *Dodge City Globe* boasted, "the Southwest will make them." Children were especially hard to keep down; for them the storms always meant adventure, happy chaos, a breakdown of their teachers' authority, and perhaps a holiday. When darkness descends, as it did that April, humor, bravado, or a childlike irresponsibility may have as much value as a storm cellar.

Whether they brought laughter or tears, the dust storms that swept across the southern plains in the 1930s created the most severe environmental catastrophe in the entire history of the white man on this continent. In no other instance was there greater or more sustained damage to the American land, and there have been few times when so much tragedy was visited on its inhabitants. Not even the Depression was more devastating, economically. And in ecological terms we have nothing in the nation's past, nothing even in the polluted present, that compares. Suffice it to conclude here that in the decade of the 1930s the dust storms of the plains were an unqualified disaster.

At such dark times the mettle of a people is thoroughly and severely tested, revealing whether they have the will to go on. By this test the men and women of the plains were impressive, enduring, as most of them did, discouragements the like of which more recent generations have never had to face. But equally important, disasters of this kind challenge a society's capacity to think—require it to analyze and explain and learn from misfortune. Societies that fail this test are sitting ducks for more of the same. Those that pass, on the other hand, have attained through suffering and hardship a more mature, self-appraising character, so that they are more aware than before of their vulnerabilities and weaknesses. They are stronger because they have been made sensitive to their deficiencies. Whether the dust storms had this enlarging, critical effect on the minds of southern plainsmen remains to be seen.

STUDY QUESTIONS

1. When did the dust storms begin and when did they end? What areas of the country did they affect the most?

2. Describe the size, color, and smell of the dust storms. How long did they last? Were they uniform?

3. Describe the impact that the dust storms had on humans and animals. How did people cope with them?

4. What kinds of destruction did the dust storms cause?

BIBLIOGRAPHY

The above selection is from Donald Worster, *Dust Bowl: The Southern Plains In the 1930s* (1979), an award-winning study that combines passion and outrage with scholarly distance and fine writing. Also valuable are Paul Bonnifield, *The Dust Bowl: Men, Dirt, and Depression* (1979) and R. Douglas Hurt, *The Dust Bowl: An Agricultural and Social History* (1981). An outstanding overview of the Great Depression is Robert S. McElvaine, *The Great Depression* (1984). In their own ways, the works of John Steinbeck, Pare Lorentz, Woody Guthrie, and Alexandre Hogue also document the era of the Dust Bowl and the Depression.

NIGHT OF THE MARTIANS

Edward Oxford

It's a truism today that the mass media influences the lives of Americans. Society is constantly barraged with questions and criticism about such issues as the quality of children's television programming, the political bias of newscasters, the ethics of television advertising, the domination of political campaigns by the media, and the decline of literacy and the written word. More than any other technological innovation, the development first of radio and then of television has transformed American life, changing the way people live and relate to one another. The first radio station in the United States began broadcasting out of Pittsburgh in 1920. Three years later there were more than 500 stations doing the same thing, and by 1929 more than 12 million families listened to the radio at home every night. The communications revolution that radio stimulated contributed to the creation of a mass, national culture.

The influence of the radio, however, did not immediately dawn on people. In 1927 the National Broadcasting Company became the first national network, and by 1933 President Franklin D. Roosevelt was effectively using the radio for his famous "fireside chats." But it was not until 1938, when Orson Welles broadcast his famous "War of the Worlds" program, that Americans realized the potential of radio to shape public attitudes. With Adolf Hitler making his designs on Czechoslovakia well known, Americans were worried that another global conflict was in the making. Battered by the frustration of the Great Depression and nervous about the safety of the world, millions of people panicked when Orson Welles described over national radio an invasion of the East Coast by Martians. In the following essay, historian Edward Oxford describes the broadcast and the controversy it inspired.

A little after eight P.M. on Halloween eve 1938, thirteen-year-old Dick Stives, his sister, and two brothers huddled around their family's radio. They were in the dining room of their grandfather's farmhouse near the hamlet of Grovers Mill, four miles east of Princeton, New Jersey. Their mother and father had dropped them off there and gone to the movies.

Dick worked the radio dial, hunting for the station that carried the *Chase and Sanborn Hour,* his—and the nation's—favorite Sunday evening program. As he scanned the airwaves, Dick tuned in the local affiliate of the Columbia Broadcasting System (CBS). A commanding voice—that of Orson Welles—riveted his attention.

". . . across an immense ethereal gulf, minds that are to our minds as ours are to the beasts of the jungle, intellects vast, cool, and unsympathetic, regarded this earth with envious eyes and slowly and surely drew their plans against us. . . ."

Dick Stives turned the dial no further. Instead, during the next hour he and millions of other listeners sat glued by their radios, convinced by an alarming series of "news bulletins" that monster aliens from Mars were invading America. Dick's village of Grovers Mill—the supposed landing site for these invaders—became the focal point of a panic wave that rapidly swept across the nation.

The program—the *Mercury Theatre on the Air* adaptation of H. G. Wells's *The War of the Worlds*—would later be remembered as the most extraordinary radio show ever broadcast. And Orson Welles, its brilliant young producer, director, and star, would be catapulted to nationwide fame overnight.

As the wonder boy of the performing arts, Orson Welles had by age twenty-three already appeared on the cover of *Time* magazine; built a considerable reputation as a radio actor; set the stage world on its ear with a *Julius Caesar* set in Fascist Italy, an all-black *Macbeth,* and a production of Marc Blitzstein's opera *The Cradle Will Rock;* and founded—with his partner-in-drama John Houseman—the revolutionary and often controversial Mercury Theatre.[1]

In midsummer 1938, the Columbia Broadcasting System, impressed by Welles's meteoric success, offered him and his repertory company a grand stage, radio—"the Broadway of the entire United States"—on which to deliver a sixty-minute dramatization each week.

Broadcast from the twenty-second floor of the CBS building in midtown Manhattan, the *Mercury Theatre on the Air* had no commercial sponsor. The show was subsidized by the CBS network, and its bare-bones budget provided no money for expensive, original plays. "We offered the audience classic works from the public domain—*Julius Caesar, Oliver Twist, The Heart of Darkness, Jane Eyre,* and such," recalls John Houseman. "Orson and I would select the book. Sometimes it was my task to fashion the original into a workable radio script."

For the last program of October, the seventeenth in their series, Welles and Houseman wanted to "throw in something of a scientific nature." They settled on an adaptation of *The War of the Worlds,* a science-fiction novel written in 1898 by British author H. G. Wells. Houseman assigned the script to a recent addition to the company, writer Howard Koch.

For the fall season CBS had moved the *Mercury Theatre on the Air* from Monday evening to the Sunday night eight-to-nine-o'clock slot, an "unsold" time period. During this hour much of America tuned in to the competing NBC Red network for the *Chase and Sanborn Hour,* which featured ventriloquist Edgar Bergen and his

---

"Night of the Martians" by Edward Oxford. This article is reprinted from the October 1988 issue of *American History Illustrated* 23. pp. 14–23, 47–48 with the permission of Cowles History Group, Inc. Copyright *American History Ilustrated* magazine.

[1]Up to this time Welles was probably best known to radio audiences as "Lamont Cranston," alias "The Shadow," on the popular Sunday afternoon mystery program of the same name. But he also appeared frequently on many other shows including "The March of Time," and was said to be earning $1,000 a week from his radio commitments alone.

wooden-headed "dummy" Charlie McCarthy. The Crossley ratings of listenership gave Charlie McCarthy a "thirty-five" (roughly 35 percent of radio listeners at that hour tuned in), while the *Mercury* usually scored about "three."

During the week before the October 30 broadcast, Welles nonchalantly put in his own typically frantic week while Houseman, Koch, and the cast struggled to ready the show. Welles spent much of his time not in the CBS studios at 485 Madison Avenue, but on the stage of the Mercury Theatre on West 41st Street, rehearsing his repertory company for the opening of a new play. He hurried back to CBS at odd hours to try out some of his lines, listen to run-throughs by the radio show's cast, and render his inimitable revisions.

Welles and his company spent much of Sunday amid a litter of sandwiches and coffee cups in Studio One, adding final touches to their version of *The War of the Worlds* and conducting a dress rehearsal with full music and sound effects.

Just before eight P.M., Eastern Standard Time, Welles, conductor-like, stood poised on his platform in the middle of the studio. He had at his command not only his loyal band of actors, but also a small symphony orchestra. Wearing a headset, the multifaceted genius was prepared to read his own lines, cue the other actors, signal for sound effects, summon the orchestra, and also keep in touch with the control room.

At the stroke of eight o'clock, he gave the cue for the start of the *Mercury* theme—the Tchaikovsky Piano Concerto No. 1 in B-Flat Minor.

For the next unforgettable hour, Dick Stives at Grovers Mill, along with several million other Americans, sat transfixed as the airwaves brought word of weird and almost incomprehensible events that seemed to unfold with terrifying reality even as they listened.

It was not as though listeners hadn't been warned. Most simply didn't pay close attention to the program's opening signature (or tuned in a few seconds late and missed it altogether): "The Columbia Broadcasting System and its affiliated stations present Orson Welles and the Mercury Theatre on the Air in *The War of the Worlds* by H. G. Wells. . . ."

Many in the radio audience failed to associate what they heard with prior newspaper listings of the drama. And, by the time a single station break came late in the hour with reminders that listeners were hearing a fictional story, many others were too agitated to comprehend that they had been deceived.

Skillfully choreographed by Welles and Houseman, the program—a play simulating a montage of real-life dance band "remotes" and news bulletins—began with deliberate calm. Millions of listeners, conditioned by recent news reports of worldwide political turmoil—and by their inherent trust in the medium of radio—believed what they heard.

Just two minutes into the show, audience perception between fantasy and reality began to blur when, following Welles's dramatic opening monologue, the microphone shifted to a "network announcer" reading an apparently routine report from the "Government Weather Bureau."

Programming then shifted to "Ramon Raquello and his orchestra" in the "Meridian Room" at the "Hotel Park Plaza" in downtown New York City.

During rehearsals for the show, Welles had insisted—over the objections of his associates—on increasing the broadcast time devoted to the fictional orchestra's soothing renditions of "La Cumparsita" and "the ever-popular 'Stardust.'" As he had anticipated, the resulting "band remote" had a disarming air of reality—and provided emotional contrast to the intensity of later news bulletins.[2]

Just when Welles had calculated that listeners might start tuning out the music in search of something more lively, an announcer broke in with a bulletin from the "Intercontinental Radio News": "Professor Farrell of the Mount Jennings Observatory" near Chicago had reported observing "several explosions of incandescent gas occurring at regular intervals on the planet

---

[2]The format was a familiar one to radio listeners. "Big band remotes"—network broadcasts featuring America's best-known dance bands as they played at one-night stands in ballrooms from coast to coast—were a staple of broadcasting during the 1930s.

Mars. . . . The spectroscope indicates the gas to be hydrogen and moving towards the earth with tremendous velocity."

The dance music resumed, only to be interrupted repeatedly during the next several minutes by other bulletins. The tempo of events—and listeners' interest—began to intensify.

From a "remote pickup" at the "Princeton Observatory," reporter "Carl Phillips" interviewed famous astronomer "Richard Pierson" (played by Welles). As the clockwork of mechanism of his telescope ticked in the background, Professor Pierson described Mars as a red disk swimming in a blue sea. He said he could not explain the gas eruptions on that planet. But skeptical of anything that could not be explained by logic, the astronomer counted the chances against living intelligence on Mars as being "a thousand to one."

Then Phillips read a wire that had just been handed to Pierson: a seismograph at the "Natural History Museum" in New York had registered a "shock of almost earthquake intensity occurring within a radius of twenty miles of Princeton." Pierson played down any possible connection with the disturbances on Mars: "This is probably a meteorite of unusual size and its arrival at this particular time is merely a coincidence."

Again the program returned to music, followed by yet another bulletin: an astronomer in Canada had observed three explosions on Mars, confirming "earlier reports from American observatories."

"Now, nearer home," continued the announcer, "comes a special announcement from Trenton, New Jersey. It is reported that at 8:50 P.M. a huge, flaming object, believed to be a meteorite, fell on a farm in the neighborhood of Grovers Mill, New Jersey, twenty-two miles from Trenton. The flash in the sky was visible within a radius of several hundred miles and the noise of impact was heard as far north as Elizabeth."

Listeners leaned closer to their sets. In Grovers Mill, Dick Stives stared at the radio and gulped.

Again the broadcast returned to dance music—this time to "Bobby Millette and his orchestra" at the "Hotel Martinet" in Brooklyn. And again the music was interrupted by a news flash. Having just arrived at the scene of "impact" on the

"Wilmuth farm" near Grovers Mill, reporter Carl Phillips, accompanied by Professor Pierson, beheld police, state troopers, and onlookers crowding around what appeared to be a huge metallic cylinder, partially buried in the earth.

About this time, some twelve minutes into the broadcast, many listeners to the *Chase and Sanborn Hour,* momentarily bored by a guest musical spot, turned their dials. A lot of them stopped in sudden shock as they came upon the CBS wavelength. The events being described seemed real to listeners—quite as real to them as reports, not many months before, that Adolf Hitler's troops had marched into Austria.

"I wish I could convey the atmosphere . . . the background of this . . . fantastic scene," reported Phillips. "Hundreds of cars are parked in a field back of us. . . . Their headlights throw an enormous spot on the pit where the object is half-buried. Some of the more daring souls are venturing near the edge. Their silhouettes stand out against the metal sheen. . . ."

Professor Pierson described the object as "definitely extraterrestrial . . . not found on this earth. . . . This thing is smooth and, as you can see, of cylindrical shape." Then Phillips suddenly interrupted him:

"Just a minute! Something's happening! Ladies and gentlemen, this is terrific! The end of the thing is beginning to flake off! The top is beginning to rotate like a screw! The thing must be hollow! [shouts of alarm] Ladies and gentlemen, this is the most terrifying thing I have ever witnessed. . . . Wait a minute! Someone's crawling out of the hollow top. Someone or. . . . something. I can see peering out of that black hole two luminous disks—are they eyes? Good heavens, something's wriggling out of the shadow like a gray snake. . . . I can see the thing's body. It's large as a bear and it glistens like wet leather. But that face. It . . . it's indescribable. I can hardly force myself to keep looking at it. The eyes are black and gleam like a serpent. The mouth is V-shaped with saliva dripping from its rimless lips that seem to quiver and pulsate. . . ."

Thirty state troopers, according to the reporter, now formed a cordon around the pit where the object rested. Three policemen carrying a white handkerchief of truce walked toward the cylinder. Phillips continued:

"Wait a minute . . . something's happening. [high-pitched, intermittent whine of machinery] A humped shape is rising out of the pit. I can make out a small beam of light against a mirror. . . . What's that? There's a jet of flame springing from the mirror, and it leaps right at the advancing men! It strikes them head on! Good Lord, they're turning into flame! [screams and shrieks] Now the whole field by the woods has caught fire! [sound effects intensify] The gas tanks, tanks of automobiles . . . it's spreading everywhere! It's coming this way now! About twenty yards to my right [abrupt silence]."[3]

Now terror was afoot. A series of voices—fictional "announcers," "militia commanders," "network vice presidents," and "radio operators"—took up the narrative. At least forty people, according to the radio bulletins, lay dead at Grovers Mill, "their bodies burned and distorted beyond all possible recognition." And in a Trenton hospital, "the charred body of Carl Phillips" had been identified.

A current of fear flowed outward across the nation. Real-life police switchboards, first in New Jersey, then, steadily, throughout the whole Northeast, began to light up: "What's happening?" "Who's attacking America?" "When will they be here?" "What can we do?" "Who are they—these Martians?"

By now, according to the broadcast, "eight battalions of infantry" had surrounded the cylinder, determined to destroy it. A "Captain Lansing" of the "Signal Corps"—calm and confident at first, but with obviously increasing alarm—described what happened next:

"Well, we ought to see some action soon. One of the companies is deploying on the left flank. A quick thrust and it'll all be over. Wait a minute, I

see something on top of the cylinder. No, it's nothing but a shadow. . . . Seven thousand armed men closing in on an old metal tube. Tub, rather. Wait, that wasn't a shadow. It's something moving . . . solid metal. Kind of a shield-like affair rising up out of the cylinder! It's going higher and higher! Why, it's . . . standing on legs! Actually rearing up on a sort of metal framework! Now it's reaching above the trees and searchlights are on it! Hold on [abrupt silence]."

In a matter of moments, a studio "announcer" gave America the incredible news:

". . . Those strange beings who landed in the Jersey farmlands tonight are the vanguard of an invading army from the planet Mars. The battle which took place tonight at Grovers Mill has ended in one of the most startling defeats ever suffered by an army in modern times; seven thousand men armed with rifles and machine guns pitted against a single fighting machine of the invaders from Mars. One hundred and twenty known survivors. The rest strewn over the battle areas from Grovers Mill to Plainsboro crushed and trampled to death under the metal feet of the monster, or burned to cinders by its heat ray. . . ."

Grovers Mill's couple of hundred real-life residents hardly knew what to make of it all. Young Dick Stives was stunned. He and his sister and brothers pulled down the shades in the farmhouse. Their grandfather shoved chairs against the doors.

Teen-aged Lolly Dey, who heard about the "invasion" while attending a church meeting, consoled herself by saying: "I am in the Lord's House." Another resident, seeing what he thought to be a Martian war machine among the trees (actually a water tower on a neighbor's property), peppered it with shotgun blasts. One man packed his family into the car, bound for parts unknown. He backed right through his garage door. "We're never gonna be needing that again anyway," he muttered to his wife.

"The monster is now in control of the middle section of New Jersey," proclaimed the voice on the radio. "Communication lines are down from Pennsylvania to the Atlantic Ocean. Railroad tracks are torn and service from New York to Philadelphia discontinued. . . . Highways to the

[3]Phillip's narrative bore a perhaps-not-coincidental resemblance to a famous eyewitness report by Chicago radio newsman Herb Morrison, who on May 6, 1937, had described the explosion and destruction of the German dirigible Hindenburg as it was about to moor at Lakehurst, New Jersey.

north, south, and west are clogged with frantic human traffic. Police and army reserves are unable to control the mad flight. . . ."

Life was soon to imitate art. A wave of terror, unprecedented in its scope and rapidity, swept across New Jersey. A New Brunswick man, bound for open country, had driven ten miles when he remembered that his dog was tied up in the backyard of his home. Daring the Martians, he drove back to retrieve the dog.

A West Orange bar owner pushed customers out into the street, locked his tavern door, and rushed home to rescue his wife and children.

Twenty families began to move their belongings out of a Newark apartment house, their faces covered by wet towels to repel Martian rays. Doctors and nurses volunteered to come to hospitals to help handle the "war casualties."

At Princeton University, the chairman of the geology department packed his field equipment and headed into the night to look for whatever it was that was out there. The governor of Pennsylvania offered to send troops to help New Jersey. A Jersey City man called a bus dispatcher to warm him of the fast-spreading "disaster." He cut their conversation short with: "The world is coming to an end and I have a lot to do!"

Meanwhile, on the radio, the "Secretary of the Interior," speaking in a voice much like that of President Franklin D. Roosevelt, announced that he had faith in the ability of the American military to vanquish the Martians.[4] He solemnly intoned:

". . . placing our trust in God we must continue the performance of our duties each and every one of us, so that we may confront this destructive adversary with a nation united, courageous, and consecrated to the preservation of human supremacy on this earth."

A Trenton store owner ran out screaming, "The world is ending! The world is ending!" Another man dashed into a motion-picture theater in Orange, crying out that "the state is being invaded! This place is going to be blown up!" The audience hurriedly ran out to the street.

A woman in a Newark tenement just sat and cried. "I thought it was all up with us," she said. A man driving westward called out to a patrolman: "All creation's busted loose! I'm getting out!"

More grim reports issued from the radio. Scouting planes, according to the broadcast, had sighted three Martian machines marching through New Jersey. They were uprooting power lines, bridges, and railroad tracks, with the apparent objectives of crushing resistance and paralyzing communications. In swamps twenty miles south of Morristown, coon hunters had stumbled upon a second Martian cylinder.

In the Watchung mountains, the "22nd Field Artillery" set down a barrage against six tripod monsters—to no avail. The machines soon let loose a heavy black poisonous gas, annihilating the artillerymen. Then eight army bombers from "Langham Field, Virginia," attacked the tripod machines, only to be downed by heat rays.

Thousands of telephone calls cascaded into radio stations, newspaper offices, power companies, fire houses, and military posts throughout the country. People wanted to know what to do . . . where to go . . . whether they were safer in the cellar or the attic.

Word spread in Atlanta that a "planet" had struck New Jersey. In Philadelphia, all the guests in one hotel checked out. Students at a college in North Carolina lined up at telephones to call their parents for the last time. When a caller reached the CBS switchboard, the puzzled operator, asked about the end of the world, said: "I'm sorry, we don't have that information."

Radio listeners soon heard an "announcer," said to be atop the "Broadcasting Building" in Manhattan, describe a doomed New York City:

"The bells you hear are ringing to warn the people to evacuate the city as the Martians approach. Estimated in last two hours three million

---

[4]Network censors, concerned that the drama might sound too factual, had earlier requested more than thirty changes in the script. Thus, although he still sounded like Franklin Roosevelt, the "President" became the "Secretary of the Interior." The "U.S. Weather Bureau" was changed to the "Government Weather Bureau," the "National Guard" became the "State Militia," etc.

people have moved out along the roads to the north. . . . No more defenses. Our army wiped out . . . artillery, air force, everything wiped out. . . . We'll stay here to the end."

Something like madness took hold among radio listeners in New York City. People stood on Manhattan street corners hoping for a glimpse of the "battle." Thirty men and women showed up at a Harlem police station wanting to be evacuated. A woman had her husband paged at a Broadway theater and told him of the Martian landings; word spread quickly and a throng of playgoers rushed for the exits.

The radio voice continued: "Enemy now in sight above the Palisades! Five great machines. First one is crossing the river . . . wading the Hudson like a man wading through a brook. . . . Martian cylinders are falling all over the country. One outside Buffalo, one in Chicago, St. Louis. . . . Now the first machine reaches the shore! He stands watching, looking over the city. His steel, cowlish head is even with the skyscrapers. He waits for the others. They rise like a line of new towers on the city's west side. . . ."

A Bronx man dashed into the street and saw people running in all directions. One New Yorker claimed he heard the "swish" of Martian flying vehicles. Another told of machine-gun fire. Atop a midtown Manhattan building, a man with binoculars "saw" the firing of weapons. In Brooklyn, a man called the police station: "We can hear the firing all the way here, and I want a gas mask. I'm a taxpayer."

An NBC executive was upset because *his* network wasn't carrying the ultimate news event. One man sped at eighty miles an hour to reach a priest before the "death rays" overtook him; his car flipped over twice, but he lived.

The program played out the drama of doom right to its end.

From atop his fictional building, the "broadcaster" continued his "eyewitness" report: "Now they're lifting their metal hands. This is the end now. Smoke comes out. . . . People in the streets see it now. They're running towards the East River . . . thousands of them, dropping in

like rats. . . . It's reached Times Square. . . . People trying to run away from it, but it's no use. They . . . they're falling like flies. . . ."

Meanwhile, in real life, Boston families gathered on rooftops and thought they could see a glow in the sky as New York burned. A horrified Pittsburgh husband found his wife with a bottle of poison, screaming: "I'd rather die this way than that!"

People called the electric company in Providence, Rhode Island, to turn off all the city lights to make it a less visible target. A motorist rode through the streets of Baltimore, Paul Revere-fashion, blowing his horn and warning of the Martian invasion.

The staff of a Memphis newspaper readied an extra edition on rumored landings in Chicago and St. Louis. In Minneapolis, a woman ran into a church yelling: "This is the end of the world! I heard it on the radio!"

Back on the broadcast, the forlorn announcer carried on: "Now the smoke's crossing Sixth Avenue . . . Fifth Avenue . . . [coughing] a hundred yards away . . . it's fifty feet . . . [thud of falling body, then only sound of ships' whistles]."

In Salt Lake City, people started to pack before heading into the Rocky Mountains. One man, in Reno for a divorce, started to drive east, hoping to aid his estranged wife. A man and woman who'd run out of gas in northern California just sat and held hands, expecting any minute to see the Martian war machines appear over the tops of trees. Electric power failed in a village in Washington; families started to flee.

In Hollywood, John Barrymore downed a drink, went to his kennels and released his Great Danes. "Fend for yourselves!" he cried.

Then, from the radio, came the mournful call of a "radio operator": "2X2L calling CQ . . . New York. Isn't there anyone on the air? Isn't there anyone?"

Forty minutes into the broadcast, Welles gave his distraught audience a breather—a pause for station and program identification.

In the control room, CBS staffer Richard Goggin was startled as telephones there began to ring.

That would only happen in an emergency. "Tension was becoming enormous in Studio One," he later recalled. "They had a tiger by the tail and couldn't let go."

For those brave enough to stay tuned, Welles was able to match the program's stunning first portion with an equally remarkable concluding sequence. In what amounted to a twenty-minute soliloquy, he, in the role of Professor Pierson, chronicled the events that followed the Martians' destruction of New York City. Welles's spellbinding voice—magnetic, doom-filled, stirring—held listeners mesmerized.[5]

In the script, a stoic Pierson, still alive in the rubble, made his solitary way toward the ruins of New York, hiding from the invaders as he went.

Along the way he met a "stranger," a former artilleryman. This survivor feared that the Martians would cage and enslave any humans still alive. The stranger was determined to outwit and outlast the Martians and, in time, to turn the heat-rays back on the invaders and even—if need be—upon other humans. And so, one day, new leaders would rule a new world.

Pierson, unwilling to join the stranger's cause, continued his lonely journey. Entering Manhattan through the now-empty Holland Tunnel, he found a lifeless city:

"I wandered up through the Thirties and Forties . . . stood alone on Times Square. I caught sight of a lean dog running down Seventh Avenue with a piece of dark brown meat in his jaws, and a pack of starving mongrels at his heels. . . . I walked up Broadway . . . past silent shop windows, displaying their mute wares to empty sidewalks. . . ."

There seemed to be little hope left for the human race. Then Pierson "caught sight of the hood of a Martian machine, standing somewhere in Central Park, gleaming in the late afternoon sun":

"I rushed recklessly across Columbus Circle and into the park. I climbed a small hill above the pond at Sixtieth Street, and from there I could see standing in a silent row along the mall, nineteen of those great metal Titans, their cowls empty, their steel arms hanging listlessly by their sides. I looked in vain for the monsters that inhabit those machines. Suddenly my eyes were attracted to the immense flock of black birds that hovered directly below me . . . and there before my eyes, stark and silent, lay the Martians, with the hungry birds pecking and tearing brown shreds of flesh from their dead bodies."

The mighty Martians had fallen: ". . . it was found that they were killed by the putrefactive and disease bacteria against which their systems were unprepared . . . slain, after all man's defenses had failed, by the humblest thing that God in His wisdom put upon this earth."

In a sprightly epilogue, Welles then explained away the whole unsettling broadcast as the Mercury Theatre's "way of 'dressing up in a sheet and saying Boo! . . . We annihilated the world before your very ears, and utterly destroyed the CBS. You will be relieved, I hope, to learn that we didn't mean it, and that both institutions are still open for business."

He tried cheerily to dispel the darkness: "So goodbye everybody, and remember . . . the terrible lesson you learned tonight. . . . And if your doorbell rings and nobody's there, that was no Martian . . . it's Hallowe'en."

The joke was on the listeners. More than one hundred and fifty stations affiliated with CBS had carried the broadcast. About twelve million people had heard the program. Newspapers estimated that at least a million listeners, perhaps many more, had thought the invasion real.

Back in Grovers Mill, disenchantment began to take hold. Twenty-year-old Sam Goldman and three pals had been playing cards when they heard that the Martians were on the move down by the mill. They had thrown down their cards and jumped into a car, ready to face the invaders. "We got there and looked around," Sam said, "and nothing was going on."

---

[5]Welles's closing narrative, fictionally dramatic in style and compressing months of events into twenty minutes, contrasted sharply with the realism of the first portion of the program. Nevertheless, many listeners apparently remained convinced that Martians had landed.

A squad of New Jersey state troopers equipped with riot guns had deployed near the crossroads. They found little more than the dilapidated old mill itself.

Nearby, in their grandfather's farmhouse, Dick Stives, his sister, and brothers talked excitedly about the "men from Mars." Then their mother and father came home from the movies and told the children about the "make believe" on radio that everyone was talking about. Dick, more confused than ever, went upstairs to go to sleep, still half-sure that what he heard was "really real."

For the players who had inadvertently just made radio history, the next hours turned into a nightmare. As soon as Welles left the twenty-second-floor studio, he was called to a telephone. He picked it up, to hear the irate mayor of Flint, Michigan, roar that his city was in chaos because of the program and that he, the mayor, would soon be on his way to New York to punch one Orson Welles in the nose.

"By nine o'clock several high-ranking CBS executives had arrived or were in full flight toward 485 Madison. We were in trouble," recalled Larry Harding, a CBS production supervisor for the *Mercury Theatre* show.

Policemen hurried into the CBS building. Welles, Houseman, and the cast were held under informal house arrest. Staffers hastily stashed scripts, memoranda, and the sixteen-inch acetate disks upon which the show had been recorded.

Welles was taken to a room on the seventeenth floor, where reporters battered him with questions about whether he knew of the deaths and suicides his broadcast had caused (none have ever been documented), whether he knew ahead of time how devastating an effect his show would have (he said he didn't), and whether he had planned it all as a publicity stunt (he said he hadn't).

Finally, at about one o'clock Monday morning, Welles and the cast were "released," free to go out into the streets of New York where not a Martian was stirring. Welles walked a half-dozen blocks to the Mercury Theatre, where, even at that hour, members of the stage company were still rehearsing their new play.

Welles went up on stage, where news photographers were lurking. They caught him with his eyes raised, his arms outstretched. The next day his photograph appeared in newspapers throughout the country, over a caption that blurted: "I Didn't Know What I Was Doing!", or words to that effect.

The next morning headlines in major city newspapers reported the hoax: "Radio Listeners in Panic, Taking War Drama as Fact" (*New York Times*); "U.S. Terrorized by Radio's 'Men From Mars' " (*San Francisco Chronicle*); "Radio Drama Causes Panic" (*Philadelphia Inquirer*); "Listeners Weep and Pray, Prepare for End of World" (*New Orleans Times-Picayune*).

Many of the listeners who had been deluded laughed good-naturedly at one another—and at themselves. Some professed not to have been taken in by what one woman called "that Buck Rogers stuff." But others turned their wrath on Welles, on the network, and on the medium that had turned their Sunday evening into a time of unsolicited terror.

CBS apologized to the public, but also pointed out that during the program no fewer than four announcements had been made stating that it was a dramatic presentation, not a news broadcast.

A subdued Welles, believing his career was ruined, dutifully followed suit. "I don't think we will try anything like this again," he stated.

For two or three days, the press would not let Welles, nor radio, off the front page. Media rivalry played its part; newspaper publishers seemed anxious to portray radio—and Welles—as villains. The clipping bureau that served CBS delivered condemnatory editorials by the pound.

While newsmen "tsk-tsked," government officials fumed. Senator Clyde Herring of Iowa, reflecting the anger of many citizens, stated his support for legislation to curb such "Halloween bogymen." The Federal Communications Commission (FCC), flooded with complaint letters, tried to find a philosophical stance somewhere between imposing severe censorship and permitting unbridled expression.

Novelist H. G. Wells cabled his disregards from London. Although he had given CBS permission

Orson Welles, besieged by reporters after the 1938 brodcast of *War of the Worlds.*
Welles expressed amazament and regret that his dramatization had created panic
among millions of radio listeners.

to air his novel, he complained that "it was not explained to me that this dramatization would be
made with a liberty that amounts to a complete
reworking of *The War of the Worlds.*"

But some columnists and editorialists began to perceive significant merit in the program. Essayist Hey-
wood Broun interpreted the broadcast as a caution-
ary tale: "Jitters have come home to roost. The peace
of Munich hangs heavy over our heads like a thun-
dercloud." *Variety,* under a headline stating "Radio
Does U.S. A Favor," described the program as a warning to Americans of the danger of unpreparedness.

In a column that turned the tide of public opinion in favor of Welles and company, Dorothy
Thompson called the broadcast "the news story of
the century—an event which made greater contribution to an understanding of Hitlerism, Mussolin-
ism, Stalinism, anti-Semitism, and all the other ter-
rorism of our time than all the words about them
that have been written by reasonable men."

Welles, to his relief, soon learned that he would
not be consigned to durance vile. "Bill Paley, the

head of CBS, brought Orson and me up on the carpet and gave us a reprimand," Houseman later recalled. "But there was ambivalence to it. The working stiffs thought we were heroes. The executives
thought of us as some sort of anarchists. But
reason—and revenues—prevailed. A few days
after the broadcast, when it was announced that
Campbell's Soup had become a sponsor, the boys
at the top began to think of us as heroes, or at least
as employable persons, as well."

Some critics continued to decry the credulity
of the American people. They spoke of the compelling power of the human voice emanating
from the upper air. Radio, ominously, seemed
able to reduce an entire country to the size of one
room; it exerted unexpected power over suscep-
tible millions.

For a book-length study titled *The Invasion
from Mars,* Princeton University psychology
professor Hadley Cantril interviewed scores of
persons who had listened to the program.
Speaking with them shortly after "that night," he

received responses ranging from insecure to phobic to fatalistic.

"The coming of the Martians did not present a situation where the individual could preserve one value if he sacrifices another," Professor Cantril concluded from his research. "In this situation the individual stood to lose all his values at once. Nothing could be done to save any of them. Panic was inevitable."

Did Welles intend the panic? Had he hoped, by means of his magnificent dramatic powers, to gain all those headlines?

Houseman dismisses such conjecture as "rubbish." He declares: "Orson and I had no clear presense of the mood of the audience. *The War of the Worlds* wasn't selected as a parable of invasion and war in the 1930s, but just as an interesting story unto itself. Only after the fact did we perceive how ready and resonant the world was for the tale. Our intent was theatre, not terror."

Welles and his players could not know that they had portrayed the shape of things to come. The program was, in a way, quite prophetic. Barely two weeks later, German foreign minister Joachim von Ribbentrop chillingly commented: "I would not be surprised if in the United States eyewitness reports are under consideration in which the 'Giants from Mars' marched up in brown shirts waving swastika flags."

Sooner than the peoples of the world could guess, a true nightmare—that of World War II—would be upon them.

Welles, of course, went on to memorable successes in motion pictures and theater. And his *War of the Worlds* broadcast became the most famous radio program of all time.

These days, the crossroads village of Grovers Mill is much the way it was that spectral night half a century ago. There are, however, signs of strangers nearby—new homes sprouting up among what had been potato fields. And futuristic shapes—sleek, glass-walled, high-technology industrial buildings—stand amid the trees.

But the old mill itself is still at the intersection of Millstone and Cranbury roads—a dot east of Princeton on the highway map. The weatherworn wooden structure, with a few of its millstones scattered about, stands lonely vigil.

Here fate tossed its random lightning-bolt. Here the "Martians" made their landing on what is now a municipal park. Nearby, ducks glide on a big, placid pond.

The former Wilson farm (the script spoke of the "Wilmuth" farm, but sightseers made do with the Wilson place) has long since been cut up into smaller properties. Here Martian-hunters once tramped across the cornfields looking for traces of the invaders.

Wayfarers from all parts of the world still occasionally wander the roads and fields of Grovers Mill. They know they will see no Martians, find no burn marks on the earth left by war machines from outer space, nor come upon charred ruins wrought by the aliens' devastation. Still, drawn by curiosity, they come and look and wonder.

Not all Grovers Mill residents find such doings fascinating. The proprietor of a nearby gas station, for example, remembers the night of the "invasion", but didn't think much of it then and thinks as little of it now. "It doesn't make sense," he says with disdain. "Never has. Never will."

But for Dick Stives, now sixty-three, the "panic broadcast" till holds disquieting memories. Not long ago he walked around the "Martian landing ground."

"When I was a kid," he recalled, "I would crawl down near the wheel of the old mill, just by the pond there, and shuck my clothes and go in swimming. It was just a pond on a farm. But now, looking at it, I have to wonder why people still come so far to find a place where something that was supposed to happen didn't happen."

"I still remember," he said, "how I felt that night, up there in the bedroom in my granddad's place, in the dark, trying to sleep, thinking about what we had heard on the radio. The nighttime would make me think about how almost anything, just about anytime, could happen anywhere—even in Grovers Mill. Things in the shadows. Things I didn't understand."

STUDY QUESTIONS

1. Describe the early career of Orson Welles. Did he realize that his "War of the Worlds" broadcast would create such a controversy?

2. Describe how the show was structured to create tension and heighten suspense.

3. How did Americans react to the broadcast? What do their reactions suggest about the power of radio?

4. In your opinion, was the broadcast unethical or dangerous?

5. How did the struggles going on in Europe affect how Americans received the broadcast?

BIBLIOGRAPHY

For discussions of the role of advertising in the 1920s, see Stuart Ewen, *Captains of Consciousness* (1976). The influence of films on American culture is ably portrayed in Robert Sklar, *Movie-Made America: A Cultural History of American Movies* (1975) and Larry May, *Screening Out the Past* (1980). Paul Carter's *Another Part of the Twenties* (1977) is an excellent description of popular social attitudes during the infancy of the radio industry. Although there is not much literature on the history of radio, see Erik Barnouw, *A Tower of Babel: A History of Broadcasting in the United States* (1966) and Francis Chase, *Sound and Fury: An Informal History of Broadcasting* (1942). The broadcast itself is discussed in Howard Koch, *The Panic Broadcast* (1970) and Barbara Leaming, *Orson Welles* (1985).

MY GUNS: A MEMOIR
OF THE SECOND WORLD WAR

Roger J. Spiller

In his preface to *Wartime: Understanding and Behavior in the Second World War,* Paul Fussell writes, "The damage the war visited upon bodies and buildings, planes and tanks and ships, is obvious. Less obvious is the damage it did to intellect discrimination, honesty, individuality, complexity, ambiguity, and irony, not to mention privacy and wit. For the past 50 years the Allied war has been sanitized and romanticized almost beyond recognition by the sentimental, the loony patriotic, the ignorant, and the bloodthirsty." Eugene B. Sledge in *With the Old Breed at Peleliu and Okinawa,* his memoir of World War II, sounded the same note. He wrote his account primarily because of "the vast difference" he discovered between what had been written about the war and what he had seen, felt, and experienced in the war.

What both writers knew was that there were really two wars—an outer war and an inner war. The outer war was the war that men, women, and children followed from the comfort of their homes; it was a war that politicians supported and military leaders planned and executed; it was the war of red arrows and blue arrows, statistics and timetables, pithy statements by commanding generals and war movies for domestic consumption. The object for those following or engaged in the outer war was the march of progress. The inner war was the war that men on the front line fought, and it was almost too horrible to talk about with anyone who had not experienced it. The object for the men caught in the inner war was survival. Sledge writes about watching the men of his unit cut by enemy machine gun fire on the beaches of Peleliu: "I felt sickened to the depths of my soul. I asked God, 'why, why, why?' I turned my face away and wished that I were imagining it all. I had tasted the bitter essence of war, the sight of helpless comrades being slaughtered, and it filled me with disgust." How, one might ask, could prisoners of the inner and outer wars discuss such experiences?

In "My Guns: A Memoir of the Second World War," Roger J. Spiller, a military historian who was born at the end of World War II, asks the central question about the inner war, "What was it like?" To hear the answer is to understand the real cost of war.

I was born in 1944, toward the middle of October, when a lot of people were getting killed for me, or blown up, or shot, or captured, or worse. Worse? "The shell hit him about here," said a veteran not long ago, remembering that time and place; "he disappeared."

The ones who survived their military service in those years eventually got their discharges, went home, went to work, raised families, and are now of an age to retire. Old age is beginning to do what the war could not, or would not. All these people, men and women, living or not, are part of what must be the most written-about generation in American history. As generations come and go, this is a particularly distinguished one, compared, say, with my own.

What, then, should one of my generation say in commemoration of those who fought in this war, most of the important things—presumably—already having been said? We know where all these people went and what they did. Any military atlas will show very large colored arrows, pointing this way and that: This is how the Australians and the Yanks traversed the Kokoda Trail to split New Guinea in half. On another page we can see Guadalcanal, an inconsiderable island, so far out of the way. Still farther on there is the campaign in North Africa and then inexorable progress across the Mediterranean to Italy, another jump into France (the "dash across France" is a perennially favorite phrase). Over in Poland, Byelorussia, and the Ukraine, the situation becomes a test of the cartographer's art; everything seems a little messier. Back in the Pacific the friendly arrows multiply and advance toward the top of the page, "stepping stones" to victory against Japan. Anyone can see how simple it is; anyone can criticize what was done, saying *this* was a better way. Why couldn't they see it then?

We have the numbers too. Nearly to a finality, we can calculate the people involved, those killed

"My Guns: A Memoir of the Second World War" by Roger J. Spiller in *American Heritage,* Vol. 42/No. 8, December 1991, pp. 45–51. Reprinted by permission of *American Heritage* Magazine, a division of Forbes, Inc. © Forbes, Inc., 1991.

and wounded ("disappeared" poses greater difficulties), where they were mostly killed or wounded, and what mostly killed or wounded them. For soldiers, artillery seemed to be the killer of killers. For civilians (let us not forget that more civilians were killed in this war than soldiers), gas or bombs, in that order. Indeed, all those matters that can be reduced to numbers have been, the tangibles as always being the most easily approached without understanding. Ships, planes, tanks, artillery pieces, "small" arms—"small" always referring to the size of the weapon and its projectile, not the damage one could do to a person—all these fill up the very large picture books found on the remainder shelves of local bookstores.

If all this leaves us less than satisfied, we can know so much about the statesman and generals of World War II that they seem like members of our own families. Their lives are so well accounted for that in the unlikely event a gap would appear in their wartime chronologies it would constitute a mystery sufficiently great to set battalions of historians into frenzied activity. The fraudulent "Hitler diaries" of a few years ago come to mind; we were nonplused that something so potentially significant could have escaped notice, so accustomed were we to knowing everything about this war.

Even a certain dislike of reading should pose no impediment to knowing about the war. Virtually every night of the year, television broadcasts some program on the war—the bigger, more visually dramatic pieces of the war, of course, but conveying a kind of recognition all the same. It is just possible that our present knowledge of the war comes mostly from this source, condensed, trivialized, and certainly very highly organized in digestible segments (one hour on "Barbarossa," the German invasion of Russia).

With all these rather insistent intrusions of war history upon our modern consciousness, it might seem strange to argue that we have lost sight of the real war altogether. That was precisely the thesis Studs Terkel meant to convey when he did *"The Good War,"* bracketing his title in quotation marks that dripped with irony. But irony turned back on Terkel: It *was* a good war even to many who participated in it, and furthermore it got better all the time as the decisiveness of the Allied victory slowly revealed itself. Our very human impulse is to negotiate constantly with our memory, to domesticate it and manage it, remembering the good parts. With every passing year the old, real war loses another round in the negotiations.

The fiftieth anniversaries of the war are upon us. As in the real war, Americans are the latecomers. Europeans have been taking notice for a good two years, but the rush of events behind the old Iron Curtain has left precious few energies for commemorating the past. If our commemorations repeat the pattern of the war itself, our consciousness of the war will build to a kind of crescendo by about 1994. How, then, at a half-century's remove, can we make a new approach on that time and its people, especially when its evidence and effect are still so much a part of us and still so meaningful to the events we see unfold on the nightly news? How do we pay proper attention to the old war and what it means without further contributing to what Paul Fussell has called the "disneyfication" of the war?

The answer for me cannot be wholly historical; such an answer implies an emotional distance from the war that I do not enjoy. My connection to this war is one of long and personal standing, and my connection to its people is so close that I dread reading obituaries for fear that one of my old war people has died. Those who made history so fresh for me are disappearing, one by one.

Exactly when I became sentient about war in general, or particularly about this war, I cannot say. It never seems to have been far away. I recall, imprecisely, photographs of relatives in uniform, well scrubbed, creased, and confident, very much younger than I thought they ever could have been. Growing up in the fifties, my friends and I always had at hand an old helmet, a shirt, or a bayonet to complement the imagination of the playground. Bloodstained items were a great premium to us. No one thought for a moment about the cost of these things. The father of one of my playmates was missing several fingers, lost in combat somewhere, torn away by a stream of machine gun fire—or so it was rumored among us. He was otherwise a calm, respectable adult presence on the fringes of childhood life, but his debility added immeasurably to his mana, a piece of secret knowledge to be conveyed in whispers on the playground. Sometimes, we played him in action, traumatic amputation and all.

Since then I have studied war more seriously, or so I think. I would like to think as well that I grew out of that childish infatuation with the play of war, but I often wonder if that is true. Once I began to study war in earnest I wondered whether I had made any intellectual progress at all. The questions that still interested me were a child's questions, really, chief among them: What is it really like? Not the war of the statesmen or the generals. Not the war of the scientists or the staff officers. Not, even, the war of the field commanders. To verge on being unkind as well as ungrateful, all these people were really office workers. I wanted to know about war at the darkest corner of its heart, that one quality that so differentiates war from all other human activity: combat itself.

For years now I have moved through the world of soldiers and soldiering as a privileged spectator, and it is from them that I have inherited a certain interest in the practicalities—what Fussell would call the *actualities*—of war, not to mention a certain impatience with the more domesticated versions of war that one finds so much in modern American life. Too, my privilege is complicated by a certain responsibility. I teach soldiers the history of war and so contribute to their vision of what war is. Soldiers, and especially professional soldiers, carry with them into their first combat an expectation of what their war will be like. My responsibility is to see that the distance between what they expect and what they get is as small as possible.

A decade and a half ago, the British military historian John Keegan wrote *The Face of Battle,* the kind of book for which historians reserve the word *seminal,* really meaning that the author created a new way of thinking about an old problem.

This photo of dead American soldiers was published in 1943, and was the first to depict American casualties. The government attempted to shield the American people from the true horror of the war, which took the lives of 300,000 American servicemen.

Keegan's view differed markedly from conventional military histories that interpreted wars from the top down. Regardless of the ways in which war had changed over the centuries, he wrote, what all wars have in common is that they are human enterprises, conducted, it is true, at extremes of human behavior and tolerance, but human all the same. Even if understanding war does require some measure of technical knowledge, it is also true that any understanding of war that does not recognize its essential humanness is flawed. The "face of battle" has always been, finally, the human face itself.

When we reduce war to an affair of numbers or great men or grand strategies, when war's humanness finds it difficult to make its way past the trivializing negotiations of memory, we have lost sight of what war is and have begun to interest ourselves in what it is not. Paradoxically, war is most human and reveals its essential character at the very place where humanness is in the greatest danger of extinction: in the killing grounds, the zones of combat where men devote every impulse of their mental and physical energy to destroying one another. Making sense of this world is a singularly demanding undertaking. And for any exploration of this world, expert guides are essential.

Those guides are all about us in the form of books, certainly, but they are about us in person as well—perhaps our fathers and mothers, our relatives, our neighbors. Only a couple of years ago I discovered that a close relative, a sweet and decent man, had done the worst kind of fighting in the Pacific and had never uttered a word about it to me—until I asked. The soldiers of the old war, notoriously laconic as they are, have begun to speak more and more. They are even beginning to return to the deadly old places where they fought, visiting comrades they left behind in the ground, or elsewhere. What they, in written and personal form, have taught me about this war is beyond calculation, perhaps even beyond my expression. I remember this war—its most important parts—through them. I think it must be, in the end, the best way of all to know a war. What have they taught me?

Twenty million Americans were examined for military service in World War II; fourteen million were accepted. Yet in World War II, as in all modern wars, the fighting part of this vast number was relatively small. Most Americans in uniform during this war knew less than nothing about combat and, what is more, were not particularly anxious to find out. The service one entered, and *when* one entered, had a great deal to do with whether one would actually fight. In the Navy the chances of engaging in seaborne combat were very high if one happened to be part of the fleets deployed to contested waters or on convoy duty in the Atlantic, and indeed the bulk of early American casualties came from just these sources. As the war wore on, the casualty rate slowed. Next came the air forces, whether Army or Navy. Like the convoy sailors, they saw combat relatively early; unlike the sailors, they did not see their casualties decline until nearly war's end. The story among the ground forces, the Marines and GIs, was precisely the reverse of the naval war: their early casualties were "light"—always in war the most relative of terms—and intensified throughout the war until, like those of the air forces, their casualties declined at the end of the war.

Regardless of the medium in which they fought, the American combatants of World War II were not relentlessly fighting. In the naval war, combat was a series of episodes that interrupted days and sometimes months of steaming from one position to another. Surely the catastrophes of naval combat could kill or wound or drown several thousand sailors at one time, and the possibility just as surely preyed upon those who manned these ships, working its own special kind of stress on them. Aerial warfare had its own particular rhythms, and for the air crews there was at least a hint of war's end in certain commands that allowed for a maximum number of combat missions for each flier. Yet on any one of their missions war's end was never far away, and what is more, the air crewmen were often unwilling witnesses to the end of someone else's war. If the "flyboys" seemed to have more opportunities to get away from their war than other combatants, as many foot soldiers grumbled, that only means we have misunderstood how their real war was composed. We do not hear the muffled sobs of fear in the squadron barracks on the night before a thousand-plane raid against Germany.

The war on the ground was predominantly the infantryman's war. Despite notable advancements in the equipment and techniques of armored warfare, this war belonged to the GI. If one is searching for a picture of those in something close to sustained combat for long periods of time, this is where one finds it. Here, too, the disparity between those who fought and those who did not seems the greatest. Of the millions of Americans sent overseas by the Army during

World War II, only 14 percent were infantrymen. Those 14 percent took more than 70 percent of all the battle casualties among overseas troops.

Even among the fighting parts of an army, a relatively small proportion actually suffered combat. The most combative of all the combat units was the infantry division. Within these American formations, combat troops of all categories counted for only 68 percent of the whole. One wartime study by a division commander, Lucian Truscott, estimated that 95 percent of his losses were sustained by his line troops. Harold Leinbaugh and John Campbell, officers of a rifle company in the fall of 1944 and into 1945, who later wrote *The Men of Company K,* put it less clinically: "We were the Willie Lomans of the war."

All this means that during World War II there existed on this planet men in all varieties of uniform who belonged to a vast military underclass, and that still millions more of their fellow citizens were in the stands, so to speak, rooting them on. They fought in the service of causes that were radically, one might even say mortally, different, but the essence of the daily lives they led was not. It consisted, as Fussell reminds us, of "the experience of coming to grips, face to face, with an enemy who designs your death." Under these circumstances, the popular wartime phrase "We're behind you all the way" takes on a rather different meaning.

Surely, then, it was the cause that made it all worthwhile. At first glance one might think that the nobility of one's cause had an important and easing effect upon those who fought in its service or even that a soldier who fights for a great and moral cause is a superior soldier, so protected by his nobility. It isn't true, and it was no closer to being true in the Second World War than in any other. Soldiering is a morally neutral act, so designed by centuries of tradition. Soldiers have fought bravely and well for the most despicable of causes, and the Second World War lasted for six years because millions of soldiers did exactly that. The great wartime cartoonist Bill Mauldin discerned among the GIs a grudging respect for the fighting qualities of enemy troops, even if they were "skunks." Some critics since the war have said that enemy troops, especially German troops, were far better soldiers than the GIs, but this is a contention far from being proved.

Assuming—only for the moment—that some enemy troops were better at their trade than American troops, should we not then view our relative lack of ability as a mark of honor, all the more indicative of sacrifice in the name of a great crusade? Then the GIs become noble amateurs or even martyrs to the cause of freedom. Surely no American armed force ever took the field for better reasons than the defeat of the Axis Powers. Was this motivation not a powerful force in our favor? Evidently not.

Field research during the war showed that frontline troops were notoriously impatient with "morale lectures" laid on by well-meaning staff. Appeals to patriotism or cause met with little response from men who were constantly on the verge of physical or mental exhaustion because their lives were threatened every day. No doubt the same well-meaning commanders and staff officers who thought troop lectures were a good idea dismissed the lack of frontline enthusiasm as unwholesome cynicism, as evidence of suspiciously low morale. Still, the troops did fight on. Why?

For most of the world's noncombatant population, the war may have been about one cause or another, but for the Willie Lomans the war was about staying alive. To ordinary men in such circumstances, no amount of morale building could offset this fundamental fact, and to such men all those who were not with them were in no position to lecture. Combat consumed too much energy to allow any left over for higher considerations of national philosophy. All the defenses their society had given them in preparation for their war—the national and popular support they received, their training and their equipment, even the official sanction to kill—were found by the soldiers to be altogether too fragile to withstand the grind of combat. The sustenance of one's own comrades, today understood by professionals as the essential cement of any combat unit, proved to be unequal to the demands of combat. Lein-

baugh and Campbell's rifle company began its war with two hundred men; by war's end combat had used up four hundred. Their casualties equaled twice their original strength. This rifle company, Leinbaugh and Campbell insist, was a wholly typical unit of its kind.

A kind of solidarity did exist on the front lines, one that commanders found threatening and attempted to suppress whenever possible; in the Great War and after, this solidarity would have been called "the brotherhood of the trench." It was a feeling best expressed by Erich Maria Remarque in *All Quiet on the Western Front* when he has his character Paul Bäumer realize that all the soldiers on the front line, friendly and enemy alike, are not fighting each other so much as they are fighting against the war itself.

My impression, but only that, is that those who fought in World War II came to this realization much sooner than their precedessors in World War I because they expected much less from this war. When the war broke out, they knew it was going to be a bad one and suffered fewer illusions about what it could do for, or to, them. Harold Bond, a young infantry officer who fought with the 36th Division in Italy, wrote years afterward: "My generation, brought up on *A Farewell to Arms, All Quiet on the Western Front,* and plays such as *Journey's End,* was not easily persuaded that modern war made any sense at all. Most certainly none of us thought any longer of glory and military heroics." For all that, Bond needed no lectures on morale to tell him why he fought: "One has to fight against a clear and palpable evil; the Nazis were both vicious and degrading, appealing as they did to the worst side of human nature." What moved Bond in the end, however, was his simpler conviction, one that was closer to war's practicalities, "that young, unmarried men should be the first to go." The *go* in Bond's memory is ambiguous. Bond seems to have meant to go overseas, but *going* could also mean never coming back, given the possibilities inherent in his particular situation. Infantry officers, especially junior ones, were a highly expendable commodity along Italy's Gustav Line in those days. A division on the

line could easily spend its complement of lieu-
tenants (137 of them) in a month or two.

And in those days, late in 1944 and early in
1945, the Allied victory was by no means a sure
thing. One reads in the histories of the war pronouncements that after a given battle—say, Stalin-
grad, or D-day, or the Schweinfurt raid, or the Battle of the Coral Sea—the Allied victory was "only
a matter of time." For those who fought, the matter of time was more than incidental; it was everything. One of Harry Brown's characters in his
novel *A Walk in the Sun* sees the war continuing
forever, one day of combat after the other, until
decades later he will fight in the "Battle of Tibet."

In late 1943 and early 1944, the war was very
much in control, the human beings fighting
against it not having arrested its murderous
progress. So the war assumed a certain monotony
for those who fought in it at sea, in the air, on the
ground, and we should not be startled to discover
a sense of futile wonderment and perhaps even fatalistic bitterness among them. Not surprisingly,
after the war ended, such feelings were sup-
pressed. While the war was on, they were very
much alive. One infantry scout in Italy remembered that "we felt simply that we had been left to
die. Men in our division gave up all hope of being
relieved. They thought the Army intended to keep
them in action until everybody was killed. . . .
All the men have hope of getting back, but most
of the hope is that you'll get hit someplace that
won't kill you. That's all they talk about."

All wars contain their own particular human
secrets. One such secret in this war was the hostility those in "the line" felt for those who were in
"the rear." The rear was both a place and an identity, it was "any sonofabitch whose foxhole is behind mine," remembers J. A. Croft, who served as
a rifleman in Leinbaugh and Campbell's Company
K. The gulf of misunderstanding that existed between those who fought and the thousands of
uniformed spectators who milled around any
combat zone most often manifested itself in brutal insensitivity. Elliot Johnson was an artillery officer with the 4th Infantry Division five days into
the Normandy invasion, when a close friend was

accidentally killed by one of his own men. Overcome by grief, Johnson sought medical aid for his
dead friend at battalion headquarters, where a
drunken colonel ordered Johnson to "get that
goddamn hunk of rotten meat out of here!" But
there were other, less dramatic evidences of ani-
mosity between the line and the rear, and indeed
no particular incident was required to keep the an-
imosity alive. The distinguished classicist Bernard
Knox, a combat veteran of *both* the Spanish Civil
War and World War II, has written only lately but
still with much feeling, "while it is true of every
war that much as he may fear and perhaps even
hate the enemy opposing him, the combat infantryman broods with deep and bitter resent-
ment over the enormous number of people in his
rear who sleep safely at night."

And so they soldiered on until they were killed
or wounded or captured or disappeared, having
little choice in the matter—or at least no choice
most cared to make. The Army recorded only
forty thousand deserters during the war, and of
these about twenty-nine hundred were actually
court-martialed. Forty-nine received the death
penalty, but only one such sentence was actually
carried out. The numbers of AWOLs—"absent
without leave," a bureaucratic rendition of the
"straggling" of older wars—was much higher, and
when the American army bypassed Paris, James
Jones reports, the city acted as a giant magnet for
ten thousand or so troops. How many of those
were actually in contact with the enemy, Jones
did not know, but that kind of behavior was much
less likely among the combat soldiers than among
those in the rear echelons.

Sometimes when talking with my students, I
ask them to calculate the number of a combat soldier's enemies, and at first they do not understand
what I mean. But the sources of mayhem in any
modern war reach dizzying numbers, and the
enemy's work is only one. The anxious trigger finger that killed Elliot Johnson's friend in Normandy was all too common. When one arms
thousands of men and confines them in a concentrated battle area, such incidents are inevitable.
Our own artillery fire, mistakenly calculated, killed

its share of friendly soldiers and probably was the source of the old artilleryman's fatalistic comment: "Looked good when it left here." Of course, the artillery could be dead on its designated target when, in a friendly version of mechanical ambush, a ground unit could walk right under it.

An additional danger threatened if one's fighting happened to involve a complicated machine. Military versions of industrial accidents were all the greater because these machines were operated in the excited atmosphere of real or potential danger. Sailors came to understand that a single enemy shell could set off a round of secondary explosions on their ships, killing and maiming far more of them than the original attack; but even when they were not under attack, the dangers of manning a modern warship were significant and ever present. In the same way, aerial combat was only one of several ways to die. "There are a variety of possible deaths which face a member of a bomber crew and each man is free to choose his own pet fear," wrote John Bennett, a squadron commander in the 8th Air force. "A tire could blow out or an engine could fail on take-off. The oxygen system or electric heating system might fail at high altitude. There is the fear of explosion or midair collision while flying formation." Or, as sometimes happened, a gunner could accidentally hit another plane in formation while testing his guns before the run to target.

Back on the ground, the killing of friends could be far more intimate. Eugene B. Sledge's memoir of the Pacific war, *With the Old Breed on Peleliu and Okinawa,* one of the best of its kind, records how one night, when a soldier became hysterical and threatened to reveal their positions, his comrades killed him with an entrenching tool because they couldn't keep him quiet any other way. "Christ a'mighty. What a pity," said one of Sledge's comrades after hearing the shovel find its mark.

Looking at the war from the vantage point of the combatants, one can easily envision one's own commander and staff as enemies. They are the ones, after all, who assist the enemy in creat-

ing the deadly environment, and if they do not look after their men, much as a doctor his patients in intensive care, the natural alienation between line and rear can sour into sullen, refractory behavior. Harold Leinbaugh saw his regimental commander on the line only once in more than a hundred days of combat, and as Leinbaugh's own confidence as a company commander increased, he was less than reluctant to see to the welfare of his company according to his own lights rather than follow the dictates of a remote command. In *Wartime,* Paul Fussell's acerbic rendition of the war that has infuriated so many spectators and no doubt has pleased just as many combat veterans, a view of the staff as being completely ignorant of war's actualities can be found throughout. "There is a 'staff solution' to the fear problem," Fussell writes, "when under shelling and mortar fire and scared stiff, the infantry should alleviate the problem by moving—never back but forward. This will enable trained personnel to take care of the wounded and will bring you close enough to the enemy to make him stop the shelling." So far so good. Then Fussell adds: "That it will also bring you close enough to put you within rifle and machine-gun and hand-grenade range is what the theorists know but don't mention. The troops know it, which is why they like to move *back.*"

All these testimonies and more leave little doubt that the real engines of combat are not mechanical but human. Fear and fatigue give combat its true character. Whether it is in the actual or the historical rear, neither is present, and so the distortions begin. Human beings are adaptable, we think, and can get used to anything; haven't they done so? Soldiers on the line did not think so. As the war went on, combatants and almost no one else knew that everyone would break under the strain of combat at some time or another, provided always he is not otherwise harmed. Break they did. At one point in the war, more "neuropsychiatric casualties" were shipped home from overseas than those who were physically injured. Significantly, these soldiers received more understanding care close to the fighting line than they did as they went to the rear, where facile moral judgments about courage were still unsullied by the realities of war.

Inevitably some of these misunderstandings of what war is really like have infected the history of the war. Misunderstanding the humanness of war, historians and other commentators have superimposed upon it judgments whose weight is too great a burden for the war to bear. Sometimes, in the soldiers' memoirs, we hear the old war strain under its modern burdens when notes of embarrassment sound about actions that in combat no one would have blinked at. For most of the veterans, however, the domestication of the war seems not to matter so much; they are mostly indifferent to the meanings we impose upon it.

Having talked with so many of these men over the years, I still find it surprising that they will talk at all to one from "the rear." It is something like asking a person to discuss his medical record. What is even more interesting is that once they do begin to talk, it is clear they see their war as the single greatest event in their lives, no matter how distinguished their postwar careers. They would agree with E. B. Sledge, the youthful combatant turned college professor, who long after his first amphibious assault against the beaches at Peleliu, still regards that event in no uncertain terms: "Everything my life had been before and has been after pales in the light of that awesome moment." Sledge's view is remarkably similar to an old friend's, well respected in his postwar profession when I first met him. In moments of confidential conversation he always turned back to the days when he flew B-17s against the Germans, his memories vivid and detailed and not at all sentimental, but more significant to him than anything he had done since.

The study of war in our colleges and universities has never been a popular subject with our professors and the academy will disdainfully ignore the anniversaries of this war if at all possible. And because the most dramatic kind of history is being made daily before our eyes, the rest of our society may find it all too easy to turn its attention away from the old war. Yet from Xenophon and Thucydides onward, war's interior landscape has posed a great mystery, and those men who made war were the most mysterious of all, their experiences perceived as impenetrable to those who were not there. The Second World War, so close at hand in time, is now only a bit more familiar to us than the wars fought by the ancient Greeks, and our limited familiarity is fading daily. Our commemorations over the next few years may postpone our forgetfulness, but eventually our most important war will take its final place in the histories, there to be investigated by the chance encounters of scholarship.

By then my old war friends will be gone as well, but their war will live with me as it always has. For one who plies a trade that makes so much of detachment, the impression of a sentiment is close to heresy, but these men of World War II will have been the closest of my friends. How close were we? Writing in *Dispatches* about a far different war in Vietnam, Michael Herr asked the same question of himself and the soldiers he encountered. How close? "But of course we were intimate," he wrote. "They were my guns. . . ."

STUDY QUESTIONS

1. What does the author believe is the best way to approach an understanding of World War II? Can an understanding of the war be rendered in statistics? Is biography or documentary the answer?

2. What does the author mean by the sentence, "Our very human impulse is to negotiate constantly with our memory, to domesticate it and manage it, remembering the good parts"? What about the phrase, "the 'disneyfication' of the war"?

3. How is war most human at the moments when human life is most threatened?

4. How did the men in different branches of the armed services experience the war?

5. How important was ideology for the men who fought the war?

6. What kind of tensions existed between front line troops and the soldiers in "the rear"?

7. How were the realities of war different from the theories of war?

BIBLIOGRAPHY

The history book that gave a human face to warfare is John Keegan, *The Face of Battle: A Study of Agincourt. Waterloo and the Somme* (1976). John Keegan, *The Second World War* (1989) is also an ideal place to begin study of World War II. Two other books that examine war, as opposed to warfare, are Paul Fussell, *Wartime: Understanding and Behavior in the Second World War* (1989), and Richard Holmes, *Acts of War: The Behavior of Men in Battle.* The literature on World War II is vast, though most of it is concerned only with individual campaigns, battles, or leaders. John W. Dower, *War Without Mercy: Race and Power in the Pacific War* (1986), details the feelings of soldiers who fought in the Pacific. Perhaps the impact of the war on the men who fought it is best experienced in the finest of the World War II memoirs and novels. E. B. Sledge, *With the Old Breed in Peleliu and Okinawa* (1981) is outstanding, a haunting memoir of fighting in the Pacific. Of the novels, three stand out: Norman Mailer, *The Naked and the Dead;* James Jones, *From Here to Eternity;* and Herman Wouk, *The Caine Mutiny.*

JOHN WAYNE GOES TO WAR

Randy Roberts

More than a decade after his death, John Wayne's movies are still enjoyed by millions of Americans. The individual names of the films are hardly important. A John Wayne Western says it all, evoking a world divided between the forces of good and evil where one man, steely-eyed and leathered by the sun, stands ready to preserve order and to punish lawbreakers. From his first major film in 1930 to his last leading role in 1976, John Wayne played the same role. He was the hero—sometimes gruff and occasionally flawed, but always there when the fighting began. He was Davy Crockett at the Alamo, the Ringo Kid on the stagecoach, the Quiet Man in Ireland, and the man who shot Liberty Valance. On screen, he fought Indians and outlaws in the West, Nazis and Japanese in World War II, communists in the Cold War, and North Vietnamese and Viet Cong in the Vietnam War. And he always won, even if he died in the process.

But John Wayne was also part of Hollywood, part of the dream factory that catered to American fantasies and myths. His wars were fought and his victories were won only in front of the cameras. During World War II when he was eligible for the draft, he chose to accept a deferment and remain in Hollywood to make movies. Like many other people in the motion picture industry, he decided that he could support America's war effort—and his own career—best by starring in movies. In the following essay, Randy Roberts examines John Wayne and Hollywood during the early years of World War II.

ecember 7, 1941. The news reached Hollywood at 11:26 on a calm Sunday morning. The Japanese had attacked American naval and air bases in Honolulu. A few people refused to believe the news. It seemed impossible, almost like another "War of the Worlds" broadcast, and they waited for the soothing voice of an announcer to tell them that it was only make believe. Everything about the day clashed with the brutal facts. The weather was perfect, even for a city where ideal weather was the norm. A cool night breeze blew off the desert from the northeast, but by 11:00 it was already in the low 70s. For the Hollywood elite, many of whom had gone to their vacation retreats in Malibu, Palm Springs, or the High Sierras, golf and swimming, not war, was on the day's agenda. Before the news reached Los Angeles, harmony reigned. Only the day before, the UCLA Bruins and the USC Trojans had played to a 7-7 tie, and that very morning a *Los Angeles Times* headline announced "FINAL PEACE MOVE SEEN."

The attack stunned Los Angeles. Responses varied. Some followed normal schedules. Thousands turned up at the "little world championship" football game and watched the undefeated Hollywood Bears, led by Kenny Washington and Woody Strode, defeat the Columbus Bulls. During the game, news updates reminded the spectators that the Bears' victory would probably not be remembered as the day's most important event. In another part of town, several hundred spectators watched Paramount Studio's baseball team defeat an "all-Jap aggregation." After the game, the FBI took the Japanese team into custody. The attack, however, disrupted most schedules. Golfers finished the holes they were playing and returned to the clubhouse. Gossips ended their conversations about Harry Warner's new granddaughter or the removal of Eddie Albert's tonsils or the antiaircraft men who had set up shop at Hollywood Park, and turned to more urgent topics. Thousands simply got into their automobiles—tanks

full and rubber treads still good—and drove aimlessly through the city, leading to traffic jams in downtown Los Angeles and Hollywood.

Soon the rumors started to ricochet like bullets. Air defense men had known the attack was imminent. Two squadrons of airplanes—that's thirty planes—had been sighted over the California coast. Japanese airplanes had reconnoitered the Bay area. Bombed the Golden Gate Bridge. Pearl Harbor was only a stepping stone. California was next. There would be an uprising of Japanese Americans. Sabotage was certain. Moved to action by the rumors as well as sound precaution, policemen went on 12-hour shifts and sent extra security guards to dams, bridges, and power stations. Most others waited for FDR's announcement that the United States was now at war.

Hollywood and the entertainment industry responded to the attack with sincere feelings of patriotism mixed with an equally sincere desire to cash in on the event. Studios abandoned a few films already in production with poorly timed themes or poorly chosen titles—the musicals *Pearl Harbor Pearl* and *I'll Take Manila* and the comedy *Absent Without Leave,* about a GI who goes AWOL. Just as quickly studios secured the copyrights for more promising titles—*Sunday in Hawaii, Wings Over the Pacific, Bombing of Honolulu, Remember Pearl Harbor, Yellow Peril, Yellow Menace, My Four Years in Japan,* and *V for Victory.* Tin Pan Alley produced topical songs within days of the attack. Although none muscled onto the Hit Parade, such songs as "Let's Put the Axe to the Axis," We're Going to Find the Fellow Who Is Yellow and Beat Him Red, White and Blue," "They're Gonna Be Playin' Taps on the Japs," "The Sun Will Soon Be Setting for the Land of the Rising Sun," "To Be Specific, It's Our Pacific," "When Those Little Yellow Bellies Meet the Cohens and the Kelleys," and "You're a Sap, Mr. Jap" expressed the angry mood of the country. The Metropolitan Opera Company, sensing that Americans did not want to see a sympathetic portrayal of any Japanese, dropped their production of "Madame Butterfly." The Greenwich Village

Savoyards followed the Met's lofty example and dumped their production of "The Mikado."

While Tin Pan Alley turned out their topical tunes and opera companies pruned their repertoires, Americans huddled close to their radios. On Monday morning and Tuesday night F.D.R. delivered his impassioned war speeches before Congress. For a few days, America—and particularly the West Coast—moved through a fog of air raid alarms, blackouts, and tense expectations. They listened as America's foreign commentators broke the news that Germany and Italy had declared war on the United States. They listened to the news that the Germans had sunk two British ships and that the Japanese had followed up Pearl Harbor with attacks in the Philippines, Hong Kong, Wake Island, Guam, and other Pacific strongholds.

Hollywood moaned that the war was a killer at the box office. Certainly flights of parochialism were the standard Hollywood reaction to any event. In 1935 when Mussolini's troops stormed into Ethiopia and the world focused on the League of Nations, a Hollywood producer asked a friend, "Have you heard any late news?" Yes, the friend replied hotly, "Italy just banned *Marie Antoinette!*" This episode of tunnel vision was surpassed in 1939 when Italy ruthlessly invaded Albania. Louella Parsons, Hollywood's leading gossip writer, began her column that week: "The deadly dullness of the past week was lifted today when Darryl Zanuck announced he had bought all rights to *The Bluebird* for Shirley Temple."

By mid-December Hollywood spokesmen complained that Americans were too interested in the war to go to the movies. Attempting to demonstrate that Hollywood *was* concerned with other events, *Variety* observed that the war had also hurt Christmas shopping, but clearly the box office crisis overshadowed all other concerns. The Wolf Man's *Variety* advertisement announced "Listen to That Box Office Howl!" but the only noise was the studio's howl of financial pain. The same was true for *The Great Dictator, Sergeant York, Citizen Kane,* and the season's other top pictures. Amidst considerable hand wringing,

Hollywood leaders speculated on the long-term impact of the war on the industry.

John Wayne shared the industry's general concern, although his worries focused more specifically on the effect the war would have on his own career. After years of struggle with bad scripts and tight budgets, by late 1941 he was moving closer to the fringes of stardom. The reviews he had received for *Stagecoach* and *The Long Voyage Home* had pushed his career to a new level. Republic's head Herbert Yates responded by searching for better scripts, assigning first-line directors, and increasing the budgets for Wayne films. *The Dark Command,* Wayne's first film for Republic under the contract his new agent had negotiated for him, reflected Wayne's new status. Yates allocated $700,000 for the film—more than any previous Republic project—and hired Raoul Walsh to direct it. He also arranged for Claire Trevor and Walter Pidgeon to star in the film with Wayne. And less than four months before the attack on Pearl Harbor, Wayne had finished his work on Cecil B. DeMille's *Reap the Wild Wind,* which Paramount had scheduled for a March 1942 release.

New agents, new contracts, better directors, better films—at the age of thirty-four Duke was a player in Hollywood. But he was not yet a major star. In late December 1941, *Variety* issued its annual review of the stars. It set down clearly where an actor or actress stood in the complicated Hollywood pecking order. At the summit of the hierarchy were the performers whose pictures earned the most money for the year: Gary Cooper, Abbott and Costello, Clark Gable, Mickey Rooney, Bob Hope, Charlie Chaplin, Dorothy Lamour, Spencer Tracy, Jack Benny, and Bing Crosby. They had helped make 1941 the best year ever for domestic box office receipts.

Next came the individual studio reports. The stars and featured performers of the individual studios were listed and briefly discussed. The major studios controlled the major talent. MGM led the pack; its stars included Gable, Rooney, Tracy, Robert Taylor, Lana Turner, James Stewart, Hedy Lamarr, Judy Garland, Myrna Loy, William

Powell, Joan Crawford, Nelson Eddy, Jeanette MacDonald, Greta Garbo, Norma Shearer, the Marx Brothers, and a host of other leading performers. If the other studios could not match MGM, they could all boast of their proven box office attractions. Warner Brothers, king of the gangster genre, had James Cagney, Humphrey Bogart, Edward G. Robinson, John Garfield, and George Raft, as well as Erroll Flynn, Bette Davis, Merle Oberon, and Ronald Reagan. Twentieth Century Fox had a group of attractive leading men and women which included Tyrone Power, Betty Grable, Gene Tierney, Henry Fonda, Randolph Scott, Maureen O'Hara, and Linda Darnell. Paramount had its comedians—Hope, Crosby, and Benny—as well as Lamour, Claudette Colbert, Veronica Lake, Paulette Goddard, Fred MacMurray, and Ray Milland. RKO featured Ginger Rogers, Orson Welles, Cary Grant, Carole Lombard, Ronald Coleman, and Gloria Swanson. Universal had a great year in 1941 thanks to the success of Abbott and Costello. And Columbia featured Peter Lorre, Boris Karloff, Fay Wray, and the recently acquired Rita Hayworth.

At the bottom of the hierarchy were the smaller studios and their performers. There dwelled Monogram. "No pretenses. No ambitious production. Just bread and butter," noted *Variety*. Its older cowboy and action stars—Jack LaRue, Buck Jones, Tim McCoy, and Bela Lugosi—kept the studio afloat. Finally came Republic. *Variety* listed Gene Autry and John Wayne as Republic's "two corking box-office assets." Wayne's reputation derived from his "loanout" status. Like Monogram, Republic produced films for theaters outside of the major distribution circles, and a star like Wayne who was used by the major studios gave prestige to the Poverty Row studio.

Wayne always a clear-thinking realist, knew where he stood in the Hollywood hierarchy. He was a star in the third-and-fourth-run theaters in the South and Southwest, in areas with more cattle than people. His success following *Stagecoach* introduced him to the first-and-second-run palaces of the East, Midwest, and West. At the end of 1941 he was nowhere near the summit of the hierarchy, far from the status of such leading men as Clark Gable, Robert Taylor, Tyrone Power, Cary Grant, Gary Cooper, or Henry Fonda. But Wayne was ambitious, and no one in the industry had his capacity for work. The facts were indisputable: his reputation was growing but not yet firmly established, and he was a thirty-four-year-old leading man. If he enlisted, would his fragile reputation survive two, three, four years in the service? How many years did he have left as a leading man? Enlistment, in the final analysis, would probably end his career.

While Wayne pondered his future and prepared for his next picture, other Hollywood stars put their careers on hold and their lives on the line. Pearl Harbor aroused deep emotions in Hollywood. During the next four years journalists and politicians would accuse the film industry of being cynical, opportunistic, greedy, and worse. The charges were often accurate. But in late 1941 and early 1942 scores of actors, directors, producers, and technicians enlisted out of a deep sense of patriotism. Like millions of other Americans, they were shocked by the Japanese attack and wanted to help win the war.

Henry Fonda, one of Duke's boon companions on vacations to Mexico, felt the pull of patriotism. He was thirty-seven—three years older than Wayne—and had a wife and three children. For all practical purposes, he was exempt from the draft. But he had a baby face, and he did not want the wives and mothers of soldiers and sailors to see him on the screen and ask, "Why isn't he out there?" Besides, as he told his wife, "this is my country and I want to be where it's happening. I don't want to be in a fake war in a studio or on location. . . . I want to be on a real ocean not the back lot. I want to be with real sailors and not extras." After he finished *The Ox-Bow Incident,* the film in which he was then starring, Fonda drove to the Naval Headquarters in Los Angeles and enlisted. No screen photographers were present; his press agent had not tipped off any reporters. Fonda wanted it simple, no different than other Americans.

John Ford, the man Duke admired the most, also felt the pull. During the late 1930s he had followed with growing uneasiness the spread of fascism in Europe. When Ford's leading writer Dudley Nichols sent him a wire of congratulations for winning the 1940 Academy Award for his direction of *The Grapes of Wrath,* Ford wrote back, "Awards for pictures are a trivial thing to be concerned with at times like these." That spring he organized the Naval Field Photographic Reserve unit, which Washington officially recognized. The forty-six-year-old Ford was ordered to report to Washington for active duty in the month before Pearl Harbor. Immediately and without publicity he left Hollywood. He left the money, the fame, the career, the glamour.

When the Japanese attacked Pearl Harbor, Ford was eating lunch at the eighteenth-century Alexandria, Virginia, home of Admiral William Pickens. He watched the Admiral take the urgent phone call. He saw the blood drain from his face. After they heard the news, Pickens' wife, Darrielle, showed Ford a scar on their home where a Revolutionary War musket ball had torn through a wall. "I never let them plaster over the hole," she said. Throughout the war and for the rest of his life Ford would remember the story. He wanted to be part of that tradition.

Tradition and patriotism pulled Jimmy Stewart into the war. Stewart's grandfather had fought for the union during the Civil War. Stewart's father had fought in the Spanish-American War and World War I. In February 1941, Stewart attempted to enlist in the Army Air Corps but was rejected because his 147 pounds was ten pounds too light for his six feet four inch frame. He went on a diet of candy, beer, and bananas. In a month he had put on the ten pounds and he was sworn into the Army. He left his $1,500–a-week movie salary for a private's wages.

Other leading men and Hollywood personalities also felt the pull. Wayne's fellow star at Republic, Gene Autry, joined the Army Air Corps. Robert Montgomery enlisted in the Navy. Tyrone Power joined the Marines. William Holden went into the Army. After the death of his wife Carole Lombard in January 1942, Clark Gable also enlisted in the Army. David Niven, Laurence Olivier, and Patrick Knowles returned to their native Britain and enlisted. Ronald Reagan, Sterling Hayden, Burgess Meredith, and Gilbert Roland all signed up. So too did directors Frank Capra, William Wyler, Anatole Litvak, John Huston, and William Keighley; producers Hal Roach, Jack Warner, Gene Markey, and Darryl F. Zanuck; writers Garson Kanin and Budd Schulberg; cameraman Gregg Toland; and thousands of other Hollywood workers. By October 1942 over 2,700—or 12 percent—of the men and women in the film industry had entered the armed forces. Some like Fonda and Stewart enlisted quietly and without fanfare. Others like Reagan and Zanuck and Gable made the process of enlistment and service an act of Hollywood. But quietly or loudly they did serve.

In 1941 professional baseball players were the only men who received as much attention and adulation as Hollywood stars. When the war started they laid down their bats and picked up service issue weapons. Joe DiMaggio, Hank Greenberg, Bob Feller, Ted Williams, Bill Dickey, Peewee Reese, and most of the other baseball legends from the 1930s entered the service. More than 4,000 of the roughly 5,700 players in the major and minor leagues served in the armed forces during the war. Some were killed or seriously injured during the conflict. Others experienced the loss of crucial skills because of a lack of practice. And even the players who returned to the big leagues after the war lost several years from a career which at best was painfully short.

Even America's popular comic book heroes enlisted in the war effort. Joe Palooka and Snuffy Smith joined the Army; Mickey Flynn enlisted in the Coast Guard; Dick Tracy received a commission in naval intelligence. Batman, Robin, the Flash, Plastic Man, Captain America, Captain Marvel, the Green Lantern, the Spirit—the cream of the super heroes—fought Germans and Japanese in the pages of thousands of comic books. The only important super hero who did not enlist was Superman—and he stayed at home for a very good reason. His creators, Jerry Siegel and Joe

Schuster, reasoned that Nazis and Japs would be no match for the Man of Steel, and with real Americans fighting and dying in the war it might denigrate their efforts if Superman defeated the Axis. To keep Superman out of the war but still show his patriotism, Siegel and Schuster had Clark Kent—a.k.a. Superman—declared 4-F. Superman's famed X-ray vision malfunctioned during his preinduction physical; instead of reading the eye chart in front of him, Superman accidentally looked through the wall and focused on the one in the next room. Shazam—4-F. Instead of fighting abroad, Superman battled Fifth Columnist activities in the States.

Movie stars and baseball stars, superheroes and boxing champions—they took their place with millions of other less famous Americans. More than any other war in America's history, World War II was a popular, democratic war. In the five years between December 1941 and December 1946, 16.3 million Americans entered the armed forces. All males between the ages of 18 and 64 had to register for the draft, although the upper age limit for service was set at 44 and later lowered to 38. One out of every six American men wore a uniform during the war. The wealthy fought alongside the poor, the single beside married men with children. Unlike the Vietnam War, relatively few men tried to avoid military service. For a man in his twenties or thirties not in uniform, the central question was, "Why not?"

It was a question John Wayne had to face for the next four years. Wayne's case was not a matter of draft dodging. Although by late 1941 Wayne's marriage was falling apart and his visits to his home and children were becoming more infrequent, he was technically married and had four children. This coupled with his age meant that he was not a prime candidate for the draft. And in February 1942 General Lewis B. Hershey, Director of Selective Service, called the motion picture industry "an activity essential in certain instances to the national health, safety and interest, and in other instances to war production." In accordance with his statement, he instructed Selective Service officials in California to grant defer-

ments to men vital to the industry. Although Hershey's order was not meant as a blanket deferment, and although the Screen Actors Guild announced that it did not want any privileged status, the California draft board was liberal in its application of the ruling. Many Washington and California officials argued that Gary Cooper was more valuable to the war effort as Sergeant York—a role he played in the top money grosser in 1941 which oozed patriotism—than as Sergeant Cooper.

The most visible Hollywood commodity in need of protection during the war was the leading man. Out of sincere feelings of patriotism or the fear of being branded as a slacker, many of Hollywood's youngest and most famous leading men enlisted. The shortage created a ticklish problem for studio public relation staffs. Leading men were supposed to project youth, sexuality, virility, and strength. But a movie star projecting those traits on the screen during the war faced the painful question, "Why isn't he in the army?" As *Daily Variety* commented, "No more he-man build up of young men as in the past, for these might kick back unpleasant reverberations. If the build up is too mighty, [the] public may want to know if he's that good why isn't he in the Army shooting Japs and Nazis. This is a particularly touchy phase and p-r has to be subtle about it." The irony of the situation was best expressed by an agent who told a producer about his latest discovery: "I've got a great prospect for you—a young guy with a double hernia."

A leading man during the war needed a good profile and an adequate voice, but more importantly he had to be either over forty, married with two or more children, or 4-F. Gary Cooper, Bing Crosby, James Cagney, John Garfield, Don Ameche, and Joel McCrea all "had a brood at home to call [them] 'pop.'" Warner Baxter, Neil Hamilton, and Nils Aster—all forty to fifty—led the new crop of "semi-romantic" leading men. Sonny Tufts, the handsome, ex-Yale football player who starred in the hit *So Proudly We Hail,* was safely classified as 4-F.

John Wayne's draft status was a family present. Like other actors with two or more children, he could have enlisted. Like his friends Henry Fonda or John Ford, he could have placed his concern for his nation above his concern for his family, status, and career. There were some aspects of his life that Wayne never spoke to the press about; some that he rarely ever even spoke to his family or closest friends about. His decision not to enlist was a part of his life that he did not discuss. Pilar Wayne, whom Duke met and married a decade after the war, said that the guilt he suffered over his failure to enlist influenced the rest of his life. Mary St. John, who worked at Republic during the war and became Wayne's personal secretary after the war, agreed. She recalled that Wayne suffered "terrible guilt and embarrassment" because of his war record. The fact that his brother Robert served in the Navy only exasperated Wayne's sensitivity. His mother, who always openly favored Robert, was not above reminding Wayne that Robert, and not Duke, had served his country during the great crisis. On the screen, Wayne was the quintessential man of action, one who took matters into his own powerful hands and fought for what he believed. Never had the chasm between what he projected on the screen and his personal actions been so great.

Throughout 1942 and 1943, as he made one picture after another and as his reputation as a leading man soared, Wayne flirted with the idea of enlistment. He was particularly concerned about his stature in Ford's eyes, and he suspected that Ford had little respect for Celluloid soldiers. His suspicion was dead right. In early October 1941, shortly after he went on active duty, Ford wrote his wife that Wayne and Ward Bond's frivolous activities were meaningless in a world spinning toward total war. "They don't count. Their time will come." Three months after Pearl Harbor, Ford again mentioned Wayne in a letter to his wife. In a letter soaked in contempt, he remarked that he was "delighted" to hear about Wayne and Bond sitting up all night on a mountain top listening through earphones for signs that the Japanese were attacking California: "Ah well—such heroism shall not go unrewarded—it will live in the annals of time."

A pattern developed in Wayne's letters to Ford during the first two years of the war. Again and again, Wayne told Ford that he wanted to enlist—planned to enlist—as soon as he finished just one or two pictures. In the spring of 1942, Wayne inquired if he could get in Ford's unit, and if Ford would want him. If that option were closed, what would Ford suggest? Should he try the Marines? Plaintively, Wayne insisted that he was not drunk and that he hated to ask for favors, adding, "But for Christ's sake, you can suggest can't you?" A year later, Wayne was still considering enlistment in his letters to Ford. After he finished one more film he would be free: "Outside of that [film] Barkus [*sic*] is ready, anxious, and willin'."

But Barkus never did enlist. Toward the end of his life, Wayne told Dan Ford, John Ford's grandson, that his wife Josie had prevented him from joining Ford's outfit. According to his story, OSS head and Ford's superior William J. Donovan had sent a letter to Wayne explaining when Duke could join the Field Photographic Unit, but Josie never gave him the letter. He also confessed that he considered enlisting as a private, but rejected the idea. How, he pondered, could he fight alongside seventeen- and eighteen-year-old boys who had been reared on his movies? For them, he said, "I was America." In the end he concluded that he could best serve his country by making movies and going on an occasional USO tour.

The problem with any discussion of Wayne's "war record" is that it depends too much on statements made by Duke and others long after the war ended. Did his wife hide Donovan's letter? There is no such letter in Donovan's public and private papers. Did he believe that he was such an American institution by 1942 that he could not enlist as a private? This statement is difficult to take at face value when one considers that Gable, Power, Fonda, and Stewart—far more important stars than Wayne—were willing to share a foxhole or a cockpit or a ship deck with seventeen- and eighteen-year-old American soldiers or sailors. Did, in fact, Wayne try to enlist? Catalina Lawrence, a script supervisor at Republic during the war who sometimes doubled as Wayne's secretary, remembers writing letters for Wayne attempting to get him in the service. "He felt so bad," she recalled, "especially after Robert was drafted into the Navy. Duke wanted to get in, but he just never could."

The closest one can come to the truth is Wayne's Selective Service record, and even here there are a few problems. The government has destroyed full individual records; all letters between Wayne and his draft board have long since been turned into ashes in official government incinerators. The skeleton of Wayne's record, however, remains. When the war started, Marion Mitchell Morrison—Selective Service Serial Number 2815, Order Number 1619—was classified 3-A, "deferred for dependency reasons." A continuation of that classification was requested and granted on November 17, 1943. Local draft boards periodically reviewed all classifications, and depending on their needs the government changed some classifications. To maintain a deferment or obtain a different deferment, a person or his employer had to file an official request. After returning the initial Selective Service Questionnaire, Wayne never personally filed a deferment claim, but a series of claims were filed "by another." Although the records have been destroyed, Republic Pictures almost certainly filed the claims. After Republic's leading money earner Gene Autry enlisted in 1942, studio president Herbert Yates was determined to keep Wayne out of uniform and in front of the camera. Therefore, in April 1944 another deferment claim was filed and granted reclassifying Wayne 2-A, "deferred in support of national health, safety, or interest." A month later Wayne was once again reclassified. With the war in Europe and the Pacific reaching a critical stage, Duke received a 1-A classification, "available for military service." This reclassification generated a series of new deferment claims, and on May 5, 1945, Wayne was once again classified 2-A. His last classification came after the war when he received a 4-A deferment on the basis of his age.

At any time during the war Wayne could have appealed his classification. At no time did he file

an appeal. Always an active man, the war years were particularly frantic for Wayne. With his career bolting forward, he worked at four different studios and starred in thirteen pictures. In addition, he divorced his first wife, met and married his second wife, and led an active social life. When he was not working, the absence of a uniform gnawed into Wayne's self-respect and sense of manhood. It was then that he wrote Ford that "Barkus was ready." But then would come another movie, another delay, another link in a chain of delays that stretched from Pearl Harbor to Hiroshima.

Perhaps in his own mind his single-minded pursuit of his career meshed with his sense of patriotism. If so, Wayne was not the only person in Hollywood who expressed such beliefs. In March 1942, shortly after the premiere of *Reap the Wild Wind,* Wayne attended a luncheon for the Associated Motion Picture Advertisers. Cecil B. DeMille addressed the audience on the subject of the role Hollywood should play in the war. DeMille, his voice charged with moral urgency, remarked, "The job of motion pictures is to help bring home a full realization of the crisis and of the deadly peril that lurks in internal squabbles. Ours is the task of holding high and ever visible the values that everyone is fighting for. I don't mean flag waving, but giving the embattled world sharp glimpses of the way of life that we've got to hang on to in spite of everything." In DeMille's mind, the civilians who worked in the motion picture industry had a job and a duty every bit as important to the war effort as the American Marines fighting on Pacific islands or American sailors battling the Germans on the Atlantic. Victory demanded unity and dedication by all Americans—at home and abroad, civilian and military.

The Roosevelt administration agreed with DeMille. Only weeks after the war began, F.D.R. announced that Hollywood had an important role to play in the war effort: "The American motion picture is one of our most effective media in informing and entertaining our citizens. The motion picture must remain free in so far as national security will permit." Unlike steel, automobiles, and other vital American industries, which were heavily controlled by the government during the war, the controls on the film industry were comparatively light. Although several of F.D.R.'s advisors counseled him to take over Hollywood production, he believed that the industry leaders would perform their duty better if they remained in charge. But the subtext of Roosevelt's message to Hollywood was clear. The studio heads could continue to make money, but their product had to serve the war effort. They had to combine propaganda within the entertainment. If they did not, then the government would take over the industry.

Washington's liaison with Hollywood was Lowell Mellett, a former editor of the *Washington Daily News* who had the good looks of an older Hollywood character actor. After considerable bureaucratic reorganization in June 1942, Mellett was placed in charge of the Bureau of Motion Pictures (BMP), which was nominally under the Domestic Branch of the Office of War Information (OWI). While Mellett, dubbed the "white rabbit" for his less than forceful character, administered the BMP from his Washington office, the bureau's Hollywood office was run by Nelson Poynter. A close friend of Mellett's as well as a newspaper man, the dark-haired, frail looking Poynter had unassailable New Deal and interventionist credentials but lacked even basic knowledge of Hollywood and film making. Nevertheless, F.D.R. charged the team of Mellett and Poynter with making sure Hollywood produced the kind of pictures deemed important to the war effort.

If he were uncertain about the process of making pictures, Poynter was very explicit about what kind of films he expected Hollywood to produce. From his tiny office in Hollywood, Poynter and his small staff compiled a blueprint to guide the motion picture industry's wartime behavior. Officially titled *The Government Informational Manual for the Motion Picture Industry,* it set down the official—and ideological—government line. The central question every producer, director, and writer should ask was "Will this picture help win the war?" Every film should contribute to that end by presenting America's effort and cause, its allies and friends, in the most generous

possible terms. The manual emphasized that the United States was engaged in nothing less than "a people's war" to create a "new world" where want and fear were banished and freedom of religion and speech were a birthright. Social democratic and liberal internationalist in its intent, the manual was designed to move Hollywood toward its ideological position.

In practical terms, *The Government Informational Manual for the Motion Picture Industry* codified a long list of "dos" and "don'ts" for Hollywood. Whenever possible, for example, films should "show people making small sacrifices for victory"—"bringing their own sugar when invited out to dinner, carrying their own parcels when shopping, travelling on planes or trains with light luggage, uncomplainingly giving up seats to servicemen or others travelling on war priorities." Americans on the homefront should be portrayed as happy, busy, productive, rationing-loving patriots, planting victory gardens, taking public transportation even when they could afford to drive, and generally pitching in to win the war. Heading the list of "don'ts" was disunity on the homefront or the battlefront. America was not to be presented as divided by any racial, class, or gender issue. Scenes of strikes or labor conflict critical of labor were frowned upon; plots which suggested that the United States was anything less than a paradise for black Americans were verboten; and resorts to ethnic or religious bigotry were censored. Similarly, the allies of the United States had to be presented as paragons of national virtue. Hollywood was instructed to use its magic to manufacture a classless Britain, an efficient and incorruptible China, and a democratic Russia. Noting the irony of Hollywood's whitewash of the Soviet Union, *Variety* commented, "War has put Hollywood's traditional conception of the Muscovites through the wringer, and they have come out shaved, washed, sober, good to their families, Rotarians, brother Elks, and 33rd Degree Mason."

During the war, John Wayne starred in movies which fit comfortably within the parameters defined by Mellett, Poynter, and the BMP. To be sure, the producers of the Wayne films occasionally clashed with the BMP, but the conflicts were usually caused by the BMP's narrow ideological interpretation of individual scenes or insistence that a specific propaganda message appear in the film's dialogue. In a larger sense, *The Government Information Manual for the Motion Picture Industry* described an America—if not a world—that Wayne already held dear. Perhaps the physical world of Hollywood was closer to the ideal presented by the BMP than any other American community. The motion picture industry was populated by WASPs and immigrants, Catholics and Jews, whites and blacks, men and women. A communist might write a screenplay which a liberal would produce and a reactionary direct, but for a time all three would be unified by a common bond—the movie. In Hollywood some of the highest paid stars were women, and a few blacks—very few—earned incomes higher than Southern cotton planters. And nowhere in America was the Horatio Alger ideal of rags to riches so religiously enshrined. Hollywood was an industry that literally manufactured modern American folk heroes. It was America's "last frontier." It was the crossroads where luck, looks, and talent intersected. And in a strange way, it was the America described in the pages of the BMP official manual. Of course Wayne believed in its message. He was its message.

John Wayne's wartime movies portrayed the BMP's message even before the bureau was created and the manual written. During the first four months of 1942, as American forces experienced painful losses in the Pacific and the Atlantic, Wayne made two pictures—*The Spoilers* and *In Old California.* Both films have similar plots. *The Spoilers,* based on the Rex Beach novel, is set in Nome in 1900 during the Alaskan Gold Rush, centers on a claim jumping scheme, and features a love triangle between Wayne, a society woman, and a dance-hall girl. During the course of the film, Wayne thwarts the claim jumping scheme as he discovers that the society woman is heartless and the dance-hall girl has a heart as pure as a Klondike nugget. *In Old California* is set in Sacramento in 1848–1849 during the California gold rush, features a land grabbing scheme, and highlights a love triangle between Wayne, a society woman, and a dance-hall girl. By the end of the film, not only does Wayne foil the land grabbing scheme and discover that the society woman is heartless and the dance-hall girl has a heart as pure as a nugget from Sutter's Mill, but he also saves the entire region from a particularly nasty typhoid epidemic.

The message of both films was also similar: defend your property with every fiber of your being. Neither film expresses any sympathy for men who traffic in appeasement or legal niceties. In *The Spoilers* two prospectors announce in a saloon that they were "just working along kinda peaceful like" when at least twenty claim jumpers forced them off their stake. What could we do, they ask. "Ya still have five fingers on your gun hand, ain't ya," comes the immediate reply. All at the bar nod in agreement to the sage advise. Even the sexual innuendo revolves around claim jumping and force. Crooked gold commissioner Alexander McNamara (Randolph Scott) plans to jump both Roy Glennister's (John Wayne) Midas Gold Mine and his woman, Cherry Malotte (Marlene Dietrich). He tells Cherry that he might "move into [Glennister's] territory." "Could be tough going," Cherry cautions. "But worth it," McNamara replies. Glennister's use of brutal force defeats both forms of aggression. In one of the longest fist fights in film history, Glennister outlasts McNamara. Force—not the impotent and even dishonest representatives of the law—proves the only solution to aggression.

The same conclusion is expressed in *In Old California.* When the good but timid citizens of Sacramento are attacked, Tom Craig (John Wayne), the otherwise peace-loving town pharmacist, asks, "Doesn't anybody fight back around here?" "Angry men defending their home," he asserts, can never be defeated. And, of course, they do triumph. Lead by the forceful Craig, "the people" overcome both the land grabbers and the typhoid epidemic. For Americans embroiled in a war to prevent land-grabbing aggression, the message of *The Spoilers* and *In Old California*—both released in the dark month of May 1942—reinforced official government statements about the causes of the war.

In Old California was little more than an inexpensive Republic formula picture. Without John Wayne, wrote the *New York Times'* reviewer Bosley Crowther, the picture "would be down with the usual run of strays." *The Spoilers,* however, received favorable reviews. "The he-men are back," noted the *New York Times.* "John Wayne is . . . virile," commented *Variety.* "John Wayne is a valuable piece of property," was the judgment of the Chicago *Tribune.* The acting characteristics which Wayne had spent a decade perfecting—the sideways glance and smile at his female lead, the tight-lipped, shark-eyed stare at his evil rival—found worthy recipients in *The Spoilers.* Dietrich's seething sexuality and Scott's oily villainy contrasted nicely with Wayne's cocky masculinity.

Wayne was maturing as an actor, and he knew it. On the set he was more self-confident. He was occasionally rude and impatient with Scott, who took a more artistic approach to his craft than Wayne. Scott, a Southerner with courtly manner, disliked Duke. On and off the set of *The Spoilers,* Dietrich occupied Wayne's attentions. The affair which had begun when Wayne and Dietrich were starring together in *Seven Sinners* had not yet run its passionate course. On and off the set they were constantly together. They dined at Ciros, the Brown Derby, Mocambo, and the Trocadero, Hollywood's trendiest restaurants. They went to sporting events and on weekend hunting and fishing trips together. Dietrich "was the most intriguing woman I've ever known," Wayne later told his wife Pilar. She shared her bedroom and ideas with Duke. And this combination of sexual and intellectual stimulation bolstered Wayne's belief in himself.

At Republic Pictures, Herbert Yates was not as interested in Wayne's emotional and intellectual growth as in his burgeoning box office power. Paramount released *Reap the Wild Wind* in March 1942, and it opened in the first-run theaters and music halls throughout the country. Respected *New York Times* reviewer Bosley Crowther saw the Technicolor epic in Radio City Music Hall. Always a generous reviewer for DeMille's films, he

was particularly lavish in his praise for *Reap the Wild Wind.* It was "the essence of all [DeMille's] experience, the apogee of his art and as jam-full a motion picture as has ever played two hours upon a screen. It definitely marks a DeMillestone," Crowther wrote. The review, and others like it, echoed like gold coins in Yates's mind. *Reap the Wild Wind* was a hit—reviewers compared it with that other breezy film, *Gone With the Wind*—and John Wayne was one of its stars, even if he was killed in the movie by a giant squid and therefore failed to win the heroine. And Wayne belonged to Yates and Republic. If Yates had been unimpressed by Duke's success in *Stagecoach* and *The Long Voyage Home,* he now fully understood the worth of his star attraction.

With profits and the war in mind, Yates put Wayne into his first war film. If it were not for the fact that *Flying Tigers* was a shameless rip off of *Only Angels Have Wings,* the film might be considered as the prototype for World War II combat films. It possessed everything but originality, a point that did not cause serious concern for an action oriented studio like Republic. Howard Hawks' *Only Angels Have Wings* (1939) contained all the motifs that film scholar Robert B. Ray has labeled as basic to Hollywood's World War II combat films: "the male group directed by a strong leader, the outsider who must prove himself by courageous individual action, the necessity for stoicism in the face of danger and death, the premium placed on professionalism, and the threat posed by women."

Only Angels Have Wings centers on a group of pilots in a South American jungle contracted to deliver the mail over a range of dangerous, stalactite mountains of unearthly appearance. In this group of flying mercenaries is a brave leader called "Pappy" who emphasizes teamwork, a man branded as a coward who has to prove his courage to win acceptance, a woman who threatens to destroy the chummy fraternity atmosphere, and pilots who share a common Hemingwayesque code of life and language. They speak with their actions, resist expressing their emotions, and demonstrate their dependency and even love in such nonverbal ways as asking for a cigarette or a match.

Flying Tigers contains all the same elements. This time the mercenary pilots are part of Colonel Claire Lee Chennault's "American Volunteer Group," flying against the Japanese for China on the eve of Pearl Harbor. Once again, the leader stresses the value of teamwork and is called "Pappy" by his men. Once again, there is a suspected coward who must prove himself, a flamboyant individualist who on the surface seems to only care about himself, and a woman who threatens the harmony and effectiveness of the male unit. There is even the same language of cigarettes and matches and painful grimaces when talk turns to matters of the heart. The similarities of plot and structure are so striking that Ray commented that "Hawks should have sued for plagiarism."

But for all the similarities—and there were many—there was a major difference. *Flying Tigers* went into production shortly after Pearl Harbor during America's darkest months in the Pacific War and dealt with the most urgent topic in the world: the war. It was filmed from May to July, 1942, months that saw the Japanese take Corregidor and the United States win the Battles of Coral Sea and Midway. *Flying Tigers* capitalized on the national mood. At a moment when the nation demanded a hero, Republic responded with John Wayne. At a time when the Americans longed for good news from the Pacific, *Flying Tigers* recounted the heroics of Chennault's "American Volunteer Group." During a crisis when the country wanted to believe the best of its allies and the worst of its enemies, the film presented Chinese straight from the pages of Pearl S. Buck's *The Good Earth* and automatous Japanese fresh from hell. In addition, the film touched the rawest of American nerves—Pearl Harbor. F.D.R.'s full war speech is replayed in the film, and the climactic scene occurs after the Japanese attack on Pearl Harbor.

The film was an ideal vehicle for Wayne. The role of the solid, quiet leader around whom all the action and all the other parts revolved played to Duke's strengths. Increasingly in his recent films

he was developing a palpable screen presence. Without talking, often without moving, he dominated a scene. In one scene, for example, the pilots listen to F.D.R.'s war speech on the radio. Slowly the camera moves in for a close-up on Wayne, who stands silent, listening to the message, a cigarette in his left hand. During the entire message, Wayne never moves. His eyes and mouth do not change expression. The only movement is the smoke drifting upward from Wayne's unsmoked cigarette. At the end of the speech, he takes a deep breath and walks off screen. Roosevelt had said it all; Wayne could only have added a trite cliché. Duke played the scene with controlled passion and complete sincerity. It is a powerful scene which underscored Wayne's screen presence.

Republic believed *Flying Tigers* conveyed the message advocated by the Office of War Information's Bureau of Motion Pictures. The film emphasized teamwork. Woody Jason (John Carroll) tells his fellow mercenaries early in the film that he is in China for the $600 a month and the $500 bonus for every Japanese plane he shoots down: "This is not our home. It's not our fight. It's a business. And, boy, I hope business is good." "It's every man for himself, isn't it," he asks just before he bums a cigarette from one man and a match from another. But by the end of the film Woody sacrifices his life in a suicide mission to save Jim "Pappy" Gordon (John Wayne). After Pearl Harbor, he realizes that China is as important as his "home street." Scenes that emphasize the importance of non-flying personnel and mechanics similarly stress the themes of teamwork and cooperation. And if that did not provide enough propaganda content, *Flying Tigers* is filled with good-hearted, loyal Chinese and cold, ruthless Japanese.

Government officials, however, had mixed reactions to the film. Harry B. Price, a government consultant on China, noted that although the film was generally of a high caliber, it left "much to be desired from the standpoint of an adequate portrayal of our Allies, the Chinese." Like so many other Hollywood films, wrote Price, *Flying Tigers* presented the Chinese as "likable, but slightly ludicrous," and there is "little in the picture to suggest that the Chinese people are human beings just as varied and many sided in their natures as Americans." In addition, the film did not explore Chennault's tactical innovations. The Bureau of Motion Picture staffer who reviewed *Flying Tigers* agreed with Price's assessment. Marjorie Thorson complained that the film's glorification of individual heroics muted its theme of teamwork and cooperation, that the Chinese are presented as harmless and slightly incompetent people, and that the major issues of the war are not discussed. She notes that although there are Chinese nurses and doctors in the movie, only American nurses are shown changing bandages and "the final decision in any matter of a flier's health is left to the *non-professional* American squadron leader . . . just being an American presumably qualifies him to make medical decisions over the head of the trained Chinese." Even worse, "no Chinese men are shown fighting." "Altogether," she concluded, the "picture attempts a great deal more than it accomplishes."

Official complaints often demonstrated an ignorance both of filmmaking and the war. Members of the "American Volunteer Group" charged that *Flying Tigers* was "unbelievably bad" because it contained several factual errors and employed two former members of the AVG as technical advisors who had been dishonorably discharged for being "suspected of perversion." Contentions that filmmakers distort history by focusing on the individual or the small group at the expense of historical reality reveal a deep misunderstanding of the industry. As for *Flying Tigers'* treatment of Chiang Kai-shek and the Chinese, blindly generous is the best description. Divided by warlordism and civil war, plagued by corruption and inefficiency, Chiang's Kuomintang government dismissed "aggressive action" against the Japanese before Pearl Harbor and after December 7, 1941, left any serious fighting to the United States. As one American military official noted in late 1941, "The general idea in the United States that China has fought Japan to a standstill and has had many glorious victories is a delusion." If *Flying Tigers'* portrayal of the Chinese is historically inaccurate, it was closer to reality than the line adopted by the BMP. And the assertion in the film that Americans provided the combat muscle in the war did reflect actual conditions.

The entire debate was irrelevant at Republic. Yates was not interested in the veracity of *Flying Tigers,* Republic was a bottom line studio, and its only concern was ticket sales. From its first preview, the film exceeded Republic's usual modest expectations. The *Hollywood Reporter* announced, *Flying Tigers* marks an all-time production high for Republic. It is a smashing, stirring, significant film. . . . It will be a record grosser in all engagements, and no theater in the land should hesitate about proudly showing it." *Variety* agreed: In *Flying Tigers,* Republic has its best picture." Even though the film was released late in the year, *Flying Tigers* became one of 1942's leading box office successes and the only picture in the top twenty not produced in one of the major studios.

No one at Republic had to search for the reason. It was John Wayne. If Republic executives needed confirmation, they found it in every major review. *Hollywood Reporter:* "John Wayne is at his peak. . . ." *Variety:* "John Wayne matches his best performance. . . ." *New York Times:* "Mr. Wayne is the sort of fellow who inspires confidence. . . ." Republic had a hit and a star. Yates was now convinced. So was the rest of the industry. And during the next three years of war, Wayne would reconfirm again and again his star status as his name alone came to guarantee box office success.

Now more than ever, Yates was determined to keep Wayne. Shortly after the release of *Flying Tigers* the film's producer, Edmund Grainger, and director, David Miller, entered the armed service. Neither would make another picture until the late 1940s. Wayne believed that he too should enlist. Yates refused to release Wayne. The loss of Gene Autry, whose contract to make eight straight pictures for Republic had to be shelved when the singing cowboy enlisted in the Army air service, devastated Yates. He told Wayne that he would sue him for breach of contract if Duke enlisted. Furthermore, Yates announced, if Wayne enlisted he would make certain that Duke would never work for Republic or any other studio again. Although Yates's threat violated government policy—every person in uniform was guaranteed their civilian job once the war ended—Wayne did not press the issue. He feared poverty and unemployment, and perhaps more, he feared losing the status he had achieved and sinking into obscurity. Always a man haunted by the ghosts of his own insecurity, he stayed out of uniform, secure in his home at Republic.

Wayne's home was Republic, but his contract allowed him to make pictures for other studios. With the scarcity of leading men becoming more pressing every month, Duke was never in greater demand. It was an ideal situation for Wayne. He was a man who never made peace with inactivity. He loved his work and he hated the time between pictures. Mary St. John, who worked as Wayne's personal secretary for over twenty-five years, said that part of his problem was that he had no hobbies, nothing to do to fill the empty days. His daughter Aissa commented that he "was a slave to his energy." On location he always awoke by four-thirty or five A.M., and even when he was not working on a picture he was up at dawn. "He never slept late. Ever," Aissa remembered. Once up, and wired by his morning coffee, he was ready for work, and when there was no work, he simply had to endure long periods of restless rest. And in 1942, such stretches were intolerable. His home life was empty, his marriage almost over, many of his friends in uniform. When he worked, his life had structure and purpose. When he was not working, he had time to mull over the irony that without serving a day in the armed forces he was becoming a World War II hero. It was during these periods that he penned "Barkus" letters to Ford.

Throughout 1942 Duke worked at a hectic pace. *The Spoilers* was shot in January and February, *In Old California* in March and April, and *Flying Tigers* in May, June, and July. While *Flying Tigers* was in post-production, Wayne moved on

to other films. Between the end of July and September he starred in *Reunion in France* for MGM, and in September and October he starred in *Pittsburgh,* another Universal film with Marlene Dietrich and Randolph Scott. Both *Reunion in France* and *Pittsburgh* were released in December. In one year Wayne had made five films, all released that same year. In addition, *Lady for the Night* and *Reap the Wild Wind* had also premiered in 1942. There were few empty periods.

Like *Flying Tigers, Reunion in France* and *Pittsburgh* were war films. *Reunion in France,* however, was a peculiar sort of war film, the product of MGM's odd but predictable slant on life. MGM, noted Warner Brothers' executive Milton Spalding, "was a studio of white telephones." Quality—or at least the illusion of quality—mattered, and studio head Louis B. Mayer spent money to obtain it. As a result, at MGM nothing was what it seemed, everything was idealized. Reality never entered the MGM lot. Women especially had to look perfect. Cameramen "had to photograph the movie queens and make them look damn good," said MGM director George Cukor. If such MGM women as Greta Garbo, Joan Crawford, Jean Harlow, Norma Shearer, Lana Turner, Greer Garson, and Myrna Loy had individual styles, they all shared a common glamour and elegance. Regardless of the role they were called on to play, they always projected beauty and glamour.

After Pearl Harbor and the start of the war, Hollywood wags exchanged jokes about how the conflict would be portrayed at MGM. "The Japs may take California but they'll never get in to see Louis B. Mayer," quipped one wit. When an industry personality remarked that the United States needed a positive slogan that articulated what the country was fighting for, a less earnest listener replied, "Lana Turner." There was a truth in both jokes. As long as Louis B. Mayer called the shots at MGM, only movies that presented a highly stylized version of World War II would be made. And as long as Mayer approved all projects, MGM would fight a war to make the world safe for Lana.

John Wayne achieved superstardom making war movies during the 1940s. Here he is pictured with Anna Lee in *Flying Tigers,* a 1942 production.

Reunion in France brought America face to face with the stark glamour of war. The film centers on the trials and clothes of Michele de la Becque (Joan Crawford), a wealthy French socialite who loses her mansion and carefree life when the Germans invade France in 1940. With the swiftness of the Nazi *blitzkrieg,* her comfortable, insulated world is shattered. Her industrialist fiancé turns collaborationist, her wealth is confiscated, and she is forced to work for her former dressmaker—a job that pays poorly but allows her to remain the best dressed woman in Paris—to pay her bills. Resisting Nazi domination, she befriends Pat Talbot (John Wayne), an American RAF Eagle Squadron flier who has been shot down and wounded behind enemy lines, and helps him escape. The film ends with Michele's

reunion with her fiancé, who turns out to be a resistance fighter in collaborationist clothing. Far from helping Germany, the industrialist had been sending the Nazis faulty war materials to foil their efforts to dominate Europe.

The BMP reacted angrily to MGM's sanitized version of the war. "If there were ever a perfect argument for OWI reading of scripts before they are shot, this picture is it," wrote BMP staffer Marjorie Thorson in her review of the film. The picture failed the war effort on a number of counts. Count one: the film presented the Gestapo as "cruel, suspicious, and sadistic" but contained a favorable portrayal of all other Germans. The German military governor of Paris is depicted as a courtly, sweet, and charming older gentleman, an echo of a European aristocracy of decency and integrity. Furthermore, the German soldiers were disciplined and polite. Count two: the film suggests that any greedy, opportunistic collaborationist may really be an upstanding, patriotic member of the French Resistance. "It is a well known fact," the reviewer reported, "that many of the great French industrialists were pro-fascist long before the present war began; that they helped the Nazis conquer France; that they are now reaping the blood-stained rewards of their betrayal." Count three: the film shows nothing of the misery that the Germans have brought to the French people. MGM portrays a France that "falls with great elegance. Everyone we see is beautifully gowned, comfortably housed, and apparently well fed." Nazi occupation of Paris, the film insinuates, only means that the swastika hangs on the railroad stations and dumpy German women get the first crack at the latest Parisian fashions. Count four: the film misses the chance to contrast Nazi and democratic ideologies. Beyond the heroine saying that democracy is not dead and will live again in France, the film fails to explore the vital issue. In the context of the film, democracy suggests only that thin French women will someday reclaim their own fashions.

The serious charges led to the final verdict: *Reunion in France* "is a very poorly conceived picture. It misrepresents France, the French underground, the Nazis. Far more serious, it unintentionally gives aid and comfort to the enemy in the peace offensive that will surely, and perhaps soon, be launched." That was the crux of the matter. The Office of War Information predicted a German peace offensive in January 1943, and it believed *Reunon in France* would work to the benefit of the Germans. At the time when the Office of War Information was pressing the BMP to get producers to seriously discuss the issues of the war in their films, MGM suggested that the war was between fat German and thin French women with fashion hanging neatly pressed in the balance. Reviewing the film, the Office of War Information's Bureau of Intelligence commented, "the most striking feature of France as shown in the picture is a genius for designing and wearing women's clothes. . . . The preservation of this genius from the bad taste of the Germans is the big issue."

Newspaper reviews agreed with the government's assessment. One review commented that Joan Crawford behaves in the film "like nobody except an MGM movie star," and the *New York Times* found Wayne "totally unconvincing as an American flyer." Most reviews emphasized that the war was a serious affair and should not be used as an MGM costume drama. The reviews, however, did not kill *Reunion in France* at the box office. It was one of MGM's top fifteen grossers for 1943. Once again, Wayne had demonstrated his worth. The message in Hollywood was clear: even a bad Wayne film made money.

Wayne's last film of 1942 was his most ambitious attempt to aid the war effort. As originally planned by agent Charles K. Feldman, *Pittsburgh,* like *The Spoilers,* was to be a vehicle for three of his clients—Dietrich, Wayne, and Scott. But it soon turned into a tribute to the industrial home front. Associate Producer Robert Fellows worked closely with the BMP to ensure that the film conveyed the government's exact propaganda message. It focuses on the Markham-Evans Coal Company, and its heroes are industrialists and workers in the coal and steel industries. In the film, Wayne plays the flawed hero Charles "Pittsburgh" Markham, a man who rose from the depths of a coal mine to the ownership of the company. In a role that Wayne was to develop more fully in such films as *Red River, Hondo, The Sea Chase, The Searchers,* and *The Man Who Shot Liberty Valance,* he portrays a man obsessed, driven by his own inner demons. Pittsburgh willingly uses anything and anyone to acquire power. On his way to the top, he abandons the woman who loves him (Marlene Dietrich) and his trusted partner (Randolph Scott). But the same ruthlessness that allowed him to rise in the coal business leads to his downfall, causing him to lose his wife, his company, and his self-worth. World War II provides a rebirth for Pittsburgh.

Once again, he rises from the mines to manage the company. Only this time he works for his nation, not himself. He is redeemed by submerging his own ego into his nation's crusade for a better world.

When Nelson Poynter and his BMP staff previewed *Pittsburgh* at Universal Studios on December 1, 1942, they were delighted. The picture was a preachy epic of coal and steel that appealed to the BMP's wordy sense of effective propaganda. It contained long semi-documentary sections of the coal and steel industries, and it rarely said anything visually that could be put into flat dialogue. But there was no mistaking its message: every American—soldier and industrial worker alike—can and should contribute to the war effort; victory would only result if "all the people" work and fight as one. The BMP applauded the results. "*Pittsburgh* succeeds in making many excellent contributions to the war information program," noted the BMP review of the film. In fact, much of the dialogue "appears to have been culled directly from the OWI Manual of Information for the picture industry. . . ." Nevertheless, the picture was "highly commended for an earnest and very successful contribution to the war effort." As far as the BMP was concerned, *Pittsburgh* was "one of the best pictures to emerge to date dealing with our vital production front. . . ."

Poynter, who had worked so closely with Bob Fellows on *Pittsburgh,* thought he had scored a real coup. Often ignored by the more important producers, Poynter actually believed that *Pittsburgh* was a good film and that his contributions to the film had been significant. As soon as he saw the final cut, he shot off a series of letters complimenting everyone involved with the movie including himself. "Magnificent. . . . It shows what can be done if the creative unit sets out to help interpret the war and at the same time put on a helluva good show," he wrote Fellows, Faldman, and several Universal executives. Poynter wrote Lowell Mellett, his BMP superior in Washington, telling him to see *Pittsburgh* and to take other Office of War Information and War Production Board people with him.

Mellett went, but he did not share Poynter's enthusiasm. "The propaganda sticks out disturbingly," Mellett responded to Poynter. Most newspaper reviewers shared Mellett's opinion. "This business of instructing and informing intrudes at times at the expense of the entertaining," noted the *Motion Picture Herald,* but the film "yields realistic results when not hampered by dialogue freighted with purpose." From West Coast to East, the reviews were the same. *Pittsburgh* was not exactly a bad film, but it was certainly "not in the inspired class," or, more to the point, it was "routine entertainment at best." In a New York theater, a cartoon entitled *Point Rationing,* which explained the use of the new rationing book, drew a more positive review than *Pittsburgh.*

The critical and financial failures of *Pittsburgh* reinforced the belief in Hollywood that if F.D.R. and alphabet agencies could get America out of the Depression, they certainly could not make a hit movie. The resistance against Poynter and his staff that was present in the industry from the beginning stiffened even more in the months after the release of *Pittsburgh.* Hollywood was right. The BMP was not film literate. Both Mellett and Poynter were newspaper men who thought in terms of words. They wanted dialogue that sounded like it was straight off an editorial page. As far as they were concerned, if a movie did not use dialogue to present the government's message, then the message was not delivered. They had difficulty thinking visually. The major studio executives realized the government approach toward propaganda would mean death at the box office. They were willing to make propaganda pictures that served the interest of the country, but they wanted to make them in their own way.

No film better demonstrates Washington's lack of understanding of movies than *Casablanca.* The classic film ran into trouble in Washington. Various sections of the Office of War Information were disappointed by the movie. Most were upset with Rick's (Humphrey Bogart's) cynicism. Others were dissatisfied with the treatment of the

French, the Germans, and the North Africans. And the last line—"This could be the beginning of a beautiful friendship"—well, as far as the OWI was concerned, it said nothing about the Atlantic Charter or why the United Nations were fighting Fascism. As film historians Gregory D. Black and Clayton R. Koppes observed, Washington "was not content to let meaning emerge from the interaction of the characters and the overall story line . . . it would have preferred a two-paragraph sermonette explaining Nazi aggression and the justice of the Allied cause."

The battle between Washington and Hollywood would drag into 1943 and would last in a more limited way for the rest of the war. It was a war fought by studio heads and producers, not actors, and as in the larger war, Wayne avoided the conflict. But his hectic activity of 1942 had begun to undermine his health. On January 21, 1943, he collapsed on a movie set and was rushed to the hospital. Doctors told him he had influenza and needed rest. That was the bad news. The good news was that his collapse was reported in the *New York Times.* Duke was a star.

STUDY QUESTIONS

1. How did the entertainment industry react to the Japanese attack on Pearl Harbor? How did the event affect Hollywood?

2. Why did John Wayne decide not to enlist when so many other leading actors enlisted in the service?

3. What role did the Roosevelt administration believe that Hollywood should play during the war?

4. Describe the goals and work of the Bureau of Motion Pictures. How did that organization try to influence the movie industry?

5. Discuss John Wayne's early war pictures. How were the enemy and the home front portrayed in these films?

BIBLIOGRAPHY

The previous essay is adapted from *John Wayne: American* (1996) by Randy Roberts and James S. Olson. Two standard biographies of John Wayne are Donald Shepard and Robert Slatzer, *Duke: The Life and Times of John Wayne* (1985) and Maurice Zolotow, *Shooting Star: A Biography of John Wayne* (1974). Two outstanding books that survey the movie industry are Garth Jowett, *Film: The Democratic Art* (1976) and Robert Sklar, *Movie-Made America: A Cultural History of American Movies* (1975). For a closer look at Hollywood during World War II see Clayton R. Koppes and Gregory D. Black, *Hollywood Goes to War: How Politics, Profits, and Propaganda Shaped World War II Movies* (1987) and Bernard F. Dick, *The Star-Spangled Screen: The American World War II Film* (1985). Richard R. Lingeman, *Don't You Know There's a War On* (1970) is an outstanding look at the home front during World War II.

PART SIX

America in the Age
of Anxiety: 1945–1960

The fallout of Hiroshima lasted many years. The most immediate result of the atomic bombs that America dropped on Japan on August 6 and August 9, 1945, was the end of World War II. V-J Day was celebrated with an emotional outpouring of relief. Most Americans believed that the United States had saved the world from the totalitarian threat of the Axis Powers. They also assumed that America would now return to its traditional foreign policy posture of isolationism. Such was not the case. World War II had made the United States the most powerful country in the world. Retreat into isolationism was impossible. During the next few years, America accepted the responsibilities that went with being a world power and replaced Great Britain as the globe's police force.

Almost as soon as the war was over, the Soviet Union emerged as America's leading rival. Joseph Stalin, Russia's leader, was by nature suspicious, and the complexities and uncertainties of Soviet politics made him even more so. He resented America and Great Britain for delaying the second front against Germany during World War II. He was also upset that the United States refused to share its nuclear secrets with the Soviet Union. Fears, anxieties, and ambitions degenerated into a new type of power conflict. Called the cold war, the object was to control, either through economic or military means, as much of the world as possible.

America originated the policy of containment as a strategy for the cold war. The policy was essentially defensive in nature, and it forced America to react to Soviet movements. Although the policy scored several notable successes—particularly in Turkey, Greece, and Western Europe—it had a number of real weaknesses. Most important, it committed American troops to prevent the expansion of Communism. In Korea and later in Vietnam, Americans came to understand the limitations and constraints of the containment doctrine.

The cold war and the fear of a nuclear confrontation shaped domestic politics as well as foreign affairs. If Americans distrusted Stalin's motives, they also questioned the actions of their own leaders. They asked pointed and complex questions, yet sought simple answers. Why had Stalin gained so much territory at Yalta? How was Russia able to develop its own atomic weapons so rapidly? Who lost China? Politicians such as Senator Joseph McCarthy of Wisconsin and Congressman Richard Nixon of California provided easy answers. They said that Communist sympathizers in the American government had worked to ensure the success of the Soviet Union. The publicity lavished on the trials of Alger Hiss and Julius and Ethel Rosenberg and the activities of McCarthy and the House Un-American Activities Committee increased the public's distrust of its own officials.

In the following section the essays deal with the fallout of Hiroshima and the cold war. Although they examine very different subjects—race questions, Korean War POWs, cigarette smoking, and television scandals—they contain a unifying theme. They all discuss Americans' attitudes toward themselves. The underlying assumption was that something deep and troubling was wrong, that the American character had changed for the worse. The search for exactly what was wrong took many different turns and helped illuminate the psychological, cultural, and social landscape of the 1950s.

READING 21

THE MAN WHO CHANGED HIS SKIN

Ernest Sharpe, Jr.

For millions of African Americans the early 1960s were years of pain mixed with glimpses of promise. Compared to white Americans, they faced a grim set of statistics. The 1960 census reported that African Americans died seven years younger than did white Americans, had half the chance of completing high school, one-third the chance of finishing college, and one-third the chance of entering a profession. On the average, African Americans earned half as much as whites and were twice as likely to be unemployed. Yet events like the *Brown v. The Board of Education* decision, the Montgomery bus boycott, and the various Freedom Rides, "sit-ins," "wade-ins," "pray-ins," and "apply-ins" sent the message that the time to change was at hand. For demanding no more than what was guaranteed them by the Constitution of the United States and a general sense of decency, African Americans were hosed, set on by dogs, arrested, beaten, and even murdered, yet they continued their march toward justice.

How ironic then, with so many examples of injustice and inhumanity toward African Americans, that many white Americans had to be told by another white American what it was like to be black. In 1959 John Howard Griffin chemically darkened his skin, shaved his head, and traveled through the heart of Dixie as a black man. He experienced humiliations large and small, occasionally feared for his life, and came to know racism on very personal terms. After a few months he returned to his white world and wrote a book about his experiences. Published in 1961, *Black Like Me* became a national sensation, selling over five million copies, angering millions of white Americans and opening the eyes of millions more. On television shows and radio programs, Griffin heard variations of the same line by whites: "I never knew what it was like to be black."

Probably Griffin never did either. In "The Man Who Changed His Skin," Ernest Sharpe, Jr. explores the life of the unusual man who passed for a brief time as black.

On a sunny November day in 1959, a tall, brown-haired Texan entered the home of a New Orleans friend. Five days later an unemployed, bald black man walked out. The name of both was John Howard Griffin, and the journey he began that Louisiana evening was to take him to a country farther than any he had ever been in, one bordered only by the shade of its citizens' skin.

For four weeks Griffin, his skin chemically darkened, posed as an itinerant black. He wandered the South, hitchhiking, seeking work, and talking and listening to people black and white. His journal of those weeks became a series of magazine articles and then a book, *Black Like Me.* In passionate first-person prose it brought home to millions of American whites the misery and injustice daily endured by American blacks. It opened eyes and seized hearts and changed minds.

It also changed lives, including Griffin's own. Abandoning a promising literary career, he devoted the next eight years to the civil rights movement. He saw authorship of a single book eclipse all his other achievements. He became for the rest of his life the man who had turned himself black. But *Black Like Me* was only the most prominent event in a life filled with drama and transformation. By the time of his death, in 1980, Griffin had left behind the sloughed skins of a dozen careers and identifies. Born to a middle-class Dallas family, he was schooled in France, where he joined in the soirées of European aesthetes and aristocrats. He served in the French Resistance and soldiered in the South Pacific, where he lived for a year as an aborigine islander. He converted to Catholicism, and he thirsted for a life of prayer and chastity even while he wrote a novel banned in Detroit for its sexual explicitness. He lost his sight, lived for ten years as a blind man, and then miraculously recovered his vision. He was a musical scholar, a religious intellectual, a working

journalist, a livestock breeder, a professional photographer, a social activist, and a controversial novelist.

And, of course, for a few weeks in 1959 he was a black man.

Griffin was a product of two disparate cultures, Texan and French, and was never totally at home in either. He was born on June 16, 1920, the second of four children. His father was a religious, hardworking wholesale-grocery salesman utterly devoted to his refined, delicate wife. Years later Griffin recalled waking each morning to the sound of his mother practicing the piano sonatas of Mozart and Schubert and Bach preludes and fugues.

When Griffin was fifteen, he came upon a magazine ad for the Lycée Descartes, a boarding school in France, and wrote to the headmaster begging for admission. He had no money, he confessed, but he would do anything to pay his way, even scrub floors. Several weeks later a reply came back: If the young man wanted to learn so badly, he was by all means welcome. Griffin presented the letter to his flabbergasted parents; they responded predictably, but he was already a person of considerable will, and he was soon aboard an ocean liner.

Griffin was a gifted student. He graduated from the lycée, then stayed in France to study medicine and the humanities. He spent his seventeenth summer at the country home of a wealthy French family. Evenings he played Ravel, Debussy, and Schubert on the phonograph or lay in bed reading Balzac, Gide, and Rabelais.

By the spring of 1939 his future seemed bright. Having decided on a career in psychiatry, he began work after his first year of medical school as an "extern" at the Tours insane asylum. A student of religious music, he conducted experiments using Gregorian chants as therapy for patients considered beyond cure. Then, in September, Germany invaded Poland. France declared war, and virtually all the medical staff at the asylum was immediately conscripted. Griffin was placed in charge of the hospital's female wing, responsible, along with eight nuns, for 120 patients. He was nineteen years old.

"The Man Who Changed His Skin" by Ernest Sharpe, Jr. in *American Heritage*, Vol. 40/No. 1, February 1989, pp. 44–55. Reprinted by permission of *American Heritage* Magazine, a division of Forbes, Inc. © Forbes, Inc., 1989.

It was a harrowing time. He was often dragged from his bed to treat wounded soldiers trucked from the front. German and Austrian Jews began trickling into the city; officially enemy aliens, many did not speak French and most lacked safe-conduct papers. As the French fell back, the young American volunteered to help the refugees. He strapped them into strait-jackets and smuggled them in an asylum ambulance to the port of St.-Nazaire for passage to England. Their faces haunted him: he never forgot the encounter with racism.

After the French surrender in 1940, Griffin himself fled. He returned to the United States and joined the Army Air Corps. Leaving for what would become a three-year stint in the Pacific, he stuffed his duffel bag full of books by Molière and Racine and scores by Mozart and Beethoven. His initial assignments were light. For a while he served as a disc jockey, broadcasting classical concerts to front-line troops. Bored, he volunteered for a post on a remote island, to set up liaison in the event of an American occupation.

He lived on Nuni, as the natives called it, for a year. His charge was not only to learn the local tongue but to gain the islanders' trust. To do so, he became one of them: fishing with the men, chewing betel nut, observing tribal customs and ceremonies, and even taking a wife. "They were one of the few truly primitive tribes left in the world," he later wrote, "in a land where there was no sense of time or goal." But life there was far from innocent. Behind the apparent languor Griffin discovered a harsh existence where children sometimes perished in brutal rites of initiation. When his year was up, he was ready to leave.

He was reassigned to Morotai, a tiny spot of land in the Moluccas close to several islands held by the Japanese. Manning the radar tent there alone one night, he was caught in an air raid and artillery barrage. He described the scene in his unpublished autobiography: "A shell shrieked downward and I threw myself to the ground. . . . The shell exploded nearby and shrapnel whizzed unseen around me. Relief and exhaustion overwhelmed my senses. . . . I wanted to lie still and

rest, to ignore some gigantic urgency in the atmosphere. A new wave of mortars, ackack explosions and shell screeches swept toward me. I hurried to my feet to run ahead of it." He didn't make it; knocked unconscious, he was at first taken for dead by medics and later rescued by an alert burial crew.

Griffin regained consciousness, apparently suffering from nothing worse than a concussion, and except for sensitivity to light and difficulty reading his mail, he quickly recovered. Sick of the service and fearful of a prolonged hospital stay, he kept his vision problems to himself. Back in the United States he was given a last physical, including a cursory eye exam. Unable to make out the results on his discharge papers, he asked another soldier to read them to him. He was staggered to learn that his vision was 20/200. He was legally blind.

He soon realized that his blindness would be more than legal. He was losing his sight completely. Specialists were unable to help; he had apparently suffered some kind of brain damage. They outfitted him with thick, dark spectacles, but they weren't strong enough. Wanting to hide his affliction, he took to reading with the help of a small, easily hidden magnifying glass.

Medicine was obviously no longer a viable profession, so in 1946 Griffin returned to France to pursue a career as a musicologist. He spent the summer at the conservatory at Fontainebleau. Each day his eyes were a little worse, but still he told no one: "I felt that losing my sight was a thing I had to do alone."

In the fall he left for Paris to visit an old school friend who had become a monk in a Dominican convent. At first he found the monastery dismal, reeking of "the odors of cabbages and onions and mop water," but distaste gradually turned to respect, and respect to reverence. "The poverty of my unlighted cell warmed with delight," he wrote. "I had imagined that men seeking union with God more or less languished in a state of mystical trauma, soaring above the baser aspects of their own daily living. But here men lived in intimacy with the things of the earth—cold, fasting, labor. . . . I saw they were men like me. I lived with them, saw them bleary-eyed at dawn, smelled them sweating after labors, and yet sanctity lay there within them."

It was to be five years before Griffin left the Episcopal Church for the Catholic, but by the time he departed the Couvent St. Jacques he was already very much converted. Moreover, he had discovered a part of himself that yearned for the devotional solitude of a monastic life. In the years to come he would often retreat to the sanctuary of monastery walls.

From Paris Griffin went to the Abbey of Solesmes, to research medieval church music. When he returned to the United States in the spring of 1947, he was twenty-six and totally blind. He was also engaged. During his year in France he had fallen in love with a woman several years his senior named Françoise Longuet.

The two faced obvious obstacles; the first was Griffin's physical helplessness. Françoise decided to remain in France for the time being. Back in Texas Griffin and his parents escaped the city's noise and hazardous traffic by moving to a farm outside Mansfield, a small town near Fort Worth. To earn an income, Griffin turned from musicology to animal husbandry. After some tutoring by teachers at Texas A&M, he purchased four Ohio Improved Chester sows and began breeding them. He also began tutoring local children in advanced piano. One of his first students was the thirteen-year-old daughter of a local insurance agent, Clyde Holland. Elizabeth Holland—"Piedy" to friends and family—was already a talented pianist. She proved an apt pupil and was soon a regular visitor to the Griffin farm.

By 1949 Griffin was earning a respectable income as a breeder of prize livestock, but his yeoman days were already numbered. That spring he met the New York drama critic John Mason Brown, who was in Texas on a lecture tour. Brown suggested that Griffin try his hand at writing; he certainly talked like a writer. Griffin, intrigued, asked how he should start. You get some paper and write, Brown curtly replied. Griffin did just that, converting a room in the barn behind his parents' house into an office. It was a cramped space, "about three long steps each way," but it suited Griffin's anchoritic temperament. It also suited his subject, a novel about a young American man studying Gregorian chant in a French monastery. Neglecting his hogs, Griffin sometimes worked all night, dictating in French on a wire recorder and later transcribing his dictation in English on his mother's ancient Underwood. In seven weeks he had completed a first draft and launched a new career for himself.

He had also precipitated a series of events that eventually changed the law of the land. He called the book *The Devil Rides Outside,* borrowing from a French proverb: "The devil rides outside the monastery walls." The six-hundred-page novel is a study of the struggle between faith and temptation, a raw, sprawling work that seems to have sprouted like a mushroom in the garden of Texas letters. In 1981 the novelist Larry McMurtry wrote of it as "a strange, strong book whose verbal energy . . . still seems remarkable after almost 30 years. In the mostly all-too-healthy and sunlit world of Texas fiction, the book remains an anomaly, dark, feverish, introverted, claustrophobic, tortured."

Issued by a fledgling Fort Worth publisher, *The Devil Rides Outside* received surprising attention for a first novel by an unknown. Reviews were mixed. "Most of the novel's sound and fury is bound up with the medieval notion that sex is the domain of Satan," complained the *Atlantic Monthly,* but the noted literary critic Maxwell Geismar was impressed. He called the book one of the best novels of the decade and dubbed its author "a Texas Balzac."

The Legion for Decent Literature, a Catholic organization, succeeded in getting *The Devil Rides Outside* banned in Detroit on the grounds that it was unfit for children and adolescents. While little in the book would shock a contemporary reader, the novel was daring for the fifties. It contains a pair of passages that describe in exactly the same language sexual climax and spiritual rapture.

Postwar censorship laws were a welter of local and state statutes, many of which, despite the historic 1934 circuit court ruling on *Ulysses,* still banned whole works based on isolated passages. In the spring of 1954 the book's paperback publisher, Pocket Books, arranged to challenge the Detroit ban. A bookstore manager was arrested for selling a copy to a police inspector; the court convicted, the bookseller appealed, and *Butler* v. *Michigan* began a two-and-a-half-year march to the Supreme Court.

Despite the praise and attention, the fall of 1952 found the thirty-two-year-old Griffin utterly miserable. After six years of delay Françoise had bitterly broken their engagement. In his grief he received solace from an unexpected source, Piedy Holland, now a seventeen-year-old high school senior. Despite Griffin's disability and the gap in their ages, the two found themselves increasingly drawn to each other. After a genteel courtship of several months, he proposed to Piedy at midnight mass on Christmas Eve. She happily accepted, and the two were married the following June after Griffin received dispensation from the Vatican for his Pacific marriage. They moved into a cottage behind the Hollands' house, and Griffin went to work on a second novel.

That fall Griffin noticed a growing numbness in his fingers. The doctor diagnosed malaria, a souvenir of his days in the tropics. The numbness progressed until by December he was not only blind but confined to a wheelchair, effectively paralyzed except in his left arm. He began taking minute doses of strychnine as a stimulant, but the prognosis was uncertain. To compound his troubles, he had been diagnosed as diabetic.

Despite these afflictions, he continued to labor on *Nuni*, a Robinson Crusoe tale of a middle-aged English professor struggling for survival on an island of savages. In his journal he wrote: "I am aware perhaps that I am putting the problems of my life into the lap of Professor Harper and I am desperate for him to solve them. I am stripping him of everything that men generally consider necessary to a man's ability to function at the human level."

Professor Harper overcame his predicament, and so, after a long ordeal, did Griffin. By May 1956, when *Nuni* was published, he was not only

Portrait of John Howard Griffin

fully recovered from the malaria but perhaps more content than he had ever been. *Nuni* was receiving favorable reviews, translations of his first novel were selling well in Europe, and he was close to finishing a third. He was the happy husband of a loving wife and the doting father of two small children. He seemed finally to have achieved a measure of peace.

All that changed one morning the following January. As with everything in his life, he described it in his daily journal:

"Wednesday, four days ago, I was walking to the house for lunch. Redness swirled in front of my eyes. Then I thought I saw the back door, cut in portions, dancing at crazy angles. I stood dumbfounded. Angles continued to dance and there was pain in the eyes and head.

"I stumbled inside, found the telephone. Somehow I got the number dialed. I heard my wife's voice.

" 'I think . . .' I began, and then collapsed into weeping.

" 'What is it? What's happening?' she asked.

" 'I think I can see.' " He could. By the time Piedy and the family physician reached the farmhouse, he was able to make out forms and colors. He was euphoric. The sight of his two-year-old daughter was "like looking at the sun—blinding me to everything else."

The strychnine, he was told, had apparently unstopped blocked blood vessels. The flow of blood in turn had unknotted twisted vessels. A month later he wrote to a friend: "We have, on this near-lethal dosage . . . brought my vision to a plu-perfect 20/15 in each eye. I am overwhelmed by details seen with the utmost clarity—every glass flaw, every pebble."

The singularity of his recovery brought Griffin national attention and some local gibes. Many in Mansfield had never taken to Griffin's cosmopolitan background and cultured air, and some suggested that maybe he had never been blind at all. *Time,* echoing the skeptics, reported in its medicine section that Griffin's recovery was unprecedented, but his blindness might have been "mainly, if not entirely, hysterical."

On February 25, 1957, a little more than a month after he regained his sight, the sun broke on Griffin again. The Supreme Court of the United States unanimously struck down the Michigan law banning *The Devil Rides Outside.* Speaking for the Court, Justice Felix Frankfurter wrote, "The state insists that, by thus quarantining the general reading public against books not too rugged for grown men and women in order to shield juvenile innocence it is exercising its power to promote the general welfare. Surely this is to burn the house to roast the pig." The decision effectively reversed an 1868 British ruling that for almost a century had remained the principal guide to Anglo-American jurisprudence on censorship and obscenity.

Moral triumphs do not pay bills, however, and the income from his novels was not enough to support Griffin and his growing family. Several months before his sight returned, he had found employment in Fort Worth as a staff writer at *Sepia,* a black monthly modeled loosely after *Life.* Griffin fit in easily at the magazine, whose publisher, George Levitan, practiced a policy of equal opportunity long before it became a national slogan.

In the fall of 1959 he began research on a piece about the high suicide rate among Southern blacks. He sent out questionnaires to black professionals, but the few who responded simply returned them blank. The article stalled. He vented his frustration on Adelle Martin, the magazine's editorial director. Why wouldn't Negroes trust him? He was on their side. Mrs. Martin, black herself, responded bluntly: Negroes knew that no matter how he tried, he would never understand. The only way he could know that it was like to be a Negro was by being one.

The remark triggered the return of an old, odd thought: If a white man became a Negro in the Deep South, what adjustments would he have to make? A few days later he proposed a series of articles to Levitan. He would dye his skin and travel the South. He wouldn't change his name or hide his background or education. He would still be John Howard Griffin—author, teacher, musicologist—but with one difference: he would be black.

The publisher warned Griffin of the dangers involved, but he couldn't hide his enthusiasm. Go ahead, he told Griffin; *Sepia* would foot the bill. Piedy was less enthusiastic. It sounded dangerous, but if he felt he had to do it, then he should. He would be gone for a month.

Two days later Griffin flew to New Orleans. He arranged to stay at the house of a friend, and the next morning he explained his project to a sympathetic dermatologist. The physician prescribed Oxsoralen, a drug usually used to treat vitiligo, a condition that causes milky patches on the skin. The process would take a couple of months. Griffin explained there wasn't time, so the physician suggested a higher dosage coupled with exposure to a sunlamp; the drug worked through reaction to ultraviolet light. There was some chance of liver damage, but as long as Griffin was monitored through frequent blood tests, he was probably safe.

For four days Griffin lay in his room under a sunlamp, his eyes protected by cotton pads. The Oxsoralen produced lassitude and nausea and didn't entirely work; by the evening of the fourth day his skin was dark but mottled. Determined to see the project through, he touched up the light patches with vegetable dye and then shaved his head. The whole process took hours. Finally he was done.

"Turning off all the lights, I went into the bathroom and closed the door. I stood in the darkness before the mirror, my hand on the light switch. I forced myself to flick it on.

"In the flood of light against white tile, the face and shoulders of a stranger—a fierce, bald, very dark Negro—glared at me from the glass. He in no way resembled me.

"The transformation was total and shocking. I had expected to see myself disguised, but this was something else. I was imprisoned in the flesh of an utter stranger, an unsympathetic one with whom I felt no kinship. All traces of the John Griffin I had been were wiped from existence."

Toting a pair of duffel bags, Griffin stepped out of the house and walked to the corner to catch a streetcar to downtown New Orleans. Trembling, he bought a ticket and moved down the aisle to take a seat in the back. No one gave him a glance. After a few moments he sighed with relief; he had passed the first test of his new identity.

He stayed the night in a shabby hotel, and the next morning he made a confidant of a street-corner shoe shine boy. The "boy," a gray-haired World War I veteran named Sterling Williams, cackled with delight at Griffin's charade. He agreed to let the writer work at his stand for a few days. Then he pointed at the giveaway brown hair on Griffin's hands. Griffin grabbed a razor from his duffel and scurried for the nearest lavatory. In his haste he almost entered a whites' washroom, forgetting he was black even as he rushed to eliminate the last sign of his whiteness.

Griffin worked as a shoe-shine boy for several days, learning when to smile, when to laugh, when to shrug, and when to be silent. One of his earliest lessons was that the friendliest customers were those looking for black women. "When they want to sin, they're very democratic," his mentor observed. After gaining some confidence, Griffin began searching for a regular job, applying for clerical work at local businesses. The responses were polite but consistent. After three days he had failed to obtain even an interview. At the end

of each day he plodded back to the shine stand, and as Williams dolloped out a supper of raccoon stew, Griffin told the old man what he already knew: nobody would hire a black man for anything but manual labor.

After a week in New Orleans, Griffin decided to travel to Mississippi, where, despite massive evidence collected by the FBI, a grand jury had recently refused to return indictments in a race lynching. New Orleans had proved outwardly affable, but as he bought a ticket at the Greyhound station, Griffin had his first encounter with the "hate stare," a cold, irrational gaze long familiar to blacks that struck Griffin like a blow in the face. It was on the bus ride that he first experienced the petty tyranny regularly visited on Southern blacks. Pulling into a small town for a rest stop, the driver let out the white passengers but ordered the blacks to stay in their seats. They grumbled and objected but complied. Griffin saw that one of the unexpected requirements of blackness was an impressive ability to hold one's urine.

He stayed in Mississippi only a few days. Overwhelmed by the oppressive poverty and climate of violence, he returned to New Orleans and then took a bus along the Gulf to Biloxi. From Biloxi he hitchhiked to Mobile, traveling beside miles of white, sandy beaches forbidden to blacks. In Mobile he again sought work and also spent much of his time seeking out the things he had once taken for granted: "a place to eat, or somewhere to find a drink of water, a rest room, somewhere to wash my hands." He had no better luck with jobs there than in New Orleans. "No use trying down here," one plant foreman told him. "We're gradually getting you people weeded out. . . . We're going to do our damndest to drive every one of you out of the state."

Unable to find a room one evening, Griffin accepted the offer of an elderly black preacher to share a thin mattress in his small, bare room. Night had come to be a time of comfort for Griffin. The strain of the day was over, and he could, like blacks throughout the South, relax in darkness's enveloping anonymity. The two men lay under quilts, gazing at the ceiling and chatting about Bible miracles. The old man was especially fond of the raising of Lazarus. When it came to prospects for Southern blacks, however, his faith was less secure. He had two sons who had gone north. He hoped they would never return.

From Mobile Griffin hitchhiked to Montgomery. The white men who gave him lifts were friendly, but invariably they turned the conversation to the same topic: "All but two picked me up the way they would pick up a pornographic photograph or book. . . . Some were shamelessly open, some shamelessly subtle. All showed morbid curiosity about the sexual life of a Negro, and all had, at base, the same stereotyped image of the Negro as an inexhaustible sex machine with oversized genitals and a vast store of experiences, immensely varied."

The situation might almost have been comic had not Griffin, despite the earthiness of his writing, possessed an almost nineteenth-century sense of modesty. He found the conversations increasingly loathsome and grew increasingly curt, a dangerous tone for a black in rural Alabama. One farmer asked Griffin if he was one of those out-of-state "troublemakers." Griffin replied that he was just passing through. The farmer patted the shotgun by his knee and gestured at the swampy forest on either side of the road. "You can kill a nigger and toss him into that swamp and no one will ever know what happened to him." Griffin nodded, "Yes, sir."

Arriving in Montgomery, Griffin found the atmosphere electric with racial tension. Blacks there seemed less passive and deferential than in other towns. The difference, he decided, was due to the influence of the city's prominent black minister, Martin Luther King, Jr. But if Montgomery's blacks seemed less defeated, its whites seemed more actively hostile. Griffin saw the hate stare everywhere. Looking into a washroom mirror, he discovered a change in his own gaze: "My face had lost animation. In repose, it had taken on the strained, disconsolate expression that is written on the countenance of so many Southern Negroes. My mind had become the same way, dozing empty for long periods."

The strain of Griffin's appropriated identity was taking its toll. He began having nightmares. Then he stopped taking the Oxsoralen pills, and his skin began daily turning lighter. His hair grew to a heavy fuzz. He decided to see if he could cross the border back into whiteness. He scrubbed off the vegetable dye, donned a dark shirt to stand off against his lightening skin, and headed for the city's white section. He strolled into a segregated restaurant and ordered a meal. "I ate the white meal, drank the white water, received the white smiles and wondered how it all could be. What sense could a man make of it?"

He returned to the black section and discovered that blacks had a subtle but definite hate stare of their own. He reapplied the dye and found himself once again accepted by one race, spurned by the other. He began zigzagging back and forth across Montgomery, shifting skins like a chameleon, deliberately testing the limits of his disguise. It was, he sadly concluded, impenetrable. He gave up and boarded the bus for Atlanta, the last station in his tracing of the black cross.

Atlanta was a surprise for Griffin. Leaving Montgomery, he had given up hope for the lot of Southern blacks, but Georgia's capital changed his mind. The city, he found, had made "great strides." He professed to see hope for the South in Atlanta, but his optimism sounds forced. Despite thoughtful interviews with black and white civic leaders and a tour of black colleges, Griffin's picture of Atlanta is overwhelmed by the shadows of New Orleans, Mississippi, and Alabama.

Nearly three decades have gone by since Griffin made his journey through the South, but *Black Like Me*'s power to move and outrage remains undiminished. Still in print, it has sold more than twelve million copies and been translated into fourteen languages. Most recently it was published in South Africa. Part of its enduring appeal comes from what seems the very transparency of the author's imposture.

It is hard to imagine a person worse suited than Griffin to pass for black. A cultural epicure who had spent his adolescence in France and lived a blind, sheltered existence for the previous decade, Griffin had remarkably little in common with most Southern whites, let alone with blacks. In the book his relations with blacks are cordial but never intimate. He practically shudders every time his ears are assaulted by jazz or the blues. Griffin was able to change his color, but not his heritage.

Which makes it all the harder to see how he pulled it off. Naturally he fooled whites; whites didn't look at blacks. But how did he dupe blacks? Surely somebody should have seen through such a thin disguise. No one did. His transformation was skin-deep, but neither whites nor blacks ever looked deeper. As readers we are in on the secret. Griffin's voice—courtly, refined, educated—is so evident throughout the book that we are amazed at the blindness of bus drivers and shopkeepers and all the others. We hear him secretly wail, "I'm just like you," at each new indignity or abuse, and we cannot believe that no one else hears him.

It is on this level of moral protest that *Black Like Me* is best known and most celebrated, as a work of civil rights advocacy and a tract on man's inhumanity to man. But also it was one of the first works of a new kind of journalism—what was called in the sixties the New Journalism—with its personal, participatory, novelistic approach. In fact, the book is arguably the genre's first masterpiece, even though Griffin was really less a journalist than a personal essayist. Judged as reporting, *Black Like Me* is an imperfect work. There is too much of the author, too little of others; too much earnest discussion of issues and too little personal observation and encounter. Assuming they had Griffin's bull-headed courage, one can imagine other writers—Norman Mailer, Tom Wolfe—rendering the experience with more nuanced insight and elegance of style.

What one cannot imagine is these masters of irony abandoning their strategic distance for the raw, racked emotion that powers Griffin's prose. *Black Like Me* is not simply a record of oppression and injustice; it is an account of painful personal discovery. Griffin began his experiment as an adventure. He assumed he would find racism, but he did not expect to find it everywhere, least of all in himself. By the end of his four weeks, he ached with hurt and humiliation. The adventure had turned into an ordeal. In discovering the brutal reality of racism, however, he also discovered compassion for the fierce stranger he had first seen three weeks before, the one with whom he had felt no kinship.

"I switched on the light and looked into a cracked piece of mirror bradded with bent nails to the wall. The bald Negro stared back at me from its mottled sheen. I knew I was in hell. Hell could be no more lonely or helpless. . . .

"I heard my voice, as though it belonged to someone else, hollow in the empty room, detached, say: 'Nigger, what you standing up there crying for?'

"I saw tears slick on his cheeks in the yellow light."

The initial installment of Griffin's series appeared in *Sepia* in April 1960, two months after the first lunch-counter sit-in and seven months before Kennedy's election. It was an instant sensation. Griffin went to New York for television interviews with Dave Garroway, Mike Wallace, and other hosts. Letters poured in—six thousand of them, mostly from Southern states, and only nine hostile.

Closer to home, friends and a few townspeople were warmly congratulatory, but most of Mansfield was silent. One night in April an effigy of Griffin—half black, half white, a yellow stripe down its back—was hung next to the downtown traffic light. A few days later a cross was burned in front of the town's predominantly black elementary school. Anonymous phone calls warned Griffin that "they" were coming to castrate him. Griffin's father came to the house to keep watch with a shotgun.

For a month the Griffins hid out in the homes of friends; in August he decided to move to Mexico. There he worked on a book version of the *Sepia* articles. Published in 1961, *Black Like Me* became an immediate best seller and was soon sold to Hollywood. (The film, a mediocre melodrama starring James Whitmore, was released in 1964.)

Griffin stayed in Mexico for nine peaceful months and began a scholarly history of the Tarascan Indians. Then, in the spring of 1961, anti-American riots erupted near his home in Morelia, and the Griffins were forced to take refuge in a Benedictine monastery. They returned north to Fort Worth.

Soon Griffin was swallowed up in the civil rights movement. He had an authority among whites and a credibility among blacks that made him a persuasive and much sought-after speaker. He lectured, marched, investigated, worked as a mediator, argued against violence, and grieved with the families of those claimed by violence. To the dismay of his literary friends, he shelved his autobiography and two nearly finished novels. What time he had for writing he devoted to essays and articles on racism, culminating with his book *The Church and the Black Man,* an outspoken criticism of the failure of the Christian churches to act on their creeds.

During this time Griffin met Thomas Merton, the Trappist monk and author of the best-selling *The Seven Storey Mountain.* The two had much in common. Both were French-educated and Catholic converts: Merton a contemplative with a lively interest in the world outside, Griffin an activist with a yearning for the cloister. Not surprisingly, a close friendship blossomed.

After Merton's death, in 1968, the Merton Legacy Trust asked Griffin to write the monk's official biography. He accepted the task gladly. Recurrent foot tumors and bone deterioration from diabetes kept him largely confined to a wheelchair, and he welcomed a return to purely literary labor. He spent the next nine years working on the book. As he had done before, he sought to understand his subject by slipping inside his skin. For nearly three years he spent two weeks out of every month at Merton's Kentucky hermitage, faithfully observing the monastic routine, a Spartan schedule of prayer and work beginning each morning at three. He discovered a tranquillity there that made these among the happiest days of his life.

By 1973 Griffin was too ravaged by diabetes to work away from home. As his health declined, the work proceeded more and more slowly. He missed his first deadline and then a second. Finally, in 1978, despite Griffin's pleadings, the Merton Legacy Trust named Michael Mott as Merton's official biographer. To compound Griffin's woes, his publisher demanded the return of its substantial advance. The settlement left him virtually bankrupt.

For the last two years of his life, Griffin was tortured by pain and despair. Emotionally he never recovered from the loss of what he thought would be his masterpiece, his contribution to the world's spiritual literature. Physically he suffered from kidney trouble, lung congestion, impaired circulation, and regular heart attacks, sometimes several a week. A bearish man, he dwindled to a hundred and fifty pounds. In 1979 his left leg was amputated and he was confined to bed.

He, Piedy, and their youngest daughter were forced to live on overextended credit cards and Piedy's secretarial job. When he could, Griffin worked on his thirty years of daily journals, with an eye toward eventual publication. Sometimes he rallied to give interviews or entertain friends or even cook a meal. But more often he had neither the wind nor the fire to do more than rest and reflect.

He died on September 9, 1980. When a friend asked the cause, Piedy said simply, "Everything." In the years since his death, a myth has spread that Griffin died from cancer cause by the Oxsoralen he had taken years before. He did not, and the suggestion of martyrdom would have offended him. He was in pain, though, in his last days, and perhaps he often thought of a favorite poem by Langston Hughes. He had used it for his most famous title:

Rest at pale evening . . .
A tall slim tree . . .
Night coming tenderly
Black like me.

STUDY QUESTIONS

1. What experiences and adventures contributed to the development of John Howard Griffin's racial attitudes? What obstacles in life did he personally face?

2. What does the novel *The Devil Rides Outside* tell us about Griffin's inner world and American society in the early 1950s?

3. Why did Griffin decide to temporarily change his skin color to better understand discrimination? Why did some people consider his experiment dangerous?

4. What conclusions did Griffin reach? What privations, small and large, did he experience? How did skin color alter the way he was received and treated by both races?

5. What impact did *Black Like Me* have on American society and American journalism?

BIBLIOGRAPHY

The best place to start a search for John Howard Griffin is in his book *Black Like Me* (1961). A good starting point for literature on the general struggles and everyday life of African Americans during the late 1950s and early 1960s is Taylor Branch, *Parting the Waters: America in the King Years* (1988). Also insightful are John Dittmer, *Local People: The Struggle for Civil Rights in Mississippi* (1994); Eric R. Burner, *And Gently He Shall Lead Them: Robert Parris Moses and Civil Rights in Mississippi* (1994); William H. Chafe, *Civilities and Civil Rights* (1980); David Garrow, *Bearing the Cross: Martin Luther King, Jr. and the Southern Christian Leadership Conference* (1986); Doug McAdam, *Freedom Summer* (1988); and Stephen Oates, *Let the Trumpet Sound: The Life of Martin Luther King, Jr.* (1982). Anne Moody, *Coming of Age in Mississippi* (1968), is also a deeply moving document of the period.

READING 22

DR. YES

James H. Jones

During the late 1940s and early 1950s, a series of unsettling events shocked Americans and disturbed their sense of postwar complacency and optimism. Communism—its spread and increased dangerousness—inspired much of the fear. In late 1949 the Nationalist leader Chiang Kai-shek and his followers fled mainland China for sanctuary on Formosa. In Chiang's place came Communist Mao Tse-tung. Although Mao's victory was predictable and the result of internal Chinese forces, Americans tended to view the "fall of China" as a victory for Soviet foreign policy. Other shocks came rapidly. In September 1949 President Truman announced that the Russians had detonated a nuclear device, thus ending the American monopoly of the bomb. And throughout the period, the trials of Alger Hiss raised questions about the loyalty of American government officials. No less sensational and disturbing was the publication of Alfred Kinsey's *Sexual Behavior in the Human Male* (1948), which quickly sold over 275,000 copies. For many Americans, Kinsey's "message" was as insidious as those of Marx and Lenin. He told Americans about themselves, about their sexual practices, fears, and desires. And what Kinsey said was not what most Americans wanted to believe. In the following essay, historian James H. Jones tells the story of Alfred Kinsey and how Kinsey's own emotional needs affected his monumental study.

In January of 1948, the W. B. Saunders Company, of Philadelphia, published "Sexual Behavior in the Human Male," by Alfred C. Kinsey. W.B. Saunders was a respectable publisher of scientific books, mostly medical textbooks. Kinsey, then fifty-three years old, had been a taxonomical entomologist—his specialty was the gall wasp—at Indiana University. The book itself weighed three pounds, cost six dollars and fifty cents (compared with the three dollars then typically charged for a new hardcover book), had no photographs or illustrations, and was loaded with charts, statistics, and footnotes. Except, perhaps, for its subject, nothing about the book suggested that it might be of general interest.

"Sexual Behavior in the Human Male" was an immediate sensation. The Kinsey Report, as it was quickly dubbed, sold more than two hundred thousand copies between January and July, 1948, obliging the publisher to run two presses around the clock in order to satisfy demand.

Reflecting on the phenomenal sales, an article in *Time* exclaimed, "Not since 'Gone With the Wind' had booksellers seen anything like it." *Life* declared, "To find another purely scientific book with a record which even approaches this, it probably is necessary to go back to Darwin's 'On the Origin of Species.'" Tin Pan Alley produced songs called "The Kinsey Boogie" and "Thank You, Mr. Kinsey," and Martha Raye produced a jukebox hit, "Ooh, Dr. Kinsey." At Harvard, where Kinsey had done his graduate work, students crooned, "I've looked you up in the Kinsey Report/And you're just the man for me." Delegates to the 1948 Republican National Convention, in Philadelphia, wore buttons that read "We Want Kinsey, the People's Choice." A cartoon in this magazine showed a woman seated in a comfortable chair looking up from her copy of the book with a quizzical expression and asking, "Is there a *Mrs.* Kinsey?" "YES, THERE IS A MRS. KINSEY," a headline in *McCall's* answered, and the accompanying article revealed her to be a home-

body who cooked and sewed, entertained the many visitors her husband brought home, and never, ever complained about his long workdays.

For the most part, the reviews echoed the tone set by Dr. Howard A. Rusk in the *Times Book Review.* Rusk, a well-known New York physician and educator, called the book "by far the most comprehensive study yet made of sex behavior." Kinsey and his co-authors, Wardell Pomeroy and Clyde Martin, had ascertained, among other things, that more than ninety per cent of the (white) males they had interviewed had masturbated, that about eighty-five per cent had engaged in premarital intercourse, that between thirty and forty-five per cent had had extramarital sex, that some seventy per cent had patronized prostitutes, and that thirty-seven per cent had experienced at least one homosexual act leading to orgasm.

In the postwar forties, Kinsey's revelations were alarming. Behind the data, some commentators suspected, was an attack on the moral code—and the institutions charged with enforcing that code—which had held American society together. Throughout, Kinsey's book was full of provocative inferences from the findings, such as his sharply worded description of members of the legal system—the "legislators and judges" whose view of sexual morality he called "largely a defense of the code of their own social level."

But the effects of the Kinsey phenomenon were just as widely perceived as salutary. Americans previously had debated such sex-related issues as prostitution, venereal disease, birth control, sex education, and the theories of Freud. But the cultural debate that greeted Kinsey's first study banished taboos that had inhibited Americans from thinking and talking about their erotic lives. Suddenly, the extent of premarital sex, adultery, and homosexuality became acceptable topics of polite conversation. Americans had been given permission to talk about sex.

In many ways, the Kinsey Report polarized the nation. The American Statistical Association was asked to evaluate Kinsey's methodology, prompted by criticism that his findings were statistically flawed. While educators and physicians

James H. Jones, "Dr. Yes" in *The New Yorker,* (August 25 & September 1, 1997).

praised him for bringing new illumination to a vexing subject, intellectuals, such as Margaret Mead, Lionel Trilling, and Reinhold Niebuhr, accused him of moral obtuseness. J. Edgar Hoover saw in Kinsey's work an implicit threat to "our way of life"—as he told the *Reader's Digest*—and ordered the F.B.I. to compile a dossier on Kinsey and his Institute for Sex Research at Indiana University.

Nearly half a century later, Alfred Kinsey remains an eminent figure in the field of sex research. In addition to providing the benchmark against which subsequent studies have been measured, the Kinsey Reports—the book on male sexuality was followed, in 1953, by "Sexual Behavior in the Human Female"—have inspired sex-education programs in high schools and encouraged several generations of sex therapists to tell their patients, "If it feels good, do it."

Because of current difficulties in fashioning accurate estimates of the extent of AIDS, Kinsey's insistence that, in his time, ten per cent of American men had had more than casual homosexual contacts is still debated, especially in the light of such recent studies as the University of Chicago's "National Health and Social Life Survey," released in 1994, which placed the number of gay or bisexual men in the American population at just 2.8 percent. Questions persist about Kinsey's personal life. At the height of the McCarthy period, two years before Kinsey's death in 1956, a special committee in the House of Representatives investigated charges that Kinsey's research served Communism by undermining the American family. More than four decades later, in 1995, Steve Stockman, a Republican congressman from Texas, introduced a House resolution calling for a congressional inquiry into charges that Kinsey had trafficked with child molesters and asking for a ban on federal funding of any sex education influenced by his work. (Like the earlier investigation, this one came to nothing.)

Kinsey was not, of course, a Communist. (He had little discernible interest in politics, and remained a registered Independent who voted Republican.) But he was not quite what he appeared to be—the genial academic in baggy tweeds and bow tie, the simple empiricist disinterestedly reporting his data. As I discovered while researching a biography of Kinsey (I have also served on the institute's scientific board of advisers), he was, in reality, a covert crusader who was determined to use science to free American society from what he saw as the crippling legacy of Victorian repression. And he was a strong-willed patriarch who created around himself a kind of utopian community in which sexual experimentation was encouraged.

In his obsessive energies and powers of persuasion, Kinsey resembled a late-twentieth-century cult leader. In other ways, he was perhaps even more like one of those protean eccentrics of the nineteenth century—a self-created visionary with a burning belief in his mission (and ability) to change the world. He found time not only to conduct the vast labors of research and writing which produced the reports, but also to make serious contributions to biology education and entomological science; to engage in physically challenging exploration in the field; to design his own house and an elaborate flower garden that served as a family classroom; to cultivate a connoisseur's knowledge of classical music and ornithology; and to change (and often dominate) the lives of scores of people with whom he came in contact.

Though hardly Victorian in his beliefs, he was decidedly Victorian in the contrast between his public life and his private life. His greatest contribution as a sex researcher was to reveal the chasm between prescribed and actual behavior and to show the high price exacted by society's sexual prohibitions. No one embodied this divide more than he did. After delving into the institute's archives, reading thousands of letters, and interviewing his associates, I concluded that Kinsey was himself beset by secrets: he was both a homosexual and, from childhood on, a masochist who, as he grew older, pursued an interest in extreme sexuality with increasing compulsiveness. His secret life was shared with a small circle of intimates, a few of whom became his sexual partners, sometimes in the name of "research." Remarkably, his activities did not prevent him from

Alfred Kinsey (seated center) surrounded by his family in Bloomington, Indiana, in September of 1953: his son Bruce (far left); his wife, Clara; and his two daughters, Joan (left) and Anne, with their husbands. Kinsey's carefully controlled public image was that of a tweedy academic and a family man.

being a devoted husband and a caring, successful father. But they almost certainly did affect the objectivity and detachment of his work as a scientist; his celebrated findings, I now believe, may well have been skewed. From the very beginnings of his research into sexual behavior, the Americans who most persistently engaged Kinsey's attention were people who were either on the margins or beyond the pale: homosexuals, sado-masochists, voyeurs, exhibitionists, pedophiles, transsexuals, transvestites, fetishists. As Saul Bellow once observed of Hawthorne's writing of "The Scarlet Letter," "there's nothing like a shameful secret to fire a man up." Not all of Alfred Kinsey's secrets were shameful, but rarely has a man been more fired up.

Kinsey was born in 1894, and spent the first decade of his life in Hoboken, New Jersey, across the Hudson River from Manhattan. Hoboken was then a drab and dirty waterfront town, and Kinsey hated it. When he looked back on his early years there, he claimed to remember only such public events as the first automobiles, the first paved streets, and the fireworks on holidays.

His parents were evangelical Protestants who practiced a fiery brand of Methodism. Theirs was an Old Testament God, who knew a person's every thought and deed and punished those who broke the Commandments. God's surrogate was Kinsey's father, Alfred Seguine Kinsey. He forbade popular music, dancing, tobacco, and drink in his household, and, as teen-agers, his three children, Alfred, Mildred, and Robert, were prohibited from dating. Alfred, the oldest, suffered from diseases—rickets, rheumatic fever, and typhoid fever—that kept him bedridden for long stretches.

When Kinsey was ten, the family moved to South Orange, New Jersey, which at the turn of the century was a well-to-do, almost rural village. There is a snapshot taken on the eve of the First World War of Kinsey in the uniform of an Eagle Scout. Sitting on a brick wall, he looks at the camera with a broad smile, sunlight glistening on his curly blond hair. His demeanor bespeaks obedience to Scouting's injunction to be courteous, respectful, cheerful, and patriotic.

In South Orange, his health improved dramatically, and he started exploring nearby hills and marshes. He pored over books of natural history and became an avid collector of butterflies. Bird-watching was a national craze, and Kinsey took part in it with the fervor other boys devoted to memorizing batting averages. At sixteen, he wrote an essay entitled "What Do Birds Do When It Rains?" He revisited the topic years later, when he wrote a best-selling high-school-biology textbook, answering the question in a chapter called "Bird Behavior":

A bird is a peculiar creature in a rain storm. While its feathers will shed water for a time, prolonged wetting soaks them and reduces their efficiency in conserving the body heat. So most birds take to the thick shelter of the bushes and trees at such a time. Only a few of them (as the robin) stay out and scold at warm rains, and a few of them (as the song sparrow) remain quite as active and cheerful as in the sunshine. . . . Parent birds usually keep their nestlings covered during a rain storm.

The passage illustrates Kinsey's approach to scientific research. In order to satisfy his curiosity, he framed simple questions that could be answered by tenacious, direct observation, even if it meant standing for hours in dripping clothes.

At Bowdoin College, in Maine, Kinsey took a double major in biology and psychology, and became a campus leader—active both in the biology club and on the debating team. He joined a fraternity, but seems not to have been especially close to his fraternity brothers, some of whom remembered him as "a loner."

Kinsey went on to Harvard for graduate study at the Bussey Institution, a major center for Darwinian "new biology." His mentor was William Morton Wheeler, the world's leading authority on the social behavior of insects and an avid taxonomist, whose lectures were based heavily on his own field observations. By the First World War, many of the brightest young scientists were casting their lot with experimental biology, electing to work in genetics, biochemistry, and the like. Only a relative handful became descriptive biologists, who relied on empirical observation to test hypotheses. In deciding to study with Wheeler, Kinsey took the less fashionable path, inspired by a love of nature and the towering example of Darwin.

Under Wheeler's supervision, Kinsey wrote his dissertation on the taxonomy of gall wasps. It was distinguished by three things that became defining features of his subsequent work: huge samples (in this case, many thousands of wasps), rigorous field work, and concise prose that gave coherence to difficult and diverse data. In 1920, Kinsey emerged from Harvard with his doctorate and a new, clear direction.

Kinsey arrived at Indiana University as an assistant professor of zoology in August, 1920. During his first months in Bloomington, he met Clara Bracken McMillen, a young woman from Fort Wayne, who as an undergraduate had been Indiana University's top chemistry student. Lively and robust, Clara, who dressed in masculine clothes and enjoyed long nature hikes, was apparently delighted on Christmas when Kinsey presented her with a compass, a hunting knife, and a pair of Bass hiking shoes. Barely two months after their first date, Kinsey proposed marriage. Clara, who considered herself a freethinker, kept him waiting for two weeks before accepting, because she feared that he was too "churchy." She need not have worried; the devout Methodist had long since begun to give way to the hard-nosed young scientist. (In later years, Kinsey stoutly declared himself an atheist.) Throughout their lives, they called each other by nicknames: she was Mac, an abbreviation of her surname; he was Prok, a contraction of "Professor" and "Kinsey."

During their honeymoon, which was mostly spent hiking through the White Mountains, they failed to consummate their marriage. Kinsey later confided to a friend that the problem was the result of both inexperience and physiology. "Kinsey wasn't altogether clear how to go about this," the friend recalled, "and Mac was completely inexperienced, as well." In Bloomington, Clara consulted a physician, who advised minor corrective surgery in her genital area. Years later, Kinsey told a colleague in the zoology department about the operation, saying that he blamed Victorian prudery for their delay in seeking help. In any case, Alfred and Clara went on to have four children—Donald, Bruce, Anne, and Joan. The oldest, Donald, who was diabetic, died at the age of three, causing the Kinseys enormous sorrow from which Clara, in particular, never fully recovered.

"I believe in marriage as an institution," Kinsey told a class of students in 1940, because "it provides for the procreation of the race and for the care of the offspring." He went on to praise the institution as "a mutual aid society which provides for the best development of two individuals. It is quite possible to walk through life alone but not as efficiently as when there is someone else to go with you to share your plans and your ambitions, to stand by when few others will support you, to help at every turn."

Kinsey's preference for efficiency over romance reflected a new "progressive" ideal embraced by many middle-class Americans between the wars: "companionate marriage," as it was called by nineteen-twenties social reformers who promoted a new egalitarianism between the sexes. Nonetheless, in some ways the Kinseys' marriage resembled the patriarchal union of Kinsey's parents. He made teaching and research the center of his life; she abandoned her interest in chemistry for domesticity. "I always realized that his work would have to come first," Clara later said. "You can't ask a man just to give up what is the driving force of his life because he is your husband."

People close to Clara considered her an equal partner in the marriage, however. Unlike many faculty wives, whose interests did not extend beyond the home, Clara was able to share her husband's intellectual life, thanks to her intelligence, her interest in the outdoors, and her undergraduate training in science. She had read marriage manuals, perused nudist magazines; like Kinsey, she had developed a local reputation as a sex expert, dispensing advice and information to neighbors and their children, not to mention her own offspring. She had become aware of her husband's homosexual inclinations—as well as his masochism—and even enjoyed, with his approval, a sexual relationship outside the marriage.

The Kinseys' "companionate" ideal extended to their children. Sex education, Kinsey argued, had to begin at home. Parents who shirked this duty, he warned, ran the risk of injuring and alienating their children, and of opening a gulf between the generations that would never close.

To inspire positive feelings about the human body, Kinsey taught by example. He would stand naked before the mirror while he shaved, making up singsong rhymes to entertain one of his children. In 1934, when the children were still youngsters—Anne was ten, Joan nine, and Bruce six— the Kinseys took a family vacation in the Great Smoky Mountains. Their cabin was isolated, next to a stream, and the family bathed nude together.

At Indiana University, Kinsey persisted in his study of gall wasps for eighteen years, with an energy that amazed his colleagues. He travelled more than seventy-five thousand miles, across the United States, in Mexico, and in Guatemala, collecting specimens by the hundreds of thousands and earning, among the small circle of scientists who did taxonomic work on insects, the reputation of a man whose devotion to research was nearly fanatical. Kinsey's work seems to have given him visceral pleasure. In contrast to the gray tone of most science writing, his monographs were filled with effusive language (one gall wasp was called "a splendid thing"). He would sit for hours, green eyeshade in place, peering through his microscope. Then, as a lab assistant recalled, he would suddenly exclaim to no one in particular, "Astounding!" or "Wow!"

It became apparent that Kinsey was an unconventional and highly opinionated scientist. During his second year in Bloomington he had started putting together material for an innovative biology textbook, to be used in high schools. He wanted to offer students what he called "a bird's-eye view" of the seven fields he regarded as essential to a basic understanding of biology—taxonomy, morphology, physiology, genetics, ecology, distributional biology, and behavior. In 1926, J. B. Lippincott published the first edition of "An Introduction to Biology," and it was successful enough, particularly in later editions, to give Kinsey considerable financial independence.

The book was distinctive in several ways: its tone was friendly, as though Kinsey were chatting with students; it exhorted young people to get out of the classroom to see for themselves how nature works; and it took a strong position on evolution, which had become a national issue in the summer of 1925, on account of the so-called monkey trial of the high-school science teacher John Scopes, in Tennessee. Kinsey's textbook laid out the basics of Darwinian evolution matter-of-factly, as though he were discussing something as uncontroversial as the life cycle of the fruit fly. The tone, which he would employ to the same effect in his books on sexuality, was intended to indicate that nothing remained for discussion: religion had lost; science had won. In the textbook, and in other writings as well, Kinsey encouraged students to think independently and skeptically. "Don't get a notion that things are true because they are in print," he advised them. A wise person had to "remember that even authorities sometimes publish things that aren't so," and to bear in mind that "what experts believe to be true may be found incorrect upon further investigation."

Kinsey's process of self-liberation was apparent on his field trips. One of the male students who accompanied him as assistants during a wasp-collecting trip to the Ozark Mountains was struck by Kinsey's casual immodesty. "He would go naked if we were in a campground," Homer T. Rainwater recalls. "He just plain didn't give a damn. Nor did he show any inhibitions about his

bodily functions." Kinsey's eagerness to talk about sex was more disconcerting. After several nights, Rainwater discerned a pattern. Kinsey would begin by sharing intimate details about his own private life. "He'd talk about his wife, and what a good sex partner she was, and then he'd go from there. He had a pretty wife, and apparently she was very accommodating, and he talked about that to us, I thought, more than was appropriate." Much to Rainwater's embarrassment, Kinsey would then ask about *his* sex life.

In later years, after Kinsey became famous, he attributed his interest in human sexual behavior to a pioneering course he developed on marriage and the family, which he began teaching in 1938. In the "Historical Introduction" to his book on men, he wrote that many of his biology students had brought him questions about human sexuality, and that when he consulted the available literature on the subject he'd been "struck with the inadequacy of the samples on which such studies were being based, and the apparent unawareness of the investigators that generalizations were not warranted on the bases of such small samples." Accordingly, he saw "ample opportunity for making a scientifically sounder study of human sex behavior," and he went on to explain, "The more recently published research provided a considerable basis for deciding what should be included in a sex history, and our background in both psychology and biology made it apparent that there were additional matters worth investigation."

Kinsey did not mention that he had been pumping students about their sex lives long before he started the marriage course. Nor did he note that it was his personal interest in the "additional matters" which had led him to examine areas of behavior that previous sex researchers knew little about, largely because most of them had not dared to ask.

No previous investigator had ever attempted what Kinsey had in mind. What he set out to do—with the university's support—was to recover every knowable fact about people's sex lives and erotic imaginings. Because he believed that people routinely hid the truth about their private needs and activities, he was all the more determined to discover what they actually thought and did behind closed doors, safe from judgmental scrutiny.

Early in his research into human sexuality, Kinsey realized that his respondents would be more trusting and coöperative if he could not only guarantee confidentiality but avoid the use of written questionnaires. Accordingly, he produced no written key to his interview, preferring to memorize the questions and the order in which they were asked. If a subject balked, or gave an answer that suddenly suggested a new area for discussion, Kinsey had to be able to leap to another round of questions, while keeping mental count of the items in each round. This enabled him to move smoothly through the hundreds of items covered in each history without losing eye contact, and insured that only he and a handful of researchers he had trained knew the specific questions asked, and the answers elicited.

Still, some kind of notation was necessary, so Kinsey devised a form and a code for recording sex histories which made his records unintelligible to outsiders. In later years, Kinsey took delight in handing visitors a sheet of paper bearing an assortment of odd-looking symbols. Explaining that the paper contained a complete record of a subject's sexual history, he would challenge his visitors to decipher it. None of them could.

While he was busy designing safeguards, Kinsey developed his interviewing skills. He learned how to read people's eyes and body language for signs that they might be holding back or lying. He taught himself to phrase questions in a straightforward manner, avoiding euphemisms that could obscure meaning. He assumed that everyone had engaged in forbidden behavior unless he or she said otherwise, and he phrased his questions so as to facilitate confession. For example, instead of asking people if they had ever masturbated he would inquire how old they were when they started masturbating. It was an approach that proved particularly effective with regard to illegal behavior.

To skeptics who wondered, in Kinsey's words, "how it is possible for an interviewer to know whether people are telling the truth, when they are boasting, when they are covering up, or when they are distorting," Kinsey snorted, "As well ask a horse trader how he knows when to close a bargain!" Over the years, Kinsey learned to employ a staccato method of asking questions, which reduced the time a subject had to think up false but plausible answers. He also made a point of maintaining eye contact, believing that it would be harder for people to lie to someone who looked them in the eye. If he suspected lying, he would stop the interview, reprimand the culprit severely, and order him to tell the truth or get out.

In June of 1939, Kinsey taught his last class of the week and left Bloomington on a new kind of field trip. Until now, he had interviewed mostly college students, family members—including Clara and their children—and friends. Yet even within this small circle, he had managed to spread the word that he would be happy to counsel people who had sexual problems. On that afternoon, he was headed for Chicago. Waiting for him was a man who had promised to introduce him to what would today be called the city's gay community.

Kinsey checked into his hotel, the Harrison, just off Michigan Avenue, and set off to interview a group of young men who lived together in a boarding house on Rush Street. Things went well. Because he showed no hint of moral condemnation, the young men were willing to trust him. Kinsey assured them that he would never divulge their confidences, and stressed that whatever they told him would benefit science. Kinsey would continue to make numerous forays into the gay subculture of other large American cities, and his reports of those experiences have an almost childlike enthusiasm. "Have been to Halloween parties, taverns, clubs, etc., which would be unbelievable if realized by the rest of the world," he wrote to a friend after one trip to Chicago. "Always they have been most considerate and coöperative, decent, understanding, and cordial in their reception. Why has no one cracked this before?"

With homosexuals, as with other subjects, Kinsey employed what statisticians call a "grab" sample—meaning that he surveyed only people who agreed to coöperate, without giving much consideration to whether their backgrounds added up to a fair representation of a particular group. He also did what is known as "snowball" sampling, which involved contacting friends and acquaintances of people who were already part of his pool or relying on the good will of an organization to get to the entire membership. He made a point of targeting groups he felt were underrepresented in other scientific samplings and who—like homosexuals—had a special attraction for him. These practices, as his critics later charged, were bound to result in a distorted representation of America's male population.

Throughout Kinsey's career, his success would turn in large measure on follow-up work. He crafted thank-you letters with care, assuring the recipients that their contributions to his research had been crucial and unique. And on rare occasions, Kinsey wrote to the parents of his subjects. Because he wanted to understand why men became homosexuals, he was eager to learn everything he could about their home lives.

Often Kinsey got caught up in the lives of the people he interviewed. To one of them, he wrote, "Your capacity for love is the thing that stands foremost in my thinking of you. Your question is a fair one—if love is extolled by poets and teachers, then what can be wrong about it in any form that remains fine and real?" No wonder these young men trusted Kinsey. This mild-mannered, soft-spoken, middle-aged scientist made it clear that he liked and respected them. Kinsey must have seemed like an approving father.

By December of 1940, Kinsey had compiled seventeen hundred histories, more than enough to establish the feasibility of his research. Convinced that he would need a hundred thousand histories for a reliable sample, he applied for a grant from the National Research Council's Committee for Research in Problems of Sex, or C.R.P.S., which was funded by the Rockefeller Foundation. The C.R.P.S. was willing to take a modest risk on helping to finance what appeared to be a promising study, and awarded him a small

grant in the spring of 1941. When Kinsey requested a larger grant the following year, Robert M. Yerkes, the committee's chairman and a distinguished Yale psychologist, arrived in Bloomington to see what Kinsey was up to. With him were George W. Corner, a distinguished embryologist at the Carnegie Institution, and Lowell Reed, a pioneering biostatistician and the dean of the School of Hygiene and Public Health at Johns Hopkins University. Kinsey promptly persuaded them that the only way they could understand his project was to submit to his interview. All three did, and emerged astonished at his skillfulness in drawing them out.

Yerkes and Corner were also treated to a demonstration in the field. For some time, Kinsey had been taking personal histories in the state's penal institutions. On this occasion, he drove his guests to the men's prison, then to the women's prison, and, finally, to a house of prostitution in the slums of Indianapolis. At each stop, his visitors watched while he conducted an interview. Many years later, Corner recalled the subject at the men's prison as having been "a major offender of some sort, I think murderous assault or something like that." Sitting face to face with the man, Kinsey abandoned the vocabulary and persona of a college professor and spoke fluently in the language of the streets. His observers were amazed by the performance, and when Kinsey was attacked by critics who questioned his ability to obtain accurate data, Corner replied, "He made me talk, and he made a Negro criminal talk, and I thought he could deal with [anyone]."

Large grants—lots of them—followed. Kinsey used the funds to build a research institute, which he filled with staff members, a library, and an archive, and for travel expenses. Over the next several years, he and his colleagues interviewed a wide assortment of people in several regions of the country. By the mid-nineteen-forties, they felt that they had compiled more than enough data to justify publication, and Kinsey was dividing his time between field work and sitting down to write the first of his explosive reports on American sexuality.

Shortly after Kinsey began writing "Sexual Behavior in the Human Male," in 1945, he collapsed—a portent of recurring health problems that he would have for the rest of his life. He attributed his condition to physical fatigue. "I have been exhausted and in bed part of the time for the last several weeks and I am glad that my traveling is over for the first half of this year," he wrote to a friend. "It has taken three years of continuous calculation on the statistics, and there is a tremendous amount of detail to work into the text that I hope will be rather easy reading."

Easy reading it was not. The strategy behind the first Kinsey Report was to shout "Science!" through an exhaustive accumulation of technical jargon and massed statistics. At every turn, Kinsey, who had refused to delegate any of the writing to others, cautioned readers not to attach too much emphasis to specific findings (while arguing that the bulk of his data was both representative and reliable), and denied any intention to influence social policy. His approach to what he liked to call "the human animal" was, he wrote, "agnostic."

Tolerance was the underlying message of the book. Kinsey bombarded his readers with the theme of sexual diversity. "There is no American pattern of sexual behavior, but scores of patterns, each of which is confined to a particular segment of our society," he wrote. He took pains to show that many forms of sexual behavior labelled criminal or rare were actually quite common. (He argued that "at least 85 per cent of the younger male population could be convicted as sex offenders if law enforcement officials were as efficient as most people expect them to be.")

Kinsey divided his book into three sections. The first part, "History and Method," contained four chapters designed to persuade readers that his research was superior to all previous studies, that his sole aim in launching his investigation was to fill a hole in science, and that his numbers were sound. The second part, "Factors Affecting Sexual Outlet," had chapters on, among other things, age, marriage, religion, and social class. To show how each of these factors affected sexual-

ity, Kinsey used the orgasm as his basic unit of measurement—that is, masturbation had the same value as intercourse. No approach could have been more subversive of traditional morality. (In a statistic that was to become celebrated, Kinsey found that the average male between adolescence and the age of thirty had precisely 2.88 orgasms per week.) The third part, "Sources of Sexual Outlet," was a catalogue of the various practices that resulted in orgasm.

For all its science, Kinsey's analysis contained considerable social commentary. Society, he argued, began its efforts to inhibit and control the sexuality of its members in childhood, with prohibitions and restrictions that continued for life. His case histories revealed that most boys had sexual experiences before reaching adolescence, and he expressed regret that preadolescents did not have more.

One of Kinsey's most provocative discoveries was that males of different social backgrounds and educational levels presented strongly dissimilar sexual histories. Young single males who had gone to high school but not beyond had the highest number of orgasms, while those who had gone to college had the lowest. Kinsey wrote, "Each social level is convinced that its pattern is the best of all patterns. . . . Most of the tragedies that develop out of sexual activities are products of this conflict between the attitudes of different social levels." He continued, "Sexual activities in themselves rarely do physical damage, but disagreements over the significance of sexual behavior may result in personality conflicts, a loss of social standing, imprisonment, disgrace, and the loss of life itself."

The chapter "Homosexual Outlet" was fifty-six pages long. Kinsey went straight to the heart of the debate over the origins of homosexuality. He rejected any connection between it and endocrinological imbalance, and dismissed conventional psychological explanations as well. "Psychologists have been too much concerned with the individuals who depart from the group custom," he wrote. "It would be more important to know why so many individuals conform as they do to such ancient custom." Homosexual behavior, he maintained, was part of the human and mammalian heritage: as a member of the animal kingdom, the human animal possessed the capacity for same-sex eroticism.

Yet Kinsey stopped short of arguing that homosexuality was biologically determined. Whether or not people engaged in homosexual behavior, he explained, depended in large measure on experience and conditioning. If their early childhood experiences happened to be with members of the same sex and if those experiences turned out to be enjoyable, there was a fair chance that the individual would repeat them, gradually forming a pattern that culminated in adult homosexual behavior.

Binary labels such as "homosexual" and "heterosexual," Kinsey argued, could never capture the rich diversity and overlapping experiences of human beings. "The world is not to be divided into sheep and goats," he declared. "Not all things are black nor all things white." Instead, he argued that human sexual behavior was fluid, and he advanced this thesis with his celebrated seven-point scale. The individuals who registered zero were exclusively heterosexual, while those who rated a six were strictly homosexual. Offered as a finely tuned instrument, the scale was designed to blend sharp distinctions and to find common ground that united people in the sexual behavior they shared. Most people fell into the intermediate categories, with private lives that combined both heterosexual and homosexual elements. Their differences from one another were matters of degree rather than of kind.

Kinsey ended the book with this disclaimer: "The social values of human activities must be measured by many scales other than those which are available to the scientist." He failed to acknowledge, however, that he had placed a thumb on the scale—that his methodology and his sampling technique virtually guaranteed that he would find what he was looking for.

From 1945 to 1947, Kinsey received dozens of inquiries from publishers who were eager to explain why their houses were uniquely positioned to present his material to the American public. Kinsey realized that it would be more prudent to

sign with a medical publisher, which catered to a professional audience, in order to forestall any charges of sensationalism or that he was trying to influence public opinion.

The task of editing Kinsey's manuscript fell to Lloyd G. Potter, the vice-president and senior editor of W. B. Saunders, and he worked closely with Kinsey throughout the summer and fall of 1947. Potter failed to note any of the instances in which Kinsey had editorialized, but his critique of the manuscript anticipated many of the complaints that would dog the book after it was published. The most serious would involve statistics.

Potter asked Kinsey for assurances that the statistical method and data in the book were, in his words, "bulletproof." He continued, "The assumption is, of course, that your findings can be applied to the United States population as a whole, but the data seem preponderantly to be collected in the eastern part of the country, and very little relates to the west and the south." Kinsey's response—that he repeatedly admitted the limits of his approach ("The calculations," he said, "are always subject to the adequacy of the sample")—was scarcely satisfactory. Still, Potter was reassured to learn from Alan Gregg, the director of the medical division of the Rockefeller Foundation, that Kinsey's statistics had been carefully reviewed by Lowell Reed, at Johns Hopkins. The real concern, said Gregg, who wrote a preface to the book, was "the general issue of freedom of scientific inquiry." He added, "I have no doubt that the book will stir up criticism. Psychoanalysis did and yet it has now become the subject of numerous books that encounter no great risk of suppression and occasion no storms."

Kinsey, in fact, turned out to be extraordinarily skillful at manipulating the media. Because of his subject, journalists had pursued him from the early years of his research. Fearing that no good could come from premature publicity, Kinsey had routinely asked officials in charge of scholarly conferences at which he spoke to omit any reference to his session in press releases. When reporters did show up, he declined to be interviewed, but told them that he would be happy to coöperate when his findings were ready for publication. "With a few exceptions, he didn't like the press," Paul Gebhard recalled, adding that Kinsey "disliked being recorded or quoted . . . [out of fear] that he could be held accountable for this and criticized."

On the eve of publication, Kinsey devised an ingenious plan for controlling the press. He would invite a select group of journalists to Bloomington. There they would receive a detailed summary of the book prior to its release date or, if they preferred, would be permitted to read the proofs. Either way, they would be free to write whatever they liked. In exchange, however, they would have to agree not to publish their articles until December, 1947—roughly a month before the book arrived in the stores—and to submit copies of their articles to Kinsey prior to publication, so that he could review them for factual accuracy.

Kinsey's policy worked as planned. Beginning in the late summer of 1947, an orderly procession of feature-story writers and reporters made the trek to Bloomington. Most of the journalists spent two or three days at the institute, and, as had many visitors before them, they saw Kinsey only as he wanted to be seen: as a middle-aged family man and a dedicated scientist, whose passion for objectivity was beyond question. With reporters sitting at his feet like schoolchildren, Kinsey told his story of how the research got started, explained his taxonomic method, and closed with deftly chosen remarks on the reliability of the data. He even persuaded many of the writers to give their own sex histories in the hope of banishing all doubts about his skills as an interviewer.

When November arrived, Kinsey was confident of success. He wrote to the pollster George Gallup, "My guess is that right now there are perhaps 100,000 people in the country who know something about our research. By the last week in November, several million will have seen magazine articles and by the middle of January there should be a very high proportion of the total population that has had information about it." The magazines fell into line: "Today, on the rustic campus of a Midwest university, a soft-spoken, keen-eyed man is quietly at work—producing a social atom bomb," *Look* announced. In language that could have come from an institute press release, *Harper's* declared, "Experts who have closely scrutinized the interviewing techniques of Kinsey and his associates endorse their scientific validity and state further that the people so far interviewed represent a fair cross section of the American population."

Although the mainstream media's reaction to the Kinsey Report was overwhelmingly favorable, the response in academic circles was decidedly mixed. As *The New Republic* told its readers, "not a few" specialists were "heating the cauldron in anticipation of the feast at which Kinsey will be the main dish." Anthropologists led the attack. Writing in the New York *Herald Tribune,* Geoffrey Gofer, a Briton, charged that "the sampling is so poor that the only reliable figures are those for college graduates in six of the northeastern states." The basic problem, Gorer argued, was that sound sampling procedures required "some carefully planned system of randomization which avoids bias on the part of the investigator." At a minimum, he maintained, Kinsey should have used "stratified sampling"—a system that rests on "the calculation that the distribution of characters being studied is directly correlated with other criteria such as age, education, religion, region, economic level, etc."

Speaking at a symposium on the book held in New York in March, 1948, Margaret Mead argued that Kinsey had atomized sex by taking "sexual behavior out of its interpersonal context" and reducing it "to the category of a simple act of elimination," and for flagrant puritanism. "Nowhere have I been able to find a single suggestion that sex is any fun, not anywhere in the book, not a suggestion," she declared. "The book suggests no way of choosing between a woman and a sheep."

In a long essay in *Partisan Review,* Lionel Trilling amplified Mead's concerns, criticizing Kinsey for failing to comprehend that sex involves the whole of an individual's character; for his seemingly willful misrepresentation of

Freudian psychology; for allowing the notion of the natural to develop into the idea of the normal; and for advancing his own peculiar views while simultaneously proclaiming his objectivity. The Kinsey Report, Trilling declared, betrayed "an extravagant fear of all ideas that do not seem to it to be, as it were, immediately dictated by simple physical fact." Even so, Trilling found much to praise in the motives behind the book. Commenting on "how very characteristically *American* a document it is," he explained, "I have in mind chiefly the impulse toward acceptance and liberation, the broad and generous desire for others that they not be harshly judged." In a conclusion that seems the fairest assessment of this curious work, Trilling remarked, "Although it is possible to say of the Report that it brings light, it is necessary to say of it that it spreads confusion."

Kinsey was especially wounded by the Gorer and Mead critiques, all the more because he suspected professional ill will and collusion. Writing to a supporter, Kinsey snapped, "The Gorer review either represents stupidity or deliberate maliciousness. He criticizes us as though our technique had been that of proportionate sample, and ignores the careful and elaborate explanation which we made of stratified sampling techniques." Kinsey rejected all negative assessments, moral and technical, of his work. He saw himself as the one scientist in the world who had uncovered the facts about human sexual behavior and had placed the truth before the public.

Another battle was more troublesome. From the moment news stories about the report started appearing, the book was linked in the public's mind to Kinsey's principal patron, the Rockefeller Foundation. For years, Alan Gregg had cautioned Kinsey against making too much of this connection. His concerns proved to be justified. The foundation found itself drawn deeper and deeper into the controversy around Kinsey's work. For the six years after the report was published, the foundation continued its support of his research, despite strong objections from some of its most powerful board members, notably John Foster Dulles and Arthur Hays Sulzberger. Although the

mixed reception in 1953 to "Sexual Behavior in the Human Female" mirrored that of the first volume, the foundation's president, Dean Rusk, decided, in 1954, under pressure from the board, to cut Kinsey loose—largely out of worry that politicians would attempt to use Kinsey as a brush with which to tar the foundation.

The battles had been hard on Kinsey. Restless and irritable, he was having trouble sleeping. The fatigue was starting to show in his face; his eyes had lost their sparkle. One colleague advised him, "It's time you let your Scotch-Presbyterian conscience drive you into taking a real vacation, for the sake of your most important program." Another friend recalled that Kinsey was plagued by "a constant sense of mortality," adding that "a great many decisions and a great deal of the spirit of the research" resulted from the fact that Kinsey "was haunted by the brevity of his life."

Kinsey had begun to build a private world that would provide the emotional support he needed. Within a select circle of staff members and trusted outsiders, he set out to create his own sexual utopia, a scientifically justified subculture whose members would not be bound by arbitrary and antiquated sexual taboos. Kinsey decreed that the men could have sex with each other, and that the wives, too, could be free to embrace whatever sexual partners they liked.

One of the outsiders, whom I'll call "Y," has given a detailed account of his experiences at the institute. Y was a handsome young professional with a diverse sexual history, which included sadomasochism and extensive homosexual contacts. When Kinsey took his history, Y was astonished by Kinsey's gift for putting people at their ease. "You were instantly . . . at peace with yourself," he recalled.

The men became friends, and during one of Kinsey's trips they met in a hotel room. "I told him I had a fantasy of having sex with him," Y recalled, "and he sort of said, 'Take off your clothes.' So I did, and we started right there." At Kinsey's invitation, Y made several trips to Bloomington for consultation and sex. Y recalled sleeping with Clara, and others, of both sexes and noted that

Kinsey was an eager participant in these sessions. Y stressed, "It wasn't all homosexual."

During his visits to Bloomington, Y always stayed at his host's house, and he observed Kinsey's strong emotional bond with Clara. "I don't think they were sexy to one another, just deeply appreciative and deeply loving," he recalled. "There was a real, durable love between the two of them. They totally accepted what the other one did."

Still, according to Kinsey's friends, there was something grim in the way he was approaching sex. He had always loved, as one friend put it, "to skate very near the edge of the cliff . . . to shock people" in order to demonstrate that he was "absolutely . . . unconstrained by moralistic forms." By the late nineteen-forties, however, his risk-taking was becoming compulsive. If the press had got a hint of what was happening, his work and career would have been ruined.

Kinsey compounded that risk by documenting, in his attic, many sexual acts on film. Not all of his colleagues and their spouses agreed to his request to be filmed. One staff wife later complained of "the sickening pressure" she was under to have sex on film, saying that she felt that her husband's career at the institute depended on her acquiescence.

Kinsey tried to justify the filming as essential to his scientific—and social—mission. Yet he also made it clear to those he took into his confidence that while they were free to enjoy the fruits of sexual liberation, they had to accept his limits on their behavior. Anyone contemplating an extramarital affair, for example, was told to clear it first with Kinsey. Paul Gebhard remembered him saying, "You've got to tell me who it is and explain it all, and then I'll tell you whether you can or can't." Gebhard added, "That edict was not necessarily obeyed."

No one felt the force of Kinsey's unyielding demands more strongly than Clara. In keeping with her behavior over many years, she did her best to throw herself into her role as the wife of the high priest of sexual liberation. Clara was filmed masturbating and having sex with a staff member.

Gebhard, speculating on why she agreed to be filmed, said, "Mac so deeply believed in the research that Kinsey was doing, I swear if he'd asked her to cut her wrists she probably would have. She idolized the man, even though she was quite free in saying he irritated her occasionally."

The writer Glenway Wescott and his companion Monroe Wheeler were two of the gay outsiders who performed in Kinsey's attic. In 1949, Wescott met Kinsey for dinner during one of Kinsey's visits to New York, and later he confided to his diary, "Kinsey is a strange man, with a handsome good sagacious face but with a haunted look—fatigue, concentration, and (surprising to me, if I interpret rightly) passionateness and indeed sensuality."

As the director of exhibitions and publications at the Museum of Modern Art, Wheeler was happy to put Kinsey in touch with dozens of gay artists and writers in the city. Through these contacts, Kinsey was able not only to add scores of homosexual histories to his collection but also to expand his appreciation of the many ways in which the homoerotic imagination informed literature and art. In return, Kinsey gave Wescott and Wheeler a standing invitation to visit Bloomington.

During one visit, the two men agreed to be filmed. Wescott had let it be known that he had most unusual orgasms—so violent that he was frequently thrown off the bed. Kinsey was eager to capture this spectacle on film, and Wescott did not disappoint him. At the critical instant, he "jackknifed," and Kinsey was ecstatic. Clara then prepared a dinner for the guests, which inspired Wescott to write in his diary, "Mrs. K is one of the greatest of cooks—if Alfred were not the hardest-working of men he would be the fattest."

Homosexual men figured prominently in the filming sessions, and Kinsey's preference was for sadomasochists. Among Kinsey's favorite subjects was Samuel M. Steward, an English professor at a Midwestern university, who had quit to become a tattoo artist and erotic writer. It took five hours for Kinsey to take his sexual history. (The average history took less than two hours.) After they had been friends for about a year, Kinsey raised the subject of filming. As Steward recalled in the gay and lesbian magazine *The Advocate,* Kinsey's "interest in sadomasochism had reached a point of intolerable tension, and he wanted to find out more." When Steward agreed to coöperate, Kinsey arranged an assignation with a freelance designer from New York named Mike Miksche, whom Steward described as "a tall, meanlooking sadist . . . with a crewcut and a great personality."

In Bloomington, Steward and Miksche put on a show that delighted Kinsey. As the sessions unfolded, various members of Kinsey's senior staff dropped by to watch. Steward was particularly impressed by Clara, whom he described as "a true scientist to the end," noting that "she sat by and once in a while she calmly changed the sheets on the workbench."

According to William Dellenback, the institute's photographer, Kinsey was becoming overtly exhibitionistic—to the point of having himself filmed, always from the chest down, while engaged in masochistic masturbation. The world's foremost expert on sexual behavior would insert an object such as a pipe cleaner or swizzle stick into his urethra, tie a rope around his scrotum, and then tug hard on the rope. Ever the teacher, Kinsey would pause just long enough to offer a brief anatomy lesson: "I remember vaguely Kinsey saying to me, 'You know, there's a little flap as you go partly up the urethra that you have to bypass, so you can't just jam the thing in,' " Dellenback recalled.

Toward the end of his life, Kinsey's boundaries shifted again—to the point where he was apparently prepared to withhold moral disapproval of adult-child sexual contacts. Wescott recalled a conversation in which Kinsey acknowledged that when he'd first started his research he considered men who had intercourse with children to be "beyond the pale"—a group for whom "there could be no sympathy." Over time, however, Kinsey seems to have tempered his views. Wescott remembered Kinsey's once telling him that of all the people he'd interviewed who had been molested as children, only a few felt that they had

been personally harmed by the experience. Kinsey's implication was that if society did not make so much of it, children would not feel harmed.

The public response to "Sexual Behavior in the Human Female" was strong enough to put Kinsey's face on the cover of *Time* in 1953. Nevertheless, his final years were not happy. Sales of the female volume were not as great as he had hoped; his research was investigated by a congressional committee amid the charges that it aided subversion. Most alarmingly, in the absence of Rockefeller funding, financial problems threatened to close his beloved Institute for Sex Research.

One evening in August, 1954, Kinsey, dejected and bitter, stood in his offices in the basement of Wylie Hall looking up at some exposed pipes just below the ceiling. On this evening, he told a close friend, he threw a rope over the pipe, tied a knot around his scrotum, and wrapped the other end around his hand. Then, he climbed onto a chair and jumped off. Shortly after this episode, Kinsey, accompanied by Gebhard and Dellenback, travelled to Peru to photograph a collection of erotic pottery. There, Kinsey took to his bed, suffering from an infection in his pelvic region. He attributed his illness to a throat infection he had contracted earlier in Los Angeles, explaining that the infection had spread to his pelvis. A physician friend, however, labelled Kinsey's illness orchitis, pinpointing the testicles as the site of the infection.

Kinsey often told his staff, "I'd rather be dead than not put in a full day's work." It was a martyr's voice. For years, he had compared himself to the great scientists of the past who had suffered terrible wrongs from the forces of ignorance. It was also the voice of the autocrat. Kinsey had always used sex research to gain control over others, and he could not bear to surrender authority to anyone. Long after Kinsey's death, Gebhard could still recall the last words his boss spoke to him: "Don't do anything until I come back."

Kinsey entered the Bloomington hospital in August, 1956. He was suffering from pneumonia, which aggravated a long-standing heart condition. On August 25th, at the age of sixty-two, he died.

The immediate cause of death was not pneumonia or a failing heart but an embolism caused by a bruise on one of his legs, which he had sustained in a fall while working in his garden.

Kinsey died believing that his crusade to promote more enlightened sexual attitudes had not succeeded. Yet in 1957, a year after his death, the Supreme Court's Roth decision narrowed the legal definition of obscenity, expanding the umbrella of constitutional protection to cover a broader range of works portraying sex in art, literature, and film. In 1960, the birth-control pill was introduced, offering a highly effective method of contraception. In 1961, Illinois became the first state to repeal its sodomy statutes. The next year, the Supreme Court ruled that a magazine featuring photographs of male nudes was not obscene and was therefore not subject to censorship. And in 1973, in a dramatic reversal, the American Psychiatric Association removed homosexuality from its list of psychopathologies. Kinsey, the anguished man of science, had prevailed.

STUDY QUESTIONS

1. Multiple contradictions marked Kinsey's life. How did he reconcile these conflicts and what do they reveal in general about the people who initiate change?

2. Who might have opposed Kinsey's work? Why were his assertions threatening?

3. Kinsey's academic heritage as an "empirical biologist" had a profound effect on his approach to the study of human sexuality. How did this background effect his beliefs on the origins of sexual preference and the relationship of class and sex?

4. The author argues that Kinsey's sexuality tainted the objectivity of his study. Considering his impact on the way Americans approach sex, does this article change his legacy?

BIBLIOGRAPHY

James H. Jones, *Alfred Kinsey: A Public/Private Life* (1997) is a recent work by the author of this piece that presents an in-depth examination of Kinsey. Two pieces that consider Kinsey's work, its effects, and its context are David Halberstam, "Discovering Sex" *American Heritage* 44 (1993): 39–58 and David Allyn, "Private Acts/Public Policy: Alfred Kinsey, The American Law Institute and the Privatization of American Sexual Morality" *Journal of American Studies* 30 (1996): 405–428. For general sexual history, see John D'Emilio and Estelle Freedman, *Intimate Matters* (1997) Martha Hodes, ed., *Sex, Love and Race* (1999).

INTELLECT ON TELEVISION: THE QUIZ SHOW SCANDALS OF THE 1950s

Richard S. Tedlow

In 1854, Henry David Thoreau wrote, "We are in great haste to construct a magnetic telegraph from Maine to Texas; but Maine and Texas, it may be, have nothing important to communicate." More than one hundred years later, Thoreau's observation, greatly expanded, is still valid. Possessing the technological means of communication is no guarantee of meaningful communication. Nowhere is this situation more evident than in the commercial television industry. In the following essay, Richard S. Tedlow examines the problems inherent in commercial broadcasting, especially as they relate to the television quiz scandals of the late 1950s. The picture he presents is not a flattering one; the object of commercial television is quite simply to sell products, not to educate or uplift its audience. The result is an industry dominated by monetary values and generally oblivious to all ethical or moral consideration. In the specific case of quiz shows, television has produced an additional side effect: it has cheapened the meaning of education and intelligence. As Tedlow cogently observed, "If any crime had been committed in the quiz show episode, it was surely the broad conspiracy to portray as genuine intellectual activity the spouting of trivia." In today's America where books of lists and trivia make the best-sellers list, Tedlow's discussion of the quiz shows has a haunting familiarity.

On the seventh of June, 1955, *The $64,000
Question* made its debut on the CBS television network. No programming idea
could have been more thoroughly foreshadowed
by previous shows. Since the mid-1930s radio had
been exploiting the American passion for facts
with contests and games. For years, small
amounts of cash or manufacturer-donated merchandise had been given away through various
formats. What was new about *Question* was the
size of the purse. The giveaway had taken a
"quantum jump"; losers received a Cadillac as a
consolation prize.

Question's format was simple. The producers
selected a contestant who chose a subject about
which he or she answered increasingly difficult
questions which were assigned monetary values
ranging from $64 to $64,000. The contestants
could quit without attempting the succeeding
plateau, but if he chose to continue and missed,
he forfeited his winnings and was left with only
his Cadillac.

By a few deft touches, the producers heightened the aura of authenticity and tension. The
questions used were deposited in a vault of the
Manufacturers Trust Company and brought to
the studio by a bank officer flanked by two
armed guards. As the stakes increased, the contestant entered a glass-enclosed "isolation booth"
on stage to the accompaniment of "ominous
music which hinted at imminent disaster" in
order to prevent coaching from the audience.
Since the contestant returned week after week
rather than answering all the questions on one
broadcast, the audience was given time to contemplate whether he would keep his winnings or
go on to the next plateau and also a chance to
worry about how difficult the next question
might be.

The program became an immediate hit. In September, an estimated 55 million people, over

twice as many as had seen the Checkers speech,
viewing 84.8 percent of the television sets in operation at the time, saw Richard S. McCutchen, a 28-
year-old Marine captain whose category was gour-
met foods, become the first grand prize winner.

Most early contestants were seemingly average
folks who harbored a hidden expertise in a subject far removed from their workaday lives. Thus
McCutchen was asked about *haute cuisine* rather
than amphibious assault. This separation was no
accident. Its purpose was not only to increase the
novelty of the show by providing something odd
to the point of being freakish but also to integrate
the viewer more intimately into the video melodrama. Everyone who had ever accumulated a
store of disconnected, useless information could
fantasize about transforming it into a pot of gold.

In a few months, *Question* had created a large
new "consumption community," Daniel Boorstin's
label for the nonideological, democratic, vague,
and rapidly shifting groupings which have characterized twentieth-century American society. Suddenly, a third of the country had a common bond
about which total strangers could converse. Paradoxically, in order to belong to this community,
the individual had to isolate himself physically
from others. Families stayed at home to watch the
show, rather than celebrating it in the company of
a large crowd. Movie theaters reported a precipi-
tous decline in business, and stores and streets
were empty when it came on the air.

Everyone whose life was touched by the show
seemed to prosper. In addition to their prize
money, some contestants received alluring offers
to do public relations work for large companies
or to star in movies. *Question's* creator, an independent program packager named Louis Cowan,
became president of CBS-TV, an indication of
how pleased the network executives were to
present so successful a show. Even the banker
who brought the sealed questions from the vault
found himself promoted to a vice presidency. But
the greatest beneficiary was the sponsor.

In March of 1955, the show was purchased by
Revlon, which soon began reaping the rewards of
well-constructed advertising on a popular televi-

Richard S. Tedlow, "Intellect on Television: The Quiz Show
Scandals of the 1950s" in *American Quarterly,* Vol. 27/No. 4
(Fall, 1979). © The Johns Hopkins University Press.
Reprinted by permission.

sion program. Several products quintupled their sales, and advertising for one had to be discontinued because it sold out nationally. George F. Abrams, the company's vice president in charge of advertising, gloated that *Question* ". . . is doing a most fantastic sales job. It certainly is the most amazing sales success in the history of the cosmetics industry. There isn't a single Revlon item that hasn't benefitted. . . ." Net sales for 1955 increased 54 percent over the previous year, and in 1956 they soared another 66 percent. When Revlon shares were first offered on the New York Stock Exchange at the end of 1955, the issue's success was "so great it was almost embarrassing."

Question's greatest liability was its own success; it spawned imitators around the world. In the United States, a spate of programs featuring endless variations of gift-giving for answering questions further retarded "TV's already enfeebled yearning to leaven commercialism with culture." Most of these have mercifully been consigned to oblivion, but one rivaled *The $64,000 Question* in the impact it made upon the nation.

The *21* program was developed by another firm of independent program packagers, Barry and Enright, Inc. The format was different, especially in having two contestants compete against each other and no limit on their winnings, but the basic idea was the same. Questions were given point values, and the points were worth money. Once again, the "wiles of a riverboat gambler" were combined with the memory of sundry bits of information which was passed off as intellectual acumen, with the result a spectacularly profitable property.

Barry and Enright leased the show to Pharmaceuticals, Inc., now known as the J. B. Williams Company, and it first appeared on NBC on October 12, 1956. Pharmaceuticals, whose most well-known product was Geritol, soon had good reason to be pleased with its quiz show. *21* did not attain quite the ratings of *Question,* but it competed successfully against *I Love Lucy,* one of the most popular programs in television history, and attracted much notice. Although its advertising director was reluctant to give complete credit to

the program for the increased sales of Geritol, it could hardly have hurt. Sales in 1957 bettered the previous year's mark by one-third.

Unlike *Question, 21* did not shun the highly educated, and one of its contestants became a symbol to the nation of the profitability of intellectual achievement. Charles Van Doren provided evidence that an intellectual could be handsome, that he could get rich, and that he could be a superstar. Like a football player, the intellectual athlete could win fame and wealth. Van Doren's family could lay genuine claim to membership in an American aristocracy of letters. Descended from seventeenth-century Dutch immigrants, Van Doren's uncle Carl was a literary critic whose 1939 biography of Benjamin Franklin won a Pulitzer Prize. His father Mark won the Prize for poetry the following year, and he was equally famous for his accomplishments in the classroom as a professor of English at Columbia. The wives of the Van Doren brothers were also literary, rounding out a remarkably cultivated quartet. Van Doren's family divided its time between a country estate in Connecticut and a Greenwich Village townhouse where guests over the years included Sinclair Lewis, Mortimer Adler, Joseph Wood Krutch, and Morris Ernst. The family was the symbol of intellectual vitality.

Van Doren established himself on the program by defeating the swarthy, seemingly impoverished previous champion Herbert Stempel on December 5, 1956, after having played three tie matches with Stempel on November 28. It was smooth sailing for the weeks that followed.

On the TV screen [Eric Goldman has written] he appeared lanky, pleasant, smooth in dress and manner but never slick, confident but with an engaging way of understating himself. The long, hard questions would come at him and his eyes would roll up, squeeze shut, his forehead furrow and perspire, his teeth gnaw at his lower lip. Breathing heavily, he seemed to coax information out of some corner of his mind by talking to himself in a kind of stream-of-consciousness. Like a good American, he fought hard, taking advantage of every rule. . . . Like

*a good American, he won without crowing.
And, like a good American, he kept on winning, drowning corporation lawyers or ex-
college presidents with equal ease on questions
ranging from naming the four islands of the
Balearic Islands to explaining the process of
photosynthesis to naming the three baseball
players who each amassed more than 3,500
hits. Charles Van Doren was "the new All-
American boy," the magazines declared, and to
millions he was that indeed. . . .*

Van Doren's victories on the quiz show brought
him greater rewards than had accrued to any of his
predecessors. He received thousands of letters
from parents and teachers around the world,
thanking him for popularizing the life of the mind.
Little services such as dry cleaning, which he had
had to pay for when supporting himself on his
$4,400 yearly salary as an English instructor at Co-
lumbia, were now donated *gratis* by star-struck
shopkeepers. Several colleges expressed an interest in hiring him away from Columbia, and he
found himself referred to in print as "Doctor" despite not yet having earned his Ph.D. And then, of
course, there was the money. Van Doren won
$129,000 during his 14 weeks on *21*. Soon after he
left, he was awarded a $50,000 contract to appear
on the *Today* show, where for five minutes each
morning he would speak of science, literature, history. "I think I may be the only person," he once remarked, "who ever read seventeenth-century poetry on a network television program—a far cry
from the usual diet of mayhem, murder, and rape."

Rumors of improper practices surfaced soon
after the quiz shows made their debut. By the end
of 1956, articles were appearing in the trade and
general circulation press discussing the "controls" exercised by the producers to keep popular
contestants alive and eliminate the unpopular.
"Are the quiz shows rigged?" asked *Time* magazine in the spring of 1957, a year in which the net-
works were investing a small fortune in them.
The answer: producers could not "afford to risk
collusion with contestants," and yet, because of
pretesting, they were able to ask questions which
they knew the contestants would or would not

know. They could thus manipulate the outcome
"far more effectively than most viewers suspect."
The report noted, however, that Van Doren "feels
certain that no questions were being formfitted to
his phenomenal mind."

A number of contestants had been disappointed
at their treatment on the shows. The most important of these, and the John Dean of this piece, was
the man Van Doren first defeated, Herbert Stempel.

Stempel's motives were very mixed. One was
money. He had quickly squandered his winnings
and failed in an attempt to blackmail more out
of producer Dan Enright. A more important reason was his bruised ego. Stempel had been forced
to portray himself as a poor boy from Brooklyn,
when in fact he had married into a well-to-do family and was from Queens. Enright insisted that he
wear ratty suits and a cheap wristwatch to project
this image and that he address the emcee, Jack
Barry, deferentially as Mr. Barry while other contestants called him Jack. He had an I.Q. of 170 and
was infuriated by having to "miss" answers he
knew "damn well." And he was beside himself at
the unearned praise accorded to Van Doren. Here
was ". . . a guy that had a fancy name, Ivy League
education, parents all his life, and I had the opposite. . . ." He would hear passing strangers remark that he was the man who had lost to this
child of light, and he could not stand it. But it was
more than greed or envy that prompted Stempel
to turn state's evidence. Even before he was ordered to "take a dive" and before he had ever
heard of Charles Van Doren, he was telling friends
that the show was fixed. Stempel knew all the real
answers about the quiz shows, and he was burst-
ing to show the nation how smart he was.

In 1957, Stempel tried to interest two New
York newspapers in the truth, but both papers refused to print what would have been one of the
biggest scoops of the decade because they feared
libel action. It is a commentary on the state of investigative journalism at the time that not until
August, 1958, after the discovery that a giveaway
show called *Dotto* was fixed, was Stempel able
to make his charges in public. At this time also,
New York County District Attorney Frank Hogan
began an investigation, and the inexorable process

of revelation had been set in motion. For almost a year, the grand jury interviewed about 150 witnesses. The producers tried to arrange a cover-up by persuading the show's alumni to perjure themselves. Many of the most well known did just that. It was one thing to fix a quiz show, however, and quite another to fix a grand jury probe. Realizing that the day of reckoning was at last approaching, the producers hurried back to change their testimony. This they did without informing the contestants, leaving them, to put it mildly, out on a limb.

For reasons which remain unclear, the judge sealed the grand jury's presentment, but the Subcommittee on Legislative Oversight (over the FCC) of the House Interstate and Foreign Commerce Committee determined to get to the bottom of the matter. Its public hearings, held in Washington in October and November of 1959, attracted worldwide attention.

On October 6, a bitter Herbert Stempel exposed the whole sordid story of *21.* He had originally applied to take part in what he thought was an honest game but was approached by Enright who talked him into becoming an actor rather than a riverboat gambler. Every detail of his performances was prearranged: his wardrobe, his diffidence, his hesitations, and his answers. He was instructed on the proper way to mop his brow for maximum effect, and he was guaranteed to sweat because the air conditioning in the isolation booth was purposely kept off. From his testimony, it became clear that Van Doren was implicated as well. On the following two days, other contestants, producer Enright, and his assistant Albert Freedman testified to the fix. No one contradicted Stempel.

In the months preceding the hearings Van Doren had consistently and ever more vehemently proclaimed that no matter what others had done, his appearances on *21* had been strictly legitimate. When Stempel's charges were first published in the papers, Van Doren was ". . . horror struck. . . . I couldn't understand why Stempel should want to proclaim his own involvement." A representative of D. A. Hogan interviewed him toward the end of the year, and he denied everything. He retained a lawyer, to whom

he lied about his involvement, and then proceeded to perjure himself before the New York County Grand Jury in January, 1959. He was assured by Enright and Freedman that they too would cover up.

Van Doren's day of reckoning came on November 2, 1959, before the subcommittee. Herb Stempel hurried down from New York City to get a seat from which he could clearly see his former adversary. Pale and jittery, Van Doren walked into the crowded hearing room and delivered himself of one of the most pathetic confessions in the history of American public speech.

He wished that he could erase the past three years but realizing the past may be immutable resolved to learn from it. When he had first contacted Barry and Enright, he had assumed that their programs were honest. Before his appearance on *21,* Albert Freedman summoned him to his apartment and, talking him into the bedroom, explained that Stempel had to be defeated in order to make the show more popular. Van Doren asked to go on the air honestly, but Freedman said he had no chance to defeat the brilliant Stempel. "He also told me that the show was merely entertainment and that giving help to quiz contestants was a common practice and merely a part of show business." Besides, said Freedman, Van Doren had an opportunity to help increase respect for intellectual life and education. "I will not," said Van Doren, "bore this committee by describing the intense moral struggle that went on inside me." The result of that struggle was history. Freedman coached him on how to answer questions to increase suspense and several times gave him a script to memorize. When Van Doren missed the questions which were slated for the evening, Freedman ". . . would allow me to look them up myself. A foolish sort of pride made me want to look up the answers when I could, and to learn as much about the subject as possible."

As time went on the show ballooned beyond my wildest expectations. . . . [F]rom an unknown college instructor I became a celebrity. I received thousands of letters and dozens of requests to make speeches, appear in movies,

*and so forth—in short, all the trappings of
modern publicity. To a certain extent this went
to my head.*

He realized, however, that he was misrepresenting
education and was becoming more nervous about
the show. He urged the producers to let him quit,
but it was only after they could arrange a sufficiently dramatic situation that he was defeated.

Van Doren's brief testimony was the climax of
the subcommittee's investigation as it was of this
scandal as a whole. Nevertheless, the hearings
continued, including an investigation of *The
$64,000 Question. Question* was also fixed, and
although the details differed from the *21* case, the
deception was no less pervasive.

It is no exaggeration to say that the American
public was transfixed by the revelation of quiz
show fraud. A Gallup poll found the highest level
of public awareness of the event in the history of
such surveys. Questioned about the shows at successive news conferences, President Eisenhower
said he shared "the American general reaction of
almost bewilderment" and compared the manipu-
lations to the Black Sox scandal of 1919. The quiz
show episode affords an opportunity to discuss
feelings toward Van Doren, the hero unmasked,
and also the general arguments which swirled
around television at decade's turn.

For Van Doren, humiliation came in the wake
of confession. Just as institutions had been happy
to associate themselves with quiz show geniuses,
they hurried to dissociate themselves when the
geniuses turned out to be hustlers. NBC fired Van
Doren, while Columbia "accepted his resignation." The actions of these two institutions were
scrutinized along with those of Van Doren in the
period following his confession.

From the first, both NBC and CBS had maintained the highly implausible stand that they were
fooled about the shows along with the public.
They unquestionably could have uncovered the
rigging had they really wanted to, and in the end
they were left holding the bag. They had lost millions of dollars and, what was worse, had suffered
what at the time loomed as a potentially mortal

blow to a very pleasant way of making a lot of
money. The popular uproar threatened to force
government to restrict the broadcasting preroga-
tives of management. In this state of affairs, Van
Doren had to go. CBS took the next step, elimi-
nating quiz shows altogether, from which NBC
refrained.

Few were surprised by NBC's stand. The network was, after all, a business, and Van Doren had
become a liability. Columbia's treatment of him
aroused different issues. Some students had no pa-
tience with him, but hundreds rallied to his defense
with petitions and demonstrations. They pointed
out that his teaching was excellent and that having
made public relations capital out of his victories,
Columbia would be craven to desert him now. The
Columbia College dean, however, maintained,
"The issue is the moral one of the honesty and integrity of teaching." The dean found Van Doren's
deceptions contrary to the principles a teacher
should have and should try to instill in his students.

The academic community holds in especial
contempt, as *Love Story* author Erich Segal was to
discover, those "willing to play the fool" for limitless publicity. In defense of Columbia's action,
political scientist Hans J. Morgenthau published
two essays purporting to show that Van Doren
had actually violated "the moral law" as handed
down from Moses, Plato, Buddha, and other wor-
thies. Apparently no such law would have been
violated had Van Doren's participation in what
thinking people very well knew was a cheap
stunt been unrigged. If any crime had been committed in the quiz show episode, it was surely the
broad conspiracy to portray as genuine intellectual activity the spouting of trivia. But while the
shows were on and winning high ratings, there
was neither from Morgenthau nor Columbia a
peep of protest.

The most devastating but also perhaps the
fairest indictment of Van Doren's role was
penned by a Columbia colleague, Lawrence S.
Hall, who demonstrated that Van Doren's confession had been as thoroughly fraudulent as his
conduct on *21*. He had not confessed because of
a letter from a fan of his on the *Today* show as he

had claimed but only because of a congressional subpoena. "To the very end he never did perform the ethical free act of making up his mind. . . . Van Doren did not *decide* to tell the truth; what he did was adapt himself to the finally inescapable necessity of telling it." Worst of all, asserted Hall, was his "concealing under [the] piously reflexive formulas" of his silken prose "the most maudlin and promiscuous ethical whoredom the soap opera public has yet witnessed."

Unlike Hall the average American seemed rather sympathetic. A Sindlinger poll asked respondents to rate those most blameworthy for the fixes. Asked to assess the responsibility of network, sponsor, producer, and Van Doren, only 18.6 percent blamed Van Doren the most while 38.9 percent blamed him the least. A substantial number even favored a continuation of the shows, rigged or not. Many man-in-the-street interviewees said they would have done no differently, and most newspaper editorials treated him extraordinarily gently.

Investigators discovered not a single contestant on *21,* and only one on *The $64,000 Question,* who refused to accept money once they learned the shows were fixed. Most were quite "blithe" about it. Pollsters at the end of the 1950s were finding the belief widespread that the individual did not feel it was his place to condemn. Moral relativism, it seemed, rather than adherence to Professor Morgenthau's moral absolutism, was the rule. So many people lived polite lies that though it may have been titillating to discover them, they were hardly worth preaching about.

Other factors, in addition to this general willingness to partake in a fraud such as the quiz shows, help explain why the outrage was muted and transient. First, as Boorstin has pointed out, television unites many people in a community, but their union is tenuous and easily forgotten. Secondly, although many were taken in by the seeming reality of the shows, they had believed and been disabused so many times in the past that the shock soon wore off. For underneath the belief in the shows there probably lingered skepticism. Robert Merton observed in 1946 that cynicism about public statements from any source,

political or commercial, was pervasive. Television was a new medium which some may have thought was simply too big to play by the rules of the old-time newspaper patent medicine advertiser. The quiz shows taught them that it was not, and some critics asserted that it was the naked selfishness of commercial radio and television, more than the machinations of particular producers or contestants, that was truly to blame. The quiz shows excited to a new pitch of intensity long-running arguments about commercial broadcasting and the public interest.

The growth of commercial broadcasting cannot be explored here at length, but suffice it to say that it was opposed every step of the way by intellectuals, educators, and journalists who deplored what they saw as the perversion of a medium of great potential for the sake of the desire of private business to push products. As early as the 1920s, when radio was first coming into its own, articulate voices spoke up against its use for advertising. Bruce Bliven thought such "outrageous rubbish" should be banned from the air, and at least one congressman considered introducing legislation to that end. Herbert Hoover, whose Commerce Department supervised the granting of broadcast licenses, felt that radio would die if it allowed itself to be "drowned in advertising chatter," but he favored self-regulation rather than government action. The Radio Act of 1927 demanded that licensees operated their stations not solely for profit but with due regard for the "public interest, convenience, and necessity."

As charted by broadcasting's foremost historian, Erik Barnouw, the ascendancy of commercial programming was established in a fit of absence of mind. "If such a system [as exists today] had been outlined in 1927 or 1934, when our basic broadcasting laws were written," he concluded, "it certainly would have been rejected." Critics believed that the quiz shows and the radio "payola" scandals that followed proved that broadcasting was too important to be left in the hands of those whose primary, if not sole, motive was to turn a profit for the stockholders.

Television executives insisted that the scandals were the exception in a generally well run industry, but critics thought they were the tip of the iceberg. In themselves, the scandals were relatively unimportant, held the *New Republic*. "A real investigation would center on the simple question: why is television so bad, so monstrous?" It was the thirst for profit which forced the industry to a state of thralldom to the ratings. It was profit which mandated such dreadful children's programming. Advertising agencies and their clients, with profit always uppermost in mind, forced absurd restrictions on what could be broadcast. When commentators complained about the astounding amount of violence on the tube, defenders warned of the danger of censorship. Critics replied that the most stultifying censorship was already being exercised in behalf of the manufacturers of the pointless nostrums of an overindulgent society. In its quest for ratings, television seemed consistently to avoid satisfying the intelligent minority.

The industry had now been caught red-handed, Walter Lippmann wrote, in ". . . an enormous conspiracy to deceive the public in order to sell profitable advertising to the sponsors." The situation which had made this shameful occurrence possible could not be allowed to survive intact. Television had "to live up to a higher, but less profitable, standard." What America needed was prime time TV produced "not because it yields private profits but because it moves toward truth and excellence." What was needed, said Lippmann, was public service television.

Industry spokesmen had traditionally defended themselves as true democrats. The president of CBS, Frank Stanton, soon after *The $64,000 Question* was first aired, declared, "A program in which a large part of the audience is interested is by that very fact . . . in the public interest." By such a standard, the quiz shows can be seen not as "cynical malpractices . . . in one corner of television," as Robert Sarnoff tried to represent them, but rather as the perfect expression of the industry.

Sarnoff recognized the charges being hurled at TV in 1959 and 1960 as the "long-familiar [ones] of mediocrity, imbalance, violence, and overcom-

mercialism." These charges had been unjustified in the past and were unjustified in 1960, but because ". . . those who press them are now armed with the cudgels represented by the quiz-show deceptions" they could not be sloughed off. Sarnoff's response was to promise careful scrutiny of such programs in the future and vigorous self-regulation. As a special bonus to the viewing public in a gesture to wipe the slate clean, he offered to donate time for a series of debates between the major Presidential candidates of 1960, which eventually resulted in the televised confrontations between Kennedy and Nixon.

Sarnoff's offer was enthusiastically welcomed by such politicians as Stewart Udall, who had been working for a suspension of equal time regulations in order to permit broadcast debates between Democratic and Republican Presidential nominees in the upcoming election. Paradoxically, the four "Great Debates" which ensued showed unmistakably the influence of the supposedly discredited quiz programs. The similarity in formats was obvious. As in *21*, two adversaries faced each other and tried to give point-scoring answers to questions fired at them under the glare of klieg lights. The debates bore as little relationship to the real work of the presidency as the quiz shows did to intellectuality. Boorstin has remarked on how successful they were ". . . in reducing great national issues to trivial dimensions. With appropriate vulgarity, they might have been called the $400,000 Question (Prize: a $100,000-a-year job for four years)." No President would act on any question put to him by the reporters without sustained and sober consultation with trusted advisors. But the American people, conditioned by five years of isolation booth virtuosity, expected the "right" answer to be delivered pithily and with little hesitation. They did not want to be told that some questions did not have simple answers—or any answers at all.

The technological advances which led to radio and television grew out of the tinkerings of amateur experimenters. These two new forms of mass communication, with unprecedented drama and immediacy, developed independently of the desire to say anything. In 1854, Henry David

Charles Van Doren, winner of $129,000 in a rigged TV quiz show, pleaded guilty to perjury in his testimony to the New York County Grand Jury and received a suspended sentence in 1962.

Thoreau wrote, "We are in great haste to construct a magnetic telegraph from Maine to Texas; but Maine and Texas, it may be, have nothing important to communicate." This observation has been yet more relevant during the last half century. Except for the military, which was always seeking more direct means for locating ships at sea and soldiers on the battlefield, no one knew what to broadcast and telecast. The federal government, dominated by the ideology of free enterprise, declined to fill this void. To be sure, regulations did prohibit certain messages over the air, but there has never been a national statement on the positive purposes of the new media which the industry was obliged to take seriously.

Businessmen soon discovered that broadcasting was a powerful instrument for increasing sales. Those advertisers who had financed the print media, including manufacturers of patent medicines, cosmetics, and cigarettes, quickly adopted the same role with radio and television. Left to their own devices, they sought programs which would constitute a congenial frame for their selling message. They soon hit upon the idea, among others, of parlor games, of which the quiz shows were direct descendants.

Such programs had been popular since the thirties, but in the 1950s, clever producers learned how to make them even more so. They combined large sums of money with the American fondness for facts, dressed up as intellectuality, and the result was *The $64,000 Question* and *21*. When these programs were exposed as frauds, a jaded public, inured to mendacity, was quick to forgive.

Critics have often complained, as they did with vigor after the scandals, that television—"a medium of such great potential"—was being so ill-used. But no one seems to have a clear vision of what that potential is. The lack of direction which characterized the early years of American broadcasting has never been overcome. Commentators such as Lippmann have won their public broadcasting system, but commercial television has not upgraded its fare in order to compete. If anything, public TV may act as a lightning rod deflecting complaints about the commercial industry by providing an outlet for those demanding alternative viewing.

For its part, the industry has usually ignored what enlightened guidance has been available in favor of traditional forms of entertainment guaranteed not to distract the viewer from the advertisements. Thus, recently, quiz and game shows have made a comeback. There has even been talk of resurrecting *The $64,000 Question*, despite the risk of reviving along with it memories of past chicanery. Such programming represents a distressing devotion to Philistinism and a failure of imagination, the solution for which is not in sight.

STUDY QUESTIONS

1. What is implied by the concept of a "consumption community"? How is this sort of a community different from any other community?

2. Compare how Charles Van Doren and Herbert Stempel were presented on the television quiz show *21*. Why was Stempel told to appear poor and deferential on the show? Is there a political statement in the images of both men?

3. How did most Americans respond to the disclosure that *21* and other quiz shows were rigged?

4. What does Tedlow mean by the concept of "moral relativism"? Is morality ever absolute?

5. What issues are involved in the debate between advocates of commercial broadcasting and proponents of public service broadcasting?

6. How were the Nixon-Kennedy television debates in 1960 similar to or different from the format of the television quiz show *21?* What does this say about the importance of television in a political campaign?

BIBLIOGRAPHY

The television industry has received far less historical attention than the film industry. This is perplexing, considering that television "touches" more people—American as well as non-American—than the movies. The fact that some movie directors have consciously cultivated reputations as "artists" undoubtedly has something to do with academic interest in their product that is not apparent with television. There are, however, several very good books on television. Among the best are Erik Barnauw, *The Golden Web* (1968), and *The Image Empire: A History of Broadcasting in the United States* (1970); Raymond Williams, *Television: Technology and Cultural Form* (1975); and Robert Sklare, *Prime-Time America: Life on and Behind the Television Screen* (1980). Also of interest are two books by Daniel Boorstin, *The Americans: The Democratic Experience* (1974), and *The Image: A Guide to Pseudo-Events in America* (1961). The Van Doren case is dealt with in Kent Anderson, *Television Fraud* (1978), and Eric Goldman, *The Crucial Decade and After: America, 1945–1960* (1960). Douglas Miller and Marian Novak discuss social and cultural developments in the 1950s in *The Fifties: The Way We Really Were* (1977).

Reading 24

SMOKING AND CANCER

James T. Patterson

For Americans who watched television in the 1960s or leafed through magazines for much of the rest of the decade, the image of a nameless man is etched in their minds. A rugged outdoorsmen, handsome and strong, framed against the equally rugged, equally strong, equally handsome American West, the land of snow-capped mountains and parched cattle country and pure virility. The man is often astride a horse, reins in his hands, a cowboy hat covering his eyes, a cigarette between his lips. The Marlboro Man, riding through the fantasies of American men and women, riding across a purely mythic American landscape toward a universal nightmare. In the early 1950s, Marlboro was a brand of cigarettes produced by Philip Morris and targeted for women. It came in a white soft pack, had a red "beauty tip" filter to camouflage lipstick, and sold under the slogan, "Mild as May." In the mid-1950s, advertiser Leo Burnett took over the Marlboro account and targeted a new audience. He dumped the white soft pack for a red hard pack, got rid of the "beauty tip" and "Mild as May" slogan, and tapped into Western iconography for the Marlboro Man. Pure West, pure American. Burnette's campaign became the most financially successful in advertising history.

By the time of Burnett's campaign, most Americans, of course, had at least a vague sense that cigarettes were related to cancer. But the tobacco industry was grimly determined to blur the growing medical evidence of the harmful effects of cigarette smoking and to tie their product to American fantasies of sex and virility. As much as any two industries, tobacco and advertising went hand and glove, each helping the other to mature and profit. In the following essay, historian James T. Patterson looks at the unglamorous side of cigarette smoking, tracing the growth of medical evidence against the habit.

No pleasure can exceed the smoking of the weed," proclaimed an advertisement from the nineteenth century. Millions of Americans agreed—among them Mark Twain, who said, "It's easy to stop smoking. I know because I've done it thousands of times." A hundred years later, Americans are bombarded with reasons for giving up the pleasure of "the smoking of the weed":

Country-western songwriter and entertainer Sollie "Tex" Williams, a heavy smoker best known for his tune, "Smoke, Smoke, Smoke That Cigarette," died after a year-long battle with cancer, his daughter said . . . her father, who was diagnosed a year ago as having cancer, smoked two packs of cigarettes a day, dropping to about a pack a day before he died. "He tried to quit, but he couldn't," she said.

Smoking causes lung cancer, heart disease, emphysema and may complicate pregnancy.

Quitting smoking now greatly reduces serious risks to your health.

Smoking by pregnant women may result in fetal injury, premature birth and low birth weight.

Cigarette smoke contains carbon monoxide.

Cigarette smoking is clearly identified as the chief, single, avoidable cause of death in our society and the most important public health issue of our time.

Cigarette consumption per person over age eighteen rose from 151 per year in 1910 to 1,485 in 1930 to a high if 4,286 in 1963; since then it has decreased, mainly after 1975, to 3,378 in 1985. Between 1935 and 1980 more than one million Americans died of lung cancer caused by smoking. Lung cancer, one medical historian commented, is "the most remarkable epidemic of the twentieth century." Government officials say that cigarette-induced ailments cost $65 billion a year by the mid-1980s, more than $22 billion for medical expenses and the rest attributed to losses of wages, productivity, and taxes. Lung cancer deaths—at least 80 percent caused by smoking—were estimated to total 126,000 in 1985, as opposed to but 2,300 in 1930 and 7,100 in 1940. These 126,000 deaths were 23 percent of cancer mortality in the United States. (Mortality from cancers of the rectum and colon, estimated at 60,000 in 1985, ranked second.) An additional 22,000 Americans died in 1985 from tobacco-induced cancers elsewhere in the body, 20,000 from pulmonary disease, and 225,000 from tobacco-related cardiovascular ailments. The grand total of nearly 400,000 represented more than 1,000 premature deaths linked to smoking a day. As one cancer researcher has commented, "it is almost as if Western societies had set out to conduct a vast and fairly well controlled experiment in carcinogenesis bringing about several million deaths and using their own people as experimental animals."

Without the increase in lung cancer, epidemiologists pointed out, age-adjusted mortality rates from malignant tumors would have declined slightly since the 1930s. But lung cancers caused aggregate age-adjusted rates in the United States to climb slowly. The villain, almost all experts agreed, was tobacco—described by John Cairns as a "fifth column in our midst." Surgeon General C. Everett Koop said in 1986 that people who smoked two packs a day had a rate of lung cancer that was as much as twenty-five times greater than the rate for nonsmokers.

If there were any promising statistics to be found in these numbers, they had to do with the tobacco habits of men. For years men had been the main consumers of cigarettes: from the mid-1920s through the early 1960s more than 50 percent of adult American males smoked. In 1985, 87,000 of the estimated 126,000 lung cancer deaths afflicted men. After the mid-1960s the percentage of adult males who smoked declined considerably—to around 33 percent in 1985—and mortality from lung cancer among white males began in 1984 to decrease for the very first time. But women, who had entered the tobacco culture later, were smoking more by this time. In the mid-1930s fewer than 20 percent of adult fe-

James T. Patterson, *The Dread Disease: Cancer and Modern American Culture* (1987), pp. 201–222.

males smoked in the United States, but during and after World War Two they, too, took up the habit in large numbers. The percentage of adult women who smoked peaked at approximately 33 percent between 1955 and 1975 and declined only to around 28 percent by 1985. By then lung cancer (at more than 38,000) for the first time seemed about to replace breast tumors as the leading source of cancer mortality among women. The American Cancer Society, drawing on evidence that had accumulated since the 1950s, reported that women who smoked while pregnant were more likely to have miscarriages, stillbirths, and premature deliveries, and to give birth to infants with serious mental and physical ailments.

These dramatic developments in smoking, and the consequent rise in mortality from lung cancer, can be traced to profound social, economic, and cultural forces in twentieth-century American life: the rise of large tobacco corporations, the flowering of mass cigarette advertising, the anxieties of world wars, the quest for masculinity, the pressure of peers, the addictive power of nicotine, the spread of female employment, the gospel of women's liberation, sheer pleasure. These and other forces helped to explain why nearly one-third of adult Americans, more than 50 million people, in the mid-1980s persisted in maintaining a habit that substantially increased their risk of premature death.

The persistence of the smoking habit is remarkable. It flourished, after all, during the very years that most Americans expressed great concern for good health, fear of death, and dread of cancer. The tobacco habit, a known risk, clashed sharply with these values. But the contradiction is not altogether surprising. Some who continued to smoke had no choice—they were addicted. Many others simultaneously celebrated competing values, such as the pursuit of personal pleasure and the quest for good health. Quitting, an investment in future gains, was a renunciation of immediate gratification. To some the sacrifice was not worth it.

The clash of values over smoking also revealed—as reactions to diseases often had—significant differences in the attitudes of America's social classes toward health, illness, and the medical

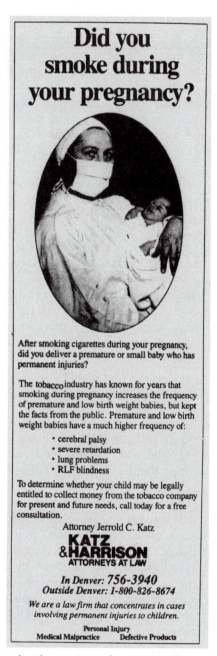

Reprinted with permission from Katz and Harrison, Attorneys at Law, 1986.

profession. Since the 1950s the clash has featured on one level a noisy battle between two well-organized interest groups—tobacco companies and health professionals. But on another level it has been a struggle between a mainly middle-class and professional alliance against smoking and a rearguard action especially strong among blue-collar and lower-class people, many of whom continue to have scant access to or faith in scientific medicine. With characteristically American independence of mind, millions of people have felt they ought to be allowed to do as they pleased, even if experts said otherwise.

In the 1920s and early 1930s, the wilderness years of cancer control, various researchers cited tobacco as a carcinogen. Their reports reinforced a popular opinion, widespread since before [President] Grant's time, that smoking was unhealthy. Grant's death, indeed, was often used (by Frederick Hoffman, among others) as proof enough of the argument. But the main concern was cancer of the mouth or throat; lung cancer was very rare.

Only in the early 1930s did many doctors begin to encounter the ailment. And only then did surgeons and pathologists start to make the connection between smoking and lung cancer. One of the first was Dr. William McNally of Rush Medical College, who stated in 1932 that "cigarette smoking is an important factor in the increase of cancer of the lungs." In 1938 Dr. Raymond Pearl, a distinguished professor of biometry, claimed in *Science* that smoking was "statistically associated with an impairment of life duration." In the same year the *Science News Letter* carried an article by Drs. Alton Ochsner and Michael DeBakey of New Orleans that asserted, "more persons are dying of cancer of the lung than ever before, probably because more persons are smoking and inhaling tobacco smoke than ever before."

Not everyone, however, agreed. James Tobey, in his popular, sensible book on cancer in 1932, spoke for many who distrusted the "rabid anti-tobacco literature" and the "fanatical reform bodies" who lobbied against smoking just as they had done—with such controversial results—against drinking. "An example of the banal attacks on to-bacco," he said, "is the frequent assertion that President Grant suffered from cancer of the throat merely because he smoked to excess." "There is no scientific evidence," he concluded, "to show that My Lady Nicotine has any deleterious effect."

Many doctors in the 1930s agreed with Tobey. Some asserted that the incidence of lung cancer only seemed to be increasing—the result of better diagnoses from X-rays and bronchoscopies. Others thought the increases real, but blamed them on atmospheric pollution or from delayed reactions to the great flu epidemic of 1918–19. Still others believed that lung cancer, which seemed mainly to afflict men, could not be caused by cigarettes, because women also smoked. And many, articulating the contemporary emphasis on "irritation," maintained that tobacco could provoke cancer only among those who overindulged and who were genetically predisposed. If there was a common denominator to these varied views, it was that cigarettes did not do too much harm if smoked in moderation. Clarence Little, summing up the evidence in 1939, concluded on behalf of the cancer society that "the more common use of tobacco is blamed by some for the frequency of lung cancer . . . It is impossible to say how accurate these opinions are."

While the experts debated, the way remained open for proponents of tobacco to push their products. In 1933 Congress approved legislation guaranteeing price supports—and long-range economic security—for tobacco farmers. This step advanced a powerful network of tobacco interests that joined the producers and marketers with governments—federal, state, and local—which derived substantial income from taxes on tobacco products.

Paramount among the tobacco lobby were the cigarette manufacturers, who spent ever increasing amounts on advertising—an estimated $50 million by 1940—to sell their wares. The new mass-circulation magazines such as *Time* and *Newsweek* became heavily dependent on cigarette advertising for revenue. The *Journal of the American Medical Association* carried cigarette ads as late as the 1950s. The battle over smoking in modern

America involved considerably more than skirmishes over scientific findings; important economic interests were also at stake.

Beginning in the late 1920s, many ads broke with the past by appealing directly to women. Cigarettes, the ads said in raising the banner of female emancipation, were "torches of freedom." Albert Lasker's "Reach for a Lucky instead of a Sweet," aimed at women's weight-consciousness. Many ads dwelt on romance and sex: "Blow Some My Way," a woman purred as she looked longingly at her man puff on a cigarette. As early as 1934 Eleanor Roosevelt showed her independence by smoking publicly. In the late 1930s women's handbags and compacts were routinely designed to hold cigarette packs. By then prominent women gladly posed for full-page color cigarette ads in the magazines. Alice Roosevelt Longworth, Theodore's daughter, praised the virtues of Luckies. "They're a light smoke," kind to the throat, she said. The syndicated columnist Dorothy Kilgallen promoted Camels. The actress Carole Lombard favored Luckies—"they're easier on the throat."

The ads, moreover, tried to make smoking look attractive: cigarettes made women sexually alluring, young men tough and masculine. The American Tobacco Company pushed a brand named "Stud," and John Wayne (who later died of lung cancer) promoted Camels. A cigarette dangled from the lips of Humphrey Bogart playing Sam Spade in "The Maltese Falcon" (1941). A sultry Lauren Bacall made her entrance in "To Have or Have Not" (1944) with the line, "Anybody got a match?" Betty Grable, the ultimate pin-up girl of the forties, posed alluringly for tobacco ads. "With the boys," she said, "it's Chesterfields." Promotions for Luckies used the acronym "LSMFT" to make the sexual connection more explicit. Lucky Strike, the ads said, "Means Fine Tobacco—so round, so firm, so fully packed."

Cigarette consumption jumped enormously during World War Two and in the late 1940s—from 1,976 to 3,552 annually per adult American during the decade. Though some of this increase reflected the growing consumption by women,

many of whom broke with traditional roles to enter the labor market, much of it was accounted for by men in the armed services. Young, far from home, often afraid, soldiers turned to cigarettes—which came with C rations—for solace amidst the pressures of war and military discipline.

So taken for granted were cigarettes to American culture in these years that the rapidly rising incidence of lung cancer, which caused 15 percent of cancer deaths by 1950, received relatively little public attention. Neither did the warnings by Ochsner and others. Many doctors, on the contrary, continued to smoke and to dismiss such warnings. As late as 1948 the *Journal of the American Medical Association* stated that "more can be said in behalf of smoking as a form of escape from tension than against it . . . there does not seem to be any preponderance of evidence that would indicate the abolition of the use of tobacco as a substance contrary to the public health."

While the AMA remained reluctant to confront the tobacco lobby for many years thereafter, others jumped in during the 1950s to forge an increasingly aggressive alliance against tobacco. Leaders in this struggle were physicians and epidemiologists who began to publish statistics connecting cigarette smoking and cancer.

One of the earliest to show concern over lung cancer was Dr. Evarts Graham, a surgeon and professor at Washington University in St. Louis. Observing great increases in lung cancers in the mid-1930s, he and his students—including Ochsner—feared a virtual epidemic of carcinoma of the lung. But Graham, a smoker himself, was slow to blame tobacco. "Yes," he told Ochsner, "there is a parallel between the sale of cigarettes and the incidence of cancer of the lung, but there is also a parallel between the sale of nylon stockings and cancer of the lung." Graham's skepticism mirrored contemporary bewilderment about the causes of lung cancer.

But Ernst Wynder, another of Graham's students, was not to be put off. He strongly suspected that tobacco was the villain, and in the 1940s he and Graham launched an epidemiological study of the subject. At the same time a group of British doctors and statisticians embarked on similar research. Both studies were "retrospective," selecting cancer patients (and others without cancer) and then asking both groups about their habits. When these studies were published in 1950, they documented significant statistical correlations between cigarette smoking and lung cancer. "Extensive and prolonged use of tobacco, especially cigarettes," Wynder and Graham concluded, "seems to be an important factor in the inducement of bronchiogenic carcinoma." The British researchers added that "smoking is a factor and an important factor, in the production of carcinoma of the lung."

Because these were careful studies, each involving hundreds of cases of lung cancer, they attracted a fair amount of attention in medical circles. But the researchers tended to stop short of asserting a causal connection between smoking and lung cancer. Other factors, they noted, might also cause the disease. Moreover, Graham and others admitted that they did not know what was carcinogenic about tobacco. Some people wondered if the carcinogenic effect came from insecticides, not from the tobacco itself. The researchers also faced criticism of their methods, for retrospective studies depend heavily on the recollections of patients. For all these reasons the early studies fell short of persuading the doubters.

But the studies were too alarming to be ignored, and over the next few years laboratory researchers showed that tars from tobacco were carcinogenic in animals. Epidemiologists, meanwhile, began conducting "prospective" studies, one of which was funded by the American Cancer Society starting in 1951. These studies used volunteers to locate hundreds of thousands of smokers and nonsmokers and to track their health over time. As early as 1952 the researchers were shocked by the incidence of lung cancer among the smokers, and in 1954 they published the first of many reports. They found that age-adjusted death rates from lung cancer were at least three times higher among male smokers than among nonsmokers, and at least five times higher among heavy smokers.

These researchers, too, conceded that other carcinogens, such as soot or automobile fumes, might also be causing lung cancer. But they were convinced by the study that cigarettes were the major cause of the disease. E. Cuyler Hammond and Daniel Horn, the ACS researchers, had both been cigarette smokers, but they quickly dropped the habit, taking up pipes, when the statistics started coming in. "We believe," they said in 1954, "the associations found between regular cigarette smoking and diseases of the coronary arteries, and between smoking and cancer, reflect cause-and-effect relationships." The ACS joined in by urging smokers to cut consumption. By 1957 Hammond was still more certain. He asserted that people who persisted in smoking two packs a day or more died seven years earlier on the average than nonsmokers and that cigarette smoking increased the chance of fatal coronary attack by 50 percent. In that same year Evarts Graham—though he cut back in 1953 to a pack a day—died from lung cancer.

By this time a few federal officials began to join the slowly developing alliance against smoking. Among these were members of the House Committee on Governmental Operations, which conducted an investigation in 1957 of tobacco advertising, especially ads proclaiming the supposed benefits of newly marketed filter cigarettes. Led by Congressman John Blatnik of Minnesota (who was a smoker), the committee reported in 1958 that "cigarette manufacturers have deceived the American public through their advertising of cigarettes." This kind of pressure encouraged the Federal Trade Commission (which in 1955 had taken steps against ads that implied medical endorsement of smoking) to negotiate a voluntary agreement with the tobacco companies in 1960. The FTC attempted to put an end to exaggerated claims for filter cigarettes.

Perhaps more important to the antitobacco alliance was the gradual participation of the Public Health Service. Under the cautious stewardship of Surgeon General Leroy Burney, the PHS in 1956 established a scientific study group involving the NCI, the National Heart Institute, the ACS, and the American Heart Association. In 1957 the group announced that "there is an increasing and consistent body of evidence that excessive cigarette smoking is one of the causative factors in lung cancer." Venturing further in 1959, Burney singled out cigarettes as the major cause of lung cancer. The cooperation of the PHS—and under it of the NCI—with the ACS suggested that the long-standing professional alliance against cancer was gradually lining up against cigarettes.

To some extent popular magazines lined up, too. As early as 1952 *Reader's Digest,* which refused to carry tobacco ads, ran a scare story entitled "Cancer by the Carton." When laboratory scientists demonstrated the carcinogenic nature of tobacco tars in 1953, *Time* stated that they had proved "beyond any doubt" that smoking caused cancer. A month later *Life* carried a story headed SMOKE GETS IN THE NEWS. It cautioned that the findings of Graham and Wynder, whose research on cigarette tars involved animals, should not induce people to "promptly quit smoking, for this might create nervous ailments." But the article also made it clear that tar from tobacco had caused cancer in mice. It added that statistics on tobacco consumption correlated with significant increases in lung cancer among human beings. Other magazines—*Nation, New Republic, U.S. News and World Report*—also refused to take cigarette advertisements. *Time, Life,* and *Newsweek,* while profiting from big ads, reported the damaging findings of the epidemiologists and the warnings of government officials.

Through these various outlets the alliance succeeded in conveying their arguments to the public. Opinion polls as early as 1954 revealed that 90 percent of respondents had read news stories linking smoking and cancer. Polls also showed ever increasing pluralities of people agreeing that "cigarette smoking is one of the causes of lung cancer." As early as 1954 a lung cancer patient sued the tobacco companies, and the store where he bought his cigarettes, claiming that they had advertised death-dealing products. Though he lost the case, his effort received a fair amount of publicity. Suits like this one signified the rise of hostility already being directed at tobacco companies.

Perhaps the most striking insight into popular attitudes came from opinion polls taken after publication of Hammond's findings in 1957. Of those polled 77 percent claimed to have heard about them. Half of these respondents said that smoking caused cancer, a quarter that it did not, and the rest that they did not know. At that time, 42 percent of the adult population (52 percent of men, 34 percent of women) were smokers. Even this group (by a margin of 38 percent to 36 percent, with 26 percent undecided) thought smoking caused cancer.

These polls made two important things unmistakably clear: first, that smokers were more likely than nonsmokers to reject the warnings about cancer; second, that substantial majorities of the population as a whole recognized that cigarettes were unhealthy. Those who smoked, then and later, did not always know the full extent of the dangers of tobacco. Smokers who were not addicted, however, were making a conscious choice to ignore the expert advice of the alliance against cancer. Their behavior says much about conflicting values in American society.

The opponents of the antismoking campaign included first of all some determined and well-financed economic interests. In 1954, following the damaging publicity surrounding the prospective studies (which temporarily depressed cigarette sales), the tobacco companies banded together to establish the Tobacco Industry Research Committee (later renamed the Council for Tobacco Research—U.S.A.). Founders of the committee recognized that they had to fight expertise with expertise, and they contacted Clarence Little, who had been running the Jackson Laboratory in Maine since leaving the ACS. Little agreed to serve (for an annual salary of $20,000) as scientific director.

Why Little joined the committee was never entirely clear—probably it was because his scientific training in genetics led him to associate cancer with genetic predisposition. Whatever the reasons, Little, who stayed at this post until his retirement in 1971, tried to give the committee scientific respectability. He received very considerable resources. Under his direction the tobacco lobby spent an estimated $7 million on research between 1954 and 1964. Most of this work, whose findings had little to do with the effect of cigarettes on health, evoked contempt from independent scientists.

In 1958 the cigarette lobby also formed the Tobacco Institute, Inc., headed by George Allen, former director of the United States Information Agency. Relying on the skill of Hill and Knowlton, a leading public-relations firm, the institute issued a steady stream of releases refuting claims that smoking caused cancer. "We are not on a crusade either for or against tobacco," it announced. "If we have a crusade, it is a crusade for research." Allen elevated tobacco to the status of national symbol. "Through the years," he said,

tobacco is poetry and plays, novels, and essays. Tobacco is painting and sculpture for great artists. Tobacco has been comfort for the combat soldier, from Valley Forge to Korea. Tobacco is the ambassador of good will around the world. Tobacco is millions of men and women on the farms, in the factories, in stores and offices. Tobacco is a moment of relaxation from today's stress . . . For Franklin Roosevelt, it was a cigarette in a jaunty holder, for Churchill a long cigar, for Einstein, a heavy curved pipe.

Meanwhile, the tobacco companies stepped up their advertising campaigns, the costs of which rose to an estimated $148 million in 1959 (and to $314 million by 1970). Huge as these expenditures were, they were worth it to an industry whose sales were $7 billion in 1960. By then much of the advertising extolled the virtues of filter cigarettes, which the tobacco companies began emphasizing in the 1950s. The tobacco companies sponsored many of the most expensive prime-time TV shows of the 1950s and 1960s—"Arthur Godfrey and His Friends," "The Chesterfield Supper Club," "Stop the Music," and

"Your Lucky Strike Theatre." "It was just like wiring the slot machine to keep paying out a perpetual jackpot," one happy advertiser exulted. "My boy, it was like *printing money.*"

Allen, an experienced Washington insider, developed an effective political coalition to counter the enemies of smoking. This coalition included many advertising executives, magazine and newspaper publishers, and the National Association of Broadcasters, who depended heavily on cigarette ads and whose good will was valued by politicians. Some advertisers were on the board of the ACS and resisted the efforts of Hammond and others to involve the society in the crusade against smoking.

Many doctors, too, abetted the tobacco coalition. Some were heavy smokers who could not bring themselves to believe the epidemiological evidence. Others attributed the rise in lung cancer to better diagnosis. Although the AMA journal opened its pages to Hammond and other researchers, top officials of the association refused to accept the causal relationship between smoking and lung cancer or heart disease. Critics charged that the association's refusal arose from its consuming fear of national health insurance: if the AMA had opposed the tobacco interests, it would have antagonized well-placed congressmen who were needed in the fight against "socialized medicine."

The "Smoke Ring," as enemies of the coalition called it, was especially strong in Congress. Its core consisted of politicians from the tobacco-producing and -manufacturing states. Their allies on the Hill included most southerners, who joined the coalition to demonstrate their regional solidarity; Republicans, who had long worked harmoniously with southern Democrats; and conservatives, who were fearful on principle of governmental regulation. Against this formidable combination, the alliance against smoking made little political headway in the 1950s.

Furthermore, some respected researchers continued to doubt the conclusions of the epidemiological studies. Wilhelm Hueper, who still headed the environmental cancer section of the NCI, considered smoking an "unhealthy habit" but concentrated his efforts on the chemical and automobile companies. He thought the air pollution caused by these companies and their products was correlated with the rise in lung cancer. Many laboratory scientists, like Harold Stewart, chief pathologist of the NCI, refused to accept the epidemiological data until it was thoroughly confirmed by experimental research. They accepted the fact that tars from cigarettes, when rubbed into the skin of animals, were carcinogenic. But they insisted that no experiments had yet connected cigarette smoke (as opposed to tars) to cancer in animals, let alone in human beings. Doubts within the NCI itself led Surgeon General Burney and John Heller, director of the institute, to move cautiously until the late 1950s.

Another prominent cancer expert who moved cautiously was Charles Cameron, medical and scientific director of the ACS. Though he accepted the epidemiological data, he resisted the argument that cigarette smoking by itself caused cancer. Like many others at the time, he was troubled by the fact that the vast majority of smokers did not seem to develop the disease—and that a few who did not smoke also were afflicted by it. He wondered if the root cause of lung cancer lay in some predisposing factor, such as genetic makeup. Perhaps the same predisposition led many people to the habit of smoking and—independently—to a susceptibility to cancer.

The defenders of tobacco seized quickly on these and other doubts about the epidemiological case. Again and again they emphasized several points: that only a small minority of smokers ever developed lung cancer (experts later estimated that consistent smokers had between a one in four and a one in ten chance of developing it); that tobacco-induced tumors in animals differed from lung cancer in human beings; that the evidence (such as it was) connecting smoking and lung cancer rested mainly on statistical associations, not on laboratory science; and that the increased incidence of lung cancer stemmed from the aging of the population, not from tobacco. Epidemiological studies pointing a finger at cigarettes, they insisted, were flawed, in part because

their findings did not fully consider the health histories or places of residence of their subjects. Little explained in 1954, "I do not feel that a definite cause-and-effect relationship between smoking and human lung cancer has been established on a basis that meets the requirements of definiteness, extent, and specificity of data, which the seriousness and implications of the problem deserve."

While Little ordinarily assumed the high road of scientific proof, he was prepared to join Allen and others in appealing to popular feelings. The scare over cigarettes, they said, was but one of many—over packaged foods, pollution, even Coca-Cola—aroused by meddlesome reformers who had nothing better to do with their time and who resorted, Little charged, to "expensive and pressure propaganda" and "personal misrepresentations and attacks." Cigarettes, tobacco spokesmen added, calmed the nerves. If people were prevented from smoking, they would fall victim to tics, or even beat their wives. Why pick on cigarettes? they asked—after all, many things kill people!

The spokesmen for tobacco devoted special emphasis to the importance of preserving personal freedom. Smokers, they pointed out, were well aware of the "propaganda" against tobacco, yet they continued to enjoy the habit. That was not because smokers were ignorant of warnings; the polls clearly showed otherwise. Nor was it because cigarettes were addictive—this was an argument that tobacco spokesmen dismissed out of hand. Rather, it was because cigarettes gave people pleasure. Millions of Americans concurred. They stressed that they loved the taste, that cigarettes set off their meals, that smoking helped them relax. Their passion for the habit sometimes recognized no bounds. One smoker exclaimed, "they can outlaw cigarettes, label 'em poison, raise the tax, jail everyone that smokes and hang everyone that raises tobacco; but people are gonna smoke."

Indeed, the tobacco lobby implied, smokers knew better than the arrogant, patronizing "experts" who were trying to run people's lives. This was a nicely calculated, populist appeal to the enduring skepticism of many Americans about professional claims for expertise. The defenders of tobacco, like many others who had resisted the medical alliance against cancer in the past, portrayed themselves as embattled Americans resisting dictation from above. The "experts," the tobacco forces said, were obstructing the right of people to do as they pleased.

As arguments like these show, the controversy over smoking involved more than a strictly medical debate over theories and therapies, more than a struggle between well-organized interest groups. It was in a way a debate over culturally ingrained life styles and cherished values. Just as the battle against cancer in America had long been characterized by social and ideological conflict, so too were the postwar arguments over smoking and health.

The debate intensified greatly following publication in January 1964 of *Smoking and Health: Report of the Advisory Committee to the Surgeon General of the Public Health Service.* This landmark document, ordinarily known as the surgeon general's report on smoking, placed the federal government unambiguously in the camp of the alliance against smoking and prompted increasingly vocal counterattacks by the tobacco coalition in the next two decades.

Luther Terry, the surgeon general in 1964, was hardly a crusader. Until 1962 he had shown little desire to combat the tobacco interests. But he faced increasing pressure for action from a number of organizations, including the ACS, the American Heart Association, the National Tuberculosis Association, and the American Public Health Association. In response he agreed to set up an advisory committee on smoking and health. In doing so Terry acted with political sagacity. To ensure that the committee would have broad support he gave the Tobacco Institute the chance to veto prospective appointees. The ten experts finally named to the committee were chosen from a list of some 150 nominees sent in by health organizations, government agencies, and tobacco interests. None of the ten had taken a public stand on the issue. Three smoked cigarettes, two others smoked pipes and cigars.

The committee, aided by hundreds of consultants, worked diligently and secretly for a year and a half. When it was ready to issue its findings, Terry staged a televised press conference behind closed doors in the State Department auditorium. The thoroughness that went into preparation of the report, together with the theatrics surrounding its publication, assured that the document would attract wide attention in the media.

The committee members were acutely aware of the need to speak with scientific precision and carefully noted the problems involved in talking about a "cause" or "major cause" of fatal diseases. Ailments such as cancer or heart disease, they acknowledged, exhibit the "multiple etiology of biological processes." But this was practically the only sop thrown to the tobacco interests, whose contentions the committee forcefully struck down. Cigarette smoking, the report said, "contributed substantially to mortality from certain specific diseases and to the overall death rate." Cigarette smoking was "causally related to lung cancer in men; the magnitude of the effect of cigarettes far outweighs all other factors. The data for women, though less extensive, point in the same direction." The committee concluded that cigarettes were a "health hazard of sufficient import in the United States to warrant appropriate remedial action."

The committee's conclusions inevitably received wide coverage in the press. *Newsweek,* speaking for most of the magazines and newspapers, called the report "monumental." Alarmed consumers cut back sharply (though temporarily) on cigarette consumption. Other organizations, moreover, demanded governmental action against tobacco. The World Health Organization called for "restriction of advertisements for cigarettes" and "regulations to curb smoking in all places of public entertainment." The ACS, able at last to pinpoint a specific cause of a major cancer, said that "the reduction of cigarette smoking offers greater possibilities than any other available medical or public health measure for the prevention of cancer, of serious illness, of physical disability, of suffering and of premature death in this country—an astounding statement, but true."

The Federal Trade Commission, which had co-operated with the surgeon general's office in preparing the report, showed special zeal for regulating tobacco. Within a week of the report's appearance the FTC requested public hearings on a proposed trade regulation requiring warnings on cigarette ads and packages. It proposed two possible wordings. One read, "CAUTION—CIGARETTE SMOKING IS A HEALTH HAZARD: The Surgeon General's Advisory Committee on Smoking and Health has found that 'cigarette smoking contributes substantially to mortality from certain diseases and to the overall death rate.' " The other said, "CAUTION: Cigarette smoking is dangerous to health. It may cause death from cancer and other diseases." The FTC recommended a ban on "words, pictures, symbols, devices or demonstrations, or any combination thereof that would lead the public to believe that cigarette smoking promotes good health or physical well-being."

In pressing its case the FTC had the support of many in the anticancer alliance, but some influential groups either fought the FTC or stood by on the sidelines. The Agriculture Department not only refused to oppose supports for tobacco farmers but also asserted that it would need much more evidence about the role of tobacco smoke before it would think about recommending health warnings on cigarette packages. The Advertising Federation of America and the American Newspaper Publishers Association joined the cigarette companies in opposing the proposed regulations. The AMA, which accepted a $10 million research grant from the Tobacco Institute to study the health effects of cigarettes, declined to endorse either the report or the FTC's ambitious plans for regulating advertising.

The Tobacco Institute protected its flanks in other ways, too. It hired the prestigious Washington law firm of Arnold, Porter, and Fortas to defend its interests and named as its chief strategist Earle Clements, a former senator from Kentucky. Clements had been campaign coordinator for Lyndon Johnson's presidential bid in 1960. His daughter was press secretary to the first lady. As a former solon Clements had floor privileges in the

Senate. He was shrewd, conciliatory, and very influential on the Hill.

Clements played for time. Matters of such import, he explained, ought to be decided by popular representatives in Congress, not by faceless bureaucrats in the FTC. Meanwhile, the Tobacco Institute announced, the cigarette companies would undertake to police themselves. Henceforth cigarette ads would not be aimed at people under twenty-one years of age or placed in college or school media. The companies' new advertising code emphasized that commercials would not "represent that cigarette smoking is essential to social prominence, distinction, success, or sexual attraction."

Accepting such assurances, Congress contented itself with passage of the Federal Cigarette Labelling and Advertising Act of 1965. This legislation authorized federal spending on a National Clearinghouse on Smoking and Health, which later proved helpful to foes of cigarettes. The law also required cigarette manufacturers to place a health warning on packages. But it was a watered-down warning: "Caution: Cigarette Smoking May Be Hazardous to Your Health." As critics pointed out, it had little if any impact on per capita cigarette sales, which were higher in 1965–66 than they had been in 1964. If anything, the warnings on packages might protect cigarette manufacturers against law suits by cancer victims and their families. (As of early 1987 the companies had won all these suits.)

Advocates of regulation especially deplored Congress's response to the contentious issue of cigarette advertising. The act not only failed to police such advertising; it also forbade governmental agencies to require any health warnings in cigarette ads for the next four years, during which time—it was hoped—the advertising code of the companies would have stilled the controversy. To the foes of tobacco, who thoroughly distrusted the companies, this was a bitter pill. The journalist Elizabeth Drew expressed this bitterness in an article entitled "The Quiet Victory of the Cigarette Lobby—How It Found Its Best Filter Yet—Congress." She called the legislation an "unabashed act to protect private industry from government regulation."

To no one's surprise the tobacco companies' advertising code had little impact on the nature of cigarette commercials. The enemies of smoking thereby intensified their efforts after 1965. A young New York lawyer, John Banzhaf 3d, was instrumental in getting the Federal Communications Commission to apply the so-called Fairness Doctrine to cigarette commercials. Though many opponents of smoking showed little enthusiasm for this effort—even the ACS, which relied on broadcasters for free air time, was cool to his plans—Banzhaf and the antismoking lobby persevered. After extended legal maneuvering, the FCC agreed in 1967 to act. Henceforth, the commission ruled, radio and television stations would have to run one anticigarette message for every three aired by the tobacco companies.

At first Banzhaf and his newly formed lobby, Action on Smoking and Health (ASH), found that broadcasters simply evaded the rule. The FCC, with only a small staff, could not begin to monitor the stations. ASH therefore concentrated on monitoring one station, WNBC-TV of New York, whose messages ran closer to ten to one on behalf of cigarettes; the antismoking spots mainly appeared between 2 and 6:30 A.M. When ASH shared its findings with the FCC in 1968, the agency stepped up its pressure. Forewarned, WNBC and other stations made a better effort, especially after courts affirmed the Fairness Doctrine in late 1968.

For the next two years the FCC ruling greatly heartened the foes of tobacco. The ACS and other health organizations created anticigarette messages, which were broadcast in what was estimated to be more than $40 million in free air time. The ads were meant to be hard-hitting. One ran a caption, "This is life," next to a group of people having fun. Then someone lit up a cigarette. The fun ended abruptly, and a new caption read, "This cuts it short." Another depicted a tough Marlboro man coughing uncontrollably as he stood at the bar of a saloon. A clean-cut, nonsmoking cowboy then pushed him aside. The word CANCER appeared on the screen, accompanied by the voice-over, "Cigarettes—they're

killers." Perhaps the most moving of these messages came from the actor William Talman, the gravel-voiced district attorney on the Perry Mason television show. In a prerecorded message Talman introduced his family to television viewers, revealed that he had lung cancer, and warned people not to smoke. "If you haven't smoked," he said, "don't start. If you do smoke, quit! Don't be a loser." By the time the message appeared on the air, Talman had died, one of many prominent Americans—Nat King Cole, Edward R. Murrow, and Walt Disney were three others—to succumb to lung cancer between 1964 and 1970.

To the tobacco lobby these antismoking spots were extraordinarily threatening. For the first time in modern history the annual per-capita cigarette consumption of American adults moved downward for an extended period of time—from 4,197 in 1966 to 3,969 in 1970. The foes of tobacco then set out to toughen the 1965 law by changing the message on cigarette packs from "Caution: Cigarette Smoking May Be Hazardous to Your Health" to "Warning: The Surgeon General Has Determined That Cigarette Smoking Is Dangerous to Your Health and May Cause Cancer and Other Diseases."

The foes of smoking also took steps to include in new legislation a ban on radio and television cigarette advertising. As in 1965, however, they underestimated the Tobacco Institute. Deeply worried by the anticigarette messages on radio and television, the tobacco forces resolved to compromise. It was better, they thought, to surrender their radio and television commercials than to allow continued airing of the opposing point of view. They recognized that such a ban would not affect their appeals on billboards or in the print media, which happily anticipated much increased advertising revenue. Though the broadcasters fought the proposed ban, their allies deserted them, and the ban passed the Congress in 1970. It went into effect on January 2, 1971, a date established so as to permit cigarette advertising—for the last time—during broadcasts of the football games on New Year's Day.

The legislation also required the companies to relabel their packages. The new message was slightly more explicit than the caution which had been required since 1965, but less alarming than the one desired by the antitobacco forces. It read: "Warning: The Surgeon General Has Determined That Cigarette Smoking Is Dangerous to Your Health." The companies had managed to prevent mention in the warning of the dread word "cancer"—or of any other smoking-related diseases.

This hotly contested legislation, the Public Health Cigarette Smoking Act of 1970, clearly indicated the political and economic power of the tobacco lobby. The cigarette companies were now free from worry about antismoking messages on radio and television. Relieved, they increased their advertising on billboards and in magazines and newspapers. *Life*'s first three issues in 1971 carried 22 pages of cigarette advertising, all in color. The companies also employed slightly more sophisticated and subtle appeals, such as promoting Virginia Slims tennis tournaments. Perhaps because of these changes, cigarette consumption moved upward again after the decline in the Fairness Doctrine years. Between 1971 and 1976 annual consumption averaged nearly 4,100 per adult, compared to the low of 3,969 in 1970. Total sales increased from 534 billion cigarettes in 1970 to 610 million in 1976.

STUDY QUESTIONS

1. What influences brought about the emergence, decline, and reemergence of cigarette smoking in America?

2. How have individual rights and community responsibility shaped the debate on smoking and health?

3. The author argues that tobacco use persists despite common knowledge about the dangers of smoking. What allows this?

4. Is there an "American" way to smoke?

BIBLIOGRAPHY

For opposing views on tobacco and public opinion, see Jacob Slocum, *For Your Own Good: The Anti-Smoking Crusade and the Tyranny of Public Health* (1998) and Philip J. Hilts, *Smokescreen: The Truth Behind the Tobacco Industry Cover-up* (1996). General works on tobacco include Jordan Goodman, *Tobacco in History: The Cultures of Dependence* (1994) and Victor G. Kiernan, *Tobacco: A History* (1991). Stephen Lock, L.A. Reynolds, and E.M. Tansey present a global collection of essays on smoking in *Ashes to Ashes: The History of Smoking and Health* (1998).

PART SEVEN

Coming Apart: 1960–1990

The era began innocently enough. In an extremely close election, John F. Kennedy defeated Richard M. Nixon for the presidency and quickly became one of the most admired men in the country. Blessed with brains, charisma, money, and a lovely young family, Kennedy epitomized America, particularly the rise and triumph of the immigrant. In public rhetoric, he cultivated a tough idealism, one that offered a courageous challenge to the Russians and hope for democracy and prosperity in the rest of the world. When Kennedy assumed the presidency in 1961, Americans believed their moral hegemony would last forever. They believed that their values deserved to govern the world by virtue of their success—an equality of opportunity and a standard of living unparalleled in human history. In closing his inaugural address, Kennedy even invoked the divine by claiming that "God's work must truly be our own."

What few people realized was that Kennedy was sitting on a powder keg, both at home and abroad. His liberal idealism, so self-righteous and yet so naive, barely survived his own life. From the mid-1960s through the mid-1970s, the country passed through a period of intense turmoil and doubt. Smug convictions about the virtues of equality and opportunity in the United States succumbed to the shrill criticisms of racial, ethnic, and gender groups. Beliefs in the virtues, safeguards, and stability of the American government were shattered by the lies exposed in the controversies over Watergate and the Pentagon Papers. By the late 1960s and early 1970s the explosion in oil prices, the appearance of stagflation, and the worries about the future of the environment all undermined the prevailing confidence about the American economy. Finally, the moral complacency so endemic to Kennedy liberalism died in the jungles of Southeast Asia. Like few other events in American history, the Vietnam War tore the country apart. At home, America was characterized by bitterness, demonstrations, and widespread disaffection from the country's leaders. A counter-culture of young people scornful of conventional values appeared, and the symbols of their rebellion were drugs and rock and roll. As far as world opinion was concerned, the country seemed to be a superpower out of control, employing the latest military technology in a futile effort to impose democracy on a nation barely out of the stone age.

Between 1964 and 1977, four American presidents struggled with these over-whelming problems. Lyndon Johnson's Great Society was eventually destroyed by what he called "that bitch of a war." Richard Nixon left the White House in disgrace after the Watergate tapes proved his complicity in perjury and obstructing justice. Gerald Ford failed in his WIN campaign—whip inflation now—and then watched helplessly as the last Americans, fleeing the invading North Vietnamese and Viet Cong troops, took off in helicopters from the roof of the United States embassy in Saigon. Jimmy Carter left the White House in 1977 after trying unsuccessfully to get Americans to accept the idea of austerity, shortages, and reduced expectations. The hostage crisis in Iran seemed the final symbol of American impotency. Not until the late 1980s, with Vietnam receding into history, oil prices dropping, inflation subsiding, Ronald Reagan in the White House, did the United States recapture its legendary optimism about the future.

READING 25

KENNEDY LIBERALISM

David Burner and Thomas R. West

On the morning after his election in 1960, no one had any idea of how completely John F. Kennedy would capture the American imagination. When he stated in his inaugural address that "the torch has been passed to a new generation of Americans," he became the symbol of a youth culture that would soon come to dominate American society and politics. By the early 1960s the first of the post-World War II baby boomers graduated from high school. Soon they filled colleges and universities, spearheading the crusades against racism, environmental pollution, and the Vietnam War. Raised during a time of unprecedented prosperity, and extraordinarily idealistic in outlook, they needed a political figure they could idolize.

John Fitzgerald Kennedy, for a brief period of time, became that idol. He had been tested in battle against the Japanese during World War II, and his exploits as commander of PT-109 had made him a hero. Kennedy had all the ingredients for stardom. Young and athletic, he exuded sexuality, at least for a major politician. His wife Jacqueline also enjoyed star qualities. Sexually appealing herself, she was at the same time refined and elegant. Small children romped in the White House for the first time since the administration of Theodore Roosevelt, and the public loved it. JFK's tragic death in 1963 only further endeared him to the American public.

However, by the early 1970s Kennedy's image was changing. He was accused of having been lukewarm on civil rights, a belligerent "cold warrior," and a friend of the business community. Rumors of his sexual escapades with several women became national gossip. Instead of the young hero trying to shape a new world, Kennedy began to look like a calculating politician obsessed with the possibility of his own greatness. In "Kennedy Liberalism" David Burner and Thomas R. West look at the record of the Kennedy administration in the area of civil rights, analyzing the political environment in which the young president operated and the extent to which his own views shaped—and limited—the federal response to the civil rights movement.

It was so sudden. The front of a bus where no black person had dared to sit, a lunch counter operated by and for the South's master race, a white Southern high school class—each had a black occupant free in that instant of centuries of subordination. The country had seldom known such freedom: the stepping across of an invisible line that had been a chasm, a moment astonishing in its revelation that a new thing could happen so quickly.

In 1960, before Kennedy's election, black and white students defied segregation ordinances by drinking coffee together at Southern lunch counters. A year later freedom riders were assaulted on their peaceable, though morally revolutionary, bus journey through the South. In the fall of 1962 the governor of Mississippi raged, for Mississippi public consumption at any rate, and mobs took over the campus of Ole Miss in answer to the enrollment of the first black student, and Kennedy, who delivered a speech that denounced not prejudice but the violation of the Constitution, sent marshals and troops to the campus. In Birmingham the following spring fire hoses and police dogs were turned upon children, and in September a fire bombing killed four black children in a Sunday school class in the basement of a Baptist church. Even before that bombing civil rights activists had compelled segregation to disgrace itself so publicly that a President with any claim to Democratic liberalism had to call for a legislated end to the discredited system. Southern white liberals, meanwhile, having finally encountered a movement that forced them to choose between their regional loyalty and their consciences, between their doubts about the efficacy of efforts for social change and their hopes for it, were turning with relief to desegregation. They, like the black community, were among the liberated. John Kennedy responded as circumstances, politics, and morality required.

"Kennedy Liberalism" from *The Torch is Passed: The Kennedy Brothers and American Liberalism* by David Burner and Thomas R. West. Reproduced by permission of the authors.

Television brought the civil rights movement before the public, and without it the 1960s would be unimaginable. That medium is faulted today for replacing the most subtle, analytical, and elegant means of conversation, the written word. But for a time two decades ago television became an instrument of analysis, making possible one of the most remarkable experiences of self-awareness and self-criticism in the nation's history. The nineteenth-century abolitionists, in contrast, had been forced to rely on a religious and Victorian moral rhetoric that defined the evil of slavery but seldom could describe its psychological and moral corruptions as precisely as do the best parts of *Uncle Tom's Cabin.* And for generations after abolition, white American politics rarely discussed racism at all except, of course, to approve of it. When the advent of television as a mass medium almost exactly coincided with the earlier days of the civil rights movement, it gave to a whole nation, perhaps even to blacks and to Southern whites as never before, clear images of the racial issue as immediate, national, morally inescapable. That is not to say that television itself is the best vehicle of criticism and analysis; brief, violent images on a screen—black protesters falling under the force of fire hoses, white mobs screaming at black children entering public schools—are not in themselves more conducive to intelligent political thought than the images of Iranian crowds that in 1980 endangered rational discussion of foreign policy in this country. But in the early 1960s the images on the screen worked with the civil rights movement itself, with a responsiveness on the part of politicians, and with such reflective writers as James Baldwin to elevate rather than to degrade the public consciousness.

Television, meanwhile, made for the ersatz familiarity with which the Kennedy family entered millions of American homes, and it was just the right family: beautiful, well mannered, well favored. TV allowed Kennedy to be so visible to the public as a whole that he seemed to be outside the party structures and the backroom maneuverings that his people managed so well.

It is easy to forget that during the early days of television another older visual medium was in its prime. Photojournalism, along with photography in general, can be at once brief and analytical; it can study the exact placement of individuals in a crowd, the look on a black child's face, the twist of hatred on the face of a white woman. During the Birmingham civil rights crisis President Kennedy commented that a photograph of a German shepherd leaping at a black woman made him "sick." Photojournalism, like television, cannot look into the ambiguities that the word can explore; it needs dramatic events, striking figures, exact moments of pain and triumph, or larger cultural events that express themselves flamboyantly. And in the 1960s Selma, Vietnam, Haight-Ashbury, and the photogenic Kennedys supplied precisely the materials with which it could do its most effective work.

The Kennedy forces knew the power of a good visual image. John Kennedy had seen Democratic governor Paul Dever of Massachusetts go down to defeat in 1952 because on television he came across as a cartoonist's rendering of an old pol, and the President knew what his own election had owed to the television debates. The administration was friendly to the press cameras. Kennedy opened his press conferences to live television coverage. The Executive Mansion initiated ideas for picture stories. It was at the suggestion of the White House that during the missile crisis a photographer snapped the reassuring picture through a rainy window of the President in thought.

In this early time of the image, President Kennedy and the civil rights movement were the most important subjects of television and photojournalism, and while the media were studying both, each was doing something for the other. At the push and tug of events, President Kennedy lent to the movement enough of the protection of the federal government to make it slightly freer to operate in the South, and his presidency made the preliminary decisions that would grow into the important legislation of the Johnson years. And civil rights would eventually bestow on the Kennedy administration a moral meaning beyond anything the government had at first planned for.

Kennedy liberalism was born in the presumption, which turned itself into a fact, that there was in John Kennedy's person and programs a force for social reformation. Black leaders increasingly looked to him for whatever he had to offer, whether it was the tangible support of marshals and federal troops in the South when their presence was essential, the partial symbolic desegregation in 1962 of federally funded public housing, or in 1963 Kennedy's espousal of civil rights legislation. Opponents of the civil rights movement, in their very fear that the President favored the rights cause, contributed to defining him as the embodiment of a liberalism that would go beyond the established New Deal programs. Liberal intellectuals could think that a youthful Harvard graduate with a beautiful and socially accomplished wife must be one of them.

Apart from Kennedy's major activities in foreign affairs, it is his performance in the civil rights controversies that has led to the most extensive judgments of him, favorable and condemnatory. That this should be so is a commentary on the early sixties. No President before John Kennedy, Abraham Lincoln included, could meet more than the smallest test for racial justice, or for forthright public discussion of the racial issue, on the terms that are now acceptable. But then no President had been put to the test by any movement as highly visible as the civil rights forces of the sixties. Kennedy's presidency coincided with the early years of a rights activism that demanded an absolute and uncompromised equality, a disappearance of private as well as official discrimination, an end to stereotypes and to the whole range of cruelties that had attended racism in this country. The Kennedy administration connected with that movement—furthering it, Kennedy's supporters say, dragged along, as more skeptical commentators insist, or growing with it. But it is at least beyond dispute that the administration's activity for civil rights differed fundamentally in character from that of the protesters in the Southern streets and the rights workers in the Southern back country. Not one but two forces were arrayed against segregation, one of them hesitant, legalistic, calculating, while the other acted out of a simple and relentless moral witness. The result of the administration's caution is that in the presence of the rights workers and demonstrators it looked timid and temporizing; the result of its activity is that the rights movement gained a solid body of federal practices to supplement the sit-ins, the freedom rides, and the marches.

Kennedy brought to his presidency a record of compromise and expediency on civil rights. As a senator coming to national prominence he had seemed scarcely aware of the Supreme Court desegregation decision of 1954 and the Montgomery bus boycott. For a northern liberal, Kennedy's record in the Senate was, even on balance, unsatisfactory. He said of Little Rock that a greater planning and leadership on Eisenhower's part could have prevented the trouble. In his vice presidential and presidential campaign he sought support from the South's most truculent segregationist governors. Kennedy omitted civil rights from a list of the "real issues of 1960" that he presented near the beginning of his presidential contest. His sympathy call to Coretta Scott King while her husband sat in a Georgia jail was a gesture of great political value, but there is no evidence that it was anything more. During the weeks after the election he created a number of task forces to make recommendations on pressing national problems, but he appointed none on civil rights. The pessimism of a conservative oddly coexisted, even in Kennedy's words, with the vocabulary of will and action. "There is always some inequality in life," he observed at a press conference in Greenfield, Massachusetts, on March 21, 1962. "Some men are killed in war, and some are wounded, and some men never leave the country, and some men are stationed in the Antarctic and some men are stationed in San Francisco. It is very hard in military or personal life to assure complete equality." Such pessimism Kennedy could also bring to the rights question.

Harris Wofford was, by Robert Kennedy's explanation, "so committed to civil rights emotion-ally" that the administration decided against appointing him assistant attorney general in charge of civil rights in the Justice Department. Wofford instead became a White House assistant on civil rights. He was to say of the position in retrospect that what President Kennedy had most liked about it, and he had least liked, was his task of serving as a buffer between the President and the civil rights forces. For the civil rights position in the Justice Department Byron White, the conservative Rhodes scholar from Yale, friend of Kennedys, and future Supreme Court justice, recommended Burke Marshall, another Yale Law School graduate and a member of a distinguished corporate law firm in Washington, D.C.

Marshall, like so many educated Americans, understood the moral problem and was a patient negotiator. He also brought to the job a liberal record; he had been a member of the American Civil Liberties Union and an originator of the idea of federal registrars who could insure enrollment of Southern black voters. But he believed in the ways of compromise and agreement and despaired of addressing the question of civil rights with the means available to a federal system of government. Marshall later opposed the Civil Rights Commission's plan to hold hearings in Mississippi that would publicize conditions there, and he opposed the commission's wish for a halt in all federal money to that and other states. He was also to observe that a major nationwide effort for integrated housing would have been too frightening. In *Federalism and Civil Rights,* published in 1964, Marshall concludes that the central government's police power cannot deal effectively with the complex race problem. And for generations, legal and social conservatives, following similar reasoning, had refrained from using governmental power to challenge unjust social institutions, so the injustice, in all its complexity, remained. The moralistic and relentless Robert Kennedy was making use of legal power, first against radicals in the Redbaiting days of the early 1950s and then against labor racketeers, long before he discovered a real "enemy within" that had long made a mockery of American ideas of justice. Yet even Burke Marshall could draw limits to compromise. He was later to observe that while some liberals were too aggressive for civil rights, others, such as Hubert Humphrey, were too conciliatory.

The earliest of the administration's measures were symbolic acts of integration. Having seen no blacks in the Coast Guard contingent of the inauguration march, Kennedy instructed the academy to recruit more. The government increased the number of blacks at social functions, desegregated the White House press and photography pools, and multiplied the appointment of Negroes to important government posts. In the spring of 1961 Secretary of Labor Arthur Goldberg attacked the practice of racial segregation in private clubs. Afterward the economist John Kenneth Galbraith, Kennedy's ambassador to India, resigned from Washington's Cosmos Club, an association of writers, scientists, and other professional people, when the club, which at the time had no black members, refused to admit the columnist Carl Rowan. At the resignation the name of John Kennedy, whom Galbraith had been sponsoring for membership, was automatically withdrawn. When for a time later in the sixties a scornful anger became the moral fashion among leftists, black and white, the well-meaning social gestures of white liberals fell victim to a studied contempt. But that has gone the way of other fashions, and it is perhaps now safe to suggest that the efforts of the Kennedy liberals to extend the common civilities had some role in the rights revolution.

Soon after two black students had integrated the University of Georgia, Attorney General Robert Kennedy in 1961 gave a speech there depicting the two as freedom fighters. (The phrase recalls the Hungarian insurgents of 1956; that is how strongly the struggle against communism gripped the imagination of the times and the Kennedys.) At the university Kennedy announced his intention to work for racial justice, and his speech decried inequities in the North as well as in the South. It was the first time a modern attorney general had spoken in the South for civil

rights. Robert Kennedy's Justice Department made or was forced to make many of the day-to-day decisions bearing on civil rights. He brought in a handful of black attorneys, along with Archibald Cox as solicitor general, Ramsey Clark, John Doar, John Seigenthaler, and many others of note. But Robert shared Burke Marshall's caution about sudden federal assaults on local customs. It was the demonstrators and the rights workers, and more particularly the assaults on them, that pushed the Justice Department forward.

The freedom riders, organized by James Farmer's Congress of Racial Equality, pressed the cause of civil rights. CORE's northern black and white demonstrators, beginning in the spring of 1961, went through the South in busloads, defying segregation of terminals enforced by state and local officials. Farmer, before the trek through the South, sent an itinerary to the President, Robert Kennedy, and the FBI, in addition to Greyhound and Trailways, and got no response. The attorney general did not like the freedom rides and tried to discourage them. Possibly the lawyer and politician in him, which in other cases his anger could overwhelm, predominated at the moment, recoiling from tactics of confrontation and defiance of local officials. If so, freedom riders would have had a ready response. Their intention was to compel the enforcement of the law, for the Supreme Court decision in *Boynton* v. *Virginia* had declared illegal any segregation in interstate bus and train terminals. The freedom riders were aware of the violence their journey might provoke but calculated that the violence would make the federal government intervene. That is precisely what Robert Kennedy did not want forced upon him.

The attorney general did not get the peace he had wished for. When a freedom bus was firebombed in Anniston, Alabama, he ordered the FBI to investigate the arson. Bull Connor, the hostile chief of the Alabama police, was directed to protect the riders in Birmingham. On May 21 patrolmen and police helicopters escorted them to Montgomery. Governor John Patterson had promised continuing protection. The governor was not an unenlightened Southern politician. He had acquired his political prominence when, upon becoming Alabama attorney general in 1954, he finished cleaning up vice-ridden Phenix City, completing the work for which his father as a district attorney had been murdered. More recently he has revealed sufficient contrition, or at least embarrassment, about racism to observe that while he did use the race issue in campaigning for governor, he would have preferred not to do so. Yet he was sufficiently of his own culture that he could not bring himself to act promptly in defense of the riders. When the riders arrived in Montgomery, a mob set upon them. John Seigenthaler, the Justice Department official and friend of Robert Kennedy, was clubbed as he was trying to protect a female demonstrator, and he lay unconscious for about twenty-five minutes. The FBI, meticulously staying within the letter of its mandate, as it sometimes did to its own advantage, stood by and took comprehensive notes. (Therein the bureau acted consistently with its inconsistent conduct during the civil rights years, when it was censorious of the movement, legalistically slow to discover violations of racial justice, and at times energetic in support of civil rights.) That evening some fifty marshals tried to protect Martin Luther King and civil rights supporters as King led a vigil in the city's First Baptist Church until Patterson at length discovered his responsibilities, declared martial law, and sent the National Guard. Nicholas Katzenbach, an assistant attorney general in Robert Kennedy's Justice Department, has remarked in another connection that neither he nor his chief liked to take away from local officers the job of protection, for they knew how much that is resented. But local authority, in Montgomery and elsewhere in these violent times, refused to act on its obligations, so there was to be street war, of sorts, between the Justice Department and the segregationists.

But in 1961 Robert Kennedy remained aloof from the tactics of confrontation and peaceful rebellion that gave to the civil rights movement its distinctive character. Byron White, who thought that blacks needed a higher standard of living rather than civil rights, explained at a press conference in Birmingham that marshals would not intervene if the police arrested the freedom riders: "I'm sure they would be represented by competent counsel." Robert actually countenanced the arrest of riders in Jackson, Mississippi, on whatever charge the local officers used against violators of segregation. Apparently he thought that the arrests would rescue the riders from the dangers they were inviting upon themselves. "Do you know," he exclaimed to Wofford, "that one of them is against the atom bomb—yes, he even picketed against it in jail!" After the arrests the attorney general urged a cooling-off period; he cited the forthcoming summit conference between the United States and the Soviet Union. Martin Luther King, Jr. agreed to a momentary respite. But hundreds of arrests followed later in the summer.

The administration was unwilling to make demands on Congress. The President appointed to Southern federal districts, especially in the deep South, judges so traditionalist that they obstructed the work of his brother's civil rights lawyers. He was, of course, constrained in his selections by the custom, almost never violated, of obtaining approval from the states' Democratic senators. The political commentator Tom Wicker has argued that Kennedy could have risked presenting Congress with a civil rights bill early in his administration. Republicans, he contends, would have had no good reason to oppose it, and Southerners were already as alienated as they could be, antagonized by the liberal rhetoric of the presidential campaign, by the administration's support of the fight to widen the membership of the House Rules Committee, and by liberal legislation having the endorsement of the White House. But when Senator Joseph Clark of Pennsylvania and Representative Emanuel Celler of New York introduced six bills to implement the Democratic platform of 1960 on civil rights, the White House disavowed the very bills Kennedy had asked for during the campaign.

Almost as cautious about the use of executive power, the administration canceled no contracts for reasons of job discrimination. Speaking of such new regulations as withholding federal funding from highway construction that practiced discrimination in working conditions, the President once urged that the rules be enforced only when essential. In 1961 the NAACP had proposed that the government withhold funds from states using them in a discriminatory way. The report of the Civil Rights Commission recommended that Kennedy explore his authority to hold back funding from Mississippi. The President, calling the idea "unbelievable" and "almost irresponsible," urged the commission not to make its statement public. At a press conference he said that he neither had nor should have the authority to stop funds going to recalcitrant states. "They ran away from it," Roy Williams said of the scheme, "like it was a rattlesnake." Yet the Civil Rights Act of 1964 was to give the President the power Kennedy had rejected. In 1960 Kennedy had attacked the previous administration for tolerating segregation in federally funded housing. But it was almost two years before he acted on his promise to eliminate it with "a stroke of the presidential pen" (he had received thousands of pens and floods of ink through the mail), and even then he acted circumspectly, burying the order in the midst of public announcements covering other subjects and phrasing it to apply only to future FHA and VA mortgages. Probably he knew that the desegregation of suburban housing was a dangerous issue; it took Lyndon Johnson until 1968 to get any legislation on the subject, and suburban desegregation is still notoriously slow to proceed.

Three times the Civil Rights Commission was ready to hold hearings in Mississippi, and three times Robert Kennedy stopped the hearings, claiming that impending legislation would be endangered. Even while pushing voter registration, the attorney general feared race riots in the South and thought that hearings might set them off. He complained, Wofford recalls, that the commission was not objective: "It was almost like the House Un-American Activities Committee investigating Communism." The commission, disregarding the wishes of the President and the attorney general, published a report on violations of civil rights in Mississippi.

Robert Kennedy and his Justice Department did take or respond to initiatives in the furtherance of civil rights. When King and other civil rights leaders involved in the freedom rides complained to him that the Interstate Commerce Commission was not enforcing the Supreme Court declaration in terminals, he had explained to them that the commission was both independent and slow to move, but in the wake of the rides, he disproved his claim, persuading the ICC to forbid discrimination. By the end of the year every airport and nearly every bus and railroad station had been desegregated. Hoping that the voter registration movement for black Southerners would bring less violence than the freedom rides, the attorney general joined in the call for the project, which the NAACP announced to the press in a statement that included the phrase "ask what you can do for your country." The need was plain: in Mississippi the percentage of blacks registered to vote had been declining for seventy years even as literacy among Negroes had been steadily rising. When the question of voter registration became central, Burke Marshall's civil rights division sent lawyers into the South to investigate violations of voting rights, and in another innovation he permitted them to initiate actions, which numbered about seventy by late 1963. Government lawyers went into Fayette County in Tennessee to sue landlords who had forced black sharecroppers off their land for trying to register for the vote, and the Agriculture Department gave food to the dispossessed.

The voter registration campaign, which put the administration at odds with white supremacists it had appointed to federal courts, was in its defense of traditional constitutional rights an eminently conservative program; and even Americans relatively indifferent to race issues could acknowledge its justice. It therefore accorded with the streak of caution that had marked Robert Kennedy's initial management of the race problem. But in the self-consciousness and militancy it awakened in black Southerners, in the political organization it spawned among them, and in the power base it ultimately provided, the voter registration project was revolutionary.

John Kennedy's administration as a whole was moving incrementally and yet at a rate unprecedented within this century on the issue of civil rights. In the early sixties motor travelers between Washington and the Northeast still had to use Route 40 in Maryland, and those travelers sometimes included diplomats from the new African nations. The government, its attention fixed on international politics, successfully urged the state of Maryland to pass a public accommodations law and persuaded the governor to apologize to a black diplomat who had been turned away from a restaurant. In the days when the District of Columbia still practiced much de facto segregation, the President appointed the first black District commissioner. He also made some notable selections of blacks elsewhere, choosing for the court of appeals Thurgood Marshall, who had argued the great school desegregation case of 1954. Kennedy strengthened the President's Commission on Equal Employment Opportunity, charged with working for more equitable hiring in the government and in the firms with which the government did business. It won some voluntary agreements from business contracting with the government to survey and improve their hiring practices. President Kennedy asked Congress to forbid literacy tests for voting, and at his behest the national legislature sent to the states the Twenty-fourth Amendment, outlawing the poll tax. The government warned universities receiving federal money for language institutes that the program funding would be contingent on an absence of discrimination; as a result, a half dozen schools withdrew. Washington also resolved to withhold federal aid from segregated school districts in areas "impacted" by federal installations. The President appointed Robert C. Weaver as housing administrator and worked hard but unsuccessfully to have his office raised to cabinet status. To the Civil Rights Commission, which President Eisenhower had made a more effective body than had been expected, Kennedy made some appointments that strengthened its activist character, and the commission, of all government agencies the most aggressive on the rights issue, was a goad to the administration.

The administration, in sum, was sending contradictory signals, and that may have given hope to elements in the South of winning a battle that they had already lost. The presidency had chosen to act with some responsiveness to that first moment in American history when it appeared possible that racial equality could actually prevail, and now rather than in an indefinite future to which Americans of good will could look wistfully. That may explain both the activity and the reticence of the administration. It was active because an increasingly insistent segment of the black population and numbers of white allies were urging it into action and because a growing number of white Americans were showing that they would not, at the slightest progress toward integration, turn into a mob. And the administration could afford to be reticent, prepared to compromise for the sake of keeping its friendship with white Southerners, because it believed that the revolution in attitudes and practices had its own momentum. Every small gesture on the part of the government made the revolution appear, and therefore be, all the more an irresistible reality. The Kennedy presidency might have gone its entire tenure in the way it and events had set, forceful enough to win popularity among black Americans, politic enough to keep the popularity among Southern whites that opinion polls registered for it until mid-1963. But in the end violence by Southern bigots brought the President to speak and act against racial injustice with a militancy that he may once have intended only for confrontation with communism.

In the autumn of 1962 James Meredith pursued his plans to enter the University of Mississippi, its first black student. He has recalled that he might not have applied to the University of Mississippi had Kennedy lost the 1960 election. Meredith worked out his plan on his own, claiming later to have received inspiration from the cadences of John Kennedy's inaugural address—which said not a word about civil rights. At least not intentionally. The famous Lincolnesque phrase borrowed by Kennedy—"We shall have to test anew whether a nation organized and governed such as ours can endure"—looked to foreign affairs, but events played it out in the deep South.

After resistance from the state a federal court ordered Meredith's admission. On the night preceding his enrollment Assistant Attorney General Nicholas Katzenbach was on the campus at Oxford, Mississippi, along with Justice Department marshals armed with tear gas. For several hours marshals were under siege in a pitched battle, while Governor Ross Barnett, instead of sending sufficient police or militia forces, declined to deviate from his public posture of antagonism to integration—though his phone conversation with the President in the evening reveals a worried and hesitant man hoping for some solution: he told Kennedy that his defiant words were directed "just to Mississippi."

The President, still unaware of the violence, went on television, urging compliance with the court order, appealing to sportsmanship on the gridiron and to Southern honor won in battle. That evening—that terrible evening, in Robert Kennedy's memory—Washington learned that two people had been killed on a campus in anarchy. The White House waited and fretted while federal troops sent by the President took much longer to arrive at Ole Miss than he had expected. Katzenbach asked over the phone whether the marshals could fire on the rioters. No, answered Kennedy, except to protect Meredith. That evening Bobby thought of the killing that might take place, and he thought of the Bay of Pigs. So did the President. "I haven't had such an interesting time since the Bay of Pigs," he said. And Robert composed a bulletin: "The attorney general announced today he's joining Allen Dulles at Princeton University." John Kennedy spoke of *Seven Days in May,* the taut 1962 thriller about a general who tries to overthrow a President to prevent a conciliatory arrangement with the Soviet Union. "The only character that came out at all was the general," said Kennedy. "The president was awfully vague." The novel's general reminded Robert of General Edwin Walker, who had been retired from a European command after his broodings about communism seemed to be prodding him toward making his own separate war on it. Robert's association was apt on that

night of Ole Miss: Walker, by now connecting communism with integration or both with the crumbling of Western civilization, was among the rioters. In the end the federal soldiers quelled the mob. Walker was arrested on a federal warrant charging him with seditious conspiracy and insurrection for spurring the rioters, but the government did not get an indictment. The army remained on the campus for months. It had taken some 23,000 troops to do the job.

Robert Kennedy was to remember that after Ole Miss the President said that he would never again believe stories about terrible federal troops in the Reconstruction era. Yet the federal government was so new to the task of enforcing civil rights that Burke Marshall had worried about whether the President had the constitutional authority to send troops without first calling on the governor to act.

The following spring Vivian Malone and James Hood entered the University of Alabama under the protection of federal soldiers. In Alabama, where the attorney general went to prepare for the integration, a state trooper jabbed him with a nightstick, and he was asked at a press conference if he was a member of the Communist party. In a remarkable effort that recalls the administration's earlier mobilizing of its resources in a war with the steel industry, cabinet members and directors of agencies called 375 business executives in Alabama to request that there be no more trouble. Similar calls were to be made to Birmingham businessmen later in 1963 with reminders that the economies of Little Rock and Oxford had suffered after racial troubles there.

The impending riot at Ole Miss had put President Kennedy for the first time before the national television audience on the subject of civil rights. Yet conceivably for strategic reasons at a moment when the threat of violence was the immediate problem, he had stressed not racial justice but obedience to the Constitution. Events the next spring so intruded the race issue into the national consciousness that a moral vocabulary was at last inescapable.

Federal efforts in deeply segregated Birmingham had been virtually unavailing; aside from the

Civil rights demonstrators in Birmingham, Alabama, were met with cruel resistance by vicious police dogs, clubs, electric cattle prods, and fire hoses.

post office and Veterans Administration hospital, blacks held fewer than one percent of federal jobs in the area. George Wallace, now Alabama governor, was moving into the leadership of Southern segregationists. The strategy of the rights workers in 1963, the only workable one, was to confront the city with massive demonstrations. What transpired placed an overwhelming demand on the national conscience: police dogs, electric cattle prods, fire hoses, and rioting. Burke Marshall, at his best when the patient arts of negotiation were required, talked endlessly with white business leaders and won at least a segment of civic opinion to the cause of peace. The administration, meanwhile, had entreated King to call off the demonstrators on the ground that they were hindering the negotiations with the whites, as the two Kennedys, never pleased with the tactics of confrontation, had wanted him in 1962 to ease off in Albany, Georgia, so that a moderate Democratic candidate for governor might win.

Kennedy, foreseeing the "fires of frustration and discord . . . burning in every city, North and South," responded as the occasion demanded. By now he, the churches, a majority in Congress, and much of the nation had awakened. Kennedy on June 11 gave an eloquent address on television: "I ask you to look into your hearts—not in search of charity, for the Negro neither wants nor needs condescension—but for the one plain, proud and priceless quality that unites all as Americans: a sense of justice."

That same night in Mississippi a white racist murdered the civil rights leader Medgar Evers. His was only one of innumerable murders of black people since the coming of slavery to the continent, but now there were awakened media to give the killing nationwide prominence.

Shortly after his television talk the President, who had presented to Congress a mild civil rights bill after Ole Miss but before Birmingham, requested the national legislature to place a partial ban on discrimination in public places, empower the Justice Department to sue for school desegregation upon a request that it do so, and give the executive broader authority to withhold funds from federally assisted programs in which discrimination occurred. The President, who had been politic enough not to want Johnson to speak out inordinately on the race issue, was bold enough to deliver his historic speech against the judgment of most of his White House advisers. Johnson had argued for some preparatory work to soften up Congress. Afterward civil rights leaders persuaded Kennedy to strengthen the proposed legislation to give the attorney general power to intervene in all civil rights cases. The Civil Rights Acts that followed his death were to go well beyond the initial Kennedy program.

Though the President never perhaps came to see the issue as absolutely and morally central— he told a press conference that tax reform was more important than anything else—he did work hard to pass the legislation, meeting with some 1,700 people that summer. After House liberals tried to revise his legislation with provisions that the administration feared would bring its defeat, Kennedy persuaded conservative Republican leader Charles Halleck to agree to a moderate version and thereby, according to the recollections of Robert Kennedy and Burke Marshall, presented the liberals with a political situation so promising that holdouts came over. If they had compromised their virtue, Halleck, in the view of many conservatives, had compromised his. He found a furled umbrella on his desk in the House. Senator Everett Dirksen made passage nearly certain by agreeing on November 2 that the Republican leadership would not support a filibuster. By the time of the President's death the bill had already cleared its most difficult hurdle, the House Judiciary Committee.

Martin Luther King, Jr. was to comment privately in an oral history that at the President's directions Robert Kennedy had done much more than his office of attorney general obliged him to do. But he remarked before Kennedy's June 1963 speech that while the President had perhaps done "a little more" for blacks than Eisenhower, "the plight of the vast majority of Negroes remains the same." When 250,000 people under King's leadership marched on Washington that August in support of the proposed legislation, John Kennedy first tried to dissuade them and then avoided addressing the assembly. Burke Marshall, however, has claimed that the attorney general did much of the real work of organizing the march: providing water and toilets (which a government is virtually obligated to do anyway) and insuring—whatever this means—"that the character of the people who were coming was in close touch with the police." Upon learning that John Lewis of the Student Nonviolent Coordinating Committee was going to give an inflammatory speech—"It attacked the President," Robert laments—the theologically conservative but socially progressive Roman Catholic archbishop of Washington, Patrick O'Boyle, was going to decline to participate. Marshall went to Walter Reuther, who enlisted the help of King, James Farmer of CORE, and others to persuade Lewis to temper his speech, which satisfied O'Boyle. The final version omitted the announcement that the civil rights forces would "march through the South, through the Heart of Dixie, the way Sherman did." The contrast is inviting: the heroic and visionary rights activists in a triumphant moment; the worried administrators who rushed about to keep everything safe and orderly. The generation of the sixties reveled in such contrasts. But if the movement that called the march could reach beyond the caution that guided the administration, the government, by keeping O'Boyle in the march, rendered the demonstration a service.

On August 28 King addressed the marchers: "I have a dream that one day on the red hills of Georgia the sons of former slaves and the sons of former slaveholders will be able to sit down together at the table of brotherhood. I have a dream that one day even the state of Mississippi, a desert state sweltering with the heat of injustice and oppression, will be transformed into an oasis of freedom and justice. . . . I have a dream that one day the state of Alabama . . . will be transformed [and] little black boys and black girls will be able to join hands with little white boys and white girls and walk together as sisters and brothers." John Kennedy never gave voice to such a dream. But he allied himself with King's, and the alliance brought forth after his death the great civil rights legislation of the mid-1960s. Congress approved the first law in 1964, and others followed in 1965 and 1966.

Robert Kennedy's later commentary on the administration's race policies gives a plausible, though self-interested, justification of the caution. State by state, he was to claim, the government had to accommodate Southern senators on federal judicial appointments. The reason the administration did not send more civil rights legislation to Congress, by his explanation, is that there was so little effective demand for it. In 1962 the attorney general went to the Hill to testify for a bill that would insure voting rights for people literate at the sixth-grade level, but interest in it was insufficient. Robert was wary of expanding the power of the federal government to defend civil rights, believing that a gradual resolution of issues was healthier than sudden confrontations of the South by rights workers under federal protection. His idea of a well-managed policy was the federal pressure and discussion that brought about the desegregation of rail and air terminals. The strategy-tempered idealism of the administration, as Robert's recollections present it, was typified in the determination to protect the right to vote: the federal government had the authority, accomplishment would bring much good, and there could be relatively small opposition to so clearly fundamental a right.

Robert Kennedy's observations in his oral history on the House liberals who tried to stiffen the administration's civil rights bill (which include his comment that the epithet sons of bitches that his father had applied to businessmen applied also to liberals) put neatly the difference between two perceptions of morality. The liberals preferred failure to a reasonable bill. "An awful lot of them, as I said then, were in love with death," the motive,

perhaps, that some of them had for liking Adlai Stevenson; they thought only of their own goals, not of the needs of others. This moralistic denunciation of liberal moralism comes from a man in whom virtuous anger seemed forever close to eruption. It may not be a just interpretation of the House liberals of 1963, and it does not take into account the demonstration provided by the civil rights activists that a will to strain beyond the limits of the sensible and the possible may have the practical effect of widening the limits. But Robert Kennedy makes a good moral case against the virtuousness that thirsts after purity. The argument is also applicable to those right-wingers who were offended at President Kennedy's attempts to reach accommodations with the Soviet Union. And it is applicable later in the decade to the seekers after purity whose antiwar, antiliberal, antigovernment, and anti-American convictions could express themselves only in superlatives chasing after superlatives. In those days could be heard the most tremendous denunciations of the United States as a genocidal country and of its people as rotting in corruption, as if any accusation more measured would be a compromise.

George McGovern has commented that President Kennedy's respect and desire for power led him to conserve it for essential uses and to refrain from expending it on anything that could dissipate it. If the observation does not describe the President who agreed to the Bay of Pigs, it does suggest the administration that finally spoke for a sophisticated understanding of the architectures of world power. Kennedy had something of the sense of federal power as a force to be calculatingly and subtly deployed against racism. And the other, contradictory component of John Kennedy's feeling for power, his tendency to react to crisis rather than to the stubborn detail of a problem, may be further explanation for the peculiar pace of his dealings with the race question: conciliatory, slow, incremental reform punctuated in the end by dramatic televised responses to the great civil rights events of the day.

STUDY QUESTIONS

1. Why was television so important to the success of the civil rights movement in the 1960s?

2. During his presidency, John F. Kennedy was extraordinarily popular with African Americans. Why? Did his record on civil rights justify that popularity?

3. What role did Robert Kennedy play in the administration's approach to civil rights?

4. Explain the major achievements of the Kennedy administration in the civil rights area.

5. Historians and critics have labeled John F. Kennedy as a conservative, a radical, or a moderate. Based on his civil rights record, what would you say about Kennedy's political philosophy?

BIBLIOGRAPHY

For favorable portraits of Kennedy and his administration, see Arthur M. Schlesinger, Jr., *A Thousand Days* (1965); Theodore M. Sorensen, *Kennedy* (1973); Herbert Parment, *Jack: The Struggles of John F. Kennedy* (1980), and *JFK: The Presidency of John F. Kennedy* (1983). Also see Henry Farlie, *The Kennedy Promise* (1973). For harsh criticisms of the Kennedy administration, see Bruce Miroff, *Pragmatic Illusions: The Presidential Politics of John F. Kennedy* (1976) and Garry Wills, *The Kennedy Imprisonment* (1982). For views of the Kennedy family, see Doris Kearns Goodwin, *The Fitzgeralds and the Kennedys: An American Saga* (1987) and Nancy Gager Clinch, *The Kennedy Neurosis: A Psychological Portrait of an American Dynasty* (1973). David Burner's *John F. Kennedy and a New Generation* (1987) is a short but excellent biography. For studies of the civil rights movement of the 1960s, see Carl Bauer, *John F. Kennedy and the Second Reconstruction* (1977) and Harris Wofford's *Of Kennedys and Kings* (1980). Also see Robert E. Gilbert, "John F. Kennedy and Civil Rights for Black Americans," *Presidential Studies Quarterly* 12 (Summer 1982), pp. 386–399; and Thomas Reeves, *A Question of Character: A Life of John F. Kennedy,* (1991).

VIETNAM IN THE COMIC BOOKS
Bradford Wright

Recent American historians view the Vietnam War as one of the seminal events in United States history—a period that shaped American military and foreign policy as well as American culture. Even the most cursory survey of books, films, and television programs over the past twenty years, to say nothing of the news media, illustrates how influential the Vietnam War has been in shaping American thought. Like no event since the Civil War, Vietnam divided Americans into opposing camps and inspired a sharp, acrimonious debate about national values and the nation's destiny. On many levels, that debate continues today. What is becoming increasingly clear is just how deeply the Vietnam War has affected American life. Perhaps the best way of demonstrating the impact of Vietnam is to look at popular culture—and no dimension of popular culture is more popular than comic books. In the following essay, Bradford Wright discusses how the comic book industry in the United States dealt with the war in Vietnam.

The comic-book industry thrived during the early 1950s, largely due to the popularity of crime and horror comic books that featured graphic violence, sexual overtones, and other adult themes. Parents, psychologists, government officials, and other concerned groups suspected that comic books contributed to a rise in juvenile delinquency. The public crusade against comic books resulted in a U. S. Senate investigation into the industry in 1954, after which the publishers established the self-censoring Comics Code Authority. In order to ensure the national distribution of their comic books, the code required publishers to adhere to the standards, which have been described by one of the code's proponents as "the most stringent for any media." The code was intended to uphold the principles of "good taste" in comic books and to preserve the medium as a "wholesome form of entertainment." Among the code's standards was the provision that "policemen, judges, government officials, and respected institutions shall never be presented in such a way as to create disrespect for established authority." The code, therefore, dictated that comic-book stories after 1954 would be not only sanitized and juvenile, but devoid of social and political criticism as well.

The establishment of the Comics Code Authority had an immediate and depressing effect on the comic-book industry as a whole. Many publishers who had relied upon themes forbidden by the code were unable to distribute their comic books and went out of business within a few years. The industry was further hurt by the rise of television, which had more to offer discerning teenagers and young adults than the code-approved comic books. The *New York Times* reported that by 1962 annual comic-book sales had dropped from 800,000,000 in 1952 to 350,000,000 in 1962. The comic-book industry, which had once consisted of over fifty publishers, began the 1960s with fewer than a dozen publishing houses.

The code did not affect all publishers equally, however, and some were not hurt by it at all. DC Comics survived the 1950s in good shape, and by 1962 it had acquired 30 percent of the market. DC had never participated heavily in the controversial crime of horror trends, and the content of its comic books was restrained even before the code, featuring such widely recognizable characters as Superman, Batman, and Wonder Woman. Throughout the 1950s these titles remained targeted at an unsophisticated juvenile readership and were, therefore, unchanged by the editorial standards of the code. DC was also probably hurt less by television than other publishers because the popularity of the televised *Adventures of Superman* may have actually boosted the sales of Superman comic books. In 1956 DC initiated what comic book historians have termed the "silver age" of superhero comic books by reviving some of its stock superheroes from the 1940s and giving them revised origins with more contemporary settings. The popularity of titles like *The Flash, Green Lantern,* and *The Justice League of America* helped reestablish the superhero comic book as the industry's most popular genre of the 1960s.

The Dell Publishing Company was one comic-book publisher that may have actually benefited from the establishment of the code. Dell's top-selling comic books were its "funny animal" titles that featured characters from the cartoons of Walt Disney and Warner Brothers. The company was proud of its reputation for producing clean, wholesome comic books that were held up as positive examples by those who criticized the rest of the industry. The president of Dell was one of the few publishers who refused to submit their comic books to the Code Authority, because Dell already maintained its own code for decency and good taste. The company thrived during the late 1950s, selling more comic books worldwide than any other publisher, but circulation dropped dramatically in the early 1960s. Dell's attempt to diversify its publishing operation by producing titles in genres such as war and science fiction failed to capture a large audience, and the company remained a second-rate publisher until it left the comic-book field in 1973.

Marvel Comics had been among the most prolific of comic-book publishers since its entry into the field in 1939. During its first two decades, Marvel followed changing industry trends, publishing titles in every comic-book genre. Marvel's war and horror comic books were its most visible titles prior to the code. The former were inspired by the Korean War and have been described by one writer as perhaps the most anti-communist of all 1950s war comics. The latter were among those specifically condemned by the U. S. Senate investigation into the industry. Marvel entered the 1960s as a much smaller publishing operation, whose most notable comic books were fantasy stories inspired by Saturday matinee monster films. That the *New York Times* failed even to mention Marvel in its report on the status of the industry in 1962 attests to the publisher's small share of the market.

The publisher of Marvel Comics noticed the success of DC's superhero titles and asked his staff to put out a comic book featuring a team of superheroes modeled after DC's *The Justice League of America.* Stan Lee, who served as Marvel's comic-book editor, art director, and head writer, conceived a comic book that actually bore little resemblance to any DC comic. Lee, working with writer Jack Kirby, created an experimental group of superheroes who displayed a depth of characterization beyond anything that had yet been attempted in the genre. The "Fantastic Four" were portrayed as human beings with diverse personalities and human failings who had accidentally acquired superpowers. One member of the group, Ben Grimm, gained his superstrength at the expense of his humanity, when "cosmic rays" transformed him into a hulking, orange, rock-skinned monster. Grimm, calling himself simply "the Thing," was overtly envious of, and hostile toward, his friends and teammates who retained their human appearance. The Thing was a new kind of superhero for the 1960s—one who was deeply alienated from and resentful of the society that he was sworn to protect.

The success of *The Fantastic Four* prompted Marvel to produce another innovative superhero comic book. *The Incredible Hulk* featured Dr. Bruce Banner, a mild-mannered physicist reminiscent of Dr. Jekyll, who periodically transforms into a tremendously strong, green-skinned brute. The Hulk's bestial nature and his hatred of the human race, which constantly hounds him, make him an outsider far removed from the traditional ideal of a superhero.

Spider-Man was destined to become Marvel's most popular character. Peter Parker is a shy, socially inept high school science student whose only family and friends are his elderly aunt and uncle. He accidentally gains the proportionate powers of a spider when he is bitten by a radioactive spider at a science demonstration. Upon discovering his powers, however, he is not inspired to use them to help mankind, but instead seeks personal fame and wealth. After his debut performance on television, Spider-Man witnesses a fugitive escape from a pursuing police officer. When the angry policeman asks him why he did not help stop the criminal, Spider-Man replies that he is looking out only for himself. Soon thereafter, Parker discovers that his beloved Uncle Ben has been killed by a burglar. He tracks the murderer down only to discover that the killer is the very fugitive whom he had allowed to escape earlier. Only then does he realize that "with great power comes great responsibility," and he pledges himself to a life of crime fighting. Here was a young superhero whose service to society was motivated not by a noble heroic ideal, but rather by an intense sense of personal obligation born of guilt. This set the tone for the *Spider-Man* comic book series, in which the hero had to contend with society's problems, phobias, and his own self-pity as often as he had to battle supervillains.

These and other comic books injected a renewed vitality into the industry, which had stagnated since the establishment of the code. Working within the constraints of the code, Stan Lee brought a sense of contemporary realism to superhero comic books despite the obviously fantastic premise of the genre. In this sense, the Marvel comic books were very different from DC's. While DC stories were set in such mythical locations as "Metropolis," "Gotham City," and "Star

City," Marvel superheroes operated in and around New York City. DC editorial policy dictated that its comic books would appeal almost exclusively to a juvenile audience, but Stan Lee searched for an older readership. Lee maintained that it was possible to capture a postadolescent audience without alienating the younger readers by presenting comic-book stories on two levels: "color, costumes, and exaggerated action for the kids, [and] science-fiction, satire, and sophisticated philosophy for the adults and near-adults."

This creative strategy brought success to Stan Lee and Marvel Comics. Although Marvel remained well behind DC in overall sales, the gap between the two publishers narrowed considerably throughout the 1960s. Marvel also won a devoted following among older readers. The popularity of Marvel Comics on college campuses was noted by *Esquire* magazine, which reported in 1966 that Stan Lee had become a popular visiting lecturer. Another issue noted that Spider-Man and the Hulk ranked alongside Bob Dylan, Ché Guevara, and Malcolm X as the most popular revolutionary figures among the collegiate New Left.

Marvel Comics employed a realism in both characterization and setting in its superhero titles that was unequaled in the comic book industry. Marvel Comics were the most popular among college students—a socially aware audience that Marvel strove to retain. For these reasons, the Marvel comic books, more than any other, serve as a barometer of the changing political and social mood during the Vietnam War. They will be dealt with in greater detail later in this chapter.

The Dell Publishing Company was the first to portray the Vietnam War in comic books. *Jungle War Stories* featured tales set in South Vietnam as early as July 1962, marking one of the war's earliest appearances in American popular culture. Unlike most Dell titles, which were targeted at young children, this war comic book aimed at a slightly older readership. Each issue of *Jungle War Stories* consisted of three or four short war stories that usually featured soldiers of the U. S. Special Forces. The emphasis of these stories was not on characterization—of which there was virtually none—or even on action. Above all, they sought to educate the audience about America's increasing involvement in the Vietnam conflict. Because the series ran during the earliest stage of American military involvement, it is likely that many of the teenagers who read the comic book gleaned from it their initial knowledge of the Vietnam situation. *Jungle War Stories* was a careful and deliberate propaganda effort for American policy in Vietnam.

The early issues of *Jungle War Stories* were devoted primarily to an explanation and justification of the U. S. presence in South Vietnam. One such story, entitled "Day of Reckoning," was unusual in that it was told from the viewpoint of a Russian military advisor to the Vietcong. The protagonist, who is referred to only as "Comrade," recounts the history of his life to some of his Vietcong troops. His life has been an endless frustration. As a boy he was chosen by the "Party" for special training in guerrilla warfare. It was a promising start for a career, because "this was the first step of the communist ladder." He was given his first great opportunity to prove himself when "the movement swept over China." He leads an attack against some of Chiang Kai-shek's supply junks, but his ambush is defeated when the supposedly "helpless" ships return fire with American-supplied machine guns. "Curse the Yankee. . . . Curse him!" exclaims the Comrade. Later he seeks to redeem himself in the eyes of his superiors by aiding the Communist guerrillas in Greece, but again he is frustrated by "American weapons speaking from the hands of Greek Government troops." Likewise, his efforts in the Malayan insurrection fail due to "Yankee arms." The Comrade angrily concludes, "It was the Yankee weapons that ended all hopes!" The Soviet's ravings are cut short by a Green Beret airborne assault on his position. The Vietcong are defeated, and the Comrade meets a fitting end when he himself is killed by American soldiers. The message in this story is that American military aid to South Vietnam is needed to confront the Communist Menace, which must be contained. The story supports the Truman Doctrine and suggests that Communism is a monolithic threat. It even hints that defeat in Vietnam might compel the Soviet "comrades," who are apparently directing the insurrection, finally to realize the futility of their efforts.

South Vietnam, however, needed more than just American weapons to stop the Vietcong. American military advisors were needed to instruct and lead the Army of the Republic of Vietnam (ARVN), which could not do anything right on its own. *Jungle War Stories* made this point clear as early as issue number one. In the first story, American Green Berets parachute into Phu-Yen province in order to lead some ARVN troops and soon conclude that "these people got no belly for fighting the Viet Cong guerrillas." Under American leadership, however, the South Vietnamese score their first success against the Communists.

The South Vietnamese civilian population similarly needed American guidance to put them on the path to victory and peace. In "A Walk in the Sun," some Green Berets come to a village with orders to move the inhabitants to a nearby strategic hamlet. Upon arriving in the village, one American soldier comments to another that "it's a crazy mixed-up war." His friend agrees, adding, "Half the peasants want no part of it . . . either side." He concludes that "there'll always be folks who figure the world owes them a living." Later, the Americans are confronted by the village leader, who tells them, "The sides of this cursed war are like grains of rice . . . no difference!" As the villagers are led through the jungle by the Americans, they witness some scenes that make a strong impression upon them: entire villages burned and destroyed by the Communists, contrasted by scenes of Green Berets giving medical attention and food to injured peasants. When the group finally arrives at the strategic hamlet, the Vietnamese peasants have undergone a profound change of attitude. The village leader acknowledges: "We were fools. You [Americans] showed us that today as you fed our hungry, buried our dead and saved our children from [the Vietcong's] horrors." He pledges the villagers' allegiance to the South and the American leadership, promising to "do our part to fight the Red dogs."

The Green Berets had won the hearts and minds of the Vietnamese people.

Not all Vietnamese were so quick to come to this conclusion, however. The South Vietnamese population remained deeply divided, and this was reflected in the comic book as well. "The Year of the Cat" is set in a village that is about to be turned into a strategic hamlet. It features two villagers—a female Songtoi and her lover, Van Xuan. Songtoi is angered by the Americans' presence in her village. Moreover, she is unhappy with the Saigon regime. She tells her lover: "Those with intelligence realize how evil the [South] Vietnamese are! And unworthy of our allegiance." Van Xuan remains committed to the South, arguing that "the government helps arm us so that we can defend ourselves against the raids of the Viet Cong!" Songtoi defends the ruthless tactics of the Communists by claiming that "people must be forced to accept what is just for them!" She eventually leaves her lover, joins the Vietcong, and is killed when they launch an unsuccessful attack on the village. Van Xuan mourns her death, but he is pleased with the battle's outcome: "It is good that the [South] Vietnamese armed us for such a time!"

It is interesting to note that both the loyalist Vietnamese and the Vietcong refer to those loyal to the Saigon regime as simply "the Vietnamese." South Vietnam is simply "Vietnam." In this sense the Vietcong are portrayed not as Vietnamese but as an exterior threat to the legitimate government and people of the South—the only true Vietnam.

In addition to the regular war stories, *Jungle War Stories* often contained pages of straightforward information on the Vietnam conflict. One such page, entitled "The Enemy in Vietnam," described the Vietcong guerrilla as a "scrawny, unkempt 100-pounder who barely comes up to the average G.I.'s shoulders." Despite his diminutive size, though, the enemy is "cruel, cunning and tough" and capable of traveling "up to forty miles a day on fabric rubber-soled shoes." This "fact page" went on to describe some of the tactics employed by the Vietcong. According to the comic book, the Communists would have children play "for days on end" near a fort that is targeted for an attack so that "the coming and going of its personnel can be carefully noted." Supposedly innocent Vietnamese children, therefore, may actually work for the enemy—an ambiguous foe indeed. Information pages like this one usually contained a combination of established facts and unsupported assertions. One, entitled "Viet Cong: The Face of the Enemy," introduces the reader to Vo Nguyen Giap, "the little-known author of the master plan for conquest by subversion." Vietcong tactics, as directed by Giap, include "a brutal succession of village burnings, road minings and bridge burnings . . . together with the capture of vital rice barges and incessant extortion of money and food from Vietnamese peasants." According to the comic book, "Viet Cong soldiers are frequently hard to distinguish from the rest of the Vietnamese population because of the typical black pajamas which they wear." While this information could have been read in the *New York Times,* the next panel states: "Reminiscent of the brutal war in North Korea is the 'Human Wave' technique practiced by the Viet Cong. Accompanied by the wild blowing of bugles, the North Vietnamese Communists attack in overwhelming numbers." This claim bore less resemblance to the true military situation in Vietnam than to the racist notion that Asians, whether they be Japanese, Chinese, North Korean, or North Vietnamese, must employ their "overwhelming numbers" on the battlefield in order to compensate for their inferiority as individual soldiers and human beings. In any case, this juxtaposition of fact and assertion in *Jungle War Stories* would have made it difficult for the otherwise uninformed reader to distinguish what was true and what was false about the situation in Vietnam.

The Vietcong in *Jungle War Stories* are portrayed as a dangerous and treacherous foe, more likely to cut their adversary's throat from behind than assault him frontally. In one story, the Vietcong take over a village and masquerade as the inhabitants in order to fool the U.S. Special Forces and the ARVN. In the next issue the Communists again disguise themselves, this time as ARVN soldiers, in order to deceive an American pilot. The next issue's story, entitled "The Enemy Has Many Faces," tells how the Vietcong, disguised as Buddhist monks, try to infiltrate a strategic hamlet. This absurd premise is taken even further in another story when the Vietcong kidnap some Vietnamese children and masquerade as their teachers in order to sneak into a school on the outskirts of Saigon. The point, which is overstated in these stories, is that the enemy in Vietnam can appear in any number of forms. What appears to be a harmless villager, teacher, or other Vietnamese civilian may well be a Communist waiting to stab a trusting American in the back. The series suggested that it was difficult to tell friend from foe in the Vietnam War.

The American soldier in *Jungle War Stories* exhibited superior qualities of military prowess, humanitarianism, and leadership. The troops of the U.S. Special Forces were usually featured as the protagonists in the stories. Several Green Berets, in particular, appeared as recurring characters, but their individual personalities are so shallow and indistinguishable from one another that the reader is not able to identify with any of them. Their deeds are not portrayed as individual accomplishments, but rather are representative of the entire American military effort in Vietnam. A page entitled "Vietnam Battle Facts," which appeared in a 1963 issue, stated simply that "our job in Vietnam is to supply and instruct [the South Vietnamese] in ways of halting the Red guerrillas' terror." The Green Berets pursue this directive successfully, whether they are organizing militarily incompetent ARVN troops or winning the hearts and minds of the population with the Strategic Hamlets program.

"The Attack Begins," proclaimed the cover of the January–March, 1965, issue of *Jungle War Stories.* The inside cover of the comic book displayed a picture of the *USS Maddox,* flanked by North Vietnamese gunboats. It briefly described the Tonkin Gulf incident as "the first major naval engagement of the Vietnam conflict."

The nature of the war had clearly changed, and the increasing American involvement in Vietnam was reflected in *Jungle War Stories*. The Green Berets were no longer as concerned with training and leading the South Vietnamese as they were with winning the war. American GIs were now fighting alongside the Special Forces. As early as 1965, the comic book drew attention to difficulties that would continue to frustrate the American military effort for the duration of the war. In one story an American pilot is forced to abandon his pursuit of retreating Vietcong soldiers when they cross the border into Laos. The Vietcong laugh at the American's predicament, noting "a little thing like a border . . . saps their strength and turns them into cowards." When the pilot returns to headquarters, he complains that "if that crazy [border is] gonna stop us every time we chase . . . well that's a dang fool way to fight a war!" As early as 1965, the series hinted that the war might be lost because government policy tied the hands of our troops.

The South Vietnamese themselves were portrayed as a significant obstacle to victory. The ARVN had always appeared as confused and inept in the series, but by 1965 the South Vietnamese leadership was seen to be dangerously corrupt, incompetent, and jealous of their American allies. In "Frontal Assault," the South Vietnamese military commanders devise a plan that they keep secret from the Americans because they want to "show our American colleagues that we Vietnamese can work out a battle scheme just as clever as [the Americans] might suggest." The plan, of course, fails miserably. Later, the American commanders discover that this and other ARVN military fiascos have come about because the plans were leaked to the enemy by a spy among the ARVN planning staff in Saigon. If the United States was going to win the war in Vietnam, according to this comic book, it would have to do so not with the help of its South Vietnamese allies, but in spite of them.

A curious item appeared in the April–June 1965 issue of *Jungle War Stories*. "A Letter from Vietnam" was a one-page letter from "Jim," an American serviceman in South Vietnam, to his teenage brother, "Billy." There were no accompanying pictures or explanation for the letter, and it is not clear whether it was fictional or an actual, reprinted letter. In it the soldier writes of his close friend Johnny, who, while stationed in Vietnam, spent his free time studying in order to earn his high school diploma. The soldier then describes an incident in which Johnny was killed in action before he had received his diploma. Jim urges his young brother to stay in high school until he earns his diploma and then to go to college. The last line of the letter reads, "I just don't want my kid brother to waste his life when it isn't necessary."

This downbeat letter was highly uncharacteristic of the usual content of *Jungle War Stories*. In one page, Dell offered a pessimistic account of a war that was crueler than anything that had been depicted in its comic books. The first comic-book publisher to come out in support of the American effort in Vietnam was also the first to discourage enlistment, however obliquely. With the rapidly escalating U.S. presence in Vietnam in 1965, it is possible that the staff at Dell feared the possible success of their own propaganda.

Because Dell did not give public credit to its comic book writers, it is not known whether there was a change of view in one writer's mind or a change in the creative staff behind *Jungle War Stories*. Whichever the case, the tone of the comic book shifted slightly after 1965. "Face of the Enemy," appearing in the same issue as "A Letter from Vietnam," tells of an American pilot who is forced to bail out over North Vietnam. He encounters a Communist soldier, who does not capture or kill the American but instead leads him safely back to the South Vietnamese border. The Communist returns to the North, where he maintains that he is doing his best to end the war, "for the benefit of all Vietnam." Never before in the comic book had the enemy been depicted with such humane characteristics.

Another story, "Big Surprise," features no Americans. It is about a South Vietnamese member of the Civilian Irregular Defense group, who is portrayed as a hero—albeit a reluctant one—who defeats a company of Vietcong single-handedly. His success is a result of accidental circumstances—he deceives the enemy because his appearance is identical to that of their commander—but, nevertheless, for the first time the South Vietnamese have demonstrated that, with a little luck, they can defeat the enemy without American help.

With the July–September 1965 issue, Dell changed the title of *Jungle War Stories* to *Guerrilla War,* a more appropriate title for a Vietnam War comic book, but the series was canceled by the beginning of 1966. The contribution of *Jungle War Stories* and *Guerrilla War* to the comic-book field was marginal. The series lasted only fourteen issues and was greatly overshadowed and outsold by the more popular superhero titles of Marvel and DC. Still, the series was significant for several reasons. It represented the first attempt by a publisher to portray the Vietnam conflict in comic books, and it did so several years before the Gulf of Tonkin Resolution truly made Vietnam an American war. The comic book was also the closest that the industry came to a propaganda effort in support to American policy in Vietnam. It should be noted that *Jungle War Stories,* like all privately published comic books, was in no way licensed by the U. S. government for propaganda purposes. Indeed, the comic book contained some themes and ideas, such as the unfavorable portrayal of our South Vietnamese allies, that would not have been encouraged by the Johnson administration. Still, by incorporating an impressive amount of information into the comic books—whether it was true or not—the creators of *Jungle War Stories* gave even their fictional features an air of authority that could lead the reader to believe that these stories, which usually followed the official government line, were an accurate reflection of the situation in Vietnam. It is impossible to determine what influence this series had upon its adolescent audience, but it is likely that many readers who came of age during the height of the Vietnam War initially learned of the conflict in the pages of this comic book.

The last significant point to make about *Jungle War Stories* is that it was the first Vietnam War comic book to fail commercially. Although the series lasted for over three years, a run of only fourteen issues is a fair to poor one by industry standards. That the title was canceled at the same time that the American military presence in Vietnam was nearly 200,000 strong and growing is probably not a coincidence. The more that people were bombarded by images and information about the war in the mass media, the less they wanted to be exposed to it in escapist popular entertainment. Whether its cancellation was a result of a conscious editorial decision or falling sales or a combination of both, the demise of *Jungle War Stories* was an early indication that the Vietnam War would be difficult to sell to the American people.

Subsequent efforts to portray the Vietnam War in comic form were also short-lived. The Green Berets continued to be the popular protagonist for Vietnam War comic books. Robin Moore's well-received novel *The Green Berets* and Sgt. Barry Sadler's hit song "Ballad of the Green Berets" seemed to demonstrate the marketability of the U.S. Special Forces. According to Robin Moore, he was approached in 1966 by General Yarborough, the commander of the J. F. K. Special Warfare Center at Fort Bragg, to start a comic strip "extolling the heroism of the Green Berets." Moore, working with artist Joe Kubert, an illustrator who had done work for DC's line of war comic books, produced a syndicated newspaper strip entitled "Tales of the Green Beret," which was based upon Moore's novel. Although Kubert maintained that he and Moore were not "taking any side, either hawk or dove," the strip read like propaganda for the Johnson administration's Vietnam policy.

The "Tales" strip was not well received. Newspapers that carried it began to drop the strip when they received complaints from readers. Some deplored the strip's "paramilitary bloodthirstiness," while others complained that it played "propaganda on the comic page." Newspaper editors also feared reader indifference. As the managing editor of the *Charlotte Observer*

WRIGHT Vietnam in the Comic Books **307**

put it: "People were reading about the war on the front page and throughout the newspaper. By the time they got to the comic page they wanted relief." Joe Kubert admitted that portraying the Vietnam War in comics created problems of reader empathy, because the United States in Vietnam was "the big guy fighting the little guy and the American has always been for the underdog."

"Tales of the Green Beret" was terminated by the end of 1967. Robin Moore blamed the cancellation of his strip on "the left-leaning portion of the academic community [who] . . . waged a vituperative campaign against the newspapers carrying [it]." Efforts by the comic-book industry to portray the Vietnam War in its publications, however, met with a similar lack of success. Dell tried once again to sell the war to readers with its own comic-book adaptation of Moore's "Tales" strip. Dell's *Tales of the Green Beret* depicted the bitter fighting in Vietnam in a more grim and realistic manner than did *Jungle War Stories.* In one story a Green Beret is even prepared to kill innocent Vietnamese civilians in order to get at the Vietcong, claiming that there was "no such thing as a non-combatant in this war!" The comic book, which proclaimed on the cover of its first issue that "if we must fight . . . we will win!," was a loser with readers. Dell published only five issues of *Tales* over a period of two and a half years before it canceled the title.

The Milson Publishing Company was a short-lived operation that tried in 1967 to capitalize on the public fascination with the Green Berets and the popularity of superhero comic books. Milson's *Super Green Beret* featured a teenager who turns into a full-grown superpowered Green Beret soldier when he dons a magical green beret. This, the most absurd of all Vietnam War comic books, failed miserably. It lasted only two issues, and Milson folded shortly thereafter.

DC and Marvel, the two leading publishers by 1968, avoided the Vietnam War for the most part. DC published five war comic books, but only one of them ever featured stories set in Vietnam. From the start of 1966 to the middle of 1967, *Our Fighting Forces* starred Captain Hunter, a retired

Green Beret who has been captured by the Vietcong. Although Captain Hunter frequently encounters the Vietcong, the search for his brother, not the war itself, motivates him and serves as the dramatic focus of the series. The published reader response to the "Captain Hunter" feature was generally favorable, but some maintained that the Vietnam War belonged in the newspapers and not in comic books. Others criticized the writers for portraying Captain Hunter as being too preoccupied with finding his brother at the expense of helping America win the war. Hunter, ultimately unable to appeal to either hawks or doves, found his brother and was banished from *Our Fighting Forces.* Such a theme was consistent with the other DC war comic books featuring stories set during World War II, a more popular war with a clearly defined purpose.

Marvel's only 1960s war comic book was also set in World War II. *Sgt. Fury and His Howling Commandos* featured a cast of diverse characters who starred in action-packed adventures that, as one writer has noted, "read like an unintentional parody of bad war movies." The 1967 *Sgt. Fury King-Size Special,* however, was set during contemporary times and featured Fury and his commandos in Vietnam. Fury, now the head of SHIELD—a high-tech espionage agency modeled after television's "UNCLE"—is approached by President Johnson to undertake a secret mission into North Vietnam in order to prevent what Washington believes is an attempt by Hanoi to build a hydrogen bomb. Fury then recruits the old members of his World War II commando unit from their civilian lives. Johnson insists that the mission must be performed by civilians, because "we cannot afford to risk escalation of the war by having our troops invade North Vietnam."

The reunited "Howling Commandos," now middle-aged but apparently still capable of taking on the Vietnamese, parachute into Haiphong in order to sabotage the suspected nuclear weapons plant. Outside the factory, two North Vietnamese sentries are having a conversation; one asks the other if he thinks that the Americans might invade the North. The soldier laughs and replies: "But of course not . . . I hear that many of them would rather invade Washington!" While the comic book implied that the American war effort might be threatened by domestic dissent, it was certainly not in danger of being defeated militarily by the enemy. The North Vietnamese soldiers in the story are hopelessly inept. An entire North Vietnamese battalion is unable to prevent the escape of any one of the seven Americans who successfully complete their mission. Indeed, the Vietnamese enemy is remarkably similar to the bungling Germans who were the prototypical antagonists in the regular Sgt. Fury series. While the idea of American civilians conducting covert missions in Vietnam was revived with popular success in the 1980s with movies like *Rambo* and *Missing in Action,* the comic book audience was not ready for it in 1967. Marvel, highly conscious of its sales figures and reader response, was not impressed enough with the reaction to the story to publish a similar comic book. Sergeant Fury returned permanently to the more familiar and more marketable Second World War.

The failure of Vietnam War comic books to command the interest and support of readers was similar to the trouble that the Johnson administration had rallying popular support for its Vietnam policy. The Vietnam conflict was a grim struggle for unclear objectives against an enemy that was not well defined. The American Green Beret was marketed in comics as the ideal heroic figure in an otherwise inglorious war. Readers, however, identified more with the superpowered comic book heroes who at times seemed more believable than their counterparts in the war comic books. While Vietnam War comic books represented only a very marginal portion of the industry's output during the 1960s, the war itself had a tremendous impact on American society that was, in turn, reflected in the more popular and prolific superhero comic books.

Marvel comic books are the most useful for the purpose of this chapter, because they differed from those of DC and other publishers in some key respects. Marvel was the first to publish code-approved comic books that appealed to an audi-

ence that was more sophisticated than the code presumed. Feedback from this older readership, which included an avid following among college students, was an important factor determining the content of the comic books. Unlike the DC superheroes who remained entrenched within the realm of fantasy for much of the 1960s, the Marvel superheroes were placed in identifiable contemporary settings like New York City, the New Mexican desert, or even Vietnam. Marvel was also the first publisher to give any of its superhero comic books a political focus during the Vietnam War period. An analysis of these Marvel comic books and the reader response to them will illustrate the degree to which they reflected the contemporary American political and social mood between 1963 and 1975.

Stan Lee wrote in 1975 that "Marvel Comics has never been very much into politics. . . . We have no official party line—I issue no editorial edicts as to what the political tone of our stories should be." Marvel comic books of the early 1960s, however, frequently had a political focus that followed the line of the Johnson administration. The early superhero plots, which were written almost exclusively by Lee, regularly featured the hero as the defender of American interests against evil Communist forces.

The Hulk in his first appearance prevents a spy named Igor from stealing the formula for America's secret "Gamma-ray bomb." In subsequent issues the Hulk battles Soviet troops that seek to capture him, and Red Chinese forces under "General Fang" that try to overrun a peaceful Himalayan nation. Comic book historians have pointed out that these stories were inappropriate for this comic book because "the [Hulk] was cast as an antihero with no concern for human society [but] Lee insisted upon pitting him against evil communists." Thor was another Marvel superhero who was made to endure a series of implausible adventures laden with the clichés of Cold War propaganda. In one issue, the Norse God of Thunder helps the inhabitants of a fictional Latin American nation overthrow a ruthless Communist dictator. Later he thwarts a Soviet plot to capture some top American scientists. In another story, Thor even defends an Indian outpost against an attack by the Red Chinese.

On one occasion, in 1965, Thor's adventures took him to the jungles of Vietnam. After being knocked unconscious by a Vietcong mortar shell, the Thunder God wakes up to find himself in the hut of a Vietnamese family. The villagers think that Thor is a "messenger of Buddha" who has been sent in answer to their prayers to "destroy the guerrillas" who have been terrorizing them. Looking about the village, Thor observes that "there is little food. . . . The Red guerrillas have brought famine to the land." He sees some American helicopters on patrol but notes that "they are so few, and the communist foe is so many . . . and so cunning."

The villain in the story is a ruthless Vietcong commander whose troops routinely round up hostages from captured Vietnamese villages. Among those captured is the family that aided Thor. It is revealed that the Vietcong officer is actually the family's eldest son, who had abandoned them years earlier in order to join the communist cause. The younger brother, who remains loyal to the Saigon regime, accuses the elder of betraying his family by "serving the Red terrorists." The Communist shoots and kills his brother in a fit of rage, shouting: "You do not matter! Nobody matters! Only the communist cause is important! People mean nothing! Human lives mean nothing!" Thor eventually rescues the family and defeats the Vietcong. The commander, overcome with grief as a result of his actions, comes to his senses, renounces communism, and commits suicide. His last words are: "It was communism that made me what I am . . . that shaped me into a brutal, unthinking instrument of destruction . . . may it vanish from the face of the earth and the memory of mankind!"

At the end of the story Thor vows, "I shall return, and when I do, the hammer of Thor shall be heard in every village . . . in every home . . . in every heart throughout this tortured land!" Despite his dramatic pledge, however, the Thunder God never did return to Vietnam. It is possible

that even at this early stage of the conflict, comic book readers understood that the situation was far more complex than this cliché-ridden plot suggested. Perhaps the 1960s readership was too sophisticated to accept the kind of simplistic scenarios that had been popular in the comic books of World War II. In any case, the Thor comic book with its trappings of Norse mythology was a highly inappropriate vehicle for conveying political messages.

Another Marvel superhero was much better suited for this. Stan Lee created "Iron Man" in 1973 and gave the character and the series a political focus that it would retain, in one way or another, throughout the Vietnam War years. A brief analysis of the "Iron Man" series during this period will illsutrate how the political tone of the comic book changed according to the evolving political and social mood of America.

The origin of Iron Man was set in South Vietnam. Anthony Stark is introduced as a millionaire industrialist and scientist who invents and manufactures weapons for the U.S. government. He travels to South Vietnam in order to demonstrate his latest invention to some high-ranking American military advisors. While accompanying a group of ARVN soldiers into the jungle to observe his weapons in action, Stark accidentally sets off a Vietcong land mine, which leaves him critically wounded. When he awakens, Stark discovers that he has been captured by Vietcong forces led by a ruthless tyrant named Wong Chu. The Communists know that a piece of shrapnel lodged near Stark's heart gives him only days to live, but they convince him to construct a weapon for them in return for an operation that will save his life. Stark agrees to build a weapon, but he secretly plans not to turn it over to the Communists, but to use it for himself. The "weapon" that Stark constructs is actually a suit of armor that keeps his heart beating and gives him augmented strength, among other powers. Taking the name "Iron Man," Stark escapes, defeats the Vietcong, kills Wong Chu, and destroys the Communist base. Like other Marvel superheroes, however, Iron Man pays a price for his new powers—he must forever wear the metal chest plate under his clothes in order to keep his heart beating.

The elements in this story set the tone for future Iron Man comic books. The Communist villain Wong Chu is the epitome of evil: ugly, rotund, and smoking cigarettes, he has no concern whatsoever for human life. The Red guerrilla cares nothing about the Vietnamese people. Even the advancement of communism is important only as a means to achieving personal power. Tony Stark, meanwhile, is the very symbol of America, a noble hero helping the South Vietnamese with his superior wealth and technology. Marvel's portrayal of the Vietnam conflict is not only childishly simplistic, but ethnocentric as well. The war is not so much a Vietnamese phenomenon as it is a battleground in the greater global struggle between the democratic West and the Communist East. Vietnam is a domino that America must not allow to fall.

Tony Stark devoted both of his lives to keeping the United States ahead in the Cold War. As Stark the industrialist and inventor, he builds new weapons like his "atomic naval cannon" for the Defense Department. In his Iron Man identity, he battles "America's enemies from within and without." His efforts as both Stark and Iron Man were appreciated by the government officials with whom he often worked. In one story, Iron Man is thanked by an FBI agent for thwarting a "commie spy ring." Later, a general at the Pentagon compliments Stark on his latest invention: "The Reds would probably give up half of Asia if they could steal the plans of what you've invented so far." No other superhero was so closely associated with the U.S. government.

Iron Man fought a series of Communist villains in battles symbolic of the struggle between the West and the East. Among these adversaries were the Red Barbarian—a Soviet general who works directly for Comrade K; the Crimson Dynamo—Iron Man's armor-clad Soviet counterpart; the Black Widow—a Soviet spy and seductress; and the Titanium Man—another armored Soviet supersoldier. Even Nikita Khrushchev made on occasional appearance; he once worked out a plan

to sabotage Stark industries so that "the U.S. would lag behind . . . in the arms race." In each of these stories, Iron Man triumphs on behalf of the U.S. government. Even when things went badly, the armored hero maintained his patriotic zeal. Once, when he was captured, he defiantly exclaimed: "If this is to be my finish, I'll show how an American faces death! I'll show that nothing can shatter the faith of a man who fights for freedom!"

From time to time Iron Man would return to the war-torn country where his heroic career was born. In a 1967 story he thwarts a plot by the Titanium Man and a Red Chinese villain called Half-Face to score a Communist propaganda victory by destroying a peaceful Vietnamese village at night and making it appear that American bombers were responsible for the carnage. Iron Man saves the village, preserves America's good international reputation, and takes the opportunity to smash some Vietcong in the process.

For the most part, though, Iron Man left the fighting in Vietnam to the American military, while he engaged Communist enemies in a more symbolic show of support for U. S. policy. When the Titanium Man issued a public challenge to Iron Man, Stark felt compelled to accept, because it was a "matter of national pride and prestige." He defeats his much larger Soviet foe and exclaims: "You thought you'd just have to flex your muscles and show your strength, and your enemies would fall by the wayside!. . . You made the worst mistake any Red can make . . . you challenged a foe who isn't afraid of you!" Iron Man's stand underscored the need to preserve American prestige by containing the Communist menace however and wherever it threatens American interests.

Two things happened in 1968 that forever changed the political tone of the *Iron Man* series. One was the Tet Offensive. The other was the expansion of the Marvel Comics publishing operation. The magnitude of the National Liberation Front offensive stunned the American people and called into serious question the administration's entire Vietnam policy, which had been so doggedly defended by Iron Man. Disillusioned Americans, especially among the young generation, felt that they had been misled and misinformed by the government. It would have been commercially unwise to present the same government line in a comic book. At the same time, Marvel's financial success allowed the publisher to expand and hire new writers and artists. *Iron Man* was one of the titles that was handed over to these new young comic-book writers, who tended to be politically liberal. The content of *Iron Man* comic-books was thereafter affected by changes in both the Marvel staff and the mood of comic-book readers.

After 1968 all Cold War themes were abandoned in the *Iron Man* series. Even when Soviet foes like the Crimson Dynamo returned, they acted more like other apolitical supervillains than the Communist stereotypes that they had once been. Iron Man himself spent less time working for the U.S. government and turned his attention inward toward such domestic issues as race relations and pollution control. The new writers played upon the Tony Stark/Iron Man character as a well-meaning but misdirected defender of the establishment. He is pitted against a new enemy called the Firebrand, who claims to have been "an all-American boy who started out to make this nation a better place . . . sat in for civil rights, marched for peace, and demonstrated on campus, and got spat on by bigots, [and] beat on by 'patriots' ". Firebrand whips up riots and hysteria among young demonstrators because he has concluded that America "doesn't want to be changed. The only way to build anything decent is to tear down what's here and start over."

Although Firebrand was portrayed as a dangerous villain, his message elicited some reader empathy. One letter pointed out that "while Firebrand was marching, trying to bring about a more peaceful world, Stark Industries was probably building weapons for Vietnam where we 'destroyed a city in order to save it'." Before 1968, most of the printed response to the series did not comment on the hero's politics, although an occasional letter praised his patriotism: "Not since

George M. Cohan has anyone so waved their country's flag—and it wouldn't hurt if there were more of this sort of thing." By the early 1970s, however, *Iron Man's* readers became increasingly concerned with the character's political stance. One wrote that "Tony Stark is going to have to do some pretty big restructuring of his life to avoid being classified as an enemy of the people." Another insisted that "the time is right for Tony Stark to quit being a weapons manufacturer." Although some conservative readers did not object to Iron Man's role as a defender of authority, most of the printed mail demanded a change.

Anthony Stark was, according to one reader, "a profiteering, capitalistic, war-mongering defense contractor . . . [who] produces devices to kill people." Recognizing that the political mood of their readership had shifted, *Iron Man's* writers tried to improve the hero's image. In one issue, Iron Man argues with a right-wing U.S. senator who claims that "there's a new breed of people in this country today. . . . who want to destroy the government that made America great." Iron Man counters that the American people, not the government, make the country great. The senator then calls him an anarchist. This was a change, indeed, from the superhero who once claimed that "no one has the right to defy the wishes of his government."

Iron Man's political about-face is confirmed after a student demonstration outside of Stark Industries turns into a riot, and the crowd is fired on by Stark's own security force. The demonstrators cry out, "it's another Kent State!" and stone Iron Man when he arrives on the scene. He criticizes the students for "preaching peace while resorting to violence," but one of them justifies their action as "the only way we can make your generation hear us." These events leave the hero deeply disturbed. He later reevaluates his image as a defender of government policy and a weapons manufacturer: "I designed . . . weapons that can be used to kill the people . . . to save another. . . . I find myself pondering every action I ever made." Finally, Stark resolves to end his corporation's association with weapons research and development and to diversify into areas such as pollution control and consumer goods.

A powerful story entitled "Long Time Gone" serves as a fitting epilogue for the political metamorphosis of Iron Man. Published in 1975 simultaneously with the fall of Saigon, the story opens with Tony Stark sitting alone in his office, pondering his own experiences in Vietnam. Looking into a mirror, he questions himself and searches his soul for the answers: "As Iron Man you beat the commies for democracy without ever questioning just whose democracy you were serving . . . or just what those you served intended to do with the world once you'd saved it for them. Vietnam raised all those questions . . . like: what right had we to be there in the first place?"

Stark relives through a flashback sequence a time when, as Iron Man, he observed the horrors of the Vietnam War firsthand. He sees confused and weary American troops fight and die. He sees a high-tech artillery piece of his own design lay waste to a village, killing enemy and innocent alike. He comes across a blind Vietnamese boy who has been orphaned by the day's fighting. Moved to tears by the death and carnage that have resulted in part from his own action, Iron Man buries the dead in a mass grave and marks it with the epitaph "Why?" Returning to the present, Tony Stark don his Iron Man armor, strikes a dramatic pose, and pledges "to avenge those whose lives have been lost through the ignorance of men like the man I once was . . . or I will die trying!" The end of the Vietnam War brings with it Iron Man's final repudiation of the government actions that he had once so zealously defended.

It would seem that a comic book featuring a star-spangled hero named Captain America should have been an appropriate series for a political focus. In 1964, Marvel revived this World War II comic book hero, who was a living symbol of patriotism and the American ideal. Stan Lee, though, seemed unsure of what to do with the Captain America character. Captain America confronts apolitical villains in New York for a few issues. Then he travels to Vietnam—not to fight alongside American troops as he did in the Second World War, but to rescue a friend who has been captured by the Vietcong. While American objectives in the war remained ambiguous, a rescue mission presented the hero with a clear and attainable goal. While he's there, of course, he battles some Communists, who are portrayed much like the other evil Red caricatures of early Marvel Comic books. Beyond this, however, there is no mention of the need to defend South Vietnam from the Communist threat, a message that was overstated in the *Iron Man* comic book.

After his brief adventure in Vietnam, Captain America is sent back to World War II, where he once again battles Hitler's hordes for nine issues, before returning to contemporary times. In an effort to find the proper tone and setting for Captain America, Stan Lee had unintentionally portrayed the patriotic hero as an appropriate symbol of a confused America that preferred to relive past glories, rather than recognize and adapt to the new world situation.

Captain America, more than any other comic book, generated a political controversy among its readers. As early as 1965, a letter from an American serviceman suggested that "the war in Vietnam would make an endless amount of adventures for . . . Cap." Lee responded, though, that other readers wanted Captain America to stay out of Vietnam. After 1968 the difference in opinion over the hero's role became more pronounced. Some readers argued that Cap should stop being a defender of the Establishment. One letter asserted, "It would fit the standards of today . . . if [Captain America was] more liberal." Another, more sophisticated response pointed out that Cap "is a very strange mixture of individualism and statism, in that when he lectures on freedom, he seems to be talking about the nation rather than the people who make it up."

Marvel also printed letters from those who continued to urge Captain America to go to Vietnam. One of these stressed that "Captain America should be devoted to uniting our nation against foes who are killing our soldiers in Vietnam. Regardless if . . . our foreign policy is right or wrong, we should stand behind the men who are dying to preserve our liberty." Stan Lee maintained, however, that informal polls taken by Marvel over the years indicated that the great majority of readers wanted Cap to stay out of the fighting in Vietnam.

Stan Lee wrote most of the *Captain America* comic books until 1972. By then the tone of the character had changed in a way similar to that of Iron Man's. Lee wrote in 1971 that Captain America "simply doesn't lend himself to the John Wayne-type character he once was. . . . We just cannot see any of our characters taking on a role of super-patriotism in the world as it is today." Consequently, Captain America went through a period of soul-searching and self-doubt about his role in the Vietnam era:

Throughout the world, the image of Captain America has become a symbol . . . a living embodiment of all that democracy stands for. But now . . . there are those who scorn love of our flag . . . love of country . . . those to whom patriotism is just a square, out-moded word. Those who think of me . . . as a useless relic . . . of a meaningless past. . . . This is the day of the antihero . . . the age of the rebel and the dissenter. It isn't hip to defend the establishment . . . only to tear it down. And in a world rife with injustice, greed, and endless war . . . who's to say the rebels are wrong? . . . I've spent a lifetime defending the flag . . . and the law. Perhaps . . . I should have battled less . . . and questioned more.

Stan Lee maintained that because Americans could not agree on a common enemy in Vietnam and because the administration's objectives were unclear, "Captain America would not be serving America by taking sides. For the sake of unity, Cap [remained] on the home front." Therefore, when Captain America does go to Vietnam in one story, he avoids conflict with either side and tries only to facilitate the peace negotiations. Captain America, instead, turned his attention toward America's domestic concerns. Together with his black superhero sidekick the Falcon, who leads a civilian life as a social worker in Harlem, Captain America tackled such problems as inner-city crime, poverty, and social dislocation. The Captain Amer-

ica of the 1970s symbolized a nation, weary of confusing and painful overseas adventures, that had turned inward to confront serious domestic ills, brought on, in part, by a decade of war.

Captain America's disassociation from the U.S. government was completed after the revelations of the Watergate scandal. The hero discovers that an organization called CRAP—the Committee to Regain America's Principles—led by a man named Quentin Harderman, is actually a front for the "Secret Empire," a fascist organization that seeks to overthrow the U.S. government. Tracking down the mysterious leader of the Secret Empire leads Captain America to the White House and the Oval Office. Although the face of the villain is obscured in shadow, the reader is left with little doubt as to the true identity of the man who sought to overthrow the U.S. Constitution. Captain America is so stunned and dissillusioned that he temporarily changes his name to "Nomad—the man without a country." He later readopts the name Captain America, however, and pledges to help restore legitimacy to the perennial American ideals of freedom and democracy that have been corrupted by a self-serving government.

The radical shift in the political tone and character of *Iron Man* and *Captain America* was a result of changes in popular American values and changes in the comic-book industry itself. After 1968 it became fashionable among the younger generation to oppose the Establishment, which had brought America the Vietnam War. The culture of dissent, which was reflected in popular music and film, was also mirrored in comic books. Cognizant of the views held by the majority of their readers, Stan Lee and the new generation of comic book creators abandoned the Cold War clichés of early Marvel stories. Evil communist caricatures were replaced by villainous right-wing authority figures. Before this could happen, however, Marvel had to confront an authority figure of its own—the Comic Code Authority.

By the beginning of the 1970s it had become clear that the comic book audience had outgrown the naive presumptions of the code. The code's insistence that "in every instance good shall triumph over evil" and that "policemen, judges, government officials, and respected institutions shall never be presented in such a way as to create disrespect for established authority" could not be taken seriously by a generation that had watched the Chicago police riot of 1968, read about the Pentagon Papers, and followed a war that defied such simplistic concepts as "good" and "evil."

Adapting to growing reader sophistication led Marvel to brush against certain code restrictions. A character called Tribune, who appeared in the *Daredevil* comic book, was typical of the new right-wing comic book villains. The Tribune is a self-styled judge, jury, and executioner who "convicts" and sentences to death antiwar demonstrators, draft dodgers, and anyone else whom he judges to be a "commie pinko." In the *Spider-Man* comic book, a character named Sam Bullitt is introduced as a retired police officer who runs for New York City district attorney. His platform is one of "law and order" that promises to stamp out "left-wing anarchists who are trying to destroy this great proud nation of ours." It is revealed that Bullitt is not only a crypto-fascist, but also a crook with ties to organized crime. Although these story lines were not technically in violation of the code, because the Tribune is not really a judge and Bullitt is not an acting policeman or an elected official, they clearly presented the authority figure as an antagonist and thus ran contrary to the spirit of the code.

In 1971 Stan Lee wrote several issues of *The Amazing Spider-Man* that dealt with the problem of drug abuse. The code implicitly forbade any mention of drugs in comic books, and the stories were rejected by the Code Authority. Lee published the comic books without the authority's seal of approval, and they sold well in spite of it. Marvel's successful defiance compelled the Code Authority to revise its outdated standards. Among the provisions that were dropped was one that forbade the unfavorable portrayal of authority figures. Comic-book writers at both Marvel and DC, which together accounted for about two-thirds of all comic books sold at that time, took advantage

of the liberalized guidelines to produce stories that were more reflective of the concerns of American society.

The Comics Code Authority was established in 1954, when it was unpopular and unwise to criticize traditional American values and institutions. By 1971 the Cold War consensus had broken down, and it had become popular to question authority and to challenge the Establishment. The young generation's disillusionment and alienation during the Vietnam War years gave rise to the culture of dissent, which was reflected in the superhero comic books of Marvel and, by this time, of DC as well. The contemporary media took notice of the comic-book industry's trend toward relevance but pointed out that its new social awareness was self-conscious and self-serving as well. Slumping sales by the end of the 1960s led the major publishers to do market surveys of their collegiate readership. Whatever their motivations, the comic-book creators' attempts to reflect contemporary values and concerns forced a revision of the code, which ultimately broadened the potential of comic-book as a medium and an art form.

Comic books since the end of the Vietnam War have tended to deal with the conflict in a manner similar to that of other popular entertainment media. The Vietnam veteran in comic books has generally been portrayed as a figure who is left alienated from society by his Vietnam experience. The first veteran to return from the war was Flash Thompson, a supporting character in the *Spider-Man* comic book. Flash, a friend of Peter Parker (Spider-Man), is an all-American boy—a high school football star, voted most likely to succeed, popular with his classmates and with women in particular. He forsakes a college football scholarship to serve his country in the Vietnam War. When he returns, Flash is a very different character. He has trouble adjusting to civilian life. He keeps to himself and snaps at his friends when they offer to help him. Later, it is revealed that Flash is deeply disturbed by his participation in a war that had victimized the peaceful Vietnamese people. Flash never really could readjust to American society after the war. By

1986 he had bounced "from one dead-end job to the next," suffered a failed relationship with a Vietnamese American woman, and felt betrayed by his friends who had stayed at home during the war and enjoyed more happiness and success than himself.

While Flash Thompson's war experience left him embittered and depressed, another comic book veteran has suffered an even deeper alienation. Frank Castle was a captain in the U.S. Marine Corps who served in Vietnam for five years. Soon after the end of the war, his wife and children are murdered by the mob after they accidentally witness a gangland killing. The traumatized marine hunts down and kills the murderers himself, and thereafter, armed with a Vietnam-era M-16, assorted pistols, knives, and grenades and calling himself "the Punisher," he wages a one-man war against crime. The Punisher's ruthless and sometimes psychotic vigilantism frequently brought him into conflict with superheroes as well as criminals during the 1970s, when he was first introduced. In the 1980s the Punisher was revised slightly into a more heroic and sympathetic figure, and he had become one of Marvel's most popular character. Mirroring popular films like *Rambo* and *Missing in Action,* the Punisher acts outside of the law, because his experience in Vietnam has taught him that the government cannot or will not get the job done. The streets of New York become a war zone, criminals are the elusive enemy, and the Punisher is the soldier who is forever fighting his own personal war against crime.

Compared with World War II and Korea, the Vietnam War itself elicited a marginal response from the publishers. Few Vietnam War comic books were published, and none succeeded commercially. To avoid alienating any segment of their politically divided readership, Marvel and DC rarely mentioned the Vietnam War in their contemporary comic books. The impact that the war had on American society, however, was reflected in the content of these comic books and was ultimately recognized by the revised Comic Code Authority. The national consensus that had united America during World War II and the Cold War dissolved during the Vietnam War. The diversity of view on the war was mirrored in the comic books, ranging from the propaganda of *Jungle War Stories* to the antiwar and anti-Establishment Marvel comic books of the early 1970s. Considering the preponderance of the Vietnam War in the American media overall, though, the comic-book industry's treatment of the conflict was quite restrained. In final analysis, comic books, indeed, reflected America's subconscious wishes: some endorsed the war, and others criticized it, but many simply offered readers an escape from the tragedy of Vietnam.

STUDY QUESTIONS

1. What was "the code" and how did it affect the comic-book industry?

2. Describe the publishing objectives of Dell Comics and Marvel Comics in the early 1960s.

3. In the early stages of the Vietnam War, how did Dell Comics and Marvel Comics portray the conflict?

4. How did *Jungle War* Stories change in its portrayal of the Vietnam War in the late 1960s?

5. How was Marvel Comics unique in the comic-book industry and how did it portray the Vietnam War from the mid-1960s to mid-1970s?

6. Describe the evolution of the Iron Man character.

7. Describe the political controversy in the comic-book industry over Captain America.

BIBLIOGRAPHY

William W. Savage, Jr., in *Comic Books and America, 1945–1954* (1990), studies the comic-book genre in the Cold War. For a general discussion of the history of the comic book in the United States, see Joseph Witek, *Comic Books as History* (1989) and Michael Benton, *The Comic Book in America* (1989). Will Jacobs and Gerard Jones, *The Comic Book Heroes* (1985), is a useful survey of the primary comic characters. Stan Lee, *Origins of Marvel Comics* (1974), provides a history of one of the giants in the industry. There is a wealth of excellent published material on the impact of the Vietnam War on American films, television, and literature. For the best of these materials, see Philip Beidler, *American Literature and the Experience of Vietnam* (1982); Timothy J. Lomperis, *"Reading the Wind": The Literature of the Vietnam War* (1987); Albert Auster and Leonard Quart, *How the War Was Remembered: Hollywood and Vietnam* (1988); Peter T. Rollins, "The Vietnam War: Perceptions Through Literature, Film, and Television," *American Quarterly,* 36 (Fall 1984), 419–432; and Deborah Ballard-Reisch, *"China Beach* and *Tour of Duty:* American Television and Revisionist History of the Vietnam War," *Journal of Popular Culture,* 25 (Winter 1991), 135–150.

READING 27

THE BEATLES' REVOLUTION

John Weiner

In the winter of the year 2000 the top selling CD was a collection of number one hits of the 1960's British group the Beatles. In addition, one of the leading selling books was a year-by-year chronicle of the Beatles. Two questions arise. First, who were these Beatles; and second, why are they still important? Why, more than thirty years after they disbanded their group, are they still the one group that seems to be different from the rest? Why in an age of instant fame, when one day's teen idol is the next day's where-are-they-now, has the fame of the Beatles remained?

They were four lads from Liverpool—John Lennon, Paul McCartney, George Harrison, and Ringo Starr—who came together, developed a unique look and style, enjoyed brilliant promotion and management, and achieved success and riches beyond their widest, most inflated dreams. Singings such songs about adolescent love as "Love Me Do," "Please Please Me," "She Loves You," and "I Want To Hold Your Hand" they conquered Great Britain and Western Europe then came to the United States and overpowered America. Their February 1964 appearance on *The Ed Sullivan Show* was sensational, and for the rest of the decade they remained the top cultural story. What made them truly unique was that they made it to the top of their world and then grew and changed and experimented—with musical styles, with drugs, with religions, and with politics. Being themselves revolutionary, they tried to deliver revolutionary messages through their songs and lives. In the following selection historian Jon Wiener discusses who the Beatles were and what they became.

Sgt. Pepper and Flower Power

Songs about childhood: that was the first project John and Paul undertook in 1966. Each did one, and the Beatles put more effort into recording them than they had given to most of their albums. The songs came out as opposite sides of the same single, with Paul's "Penny Lane" on the A side. He sang sweetly and affectionately about the "blue suburban skies" of his childhood shopping center.

John's feelings about his childhood were not sweet. His childhood experiences hurt him. How badly he would not be able to say until the *Plastic Ono Band* album in 1970. But the song he recorded at the end of 1966 represented a step in that direction: "Strawberry Fields Forever."

The song was part of his first attempt to move beyond the Beatles. He wrote it in Spain, during the shooting of *How I Won the War.* He worked on the song for six full weeks—"time to think," he called it.

When he sang "I'm going to Strawberry Fields," he was singing about a real place in Liverpool: a grim orphanage. It was not far from his Aunt Mimi's, with whom he lived from the age of five, after his father abandoned him and his mother decided to have his aunt raise him. His sense of loss over these childhood traumas was expressed for the first time in the song. He was taking his first steps toward the awful screams "Mama, don't go / Daddy, come home" on the opening track of the *Plastic Ono Band* album.

When he sang "Nothing is real," he was doing something he had never done before: naming the childhood feeling that had intensified during his life as a Beatle. The line anticipated the project of "becoming real," which he declared in 1970. But in 1966 he couldn't imagine overcoming that sense of unreality. He could barely express his feelings of isolation—"No one I think is in my tree"—and hopelessness—"it doesn't matter much to me."

Few understood what John was doing. He wanted it that way. He had carefully concealed his ideas in a dizzy, dreamy *tour de force* of sound that saturated the listener with music. But the Beatles had ceased to exist as a band on that song; John was alone, his music coming from electronic devices in the recording studio, not from the Fab Four. The promotional video for the song helped conceal John's real purpose, opening with the Beatles romping in a big field on a beautiful sunny day. He knew what people wanted from the Beatles: their playful optimism, not the terrifying truth about his feelings of abandonment, isolation, and hopelessness.

After the Beatles released "Strawberry Fields Forever," Paul got an idea for a new album: bring the songs together around a single concept. The Beatles would assume the identities of another band, old-time music-hall entertainers, and the music on the album would take rock on a tour of popular styles of the century: marching bands, circus music, folk songs, jazz hits, the new psychedelic sounds. They would create dazzling effects in the studio, effects that had never been put on a pop album before.

Sgt. Pepper's Lonely Hearts Club Band, with its rich variety of sounds and feelings, seemed to show that rock had become broad enough and free enough to express anything. Greil Marcus, writing on rock for the San Francisco underground *Express Times,* recalled listening to an advance copy with friends: "You mean this thing is going to be in the stores, we can buy it, listen to it ourselves?" The album made history in a dozen ways: it brought art in pop; it mixed good-time rock and roll with thoughtful ballads; its cover—a collage of the Beatles surrounded by heroes and celebrities—was amazing; its budget—$75,000—and sales—2.7 million in the United States—were unprecedented. But John's work on the album pulled him off the road leading from *How I Won the War* to the radical art of the *Plastic Ono Band* album. For him *Sgt. Pepper* was a step backward.

The album was mostly Paul's. He was the principal composer of seven of the twelve songs. "She's Leaving Home" was a gem of realism, and

Jon Wiener, *Come Together: John Lennon In His Times* © 1984 Jon Wiener. University of Illinois Press, pp. 33–57.

his whimsy was never more delightful than on "Lovely Rita" and "When I'm Sixty-four."

After the reprise of the "Sgt. Pepper" theme, after the end of the music-hall performance, John sings about real life, right now, with its loneliness and horrors. "A Day in the Life" presents a vivid contrast to the playful optimism of the rest of the album.

The opening line took on a terrible new meaning after John was killed: "I read the news today oh boy." The "oh boy" seems too real: sad, vulnerable, and puzzled. The lyrics represent a kind of dream journalism in which the facts of an ordinary day do not connect. John tells how terrible events are presented by the media as a form of entertainment, leaving the viewer feeling confused, isolated, anxious, and filled with dread. The images are concise and chilling: a suicide in a car, crowds that stand and stare and then turn away. John sings with a controlled intensity. His voice is at first subdued; soon it almost cracks with despair. The insistent beat disintegrates. The music reaches a crescendo of dissonance.

Paul's bridge interrupts: the narrator awakens, and with a routinized, nervous energy, gets ready to go to work, where he falls back into his "dream." John returns with more of the day's news: "four thousand holes in Blackburn, Lancashire." Later he explained this image as coming from a newspaper article on potholes in the street, near the article describing the man who committed suicide. The newspaper regards the terrible suicide and the insignificant potholes equally as "news." Sgt. Pepper's band ended its concert complimenting its "lovely audience." John then describes the audience in the Albert Hall as "holes," lifeless and empty.

His response to these terrifying images is to propose to turn us on. But this trip will not be fun, it will not be getting high with a little help from our friends. This is turning on in pain and defeat, to escape the misery of "a day in the life." At the end John's terror and despair have turned into an irrevocable hopelessness. The music culminates in a dissonant, formless, nightmarish orchestral crescendo, ending with a forty-three-second chord of utter finality.

John's other songs included "Good Morning, Good Morning," which hinted at his dark feelings, and then denied them: "I've got nothing to say but it's okay." He contributed the weakest song on the album, "Being for the Benefit of Mr. Kite." Its elaborate circus sound effects only emphasized that it lacked something. The song of John's that caused the most excitement was "Lucy in the Sky with Diamonds." It was psychedelic.

John had fun telling straight reporters the song's title came not from the initials LSD, but from something his four-year-old son Julian had written. The reporters didn't really need to ask. If they had read the words on the jacket sleeve, they would have seen that the song described an acid trip. If they had actually listened, they would have heard John's effort to simulate a trip with sounds. The music captured some of the swooning euphoria of the acid experience, but the lyrics were cloying, even in 1967: "rocking horse people eat marshmallow pies."

The line about "flowers that grow so in-credibly high" did provide a nice image for a central chapter in the history of youth culture: flower power and psychedelia. LSD, its advocates promised, brought a new kind of experience and knowledge. It broke down the barriers that separated people from the rich, hidden utopia within themselves. It gave people an immediate, sensuous experience of colors and sounds, and promised a direct, authentic knowledge of the self and others. It revealed the extent to which bourgeois culture locked people into drab routines, cutting them off from their true feelings and perceptions. It exposed the isolation and repression of daily life in straight society. It brought emotional experiences so intense you would never be the same afterward.

There was also the possibility that this experience would be too intense, this self-knowledge too frightening, unbearable: the "bad trip." People had killed themselves on bad trips, people had gone into mental hospitals when they came down. For John, with his feelings of isolation and hopelessness, taking LSD required either recklessness or courage.

When John took it, and thereby joined the counterculture elite, he wanted to make music out of his experiences. Bob Dylan had shown it could be done in "Mr. Tambourine Man," which conveyed the dreamy quality of one kind of marijuana high. John set out to do the same for LSD. His song "Tomorrow Never Knows" on *Revolver* described the psychedelic quest for knowledge with strange, distorted sounds that had nothing to do with rock music; violin snatches, barrelhouse piano, tapes running backward. The lyrics were paradoxical and stirring: "Play the game existence to the end / Of the beginning." "Lucy in the Sky" emphasized simply the visual weirdness induced by LSD—the marmalade skies. This was the acid trip at its most trivial.

The way to self-knowledge through LSD was to dissolve the ego, to let go of desire and ambition, John explained in "Tomorrow Never Knows." You found yourself by losing yourself. This approach combined a life-affirming optimism with a profound passivity. For some, LSD provided an intense form of recreation; for John it was the basis of a completely serious search for himself. As critics Robert Christgau and John Piccarella put it recently, he "went with the flow down into the flood."

Although this search for self-knowledge through LSD was an honorable one, it didn't work for John. Three years later in *Lennon Remembers* he explained, "I got the wrong . . . message on acid—that you should destroy your ego. And I did, you know." It nearly brought him to disaster. But at the end of his LSD experiences, isolated from the Beatles, with his defenses broken down, he would be compelled to return to basics, to start over.

During the summer of 1967, however, none of this was clear. The Beatles as a group stood not only for the quest for self-knowledge through LSD but for "flower power." Flower power seemed hopelessly apolitical to New Left activists, but it represented a profound cultural revolution. The hippies rejected virtually all of bourgeois society; its sexual repression, private property, individualism and competition, authoritarian family, defini-

tions of masculinity and femininity, linear logic, and compulsive cleanliness. Flower power asserted a utopian politics. Its communes brought to life an alternative community and culture on the fringes of the straight world. This community valued play over work, spontaneity over order, shared poverty over individual acquisitiveness.

Flower power opposed the politics not only of the mainstream but also of the left. Hippies saw the confrontation tactics and mass demonstrations of the antiwar movement as a mirror of the status quo: they addressed the same issues, sought the same kind of power, reproduced the straight world's forms of domination and repressive work routines.

Despite this explicit rejection of political activism, the hippies contributed to the development of the New Left—perhaps in spite of themselves, and typically without any conscious intention. They expanded the arena of the political. The government's foreign and domestic policies were not the only, or even the most important, forms of oppression that had to be challenged. Domination in the family, the oppressive organization of work and play, sexual repression—the hippies insisted that a radical movement had to address these issues of personal life, had to pursue a politics of liberation.

They insisted also that the challenge to bourgeois society had to go beyond criticism and protest. The values of the counterculture had to be put into practice every day. The radical project was not just for some distant future; the work of creating a new society had to begin immediately, in the interstices of the old one.

The forms of protest with which the hippies confronted straight society were playful, imaginative, and improvised. When buses brought tourists to stare at Haight-Ashbury in 1967, hippies ran alongside holding up mirrors. Hippie street life emphasized the put-on; hippies were happy to shock straight people. This style made its mark on the movement's tactics. It demonstrated how new forms of protest and resistance could be created. It expanded the definition of the political act.

Hippies understood that revolutions require a transformation not only of social and political organization but also of consciousness. They understood better than the early New Left that society exercised domination not just over the organization of daily life but also over forms of thought. Thus they sought to create new kinds of subjectivity, to liberate the imagination. Over the next several years John would embrace each of these central themes of the counterculture and work to bring them into New Left politics.

During the summer of *Sgt. Pepper,* however, these links between the counterculture and the New Left remained murky for John and for everyone else. The underground press began to express the values and concerns of both movements, but was not yet making any sustained effort to examine the areas of antagonism and alliance. The first underground papers—the Los Angeles *Free Press,* the Berkeley *Barb,* New York's *East Village Other*—were satisfied to mix articles about the drug culture, sexual freedom, police brutality, macrobiotics, and protest demonstrations with record reviews. A serious debate about sixties music and politics would not begin for another year, and it would be provoked by John and his song "Revolution." In the meantime, virtually everyone loved *Sgt. Pepper.*

Robert Christgau, who would lead in developing the self-consciousness of the New Left and the counterculture about music and politics, was writing in a music magazine called *Cheetah* at the time. He called *Sgt. Pepper* "the best rock album ever made" because of its "exploration of the formal possibilities" of "aboriginal rock and roll," and because it served as a "catalyst for the entire youth movement." The youth movement, he wrote, "sadly, perhaps, is not about overthrowing society. It is about living with it, coping. . . . While part of me feels ashamed every day for my own society, another part of me is very much of that society."

The Beatles' right-wing critics argued that *Sgt. Pepper* was communistic. The proof, they said, was on the album cover, where among the figures standing behind the Liverpool lads they found Karl Marx. The critics failed to note that Marx stood next to Oliver Hardy and behind an Indian guru who has never been identified. And Marx was the only political figure. The other radical heroes of the decade—Fidel, Che, Mao, Ho Chi Minh—were absent. But the immediate predecessors of the counterculture were there, those antagonists of bourgeois respectability, Lenny Bruce and William Burroughs.

Sgt. Pepper found listeners in the most unlikely places. A writer for *Christian Century* recalled that "With a Little Help from My Friends" was played at "an underground Eucharist service" held by a group planning a Lutheran conference on war and racism. The worship leader explained that "while many people thought 'friends' were drugs, Beatles lyrics usually had more than one meaning, and people who were sticking their necks out on the Vietnam issue would indeed need 'a little help from their friends' "

Time magazine devoted a cover story to *Sgt. Pepper.* The Beatles' early music had "blended monotonously into the parched badlands of rock," the magazine declared with breathtaking ignorance. But *Sgt. Pepper* had changed all that. It turned pop music into "an art form." "A guaranteed package of psychic shivers," the record made "parents, professors, even business executives" into Beatle fans. This was supposed to be a compliment.

The *Time* story made Richard Goldstein's penetrating review seem particularly impressive. "For the first time, the Beatles have given us a package of special effects, dazzling but ultimately fraudulent," he wrote in the New York *Times.* The Beatles had turned away from their achievements on *Revolver* and *Rubber Soul,* "the forging of rock into what is real. It made them artists, it made us fans. . . . We still need the Beatles, not as cloistered composers, but as companions. And they still need us, to teach them how to be real again."

Sgt. Pepper contained no hint of the social and political conflicts that intensified through 1967. That spring, while the Beatles worked on the album, the antiwar movement in America took some big steps. Martin Luther King, Jr., finally declared, "We must combine the fervor of the civil rights movement with the peace movement." Women Strike for Peace demonstrated at the Pentagon; five thousand scientists petitioned for a bombing halt; and University of Wisconsin students forced Dow Chemical recruiters off campus. Dow manufactured napalm, the jelly dropped from American planes which clung to the skin of the Vietnamese as it burned.

Ramparts magazine revealed in March that the National Student Association had received more than $3 million from the CIA through dummy foundations. The magazine subsequently revealed that thirty other organizations and publications which claimed to be independent had been secretly funded by the CIA. On April 15 the largest antiwar demonstration to date was held in New York City, as 250,000 people marched down Fifth Avenue in a "peace parade," while 50,000 more marched in San Francisco. Heavyweight boxing champion Muhammad Ali was arrested after refusing induction into the Army. He had been denied conscientious-objector status. Boxing authorities immediately stripped him of his title as sports became politicized around the issues of war and race.

The summer of *Sgt. Pepper* was also the summer of ghetto rebellions in the United States. In mid-July Newark exploded: blacks battled police over a ten-square-mile area. After five nights, 24 blacks had been killed, more than 1,500 were injured, and 1,397 were arrested. A commission set up by the governor criticized the "excessive and unjustified force" used by National Guardsmen and police, who shot at black people indiscriminately and vandalized black businesses. A week later the Detroit ghetto exploded. Snipers held off National Guardsmen, and for the first time in twenty-five years officials summoned federal troops to quell a civil disturbance. The toll in Detroit was thirty-six blacks killed along with seven whites, over two thousand injured, five thousand arrested, and five thousand left homeless from 1,442 fires. Smaller riots broke out in Harlem, Milwaukee, Cambridge, Maryland, Minneapolis, and Chicago.

The ghetto uprisings revealed to white America the rage of the black underclass. They demonstrated the indiscriminately brutal response of white authority and suggested the tremendous gulf that separated white youth in the summer of *Sgt. Pepper,* flower power, and the peace movement from ghetto youth shouting "Burn, baby, burn." Census statistics released later in the year showed the material basis for black rage; 41 percent of nonwhite families earned less than $3,000 a year, compared to 12 percent of white families; the unemployment rate for blacks was double that for whites; most black young people attended segregated schools.

The Six-Day War in the Mideast took place that same summer. Israel launched a surprise attack on Egypt in June, responding to Egypt's military buildup, expulsion of the UN emergency force from the Sinai, and alliance with Syria, Jordan, and Iraq. Peter Brown described how the war touched the Beatles: "There was enormous pressure from the Jewish establishment in London during the war to get the Beatles to appear in a benefit concert for Israel. Brian said, 'Absolutely not.' He would never do benefits. He argued that you can't select these things wisely, so it's better not to do them at all. Our aim is to sell records, he said, so we should keep out of anything controversial. The pressures Jewish leaders applied were really pretty nasty ones. People like Lew Grade and Co. really put the old screws on Brian. It wasn't that he didn't sympathize with the cause. It was that he'd made this rule and he wasn't going to bend it, even if it affected something so close to him."

In the middle of that summer of conflict, the Beatles played a new song, written and sung by John: "All You Need Is Love." Seven hundred million people heard it in a worldwide TV satellite broadcast. It became the anthem of flower power that summer. Radicals continued to denounce John for it for the rest of his life.

The song expressed the highest value of the counterculture. In retrospect, "love" seems an absurdly naïve slogan. For the hippies, however, it represented a call for liberation from Protestant culture, with its repressive sexual taboos and its insistence on emotional restraint. John's song seemed to say that to find happiness, you didn't "need" the traditional bourgeois virtues—individualism, aggressiveness, competition, acquisitiveness. All you needed was love.

Neither the song's fans nor its critics had listened to it closely. John did not say that love would solve the world's problems. He suggested that the world's problems would take care of themselves; thus life could be devoted to love instead of to solving problems and achieving distant goals. The song presented the flower-power critique of movement politics: there was nothing you could do that couldn't be done by others; thus you didn't need to do anything about the killing in Vietnam or the oppression of America's blacks. Everyone should relax and enjoy this place and this moment. John was arguing not only against bourgeois self-denial and future-mindedness but also against the activists' sense of urgency and their strong personal commitments to fighting injustice and oppression.

As usual, New Left writers were not unanimous about "All You Need Is Love." Most objected to John's message of acquiescence in the status quo, but some found things to like in the song. The SDS paper at Cornell University argued that it conveyed a "gentleness combined with strength" that distinguished it from most of rock, which was "an assault." The movement needed more of this nonviolence, and John was pointing the way.

On the flip side was a sweet self-satire, "Baby You're a Rich Man," in which Paul asks John questions in a soprano voice. What music is he going to play in the new key he's found? They were thinking about psychedelia at the time, but that question—what to do with his new ideas—was one John would start asking himself more and more seriously.

John followed that with "I Am the Walrus," released at the end of November 1967, the wildest music the Beatles ever recorded. Later he said he understood the Walrus in the Lewis Carroll poem to be a symbol of socialism, resisting the capitalist Carpenter. He was wrong about that. The Walrus and the Carpenter were both villains, eating the poor oysters they lured to take a walk with them. That isn't what made the Walrus important to John. He remembered the lines " 'The time has come,' the Walrus said, 'to talk of many things: of shoes and ships and sealing-wax, of cabbages and kings.' " When John sang "I Am the Walrus," he was identifying with this articulate symbol of the imagination.

The first line referred to the LSD-inspired project of destroying his ego—"I am he as you are he"—and asserted the sixties communal ideal: "we are all together." In each verse, John poured out a torrent of disjointed images, ending with "I'm crying." He sang that line without expression, with a blankness that was frightening. He was hinting that LSD wasn't working for him, but he was also disguising his bad feelings in a dizzying spectacle of sounds and words, as he had done with "Strawberry Fields Forever." He was not yet able to tell the truth simply and directly.

The triumph of *Sgt. Pepper* served as a challenge to the Rolling Stones, Bob Dylan, and the rest of pop music in the summer of 1967. The Stones had started recording new material when *Sgt. Pepper* came out; they stayed in the studio another three months, working on the album that would be measured against the Beatles' masterpiece. Their work was interrupted by Mick Jagger's and Keith Richards' trials on drug charges. Two days before *Sgt. Pepper*'s release, Jagger was found guilty of possessing four amphetamine pills and sentenced to six months in prison; Richards, found guilty of permitting his house to be used for the smoking of hashish, was sentenced to one year. Even the ruling-class *Times* of London had to object, publishing an editorial titled "Who Breaks a Butterfly on a Wheel?" The Beatles jointly made a political statement, signing a full-page ad in the the *Times* three weeks after the release of *Sgt. Pepper* calling for the legalization of marijuana.

Jagger's drug bust and draconian sentence drove him to the left. "The way things are run in Britain and the States is rotten and it is up to the young to change everything," he declared after his trial. "The time is right now, revolution is valid. The kids are ready to burn down the high-rise blocks and those stinking factories where they are forced to sweat their lives away. I'm going to do anything, anything that has to be done, to be a part of what is about to go down."

Their Satanic Majesties Request, recorded between June and September and released in November 1967, had none of this anger. It was the Stones' attempt to be more psychedelic than *Sgt. Pepper,* and it was a failure. Jagger had pushed to do it, and Brian Jones had opposed it, arguing the Stones should stay true to their roots in rhythm and blues. Americans missed the pun in the title: British passports read, "Her Britannic Majesty . . . requests and requires . . ." The Stones were referring to their recent drug busts, which made it impossible for them to travel freely. They tried to hide the weakness of the music by putting a 3-D cover on the album. At least the Beatles couldn't top that.

Sgt. Pepper was loved by the counterculture and imitated by the Stones, but it was challenged by Bob Dylan. In January 1968, six months after the Beatles' album appeared, he released his first album since his motorcycle accident a year and a half earlier: *John Wesley Harding.* The Beatles' music sounded extravagant; Dylan simply strummed his acoustic guitar. The Beatles were playful; Dylan was serious. The Beatles' sources ranged from the British music hall to the Indian raga; Dylan drew strictly on American music. Even the cover of *John Wesley Harding,* a plain black and white photo of Dylan surrounded by two Native American musicians and one woodsman, was a reply to the cover of *Sgt. Pepper.* Dylan's response to the Beatles, Robert Christgau wrote in May 1968, was "salutary" and "mature."

John Wesley Harding offered not only an artistic alternative to *Sgt. Pepper* but also a political one. While none of the songs spoke directly about the war, the entire album expressed a subtle awareness of it and showed how it was affecting Dylan. The Beatles' playfulness and fantasy ignored the war's existence, while Dylan's new songs acknowledged it by trying to be real, and by playing fewer games than ever before. The best song on Dylan's album, "All along the Watch-

tower," expressed a new commitment to truthfulness and seriousness. The song opened with the old Dylan, "the joker," looking for a way out. But he had learned that life is too short for joking. New Left critics were less happy with "Dear Landlord," which seemed like his coming to terms with authority in society. But it was hard not to like the tender "I'll Be Your Baby Tonight."

Dylan himself was talking about John. "The last time I went to London I stayed at John Lennon's house," he told an interviewer. "You should see all the stuff that Lennon bought: big cars and a stuffed gorilla and thousands of things in every room in his house, cost a fortune. When I got back home I wondered what it would be like to have all those material things. I figured I had the money and I could do it, and I wondered if it would feel like anything real. So I bought all this stuff and filled my house with it and sat around in the middle of it all. And I felt nothing." He wasn't a working-class lad from Liverpool.

Meanwhile, in a different realm of popular music which for a while seemed untouched by artistic or political ambitions, the Beach Boys had been perfecting their sound, a celebration of complacent white middle-class suburban youth. Jim Miller has written sensitively about the contradictions faced by their brilliant leader Brian Wilson: "His business was the revitalization of myths he wished were true and knew were false." "California Girls" peaked at Number Two that summer. A masterpiece of white pop harmony, it later became a shampoo commercial. The Beach Boys' most ambitious album, *Pet Sounds,* somehow became obsolete when the new Beatles album appeared. After *Sgt. Pepper* the Beach Boys never got one of their songs into the Top Ten. Suddenly their records had become oldies.

During the summer of *Sgt. Pepper* the alternatives posed by soul music and soft rock became clearer than ever before. When *Sgt. Pepper* was released in June, the Number One song was Aretha Franklin's "Respect." Her album *I Never Loved a Man (The Way I Love You)* followed. More than anyone else, she brought the apocalypse of gospel to the white rock audience, singing with desperation and urgency. "Respect" was a powerfully rocking statement of feminist, black pride.

"Respect" was replaced in the Number One spot by the Fifth Dimension's "Up Up and Away," which realized its potential later when it became a TWA commercial. Smokey Robinson's greatest song, "The Tracks of My Tears," didn't get any higher than Number Nine. This was also the season of the shlock flower-power anthem that told people going to San Francisco to be sure to wear a flower in their ear.

At the end of the summer of *Sgt. Pepper* the Beatles seemed to have everything: they were a critical and popular triumph, they had the power to do anything they wanted. Then manager Brian Epstein died of an accidental overdose of sleeping pills. He was thirty-two years old and a millionaire. "I knew we were in trouble then," John said later in *Lennon Remembers*. "I thought, 'We've fucking had it.' "

From Brian Epstein to the Maharishi

John feared the future after Brian Epstein's death because he knew how important Epstein had been in taking those Liverpool tough guys and turning them into the Fab Four. Epstein came from a prosperous family of provincial Jewish merchants. The family store sold furniture and lamps, pianos and sheet music. As a child in local private schools, Brian was the victim of anti-Semitism. As an adult, Epstein had the misfortune to be gay in a social world where that was taboo. Forced to lead a double life, respectable businessman by day and homosexual by night, he was intermittently attacked by "queer-bashing" gangs of tough youths and occasionally subjected to blackmail and extortion.

Epstein, an energetic young businessman, persuaded the family to open a big record store and make him manager. When Beatle fans started asking for their records, Brian decided to find out what the excitement was about. He went to see them downstairs at the Cavern Club in November

1961; he was twenty-seven years old at the time. He called his book describing how he discovered them *A Cellarful of Noise;* Eric Idle of Monty Python parodied it as *A Cellarful of Goys.* Epstein signed a formal contract to manage the Beatles in December 1961.

The Beatles before Brian had been shaped by the material conditions of music-making in the rock clubs of Hamburg, West Germany. They spent a good part of the years from 1960 to 1962 working on Hamburg's Reeperbahn, with its strip clubs, prostitutes, and brawling sailors. Playing eight hours a night, the Beatles developed a loud, hard, exuberant style and a raw, desperate look. They had to play loud to drown out the drunks, they had to keep playing during the fights, and the crowds demanded a wild stage show. The Beatles could "make show," as the Germans put it—especially John, who screamed and leaped around the stage. "We'd been meek and mild musicians at first," drummer Pete Best said later. "Now we became a powerhouse."

The live recording made at the Star Club in Hamburg in 1962, released in 1977, suggests the energy with which the Beatles made show. Its twenty-six songs also indicate that the Beatles began as rock and roll purists. John's songs included Chuck Berry's "Sweet Little Sixteen," the Isley Brothers' "Twist and Shout," and Gene Vincent's "Be-Bop-A-Lula." Paul did Little Richard's "Long Tall Sally" and his "Kansas City" medley. John and Paul covered Phil Spector's first hit, "To Know Him is to Love Him," and sang a Lennon-McCartney original, "I Saw Her Standing There." Paul also displayed a taste for sentimental shlock: he sang "A Taste of Honey," "Besame Mucho," and "Falling in Love Again" for the Hamburg drunks.

The Beatles regarded their audience as adversaries. John recalled later that he "used to shout in English at the Germans, call them Nazis and tell them to fuck off." The louts just clamored for more. British sailors sometimes stopped by; they weren't much better. "After a few drinks," John recalled, "they'd start shouting 'Up Liverpool!' "

John and the other Beatles returned to Liverpool from Hamburg, as Eric Idle said in his parody

The Rutles, "full of experience and pills." In March 1961 they made their first appearance at the Cavern Club, which would serve as their base as they became Liverpool's top group. The audience consisted of local teenagers instead of drunken sailors, but the working conditions there resembled Hamburg's: the music had to be hard and loud, the beat had to be strong.

Already the Beatles were distinguishing themselves from other local groups. "When we got back from Hamburg," John later said, "every group had a lead singer in a pink jacket. We were the only group that didn't have that one guy out front. . . . That was how we broke through: by being different." A group without a leader, they created their music collectively—a rare phenomenon that explained part of their magic and contributed to their appeal. The communal aspect of their artistic work, which would become so significant a symbol of the sixties, was already part of the Beatles before Brian.

Before Brian Epstein appeared on the scene, the Beatles had taken some important steps. They developed their collective identity and their loud and hard style, they practiced on the classics, they lived the life of drugs, sex, and rock and roll. But the most important steps in their musical and cultural development lay ahead. The Hamburg tapes contain none of Lennon and McCartney's musical inventiveness or lyrical brilliance and little of the originality with which they would soon transform pop music. Their character as individuals in a group had not yet developed. The Beatles before Brian remained old-fashioned working-class tough guys.

Epstein got them an audition at Decca Records, at which they sang the Coasters' "Searchin'." A man named Dick Rowe turned them down. A year later Paul said, "Rowe must be kicking himself now." John replied, "I hope he kicks himself to death."

In July 1962 Epstein convinced George Martin of EMI to sign the Beatles to its Parlophone subsidiary. Martin, who would play a major role in creating the sound of their later albums, had worked on the *Coon Show,* one of John's favorites. In his first move he got rid of the Beatles'

mediocre drummer, Pete Best. The Beatles replaced him with Ringo, whose identity as the sad and lovable one masked a genuine musical talent.

Epstein now insisted the Beatles give up their leather outfits and their tough-guy appearance. When their first album, *Please Please Me,* appeared in March 1963, the cover showed them smiling in cheap new suits, looking clean, eager to please, and distinctly working-class. Eight months later *With the Beatles* came out, and Epstein had transformed them again. The Beatles wore black turtleneck sweaters, looked serious, and appeared in an arty shot with dramatic lighting and a grainy print. They looked like bohemian students, thoroughly middle-class.

They gave up their macho image, not because they were drawn to a less sexist conception of themselves, but because they wanted to win middle-class fans, to make money; as John said in *Lennon Remembers,* to "make it very, very big." If their motives were less than noble, the cultural consequences of their transformation were nevertheless positive: they helped loosen the straitjacket of conventional sex roles. The definitions of masculine and feminine that prevail in our society do not come directly from nature. Young people have to be taught what they mean, and rock plays a central role in this cultural process. Pop music provides a way for young people to express their sexuality, but it also tends to reinforce sexual stereotypes, and to deny the existence of alternative sexual identities. In this way rock operates also as a form of sexual control.

The Beatles challenged the way rock constructed male and female sexuality. Before the Beatles, rock organized sexuality around two poles: "cock rock" and "teenybop." Cock rock was (and remains today as "heavy metal") an explicit, crude expression of male sexual domination. The performers constantly reminded the audience of their prowess. Plunging shirts and tight pants prominently displayed male bodies. Microphone stands and guitars served as phallic symbols. The music itself was structured to suggest arousal and climax; the lyrics, and especially the vocal style, were assertive and arrogant. Women were portrayed as sex objects, or as possessive, endangering the freedom of men. The sexual meanings of cock rock were especially clear at live concerts.

Teenybop was consumed almost exclusively by girls. The male teenybop idol—Paul Anka provided the best example in the pre-Beatles era—was vulnerable, needy, and full of self-pity. He was young, soft, pretty and puppy-like, romantic, and easily hurt. Most important, he was anxious to find true love. He sang about feeling lonely. He was often let down or stood up. He needed a sensitive and sympathetic soulmate. For teenybop fans, pinups, posters, and TV appearances had almost as much significance as live performances.

The Beatles challenged the cock rock/teenybop division. They were something new: as rock theorists Simon Frith and Angela McRobbie wrote, "neither boys-together aggression nor boy-next-door pathos." Their personae suggested that the ideal male was no longer the tough, crude, and emotionally distant person, nor was he the lonely, pretty boy next door. He didn't take himself completely seriously, the way the traditional male did, and he was smarter, more energetic, and warmer.

Guardians of traditional sex roles objected to the Beatles' departure from the stereotyped male identity. Within the traditional framework, this could only be interpreted one way; thus the Beatles were denounced for being "feminine." That was wrong; they never acted like women.

Undoubtedly the Beatles remained deeply sexist in their own relationships with women at this time. And undoubtedly the Beatles' new sexual identities were part of a larger cultural change. But the Beatles helped construct a new nonmacho male sexuality when other rock stars didn't.

The construction of this new ideal male figure was not John's project. The idea seems to have come from Epstein, who was gay, and whose only conscious purpose was to make the Beatles more popular. He was not shaping them into his own idea of male sexuality; he was drawn to the exaggerated macho style, and, in any case, he kept his work and his sex life completely separate. Other groups had gay managers whose sexual preferences did not affect the way their music was presented. Nevertheless something about Brian's own break with conventional sexuality may have contributed to the way he shaped the Beatles' new sexual identity.

The Beatles' challenge to rock's organization of sexuality was less than relentless, especially in their early songs. Lennon and McCartney's lyrics often respected teenybop romantic conventions. Boys and girls held hands and fell in love, and John often promised not to be too sexually aggressive: "I'll be good like I know I should," he sang, and "I'm happy just to dance with you."

However, John also wrote a series of songs making obvious sexual demands, a theme from cock rock. In his very first song, he told his girl, "Please please me." His next song pleaded, "Love me do." John's raucous and passionate "I Want to Hold Your Hand" was a masterpiece of sexual frustration: when he touches her, he can't hide his "love," she's got "that something," and when he "feels that something," he wants to—hold her *hand,* sung with a head-shaking falsetto cry. Another of John's early songs triumphantly announced that he had discovered how to get girls to give in; All he had to do, he declared, was tell them the words they wanted to hear.

In John's early songs he concealed his bad feelings beneath teenybop conventions. He repressed his fears, his anger, and his depression, along with the vague wishes for peace and freedom that he would express in the next few years. The bad feelings he sang about were limited to the misery of the teenybop idol who had lost his girl. The once exception to these clichés was "There's a Place," in which he confessed that, when he felt "low," he went to a place where "there's no time and I'm alone." "It's my mind," he declared, a line whose awkwardness testified to its truthfulness. This idea would grow in significance in his music and his life over the next decade.

The Beatles' challenge to the conventions of cock rock and teenybop triumphed not just because of their personae but also because of their music. They broke out of three-chord cock rock and four-chord teenybop. Their songs brought in minor chords and unexpected sevenths, and had many more changes than guitar-players were used to. "All my Loving" had six chords; the next year "A Hard Day's Night" had eleven. Bob Dylan recognized Lennon and McCartney's creativity: "Their chords were outrageous," he said, "just outrageous." And they played their outrageous chords over a rough R&B beat. The Beatles sounded new and exciting because their songs had a structure that really was new and exciting.

The Beatles musical triumph over cock rock and teenybop also depended on John's and Paul's singing. They sounded exhilarating, joyous, exuberant. Their singing style was not, however, as original as their music-writing; they had learned the screams, shouts, and falsetto cries of gospel-rooted R&B, and practiced the sweet, close harmonies introduced by early Motown and girl groups. The escalating cries of "Come on!" in "Please Please Me" and the call-and-response shouts of "Yeah!" in "It Won't Be Long" were pure R&B. Their vocal style thrilled a white audience that had not yet discovered the new black music, with its total release and wild expression of feeling.

Little Richard, who played on the same bill with the Beatles in Liverpool in 1962, was quoted in the newspaper *Mersey Beat* as saying, "Man, those Beatles are fabulous. If I hadn't seen them I'd never have dreamed they were white. They have a real authentic Negro sound." That was almost exactly what Sam Phillips said he found in Elvis: "Someone with the Negro sound and the Negro feel." There is no reason to believe Little Richard actually said the words attributed to him by *Mersey Beat,* or that if he said them, he meant them, but still the parallels are striking. The Little Richard quote wouldn't have been published unless it expressed the way the Beatles wanted to be seen and heard. But the Beatles didn't simply cover black hits; they incorporated the black vocal-group style into their own distinctive songs. John never tried to "sound black"; he was proud to sing with his Liverpool accent.

The Beatles music was created under conditions that gave them a degree of artistic autonomy rare in the world of pop music. Because they wrote their own songs, they were free from the grip of the hack songwriters and A&R men of the music-publishing industry. Because they accompanied themselves, producers had less power over how they sounded. Because they had served a long apprenticeship, and because they tried out their songs in front of live audiences before recording them, they knew what made their music work better than producers and executives did. As a result, under Epstein's management their music was really theirs; its passion and exhilaration were authentic.

Finally, the Beatles triumph was part of a larger cultural change. In the last week of August 1963, the pop charts blossomed. The Beatles released "She Loves You," with John singing lead. In the United States new black music was gaining a white audience; that same week the Number One song was Little Stevie Wonder's "Fingertips, Pt. 2." And Number Two was Bob Dylan's "Blowin' in the Wind," sung by Peter, Paul and Mary. The same week, 200,000 people joined the march on Washington and heard Martin Luther King's "I have a dream" speech. The sixties were beginning.

In his most candid interviews, John repeatedly said that the Beatles under Epstein "sold out." That seems a harsh judgment, influenced perhaps by a facile contrast with Mick Jagger. But when Jagger played the part of rock's bad boy, he wasn't doing it to uphold a principle; he was reproducing a cock-rock stereotype. When the Beatles moved from being leather-clad tough guys to gentler and smarter people, they weren't selling out; they were constructing an alternative to the macho stereotype, and their music was expressing a wider range of feelings than rock and roll had ever expressed before.

However, when Epstein reshaped the Beatles' identities, he did force John to give up one important part of himself: his anger. That does not seem to have been true of any of the other Beatles. It's not clear that they gave up anything. But John was a genuinely angry young man. His anger may have been inchoate, expressed through the stereotypes of working-class macho, but it was real. When he played the cheerful wit, he had to repress a vital part of himself. And he couldn't do it for very long. It made him depressed. When he finally went into therapy, he learned to draw on his anger to create his greatest music.

John never had a close relationship with Brian, except during one brief period in 1963. In April John's wife Cynthia gave birth to their son Julian. Cynthia wrote in her memoirs, "It was a week before I saw my husband." John had been on tour; the Beatles had just that week achieved their first British Number One song, "Please Please Me," on which John sang lead. Cynthia remembered John's arrival as "a wonderful moment."

" 'He's bloody marvelous, Cyn. . . . Who's going to be a famous little rocker like his Dad then?' " But a crowd began to gather, and "very quickly . . . John was beginning to feel trapped.

"Before he left he told me that Brian had asked him to go on holiday to Spain with him and he wanted to know if I objected. I must admit that the request hit me like a bolt out of the blue. . . . I was well aware that John deserved a holiday. He had just completed a tour and recording sessions. I concealed my hurt and envy and gave him my blessings. He was delighted and left me a happy man."

In 1980 an interviewer asked John about this trip with Brian. "It was almost a love affair, but not quite," he said. "It was never consummated. But we did have a pretty intense relationship. And it was my first experience with someone I knew was a homosexual. . . . We used to sit in cafés and Brian would look at all the boys and I would ask, 'Do you like that one? Do you like this one?' "

John was touchy about homosexuality when he returned. Several weeks later, at Paul's twenty-first birthday party, John picked a fight with a local disc jockey who had helped them get several bookings. Later he explained to Hunter Davies, his official biographer, "I smashed him up. I broke his bloody ribs for him. I was pissed at the time. He'd called me a queer."

The spring of 1963 was filled with significant events for John; his first child was born the same

week that he had his first nationwide hit song. It must have given him an intense sense of his own potency. The excitement of life on the road with the boys, a male adolescent fantasy come true, stood in sharp contrast, however, to the utter conventionality of Cynthia and the life she promised him. Her memoir conveys this clearly if inadvertently: John felt trapped by the crowded room, she says, but also he felt trapped by the prospect of his new role as father in a traditional household.

To escape this fate, at least briefly, John eagerly went off with Brian. If Brian found John attractive, John wasn't necessarily interested in a sexual relationship with him. Brian was twenty-nine, six years older than John. That six years separated two generations. Brian grew up before Elvis, before rock and roll. He dressed in business suits. He was in charge of the Beatles' business. He took care of them while they played music. John, faced with the prospect of being a father to Julian, preferred to go away with Brian, who had been a good father to him. For John, Brian's homosexuality may not have been as important as his status as an adult, one who didn't need John to grow up, who liked him as a youth.

After the Beatles gave up touring in 1966, a year before Epstein's death, they hardly ever saw him. Part of Brian's misery that year arose from his sense of uselessness in his work as the Beatles' manager, and part arose from despair over his doomed love affairs. "I'm no good with women," he once told his assistant, "and I'm no good with men."

By the early seventies John learned through Yoko how traditional sex roles oppressed women, and how the same ideology and power structure that oppressed women also oppressed homosexuals. In 1973 he contributed a poem and a drawing to *The Gay Liberation Book*. That took courage; virtually all of the other celebrity contributors—Gore Vidal, Allen Ginsberg, Paul Goodman—were themselves gay. John's knowledge of Epstein's suffering must have been in his mind when he decided to support gay liberation.

John and the others learned of Epstein's death while they were beginning another major step away from the conventional life of rock super-stars: receiving instruction from the Maharishi Mahesh Yogi. John hoped meditation would do what LSD hadn't, bring him closer to truth and re-ality. Meditation also promised to provide some relief from his depression. "Through meditation I've learned how to tap energy that I've had in me all the time," he told talk-show host David Frost. "Before I could only reach this extra energy on good days when things were going well." With the enthusiasm of a convert, he recommended it to everyone. "Not just a special few, or brainy people or cranks, but everyone." John's song "Across the Universe" sought to convey the expe-rience of meditation, admitting its fatalism and pessimism—"Nothing's gonna change my world." Years later he explained that meditation had offered a much-needed escape from life as a Beatle. "Somebody had a place in which I could withdraw," he said.

Going to India was George's idea. John and George had consistently been the radicals among the Beatles. They had insisted on denouncing the war in Vietnam; they took LSD first. John never drew back from new experiences the way Paul did. He wanted to find answers to the questions that troubled him, and he wanted relief from the unhappiness of Beatle life. He went to India, with the rest of the group.

Ringo left first, discreetly claiming the "food" didn't agree with him. John didn't change his mind about the value of meditation until the Ma-harishi was accused of sexual misconduct. In *Lennon Remembers* John explained what hap-pened when they told him they were leaving. He asked, " 'Why?' I said, 'If you're so cosmic, you know why.' . . . And he gave me a look like 'I'll kill you, you bastard.' "

Mick Jagger had from the beginning called the Maharishi a "bloody old con man." Jagger told Keith Richards, "I can understand George falling for all that peace, love, and pay-the-bill crap, but not John. I'd always thought John was a bright lad."

John had spent less than eight months as a follower of the Maharishi—from August 1967

until April 1968—a brief period, especially in light of the media attention that relationship re-ceived. John never said the climactic trip to India had been a mistake. "I did write some of my best songs while I was there," he said, point-ing to "Yer Blues" and "I'm So Tired." "The ex-perience was worth it if only for the songs that came out."

During the time he spent meditating with the Maharishi, John's political interests continued to develop. In October 1967, two weeks after John appeared with the Maharishi on the *David Frost Show, How I Won the War* opened in London. At the premiere John explained his reasons for mak-ing the film: "I hate war. If there is another war I won't fight and I'll try to tell all the youngsters not to fight either. I hate all the sham." That political statement was the strongest he'd ever made.

Two days after the premiere, 100,000 people marched on the Pentagon. The Sunday newspa-pers reported both events. It was a fortuitous co-incidence: the new kind of antiwar film that Lennon made with Lester found a counterpart of sorts in a new kind of political action. Both con-sciously sought to break the barriers of conven-tional definitions, to find new ways of declaring an antiwar position, to seek a transformation not only of government policy but also of the forms of political expression.

In 1968 sustained debates began to appear in print that explored the Beatles' meaning and sig-nificance for the New Left and the countercul-ture. Two years before, discussions of the Beatles had been confined to mainstream magazines like *Time* and *Look;* the teen and fan magazines also wrote about them. The mass media had defined the audience for articles about the Beatles as puz-zled parents and dumb fans; no self-conscious youth culture existed in print. That began to change in 1967, as the growing underground press wrote about *Sgt. Pepper,* but those articles mainly celebrated the Beatles' music.

The English took the lead early in 1968, when the *New Left Review* ran a debate about the alter-native forms of personal and political engagement offered by the Beatles and the Rolling Stones. The prevailing view of the Beatles as "original, mature, serious, and thoughtful" was challenged by Alan Beckett. He argued that their music had "a dangerous tendency towards denial that there is anything difficult in relationships."

The Stones' music, in contrast, with its "arrogance, brutality and narcissism," constituted "a completely justifiable and welcome attack on the amorous clichés of popular music" and especially on the Beatles' kind of "facile intimacy." The Stones' music could have a "constructive, liberating effect on the individual," because it is "only when such feelings have been isolated, recognized and incorporated into the self, that they can be transmuted." The Stones' *Satanic Majesties,* however, which had been released a few months earlier, he judged a failure. Its attempt at psychedelic music resulted in "hackneyed imagery" that stood in sharp contrast to John's authentic accounts of the psychedelic experience, "Strawberry Fields" and "I Am the Walrus."

In a second *New Left Review* piece Richard Merton argued that the Beatles "have never strayed much beyond the strict limits of romantic convention. . . . Central moments of their *oeuvre* are nostalgia and whimsey, both eminently consecrated traditions of middle-class England. Lukacs's pejorative category of the 'pleasant' which dulls and pacifies fits much of their work with deadly accuracy." Here Merton was pointing to Paul's special contribution.

As for the Stones, their music is "about sexual exploitation, not narcissism," he argued. "The enormous merit—and audacity—of the Stones is to have repeatedly and consistently defied what is a central taboo of the social system: mention of sexual inequality. They have done so in the most radical and unacceptable way possible: by celebrating it. The light this black beam throws on the society is too bright for it. Nakedly proclaimed, inequality is *de facto* denounced."

Yet another *New Left Review* writer challenged this conclusion. "Who does the denouncing?" Michael Parsons asked. "Merton seems to mean that the Stones, by presenting us

with a blatant and undisguised statement of male domination and exploitation," enable us to recognize and denounce it. But, he argued, we should not assume that the Stones adopt the same critical attitude that we do. Merton responded that "an artist's private purpose is not determinant of the objective meaning of his work. . . . Celebration of inequality is incompatible with it, because it taunts the oppressed to liberate themselves. The insistently jeering note of so many Jagger/Richards compositions is a form of solidarity."

The debate on sixties music and politics thus portrayed the Stones and the Beatles as representing antagonistic social and cultural stances: "The Beatles want to hold your hand, the Stones want to burn your house" was the way one rock writer summed it up. But this argument overlooked the way those differences had been created by the media. The musical origins of the two groups were virtually identical. "Both of us came out of the same Chuck Berry, Little Richard, Elvis Presley school of music," Keith Richards admitted in 1981. "I think a lot of the difference between us was imaginary," the creation of Brian Epstein and Stones manager Andrew Oldham, both geniuses of public relations.

Jagger and Lennon did many of the same songs in 1963 and 1964: both sang Chuck Berry's "Carol," both sang Barrett Strong's "Money," both covered Arthur Alexander (Jagger did "You Better Move On," Lennon did "Anna" and "Soldier of Love"); both did Jerry Leiber and Mike Stoller songs (Jagger did "Poison Ivy," Lennon did "Some Other Guy"); both covered Motown men—Jagger sang Marvin Gaye's "Hitch Hike" and Lennon sang Smokey Robinson's "You've Really Got a Hold on Me." And Jagger sang a Lennon-McCartney composition: "I Wanna Be Your Man."

There were differences in the musical taste of the two groups. The Stones played Chicago blues—Jimmy Reed, Muddy Waters, and Little Walter—while the Beatles did more recent R&B: Little Richard, Larry Williams, and the Isley Brothers. The Beatles concentrated on cover versions of established black hits, while the Stones became connoisseurs of obscure black music; their cover of Slim Harpo's "King Bee" was emblematic. And the Stones never would have done "Till There Was You" or "A Taste of Honey." Public relations did not explain that. The difference between Brian Jones and Paul McCartney did.

Because the early Stones' similarities to the Beatles seemed stronger than these differences, because they too covered American black hits and had "long" hair, the Stones feared they would be cast as "Beatle look-alikes." It was a sensitive point. When a reporter asked if the Stones' hairstyle owed anything to the Beatles, Jagger replied defensively, "Art students have had this sort of haircut for years, even when the Beatles were using hair cream."

Stones manager Andrew Oldham saw the way out of the "Beatle look-alike" dilemma. He would cast the Stones as the antithesis of the Beatles. Jagger, Richards, Jones, Bill Wyman, and Charlie Watts would be turned into a tough, defiant working-class group. If even Mum liked the Beatles, the Stones would become the group parents loved to hate. The media went for it. The London *Daily Mirror* ran a headline in March, "Would You Let Your Daughter Go with a Rolling Stone?" The first Associated Press report in the United States called them "dirtier, streakier and more disheveled than the Beatles."

The irony was that the tough, defiant, proletarian-looking Stones came from bourgeois families. Jagger's father had been a teacher. The Jagger home had "an atmosphere of middle class 'gentility,' " their 1965 official biography stated. While John had flunked every subject in his O-level examinations at age sixteen, Jagger passed seven of his, and did even better on his A-levels two years later. "Mick seemed destined for a steady office job," his mother recalled. "That was why he went to the London School of Economics to study accountancy."

Brian Jones did even better in school, passing his O-levels in nine subjects a year early and doing well on his A-levels. "He sometimes talked of becoming a dentist," his mother said. Keith Richards came from a background closer to John's: son of an electrical engineer, he was a "problem" student and a Teddy boy. He went to art college dreaming of becoming a rock musician. While the Beatles worked their way from Liverpool to London, Jagger attended LSE and his band played in suburban Richmond.

At the same time that Jagger was assuming his working-class tough-guy role, another identity for the Stones was being shaped. *Vogue* magazine featured Jagger in 1964 in a portrait by David Bailey, the hippest high-fashion photographer. Jagger's group, the accompanying article said, was "quite different from the Beatles, and more terrifying. 'The effect is sex,' wrote one observer, 'that isn't sex, which is the end of the road.' " Before the Stones had their first Number One single, Jagger was being portrayed as fashionable and hip, mysteriously androgynous, and on his way to becoming one of high society's "beautiful people." In 1964 such a portrayal of John Lennon or any of the other Beatles was unimaginable.

That July the Stones' "It's All Over Now" became their first Number One British single, replacing the Animals' "The House of the Rising Sun" on the charts. At concerts in England their fans rioted regularly. In Blackpool, not far from Liverpool, the biggest rock riot in British history broke out at a Stones concert: fifty were injured, seventy police were called to fight fans, who ripped out the theater's chandeliers and tossed a Steinway grand piano off the stage. Riots also broke out in Paris following the Stones' concert. Police arrested 150. John must have been envious.

Thus, while the Beatles' manager insisted that John Lennon give up his anger to become "really big," the Stones' manager insisted that they act angry. This left John with the sense that he had sold out and that the Stones were more authentic rock and roll rebels. In retrospect, the Stones seem to have been playing the stereotyped cock rock role while the Beatles took more risks in challenging sexual conventions. But this difference became clear only in the seventies with the development of feminism.

As the New Left and the counterculture became more self-conscious and articulate in the late sixties, the Beatles and the Stones came to represent the real alternatives young people faced: they could sell out and accommodate themselves to adult, bourgeois society, or they could defy it, seeking to change both society and themselves. In 1968 John Lennon himself could no longer escape that choice.

STUDY QUESTIONS

1. What intrinsic themes or mechanics shaped *Sgt. Pepper?* How was *Sgt. Pepper* associated with "flower power?"

2. Social and political conflict marked the summer of 1967. What was John Lennon's answer to these events? How and why was it misunderstood or misappropriated?

3. How did John Lennon's desire for "reality" conflict with the "escapist" nature of the Beatles during the creation of *Sgt. Pepper's?* How did this compare with the relationship between hippies and the New Left?

4. How did other rock acts react to the release of *Sgt. Pepper?* What do their responses reveal about an all-inclusive subculture?

5. How did Epstein help the Beatles forge a new male identity? What elements of "cock rock" and "teeny bop" did they incorporate in this new model?

6. What did the Beatles' experiences with Maharishi expose?

7. What competing alternatives did the Beatles and Rolling Stones offer, and what do they reveal about New Left's process of internal definition?

BIBLIOGRAPHY

To examine the Beatles and John Lennon, see Sam Leach, *The Birth of the Beatles and Rocking City* (1999), Ian Macdonald, *Revolution in the Head: The Beatles' Records and the Sixties* (1998), Mark Heartsgood, *"A Day in the Life": The Music and Artistry of the Beatles* (1996), George Martin and William Peterson, *The Summer of Love: The Making of Sgt. Pepper* (1995) and Jon Fitzgerald's "When the Brill Building Met Lennon-McCartney: Continuing Change in the Early Evolution of the Mainstream Pop Song" *Popular Music and Society* 19 (1995): 59–77. For an examination of "hippies," see Timothy Miller, *The Hippies and American Values* (1991). For background on the New Left, see Peter B. Levy, *The New Left and Labor in the 1960's* (1994), Doug Rossinow, "The New Left in the Counterculture: Hypotheses and Evidence *Radical History Review* 67 (1997): 79–120, Paul Lyons, *New Left, New Right, and the Legacy to the Sixties* (1996), Richard J. Ellis, "Romancing the Oppressed: The New Left and the Left Out" *Review of Politics* 58 (1996): 109–154. Paul Friedlander considers social aspects of Rock and Roll in *Rock and Roll: A Social History* (1996); also helpful is David P. Szatmary's *Rockin' in History: A Social History of Rock and Roll* 4th ed. (2000).

READING 28

LIBERALISM OVERTHROWN
Matthew Dallek

In 1964 Barry Goldwater, a Republican senator from Arizona, ran for the presidency on a platform that seemed singularly out of step with the times. At a moment in American history when liberalism was nearing its high point, when more government was seen as the answer to the country's many problems, Goldwater called for a drastic reduction in the size and scope of the federal government. The government in Washington, he suggested, had already become too big, too fat, and too complacent, and he meant to change all of that. "I have little interest in streamlining government or making it more efficient, for I mean to reduce its size," he wrote. "I do not undertake to promote welfare, for I propose to extend freedom. My aim is not to pass laws, but to repeal them."

His Democratic opponent Lyndon Johnson scoffed at Goldwater's proposals. He promised a Great Society, with Washington playing the role of Big Daddy. "I just want to tell you this—we're in favor of a whole lot of things and we're against mighty few," Johnson said in speech after speech. He favored federal dollars for Medicare, Medicade, regional redevelopment, urban renewal, and education. Responding to his measured tones—and perhaps frightened by Goldwater's seeming stridency—Americans voted in large numbers for Johnson. As Johnson carried over 60 percent of the popular vote, journalists wrote obituaries for Goldwater's conservative movement. A *Time* magazine writer prophesied, "The conservative cause whose championship Goldwater assumed suffered a crippling setback. . . . The humiliation of their defeat was so complete that they will not have another shot at party domination for some time to come."

But the movement was not dead. As Matthew Dallek shows in "Liberalism Overthrown," the election of 1964 just showed the conservative movement how to win. In 1966 a new candidate—polished smooth by years in Hollywood and a sharp staff of advisors—assumed the lead of the movement. In that year in California conservatism and liberalism battled once again for domination.

The rain had been pelting for hours when the mourners gathered in St. Cecilia's Roman Catholic Church, in the Sunset district, but now the skies cleared as four National Guard helicopters clattered overhead in a "missing man" formation as scores of dignitaries—governors and representatives, senators and aides from Sacramento and Washington, Los Angeles and New York—stared gravely at the casket, draped in the red and white state flag. It was February 17, 1996, and Edmund G. ("Pat") Brown, the liberal former governor of California, was being buried in San Francisco.

The mourners were burying more than a man; they were burying a political era. The decades-long liberal consensus that had begun with the New Deal had faded years before. But Brown's passing offered friends and foes alike a chance to reflect upon that time.

As word of his death spread, the telephone at the Brown family home rang with calls from around the nation. Kathleen Kelly, one of Pat Brown's ten grandchildren, walked outside the modest three-bedroom house in Benedict Canyon to address the reporters gathered in front. "My grandfather, I think, represented to so many people a compassion and a justice that we are just not seeing in this political era," Kelly said. A political commentator named Sherry Bebitch Jeffe had been in New Hampshire covering the Republican presidential primary when she heard of Pat Brown's death. "This place today," she said, "is one million light-years away from where California politics and government were back then. Here I am following a group of men, including the incumbent, who are competing against everything that Pat Brown stood for . . . active government, government that could make civic life better for everyone. That is all under deconstruction right now, on all sides of the political spectrum."

Why did liberalism fail? For the past thirty years that question has dominated many discussions of American politics, and the search for answers has become something of a national obsession. Conservative politicians, such as Newt Gingrich, tend to blame student radicals and pushy minorities for wanting too much too fast. Liberals generally either fault a white racist backlash or, when the issue is raised, act as if they were discussing sexual matters with their teenagers: They prefer to avoid the subject (remember Michael Dukakis in 1988?).

Scholars and journalists have also offered numerous explanations, and their studies of the civil rights movement, the Great Society, the New Left, and Vietnam have done much to answer the question, but most have missed a central reason: the rise as early as the 1960s of a well-organized, popular conservative movement bent on winning political power.

The best studies of the 1960s—Allen Matusow's *The Unraveling of America,* John Morton Blum's *Years of Discord,* and William Chafe's *The Unfinished Journey*—pay little or no attention to the rise of the right, one of the most important developments of the decade. Instead, these books divide the politics of those years into neat categories, describing, in order, the triumph of New Deal and Great Society liberalism, left-wing challenges to liberalism, and the disintegration of the liberal coalition. If they mention conservatism at all, it is usually only after 1968, and the one serious study that deals with both liberals and conservatives—Thomas Byrne Edsall's *Chain Reaction*—minimizes the role conservatives played in their own victories and argues that racial backlash was the main key to the rise of the right.

Previous interpretations of liberalism's collapse are not wrong, but they are incomplete: None of them capture the complexity of the political transformations that took place in the 1960s. The decline of liberalism and the rise of the right were not, as many have suggested, two separate developments. Rather, they were inextricably intertwined, and to understand the sudden, dramatic shift, we need to examine how liberal failures and conservative successes worked hand in hand to reverse a long-standing political balance of power.

"Liberalism Overthrown" by Matthew Dallek in *American Heritage,* Vol. 47/No. 6, October 1996, pp. 39–60. Reprinted by permission of *American Heritage* Magazine, a division of Forbes, Inc. © Forbes, Inc., 1996.

We also need to look back past the convulsions of the last thirty years and revisit a time that was so different—politically, ideologically, socially—from our own that it seems, as Pat's son, Jerry, put it, "like a different country." The time was 1966; the place, California. That year Pat Brown was being challenged by a bumptious political upstart from Southern California, Ronald Reagan.

Brown should have won. He should have won because he was a popular two-term incumbent, the economy was booming, migrants were thronging the West, hailing his state as the promised land, and he had accomplished more than any of his predecessors. In previous races he had defeated two of the Republican party's political titans, the Senate minority whip William Knowland and former Vice President Richard Nixon. That last victory had earned him the nickname "the Giant Killer."

And Ronald Reagan, his likely opponent in the 1966 general election, was no Richard Nixon. A fervent right-winger, a mediocre actor, and, most encouraging, a political novice, Reagan seemed easy prey for the Giant Killer. Surely, the governor thought, his constituents would never put someone with such scant experience and such shallow, extreme views in charge of the most populous state in the nation, would never reject a liberal, progressive philosophy for an antiquated conservatism more appropriate to the nineteenth century. The forces of history seemed once again to be on his side.

Pat Brown was a Catholic, a Californian, and a career politician. Above all, he was a liberal. But he hadn't always been one. Born in San Francisco in 1905, a year before the great earthquake razed the city, Edmund G. Brown early developed an interest in politics. In the seventh grade he delivered a "give me liberty or give me death" speech on behalf of World War I Liberty bonds so rousing that classmates started calling him Pat, short for Patrick Henry. The name stuck.

In 1928 Brown ran for the state assembly as a Calvin Coolidge Republican. Soundly defeated, he returned to his fledgling law practice in San Francisco. A few years later, as the Great Depression

settled on the nation, he began to question the wisdom of his laissez-faire philosophy. His high school chum Matthew Tobriner (a future state supreme court justice) told Brown to wake up; F.D.R.'s victory was no ordinary political event but the beginning of a new political era. Tobriner gave Brown copies of *The New Republic* and quoted the columnist Walter Lippmann on the need for economic reform. In 1934, with farm prices at record lows and twenty million Americans out of work, Pat Brown became a Roosevelt New Dealer.

The switch was not unusual. Like many young men of his generation, Brown had come to believe that the ideas of Coolidge, Harding, and Hoover held little hope for the unemployed millions. Those ideas, Brown said years later, represented "an appeal for human selfishness. . . . I never regretted the change, not for a minute."

He had little reason to. As a moderate Democrat he built a political résumé second to none: In 1943 he was elected San Francisco district attorney, seven years later he became the state attorney general and earned a reputation as a tough law-and-order man, and in 1958 he became governor of California—just the second Democrat to hold that post in the twentieth century.

Although his predecessors were virtually all Republicans, they were also, like him, liberals. Hiram Johnson, the progressive governor who dominated California politics from 1911 to 1917, was one of the great crusaders of the era; he rid the state of the corrupting influence of the Southern Pacific Railroad and won passage of such landmark-political reforms as the referendum, recall, and initiative. During his tenure brothels were banned, racetrack gambling outlawed, workmen's compensation laws enacted, and eight-hour days adopted. Earl Warren shared Johnson's vision. Governor from 1943 to 1954—the longest tenure in state history—Warren built highways, housing, schools, prisons, mental health facilities, and parks, and in so doing met the needs of the three million new residents who moved to California during his incumbency.

But in California no one more incarnated the forces of liberalism than Pat Brown. He helped build the largest and most prestigious state university system in the country as well as the California water system, which each day brought two billion gallons of the precious liquid from the rainy north to the arid south. He won passage of fair housing legislation, established a Fair Employment Practices Commission, reformed state labor laws, increased unemployment insurance, and expanded welfare benefits. He believed in the ability of government to improve the human condition—a central tenet of postwar liberalism—and he brought the state into unprecedented areas of California society.

"Think big," Pat exhorted fellow Californians in his 1962 race against Richard Nixon. In the boom years of post-World War II America, many politicians thought big. But in vision and public works, none thought bigger than Pat Brown.

In early 1966 Brown felt so good about his chances against Ronald Reagan that he did what many politicians in his position would have done: He played dirty to help Reagan get the Republican nomination. George Christopher, the moderate Republican former mayor of San Francisco, who was challenging Reagan in the primary, had been convicted in 1940 of violating milk-pricing laws. It was a minor transgression and had done little damage to Christopher's political career. Until 1966. The Brown campaign got wind of the scandal, and in the two months before the June primary Brown's people spoon-fed the story to reporters. In early May the governor's team hit pay dirt when the syndicated columnist Drew person wrote two ferocious articles about the milk control law violation. "Pearson's putrid piece . . .," one prominent Christopher supporter said, "can be laid right at the door step of Pat Brown's political outhouse. Brown, of course, wants to . . . destroy George Christopher, and thus have Ronald Reagan nominated." Don Bradley, one of Brown's top campaign aides, responded: "Mr. Christopher is a cry baby. . . . George Christopher's arrest record . . . [is a matter] of public record which Mr. Christopher has yet to explain adequately.

Mr. Christopher has been ducking the truth for years." It was a blow from which Christopher's candidacy never recovered.

It was also a classic miscalculation. In the 1950s and 1960s liberal politicians and journalists dismissed conservatives as "kooks" and "crackpots" with no hope of winning political power. "Republicans," a typical article read in 1966, "try to make the voters afraid of the world." Right-wingers, another explained, like to "complain about the twentieth century." Pat Brown could not have agreed more. In 1964, during the fight over Proposition 14, a move to repeal the Brown-endorsed Rumford Fair Housing Act, the governor described his conservative opponents as fascists: "There have been echoes in this state of another hate binge which began more than thirty years ago in a Munich beer hall. These echoes come from a minority of the angry, the frustrated, the fearful. They do not represent California or its people. But what they do represent—the spasm reaction of hatred—does exist not only in California but elsewhere in our nation and in our world."

When Brown heard Reagan might oppose him, he was at once incredulous and delighted: "Ronald Reagan for Governor of California?" Brown wrote in 1970. "We thought the notion was absurd and rubbed our hands in gleeful anticipation of beating this politically inexperienced, right-wing extremist and aging actor in 1966." In January 1965 one of Brown's secretaries sent Jack Burby, his press secretary, an article predicting that Reagan would run for governor. "Bring him on," Burby scribbled in the margin.

But before Brown could do battle with Reagan, he had to contend with Sam Yorty, the maverick mayor of Los Angeles, who was running against Brown in the Democratic primary. Yorty was the George Wallace of California politics, an acid-tongued conservative Democrat, who had become known for his scalding attacks on liberal elites. In early 1966 Yorty concentrated his fire on Pat Brown: The governor coddled left-wing radicals, did nothing to halt the proliferation of drugs, stood by while Communist agitators fomented riots on campus, and had lost touch with the common man.

Worst of all, Brown had failed to crack down on black rioters in Watts. Imposing law and order, Yorty thundered, was the only way to quash the violence in South Central L.A. Yorty's police chief backed him all the way. "We are interested," Chief William Parker declared, "in maintaining order." When Watts erupted, Parker explained the disorder this way: "One person throws a rock and then, like monkeys in a zoo, others started throwing rocks." Yorty returned the favor to the chief posthumously when at Parker's funeral in 1966 he crooned, "God may not be dead, but his finest representative on earth has just passed away."

Berkeley was also a favorite subject of the mayor. During the campaign a reporter asked Yorty what he thought of a report on the situation there recently issued by a state senate committee. He hadn't had a chance to analyze it, Yorty responded; then, said the San Francisco *Chronicle,* he "launched into a lengthy dissertation on 'filth' on the campus."

There are times in American history when events are so unsettling, so disruptive to the normal patterns of social interaction, that they shake the political foundation to its core. In 1919 race riots, widespread labor unrest, the battle over women's suffrage, and the rejection of Wilson's cherished Versailles Treaty helped end two decades of progressive reform and usher in the new era of retrenchment that Warren G. Harding called a "return to normalcy." Normalcy ended in 1932, when Franklin D. Roosevelt, with no firm ideas about how to govern, began to forge a new political coalition that brought workers, blacks, and Southern whites together in the belief that government had the capacity to improve their lives. And in 1966 the third great political upheaval of this century began.

In California the new era might be said to have begun on October 1, 1964, when police at the University of California, Berkeley, arrested Jack Weinberg, a former student, for setting up a civil rights table on campus. The police were about to drive Weinberg off to jail when several hundred students surrounded their car. The standoff lasted

for thirty-two hours, and it not only launched the Free Speech Movement but also marked the beginning of almost a decade of student protest. Ten months later, on a scorching summer day, the black ghetto of Watts some three hundred miles south of Berkeley exploded in violence. When the riots finally subsided, the statistics told the story: thirty-four dead, one thousand injured, four thousand arrested, two hundred million dollars in property damage, and sixteen thousand law enforcement officials deployed.

Watts and Berkeley were the two most visible issues in California in the mid-sixties, but there were plenty of others to reinforce the sense that disorder and immorality were taking over. In 1965, just one year after Californians had voted overwhelmingly to repeal Pat Brown's Fair Housing Act, the state supreme court declared the repeal measure unconstitutional and reinstated the antidiscrimination law. At Berkeley protests against the Vietnam War popped up, and a short-lived Filthy Speech Movement, in which students took turns shouting "F—!" over loudspeakers in Sproul Plaza, raised the specter of "educational anarchy." Residents read stories about LSD, saw photos of unkempt hippies parading the streets of San Francisco, and were told that their state had the good fortune to be producing 60 percent of the nation's "booming smut trade." One conservative activist vividly summed up many Californians' feelings about the last: "This crud falls into the hands of teenagers and younger persons . . . and the worst stuff comes in books like 'Seed of the Beast,' which describes sexual intercourse between animals and humans, and 'Queer Daddy,' which contains vivid descriptions of almost every other kind of perversion. . . . The message . . . is that if you haven't practiced homosexuality, you just haven't lived."

The polls showed that nine out of ten Californians disapproved of antiwar demonstrations; they identified "crime, drugs, juvenile delinquency" as the most pressing issue confronting their state; "racial problems" came in second; "student discipline at the University of California," sixth.

Berkeley was a particular sore point. Tuition was free there, and the university was widely seen as the crown jewel in the state's educational system. So when *The Saturday Evening Post*— that citadel of middle-class values—reported that "on the sunny, seemingly serene Berkeley campus, rebellion is fashionable and it is widely believed that half the student body has experimented with marijuana," tax-payers were upset. Berkeley Citizens United, a local conservative group, issued a mock U.C. curriculum in which the entering class could look forward to taking "Riot 101, Russian Language 101, and Dirty Books 101," while sophomores were required to devote two minutes per week to "Personal Hygiene" and eleven hours to "Draft Dodging, Troop Train Delaying, and Composition (4-Letter Words)." Those fortunate enough to make it to their junior years could take "Police Car Sit-In 331, Car Burning Lab, and Public Speaking Lab (Yelling and Shouting)."

At other times—say, in the 1950s—Sam Yorty might have come across as a mere hooligan, flinging wild political charges that bore little relation to the larger scene. But in the mid-1960s his attacks on the liberal establishment range true for increasing number of Californians.

In the early weeks of the primary Brown simply ignored Yorty. Then, when the mayor seemed to gain in the polls, he went on the attack: "This little man has flipped his lid. Yorty thinks everyone is against him. . . . [The] psychiatric term for this . . . [is] paranoia—and I think this is the best way to describe the Mayor of Los Angeles." But Brown never campaigned vigorously against Yorty; he dismissed him and saved his money for the general election.

When the primary returns came in on June 7, Brown was shaken. He had won, of course, but it was a near thing. Yorty had received almost a million votes, 38 percent of the Democratic total. One thing was immediately clear: If Yorty's supporters decided to vote for Ronald Reagan, the Republican nominee, in the general election, Brown would probably lose. Though a massive defection of voters from one party to another was

unlikely, the governor was worried; he had to keep Yorty Democrats in the party fold.

The California Democratic party's leaders gathered less than a week after the primary to discuss their strategy for the general election, and they came away from the meeting confident that liberalism was alive and well. Reagan, who had walloped Christopher by more than seven hundred thousand votes, had "got a free ride" during the primaries, Robert L. Coate, the Democratic state chairman, announced. That would soon change, Eugene Wyman, California's Democratic National Committeeman, predicted, when the actor was exposed as a "staunch defender of the far right . . . a disgrace to the Republican Party and a threat to the politics of moderation which has given this state wise and able leadership in the past two decades."

In 1964 Lyndon Johnson and the Democratic party had succeeded in painting Barry Goldwater as an extremist who would jeopardize national security and gut popular federal programs. In 1966 Pat Brown and his Democratic supporters thought they could do the same thing to another fierce conservative who despised most government involvement in the marketplace and took strong law-and-order stands on crime, social unrest, and immorality.

But by the mid-1960s Ronald Reagan was not, nor did he appear to be, an extremist. Reagan spent much of the 1950s sharpening his conservative philosophy as a spokesman for General Electric; he travelled from plant to plant, promoted the company's image, and spoke to workers and businessmen about the evils of high taxes and big government. "The Speech," as his standard talk came to be called, interspersed lively and entertaining stories with political tidbits about the wonders of the free-enterprise system.

The year 1964 proved pivotal for both Ronald Reagan and the conservative movement. Having already become a well-known figure in California right-wing circles, he agreed to serve as state cochairman of Citizens for Goldwater. His big moment came in the closing days of Goldwater's campaign. In a last-ditch effort to sway voters,

Reagan went on national television to speak on behalf of Goldwater. The speech, "A Time for Choosing," did little to help the Republican presidential candidate, but conservatives found Reagan's performance so stirring that they immediately hailed him as one of the rising stars of the Republican right.

Holmes Tuttle and Henry Salvatori, two wealthy Southern California businessmen, liked what they saw so much that they asked Reagan to run for governor in 1966. Don't just say no, Tuttle pleaded; take some time to think about it. Reagan agreed, and the Friends of Reagan, the campaign's fund-raising arm, was organized. From the outset the candidate had the backing of many wealthy Angelenos. More important, he had shrewd political advisers who thought they knew how a conservative could win the governorship. Stu Spencer and Bill Roberts, California's top political consultants, advised Reagan to avoid ill-tempered remarks and to work with moderate Republicans; they designated him a "citizen-politician" and started calling his reform program the Creative Society, in hopes of blunting voters' fears of conservatives as out-of-touch nay-sayers; and they hired two behavioral psychologists, Kenneth Holden and Stanley Plog, to help Reagan with the issues. "He knew zero about California when we came in, I mean zero," Plog recalled, but Reagan was a quick study and knew how to convey his ideas in a clear and forceful manner.

He was also careful to avoid the more radical ideas and statements that had so harmed other conservatives. Goldwater, during his presidential campaign, had threatened to "lob [missiles] into the men's room at the Kremlin." During his race Reagan spoke of a better California. "Our problems are many," he said in the speech announcing his candidacy, "but our capacity for solving them is limitless." When pressed about his support from radical right-wingers, Reagan explained that *they* were buying *his* philosophy, not the other way around.

The only time he appeared to be a genuine fire-breathing radical came in March 1966, during a debate with George Christopher in front of the Negro Republican Assembly. Ben Peery, a black

Los Angeles businessman, asked Reagan how he could solicit black votes after having opposed the 1964 Civil Rights Act. When Christopher expressed similar doubts, Reagan, who had been under attack all day, threw down his note cards. "I resent the implication that there is any bigotry in my nature," he shouted. "Don't anyone ever imply I lack integrity. I will not stand silent and let anyone imply that." Then he stormed out of the debate, muttering, "I'll get that S.O.B."

Holden, who was in the audience, watched appalled, then managed to reach Reagan at home and pleaded with him to return to the event: "Why don't you come back and have a drink with the delegates? It will ease a lot of hurt feelings." Reagan eventually did so, but his advisers were aghast. Nothing frightened them more than the charge of extremism. The issue had helped sink Goldwater in '64, and it could do the same to Reagan in '66. Another outburst, they warned, could doom his campaign and end his political career. Reagan promised that it would not happen again.

It didn't. In August 1966 California Democrats released a twenty-nine-page paper, "Ronald Reagan, Extremist Collaborator." Reagan was not a moderate Republican, it claimed, but actually a dangerous radical, his campaign was "riddled" with members of the John Birch Society, he accepted money from extremist groups, and he opposed government programs like Social Security and federal aid to education. Serious charges, but they didn't stick. When Democrats presented Reagan with a press release claiming that Spencer-Roberts—his own political consultants!—had once identified him as an "extremist," the candidate coolly called the move a "diversionary tactic to avoid campaigning on the issues." In the end Reagan just seemed too good-looking, too upbeat, and too witty to be a member of any lunatic fringe.

He had, in short, all the markings of a candidate with a finely tuned political campaign, something that conservatives, for all their ideological fervor, were unaccustomed to. He also represented a movement that, by the mid-sixties, was hell-bent on winning political power.

After the election was over, the Los Angeles *Times* reported: "Don Bradley, the governor's campaign chairman, said Brown was the victim of a national movement toward conservatives that resulted from voter resistance to Negro gains." Race, of course, has almost always played a central role in American politics. In the eighteenth century the Constitutional Convention nearly disbanded over the issue of slavery; less than a century later the question re-emerged with such force that it took six hundred thousand American lives to settle the issue; in this century the great black migrations from the rural South to the urban North helped thrust civil rights to the center of national debate; and in the 1960s the growing disillusionment with the black struggle for freedom gave conservatives a powerful issue with which to pry lower-middle-class Americans from the Democratic coalition.

Reagan's campaign was no exception. His stances on fair housing, urban riots, crime, and welfare all appealed to whites increasingly resentful (and fearful) of blacks and members of other minorities who seemed to be getting "special privileges." Race was a central issue. But it was not, as some have suggested, the only one. Rather it fitted into a larger set of ideas about the iniquities of big government. The two issues were so intertwined that to understand Reagan's campaign—and the rise of the right—we must understand how the issue of race fitted in with and reinforced conservatives' broad antigovernment message.

Throughout the campaign Reagan repeatedly charged that the bureaucratic welfare state coddled minorities, raised middle-class taxes to meet the growing costs of welfare, threatened individual liberty, and failed to impose order on the small but dangerous numbers of radicals, dissidents, and criminals. In 1966 events helped reinforce Reagan's ideas.

No issue was bigger than public morality—law and order—and Reagan rarely wasted an opportunity to expound on liberal shortcomings in this area. Berkeley, much to his campaign's delight, stayed in the news throughout 1966. In the first

Edmund "Pat" Brown campaigning

week of May the state senate Sub-Committee on Un-American Activities released a long-awaited report on the University of California. A few days later Reagan appeared at the Cow Palace in San Francisco and explained before a cheering throng that he had not yet seen that report; then, suddenly, he whipped out a different one on Berkeley, from the Alameda County district attorney's office (where the future Attorney General Ed Meese worked), and said, "The incidents are so bad, so contrary to our standards of decent human behavior, that I cannot recite them to you from this platform in detail." But he went right on to describe—in detail—a dance at Berkeley sponsored by an antiwar group.

"The total crowd was in excess of 3,000, including a number of less-than-college-age juveniles," Reagan began. "Three rock 'n' roll bands were in the center of the gymnasium playing simultaneously all during the dance, and all during the dance movies were shown on two screens at the opposite ends of the gymnasium. These movies were the only lights in the gym proper. They consisted of color sequences that gave the appearance of different-colored liquid spreading across the screen, followed by shots of men and women[;] on occasion, shots were of the men's and women's nude torsos, and persons twisted and gyrated in provocative and sensual fashion.

The young people were seen standing against the walls or lying on the floors and steps in a dazed condition with glazed eyes consistent with the condition of being under the influence of narcotics. Sexual misconduct was blatant."

This moral decline, Reagan continued, had began in 1964, "when the so-called free-speech advocates, who in truth have no appreciation for freedom, were allowed to assault and humiliate the symbol of law and order, a policeman, on the campus; and that was the moment when the ringleaders should have been taken by the scruff of the neck and thrown out of the university once and for all." The audience cheered.

Almost all the issues, in fact, fitted in with Reagan's promise to restore order. On Vietnam? Reagan proposed simply that we "go in there and do it." Antiwar demonstrators? Charge them with treason. Urban riots? Just invoke the law. Crime? Lock criminals in jail, and don't handicap the police.

Meanwhile Reagan used racial issues to draw attention to what he saw as the dangerous excesses of big government. His position on California's Fair Housing Act was typical. The law, he charged, embodied the dangers of an expansive and encroaching government. Yes, he said, he despised bigotry just as much as the next guy, but in the end the government had no right to tell people how to sell or rent their property. In 1966 welfare and taxes also became hot political issues. There were, Reagan said at one campaign stop after another, people moving to California not for the opportunity to work but for the chance to get on welfare: "You have to live in California for five years to be governor, but you can get on welfare in twenty-four hours."

Throughout the campaign Brown was on the defensive. Reagan called him "soft" on black rioters, campus degenerates, drug dealers, and hippies. As Berkeley imploded, Brown seemed indecisive. During the Free Speech Movement, for example, when students occupied Sproul Hall, he hesitated before calling in the cops to arrest them as trespassers. A local radio station interspersed its coverage of the arrests with a commencement address Brown had given at the University of

Santa Clara a few years earlier. "Thank God," the governor had said that day, "for the spectacle of students picketing. . . . At last we're getting somewhere. The colleges have become boot camps for citizenship, and citizen-leaders are marching out of them. . . . Let us stand up for our students and be proud of them."

Pat Brown was a decent man. He cared about people, and he governed with the hope of improving their individual lives. But his sympathy for civil rights and student grievances and his concern for the growing urban poor gave voters the impression that he had encouraged many of the disruptive elements that had thrown California into its present turmoil. Even when he took decisive action—like calling out the National Guard to quell riots in San Francisco and Oakland—people wondered how he had let things get out of control in the first place. What, voters asked Reagan during the campaign, would he do "about those bastards at Berkeley"? More, he invariably replied, than Pat Brown ever would.

Nor could Brown count on the support of the more liberal members of his party. The Vietnam War and urban riots saw to that. As a staunch supporter of President Johnson's Vietnam policy, the governor had an unprecedented problem on his hands in 1966: Si Casady, the head of the California Democratic Council (CDC), the party's largest volunteer organization in the state, was encouraging young men to burn their draft cards. Under pressure from the White House, Brown forced Casady to resign. But the problem didn't go away. Students who in other times could have been counted on to hand out leaflets and knock on doors for the Democratic nominee continued to protest the war, and even its more moderate opponents had trouble getting excited about re-electing a man so strongly identified with the policy-makers in Washington.

The social upheavals of the early and mid-sixties had transformed the political climate. By 1966 Reagan's anti-government ideology had come to appear moderate, rational, and a force for order. Brown, by contrast, seemed allied to the radical left and the increasingly militant civil rights leadership. The governor admitted himself that he was caught in a "political vise" between a growing left-wing movement that attacked liberalism for not going far enough and a conservative revival promising, among other things, to restore order. It was not a good position to be in, because in 1966 the political center—which, as the historian Arthur Schlesinger, Jr. once put it, is "vital" to the preservation of freedom—collapsed.

During the desultory final days of the race, his lead gone, Pat Brown remained uncomprehending. "Why, oh, why, my friends," he pleaded, "would you turn this state over to a man who has never fought before a city council or a board of supervisors?" At a night rally in San Bernardino, when the electricity failed, Brown said, "They can cut off the electricity, but they can't shut up the greatest governor California has ever had."

On November 8, 1966, Reagan beat Brown by almost a million votes. Four years earlier, when Brown had defeated Nixon, the former Vice President, in a spasm of indignation and anger, had lit into the journalists arrayed before him. "You won't have Nixon to kick around anymore, because gentlemen, this is my last press conference." Brown was determined to avoid repeating that fiasco. When the votes were finally tabulated, he went before his deflated supporters and thanked California "for giving me eight wonderful, marvelous years." When he finished, his advisers suggested he leave through a rear exit. Instead the governor stepped down from the podium and plunged into the crowd of loyal supporters. Then he walked out to his limousine, climbed inside, and started to cry.

Sam Yorty had other plans that night. The maverick mayor had refused to endorse either candidate during the campaign, but as soon as Reagan's victory was assured, he left little doubt about where his sympathies lay; he hurried over to the hotel where the victory celebration was under way and congratulated the governor-elect.

Individual communities also told the story that day. Norwalk was one of the many Democratic working-class suburbs that had sprouted in recent years along the Pacific coast, and on Election Day

1966 Norwalk was one of many Southern California Democratic communities that voted overwhelmingly for Ronald Reagan.

Norwalk's rejection of Pat Brown is, on one level, strange. Three out of four voters were registered Democrats, and residents had traditionally favored liberal government programs like Social Security and workmen's compensation. And the government had done much to ensure the city's economic well-being; many residents worked at nearby defense and aerospace plants, and the Metropolitan State Hospital employed fourteen hundred men and women.

Yet on another level Norwalk's support for Reagan was not strange at all. The city had been conceived in a revolt against government. Like those of many nearby bedroom communities, Norwalk's residents resented the Los Angeles board of supervisors; simple street repairs sometimes required weeks of fighting with the county bureaucracy. The people of Norwalk wanted to control their own affairs, and in 1957 they won a charter from the county and incorporated. By the mid-sixties their grievances with government had reached the boiling point: Taxes were too high, the welfare state seemed out of control, the fair housing law was raising fears of lower property values and higher crime rates (in 1966 only three black families lived in the town), and the counterculture, the new left, minorities, and liberals seemed to have dedicated themselves to the common purpose of flouting the values that Norwalk residents held dear. Government had become a remote institution out of touch with the needs of ordinary citizens.

Why did Californians revolt against liberalism? Most studies of the sixties suggest that liberalism and conservatism were two separate, isolated political movements whose paths did not cross until the end of the decade, when liberals were already in retreat. Most books on the politics of this decade focus on some aspect of the American left: the civil rights movement, the counterculture, the antiwar movement. Studies of liberalism, of which there are surprisingly few, tend to explain the demise of the New Deal coalition as the result of internal weaknesses: failure in Vietnam and the limitations of the Great Society reforms. The few detailed studies of modern conservatism (which only recently has been recognized as a serious political movement worthy of scholarly attention) similarly emphasize changes within the movement—the growing number of right-wing organizations, the repudiation of extremists, and conservatives' use of social issues—to explain the right's success.

These accounts are important, but they don't explain—at least not entirely—how conservatism replaced liberalism as the dominant force in American political life. It is true that student protests, urban riots, pornography, and antipathy to civil rights did much to discredit liberalism. Liberal Democrats, after all, were the party in power, and on their watch things seemed to fall apart.

But liberalism failed for two other, lesser-known reasons. It collapsed first because the white working and middle classes, men and women in communities like Norwalk, had come to mistrust—and at times despise—what they had held in high regard since the 1930s: centralized government power. In the thirties liberals had used government to establish a lifeline for the millions of Americans left bewildered and impoverished by the Great Depression, but by the 1960s unprecedented prosperity, partly the product of liberal reforms, had given rise to a new middle class that was hostile to high taxes and to many of the social programs they financed. This newly minted middle class expected liberals to denounce immorality and social disorder, to speak out for traditional values, and to stop paying so much attention to the dispossessed—the poor, the minorities, the radicals. On all these counts this restive majority found liberals wanting. The white backlash was the most visible, and perhaps the most potent, issue feeding the new anti-

government mood. But it was also part of a larger revolt, a much deeper disillusionment with liberal government and those who championed it.

Liberalism failed also because—and this is rarely acknowledged—conservatives had transformed themselves into powerful political contenders armed with a devastating critique of their opponents. In the mid-sixties the conservative movement emerged as a smoothly running political machine; it had repudiated extremism, developed a more positive political platform that stressed the efficacy of individual initiative, and found a middle class receptive to its message. By the mid-sixties the right was able successfully to portray liberals, the supposed champions of the common man, as elitists who had lost touch with the needs and aspirations of ordinary Americans.

The campaign between Pat Brown and Ronald Reagan shows that we can't understand the failure of liberalism without understanding the rise of the right. Brown's and Reagan's careers were not always linked, but their fates were. Brown became governor at a time when conservatives were just beginning to find a coherent political voice; his policies helped galvanize the movement, and his failure to resolve the social crises of the decade paved the way for Reagan's victory in 1966, a victory that came in part from years of conservative organizing.

Thirty years ago this November Pat Brown's political career—and the liberalism it epitomized—came to an abrupt end. As a politician Brown had his flaws: He wasn't terribly charismatic, he was not a man of powerful intelligence, he had been in office eight long years, and he looked bad on television. But in 1966 he possessed one crippling defect: He was a liberal. And when Pat Brown went down, so did the philosophy that he had clung to throughout his adult life. It has never really recovered.

STUDY QUESTIONS

1. For which values and policies did Pat Brown stand? Why did he think that he would have little trouble winning reelection in 1966?

2. Was California's history in the 66 years of the twentieth century one of liberalism or conservatism?

3. How did liberals and conservatives differ in terms of political philosophy and public policies?

4. What issues dominated the primaries and the gubernatorial race? What role did race play in the election?

5. How did Reagan's advisors shape his image to appeal to voters? How did Democratic politicians attempt to shape a negative image of Reagan as a wild-eyed radical?

6. What best explains the decline of liberalism and the rise of conservatism in the 1960s?

BIBLIOGRAPHY

The rise of Reanald Reagan, and especially his role in the modern conservative movement and the California gubernatorial race of 1966, has received considerable attention in the last decade. Lou Cannon, *President Reagan: The Role of a Lifetime* (1991) is outstanding, as are Garry Wills, *Reagan's America* (1988) and Robert Dallek, *Ronald Reagan: The Politics of Symbolism* (1984). Robert Alan Goldberg, *Barry Goldwater* (1995), examines not only Goldwater but the movement he helped to launch. The decline of liberalism and the rise of conservatism are also detailed in Thomas Ferguson and Joel Rogers, *Turn Right: The Decline of the Democrats and the Future of American Politics* (1986) and Steve Fraser and Gary Gerstle, *The Rise and Fall of the New Deal Order* (1990).

PERFECT BODIES, ETERNAL YOUTH: THE OBSESSION OF MODERN AMERICA

Randy Roberts and James S. Olson

The message comes at Americans from every direction, every hour of the day. Cher appears on television touting the miraculous benefits of the President's First Lady exercise salons. Lynn Redgrave comes on a few minutes later delivering superlatives about Weight Watchers's frozen entree foods. Jane Fonda's exercise videotapes confront shoppers in supermarkets and video stores. Victoria Principal and Raquel Welch write diet and fitness books, both of which become best sellers. Plastic surgeons advertise in newspapers and on television, urging Americans to get rid of what they hate or acquire what they want for their bodies. Every issue of *Family Circle, Woman's Day,* and *The Enquirer* contains some new article about the latest weight-loss panacea.

Sports programming dominates television, as if Americans have an insatiable need to watch football, baseball, basketball, bowling, bodybuilding, and a host of other competitions. Future linguists and anthropologists will study what have become the highlights of contemporary American popular culture—diet sodas, low-calorie beers, Lean Cuisine, sugarless gum, half-the-calories bread, Nautilus, jogging, Iron Man marathons, "fun runs," tennis, bicycling, 10 K races, Superbowls, play-offs, World Series, Grand Slams of golf and tennis, Little League, Pop Warner football, and championship after championship.

Modern America is not the first society to indulge in the emptiness of narcissism, but no other society has ever had such resources to spend on a fruitless crusade to prevent aging and deny death. In "Perfect Bodies, Eternal Youth: The Obsession of Modern America," Randy Roberts and James S. Olson examine the preoccupation with health, fitness, and youth in the United States, explaining how and why the members of an entire culture have become infatuated with their own bodies.

Fewer and fewer people these days argue that running shortens lives, while a lot of people say that it may strengthen them. If that's all we've got for the time being, it seems a good enough argument for running. Not airtight, but good enough.

—Jim Fixx

It was a perfect July day in Vermont—clear and cool. Jim Fixx, on the eve of a long-awaited vacation, put on his running togs and headed down a rural road for his daily run, expecting to do the usual twelve to fifteen miles. At fifty-two years of age, Fixx was a millionaire, the best-selling author of *The Complete Book of Running*, and the reigning guru of the American exercise cult. In 1968 he had weighed 214 pounds, smoked two packs of cigarettes a day, and worried about his family health history. Fixx's father had died of a heart attack at the age of forty-three. So Fixx started running and stopped smoking. He lost 60 pounds and introduced America to the virtues of strenuous exercise: longevity, freedom from depression, energy, and the "runner's high." He regularly ran 80 miles a week. When he hit the road on July 21, 1984, Fixx weighed 154 pounds and seemed the perfect image of fitness. Twenty minutes into the run he had a massive heart attack and died on the side of the road. A motorcyclist found his body later that afternoon.

Fixx's death shocked middle- and upper-class America. Of all people, how could Jim Fixx have died of a heart attack? Millions of joggers, runners, swimmers, cyclists, tri-athletes, walkers, weight-lifters, and aerobic dancers had convinced

From Randy Roberts and James S. Olson, "Perfect Bodies, Eternal Youth: The Obsession of Modern America" in *Winning Is the Only Thing*. The Johns Hopkins University Press, Baltimore/London, 1989, pp. 213–34. Reprinted by permission.

themselves that exercise preserved youth and postponed death. It was the yuppie panacea; "working out" made them immune to the ravages of time.

The autopsy on Fixx was even more disturbing. In spite of all the running, his circulatory system was a shambles. Fixx's cholesterol levels had been dangerously high. One coronary artery was 98 percent blocked, a second one 85 percent blocked, and a third one 50 percent blocked. In the previous two to eight weeks, the wall of his left ventricle had badly deteriorated. On that clear Vermont day, Jim Fixx shouldn't have been running; he should have been undergoing triple-by-pass surgery.

Even more puzzling, Fixx had been complaining for months of chest pains while running—clear signs of a deadly angina, the heart muscle protesting lack of oxygen. Friends had expressed concern and urged him to get a check-up. He resisted, attempting to will good health. In January 1984 he had agreed to a treadmill test, but he skipped the appointment that afternoon, running 16 miles instead. Why had someone so committed to health ignored such obvious warnings? How had sports, exercise, and fitness become such obsessions in the United States?

Modern society was the culprit. In an increasingly secular society, church membership no longer provided the discipline to bind people together into cohesive social groups. Well-integrated neighborhoods with long histories and strong identities had given way after World War II to faceless suburbs. Corporate and professional elites tended to be highly mobile, relocating whenever a pay raise was offered. The new American community had become fifty suburban homes and a 7-11 convenience store. New organizations, especially business and government bureaucracies, had assumed power in the United States, but those were hardly places where most Americans could feel comfortable and in control. Blessed with money but deprived of community in the 1970s and 1980s, Americans began to use sports to rebuild their sense of community and fitness and to define individual happiness and individual pleasure, creating a culture of competitive narcissism supported by a host of therapeutic panaceas, such as EST, psychotherapy, Scientology, and strenuous exercise.

For individuals, families, groups, and communities, sports had become a new cultural currency, a common ground upon which a diverse people could express their values and needs. Unlike European society, where such traditional institutions as the church, the aristocracy, and the monarchy had maintained order through established authority, America had been settled by lower-class working people and small farmers. The traditional institutions anchoring European society were absent. Without those same moorings, America had always confronted the centrifugal forces of individualism, capitalism, Protestantism, and ethnicity, using the culture of opportunity to stave off social disintegration. Social mobility, the westward movement, the abundance of land, and ruralism helped stabilize a highly complex society.

But in the twentieth century, when industrialization, urbanization, and the disappearance of the frontier changed the definitions of opportunity and progress, the values of individualism, community, and competition had to find new modes of expression, and sports became a prominent one. At the local, regional, and national levels, sports evolved into one of the most powerful expressions of identity. Outside observers marveled, for example, at the "religion" of high school football in the more than eleven hundred independent school districts of Texas. When viewed simply as sport, of course, the obsession with football seems absurd, but when viewed in terms of community identity, it becomes more understandable. In hundreds of rural areas, where scattered farms surround tiny county seats, the local high school, with its arbitrarily drawn district lines, was the central focus of community life. Rural Texans passionately opposed school district consolidations, even when it made good economic sense, because it threatened the high school, high school football, and community

identity. For hundreds of small Texas towns—and rural areas throughout much of the rest of the country—high school athletics was literally the cement of community life.

It wasn't just high school sports which provided new identities in the United States. After World War II, social and economic pressures worked against the nuclear family. More and more women were working outside the home; more and more men were working at job sites long commutes from the suburbs; and divorce rates were way up. Childhood play became less spontaneous and more organized as schools, government, and communities assumed roles once played by the family. The most obvious consequence was the appearance of organized youth sports. Little League grew by leaps and bounds beginning in the 1950s; child's play, once the domain of the home and immediate neighborhood, became a spectator sport complete with uniforms, umpires, scoreboards, leagues, play-offs, drafts, and championships. By the 1980s, Little League was competing for time with Pop Warner football, Little Dribblers basketball, soccer, and swimming, with organized competition beginning in some sports at the age of three. In 1987 sports sociologists estimated that thirty million children under sixteen years of age were competing in organized sports.

Sports functioned as identity on the regional level as well. In an age when television, movies, and mass culture threatened regional distinctiveness, sports emerged as the single most powerful symbol of localism and community loyalty. That was obviously true of high school and college sports, but even in professional sports, when ownership shifted away from local businesses and entrepreneurs to conglomerates and national corporations, the regional identity of teams remained critically important to gate receipts and television revenues. The rivalries between the Chicago Bears and the Green Bay Packers, or the Boston Red Sox and the New York Yankees, or the Boston Celtics and the Los Angeles Lakers, filled stadiums, arenas, and living rooms with fans desperate for the home team to win. Five hundred years ago, European cities dedicated all their surplus capital over the course of 100 to 200 years to build elaborate cathedrals to God. In the United States during the 1970s and 1980s, the modern equivalent of the medieval cathedral was the domed stadium. For sports, not for God, American communities would sell bonds and mortgage themselves for the next generation.

Even on the national level, sports competition reflected and promoted American nationalism. Sports was a mirror of federalism, at once local in its community loyalties but national in its collective forms. The 1984 Olympic Games in Los Angeles did not just expose a rising tide of patriotism and national pride; they became a major force in stimulating a new American nationalism. Unlike the recent Olympic Games in Montreal, Moscow, and Seoul, the Los Angeles Games did not accumulate billion-dollar deficits and require the resources of national governments to prop them up. In 1984, "free enterprise capitalism" organized and conducted the Games, used existing facilities, and turned a profit. The Los Angeles Coliseum was filled with flag-waving Americans cheering every native athlete winning a medal. On television back home, Europeans watched the proceedings with astonishment and not a little fear, worrying about the burst of American patriotism, nationalism, and even chauvinism. Nearly a decade after the debacle in Vietnam, American pride and optimism were on the rebound, and the 1984 Olympic Games was center stage for the resurrection of the American sense of mission.

Modern sports in the United States also provided a sense of identity cutting across class, racial, and ethnic lines. In penitentiaries throughout the country, intense struggles were waged every evening over television and radio programming, black convicts wanting to watch soul stations and black sit-coms and whites demanding MTV or white sit-coms. But there was no trouble or debate on Sunday afternoon or Monday nights during the fall. It was football, only football, and blacks and whites watched the programs with equal enthusiasm. On Monday evenings in the fall, whether in the poorest ghetto tenement of

the South Side of Chicago or the most tastefully appointed living room in the Lake Forest suburbs, televisions were tuned in to football, and discussions at work the next morning revolved around the game, who won and who lost, and why.

For ethnic minorities and immigrants, sports similarly became a way of identifying with the new society, a powerful form of acculturation. During the 1980s, for example, Los Angeles became the second largest Mexican city in the world, behind only Mexico City in Spanish-speaking population and larger now than Guadalajara in terms of Mexican residents. At Dodger Stadium in Los Angeles, Mexicans and Mexican Americans became an increasingly large part of the evening box office, helping to sustain Dodger attendance at its three million-plus levels each year. In September 1986, when Dodger pitcher Fernando Valenzuela won his twentieth game of the season, the Spanish cable network SIN broke into its regular programming nationwide for live interviews. The fact that sports was making its way to the headlines and front pages of major newspapers was no accident in the United States. It had become, indeed, a new cultural currency in modern America, a way to interpret change and express traditional values.

Women, too, used sports as vehicle in their drive for equality and identity. The development of women's and men's sports in America has varied considerably. From the first, men's sports have emphasized fierce competition and the ruthless pursuit of expertise. Early male and female physical educators, however, believed women were uncompetitive and decided that women's sports should promote a woman's physical and mental qualities and thus make her more attractive to men. They also believed that sports and exercise should sublimate female sexual drives. As renowned nineteenth-century physical educator Dudley A. Sargent noted, "No one seems to realize that there is a time in the life of a girl when it is better for her and for the community to be something of a boy rather than too much of a girl."

But tomboyish behavior had to stop short of abrasive competition. Lucille Eaton Hill, director of physical training at Wellesley College, urged women to "avoid the evils which are so apparent . . . in the conduct of athletics for men." She and her fellow female physical educators encouraged widespread participation rather than narrow specialization. In short, women left spectator and professional sports to men. Indeed, not until 1924 were women allowed to compete in Olympic track and field events, and even then on a limited basis.

During the 1920s the tennis careers of Suzanne Langlen and Helen Wills were used to demonstrate the proper and improper pursuit of victory by athletic women. Tennis, for the great French champion Langlen, was not only a way of life: it was life. Her only object on a tennis court was to win, and between 1919 and 1926, when she turned professional, Langlen lost only two sets of singles and won 269 of 270 matches. But at what cost? Bulimic in her eating habits and subject to dramatic swings in emotions, she suffered several nervous breakdowns and lived in fear of losing. In addition, male critics noted that, far from keeping her looking young, tennis cruelly aged Langlen. Journalist Al Laney remarked that by the mid-1920s Langlen looked thirty years older than she actually was and that her complexion had turned dull and colorless. Her friend Ted Tinling agreed that before she turned twenty-five, "her face and expression had already the traces of deep emotional experiences far beyond the normal for her age."

In contrast, Helen Wills was a champion of great physical beauty. Before Wills, Americans tended to agree with journalist Paul Gallico that "pretty girls" did not excel in sports and that outstanding female athletes were simply compensating for their lack of beauty. Summarizing this school of thought, Larry Engelmann observed: "Athletics was their way of getting attention. If Suzanne Langlen were really beautiful, for instance, she wouldn't be running around like crazy on the tennis courts of Europe. She would have been quietly at home, happily married. Athletics proved a refuge and a last chance for the desperate female ugly duckling."

Yet Wills was beautiful, and she was great, winning every set of singles competition she played between 1927 and 1933. Journalists explained Wills's success and beauty by stressing the fact that tennis was only a game for her, not a way of life and certainly not life itself. Losses did not worry her. She always appeared composed. "My father, a doctor," she explained, "always told me not to wince or screw up my face while I was playing. He said it would put lines on my face." And no victory was worth a line.

Women were not fully emancipated from the older ideal until the 1970s, when they asserted their right to be as ruthless and competitive in athletics as men. Tennis champion Billy Jean King symbolized on the court as well as off this new attitude. Like Langlen, she single-mindedly pursued victory. And she was no more concerned with sweating and grimacing than Pete Rose. Unlike Wills, King was not interested in art or starting a family. When asked why she was not at home, she replied, "Why don't you ask Rod Laver why he isn't at home?" It was as eloquent a statement of athletic liberation as could be asked for.

To develop fully as an athlete, King had to earn money. Along with Gladys Heldman and Philip Morris Tobacco Company, King helped to organize the Virginia Slims women's tennis circuit in 1971. That year she became the first female athlete to earn $100,000 in a single year. More importantly, she labored to get women players a bigger share of the prize money at the major championships. In the early 1970s women's purses at Wimbledon and the U.S. Open were about 10 percent of the men's. By the mid-1980s the prize money split was equal. As if to punctuate the point that women's tennis had arrived, King defeated the former Wimbledon triple-crown champion (1939) Bobby Riggs 6-4, 6-3, 6-3, in a highly publicized match in the Houston Astrodome in 1973.

Even more important than King for the future of women's athletics was Title IX of the 1972 Educational Amendments Act. It outlawed sexual discrimination by school districts or colleges and universities which received federal aid. Certainly, athletic budgets in high schools and universities are not equally divided between male and female athletics. But women have made significant gains. Before Title IX less than 1 percent of athletic budgets went to women's sports. By the 1980s that figure had increased to over 10 percent. No longer is there a serious argument over the road women's sports should travel. Instead, the battle is over what portion of that pie they should receive.

But it wasn't just countries, cities, colleges, small towns, high schools, and ethnic groups which turned to sports in the 1980s as the most powerful way of defining their values. The most extraordinary development in contemporary popular culture was the extent to which individuals turned to athletics, exercise, and body image as a way of finding meaning in an increasingly dislocated society. In the mid-1980s, a Louis Harris poll indicated that 96 percent of all Americans found something about their bodies that they didn't like and would change if they could. Harris said that the "rampant obsessions of both men and women about their looks have produced an obvious boon for the cosmetics industry, plastic surgery, diet doctors, fitness and shape advisers, fat farms, and exercise clubs." The cult of fitness and the cult of individual happiness went hand in hand. Politicians used international sports at the Olympic level to confirm the superiority of various political systems or prove the equality of their Third World cultures; they mustered professional sports to project the quality of life in major American cities; collegiate sports touted the virtues of different universities; and in the 1970s and 1980s, millions of Americans embraced the cult of fitness to discover the meaning of life, retreating into the fantasy that they are how they look.

The cult of fitness and preoccupation with physical appearance first emerged in the United States during the John Kennedy administration. In the election of 1960, Kennedy used television as it had never been used before when he challenged Richard Nixon to a series of debates. Kennedy faced formidable odds. Young, handsome, and wealthy, he was considered perhaps too young, too handsome, and too wealthy to

make an effective president. His Roman Catholicism seemed another albatross. Behind the polls, Kennedy needed a boost. The televised debates were perfect.

Nixon arrived in Chicago for the first debate looking tired and ill. He had injured his knee six weeks before, and a hospital stay had weakened him. On the eve of the debate a chest cold left him hoarse. He looked like a nervous corpse—pale, twenty pounds underweight, and haggard. Make-up experts suggested covering his heavy beard with a thick powder, but Nixon accepted only a thin coat of Max Factor's "Lazy Shave," a pancake cosmetic.

Kennedy looked better, much better. He arrived at Chicago from California with a suntan. He didn't need make-up to look healthy, nor did he need special lighting to hide a weak profile. He did, however, change suits. He believed that a dark blue rather than a gray suit would look better under the bright lights. Kennedy was right, of course, as anyone who watches a nightly news program must realize. Once the debate started, Kennedy intentionally slowed down his delivery and watered down his ideas. His face was controlled and cool. He smiled with his eyes and perhaps the corners of his mouth, and his laugh was a mere suggestion of a laugh. Although Nixon marshalled a mountain of facts and closely reasoned arguments, he looked bad. Instead of hearing a knowledgeable candidate, viewers saw a nervous, uncertain man, one whose clothes didn't fit and whose face looked pasty and white. In contrast, Kennedy *looked* good, scored a victory in the polls, and went on to win the election by a razor-thin margin.

The first president born in the twentieth century, Kennedy had claimed in his inaugural address that "the torch had been passed to a new generation of Americans . . . tempered by war, disciplined by a hard and bitter peace, proud of our ancient heritage." Life around the White House soon reflected the instincts of a new generation. It wasn't just little Caroline and later John-John frolicking on the White House lawn. The Kennedys were fiercely competitive and obsessed with sports. At the family compound at Hyannisport or Robert Kennedy's "Hickory Hill" home in Virginia, the days were filled with tennis, golf, sailing, isometric exercise, swimming, horseback riding, badminton, and a brutal form of touch football, which overweight and overaged visitors dreaded, since the Kennedys expected everyone to give it a try. An atmosphere of youthful virility surrounded the Kennedy administration. To impress the Kennedys, one associate remembered, you had to "show raw guts, fall on your face now and then. Smash into the house once in a while going after a pass. Laugh off twisted ankles or a big hole torn in your best suit."

The whole country became infatuated with the sense of vitality, and the fifty-mile hike became the symbol of fitness. Marine Corps commandant General David M. Shoup, whom Kennedy especially admired, accepted Kennedy's challenge to see if his Marines could duplicate a feat of Theodore Roosevelt's 1908 Marines—march fifty miles in less than twenty hours. Shoup met the challenge, as did Attorney General Robert Kennedy, who walked his fifty miles along the path of the C & O canal. Kennedy's secretaries took up the challenge, and once the newspapers had picked up the story, tens of thousands of Americans tried it too. The spring of 1963 became the season of the fifty-mile hike.

These were also years of giddy infatuation with the Mercury astronauts, whose crew-cut fitness first came to public attention at their introductory press conference in 1959. All of them were military pilots, and John Glenn of Ohio emerged as their leader. Square-jawed with ramrod perfect posture, Glenn had a personality and value system to match. He was the ultimate "goody-goody," and America loved him. The country was also astounded at his daily fitness regimen—vigorous calisthenics followed by a two-mile jog along the beach. Two miles—every day! Even when it rained.

If John Glenn was the leading jogger of the 1960s, the scientific father of running was Kenneth Cooper, an Air Force physician. A high

school track star in Oklahoma City, Cooper finished medical school and joined the Air Force as a physician at the School of Aerospace Medicine in San Antonio. He tested fitness levels in thousands of potential Air Force pilots and in the process developed new standards of conditioning. To really benefit from exercise, Americans had to get their heart rate above 130 beats a minute for a sustained period. Jogging, running, racquetball, squash, cycling, walking, and swimming were the best exercises.

To please an increasingly technical, postindustrial clientele whose faith in science was unrivaled, Cooper even charted fitness, providing a quantified methodology to guarantee fitness. An aerobically fit person had to "earn 30 points a week." He or she could do this by walking three miles in no more than forty-one minutes five times a week; by swimming 700 yards in fifteen minutes five times a week; or by running a mile in eight minutes only twice a week. To measure fitness, Cooper recommended the "twelve minutes test." If a person can run or walk less than a mile in twelve minutes, he or she is in "very poor shape"; 1 to 1.25 miles is "poor"; 1.25 to 1.5 miles is "fair"; 1.5 to 1.75 miles is "good"; and more than 1.75 miles is "excellent." Cooper also warned people to watch out if their pulse rate exceeded 80 beats a minute. Fewer than 60 beats was "excellent." Vigorous exercise would reduce the heart rate. In Cooper's own words, "You might just save your heart some of those 20,000 to 30,000 extra beats you've forced on it every day."

The country was more than ready for Cooper's message. Early in the 1960s the first of the baby-boom generation hit college. The "don't trust anyone over thirty" culture had appeared, protesting war and inequality and proclaiming the virtues of brotherly love and sexual liberation. In 1961 half the American population was under thirty. By 1964 the median age had dropped to twenty-seven and in 1966 to twenty-five. America fell in love with youth, health, sex, and pleasure. Hippies, protests, "love-ins," "teach-ins," Woodstock, drugs, rebellion, and loud, self-righteous rejections of materialism emanated from college campuses.

But in 1967 the first baby-boom class graduated from college. The transformation of hippies into "yuppies" was underway. By 1971 those 1946 babies were twenty-five years old. The cruel tricks of gravity and heredity commenced. Bellies started to thicken, hairlines to recede. Women with babies looked despairingly at abdominal stretch marks and the faint beginnings of "crow's feet." The youth culture still survived, but individual youth was proving to be a temporary state. Middle age loomed as large as death.

Dr. Kenneth Cooper had the answer. Late in 1968, he coined a new word and wrote a book by the same name—*Aerobics.* By 1972 the book had sold nearly three million copies to anxious yuppies bent on postponing the inevitable. By the early 1970s, Cooper had an estimated eight million Americans, including astronaut John Glenn, adding up their weekly points, counting their pulse, testing their speed, taking their blood pressure, and weighing their bodies.

Throughout the 1970s and 1980s the cult of fitness reached extraordinary dimensions in the United States. More than twenty million Americans regularly exercised, and along with the running boom came a boom in racquetball, tennis, swimming, cycling, weightlifting, and "aerobic" dancing. In 1970 only 125 people entered the first New York City marathon, which took runners over a 26-mile course through all four boroughs; but in the 1986 marathon, 20,000 officially entered the race, and 19,412 finished it. The race was so popular that organizers had to reject thousands of applicants. Marathons became common events on every weekend all across the country.

The triathlon endurance was an even better gauge of the fitness cult. Known as the ultimate of the "ultrasports," the triathlon combined a 2-mile swim with a 112-mile cycle ride and a 26-mile run. In 1986 more than one million Americans competed in triathlon events around the country. And in what can only be considered the absurd limit of the fitness craze, Stu Mittleman won the "Sri Chinmoy 1,000 Mile Marathon" in New York City in 1986. His time of just under fifteen days "was my best ever."

The cult of fitness was rivaled only by the obsession with youth and body image which swept through American culture in the 1970s and 1980s. To be sure, this was nothing new. Americans had long been preoccupied with their bodies, and attempts to stay young had centered on staying thin, as if slenderness were in itself a foundation of youth. In the 1860s Harriet Beecher Stowe had written: "We in America have got so far out of the way of a womanhood that has any vigor of outline or opulence of physical proportion, that, when we see a woman made as a woman ought to be, she strikes us as a monster. Our willowy girls are afraid of nothing so much as growing stout."

To stay thin, nineteenth-century American women dieted and corseted their bodies. "It ain't stylish for young courting gals to let on like they have any appetite," admitted one female. And through tightlacing their corsets, women could maintain the proper girlish waistline of eighteen inches, with only such acceptable side effects as headaches, fainting spells, and uterine and spinal disorders.

If tightlacing and dieting led to serious health problems, illness was in itself admired. Consumptive women were romanticized and imbued with spiritual qualities. Little Eva in *Uncle Tom's Cabin,* Beth in *Little Women,* Mimi in *La Bohème*—all were thin, romantic consumptives who radiated spirituality and sensuality. Perhaps the ideal was the romantic ballerina—thin, ethereal, pale, pure, as certain to die young as poor broken-hearted Giselle.

Throughout the twentieth century, thinness has largely remained the feminine ideal, although sickliness generally declined as an attractive characteristic. The Gibson Girl of the turn of the century touted athletics, and during the 1920s the

According to tradition, the marathon commemorates the messenger who, in 490 B.C., ran 20 miles to Athens with news of the Greek victory at Marathon. Running marathons has gained popularity in recent years: in 1986 some 20,000 runners entered New York City's marathona and 19,412 finished it.

flapper exuded energy, vitality, and youth. And if the breast-bound flapper did not survive the 1929 stock market crash, an emphasis on thinness did. Indeed, only during the 1950s, when Marilyn Monroe was at her height, was there a serious challenge to the slender ideal.

Post-World War II culture has enshrined both thinness and youth for men as well as women. Advertisers have aided the process. Since photographers maintain that clothes look best on lean bodies, leading fashion models have always been thin and generally young. But since the 1960s, advertisers have used youth and thinness to sell other products as well. The evolution of Pepsi-Cola slogans illustrates this point:

1935: "Twice as Much."
1948: "Be Sociable—Have a Pepsi."
1960: "Now it's Pepsi for those who think young."
1965: "The Pepsi Generation."
1984: "Pepsi: The Choice of a New Generation."

Appeals to abundance ("twice as much") and social interaction ("be sociable") were replaced by the promise of eternal youth. As if to reinforce this appeal, Pepsi paid magnificent amounts to two thin, youthful Michaels as spokesmen: Michael Jackson and Michael J. Fox. Far from being sociable, Jackson is a virtual recluse, obsessed with personality change through plastic surgery. And Fox, as sure as Peter Pan, is the perpetual adolescent.

To fit the culture's procrustean mold, advertisers encourage Americans to binge and purge, consume and diet. Consume because "you are someone special" and "you can have it all." Diet because "you can never be too thin or too rich." In his perceptive book *Never Satisfied*, Hillel Schwartz argues that "dieting is an essentially nostalgic act, an attempt to return to a time when one *could* be satisfied, when one *was* thinner, when the range of choices in the world neither bewildered nor intimidated. To restrict one's range of choices, as all dieters must do, is not so much deficient as it is regressive. . . . Imagining a miraculous future, the dieter is always looking back."

In a secular, materialistic age, dieting has become an ascetic religion. Seventeenth-century poet and preacher John Donne wrote, "The flesh that God hath given us is affliction enough, but the flesh that the devil gives us, is affliction upon affliction and to that, there belongs a woe." To be fat in America has become a religious as well as a secular sin. Christian diet books emphasize John 3:30—"He must increase, but I must decrease."

In 1957 Charlie Shedd in his *Pray Your Weight Away* confessed, "We fatties are the only people on earth who can weigh our sin." His book inspired some Christians to lose weight and others to write diet books. Such works as Deborah Price's *I Prayed Myself Thin,* John Cavanaugh's *More of Jesus and Less of Me,* Reverend H. Victor Kane's *Devotion for Dieters,* and Francis Hunter's *God's Answer to Fat—Lose It!* emphasized that godliness is in league with thinness. Capturing the temper of her times, columnist Ellen Goodman wrote in 1975 that "eating has become the last bona fide sin left in America." And on this point, religion and secular humanism are in complete accord.

The fitness boom and body-image obsession financed a huge growth industry. To support their new interest in fitness, Americans needed equipment and clothes—shoes, shorts, shirts, racquets, bicycles, balls, paddles, bats, cleats, gloves, goggles, weights, scales, blood-pressure cuffs, timing watches, clubs, socks, headbands, wristbands, and leotards. Between 1975 and 1987 sporting goods sales in the United States increased from $8.9 billion to $27.5 billion. Americans spent $4 billion on athletic shoes alone in 1987. Health clubs, once the domain of the wealthy and a small clique of bodybuilders, multiplied in number from 350 in 1968 to more than 7,000 in 1986. Gross revenues in 1987 exceeded $650 million.

Exercise and fitness revenues were matched by those of the weight loss industry. Jean Nidetch founded Weight Watchers in 1962 and eventually franchised it, making sure that group leaders had

been through the diet program and reached "maintenance" levels. Attendance doubled between 1983 and 1987, the gross revenues went past $200 million that year. Sybil Ferguson's Diet Center, Inc., founded in 1969, had two thousand franchises in 1987 and nearly $50 million in gross revenues. Americans spent $6 billion for diet soda in 1986, $5 billion for vitamins and health foods, and $350 million for diet capsules and liquid protein. The President's Council on Physical Fitness estimated that 65 million Americans were dieting in 1987. Diet Coke, Diet Pepsi, Diet Dr. Pepper, Lean Cuisine, Bud Light, Miller Lite, "lite" bread, sugarless gum, NutraSweet, Cambridge, and a host of other diet products entered American popular culture.

What dieting and exercise couldn't fix, plastic surgery could. Americans went on a plastic surgery binge in the 1980s—not to repair real damage to their bodies or birth defects, but to improve their appearance cosmetically and recapture the illusion of youth. In 1987 more than 500,000 Americans underwent cosmetic plastic surgery. The most popular procedures were abdominoplasty (tummy tucks), breast augmentation, liposuction (fat removal), blepharoplasty (eyes,), and rhinoplasty (nose). Plastic surgeons were also beginning to perform "total body contour" procedures. To postpone middle age, yuppies made plastic surgery a $3 billion industry.

Americans also changed a number of their habits in the 1970s and 1980s. Cigarette consumption began to decline in 1982. In 1965, 52 percent of men and 34 percent of women smoked. By 1985 only 33 percent of men and 28 percent of women smoked, and at the end of 1987 the American Cancer Society estimated that only 27 percent of Americans were still smoking. Per capita whiskey consumption dropped nearly 20 percent between 1976 and 1986 as Americans turned to lower-alcohol-content beer and wine coolers. Beef and pork consumption dropped in favor of chicken and fish when cholesterol-conscious Americans turned away from "red meat." Caffeine was also suspect. Americans under twenty-five drank only a third of the coffee their parents did; sales of decaffeinated coffee and drinks like Pepsi Free and Pepper Free symbolized the new health consciousness.

The results were impressive, even though some of the gains had to be attributed to better drug therapy, the rise of heart bypass surgery, and improvement of cardiac care units in American hospitals. But the bottom line was that between 1950 and 1985, the death rate per 100,000 people from cardiovascular and cerebrovascular disease declined from 511 to 418, a dramatic improvement. The cult of fitness seemed to be paying dividends.

But there was an underside to the cult of fitness, an obsessive perfectionism which was the antithesis of good health. Jim Fixx and his daily runs in spite of chest pains were one example. Kathy Love Ormsby was another. The North Carolina State University junior, who held the U.S. collegiate women's record for 10,000 meters, had difficulty dealing with failure. In the 1986 NCAA championships, after 6,400 meters, she was struggling along in fourth place, running a bad race. Then, as she approached a turn, she decided to keep going straight. She ducked under a railing and ran straight past Wisconsin team coach Peter Tegen. "It was eerie," he said. "Her eyes were focused straight ahead." She kept going—out of Indiana University's track stadium in Indianapolis, across a softball diamond, over a seven-foot fence, down New York Street, toward the bridge that spans the White River. Seventy-five feet onto the bridge she stopped, climbed over the railing, and jumped. After falling thirty-five feet, she landed on the soggy ground close to the river. She broke a rib, collapsed a lung, and fractured vertebrae. The doctor who attended her said that she would be permanently paralyzed from the waist down: "Given the distance that she fell, she's very lucky she's not a quadriplegic," Dr. Peter Hall noted. "She could have easily died."

Why? Ormsby was a high school valedictorian, a straight-A student, the record holder for the 800, 1,600, and 3,200 meters. At North Carolina State

she was a track star and promising premed student. She was raised in a strong Christian family and was deeply religious herself. After her record-breaking 10,000-meter run, she told a reporter: "I just have to learn to do my best for myself and for God and to turn everything over to Him." Her leap had turned everything over to Him.

Some observers blamed Ormsby's consuming pursuit of perfection. Others blamed the pressure of world-class sport competition. Her father commented, "I believe . . . that it had something to do with the pressure that is put on young people to succeed." Certainly society's emphasis on the importance of sports places tremendous strains on young athletes. Often isolated from the world outside gyms and tracks and stadiums, they begin to think that their world has real, lasting meaning. Failure, then, becomes equated with death itself.

Such obsessive perfectionism also affected millions of other people, only a tiny fraction of whom were competitive athletes. For many people, exercise and weight loss became forms of psychological discipline, proof that the individual was in charge of his or her life. A 1986 Gallup Poll estimated that three million Americans, most of them women, suffered from eating disorders—anorexia nervosa and bulimia. In anorexia nervosa, victims virtually starve themselves to death, using laxatives, exercise, and absurdly low calorie intake to lose body weight. Most psychologists attribute the eating disorder to a sense of powerlessness in the victim. They strive for a sense of weightlessness, and in that weightlessness they find a sense of control missing from other areas of their lives. In 1984 the soft-rock vocalist Karen Carpenter brought the disease to national attention when she died of a heart attack induced by extreme weight loss. Even when their weight drops below 85 pounds and they resemble concentration camp victims, anorectics still look in the mirror and see themselves as fat, with round faces and flabby skin. Breasts disappear, menstruation stops, and their bodies return momentarily, just before death, to preadolescence.

Bulimia is a related disorder. The Gallup Poll concluded that nearly 10 percent of all American women between the ages of sixteen and twenty-five practice bulimia, an eating disorder characterized by huge calorie intake followed by self-induced vomiting. The Food and Drug Administration said that bulimic episodes may last up to eight hours, with an intake of 20,000 calories (an equivalent of 210 brownies, or 6 layer cakes, or 35 Big Macs), involve 25 to 30 vomiting episodes, and cost up to $75 a day for food purchases. If untreated, the disease causes irregular heartbeats, cramps, fatigue, and seizures by destroying the body's electrolyte balance. The gastric acid from vomiting will also erode teeth away.

In a country which historically has been keenly competitive and has periodically affirmed a belief in perfectionism, the idea of a better life through sports has been carried to obsessive lengths. Often the object of physical fitness has not been to produce health and well-being but to test or even to escape the limits of one's body. Ultra-distance runner Stu Mittleman, one of the leaders in his field during the 1980s, was the epitome of this tendency. For him a 26-mile marathon was unsatisfactory, a flat, almost meaningless endeavor. The 100-mile event was better, and in the early 1980s he established the American record with a 12:56:34 run. Better still was the six-day event, in which his 488 miles was also an American record.

In ultra-distance running Mittleman saw man rediscovering his lost past. "Our culture forces us to eliminate sensory input so that we can cope," he observed. "Sports re-sensitizes. I want to live life intensely. . . . Long slow running has a heritage in hunting and gathering. Sprinting is based on retreat, on flight." Life, then, is best experienced at the limits of endurance, well past what is good for one's health. Yet, sometimes even that does not seem enough. As Mittleman told an interviewer, "I plan to do a 12-hour run tomorrow. You know, it seems like so little now."

Among world-class athletes, performance is more important than health. During the nine-

teenth century athletes occasionally took drugs to enhance their performances. Cyclists, in particular, used drugs to extend their pain and endurance barriers. As early as 1869 some cyclists used "speed balls" of heroin and cocaine to increase endurance. Others used caffeine, alcohol, nitroglycerine, ethyl ether, strychnine, and opium to achieve the same effect.

Of course, not all athletes survived such experimentation. And in the twentieth century, as drug use became more frequent, the casualty rate climbed. In 1960 Danish cyclist Knut Jensen collapsed and died during the Rome Olympics. He had taken amphetamines and nicotinyl tartrate to improve his chances of victory. In 1967 Thomas Simpson died during the ascent of Mount Ventoux in the Tour de France. Amphetamines were discovered in his jersey pockets and luggage.

Since World War II, however, stimulants have done less damage than muscle-building drugs. During the 1920s American scientists isolated the male hormone testosterone. By the 1940s testosterone was being hailed as a potential fountain of youth. Science writer Paul de Kruif in *The Male Hormone* (1945) noted that the newly developed synthetic testosterone "did more than give [the subjects] more energy and a gain in weight. . . . It changed them, and fundamentally . . . after many months on testosterone, their chest and shoulder muscles grew much heavier and stronger. . . . In some mysterious manner, testosterone caused the human body to synthesize protein, it caused the human body to be able to build the very stuff of its own life." There is evidence that during World War II testosterone was administered to German storm troopers to increase their strength and aggressiveness.

In 1945 de Kruif speculated, "It would be interesting to watch the productive power of [a] . . . professional group [of athletes] that would try a systematic supercharge with testosterone." By the 1952 Helsinki Olympics the Soviet Union had embarked on just such a campaign. That year Soviet weightlifters won seven Olympic medals, and U.S. Olympic weightlifting coach Bob Hoffman told reporters, "I know they're taking the hormone stuff to increase their strength."

At the 1954 World Weightlifting Championships in Vienna, a Soviet team physician confirmed Hoffman's belief. Upon returning home, Dr. John Ziegler, the U.S. team physician, acquired some testosterone and tested it on himself, Hoffman, and several American lifters. Concerned about the hormone's side effects—heightened aggression, increased libido, prostatic problems, and hirsutism—Ziegler approached the CIBA pharmaceutical company about producing a drug that would have testosterone's anabolic (muscle-building) effects without its androgenic (masculine characteristics) problems. The unsatisfactory result was the anabolic steroid Dianabol, a drug intended to aid burn victims and certain post-operative and geriatric patients.

Dianabol soon became the candy of the athletic world. By the 1960s nearly every world-class weightlifter was taking some form of anabolic steroid. In fact, steroids became the *sine qua non* of lifting. American superheavyweight weightlifting champion Ken Patera announced in 1971 that he was anxious to meet his Russian counterpart Vasily Alexiev in the 1972 Olympics: "Last year, the only difference between me and him was that I couldn't afford his pharmacy bill. Now I can. When we hit Munich next year, I'll weigh in at about 340, maybe 350. Then we'll see which are better—his steroids or mine."

Track and field athletes, football players, and bodybuilders similarly improved their performances with the aid of drugs. Jay Sylvester, a member of the 1972 U.S. Olympic track and field team, polled his teammates and found that 68 percent had used steroids to prepare for the Games. They believed that without them they would be at a competitive disadvantage. The same was true in football. One San Diego Charger player told team psychiatrist Arnold J. Mandell, "Doc, I'm not about to go out one-on-one against a guy who's grunting and drooling and coming at

me with big dilated pupils unless I'm in the same condition."

Testosterone and anabolic steroids have led to athletes' experimenting with other performance-enhancing drugs. One of the more popular recent additions to this drug array is human growth hormone (hGH), a hormone manufactured from the pituitary. As the authors of *The Underground Steroid Handbook* claimed, hGH could "overcome bad genetics. . . . We LOVE the stuff." Of course, it may also cause elongation of the chin, feet, and hands; thickening of the rib cage and wrists; and heart problems.

Risk is part of taking drugs. Anabolic steroids can cause a rare, fatal type of kidney tumor, high blood pressure, sterility, intestinal bleeding, hypoglycemia, heart problems, acne, a deepened voice, and a change in the distribution of body hair. Steroids and testosterone also make users more aggressive and irritable. One NFL player confessed that testosterone "definitely makes a person mean and aggressive. . . . On the field I've tried to hurt people in ways I never did before. . . . A lot of guys can't handle it. I'm not sure I can. I remember a while back five of the guys on our team went on the juice at the same time. A year later four of them were divorced and one was separated. I've lost a lot of hair from using it, but I have to admit it's great for football. . . . I lost my family, but I think I'm a better player now. Isn't that a hell of a trade-off?"

By the 1970s steroids had become part of America's drug culture, and athletes asserted the right to decide what could or could not go into their own bodies. Frederick C. Hatfield in *Anabolic Steroids: What Kind and How Many* (1982) wrote: "As pioneers, these athletes carefully weigh the risk-to-benefit ratio and proceed with caution and with open minds. Can there be much wrong with getting bigger and/or stronger?" Users, then, have been transformed into pioneers, "adventurers who think for themselves and who want to accomplish something noble before they are buried and become worm food."

Ironically, however, most of the users are not world-class athletes. In the 1980s use of steroids expanded out of the realm of world-class athletes to college and high school playing fields. An estimated one million young American men and women were consuming large amounts of anabolic steroids in 1987. The praise they received for "bulking up" was irresistible. When they reduced steroid use and lost muscle tissue, friends immediately commented on how "much smaller you are," and they would return to the pills. Like bulimia and anorexia nervosa, anabolic steroids were addictions linked inseparably with body image.

Steroid use was most pronounced in the subculture of body building. Most of these men and women are not competitive athletes trying to break a world record or win an Olympic gold metal—"to accomplish something noble"—but people who want to look "pumped." Like dieting and cosmetic surgery, steroid use has become a means to a better-looking body, and looks—not health—is the real objective.

The quest for the "ideal" body has been taken to its furthest pharmaceutical extremes by bodybuilders. Not only do they take steroids to build up muscle mass, but they also diet and take diuretics to achieve maximum muscular striation, or the "cut up" look. For weeks or even months before an important competition, bodybuilders eat as little as 1,000 calories a day and still work out eight or more hours a day. The result may be "the picture of health," but there is no reality behind the image. As one professional commented, "When we walk on stage we are closer to death than we are to life." And after a contest, in a bulimic binge, bodybuilders "pig out," often putting on fifteen pounds in one evening of eating.

Furthermore, to support their quest, many bodybuilders resort to homosexual "hustling." In theory, male bodybuilders have enshrined heterosexuality. Charles Atlas advertisements emphasized that the prize for the biggest biceps was the woman in the bathing suit. *Muscle and Fitness,* the leading body-builder magazine, reinforces this mythology by always picturing beautiful women hanging onto the biceps and thighs of "pumped," oiled men. "Ya know," said *Muscle and Fitness* editor Joe Weider, "in every age the women, they always go for the guy with the muscles, the bodybuilder. [The women] never go for the studious guy."

In fact, gay men have been a continual source of financial support for bodybuilders. Since serious bodybuilding is a full-time pursuit, the men involved need some source of income. Anthropologist Alan M. Kline estimated that 50 to 75 percent of southern California bodybuilders "hustle" the gay community for living expenses. Hustling ranges from posing for "beefcake" photographers and dancing nude at all-male events to pornography and sexual acts. Most bodybuilders, however, insist that they are not homosexual, that they have to hustle only to finance their bodybuilding habit. And besides, they insist, almost everyone does it. "People don't realize," noted one bodybuilder, "that in any given line-up of twenty competitors ten are hustling."

Many serious bodybuilders sacrifice heterosexual relationships as well as good health for their obsession. As one admitted, "On any given day I can go out with a woman, but it is not very satisfying. . . . Women demand time. I don't have that right now." Time, commitment, women, and even other men—all are obstacles to be mastered or avoided in the pursuit of a narcissistic ideal. To echo Michael Jackson's popular 1988 song, life for these bodybuilders starts and ends with the man in the mirror.

By the end of the 1980s, sports had become the secular religion of America. The stadiums, tanning salons, health spas, and gymnasiums had become the new cathedrals; jogging, running, aerobic dancing, cycling, weightlifting, and dieting the new rituals; and televised events, newspapers, radio talk shows, and sports and health magazines the new liturgics. The most obsessive athletes have a disciplined devotion that even the most ascetic medieval saints would have envied.

Alberto Salazar, the world-class marathoner, bragged about his willingness to run 105 miles a week on stress-fractured legs. In the heat of one marathon, he kept running even when his body temperature had reached 108 degrees, collapsed in heat prostration, and while being packed in ice, received the last rites of the Roman Catholic Church.

Sports in the 1980s holds out secular salvation for nations, communities, and individuals. In competition and fitness, they locate the holy grail, the meaning of life in a world where God, church, and state no longer reign supreme. In *The Complete Book of Running,* Jim Fixx wrote: "It is here with my heart banging against my ribs that I discover how far beyond reason I can push myself. Furthermore, once a race has ended, I know what I am truly made of. Who can say how many of us have learned life's profoundest lessons while aching and gasping for breath?" On that Vermont road in 1986, with his body aching, his lungs gasping for breath, and his heart pounding against his ribs, Jim Fixx may have discovered the meaning of life.

STUDY QUESTIONS

1. Why did sports assume such an important dimension in American culture after World War II?

2. To what extent does sports in America reflect the aggressive, competitive spirit of the large culture?

3. What are the advantages and disadvantages to the new American obsession with sports?

4. In rural areas, why are high school sports so important to the community?

5. Why has plastic surgery become so popular in modern America?

6. How can anorexia nervosa and bulimia be seen as cultural, not merely physical, extremes?

7. What does the concept *cultural currency* mean? How do sports assist American society in transcending ethnic and religious divisions?

8. What is the connection between the cult of fitness and the post-World War II baby boom generation of yuppies?

BIBLIOGRAPHY

For an extraordinary look at American values in the contemporary period, see Christopher Lasch, *The Culture of Narcissism: American Life in the Age of Diminishing Expectations* (1975). Also see Peter Clecak, *America's Quest for the Ideal Self* (1983). Randy Roberts and James S. Olson analyze the American obsession with sports in *Winning Is the Only Thing* (1989). Studs Terkel's *American Dreams: Lost and Found* (1980) is an oral history of how Americans coped with the social and economic changes of the 1970s and 1980s. Hillel Schwartz's *Never Satisfied: A Cultural History of Diets, Fantasies and Fat* (1986) is an outstanding examination of the American preoccupation with youth and body image. Also see Kim Chernin, *The Obsession: Reflections on the Tyranny of Slenderness* (1981). For the dangerous, pathologic dimension of weight consciousness in history, see Rudolph M. Bell, *Holy Anorexia* (1985).

Photo Acknowledgments